1915
THE DEATH OF INNOCENCE

Also by Lyn Macdonald

They Called It Passchendaele
The Roses of No Man's Land
Somme
1914

1915
The Death of Innocence

Lyn Macdonald

BCA

LONDON NEW YORK SYDNEY TORONTO

This edition published 1993
by BCA
by arrangement with
HEADLINE BOOK PUBLISHING

CN 2945

First published in Great Britain in 1993
by HEADLINE BOOK PUBLISHING

10 9 8 7 6 5 4 3 2

Typeset by
Letterpart Limited, Reigate, Surrey

Printed and bound in Great Britain by
Mackays of Chatham PLC, Chatham, Kent

Contents

Author's Foreword and Acknowledgements   vii

List of Maps   xi

Part 1: 'We're here because we're here, because we're here . . .'

Chapter One   3

Chapter Two   16

Chapter Three   38

Chapter Four   49

Chapter Five   59

Part 2: Into Battle: Neuve Chapelle

Chapter Six   75

Chapter Seven   87

Chapter Eight   99

Chapter Nine   114

Chapter Ten   130

Part 3: 'This is the happy warrior – this is he!'

Chapter Eleven   147

Chapter Twelve   169

Chapter Thirteen   182

Chapter Fourteen   196

Chapter Fifteen   211

Part 4: The Desperate Days

Chapter Sixteen   231

Chapter Seventeen   246

Chapter Eighteen   258

Chapter Nineteen   269

Chapter Twenty   280

Chapter Twenty-One   295

Chapter Twenty-Two   311

Part 5: 'Damn the Dardanelles – they will be our grave'
Chapter Twenty-Three   331
Chapter Twenty-Four   342
Chapter Twenty-Five   355

Part 6: Slogging On: The Salient to Suvla
Chapter Twenty-Six   379
Chapter Twenty-Seven   396
Chapter Twenty-Eight   413
Chapter Twenty-Nine   428
Chapter Thirty   442

Part 7: Loos: The Dawn of Hope
Chapter Thirty-One   459
Chapter Thirty-Two   478
Chapter Thirty-Three   496
Chapter Thirty-Four   512
Chapter Thirty-Five   532
Chapter Thirty-Six   552

Part 8: The Dying of the Year
Chapter Thirty-Seven   571
Chapter Thirty-Eight   585

Bibliography   603
Author's Note   606
Index   611

Author's Foreword
and Acknowledgements

In the chronicle of the Great War the resonant names of great battles – Mons, Somme, Passchendaele – have echoed down the years. But although the Battles of Neuve Chapelle, Ypres, Loos were far from insignificant and have received some attention from historians (and the Gallipoli campaign has received a great deal), 1915 as a year has been strangely neglected.

Looking back in harsh hindsight 1915 appears to be a saga of such horrors, of such mismanagement and muddle, that it is easy to see why it coloured the views of succeeding generations and gave rise to prejudices and myths that have been applied to the whole war. But it was a year of learning. A year of cobbling together, of frustration, of indecision. In a sense a year of innocence. Therein lies its tragedy.

The battles of the early months of the war in 1914 were not 'battles' in any sense that Wellington would have understood. From the British point of view Mons, the Marne, the Aisne and the First Battle of Ypres were rather struggles for survival, and by January 1915 their names had already passed into legend. The incomparable Regular soldiers of the original British Expeditionary Force had suffered ninety per cent casualties and to all intents and purposes it was no more. The few who were left or had been hastily brought back from foreign stations held the line through the winter, together with the erstwhile 'Saturday Afternoon Soldiers' of the Territorial Force. The line ran through the Flanders swamps. The men who held it fought the wet; they fought the snow, the rain, the cold; they fought the floods and the mud. Ill-equipped and with pathetically small supplies of ammunition, they fought the Germans. And they waited – for the coming of spring, for the promised reinforcements, and for the better weather which would herald the start of the offensive that would surely break the German line and send them roaring through to victory.

The first months of 1915 were a time of hope, of wide-ranging plans and far-reaching ideas which were destined to end, at best, in stalemate and in another gallant litany of fortitude and loss – Neuve

Chapelle, Aubers Ridge, Festubert, Gallipoli, Ypres (always Ypres!) and Loos. By the end of the year all the old ideas of warfare had been swept away, although some of those responsible for the conduct of the war were slow to realise it. It was the year that brought the new armies they called 'Kitchener's Mob' into the fight, sent the Anzacs to Gallipoli, the Canadians to Ypres. By the end of it there were some who already felt that the war had taken on a momentum of its own. It was a long time before the lessons of 1915 were learned and applied, for it was cursed with partial victories which implanted the idea that in better circumstances, with more ammunition, more men, better communications, more detailed planning, with firm leadership and with a modicum of luck, the enemy's resistance could be finally crushed.

Words like gallantry, endurance and patriotism have an old-fashioned ring about them which strikes discordantly on modern ears. It is easy to dismiss the soldiers as gullible victims, the generals and their political masters as incompetent dolts, the nation as a whole as unprotesting sheep blind to the realities which, eighty years on, a generation that believes itself to be endowed with superior sensibilities is quick to appreciate and condemn. To subscribe to this point of view is to show little understanding of human nature and the spirit of the times. We cannot alter history by disapproving of it. I hope that, by setting events in context, this book might add a little to the understanding of how and why things happened as they did. As always, my intention has been to 'tell it like it was', to tune in to the heartbeat of the experience of the people who lived through it. In the end it is the people who matter.

My thanks, as always, must go first to the Old Soldiers who have told me their stories personally, written them down, or often vividly described what happened as we stood on the battlefields during one of my many trips to Flanders in their company. Many whose stories appear in this book have, alas, not survived to see them in print. Time is running out, and it is all the more important that we should listen, and listen carefully, before the curtain finally falls on the generation who experienced the Great War that was the watershed of the tumultuous twentieth century and the bridge between the old world and our own.

It was a literate generation of inveterate letter-writers and diary keepers, and it is almost impossible to list the staggering number of people who have so very kindly sent me collections of letters, diaries, photographs, papers, belonging to their families or, occasionally, rescued from abandonment in antique shops. The latter give me particular pleasure – Corporal Letyford's diary, from which extracts have appeared in *1914* as well as in this book, is just one example. I like to think he would have been pleased. My thanks to Andrew Taylor, to Ian Swindale for Pte. Harry Crask, to Dr R.C. Brookes for Pte. Bernard Brookes, Brenda Field for the memoir of Trooper Harry Clarke, R. A. Watson for Alan Watson's diary, and to the many other people who have so generously endowed me with valuable contemporary written material and given me permission to make use of it. It goes without saying that my archive of first-hand material, written and oral, will in due course (on my demise or retirement) be passed to the care of the Imperial War Museum for the benefit of future students and historians.

My thanks are also due to the Imperial War Museum, and in particular to Roderick Suddaby, Keeper of Documents, for his great interest and assistance in the preparation of this book and for making available unpublished material which makes a considerable contribution to its scope. Also to my friend and colleague Mike Willis, whose knowledge of the photographic archive is second to none, for his invaluable assistance with the illustrations.

Many people have assisted in interviewing the Old Soldiers, and I must especially thank Barbara Taylor, Colin Butler, Chris Sheeran, and Eric Warwick. Others have helped enormously with the research in parts of the world which were not immediately accessible to me. I should like in particular to thank Elspeth Ewan in Scotland for local research in pursuit of extra information on Jim Keddie, Bill Paterson in Edinburgh, and Vivien Riches, who was my assistant a long time ago and who has maintained her interest since moving to Australia, where she found and interviewed the Australian veterans of Gallipoli.

My French and Belgian friends have, as always, taken a great interest and, by sharing civilian recollections, added another dimension to the story of 1915. Yves de Cock generously made available his research on the gas attack. My friend Stephan Maenhout introduced his 'Tante Paula' (Mevrow Hennekint née Barbieur) who told the story of her family in 1915. I must pay particular tribute to the senior members of my own much-loved French family, Pierre and Germaine Dewavrin, who have added so much to my understanding over the years, and whose recollections of 1915 appear in this book.

Colonel Terry Cave most kindly helped with information on the Indians; Peter Thomas of P & O and Vivien Riches in Australia between them researched different aspects of the story of the *Southport*; and Lord Sterling, Chairman of P & O, also deserves my gratitude for his interest and for his generosity to the Old Soldiers.

I must also thank Rennie McOwen and many readers of the *Edinburgh Evening News* who responded overwhelmingly to his request and showered me with unique photographs and personal recollections of the Royal Scots rail disaster. Anne Mackay of the Scottish Music Information Centre took a great interest and went to considerable trouble to supply me with the words of 'The March of the Cameron Men' which, to our shame as Scots, neither General Christison nor I could wholly remember.

Of all my books on the First World War *1915* has been the longest and most complicated to write. (My publisher, Alan Brooke, remarked 'It's taken as long as the war itself!') With the deadline looming the last few months have been trying for my family. I must thank my husband, Ian Ross, for suffering almost in silence, for his constant interest and support, and for all the take-aways he brought home when there wasn't any dinner!

I have been blessed with colleagues over the years who have given unstintingly of their time, interest and support. Some are mentioned above. Tony Spagnoly is always available for interesting discussion and gave much appreciated help with the maps; and John Woodroff, my military researcher, deserves my warmest thanks for answering a million queries on corps, divisions, battalions and individual soldiers – plus many other topics – and he very occasionally took as long as five minutes to come up with the answer.

Last, but by no means least, I must thank my stalwart assistant Sandra Layson, not just for her competence and efficiency, but for her bright presence, her sharp appreciation, her support and sympathy – evidenced by the occasional tear over the 'sad bits' – and for a great deal of extremely hard work.

Lyn Macdonald
London, 1993

List of Maps

The Western Front 1915   8

The Front, Ypres to Vimy 1915   32

The Battle of Neuve Chapelle   80

Neuve Chapelle: German positions, 11 March   100

Neuve Chapelle: The line at the end of the battle   133

The Ypres Salient 22 April 1915   175

Ypres: The Gas Attack   191

Ypres: The Salient after Retirement   274

Ypres: Bellewaerde and Frezenberg Ridge   281

Aubers Ridge   296

The Eastern Mediterranean   343

The Gallipoli Peninsula   343

Gallipoli: Helles and the Southern Sector   357

Gallipoli: Gully Ravine, 28 June 1915   366

Gully Ravine: Final line 5 July   366

Gallipoli: Anzac   436

Gallipoli: Suvla Bay and Anzac   443

The Battle of Loos   497

Loos, 26 September   533

Loos, 14 October   533

Part 1

~

'We're here because we're here, because we're here . . .'

Oh, the rain, the mud, and the cold
The cold the mud and the rain.
With weather at zero it's hard for a hero
From language that's rude to refrain.
With porridgy muck to the knees
With the sky that's still pouring a flood,
Sure the worst of our foes
Are the pains and the woes
Of the rain, the cold and the mud.

Robert Service

Chapter 1

Across the chill wasteland that was Flanders in winter the armies had gone to ground. During the short hours of murky daylight, rifles occasionally crackled along some stretch of the line. From time to time a flurry of rooks, startled by a shot that ricocheted through a wood, rose cawing from the trees to wheel in the grey sky. Here and there, when some half-frozen soldier drew hard on his pipe, as if hoping its minuscule glow might keep out the cold, a stray puff of smoke would rise to mingle with the ground-mist that lay most days above the bogs and ditches. In Flanders, where the merest rise counted as a ridge and the smallest hill was regarded as a mountain, vantage points high enough to give a bird's-eye view were rare, but on a quiet day even a vigilant observer standing almost anywhere above the undulating length of the front line would have been hard pressed to detect any sign of life and, apart from the odd burst of desultory fire, any evidence that the trenches were manned at all.

On the British side the fire was desultory because bullets were too precious to waste, and also because the soldiers were disinclined to shoot. Nineteen fifteen had swept in on the back of a gale, and high winds and violent rainstorms continued to torment the men in the trench line for day after dreary day. Peering across the parapet, enveloped in a clammy groundsheet that mainly served to channel the rain into rivers that trickled into his puttees and seeped downwards to chill his feet, contemplating the ever-worsening state of the rifle that rested on the oozing mud-filled sandbags, the last thing a soldier wished to do was foul the barrel by firing it if he could help it. Cleaning the outside was bad enough, and no sensible soldier was belligerent enough to wish to spend hours cleaning the bore for the sake of a few pot-shots in the general direction of the enemy.

Such belligerence as there was at present was largely directed by officers towards their own troops. Authority on both sides of the line had strongly disapproved of the Christmas spirit of goodwill that had brought the front-line soldiers of both sides out of their trenches to swap greetings and gifts, and the rebukes that had passed down the chain of command through discomfited Brigadiers, Colonels and Majors to the rank and file, had left them in no doubt that such a thing must not occur again. But it was good while it lasted.

Parcels had arrived by the trainload from Germany and by the boatload from England, from places as far apart as Falmouth and Flensburg, Ullapool and Ulm. So many trains were required to bring the flood of Christmas mail to France from the Fatherland that German transport and supply depots were seriously disrupted, and even officers at the front complained that crowded billets and narrow trenches were becoming dangerously congested, for goods and parcels were showered on the troops by legions of anonymous donors as well as by friends and families. In most Germans towns and villages committees had been formed to raise funds and send Christmas parcels, *Weinachtspaketen*, to the troops. The more sentimental called them 'love parcels' – *Liebespaketen* – and at least one recipient, fighting for the Kaiser in the comfortless trenches of the Argonne was struck by the irony of the name. He expressed his thoughts in a plaintive verse that appeared in one of the many columns of thank-you letters in a German newspaper whose readers had been particularly generous. 'So much love,' he sighed, 'and no girls to deliver it!'* Even the Kaiser sent cigars – ten per man – in tasteful individual boxes inscribed 'Weinachten im Feld, 1914'.

The British soldiers had also received a royal gift (a useful metal box from Princess Mary, containing cigarettes, or pipe tobacco, or chocolate for non-smokers); they had plum puddings sent by the *Daily Mail*, chocolate from Cadbury, butterscotch from Callard & Bowser, gifts from the wives of officers of a dozen different

---

*   Notschrei Aus Den Argonnen

Liebeshandshuh' trag' ich an den Händen,
Liebesbinden warme meine Lenden,
Liebestabak füllt die Liebespfeife,
Morgens wasch' ich mich mit Liebesseife,
Liebesgabendankesagebriefe,
Warmt der Liebeskopfschlauch nachts den Schädel
Seufz' ich: 'So viel Liebe – und kein Mädel!'

I wear love's gloves on my hands,
Love's leggings warm my thighs,
Love's tobacco fills love's pipe,
In the mornings I wash with love's soap,
For loving gifts a thank-you letter,
Warm is love's cap against my skull.
I sigh to myself: 'So much love – and no girl!'

able. The Lord Mayor's Juvenile Fancy Dress Party had gone ahead as usual, but this year the frivolous columbines and harlequins, the troops of elves and fairies, so popular in peacetime, had been ousted by fleets of juvenile sailors, contingents of small red-caped nurses, battalions of miniature soldiers shouldering toy rifles – even a six-year-old admiral, wearing a small cocked hat and sporting a little sword.

A field service uniform, complete in every detail but scaled down to fit children from six to twelve, could be bought at Gamages store for as little as five shillings and eleven pence. Hundreds were sold, over the counter and by mail order, and the sight of khaki-clad tots trailing at the heels of self-satisfied adults became as common in the streets and parks as the sight of youngsters in sailor suits.

Having been brought up in the belief that the security of the British Empire could safely be left in the hands of its army – trained, drilled and disciplined to the highest standards of competence – confident that the shores of their islands were protected by a navy that ruled the oceans of the world, the British public was inclined to take a complacent view of the war. A whole century had gone by since a European power had seriously threatened Britain's shores, and it had been a century of unprecedented prosperity and expansion. It had also been a century of progress, and it was popularly believed by every Briton, from the monarch to the man in the street, that the British system of democratic government, wise administration and spreading enlightenment was an example to the world. It was a century in which full-scale wars had been far-off affairs, and warring tribes and upstart nations had been easily swatted down. It was hard to break the habit of believing that this state of affairs was based on a natural law of superiority and would continue forever. True, there had been some unfortunate setbacks in the progress of the war so far, but even Waterloo had been described by the victorious Duke of Wellington as 'a damned close run thing'. The centenary of the Battle of Waterloo would fall in June 1915; by a happy chance, Wellington's own pistol had come up for sale and a group of well-wishers had bought it as a New Year's gift for his successor, Sir John French, now in command of Britain's army in the field. Few people doubted that 1915 would be another *annus mirabilis*, that Sir John French and his allies would soon have the Kaiser on the run and would defeat him as decisively as the great duke and his allies had defeated Napoleon a hundred years before.

But to those who took a long, hard and realistic look at matters as they stood it was clear that on the western front there was deadlock. The great autumn battles had brought the Germans to a standstill and the armies now faced each other in a long line of trenches that began among the sand dunes of the Belgian coast, snaked across the

7

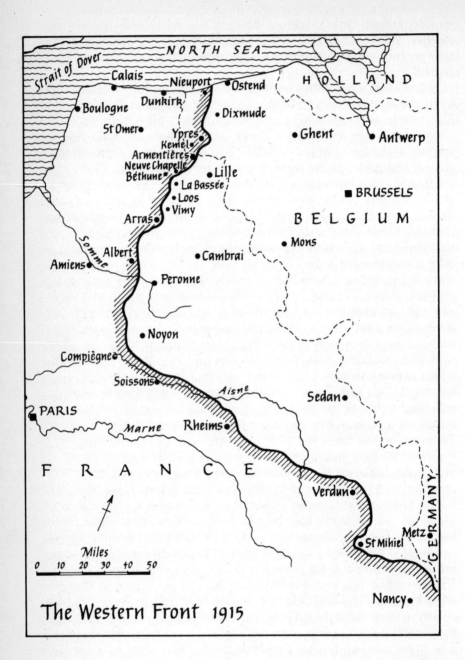

The Western Front 1915

face of France and ended within sight of the mountains of Switzerland. And there, it seemed, the German invaders intended to stay. They were assiduously digging in – not just a single line of entrenchments, but a second behind the first, and behind that another. With well-sited machine-guns and well-disciplined rifle fire their positions were virtually impregnable and in the No Man's Land beyond their line, the bodies of the men who had tried to breach it had been lying since November. They were the proof, if proof were needed, that the war that had been anticipated and prepared for had been fought and was over. Nobody had won. Slowly the realisation began to dawn that the armies must now prepare for a war that no one had anticipated and for which they were ill equipped. All that anyone could be sure of was that this war would be different from any that had ever been fought before. The machine-guns would see to that. The Germans were outnumbered in places by as many as three to one but, thanks to machine-guns liberally sited along their trenches, they could repel attack after attack. Not for nothing was the machine-gun called Queen of the Battlefield. Soon, they would be calling it the Grim Reaper.

The machine-gun was hardly a new-fangled 'wonder-weapon'. It was not even a new invention. The first hand-cranked versions had been used more than half a century earlier during the American Civil War and the pioneers of the expanding British Empire were quick to realise its usefulness. It could inflict such carnage on an army of native warriors armed with shield and spear that their chiefs could be speedily persuaded to part with land and mineral concessions. A single Gatling could bring a whole troop of horsemen to book. Against primitive weapons, a couple of them could win a small-scale war. One anti-imperialist spokesman summed it up in an ironical verse:

> Onward Christian Soldiers, on to heathen lands,
> Prayerbooks in your pockets, rifles in your hands,
> Take the glorious tidings where trade can be done,
> Spread the peaceful gospel – with a Maxim gun.

But, as a weapon of conventional warfare, the machine-gun had not found favour with the hierarchy of the British Army. Some people in Germany had been quicker to appreciate its possibilities – and almost the first had been the Kaiser himself.

The Kaiser's passion for his Army was equalled only by his obsession with his Navy, and his dearest desire was that both should match the Army and Navy of Great Britain, and even surpass them in strength and magnificence. Military matters occupied a large part of the Kaiser's attention. Soon after he came to the throne in 1888 he had decreed that court dress would henceforth be military

9

uniform, and heaven help the officer, even the long-retired officer approaching his dotage, who appeared in the Imperial Presence wearing mufti. Unless he was hunting, the Kaiser himself seldom wore civilian clothes, and he had once gone so far as to order that the officers of a Guards regiment should be confined to barracks for two weeks on hearing that they had dared to attend a private party in civilian evening dress.

The Kaiser himself had uniforms for every occasion, many designed by himself, and it was even whispered that he had a special uniform, based on that of an Admiral of the Fleet, for attending performances of *The Flying Dutchman*. The joke had a ring of truth. In the first seventeen years of his reign he had introduced no fewer than thirty-seven alterations to the uniform of the army until it was brought discreetly to his notice that, although military tailors were prospering, some officers were having serious difficulty keeping up with the expense.

The Kaiser was interested in everything, had opinions on everything, particularly on military subjects, and he never tired of expounding his views. His mouth seemed as large as the waxed moustaches that bristled across his face, and it seemed to some of his long-suffering ministers that the Kaiser's mouth often appeared to be functioning independently of his brain. They had thought so at the time of the Boxer Rebellion when Germany proposed the dispatch of an international force to China after the seizure of foreign embassies in Peking. The Kaiser travelled to Wilhelmshaven to give his personal farewell to the German contingent and the manner in which he harangued the troops on the quayside had caused even the most loyal of his ministers to quail. The Kaiser wanted revenge. He wanted blood. He wanted Peking razed to the ground. He commanded his troops to show no mercy and to take no prisoners. He reminded them (inaccurately) of their forebears who had fought under Attila the Hun and urged them to follow their example. They must stamp the name 'German' so indelibly on the face of China that no Chinese would ever again dare to look a German in the face.

This bravura performance was unrehearsed and even though Germany had suffered a gross insult at the hands of the nationalists (the German ambassador had been murdered) the Kaiser's language and demeanour caused his military entourage deep disquiet.*

---

* The German expedition had been the Kaiser's own idea. But his force had hardly set sail when word arrived that order had already been restored by a mixed force of British, Japanese and Russians. The situation was back to normal long before the German troops reached China. The Kaiser was furious.

The episode was disturbing, even allowing for the fact that this first whiff of military adventure in his twelve years' peaceful reign had gone slightly to the Kaiser's head. Now he was set on a mammoth programme of costly shipbuilding to quadruple the navy, was planning a huge expansion of the army, and had recently assumed the rank of Field Marshal, asserting that he had been begged by senior officers to do so. Now that he held this high-ranking position, he airily announced, he might easily dispense with the services of a General Staff. No one was quite sure if the All-Highest was jesting. But his opinion of his General Staff officers was expressed in terms that left no room for doubt. They were a bunch of old donkeys, the Kaiser raged, who thought they knew better than he did just because they happened to be older than himself – and at forty-one he was hardly a child!

The fact was that despite the military upbringing, obligatory for Hohenzollern princes, despite his pretension to military knowledge, the outwardly respectful members of the General Staff were deeply wary of their Kaiser and his meddlesome ways. Let him design dress uniforms for his regiments, let him order parades and reviews, let him play at manoeuvres – let him do anything at all with the Army that would keep him harmlessly amused, but prevent him at all costs from doing anything that would upset the long-established status quo.

But there was a grain of justification for the Kaiser's impatience with his senior Generals, for among the torrent of half-baked notions that poured with inexhaustible energy from his restless brain there was an occasional flash of insight or an idea worth considering. The machine-gun was one of them and, like so many things the Kaiser admired and envied, it had come from England. He had first seen one years before when he had attended the Golden Jubilee celebrations of his grandmother, Queen Victoria.

It was the glorious summer of 1887 and for the whole of June it was 'Queen's Weather' – day after day of cloudless skies and brilliant sunshine. There was a large gathering of European royalties, most of them related to each other and to the Queen. There were maharajahs from India, gorgeous in silk brocades and bedizened with jewels; there was the Queen of Hawaii, and the heirs to the exotic thrones of Japan, Persia, Siam, and when the Queen rode to Westminster Abbey in an open carriage drawn by six white horses, no fewer than five crowned heads and thirty-two princes rode in her procession. Silks shone, plumes nodded, jewels flashed, orders and medals glistened in the sun, harnesses burnished to blinding radiance gleamed and glinted on horses groomed to look hardly less magnificent than their riders. Even the Queen, though simply dressed, wore diamonds in her bonnet. London had never seen such a display and the crowds went wild.

Queen Victoria's children and grandchildren had married into every royal house, every dukedom and principality of united Germany, from the mighty ruling house of Prussia downwards, and a host of Hohenzollerns and Hesses, Hohenlohes, Coburgs and Battenbergs, with her British blood mingling with Albert's German blood in their veins, were living proof of the ties of friendship and brotherhood that bound the two nations. On this most glorious day of Queen Victoria's glorious reign it was unthinkable that those ties could ever be severed.

The Queen's eldest daughter, the Crown Princess of Prussia, drove with the Queen in her carriage. In front rode her husband the Crown Prince and some distance behind, in strict order of precedence, rode the future Kaiser, their twenty-eight-year-old son, Prince William of Prussia. Prince William was vexed. He was not pleased with his position and while he was a little too much in awe of his grandmother the Queen-Empress to complain to her directly, he let it be known that in his opinion a Prince of Prussia, although at present only the son of a Crown Prince, deserved to rank before princes and even kings of duskier complexions who ruled over less eminent domains.

William was always an awkward presence in the royal circle and the Queen, when confiding her dread of entertaining 'the royal mob' to her daughter, had made no bones about the fact that she would prefer him not to come: 'I did not intend asking Willie for the Jubilee, first because Fritz and you come, and secondly because . . . we shall be awfully squeezed at Buckingham Palace . . . and I fear he may show his dislikes and be disagreeable. . . . I think Germany would understand his remaining in the country when you are away on account of the Emperor at his age.'

The Prince of Wales, on the other hand, was quick to appreciate that the age of the German Emperor was very much to the point. He was over ninety and he was frail. Inevitably he must die soon. His heir, Prince William's father, was dying too. This fifty-six-year-old Crown Prince (who was, in the words of his mother-in-law, Queen Victoria, 'noble and liberal-minded') had been waiting thirty years for the throne and with it the opportunity of bringing much-needed reform to autocratic government in Germany. Now he was mortally ill with cancer of the throat and, like it or not, the chances were that Prince William would soon be Kaiser. Ever the diplomat, the Prince of Wales talked his mother round to the view that for the sake of future relations with the German Empire it would be unwise to offend its Emperor-to-be. The Queen relented, but held the Prince of Wales responsible for 'keeping William sweet'.*

---

* The old Emperor died the following March just before his ninety-first birthday, and in June of that year (1888), after his father's sad reign of a hundred days, William became His Imperial Majesty Kaiser Wilhelm II.

12

'Keeping William sweet' was a matter of keeping him occupied and, if possible, flattered. The Jubilee programme fortunately included almost enough parades, reviews and tattoos to satisfy even Prince William's passion for military pageantry, and they would keep him busy for some of the time; for the rest of it, his uncle shrewdly guessed that nothing would keep his nephew sweeter than arranging for him to inspect a few regiments. From the future Kaiser's point of view the highlight of this agreeable programme was the day he spent with the Prince of Wales' own regiment, the 10th Royal Hussars, at their barracks in Hounslow. The visit was a huge success and the future Kaiser came back full of it. In particular, he was impressed by a delightful novelty the like of which he had never seen before. It was the regimental machine-gun and it was the private property of the Commanding Officer, Colonel Liddell. The previous year he had purchased it out of his own pocket from the Nordenfeld Company and had it mounted on a light two-wheeled carriage that a horse could gallop into action. Prince William had been charmed. He inspected the regiment, rode with it in the morning, lunched in the officers' mess, rode out again in the afternoon and, as a grand finale to the day, even joined the Hussars in a wild cavalry charge. The Prince made a flattering speech before his departure and soon after he returned to Berlin sent his signed photograph, in the uniform of his own Hussars of the Guard, in appreciation of the splendid day he had spent at Hounslow. That was not all. Four invitations were dispatched by his grandfather, the German Emperor. They were addressed to the Colonels of the four regiments the Prince had inspected during his visit and invited them to spend three weeks as the Emperor's guests in Berlin.

When the four Colonels travelled to Berlin, they took with them a wonderful present by command of the Prince of Wales. It was a machine-gun, just like the one William had admired at Hounslow, complete with an identical 'galloping carriage'. It capped William's pleasure in what were to be three blissful weeks. With his parents wintering in Italy in the vain hope of improving his father's health there was no one in Berlin to cramp his style. Under the rheumily indulgent eye of his aged grandfather, who found this young turkey-cock more to his taste than his gentler, liberal-minded heir, William could strut and show off to his heart's content.

Like his uncle, the Prince of Wales, Colonel-in-Chief of the 10th Royal Hussars, Prince William had a cavalry regiment of his own. They were the Hussars of the Guard, the crack Garde Husarien Regiment, and he instantly whisked the two Cavalry Colonels off to Potsdam to enjoy the hospitality of his regiment for the duration of their visit. It gave him huge pleasure to show off his troops, to ride with the British officers as his horsemen drilled, to escort them on inspections of the stables and the barracks, to ride out with them on manoeuvres, to fight mock battles, to entertain his visitors at formal dinners in the mess and at the Palace, to present them to his grandfather the Emperor. At all these events the new machine-gun had pride of place, trundling through manoeuvres on its carriage driven by Corporal Hustler of the British Hussars, or standing on the parade ground with a cluster of Prussian Hussars listening respectfully as Hustler, or occasionally Prince William himself, explained its finer points. Hustler was to stay on for several weeks to instruct a nucleus of Prussian troopers in its use. But, by the time of the last grand review on the eve of the British Colonels' departure, when the machine-gun bowled past the Emperor and his guests at the head of the regiment, quite a number of the men had already mastered the art of firing it, and Prince William was well pleased.

But already in 1887 the clumsy hand-cranked Nordenfeld was obsolescent. Before long it was replaced by the quick-firing fully automatic Maxim and the new Kaiser brought even the 'old donkeys' of his General Staff round to the view that a few more machine-guns in other regiments would not come amiss. By the turn of the century the German Army possessed more of them than any other in Europe – and once they had taken up the idea they made the most of it. Machine-gunners were highly trained, there were inter-regimental competitions to keep them on their toes and, as a further incentive, prizes for the winners, who each received a watch inscribed with the Kaiser's name and presented as his personal gift. The standard of firing was high and every German machine-gunner was a marksman.

In the British military establishment there were men who grasped the significance of this new weapon – the great Sir Garnet Wolseley as early as 1885, General Allenby as late as 1910, and in the years between there were others who urged and lobbied, pleading the case for machine-guns. A few were grudgingly purchased, but the High Command remained unconvinced.

To these professional minds – trained long ago to study ancient battles, schooled in the belief that the classic practices of war were inviolable – the idea of the machine-gun as a short-range weapon for the use of infantry did not come easily, for the infantry were still expected to charge cheering with the bayonet, clearing the way for the cavalry to dash gloriously past and take up the real battle. The General Staff were cavalrymen almost to a man, and if they bothered to think of machine-guns at all they thought of them as highly over-rated weapons. Even when they blazed into action in the Russo-Japanese war, even when Sir Ian Hamilton as British Military Observer reported on their devastating effect, the British General Staff remained unmoved.

14

The assessment of supplies of equipment and ammunition likely to be required in any foreseeable circumstances had been fixed in 1901 at the end of the Boer War. In 1904 it was reviewed and confirmed. That year Vickers supplied the British Government with ten machine-guns for the use of the British Army. By 1914 when Great Britain went to war with Germany, this standard annual order had not been increased. By now the *Infantry Training Manual* devoted just a dozen pages to machine-guns, and the *Cavalry Manual* still enjoined that 'it must be accepted as a principle that the rifle, effective as it is, cannot replace the effect produced by the speed of the horse, the magnetism of the charge, and the terror of cold steel'.

This principle was still held sacred by the army commanders when the British Army went to war with Germany in 1914. By the turn of the year when the bogged-down armies were standing face to face across a dreary stretch of Flanders mud, they had seen no particular reason to change their view. Winter was always a time of breathing space. Soon the spring would come, the armies would be on the move and the cavalry would come into its own.

Chapter 2

There were new graves in the burgeoning cemeteries behind the lines where they had buried the missing of the autumn battles whose bodies had been recovered during the Christmas truce. During January, as the sad parcels of belongings reached home and the last sparks of hope were extinguished, a series of poignant letters appeared in *The Times*, under the heading 'Swords of Fallen Officers'. Officers who had gone with the Regular Army to France had gone equipped and accoutred almost as elaborately as their military ancestors had gone to Waterloo, and there was much heart-burning when their effects reached home and their swords were found to be missing. It was hard for mourning relatives to accept the most likely explanation that these prized possessions had been pilfered en route and the tone of the letters from bereaved fathers left little doubt of their firm belief that their sons had died charging the enemy trenches, sword in hand:

My late son's sword may have been picked up and forwarded to someone else. It is a Claymore, No. 106,954, made by S. J. Pillin, and has embossed on it the battles of the regiment and 'DCM from DFM'.

•

I am a fellow-sufferer, having received the effects of my late son, admirably packed but minus the sword, to my great sorrow and disappointment.

•

I would like to endorse the letter from 'The Father of an Officer Killed in Action'. The pain caused to relatives by non-receipt of a lost one's sword is great.

•

To any private soldier, English or Indian, who may have found the sword and returns it to me through his officer, I will send a present of £5.

•

We are all giving of our best and dearest for our country, and the least we ask for is that those precious relics should be restored to us.

●

The colonel of my son's regiment kindly wrote and told me it had been sent to the depot some days before, but I can hear nothing of it, so I suppose it has gone with the others, but where? There does not seem much demand for swords at the Front; if there was, I would not grudge it.

●

It is suggested to me that when my son was struck down he may have been carrying the sword in his hand, and it fell into the wet trench and sank – not improbable.

But it was spades not swords that were wanted in the trenches. And manpower. And muscle-power. And hard grinding labour. The brunt of the work fell on the Royal Engineers.

The 5th Field Company, Royal Engineers, had been out since the beginning. They had dug the Army out of Mons, they had dug trenches for the infantry throughout the long retreat, blown bridges over rivers in full view of the Germans when the last of the infantry had safely crossed, and, when the tide had turned, they built pontoon bridges across the same rivers to take the infantry back, first to the Marne, then to the Aisne, and finally along the long road north as they raced the Germans back to Flanders. The engineers had toiled again at Ypres, digging trenches for reserves and supports and, always under shellfire, throwing up entanglements of barbed wire to protect them. And when the Germans attacked and the troops were pushed back, as the front line gave way, and battalions were decimated, the engineers had gone into the trenches and helped the thinning ranks of infantrymen to beat the Germans off. The 5th Field Company had been in at the kill when the last wavering line faltered and briefly gave way, when the Prussian Guard streamed through and every man was needed to try to stop them. In retrospect it had been their moment of glory, for the sappers had flung down their spades, picked up their rifles, formed up with the ragged remnants of the infantry, fixed bayonets and charged into Nonnebosschen Wood to drive the Germans back. It had not seemed very glorious at the time – but it had saved the day.

Now the infantry were returning the favour by turning out working parties night after night to labour alongside the sappers constructing defences. Working in the flooded marshland to the south of Armentieres where the River Lys, swollen by incessant rain, wound across the waterlogged plain and overflowed to mingle with a thousand streams and ditches, even the battle-hardened veterans who had been out since the start of the war agreed that this

17

was the worst yet. It was a waterscape rather than a landscape. Trenches filled up with water as fast as they were dug and the culverts and dams they made to divert it merely channelled the flood to another trench in another part of the line. They built bridges across watery trenches that collapsed into the stream with the next rainstorm in a cascade of mud as the sodden banks that supported them gave way. They took levels, drew up plans, set up pumps, but still the water rose. The trenches were knee deep in it. The men who manned them, soaking, shivering, plastered from head to foot with mud, reflected bitterly that it was not so much the Germans as the weather that was the adversary.

Lt. C. Tennant, 1/4 Bn., Seaforth Highlanders (TF), Dehra Dun Brig., Meerut Div.

Water is the great and pressing problem at present, the weather has been almost unprecedently wet and the whole countryside is soaked in mud and like a sponge. Owing to its flatness it is generally impossible to drain the trenches and in many cases those now being held were only taken in the first instance as a temporary stopping place in the attack. A battalion would dig itself in at night – perhaps improve an ordinary water ditch with firing recesses – in the expectation of getting on a bit further the next day. The change and chance of war has caused these positions to become more or less permanent and every day of rain has made them more and more unpleasant until now the chief question is how to keep the men more or less out of the water. In a summer campaign it would not matter, but when a hard frost sets in at night, and we have had several (luckily short) spells, frostbite sets in at once and the man is done for so far as his feet and legs are concerned. Our own British troops have stood it wonderfully well but some of the Indian regiments have suffered pretty severely in this respect. As you may well imagine some of these trenches that have been held for a long time are in a pretty grizzly state.

In the fight against the elements there was little energy to spare for fighting the enemy and, in any event, in such conditions attack was all but impossible. It was obvious that the Germans were in the same plight and on frosty nights, when the clouds cleared and the light from a hazy moon rippled on lagoons of ice and water spread across the morass, when the machine-guns fell silent and only the occasional smack of a bullet cracked in the frosty air, the Tommies could hear the splosh and thud of boots and spades in front and see the Germans silhouetted fifty yards away engaged on the same

18

dreary task, bailing and digging, and doubtless cursing, just as they were themselves.

Day after day throughout the cheerless month of January, Corporal Alex Letyford recorded a terse catalogue of miseries in the pocket diary he kept wrapped in oilcloth to protect it from the wet.

Cpl. A. Letyford, 5th Field Coy., Royal Engineers.

1.1.15 At 6 p.m. (in dark) go to the trenches making culvert and dams. Trenches knee-deep in water. We work until 3 a.m.

2.1.15 6 p.m. off to the trenches. I take some men and make dam to prevent water coming from German trench and return at 5 a.m.

3.1.15 Parade at 6 a.m. March to trenches. We dig communication trenches and are fired at the whole time. Work until 6 p.m.

4.1.15 During the day we build stables near billet for our horses. At 6 p.m. we go to the lines and trace out redoubts. Rather risky work as we are only eighty yards from the Germans who are doing a lot of sniping from their lines. We also make a bridge across our front line. Four feet of water in this part of the trench line. Return to billets about midnight.

5.1.15 Spend the morning trying to dry out our clothes. We are all covered in mud from head to foot. At 6 p.m. I go with Captain Reed to the trenches and fix six pumps. Wading about in water to our waists until 2 a.m.

6.1.15 We go up at 8.45 a.m. and improve trenches for reserves.

7.1.15 Go out at 3 a.m. and make a bridge in the line of trenches about a hundred and fifty yards from Fritz. Return at daylight and rest remainder of day.

8.1.15 Again at work on the reserve trenches. At nightfall I remain with eight men and make the bridge again, it having been knocked into the stream. It rains nearly all the time and the enemy torment us with their Very lights and sniping. Return at 9 p.m.

9.1.15 Parade at 8 a.m. I take four men to dig communication trench. Work until 5 p.m. and reach billet at 6.30 p.m. The trenches are now waist-deep in water, part of section returned early, being soaked through, breast-high. My party had to run the gauntlet on returning across the open in preference to coming through the trenches!

The journey was slow and hazardous, because it was impossible to accomplish it silently. The sound of splashing and sliding, the clink of tools, an inadvertent cry as a bridge collapsed or someone plunged into a water hole, were a sure sign that men were on the move, and the enemy flares would hiss into the sky, bathing the lines in incandescent light that showed up every tree, every twig, every man who was caught in its glare. Then machine-guns would spit from their hidden posts and snipers take aim at such targets as they could see before the rocket burned out and plopped, sizzling, back to the sodden earth. It lasted seconds but, to the men standing motionless for fear of being spotted, it seemed an eternity.

Even quite far behind the front line it could be as dangerous by day, for the 'line' was hardly a line at all, but a succession of outpost trenches cut off by the water-filled dykes that crisscrossed the flooded land. Under the cover of mist and darkness it was easy enough for snipers to slip through and find hideouts convenient for taking pot-shots at unsuspecting or unwary soldiers. In the lines themselves, marooned all day in barrels begged from breweries to provide reasonably dry standing, sentries kept a sharp look-out, but snipers were devious and some, more courageous and ingenious, were skilled in the arts of disguise and deceit. Stories of spies and snipers abounded – and some of them were true.

Lt. R. Macleod, V Bty., RHA, 2 Indian Cavalry Div.

We had a little spy hunt the other day. We shifted our billet to a new place. On going into the loft we discovered a little observation place very neatly made in the roof. There was a place where two tiles could be easily slid up, giving a very good view over part of the country. (The rest of the tiles being cemented down.) There was also a supply of provisions concealed up there. At the back of the house there is a large barn, apparently filled with straw. On examining the place it was found that the straw was hollow, and contained a small room with a passage leading to it through which a man could crawl. There was also another passage leading out to a trap-door very cunningly concealed under a heap of straw above a cow stall. No spy has been near the place since. We only discovered the presence of the room and passage by walking on top of the straw, and finding it giving way under our feet.

20

Major Elliot-Hill had an even more thrilling encounter.

I was riding along a quiet country road when I heard a report from a rifle. I dismounted, tied my horse to a tree, and had a good look round. Presently I saw what at home we would call a farm labourer working at a turnip clamp in a field. Keeping out of his sight I rode back to the farm house where we are billeted and borrowed some not-very-savoury farm labourer's clothes. I went back on foot and started walking up the ploughed field towards him as if I was very interested in the straightness of the furrow, but I was actually more interested in my automatic revolver. When I got within reach of the fellow I tackled him. It was a fairly good struggle but I overpowered him and managed to march him back and hand him over to the authorities. They were not much inclined to take me seriously at first, but they locked him up anyway. They soon changed their tune when we went back to the turnip clamp and found a rifle and fifty rounds of ammunition hidden in it.

News of such morale-boosting exploits was made much of in letters home, and although the stories were mostly based on hearsay, much embellished, and usually owed more to the writer's imagination than to hard facts, they were frequently passed on to the local newspapers in which 'Letters from the Front' were a popular feature. A favourite story, current in the early days of January, told of a heroic Tommy who went into a barn to fetch straw and bumped into two fully armed Germans. Keeping a cool head he pointed the only weapon he had – a pair of wire-cutters – and shouted 'Hands up!' The Germans obligingly dropped their rifles, raised their hands, and meekly allowed themselves to be taken prisoner. The public loved such stories. If British brawn was not yet sufficient to defeat the Germans the assurance that British brain could be depended on to dupe them was the next best thing.

The best of all stories of duping the Germans had just reached Britain from Australia and caused much gloating and excitement. It concerned the tramp steamer *Southport*, out of Cardiff – but a long time out, because the *Southport* belonged to the raggle-taggle fleet of tramp steamers that sailed the oceans of the world, picking up contracts and cargoes where they could. It was sometimes years before such a ship returned to its home port and, unless there were children to keep her at home, the captain's wife, as often as not, accompanied her husband on the voyage. Some, like Captain Clopet's wife, had circled the globe several times. Early in 1914 Mrs Clopet had crossed the Atlantic and had passed two pleasurable weeks in New York while the *Southport* unloaded and took on a cargo of American machinery. She had endured the gales of the south Atlantic, rounded the Cape of Good Hope to Durban, supervised the loading of provisions and shopped personally for the fresh fruit and other dainties that would ensure Captain Clopet's domestic comfort on the long onward haul to Australia. It was May before they got there, and early June before the *Southport* sailed on to New Zealand with a cargo of coal. Having plied her leisurely way from Auckland to Wellington and on to Dunedin she turned north for Ocean Island in the Pacific to load phosphates bound for Rotterdam. At Ocean Island orders were changed and the *Southport* was to sail on to Nauru to take on a cargo of phosphates for Stettin, but bad weather, and congestion in the harbour, made the task impossible and Captain Clopet was forced to return to Ocean Island and then sail on an inter-island hop to the Gilberts, picking up small workaday cargoes as he went to fill the time.

The *Southport* was not the most ramshackle of freighters – she was only fourteen years old, she was more than three thousand tons, had a crew of twenty-three and her single deck was lit by electricity, which was a welcome improvement on the lanterns and candles of Captain Clopet's youth, but she had no modern refinement so sophisticated as radio. For all she knew of the outside world as she hopped between the atolls of the Pacific Ocean, she might as well have been sailing on the moon. The only thing for it, decided Captain Clopet, was to make for Kusaie in the Caroline Islands where the fast mail-ship *Germania* called every two months. She would be arriving any day now. She might well be bringing him new orders as she had done in the past, and at least she would be able to replenish their scanty supplies to tide them over until orders arrived. The *Southport* anchored in the bay at Kusaie on 4 August. That day, twelve thousand miles away, Britain declared war on Germany.

Fresh water was obtainable and that was a relief, but there was no food on the island, for a cyclone early in the year had destroyed the crops, killed cattle and pigs, and the natives were subsisting on roots and coconuts. There was nothing to be done but to cut the ship's rations and wait, day after day, for the arrival of the overdue *Germania*. The *Germania* never came. But, on 4 September, the *Geier* did. She was a German warship, and she had every right to be there because the Caroline Islands were German, and although German rule was limited to collecting from King Sigrah an annual tax of six marks per head of his subjects, the German flag flew in the tiny township outside the mission church. This circumstance was of no concern to the crew of the *Southport* who had not heard a hint of the international tensions that had bubbled to the surface in Europe during their absence, nor did they have the faintest idea that Britain

22

was at war with Germany. The crew crowded on deck, cheering the *Geier* as she sailed into the anchorage. The captain and his wife were ashore and it was Chief Officer Dodd who ordered the ship's ensign to be dipped and who waited on deck, beaming in welcome, as a cutter from the battleship approached. He attached no significance to the fact that the *Geier*'s guns were trained on his vessel, and he was only slightly surprised to see that the boarding party was armed to the teeth and looking far from affable. The German officer saluted correctly then, speaking English, but without so much as wishing him a good day, dropped the bombshell.

Chief Officer C. Dodd, SS Southport.

He said, 'Of course you know that war has broken out between Britain and Germany?' I said, 'No.' The German said, 'Oh yes. We have been fighting about a month.' I said, in as casual a manner as I could muster, 'I suppose we are prisoners of war then.' The officer made no reply. He said he preferred to wait until the captain arrived on board. But he was perfectly polite. There was nothing domineering about him, but he posted the armed guard around the ship, and they looked none too friendly. Then he wanted to know what provisions we had but when I told them of what straits we were in for tucker ourselves, they didn't bother. Still, they went over the ship with a fine toothcomb and spent a long time in the engine room, fiddling about with things, which the chief engineer didn't like at all. We were all dumbfounded. Then the captain came back and had a long talk with the officer.

Capt. A. Clopet, SS Southport.

The upshot was that our flag was hauled down and the German flag hoisted for half an hour while the Germans read me the proclamation that my ship had been seized in the name of the Kaiser. They left the guard on board and stayed in the bay for two days. Next day another ship sailed in. It was the German merchant steamer *Tsintau* of Bremen and they sent the steamer alongside the *Southport* and took a great deal of our coal. Soon afterwards an officer in command of marines on the *Geier* came on board with another party whose job was to put the engines out of commission to prevent us putting to sea. They removed nearly all the eccentrics and other parts of the machinery and took away the main stop valve.

The officer of the *Geier* told me that he would not sink us but that we would have to remain at Kusaie until after the war was over. I pointed out to him that we were short of provisions and that the natives, on account of the cyclone, were also short of food. The officer replied that there were coconuts on the island and he said, very sneeringly, 'The people of Paris once lived on rats.' This infuriated me. I was born of French parents, although I am a naturalised British subject, and my parents were in Paris during the siege by the Germans in 1870 and they told me enough of that terrible time to make me fully appreciate the reference to rats! I told him in no uncertain terms that my men would be starved out, and I could not be responsible for what starving men might do on the island. That gave him second thoughts, he wrote out there and then an order to King Sigrah to secure supplies of meat and so on. It said that whatever he gave me would be paid for after the war.

Not content with taking our coal the Germans on the steamer *Tsintau* took some of our kerosene oil and everything else they thought would be of use to them, although the officer on the *Geier* had obviously told them not to touch our provisions, because we had none to spare. The *Geier* also took off our boatswain and two of our firemen, who were all German and they went willingly enough, and one of our Norwegian sailors – a man with a good appetite! – left the ship voluntarily to go on the German steamer *Tsintau*. This, of course, left us short-handed but, as the German officer pointed out, since we were not going anywhere, it hardly mattered. 'The fate of your ship will be decided by a prize court,' he said, and then they sailed off in a great hurry it seemed. But his last words to me were that they would be back in a fortnight and expected to find us there when they returned.

Mrs Clopet, who had been confined to her cabin on her husband's orders for most of the last two days, was now released and accompanied Captain Clopet when he went ashore to visit King Sigrah to negotiate food supplies. He took the German order with him – for all the good it was likely to do! While the Captain was gone and the deck crew passed the time by fishing over the side in the hope of a tasty catch to augment the meagre rations, the engine-room crew got down to more serious business. Chief Engineer Harold Cox was no novice when it came to engines. He had served on ships far older than the *Southport*, and had repaired and nursed and cosseted engines that were on their last legs. Given a hammer, a hacksaw, a soldering iron, a length of tow, even a ball of string, he could repair anything and make a faltering engine sing sweetly enough to bring a ship to port. He was determined not to be defeated now and Harris and Griffiths, the 2nd and 3rd engineers, were of the same mind. While the Captain was ashore they investigated the damage.

The Captain was not in a happy frame of mind. The negotiations had been long and wearisome and the outcome only partly satisfactory. Faced with the German order, King Sigrah had been obliged, with great reluctance, to hand over supplies, but he could give no more than he had got, and all he had (and could ill spare at that) was coconuts and the roots of trees which, ground up and mixed with coconut milk, were all that his own people had to eat. Equally reluctantly the captain agreed. It was Hobson's choice. He arranged to send a party of men ashore the following day to supervise the loading of the native long-boats that would ferry this miserable provender to his ship, and returned gloomily on board. But his gloom was quickly dispelled by his chief engineer who met him with the happy news that the damage to the engines was not so great as they had feared. He believed it might just be possible to manufacture some of the missing parts and to contrive makeshift parts to replace some others, and thought that, with a little time and patience, they could get the *Southport* on the move.

It took more than time and patience. It took working round the clock, monumental effort, plus liberal applications of ingenuity and elbow grease. And it took ten days, with the thud and clanging of hammers echoing across the bay, the rasp of saws on metal, while lookouts fearfully scanned the horizon for signs of the *Geier*'s return. On the afternoon of the tenth day they managed to get up steam – the fact that it was a poor head of steam was a good deal less important than the fact that the engines would take the ship ahead, but not astern. The Captain thought he could manage. It would have been worse after all, he remarked, if it had been the other way round.

It was a feat even to get her to face outwards from the anchorage but that night in the darkness, with all her own lights extinguished, the *Southport* limped out to sea. It took them twelve days to reach Brisbane, sailing via the Solomon Islands – partly in German hands, but they had to take the risk – and they sailed at quarter power, with the crew on quarter rations. It was better than subsisting on roots.

The welcome they received in Australia almost made up for the hazards and privations of the voyage. The people of Brisbane showered them with gifts. Food was brought aboard – sacks of rice, dozens of loaves, butter, sugar and flour by the stone, ducks and chickens, whole sides of beef. In their elation the crew were, with difficulty, restrained from dumping the loathsome roots and coconuts into the harbour and persuaded to unload them in the conventional way. They were fêted and petted and treated in

25

waterside bars, and they recounted their adventure again and again and again. It took a long time to repair the engines, and a long time for the story to filter through to Great Britain. By the time it did get there in early January the *Southport* was on her way again, taking up the voyage that had been so rudely interrupted four months earlier, sailing towards the Pacific to Ocean Island to pick up her cargo of phosphates and head for Rotterdam. Mrs Clopet, who had refused the offer of a fast passage home from Australia, was still on board.*

The saga of the *Southport* enlivened many a breakfast table and similar, though less spectacular, stories of scoring off the Germans, contained in letters home were passed round, and gloated over at work parties the length and breadth of Britain, where news from the front was exchanged and gossiped over as the ladies of Britain did their bit for the war effort, rolling bandages, knitting socks, hemming khaki handkerchiefs and sewing nightshirts and flannel bedjackets for the wounded in hospital. Many such ladies made use of the pin-cushions that had enjoyed a large sale at Christmas. They were soft dolls, rather than conventional pin-cushions, shaped, unflatteringly, to represent the Kaiser, and there was certain satisfaction to be gained in giving the arch-enemy a sharp jab from time to time in the course of their work.

But anti-German feeling, innocent enough when it was confined to sticking the occasional pin or needle into the Kaiser's effigy, had a more sinister side, and one tragedy, hastily hushed up, had caused the authorities some discomfiture. It happened at Henham in Suffolk. People had been edgy ever since Scarborough had been shelled by German warships in December, and stories of spies signalling from beaches were rife on the east coast. An over-officious Chief Constable, whose suspicions were based entirely on malicious gossip, ordered an innocent schoolmaster and his wife to move, not merely out of his area, but out of Suffolk entirely. The Smiths had one son, a brilliant boy who had studied languages in France, and, more ominously, in Germany long before the war. 'Where was this son now?' the local busy-bodies asked themselves, and the answer came pat. 'Why, in Germany of course!' The rumour was embroidered as it spread. Young Smith was known for a fact to have taken German nationality and enlisted in the German Navy. Young Smith was Captain of a warship, a U-boat Commander, the

---

* The *Southport* continued her leisurely progress and survived to do her bit for the war effort. She was requisitioned by the government in May 1917 and ran the gauntlet of German U-boats to bring wheat and foodstuffs from the USA and Canada to beleaguered Britain. She continued in government service until 1919, was sold to Greece, where she was renamed *Tithis* in 1923, and broken up in Italy in 1932.

officer in charge of a fleet of fast armoured motor boats – it hardly mattered which. The Smiths lived not far from the coast, lights had been seen flashing on the beach and the only likely explanation was that this elderly couple had been signalling to their German son lurking in an enemy vessel off the coast and doubtless preparing to blow them all to smithereens. The Smiths were ostracised. Wherever they went there were wagging tongues and knowing nods, and finally the Chief Constable, acting far beyond his powers under the Defence of the Realm Act, issued his ultimatum. The following day Mrs Smith was found hanging from a beam in her kitchen. Her son, who had been teaching languages in Guatemala, was even now on his way home to join up.

When the story came out, there were some who felt ashamed, but it was easier for a bad conscience to take refuge in disbelief and righteous indignation. The slightest hint or taint of Germanism was enough to ruin the most illustrious reputation. Names were being anglicised wholesale, and an innocent misprint brought wrath down on the head of the social editor of *The Times* who was forced to grovel to the furious father of one bride-to-be and to make amends by inserting a notice free of charge among the announcements of 'Forthcoming Marriages':

Mr O. C. Hawkins and Miss Holman

An engagement is announced between Osmond Crutchley, eldest son of Mr and Mrs Thomas A. Hawkins, Glenthorne, Chealyn Hay, and Marie, eldest daughter of Mr and Mrs Ernest Holman (NOT Hofman, as stated through a clerical error in a previous announcement).
22 Gloucester Square, Hyde Park, W.

Real indignation was reserved for the judge who had the temerity to find in favour of a plaintiff accused of trading with the enemy. This unfortunate man was an American who must have regretted, in the present circumstances, that he had ever taken out British citizenship. He was manager of the London branch of an American firm which also had a branch in Frankfurt, managed by his brother. There was a large sum of money owing and, at his brother's request, the London manager had found a means of sending it to Germany via Holland. He was caught in the act and had spent six uncomfortable weeks in prison before the case came up. The judge took into account some extenuating circumstances and set him free. The extenuating circumstances, ironic to say the least, were that the Frankfurt manager had also been jailed for pro-British activities. But the irony was lost on an indignant British public who clung to

27

the axiom that there was no smoke without fire.

The Trading with the Enemy Act was a godsend to some British firms who held large stocks of German goods – as yet unpaid for – which, in the present climate of anti-German feeling, they had little prospect of selling. The matter of mouth organs was a case in point, and it was a tricky one. Mouth organs were in demand. There was a dearth of mouth organs at the front and the relatives of soldiers were scouring the shops to obtain them. They were cheap, they were small enough to be easily packed in parcels, and nothing was more likely to cheer the troops in the monotony of life in the trenches. But, mouth organs were almost exclusively of German manufacture and it would never do to boost enemy trade – even retrospectively! – by buying pre-war stocks of goods made in Germany, let alone be so crassly unpatriotic as to send them to the boys who were being shot at by the mouth organ makers themselves. Wholesalers scoured every possible neutral source of supply and eventually found enough mouth organs in Holland to fill the gap until a Birmingham firm was persuaded to take up the cause and meet the demand. This boycott of German goods, like the taboo against buying toys of German manufacture at Christmas, was not based entirely on blind prejudice, for it was widely known that the bombs which the Germans were hurling at British trenches had been made in many cases in toy factories, and that the fuses were manufactured in Bavaria by makers of clocks and watches. Cuckoo clocks were removed from walls on which they had sometimes hung for decades and anxiously scrutinised to make sure that they had originated in neutral Switzerland and not in hateful Germany, and the once-proud owners of expensive Bechstein or Steinway pianos were torn between reluctantly closing the lids for the duration of the war or trumping the enemy by abandoning Mozart and Handel in favour of British patriotic songs thumped out endlessly on their German keys.

Patriotic songs were all the rage at home and some starry-eyed idealists were a little disappointed that they were not equally popular with the troops. Some newspapers took up the cause. 'Teach them the songs of Agincourt,' suggested one enthusiastic patriot without, however, specifying what particular songs these were or where they were to be found. 'English folk songs,' suggested another, 'would be more appropriate, to be sung with gusto!' The strains of 'Greensleeves' were seldom heard on the lips of the Tommies, and if the kind of songs they sang as they endlessly route-marched round the country bore little resemblance to those such innocent civilians would have preferred to hear, it only reinforced their missionary zeal. It seldom struck them that the bawdy dirges that cheered the troops on the long training marches in all probability faithfully echoed the sentiments of the songs that had cheered foot-soldiers on the road to Agincourt centuries before.

Music was in the air. Sheet music poured from the printing presses, 'Tipperary', the hit of the previous summer which had found favour with the troops, had gone into umpteen editions, and 'Sister Susie's Sewing Shirts for Soldiers', the felicitous show-stopper of a Christmas pantomime, was threatening to overtake it in popularity. And music was all the rage in ten thousand towns and villages where several hundred thousand soldiers were in training camps from Inverness to Salisbury Plain. The fact that they were not quite soldiers yet was neither here nor there. They must be entertained, and entertained they were. Local talent was rounded up by entertainment committees as forceful as any press-gang, and in many places there were concerts once a week. Sometimes the programmes were a little above the heads of the troops. Cellists droned, violinists scraped, sopranos warbled, elocutionists spouted, basses boomed, but there was often a good feed to accompany the entertainment, kind ladies distributed cigarettes, and the troops took the bad with the good. The highlight of one concert in Jedburgh was a rendering by the local doctor's wife of 'My Little Grey Home in the West'. It had a recognisable tune, it came as a welcome change after a programme of cultural music and heroic poems, and the troops encored it three times. They were the 1/7th Battalion of the Argyll and Sutherland Highlanders and most of them had recently left some little grey home in the west of Scotland at Lord Kitchener's behest.

The tune, if not precisely catchy, was easy to play on a mouth organ and it was equally popular with soldiers holding the miserable outposts of the British line in Flanders. But the words were not appropriate, and in Flanders they had adopted their own version:

> I've a little wet home in a trench,
> Where the rainstorms continually drench,
> There's a dead cow close by
> With her feet towards the sky
> And she gives off a horrible stench.
>
> Underneath, in the place of a floor,
> There's a mass of wet mud and some straw,
> But with shells dropping there,
> There's no place to compare
> With my little wet home in the trench.

The dead cow was a realistic touch. In the one-time farmyards close up to the lines there were dead cows all over the place and not all of

them had been victims of enemy action. Private Crossingham of the
Grenadier Guards was still trying to live down the episode when he
had accidentally shot one while on sentry duty. His protestations
that the cow had failed to reply to his challenge did him no good at
all. His fame had spread throughout the Battalion and, wherever he
went, even complete strangers were apt to taunt him as he passed
with a verse of doggerel composed by a wag he would have dearly
liked to get his hands on.

> Last night at the setting of the sun,
> I shot a farmer's cow.
> I thought she was a German Hun –
> I beg her pardon now!

Despite the miseries of wet and cold and the dangers of their
day-to-day existence, the troops in Flanders had not lost their sense
of humour. The biggest laugh was raised in the leaking ruined
cottage that served as the officers' mess of the 1st Worcestershires
behind the line at Festubert. Buckling on his equipment, staring out
into the pelting rain as he prepared to take another hapless
working-party up the line, Lieutenant Roberts remarked thoughtfully, 'I went to see my Great Aunt Agnes while I was on leave. She
said to me, "Tell me, are there any picture palaces where you and
your friends can go when you get back from the trenches in the
evening?" ' And, for a time, 'off to the picture palace' became a
popular synonym for 'going out with a working-party' until the joke
wore thin.

But if the majority of civilians were isolated from the full realities
of war they were not entirely unaware of conditions at the front and
of the physical hardships the men were undergoing. Knitting
became a patriotic duty and mountains of parcels and bales of
'comforts' arrived in France by the boatload.

*CQMS, R.A., S. McFie, 1/10th (Scottish) Bn. (TF), King's
(Liverpool Regt.).*

Yesterday I drew a lot of cigarettes presented by somebody,
and a pipe per man sent by the Glasgow tramway-men, as well
as some peppermint sweets from the manufacturers. Today
again there was a supply of cigarettes, tobacco and matches as
well as a lot of tinned salmon given by the Government of
British Columbia. We have also had socks from Princess Mary,
gloves from the Archduke Michael, razors from a man in
Sheffield, etc. Also socks, body belts, cap-comforters, combs –
surely no army has ever before been so well looked after.

Pullovers, socks and mufflers were welcome enough, but what the Army needed most, and needed urgently, was sandbags. They had given up trying to dig trenches across the worst of the morass; now they were building breastworks instead, filling sandbags with earth – more often mud! – and building high protective walls with crude shanties behind for shelter and redoubts in front for protection. They needed sandbags by the thousand, by the million, and appeals went out to churches and work-groups to supply them.

Sewing sandbags was hard labour, and working with rough canvas not unlike sewing mailbags, but the women of Britain set to and turned them out by the million. Before Easter the Surrey village of Newdigate alone had sent off 1,665. But while such industry was laudable and the country was enthusiastically doing its bit, it was doing little to speed the progress of the war and it seemed to some who were in a position to take an informed, objective view that the war was proceeding in a way that was too dilatory by half and that there was an unforgivable complacency in high places.

One was Sir Maurice Hankey, Secretary to the Committee of Imperial Defence, the other was David Lloyd George, Chancellor of the Exchequer. By coincidence, and without consultation, the two men had spent the days between Christmas and New Year putting their misgivings on paper. On New Year's Day both memoranda were distributed to members of the Cabinet. In their assessment of the situation they were surprisingly similar. Lloyd George, who had recently visited France, dwelt on the apparently leisurely approach to the war and begged that the War Cabinet might meet regularly every few days rather than at intervals of two weeks or longer. He deplored the lack of policy, and criticised the generals who seemed to him to be so flummoxed by the Germans' decision to dig in that they could think of no apparent means to break the deadlock.

In Sir Maurice Hankey's memorandum he turned his mind to practical means by which the deadlock *could* be broken. Victories were needed to encourage the people at home. How were they to be achieved?

He incorporated a list of ideas. Numbers of large, heavy rollers propelled by motor engines to roll down the barbed wire by sheer weight; bullet-proof shields or armour; smoke balls to be thrown by the troops towards the enemy's trenches to screen their advance; rockets throwing a rope with a grapnel attached to grip the barbed wire 'which can then be hauled in by the troops in the trench from which the rocket is thrown'; spring catapults, or special pumping apparatus to throw oil or petrol into the enemy's trenches. He had privately gone so far as to have some prototypes made and tested.

But the results of Hankey's experiments had not found favour

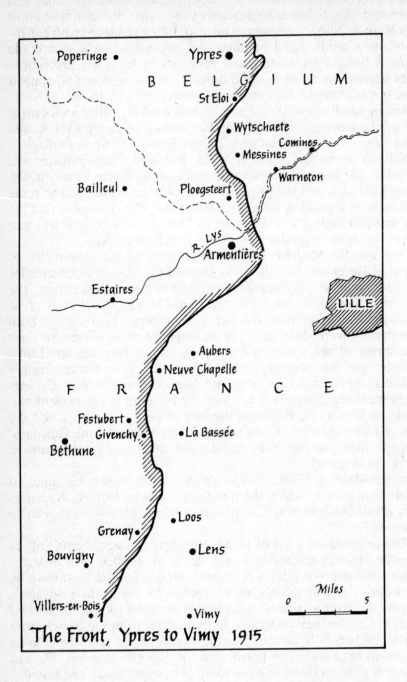

The Front, Ypres to Vimy 1915

with either the military commanders in the field or the military hierarchy at the War Office, and so far as the War Office was concerned they already had their hands full with the mammoth task of organising three hundred thousand volunteers and supervising the million and one details that would lick them into shape and turn an amorphous mass of civilians into something that approximated to an army. They were already being inundated with bright ideas from would-be inventors, but there was simply no time to give them serious consideration and, as Hankey sadly remarked, 'The bright ideas are not new, and the new ideas are not bright.' The commanders in the field had other things on their minds than the invention of unconventional new weapons. They would have been more than happy to have a sufficient supply of the old ones, and Sir John French was already confiding his disquietude to his diary:

23.1.15 There is more delay in sending these new 9.2 guns. It is said to be caused by the Christmas holidays which the men in the factories insisted on having! It appears they get very high wages and are accordingly independent! I am also somewhat disappointed in the promised supply of ammunition.

The troops themselves displayed some ingenuity in supplying the deficiency. Dumps were scoured for empty jam tins and the engineers, who had passed most of the night improving the defences in the line, spent hours during the day filling them with old nails, tamped down with gun cotton to make primitive bombs. The bright sparks of the 15th Field Company Royal Engineers of the 24th Brigade even manufactured a trench mortar. It was only a length of drainpipe soldered up at one end with a touch-hole bored above it and was ignited with a match and gunpowder. But it fired the jam-tin bombs a good distance towards the Germans and, despite a few unfortunate accidents in the course of its erratic performance, it cheered the troops wonderfully.

A battalion of the Cambridgeshires in Plugstreet Wood* acquired an even more primitive weapon – a replica of an ancient catapult, designed by a professor of history at Cambridge University. He was an acquaintance of their Commanding Officer to whom he eagerly canvassed the merits of the catapult in screeds of sketches and instructions. It could throw bombs or even boulders at a push, and it could throw them a long distance. The Romans, he added, had used an identical weapon with satisfactory results to batter down the wooden gates of rebellious cities,

---

* The unpronounceable Flemish name 'Ploegsteert' had quickly become 'Plugstreet' to the Tommies.

and he was convinced that it could be used with equal success against the German trenches. It seemed worth a try. Working parties were organised, first to scrounge suitable timber, then to construct the catapult itself. It took several days and two more nights of strenuous work to build an emplacement and dig the monster in. It was more than seven feet long, and being constructed of hefty beams filched from shell-torn buildings, it weighed several hundredweight. But the Tommies were less practised than the Romans in the art of catapulting, and any missiles they managed to fire as often as not fell harmlessly to the ground or, worse, back on their own heads. The experiment was abandoned, the Colonel tore up the design in disgust and the Tommies chopped up the Roman weapon for firewood.

But although it was impractical, the idea of the catapult as a weapon of siege warfare was not entirely inappropriate, but many months would pass and many men would die before people would understand that siege warfare was exactly what the Army was engaged in. Their faith was still vested in the cavalry, now dismounted and valiantly, if not uncomplainingly, suffering the indignities of working-parties as they waited for the breakthrough that would send them charging through the German lines, scattering all before them as they rode non-stop to Berlin.

But not everyone shared such sanguine expectations. Lloyd George had been disquieted by his recent visit to France where he had observed the effects of the impasse at first hand in both British and French sectors, and a meeting with General Joffre had given him food for thought. Joffre had been adamant that the Germans would never succeed in breaking his lines, not even if they outnumbered the French by two or even three to one, and he reminded Lloyd George that even the thinly held line round Ypres had not given way in the face of the German onslaught of recent weeks. Lloyd George took the point but, although he kept his opinion to himself, he reflected soberly that the opposite was equally true and that the allies had just as little chance of breaching the line held by the Germans.

Lt. C. Tennant.

The war in the western area has reached a pretty disgusting phase. The opposing trenches are very close to each other – in some cases not more than twenty yards apart and there we sit facing each other and killing each other by every possible means. Attacks on each other's trenches are as often as not absolutely useless. If we rush a German trench we lose an enormous lot of men in doing it and those who do get there are promptly blown up by mines left there while the enemy retires to another line of trenches a few yards to the rear from which he makes the hard-won trench untenable. Moreover, the advance, unless successful over a very long section of the line, is no use as it merely creates a dangerous salient liable to enfilade by artillery and machine-guns from the flanks. Such a position has been created just in front of us where we were from the 19th to the 24th December and our own 1st Battalion had a terrible time. The trench they were holding was a very bad one (the water up to the men's waists in places) and owing to the retiral of some Indian troops on their flank, they were left practically 'in air'. But they held on for nine days until they were relieved by another Battalion who – I'm sorry to have to say it – after two hours evacuated the trench as utterly untenable!

The hostile trenches are now in many places so close together that the war is almost reverting to continuous hand-to-hand fighting. I was told of an incident the other day when a double company (nominally two hundred men) of the HLI – after a long burst of fire repelling an attack – had only nineteen rifles working at the end of it.

But for the majority of the troops, dodging bullets and exploding shells as they shivered in the mud flats, there was nothing for it but to dig and bail, to bail and dig, slogging through the mud in the dark as they laboured to build defences.

Cpl. A. Letyford.

1.2.15 to *5.2.15* Go up to the trenches each night making continuous breastworks. Have a hundred infantry working with us each night. We lose a few of the working-party killed by snipers. Came unexpectedly on a German listening post last night whilst searching in front of breastworks.

6.2.15 I go with second relief at 9.30 p.m. Continue breast-works and meet no. 4 section, so that now the work is completed from Festubert to Givenchy. We have thus advanced about six hundred yards without fighting.

This achievement was duly noticed and reported triumphantly in the war news columns of the press. It doubtless cheered up the people at home but, to the troops, one muddy position was very much like another and, as the casualties mounted and men sank wounded and dying into the swamp, as the hospitals filled up with men sick with fever and crippled with rotting feet, a six-hundred-yard advance was nothing to write home about or even anything like sufficient compensation for their efforts.

The population of Great Britain, with a century of Empire building behind them, was accustomed to regarding even large-scale wars as distant affairs that could safely be left in the hands of professional soldiers. But now their own boys were in khaki, milling around in camps and training grounds as they prepared to go to the front, and Sir Maurice Hankey was not alone in realising that when the new armies took the field people at home would take a keener and more personal interest in the conduct of the war as they followed the fortunes of their nearest and dearest. This new army, the battering ram that was to smash the German defences, must be properly used. The new recruits were of high calibre, volunteers motivated by a desire to do something positive for their country, unlike most peacetime recruits. Few of the men who joined the ranks of the Regular Army prior to the war were drawn to enlist for love of a uniform or the seductive call of fife and drum, but they were professionals to a man, so highly trained and skilled in the arts of soldiering that they were second to none. They could fire fifteen rounds a minute, and fifteen aimed rounds at that, and six months earlier they had fired their rifles to such effect at Mons that the Germans still genuinely believed that they had been met by machine-guns. But there were precious few Regulars left, and the thinned-out ranks of the old army could never have held out since November had it not been for the Territorials who, strictly speaking, had no business to be there at all.

The Territorial Army was a mere six years old, formed in 1908 from a nucleus of the old County Volunteers and augmented by young civilians who enjoyed a bit of drill and military training of an evening or a weekend, and who looked forward all year to a free holiday under canvas at the annual camp. They called them the Saturday afternoon soldiers, they were intended for 'home service only' and, in the event of an emergency, their role was to guard the country in the absence of the standing army which might be fighting abroad. That idea had been abandoned many months ago. The Territorial Force, as its name implied, could not be sent to serve overseas, but it could be asked to volunteer – and it had volunteered almost to a man. Now the Territorial battalions of a dozen different regiments were serving in France with the remnants of the Regulars and their reserves, and although some of the early arrivals had seen action before the end of the autumn battles, most of the Territorials were champing at the bit as they waited to get on with the war.

36

Lt. C. Tennant.

The poor old Territorials have little to do except keep themselves in training and a good deal of trench digging and fatigue work. And so though we have now been within sound of the guns for nearly two months we have seen nothing of the actual fighting except digging a trench before Christmas. It is a little maddening as, however inefficient we may be as compared with our own Regulars of the original expeditionary force, we are every bit as good as the second and third line troops that Germany is now bringing up: at least we should like an opportunity of seeing how we compare! However Kitchener and French know their own job best and I am very certain that all in good time we shall get our chance. In fact our Divisional General when inspecting us two days ago as good as promised that we should get a move on after this rest.

Getting a move on was what everyone wanted to do. But the most urgent need, before they could even think of it, was for more men.

Chapter 3

The Territorial Force had been on the move for months and where they ended up depended on the luck of the draw. Some people in the higher echelons of the War Office would have preferred to keep the Territorials at home to act as a foundation on which new armies of raw volunteers could be built. But it was not to be thought of while there were trained Regulars, fit and ready to fight, now kicking their heels in foreign stations round the Empire. The first priority was to bring them home again and to send the Territorials to protect Great Britain's interests in their place. So the grand reshuffle began, troopships set sail, and the Terriers were packed off to Ireland, to Egypt, to South Africa. More than thirty battalions embarked on the long voyage to India but the optimists who had expected something resembling a holiday cruise were doomed to disappointment. The ships were packed and the accommodation was basic, particularly in vessels that had been hastily requisitioned and refitted. There were up to four 'sittings' for meals which the men ate catch-as-catch-can, squatting wherever they could find a space on a crowded deck or narrow passageway. But deck space was hard to find, for at any hour of the day there was hardly a corner that was not occupied by some sweating platoon drilling or practising musketry or signalling at the insistence of an NCO or officer who was anxious to make the most of the allotted time before the precious space must be surrendered to the next platoon on the rota. Throughout the voyage, from dawn to nightfall, the men were kept hard at it in a rigorous programme of lectures and physical training to keep them alert and fit for duty at the other end. At least there were no route-marches.

The same could not be said for the Territorials in Malta where the luck of the draw had taken Arthur Agius and his battalion as part of the 1st London Infantry Brigade which was detailed to carry out garrison duties while training at the same time for the war. They were fitter than most of the raw recruits now endlessly tramping the roads of Great Britain, footsore in civilian shoes, and the two companies that marched every four days by the coast road to the ninth milestone rather enjoyed the exercise in the mild Mediterranean climate. Their duties were important but hardly onerous, for they amounted to little more than manning the coastline in the unlikely event of an enemy attack, and keeping a sharp look-out for submarines that might threaten the sealanes and the ships of the Royal Navy.

The Londons camped under canvas and they looked forward to their four-day stints away from barracks, much as they had looked forward in peacetime to getting away from the office to the summer camp. Like life in the office, the routine at Imtarfa Barracks kept every nose to the grindstone. There were drills and lectures all day long to keep the men busy and bring the Battalion up to scratch for active service. The Londons pounded the barrack square, drilling by platoons, by companies and eventually joining up with sister battalions to drill and manoeuvre as a brigade. There were extra sessions, mostly early in the morning, for the specialist sections, the signallers, the machine-gunners, the scouts – even the band was detailed for stretcher-bearing practice from 6 to 7.30 every morning except Sundays. It was hardest of all on the officers who not only had to supervise the training of the men but had to be trained themselves in the finer arts of war. Officers' lectures were held literally at crack of dawn in the two hours before the battalion day officially began with breakfast at 8 and first parade at 8.30. There were more lectures for the officers at 5.30 p.m. while the men were enjoying tea at the end of an arduous day, and later, after dinner in the mess, the officers were obliged to write up notes and clarify their own thoughts on such matters as 'Esprit de Corps', 'March Discipline', 'Personal Hygiene', 'The Origin of the War' and 'Malta' so that they in turn could deliver lectures on these topics to their men. 'Personal Hygiene' was the source of deep embarrassment to younger officers afflicted with shyness. It was true that the lecture gave useful advice on the inadvisability of eating unwashed fruit and drinking unboiled goats' milk or water, but its real purpose was to warn adventurous soldiers of the dire consequences likely to befall any who succumbed to the wiles of prostitutes plying their trade in the back streets of Valletta. Some officers delivered this information in a manner so obscure and so ambiguous that some youthful innocents were led to believe that all feminine society was to be avoided, from the vendors who sold grapes and apples outside the barracks to the refined lady volunteers who doled out books, writing paper and cups of tea at the Floriana Soldiers' Club.

The Commanding Officer, Colonel Howells, was ultimately responsible for the whole complicated training programme and no one in the Battalion worked harder. His most exacting task – and it seemed at times to be never ending – was to instil the idea that the

Battalion was now on a war footing. The men were no longer 'Saturday Afternoon Soldiers' and the happy-go-lucky attitude, the spirit of friendly bonhomie that had bonded the battalion in peacetime simply would not do in time of war. It was a difficult message to get across. For all their enthusiasm and goodwill the Territorials were independent spirits and despite their rapidly improving skills as soldiers their attitudes were still those of civilians. The Army frowned on 'conduct prejudicial to good order and discipline' and it was the Colonel's duty to put aside his personal feelings and crack down hard.

In every Territorial battalion it was a time-honoured custom after drills, and sometimes before them, for its members to repair to the local pub for a beer with their mates, and frequently with an officer. Pubs in the vicinity of a drill-hall did good trade on Wednesdays and Saturdays – the Lilliput in Bermondsey had even given its name to the local Territorial battalion, the 12th East Surreys, universally known as 'The Lilliput Lancers'. It was too much to expect that such men would take kindly to the army regulation that sergeants might not walk out in the company of corporals when off-duty, and that corporals and lance-corporals might not walk out with privates. Colonel Howells was not the only Commanding Officer of a Territorial battalion who was having difficulty in getting this message across to his men.

But if the order was flagrantly breached, it was not because the men were insubordinate, but because they were genuinely unable to see the sense of it and could not believe that the Colonel was serious. 'But sir,' blurted one aggrieved soldier, marched into Captain Agius's company orderly room on the heinous charge of strolling out of barracks with his brother, 'we sleep in the same *bed* at home!' He was perhaps the sixth man who had been hauled up on the same charge at company office that morning, and Agius was weary. 'Seven days confined to barracks,' he rapped. But he saw the point. It so happened that his own brother, Richard, was an officer in the battalion.

Many had been workmates in civvy street. There was almost a whole platoon from Brooks' Piano Manufacturers, a contingent from Holt's Bank, a happy band of dustmen and roadsweepers from Westminster Cleansing Department, and groups of friends or colleagues from a score of sports clubs and business concerns were scattered through the battalion. In a Territorial battalion rank was something to be observed within the bounds of the drill-hall and parade-ground and in peacetime a Terrier would no more have thought of walking ten paces behind a workmate who happened to be a sergeant than of saluting the lady at the breakfast table who happened to be his mother. All ranks enjoyed the social life, mixing in free-and-easy comradeship at the 'family hops' held once a month in the drill-hall, and at the children's parties and smoking concerts at Christmas. How could they be expected to take kindly to being split up now according to the number of stripes a friend might sport on his arm?

In peacetime this camaraderie had been the strength of the Battalion – but it could be a fatal weakness on the battlefield where authority and discipline might tip the balance between failure and success. The real headache, when the Colonel clamped down, was that the NCOs, who were the backbone of the Battalion, resigned en masse rather than give in. Day after day Battalion Orders contained lists of NCOs – many recently promoted – followed by the ominous words 'reverted to private at his own request'. In the face of the Colonel's displeasure the officers detailed to supply replacements from the ranks were forced to resort to stratagems ranging from flattery to near-bribery, in their efforts to persuade men to accept a stripe. Most refused. Colonel Howells, now thoroughly exasperated and well aware that the efficiency of his Battalion could be at stake, ordered that henceforth any man 'desiring to relinquish rank' must first be interviewed by himself. But that was as far as he could insist. The men knew their rights and if persuasion didn't work there was nothing the Colonel could do but acquiesce.

The matter of rights was the subject of eager discussion in any battalion of Territorials. Most companies in a battalion of Regular soldiers would have a barrack-room lawyer, but in a battalion composed mainly of men drawn from the business and professional world every man knew his rights and saw no reason why he should not avail himself of the privilege he had enjoyed as a private individual of exercising his own judgement. Grievances were not many (the walking-out order had been the most resented) but the Colonel was appalled to receive a curt notice from Brigade. It had travelled down the chain of command from the frosty eminence of Whitehall itself and it conveyed the unwelcome news that a number of his men had complained of minor grievances direct to the War Office. This was not only a breach of military etiquette but was in breach of King's Regulations.

Wearily the Colonel ordered a special parade of each company for the purpose of hearing paragraph 439 of King's Regulations read aloud by the Company Commander. He also ordered each officer to confirm in writing that this had been done and that he, personally, was satisfied that the men understood the position. In accordance with the Army Act, complaints must be made through their captain; if the complaint concerned their captain they might approach their commanding officer, and if it concerned the commanding officer they might complain, in the last resort, to the General during the annual inspection. The Londons were not unfamiliar with King's Regulations, but in their eagerness to inform themselves of a soldier's rights, they had tended to skim over the sections that set out his obligations.

But by November the Battalion had settled down and, on the whole, Colonel Howells was not displeased with his men. They worked hard, they were cheerful and enthusiastic and they were beginning to understand the necessity of obeying the rules imposed on them by the Army. There were almost sufficient NCOs, some of the originals had even come back to the fold, and the slap-happy chumminess of the early months was giving way to pride in *esprit de corps*.

Off duty the Londons amused themselves as best they could. Football enthusiasts organised scratch games on the barrack-square, there were swimming parties and at weekends there were passes to Valletta, where the entertainment ranged from quiet afternoons at the Floriana Soldiers' Home to visits to the cinema, an occasional concert at the theatre, and the rougher attractions of bars and cafés frequently followed by a good deal of horse play on the way home. Monday after Monday a procession of soldiers who were marched into the orderly room on a charge of appearing capless on parade explained with an air of injured innocence that the cap had been 'knocked off on the last train from Valletta'. Their reward was invariably seven days CB as well as having to stump up for a replacement.

Although Colonel Howells was required to turn these amateur soldiers into professionals, and although he went by the book and doled out punishments as severely as any regimental martinet, he had a sneaking sympathy for the men who had difficulty in adapting to the new regime. Notwithstanding the harsher discipline demanded by the circumstances, the Battalion was still very much a family. Five babies had been born into the Battalion since their fathers had been in Malta and, just as they had in peacetime, these happy events had appeared in Battalion Routine Orders. Officially it was noted that the new arrivals had 'been taken on strength of the Married Establishment' and the babies' heads had been joyously wetted in celebratory pints. But there had been sadness too, and the Battalion mourned two stillborn infants and one young mother who had died in childbirth. It had grieved the Colonel that he had not been able to grant compassionate leave. The distance was too great, and there was neither time nor shipping space to spare. The Royal Navy was stretched to the limit, and the troopships that were passing the shores of Malta every day were crammed to capacity with Regulars on their way to the war. The Londons followed their progress and, watching through binoculars from the guard post at milestone 9, wondered when their own turn would come.

It had come just after Christmas, and the last days of the old year had bustled with preparation, with packing up, with kit inspections, and a grand parade at which the London Infantry Brigade had been inspected by the Governor of Malta who, now that the brigade was on the point of departure, showered them with praise and compliments. Relations between the soldiers and the Maltese had not always been so cordial. The soldiers had been convinced that everyone was out to do them down, from the hawkers of fruit who haunted the barracks to certain strait-laced Maltese ladies who had caused them to be reprimanded for bathing in the nude. Now, all was forgiven and all Valletta turned out to cheer the London Brigade on its way as it mustered on the Custom House Quay. The Grand Harbour was full of ships, dressed overall in honour of the Brigade, and, riding at anchor among them, the *Neuralia* and the *Avon* waited to take them on board.

Capt. A. J. Agius, MC, 3rd (City of London) Bn., London Regt., Royal Fusiliers (TF).

We embarked on the SS *Avon* in two parties. I was in the second lot. The *Avon* was in mid-harbour and we were taken out in a tug with a lighter on each side and got on board about 12.40 p.m. The *Avon* was a big ship, about eleven thousand tons, and very comfortable, though the saloon had been spoilt by being divided in two by wooden boarding. The officers feed on the port side and the men in the centre and to starboard. The Smoking Room is the Sergeants' Mess. Several of the men have 1st Class two-berth cabins temporarily made into four-berth. The 4th Battalion embarked after we did and we sailed about 3.30 p.m. – the *Neuralia* sailing just before us.

What an impressive scene it was! The Barraccas were crowded with people cheering and waving. All the boats in the harbour hooted. The crew of the French battleship *France* lined up on deck and cheered us as we went by, and there were two bands, one on the Lower Barracca and one on Fort St Elmo. They played 'Auld Lang Syne' as we sailed out of the harbour – and we sang, and they cheered, and the ships' sirens kept on hooting until we cleared the harbour and turned out to sea. What a send-off!

On 6 January they disembarked at Marseilles to a welcome that almost matched the send-off from Malta, and marched through streets lined with cheering crowds to entrain for the long journey north. It took a good half hour to squeeze the Battalion and its baggage on to the long train. There were two first-class coaches for the officers to share, three to a compartment, but the men came off worse. They looked in dismay at what they took to be cattle trucks – the windowless military rolling-stock designed by the practical French to be equally suitable for the transportation of supplies, ammunition, eight horses or forty men. Even with clean straw on the floor, with warm blankets and kit-bags propped up as makeshift armchairs, this accommodation was a bleak come-down from the soft berths of the *Avon*. But they were not cast down, and the humorists of the Battalion were soon busily embellishing the wide sliding doors with slogans they considered more suitable than the stencilled notice '*40 hommes. 8 chevaux*' favoured by the military authorities. *Don't breathe on the windows* ran a close second in popularity to *Non-stop train to Berlin*. Teas were dished out and a generous issue of cheese, bread, jam and bully beef, with the warning that these rations were to last over the two-day journey.

The officers, who were allowed to leave the train in batches in search of dinner, did rather better. Arthur Agius went off with Harry Pulman, Cyril Crichton and Harold Moore to the Hotel Bristol and dined sumptuously on hors d'oeuvre, bouillabaisse, and jambon aux epinards, washed down with Asti Spumante. Then, with appetites whetted by the delicious French food, they skipped cheese and dessert in favour of dashing to the shops in search of something better than army rations to sustain them on the way north.

Capt. A. J. Agius, MC.

We got back to the station at 8 and the train finally left at 8.50 p.m. We settled down very comfortably. We arranged three bunks round the compartment, Edouard and Giles on the seats on either side and I in the middle. I put a packing case in the gap and a long cushion over. In the daytime we put the seats back and we each have a corner. The fourth is our larder – on the rack the bread, cheese, bully beef, jam and water, on the seat bottles of beer and wine, sardines, butter, chocolate and biscuits and, hanging near the window, a very moist chicken and some rather warm cheese. The drawback was that, being a non-corridor coach, there were no conveniences! We washed in our canvas buckets, shaved in water in my mess tin (warmed by being put on the hot radiator) and did our teeth in our cups. We had brekker of bread, cheese, sardines and beer.

It is a most extraordinary journey! Everyone turns out to cheer us and the men are most cheerful. We reached Mâcon at

1 p.m. and stopped for forty-five minutes, so we dashed into the buffet and had a meal – two helpings of steaming omelette, vin ordinaire and café au lait. For the rest of the afternoon we had a triumphal progress. Every time the train stops there's a fearful jolt as it is braked like a goods train. Everywhere we stopped for a few minutes we had a royal reception – vociferous cheers and the men had presents of wine, fruit and cigarettes showered on them, and the donors would insist on signing their autographs in their paybooks. It was rather a wonderful sight.

At 7.15 p.m. we made a stop of nearly an hour at a place called Les Laumes Alesia where we took the opportunity of getting a meal in the local inn, very simple, but very good – soup, peas, omelette and beef as four separate courses – 2 francs 50, washed down by vin ordinaire. The men had hot coffee, over which I presided as orderly officer. We left Les Laumes about ten past eight. It was a *very* cold night, and when they changed engines they forgot to attach the heating pipe! I slept like a rock, however.

Trundling through the January night the thousand men in the wagons behind the first-class coaches that contained their officers did not notice the loss of heating since they had not enjoyed this amenity in the first place, but everyone, from the Colonel downwards, noticed that it was getting colder and colder as the train travelled north. When they woke, cramped and chilled, they were well north of Paris. There was snow on the ground and the train had swung on to the Calais line that would take them on up to Flanders. And if the freezing winter weather was hard to take after the balmy Mediterranean, if the home leave they had been hoping for was clearly not to be, it was at least some consolation that they were on their way to the real war.

In fact, they were on their way to Etaples, and when they reached there it was not much to their liking. Even in far-off Malta the troops had heard of the legendary Flanders mud, but they had hardly expected to meet it, ankle deep, as they stepped in pitch darkness on to the station platform. The passage of two battalions and numerous teams of horses coming in from the country roads had churned the snow into a mess of slush and slime and the Battalion, weighed down by heavy kit-bags, slipped and slithered and swore as they struggled to keep their footing and form up by companies in the street outside. It took the best part of an hour before they could set off in the teeth of a hail-storm to march to the camp and, although it was only three-quarters of a mile away, it was almost another hour before they reached it.

In due course the camp at Etaples would be one of the largest

45

base camps in France, but in January of 1915 it was in its infancy, a makeshift affair scarcely large enough to hold the three battalions of the London Infantry Brigade whose unhappy lot it was to inhabit the sagging tents pitched across open country beyond the sand dunes on a desolate coast. Behind them a belt of trees and the slopes of more fertile farmland gave a certain amount of shelter, but the tent lines had been badly placed with the openings towards the sea and all night they flapped and ballooned in the icy wind that whistled through every fold and crevice. With fifteen men jammed into tents meant for twelve nobody got much sleep.

Next morning, their labours cheered on by frequent showers of sleet, all three battalions spent three hours striking camp and re-positioning the lines and re-pitching the tents to face inland while company cooks, working under difficulties to keep the fires going, contrived to brew endless supplies of tea and cook hot dinners at the same time. At the end of the day the camp was much improved, and it was all to the good for, as everyone knew, they were likely to be there for some time.

There was much to be done, and it could not be done in a day. The most welcome event was the issue of warm clothing, mufflers, cardigans, caps with ear-flaps to let down against the cold, serge uniforms to replace thin khaki drill and, best of all, warm overcoats. Packs were issued to replace the peacetime kit-bags which were packed with superfluous kit and sent home. The officers' tin trunks went too, and with them the blue patrol dress worn as mess-kit in the palmy days in Malta, the Sam Browne belts of shining leather, and the swords which were now deemed by the Army to be surplus to the requirements of trench warfare. The officers were issued with revolvers instead (they had to pay for them) and from now on were to carry haversacks and wear practical webbing straps and equipment like the men. Personal kits were issued in dribs and drabs – but the battalion equipment was another matter. Day after day they waited for the transport – the general service wagons to carry rations and forage, the water-carts, the cooks' wagons, the tool-carts, the carts for small-arms ammunition, and the horses that would pull them all.

Without its wheels the Battalion was useless. Without weapons it could do nothing at all, and the few rifles that had been required for garrison duties had been left behind in Malta. It was all very well for the Colonel to receive instructions that 'training will continue' but lacking weapons, in the absence of a parade ground or even of fields that were firm underfoot, with no dry huts or marquees where the men could be assembled, and since it only stopped raining in order to snow, it was difficult to keep the men occupied let alone train them. There was nothing for it but to route-march them round the country roads hour after dreary hour, to go through the motions of practising 'company attacks' with sticks to represent rifles, flags to represent the enemy, and string to represent the trenches which, for lack of spades and shovels, they were unable to practise digging in the sodden ground. As often as possible, as a welcome diversion, the men were marched to Etaples in mud-spattered batches to wash in hot water at the fishmarket or at the gasworks. Every day brought fresh rumours and expectations but it was more than two weeks before the tools and the transport finally arrived. Last of all came the rifles.

The machine-guns arrived too, to the profound relief of Arthur Agius who had been endeavouring to train a machine-gun section without the benefit of guns to train them on. He had managed to commandeer a freezing leaky shed where he expounded as much of the theory as was possible with the aid of diagrams, but when they had gone over it a hundred times in wearisome detail and inspiration had long run out, he was reduced to sending the men off to 'practise reconnoitring'. By the alacrity with which they set off Agius had a shrewd suspicion that their intention was to reconnoitre some warm farmhouse kitchen where eggs and hot coffee could be obtained, and judiciously refrained from questioning them too closely on their return.

But now that the weapons had arrived there was plenty to do and his command was a machine-gun section in more than name. They had 4 guns, 4 wagons, 12 horses and 36 men. At last, the Battalion was ready and on 25 January they received orders to move the following day.

Capt. A. J. Agius.

We got up at 3.30. It was a beautiful night and just on freezing point. I struggled with a cold-water shave of which I felt rather proud considering the hour and the dark and the temperature. We finally paraded at 6.30 – there had been a lot to do in the meantime and it was not very easy to get it all done in the dark.

We got clear after having had quite a decent meal of bread and butter, cold bacon and tea. We reached the station about 7. The train was due to start at 8.25, though by the time we had packed in all our transport (some thirteen wagons and fifty-eight horses) it was about 8.50 before we got off. We officers were eight in a compartment and we entrained just in time, for we had only been in the train a few minutes when it began to sleet and finally turned into snow. The carriage was pretty cold.

It was pretty slow going as our speed wasn't by any means

47

fast and we made several short stops. The distance to GHQ at St Omer is only thirty or forty kilometres, but we didn't arrive until 3 p.m. We detrained and paraded in the station which took some time. We moved off at last and marched out to our billets at Tatinghem. It is about three miles out of St Omer, which is GHQ. All the roads are paved, but as they are paved with cobblestones marching is rather uncomfortable. We reached billets after about an hour's march feeling a bit tired. We were wearing equipment for the first time, including a large pack in which the men carry their worldly belongings. It feels a bit heavy on one's back. The village looks a bit desolate and a lot of the inhabitants have gone. We were a very long time getting settled and getting the men into billets. Most of them are in barns and very comfortable. My sleeping quarters are only fairly comfortable – the place is, alas, the quartermaster's stores. I have a large room which, when I arrived, contained little furniture but I managed to scrounge a washing cabinet, a chair and a table. There is a bed of sorts.

We are not yet assigned to any brigade or division and are Army Troops. We are apparently to continue training until the advance, which people say is to be in April.

But even 'a bed of sorts' and a roof overhead was a welcome improvement on the tented camp at Etaples where, since their camp beds had been sent back as 'superfluous kit', the officers' sleeping bags had rested on hard tent boards. And the men, deep-bedded on straw in barns that were dry if not warm, had no complaints. The wind was blowing from the east and from time to time they could hear a gentle thudding in the distance. It was the sound of the guns at the front, now barely thirty miles away. The men nudged each other, listened, and were thrilled. But, as they burrowed into nests of warm rustling straw, pulling rough blankets over limbs wearied by the long march, and settled themselves contentedly to sleep, not many soldiers were inclined to give much serious thought to the future.

Chapter 4

Three miles away at his headquarters at St Omer, the Commander-in-Chief, Sir John French, in consultation with his staff officers, was giving the future very serious thought indeed. There was a great deal to think about and the Commander-in-Chief was a frustrated man. He wanted to get on with the war and it seemed to him that people and events were conspiring against him. He was under pressure from two directions – by General Joffre, in command of the French armies, who required his help in mounting an offensive of his own, and by the War Council in London who appeared to Sir John French to be thwarting his every move and had, moreover, failed to keep the promises of supplying the men and munitions on which his plans depended. Part of the trouble lay in the fact that the War Council was not convinced that French's plans were sound or even if the war on the western front should be carried on in more than token terms. They were staggered by the casualties, disillusioned by the lack of any significant gains, and dismayed above all by the total failure of attacks undertaken in conjunction with the French in mid-December. They had seriously considered withdrawing the British Expeditionary Force completely, leaving a strong reserve near the French coast in case of emergency, and sending the bulk of the troops with the new armies, as they became available, to strike at the enemy in some other place where their efforts might possibly bring the war to a speedier end. Opinion was divided as to where that place should be, but the politicians were united in the view that the deadlock on the western front was absolute and that the chances of either French or British breaking through the German lines were small.

The Germans had been digging in and, even in winter conditions, with the advantage of higher, drier, ground they had managed to construct a formidable network of defences protected by burgeoning thickets of barbed wire that seemed to British observers to be expanding to forests as the winter days passed. Since the lines were continuous and there were no flanks to be turned there was nothing for it but to sit it out or even, in the last resort, to get out.

The French who were defending their own soil, and were in no position to get out, would not have taken kindly to this idea, even if anyone had had the courage to suggest it. But neither would Sir John French. Far from London and the deliberations of the War Council the British and French Commanders had been hatching plans of their own. General Joffre wished to launch an offensive that would strike at the Germans' Achilles heel – those long and straggling lines of supply that led from the heart of France across the conquered territories to the heart of Germany.

The line held by the Germans ran from the Alps across the Vosges mountains in Alsace, into Lorraine, across Champagne, swinging north through Picardy and Flanders to meet the North Sea on the coast of Belgium. It was a long, long line to keep supplied with troops and materials and behind it in places the roads and rail lines essential to German transport and communications were few and far between. Joffre's plan was to breach them in a series of piecemeal attacks on either side of the huge salient where the German line bulged deep into France. He would strike north from Reims, north from Verdun, and east from Arras, and he would keep up the pressure, gradually squeezing, always tightening his grip. It might take months, but the prize would be worth it, for if the French could slice across the salient cutting German communications as they went, the enemy would be deprived of his lifeline to the Fatherland and might well be obliged to retire and eventually give up the line.

This plan attracted Sir John French, for it fitted in well with a plan of his own. It was an idea which had met with only half-hearted approval from the War Council, which had already turned down his plan to attack with the Belgian Army up the Belgian coast along the minuscule strip of unflooded land that lay behind the sand dunes and the sea. That project had been mooted and encouraged by Winston Churchill who, as First Lord of the Admiralty, had promised naval support – but now Churchill had other fish to fry and the War Council, as a whole, had a shoal of them. Since the end of October when Turkey had entered the war on the side of the Germans, the options had increased, and it seemed that every minister had his own pet theory as to how the war should be waged. Fisher, the First Sea Lord, favoured an attack on Germany from the Baltic; Lloyd George, Chancellor of the Exchequer, favoured striking at Austria by attacking from the Adriatic coast; Lord Kitchener proposed launching an attack on the Turks from the coast of Palestine. But it was Winston Churchill who came up with the one irresistible idea. To seize the Dardanelles, to capture Constantinople and thus, at one blow, open up the Black Sea highway to the Russians, relieve the pressure on Russia's army on the eastern front, and – best of all – force open Germany's back door by way of the Danube. Not least of the attractions was that all this would be achieved by the Royal Navy who would merely be required to enter the straits and bombard the forts that protected them. Casualties would be few, and only a small force of men need be landed in the wake of the navy to secure the forts and raise the British flag. The plan had been drawn up by Admiral Carden, Commander of the Mediterranean fleet, at Winston Churchill's request, and it was more than irresistible. All things being equal, it was fool-proof.

It was put forward at a meeting of the War Council on 13 January – the very meeting at which Sir John French's plan to attempt an advance up the Belgian coast had been turned down. French had travelled to London to attend it and even he had reacted with lukewarm (and temporary) enthusiasm to Winston Churchill's plan, presented with all the force of Churchillian passion and eloquence. But he was not prepared to regard an expedition to the Dardanelles as a substitute for action on the western front, and so far as that was concerned he had ideas of his own.

Now that the plan for a coastal attack had been finally scotched Sir John French began to consider alternative plans of attack – for attack he must, if only to raise the morale of the troops 'after their trying and enervating experiences of winter in the trenches'. On 8 February he put his view cogently in a memorandum to the War Council. Nowhere had the experience of the troops been more 'trying and enervating' than in the flat lands at the end of the British line where the flooded River Lys and its tributaries seeped across the marsh. It was here the Commander-in-Chief proposed to mount an offensive. He did not accept the view that it was impossible to break through the German line, and he said so forcibly. An attack at Neuve Chapelle held out several tantalising possibilities. Not least was the chance – and French and his staff believed it to be a certainty – of capturing the Aubers Ridge that ran along the eastern edge of the valley. It was not much of a ridge, a mere four miles long, with a maximum elevation of fourteen metres at most, but it was high enough to give the Germans who held it a considerable advantage. If the offensive were launched as soon as conditions improved and the foul weather began to abate, the troops could be on top of the ridge in two days at most, and out of the slough forever.

Sir John French was encouraged in this idea by General Joffre, who informed him that, as part of his own ambitious project to breach the German salient, he proposed to launch his 10th Army to force the German front and capture the high ground to the east between Arras a few miles to the south and la Bassée where the French sector joined the British. If the British could attack simultaneously on the French left, the possibilities were boundless. Since this was exactly what Sir John French had in mind, he was delighted. But Joffre made one condition. If his offensive was to succeed, if he were to be in a position to press home his advantage, he must have more men. He had two whole Army Corps north of the British line at Ypres and he was insistent that Sir John French should now replace them with British troops and extend his own line to the north.

The Commander-in-Chief was not averse to this idea – indeed he had first proposed it himself when he had mooted his Belgian coast offensive in order to place the British Army adjacent to the Belgians. The fact was that, with a conglomeration of units and nationalities still holding the line in positions where the early battles had left them, the allied line in the north was something of a hotch-potch creating unnecessary difficulties of liaison and command. The teeming roads behind it were a constantly shifting kaleidoscope of uniforms and nationalities, for there were always troops on the move. French Cuirassiers on horseback, their once-gleaming breastplates dulled and rusting in the all-pervading damp; turbanned Indian troops hunched against the cold; foot-slogging poilus, mud-spattered in their horizon blue; Tommies, muffled up in khaki, leather jerkins and a variety of woollen caps, mufflers and mittens that would have reduced a peacetime sergeant-major to apoplexy. And in the extreme north, Belgian troops on their way to the marshes where the allied line trickled into flooded land, and where the line itself was little more than a straggle of duckboard causeways and island outposts in the morass.*

For the British to sidestep and join up with the Belgians, for the piecemeal French corps, at present between them, to go south and join up with the main French Army would obviously make sense. But, since the proposal had been put forward, things had changed. General Joffre had already reduced the force that stood between the British and the coast by more than a hundred thousand men in order to create an *armée de manoeuvre* – a flying column that could be held in reserve and thrust in to support any part of his three-hundred-mile front that might be seriously threatened. Without the support of a strong French force standing between them and the sea the British front was more vulnerable than ever and the men who held it were already strained to the limit. It would be a tall order to supply troops to replace the two corps of the French Army that stood between the British and Belgians on a front that ran eight

---

* This part of Belgium had been flooded in 1914 when King Albert of the Belgians had ordered the dykes to be opened to stem the German invasion.

miles north from Ypres, for a corps of the French Army at full strength comprised thirty-six thousand men. But it was a quiet front for the moment, and Sir John French had been confident that he could replace them and hold the line with half as many. All he required was two divisions – but they would have to be good ones, and professional to a man.

Two first-class divisions* made up from Regular battalions returned from overseas had already arrived and taken over part of the front from the French. A third (the 29th Division) now assembling in England had been promised and the 1st Canadian Division was expected to embark shortly for France. But the War Council was having second thoughts, and it was a severe blow to Sir John French when he was informed on 19 February that the 29th Division was no longer available.

Three days earlier there had been a drastic change of plan. Even as the fleet was steaming towards the Dardanelles carrying with it the hopes and aspirations of the War Council a bombshell had exploded in their midst and it had been dropped by the Admiralty Staff. They now declared that, whatever its initial success, the strength of the Royal Navy alone would not be enough to force the Dardanelles, to capture Constantinople and to force a Turkish garrison on the Gallipoli Peninsula to evacuate it without a fight. The fact was that the professional sailor and First Sea Lord, Admiral Fisher, had been pressured and out-argued by the politician Churchill, First Lord of the Admiralty. But Fisher had all along been deeply suspicious of the plan. Now the Admiralty Staff had dug in its heels and made its views known in a memorandum that amounted to an ultimatum. Admiral Sir Henry Jackson had set out the situation clearly and concisely and in his last sentence he punched the message home: 'The naval bombardment is not recommended as a sound military operation, unless a strong military force is ready to assist in the operation, or at least to follow it up immediately the forts are silenced.'

This was a disconcerting departure from the original plan, so tempting in its promise of easy victory, so seductive in its power to demonstrate to skittish Bulgaria, still teetering indecisively on the fence, that the allies were on the side of the angels and it had best join them forthwith. Reluctantly, and after much discussion, the War Council gave way. It was true that there were not many troops to spare – but there was still the 29th Division. Two battalions of Royal Marines, detailed to provide landing parties to finish off the forts after bombardment, were already on the Greek island of Lemnos (borrowed to provide a forward base)

---

* The 27th and 28th Divisions.

and it was likely that the French could be persuaded to help, for the French Government had already sent a flotilla to assist the Royal Navy in attacking the straits. Why should they not send a division also?* It was agreed to ask them, and to send such troops as could be raised to Lemnos to be on the spot to assist the navy if need be. If a real emergency arose, troops could be brought from Egypt to reinforce them. No one seemed to remember that the beauty of the naval plan was that, if it did not succeed, it could be speedily broken off and, without loss of face, be regarded as a raid – a mere growl, a baring of the British bulldog's teeth, which might be equally effective in reminding Bulgaria that, if it chose, it could snarl and bite.

The fleet was even now steaming towards the Dardanelles and would attack in three days' time. It would be at least a month before the troops could possibly get there. If it struck any member of the War Council that it would be wise to postpone the naval operations until the troops were at hand, his misgiving was overruled. They were first and foremost politicians, and they were on the brink of a demonstration that would bring vacillating Bulgaria, and perhaps Greece and Rumania as well, into the fold. There was no time to be lost. Throughout their consultations with the Admiralty it did not occur to the War Council to seek the advice of the soldiers on the General Staff. No one even thought to inform the General Staff that a military operation was contemplated.

Lord Kitchener had by no means decided to agree to the proposal that the 29th Division should be sent to the Dardanelles – but he was equally reluctant to throw his last remaining force of expert, seasoned soldiers into the maw of the western front which had already chewed up the cream of the British Army and with little to show for it. Sir John French was informed that the 46th Division would be sent in its place. Since this division from the South Midlands was a Territorial Division which, in the opinion of the Commander-in-Chief, would require more training and tutelage in practical trench warfare before it would be fit for front-line service, this well and truly threw a spanner into the works, and French was considerably annoyed. Without first-class troops it was now impossible for him to accede to Joffre's request to stretch his line and sidestep to release the French troops Joffre required to strengthen his attack. If he did so, he would have too few troops for his own

---

* General Joffre could think of many reasons why they should not and, when approached by the French War Ministry, flatly refused to spare a single man from his own armies. The components of the French division had to be found in North Africa, from a mixture of French Colonial troops.

54

offensive. As it was, the untried and inexperienced Canadians were already earmarked to take over part of the front adjacent to the line of his proposed attack in order to release troops of his own to stiffen it. This then was his dilemma: to relieve the French and abandon his offensive, or to refuse to relieve the French and go ahead with it. Alternatively he could try to persuade Joffre to change his mind or, at the very least, to agree to delay the takeover until after their joint attack had been crowned, as it surely would be, with success. Approach after approach, meeting after meeting, throughout the last days of February produced no result. Joffre was adamant. No troops, no joint attack, and that was that.

Based on what Joffre saw as the abysmal performance of the British troops in the joint December offensive when they failed to achieve the smallest result and had incurred heavy casualties Joffre held a poor opinion of their chances of succeeding. At best he looked on the British contribution to the 'joint offensive' as providing a useful diversion on his left. The breakthrough, if it came at all, would be made by his own troops – and only if there were enough of them to carry it through. Lacking French élan, in Joffre's secret opinion, the British Army could be most usefully employed in holding a static line and keeping the enemy pinned down while the French got on with the real job.

Already Joffre had modified his plans and halved his demands. He now required the British Commander-in-Chief to relieve a single corps, not two. But, without the 29th Division, even that was beyond Sir John French, and without the release of the troops that would provide him with a cast-iron guarantee of success, Joffre had no intention of committing his Tenth Army to another forlorn 'joint offensive' only to be dragged down by British failure. He would wait until the time was ripe. As for Sir John French, if he was still determined to fight, then he must fight alone.

Not far away from GHQ where their future, had they known it, was being decided in the scores of telegrams and memoranda flying between St Omer, Downing Street and Whitehall, the 3rd Londons had spent the weeks of indecision shaking down, learning to use their new equipment, and carrying out intensive training in open country. The weather was foul, and although the hours of wintry daylight were blessedly short, ploughing around the sodden, often snow-covered, fields, fighting an invisible foe in imaginary battles, was not a pastime that appealed to them. The whole of the London Infantry Brigade was there (apart from the 1st Battalion which had been left behind to assist the relief garrison in Malta) and the one bright spot in the dark February days was occasional meetings on the march with their sister battalion, the 2nd Londons. This event was eagerly looked forward to and no matter how tired and dispirited they were, it never failed to cheer them up. This was due to the doctor's horse.

When horses were issued to the officers at Etaples the medical officer of the 2nd Battalion had acquired a charger whose pure white coat would have been admired anywhere else but in France where, as his brother officers gleefully pointed out, it would present a prime target to an enemy marksman if he rode within a mile of the battle-line. Captain McHoul had taken this to heart and, with the assistance of his servant, had attempted to dye his horse with permanganate of potash. This was standard practice, but something had gone wrong and McHoul's mount had emerged from the treatment a bright canary yellow. It could be seen for miles in the open country and the 3rd Londons took a lively delight in spotting it and subjecting their sister battalion to jeers, catcalls and a barrage of chirrups and bird-whistles.

Although the 2nd Londons loyally riposted to these insults – and in good measure – every member of his own Battalion (with the understandable exception of the doctor himself) was equally tickled, and the MO was the butt of merciless leg-pulling. He took it in good enough part until Lieutenant Teddy Cooper was inspired to compose a ditty for the delectation of the officers' mess. It had many verses, leaden with ponderous humour, but it was the last two stanzas that hit home:

> Henceforward when he rode abroad
> A ribald whisper flew,
> Whilst Tommies tittered, Captains roared
> And urged a dry shampoo.
>
> The rumour was he murmured 'Cheep'
> Instead of saying 'Whoa'
> And gave it groundsel in a heap
> To make the beggar grow.

This was the last straw, and the MO resorted to desperate measures. Repeated application of a mild solution of bleach only made matters worse, for it dried out in unsightly piebald streaks, but a sympathetic farrier sergeant made up a new concoction which he assured the doctor would transform his charger from a canary to a respectable chestnut. Unfortunately, reacting to the bleach which had been generously applied, his horse emerged an interesting shade of deep violet. There was nothing McHoul could do but put up with the hilarity with as much dignity as he could muster and console himself with the thought that at least he would no longer attract the attention of an enemy sniper.

In any event there was serious business ahead. The London Brigade was about to be split up. Soon the 2nd Londons would be setting off to join the 6th Division in the trenches near Armentieres, complete with purple horse and its embarrassed rider. The 3rd had already gone. Their ultimate destination was the trenches behind Neuve Chapelle where Sir John French was gathering his forces for the battle.

Capt. A. J. Agius, MC.

9th February It was a very threatening morning, cloudy and windy, with a fierce yellow sky forewarning more wind. Our expectations were fully justified, for soon after we had started it came on to rain and hail, and the wind, which blew across from our right front, grew stronger. We made a march of ten or twelve miles. It was a beastly march, but everyone stuck it very cheerily, though wet through. Being mounted I had started with my British Warm and as the rain grew worse I slipped my Burberry on top. Yet so penetrating were the wind and rain that the wet came through.

If conditions were bad for the officers on horseback, they were a good deal worse for the men on foot, for half the battalion had just been issued with new boots and, unlike their more fortunate comrades who had received theirs a fortnight earlier, had to take to the road with no opportunity of breaking them in. In mid-afternoon when they finally stopped in the rain-lashed village of Wittes the chorus of groans and curses that came from a dozen barnyard billets was indescribable. Five hundred men were struggling to pull the soaking boots from their swollen feet. Packing the boots with straw, attempting with more optimism than success to dry them out by the flame of a single candle, merely made matters worse. By morning the new leather had hardened and shrunk and the men were in a sorry state as they set off to hobble to Ham. It was a march of fifteen kilometres. Mercifully, the gale had blown out and it was a clear sunny day; mercifully, it was to be five days before the Battalion took to the road again. It was just about long enough for the sore feet to recover.

And it was long enough for some of the officers to have a beano. It was the birthday of Captain E. V. Noël, whose initials had caused him to be nicknamed 'Evie'. Harry Pulman and Arthur Agius had struck lucky in the matter of billets. The old lady in the farm where they lodged was unusually welcoming, fussing over them like a mother and feeding them like princes, and they had been so loud in her praises that it was unanimously decided to hold Evie's birthday party there. Their hostess was charmed with the idea and determined to do them proud.

Capt. A. J. Agius, MC.

We had quite a feast! We got a table rigged up on a couple of trestles, and the old lady supplied us with linen and crockery galore. There was a linen tablecloth and a napkin each – eleven of us sat down – a large glass and a small one each, knife, fork, spoon etc. We ate hors d'oeuvres of sardines and local paté, soup (a thick, warming, village soup), then a priceless omelette and two fowls with fried potatoes and gravy. (And what a job she'd had to kill them that morning, chasing round the farmyard with a cleaver!) We ended up with birthday cake, and that was about as much as anyone could manage. We had wine, red and white, to drink and liqueurs and coffee to finish up with. There were speeches from Harry and Bertie Mathieson, to which Evie replied. After that we sang choruses. And finally, very late, we got to bed.

They had passed many jolly evenings in peacetime, and quite a few since the war, but it was generally voted that this was the best yet. It was also the last that this coterie of old companions would spend together. Ahead lay the battle, and not all of them would survive it.

Chapter 5

If there were those who had serious doubts that it was the right moment to launch an offensive, in the opinion of Sir John French there could hardly have been a better one. Even without the cooperation of General Joffre, French and his staff were confident of success. The responsibility would be in the hands of the officer in command of the First Army, General Sir Douglas Haig. His troops were to fight the battle and he and his staff were now engaged in drawing up the detailed plans that would take them to victory. Lately there had been a marked change in the enemy's tactics. The Germans seemed content to maintain their positions by standing on the defensive, and reliable intelligence reports confirmed that they had drastically reduced their manpower on the western front, and that their reserves were few. The German High Command had decided to pitch its strength at the east.

As far back as the early eighteen nineties the Germans had drawn up plans for a possible European war and had realised that, if it came, it would be necessary to fight in the east as well as the west. In 1894 France and Russia had extended their formal alliance by a military agreement that guaranteed assistance in the event of either being attacked. This meant that there were two potential enemies on the borders of the German Empire and Count von Schlieffen had drawn up a military plan to deal with them both. In August 1914 it had been put into effect.

The nub of the plan was the swift invasion of France, striking through neutral Belgium where she would least expect it, and to proceed with maximum strength in a vast encircling movement that would capture Paris, force France to sue for peace and put victorious Germany in such a position of advantage that she could safely remove her troops from France and turn her attention to defeating Russia. The peace terms would be stringent, and punitive war reparations imposed on France would fuel the German war machine at no cost to the German people. But everything hinged on speed.

Six weeks had been allowed for the defeat of France. The Germans had looked carefully at the probabilities and, calculating the vast distances that separated the regions of the sprawling Russian Empire and the difficulties of concentrating troops, taking into account the lack of roads, the scarcity of railways (which were not even of European gauge), they had concluded that at least six weeks must elapse after mobilisation before a Russian army would be able to enter the field. By that time, the German armies, fresh from victory in the west, could be moved east to join battle with Russia and win the war. So confident were the Germans of success, so anxious to commit the best of their resources to ensuring it, so sure of their assessment that Russia would be slow to take up arms, that they were equally sanguine in their conviction that the defence of the vulnerable border of East Prussia could safely be left to local *Landsturm* troops.

But the Russians were true to their obligation to support their French ally, and they took the Germans completely by surprise. On 17 August, before Russian mobilisation was halfway complete, two Russian armies had invaded East Prussia, broken the front, and advanced more than a hundred miles into German territory. This had come as a rude shock to the Germans and, long before France could be overwhelmed, they were forced to reduce the force dedicated to defeating her by three army corps which might have tipped the balance in the west, had they not been rushed back to save the situation in the east. They had arrived too late to cheat Russia of early victories which did much to hearten her allies, but a few days later they roundly defeated the Russians at Tannenberg. Russia had held her own, fighting against the Germans in East Prussia, against the Austrians to the south, against the Turks further east. But the Russians were struggling, and by January the situation was critical. There was no lack of men to fight, but they needed guns to fight with and ammunition for the guns to fire. Every day they were firing almost three times as much as the munitions factories could possibly produce and eating into reserve supplies that were now dangerously low. Above all, they needed weapons. Rifles were now so scarce that one man in four was being sent to the front without one and the Russians had to rely on retrieving the arms of men killed or wounded on the battlefield to equip the men who had come to take their place. If the Russians were defeated, and if the Germans were then able to take large numbers of troops from the east and mass them for an offensive in France, then the game would be up on the western front. It was for this reason that the War Council wished to relieve the pressure on Russia by opening an offensive in a new theatre of war where it would do Russia most good. It was also the reason behind Sir John French's fervent desire to attack in the west.

In December, eight more divisions of German infantry and four of cavalry had left the western front to fight the Russians and, they hoped, to finish them off, and Sir John French was itching to take advantage of this thinning of the German line as soon as the ground and weather conditions improved. The British troops were fewer than the Commander-in-Chief could have wished for but, just for once, and possibly not for long, they substantially outnumbered their opponents. They must grasp the nettle and seize the moment to strike. The risks would be small; the rewards would be rich.

The Aubers Ridge was a desirable objective in itself, but beyond it lay the promised land – a wide flat plateau, ideal for open warfare with little cover and none of those convenient ridges so easy for the enemy to defend. Beyond it lay the real prize, the German-occupied city of Lille, capital of French Flanders, with its satellite textile towns of Roubaix and Tourcoing. They could not be captured in a day but, given the success of the initial assault (and how could it fail?), given the assistance of the French in pushing forward (and they would surely join in!), and given the lack of large reserves of German soldiers to defend them, these important industrial towns could be captured in a campaign of two weeks. At a single blow their captive populations would be liberated and the wheels of their factories set turning to assist the allied war effort. Long before reinforcements could be brought from Germany the way would be opened to the great plain of Douai, Joffre's army would advance, his grander design would succeed and, in the west at least, the war would be won.

For the French population of the occupied towns it was tantalising to be so close to the line, lying beneath the heel of the Germans within the sound of the guns little more than twenty miles away. For the people of Tourcoing the frustration was worst of all. Drawing an imaginary triangle on the map Tourcoing would lie at the apex, as near to Ypres as to Aubers Ridge at either end of its base. In those early days of the war, every local attack, every minor action, every exchange of gunfire heard so clearly in the streets, raised hopes that the allies were on the move and liberation was at hand. But there were a few who took a more realistic view and Henri Dewavrin was one:

M. Pierre Dewavrin.

My father was always a pessimist. He had gone to a military school, the Collège Ste Geneviève. He intended to make a career in the army but, when he was only seventeen, there was a slump in the wool trade and he had to leave and help his father restore his business as a wool broker. But he always kept his interest in military matters. I had just turned twelve when we were occupied by the Germans. I remember very well that every day they used to post up the official army communiqués on the door of the Hôtel de Ville – not just their own German one, but the French and British communiqués as well, which was remarkable when you think of it.

My father used to study them for hours at a time, trying to work out what was really happening, and he always took a very gloomy view, because he knew the country well, and he knew that the so-called advances that the French or the British were proclaiming were really nothing at all. He used to discuss the situation for hours at a time. He could think of nothing else. His friends and colleagues nicknamed him 'Général' Dewavrin because he spent his days at his club for businessmen, always talking about the war. Of course, he was naturally concerned because two of my elder brothers were with the French Army and there was no news of them. He just had to try to work out for himself what was happening and there was plenty of time to talk things over because there was no work and no business to be done.

Everything had come to a standstill. The factories were shut down because the Germans were short of war material and the first thing they had done was to strip the factories and take all the copper parts from the machines, right down to the smallest components. Even if they could have run the machines without them there were no raw materials to work with, and all the workers of military age had been mobilised and were fighting on the other side of the line. In any event, no one wanted to work for the Germans. They occupied Tourcoing on the 10th of October and on the Sunday we went to mass as usual at our church, St Christophe. Chanoine Leclercq gave the sermon and I shall never forget it. He was a saintly man, and a brave man, because he defied the Germans. He reviled them, and he didn't mince his words. *He* said that the factories must close and that, whatever happened, *no one* must work for the Germans or do anything at all to help them if they could avoid it. We couldn't fight, he said, but we could show that we were Frenchmen and defy them. A few days later he was arrested and sent to Germany. He was a prisoner there for exactly four years, from 18 October 1914 to 18 October 1918. Many people were arrested and sent as hostages or prisoners to Germany. It happened in my wife's family, that is, in the family of the lady who became my wife ten years later.

Mme Germaine Dewavrin.

My father was a manufacturer of wool, in partnership with his brother. It was a huge enterprise. It was called 'Usines Auguste et Louis Lepoutre'. They had twelve factories round Roubaix and Tourcoing and two more in America, near Providence in Massachusetts. Every day between them they used the wool of ten thousand sheep – thirty thousand kilos of wool. When we were occupied, naturally all that stopped. The Germans requisitioned everything, stripped the factories bare, but my father had large stocks of wool. The Germans had taken a certain amount, but he was determined that they should not have the rest. So he hid it.

The biggest factory was in Roubaix, and it was a huge place. In one building there was a long corridor with doors leading to the store-rooms. The wool used to be delivered on wooden pallets, so the store-rooms were packed to the ceilings with wool and then the pallets were propped up against the walls all along the corridor so that the doors were hidden. But my father was denounced. One of the workers who must have had some grievance, or who wanted money, gave him away to the Germans.

Of course as children we knew nothing of all this until the Germans came to our house to arrest him. They took my father and my mother. We saw them go, surrounded by soldiers with fixed bayonets, they marched them on foot all the way to Tourcoing. It was terrible, terrible. I was ten years old, the youngest of the family, and we had an English nursery governess called Nellie Smale. She was absolutely distracted! Naturally, being English, she was terrified. She could have gone home when the war began, but she had been with our family for so many years she decided to stay. Of course, we never expected that things would go so fast and so badly. And the occupation, when it happened, came so quickly! Even so, many people were evacuated and Nellie could have gone too, but she chose not to. Then when she saw my father and mother being marched off she thought she would be taken next. She was terrified every day of the war!

My mother came home next day, but my father was taken as a hostage to Germany. Months afterwards they released him but after he had been home for a time they arrested him again and sent him back to Germany. Many, many prominent citizens and industrialists were taken hostage. I suppose it was to make an example of them and ensure the good behaviour of the people in the occupied towns. It was a very hard time. It was even harder for the people who had worked in our factories and were less well off. There was great hardship. Every municipality gave out vouchers so they could buy the food the Germans were supposed to provide, but there was very little of it.

63

M. Pierre Dewavrin.

In Tourcoing we had a large house, because we were a large family, and we could not avoid having Germans billeted from time to time. Of course, we had as little as possible to do with them, but they were in our house. Sometimes they were officers, who were very correct and polite, but when there were troop movements, we often got ordinary soldiers – sometimes as many as twenty or thirty of them sleeping on the floors and eating in our kitchen. In early 1915 they were very simple men, mostly Bavarian peasants, and their officers treated them like animals, with absolute contempt. Of course, being Bavarians, they were devout Catholics and it amazed us youngsters when we saw them cross themselves when they were handed their bread ration. We asked ourselves how the Boche could possibly be Christians!

In their communiqués the Germans had been trumpeting their successes on the eastern front. Studying them as he did, weighing up the evidence of his own ears that the sound of gunfire to the west was lessening every day as February drew to a close, 'Général' Henri Dewavrin could hardly be blamed for taking a gloomy view of the progress of the war. He would have been right in deducing that British ammunition was in short supply, but it might have heartened him to know that the British guns were silent because Sir John French was economising ammunition in order to build up a reserve for the battle that lay ahead. The field guns had been rationed to six rounds a day. The heavy Howitzers were forbidden to fire more than two.

The question of ammunition was a serious one, and for months past the sparseness of supplies reaching France had been causing Sir John French great anxiety. He was not interested in the trials and difficulties that faced the War Office, his sole concern was that supplies of guns and ammunition fell far short of the amounts that had been promised and that even if the promised supplies had been met in full they would still have fallen woefully short of the amount he required to prosecute the war with any hope of success.

It was all very well for the army to demand more guns and munitions, but it was by no means easy to supply them. For one thing, there was the question of premises. Even if empty factories were requisitioned and others turned over to the manufacture of munitions, who was to man them? In the infectious enthusiasm of early recruiting no one had stopped to reflect that the services of skilled men would be of more use to King and Country in engineering workshops than as raw recruits in the expanding ranks of the

New Armies where, for want of proper weapons, the infantry was drilling with wooden rifles and would-be gunners were learning their trade on ancient artillery pieces borrowed from museums. Some were actually obliged to practise gun-drill on a home-made contrivance, the barrel represented by a tree trunk balanced on a trestle, with two cross-sections lopped from it to imitate the wheels.

Even if all the engineers who had disappeared into the army were combed out and brought back it would not be enough, or nearly enough. Rifles were needed. Guns were needed – machine-guns, fuses, shells by the thousands, bullets by the million. Large orders had been placed at the start of the war, and there was no shortage of raw materials, but even if the existing factories had been working flat out it would have been impossible to fulfil more than a fraction of them. But they were not working flat out and, worse, there was an upsurge of industrial troubles and disputes.

Many of the jobs involved in the manufacture of munitions could have been carried out by unskilled labour, but the Amalgamated Society of Engineers had absolutely vetoed this suggestion and, in the face of such union opposition, employers were forced to turn down countless volunteers. Even within the skilled workforce itself there were restrictive practices. One man per machine was the rule, even where output could have been increased by working shifts, and no doubling up of jobs would be accepted. Nor was there any question of a single-union agreement that would allow an engineer to mend a fuse, if need be, or an electrician to loosen a bolt or tighten a screw.

The attitude of the skilled men was understandable. It took seven years of hard-grafting apprenticeship, working for a pittance, to qualify as a tradesman, and even a skilled journeyman's wage could be as little as £2 a week. The minimum wage agreement had been won only after years of struggle, and decades of exploitation in Victorian workshops were still fresh in the minds of the men who had fought for the rights and conditions they now enjoyed. Was it all to be sacrificed now? If cheap unskilled labour was swept up by the national emergency to fill the factories, might not their own jobs be swept away when the emergency was over and employers – whom they had good reason not to trust – were tempted to use the precedent to undermine the hard-won rights of skilled workers?

Employers were at the nub of the industrial trouble that came to a head in February, for the men believed that they were making huge profits from the war, and making them at the men's expense. Prices were rising, but wages were not and while employers on the one hand were urging the workforce to greater effort and ever-rising output, they were refusing, on the other, to meet even reasonable pay claims. Workers threatening to strike were vilified wholesale by the press, whipping up a frenzy of patriotic indignation. Few people stopped to consider the problems faced by the War Office or the culpability of manufacturers who, through greed or over-optimism and not least by reason of self-interest led by fear of competition, were probably most to blame. The workforce was a useful scapegoat and not many took the trouble to look at things from the workers' point of view – least of all Sir John French. And least of all the gunners standing idly by their guns in Flanders while the Commander-in-Chief gathered up a supply of precious shells for his offensive.

He was gathering men too.

During their five-day stay at Ham the 3rd Londons had been mildly surprised to be inspected by General Willcocks and welcomed 'to the Indian Army' and to find that they were to form part of the Meerut Division. 'Army' was a forgivable conceit on the part of the general, who had good reason to be proud of his troops, but it was something of an exaggeration for it comprised a corps of two infantry divisions and one of cavalry. In addition to native Indian troops each infantry brigade contained one battalion of British Regulars (as it had done in India) and each was now to be augmented by a battalion of Territorials or Special Reservists.

If wintry Flanders came as a rude shock to the 3rd Londons fresh from the mild climate of Malta, it had been considerably worse for the Indians and most of them had been there for months. The Indian troops had played an active part and proved their worth in spite of the dreary conditions, the icy chill of the northern marshes, the water-logged trenches where, vaselined and oiled to the waist, the men on outpost duty had to stand for hours with barely a glimpse of the pallid disc that masqueraded as the sun in those alien northern skies. Many had fallen in action and some in the trench-raids at which the Indians were so expert; frostbite, influenza and pneumonia had all taken their toll and recently measles and mumps, encountered in Europe for the first time, had swept through the ranks. But the cold was the worst, and the Indians could hardly remember the sensation of being warm, still less the fierce heat of the Indian plains burning under the sun they called 'the Bengal blanket'. The British public were sympathetic to the plight of the men plucked so cruelly out of their element. Tons of warm comforts had been sent and it was no unusual sight to see turbanned Indian troops hunched over tiny cooking fires, cocooned in a dozen or more khaki scarves and shawls plaited and knotted across khaki overcoats. Their khaki service dress was a far cry from the colourful silken glamour of the regimental uniforms that were the joy of the Indian Army, but the names of the regiments still rang like a litany that celebrated all the pomp and panoply of Empire – the Dogras,

66

the Baluchis, Garhwalis, the Deccan Horse, the Secunderabad Cavalry, Pathans, Sikhs, Punjabis, the Jodhpur Lancers.

They came from every corner of the Indian sub-continent and represented every caste and creed, and this presented the military authorities with certain problems. At the base camps in Marseilles and later in Orleans and Rouen it required six separate kitchens to cater for the different dietary and religious needs and although the problem had been tackled in the field by issuing rations and allowing the Indians to cook them for themselves, this system brought other difficulties. One officer, walking past such a group cooking food on the roadside, was amazed to see them tip out the contents of their cooking pot as he passed. The 'shadow of the infidel' had fallen across their food and they would rather go hungry than eat it. Even the basic army rations were unacceptable to Indian troops. To the exasperation of Captain Maurice Mascall, who was an officer in a mountain gun battery, his drivers refused to eat the biscuits he was forced to issue in lieu of scarce chapatti flour. But the drivers seemed unconcerned. They politely pointed out, when called to account, that they did not expect to survive anyway and might as well die of starvation in a state of grace than be consigned to damnation by a German bullet with a stomach defiled by impure food. 'This argument,' remarked Mascall, 'rather took the wind out of the Major's sails as he had hoped that the pangs of hunger would prove stronger than caste prejudice.'

It seldom did, and provisioning the Indians was a headache. Beef was not acceptable to many and, since pork was absolutely taboo, all France as far afield as the island of Corsica was scoured for goats, as old and tough as possible, to supply the Indians' needs. Such was their horror of anything connected with pork that exhausted Sikhs newly out of the line even refused to enter the pigsties they were allocated as temporary billets. The officers who had served with the Indian Army in peacetime understood these shibboleths but as casualties mounted and they were replaced by others with no experience of Indian troops, difficulties and misunderstandings increased.

But in Britain the Indian soldiers were hugely popular. Public imagination had been caught by the munificence of the maharajas who had offered troops, money, even lakhs of rubies, to assist the war effort, and also by the loyalty of these soldiers of the Empire who had obeyed the Empire's call to come and fight. Everyone approved when the Royal Pavilion in Brighton was turned into a hospital for Indian wounded, for what could be more appropriate and more likely to make them feel at home than its sparkling minarets and oriental decor? Money poured into the Indian Soldiers' Fund. Speakers of Indian languages – many of them retired from the Indian Civil Service – visited them in hospital. There were outings, even sight-seeing trips to London for the convalescents (including a visit to Lord Roberts' grave in the crypt of St Paul's). Everything Indian was fashionable and an oriental matinee at the Shaftesbury Theatre raised a large sum of money for the benefit of Indian troops. It featured oriental dances, songs, recitations, and tableaux, including 'an Indian Garden scene with characters represented by Indian ladies and gentlemen'. The performance was attended by several royal ladies, including the Queen Mother, Queen Alexandra, and it was voted a resounding success.

The sturdy little Gurkhas from the hill country of Nepal were just as popular. They were tough fighters, proud of their prowess and their skill with their kukris, those lethal weapons whose curved blades were honed razor sharp and which, in the opinion of the Gurkhas, were miles better than any rifle. They had been mobbed at Marseilles by girls demanding to have their fingers scratched 'for luck', and the Gurkhas had obliged, grinning with delight. It was the first time they had drawn blood, although so little had they known about the war that they had spent the last two hours of the train journey to Calcutta sharpening kukris in the belief that they would be meeting the enemy the instant they arrived.

When they finally did meet the enemy in the alien land of Flanders they had quickly adapted and shown their mettle. Killing Germans was what they were there for, and killing Germans was what they intended to do. The Gurkhas were particularly adept at scouting and patrolling, and delighted in creeping undetected to a German outpost and dispatching some unsuspecting enemy with a silent swipe of the deadly kukri.

Lt. Col. D. H. Drake-Brockman, 2nd Bn., Garhwal Rifles, Garhwal Brig., Meerut Div.

We organised a raid on the German trenches opposite our right flank where it ran into what we called 'the gap'. This was a portion of ditch which ran along our front at this place. Our right and the 1st Battalion's left ran into it.

Fifty men from each battalion were lined up in the ditch on the right flank and the signal to advance was given. The special feature of a night attack is the imperative necessity for absolute silence till you are actually ready to charge and close up to your objective – otherwise cheering too soon only gives the enemy notice of your intention and time to prepare to meet your attack. Our men crawled right up to the German parapet in silence and lay under it without being noticed. Major Taylor lay there too, watching, and when he considered the psychological moment had arrived he gave the signal to charge into the trench by firing his revolver at some grey-coated Germans he could just see walking by below him and immediately they all jumped into the German trench with an almighty yell.

I don't suppose men were ever scared so much as these Germans were, for they bolted down every handy communication trench as if all the demons in Asia were after them. I think it must have been this incident that gave rise to the yarns and pictures which one saw in the illustrated papers of men dressed like Gurkhas with drawn kukris in their mouths crawling up to the German trenches. We took six live prisoners, one of whom was wounded, and we know that two were killed. But the great thing was the moral effect which it must have produced on the enemy.

Stories of the Gurkhas abounded. One favourite told of a German soldier looking over the parapet just as a Gurkha crawled up. The kukri swished and the German sneered and shook his head. 'You missed, Gurkha!' The Gurkha replied, 'You wait, German, wait until you try to *nod* head.' Apocryphal though it was, it precisely summed up the spirit and character of the tough little hillmen. Outlandish rumours of blood-chilling deeds spread like wildfire among the Germans who soon developed a healthy respect for Asian soldiers. In some cases it amounted to outright fear and one unfortunate German who had been captured by a patrol and brought into the British line was so overcome by terror on being patted and stroked by a smiling Indian soldier that he actually fainted. The Indian was extremely put out. His intention had been to reassure the prisoner by demonstrating sympathy and friendship. But the German's imagination had been fired by lurid rumours of cannibalism and he assumed that his captor was exploring his person with a view to identifying the plumpest, juiciest cuts.

On the night of 21 February detachments of the 3rd Londons went into the trenches for the first time with the front-line battalions of the Meerut Division. Some were attached to the Gurkhas who gave them a friendly welcome. It was only possible to communicate in sign language but in quiet spells there was much displaying of kukris, which the British men were anxious to examine, and the Gurkhas were equally anxious to show off, as well as the trophies and souvenirs that were proof of the number of Germans they had bagged. Among the caps and helmets and tunic-buttons were a number of desiccated objects which on closer examination were shown to be human ears, and grinning dumbshows of throat-cutting gestures left no doubt in the mind as to how the Gurkhas had come by them.

They were treated occasionally to a short unpleasant fusillade of pip-squeaks, which the Gurkhas called 'Swee-thak's' and appeared to shrug off with a certain derision that was heartening to men coming under fire for the first time. But for once it was a bright day and the blue sky buzzed with aeroplanes, wheeling and climbing and dodging the shell-bursts as the guns sought to bring them down. It was fascinating to watch the white puff of an explosion appearing as if by magic against the blue of the sky, followed a moment later by the crack of the explosion and the whirr of the shell travelling through the air. They were British aeroplanes, and it was fortunate that the German shells failed to hit them because they were engaged on an important task. The first air cameras had just been delivered and the planes were taking advantage of the clear fog-free weather to photograph the German trenches and the fortifications behind their front line. These first aerial photographs would be flat affairs compared with the finely detailed shots that would later prove so invaluable, but they were infinitely better than nothing. The map-makers were working overtime and for the first time since the stalemate had set in the Army would have eyes, would be able to see beyond ridges and round corners, and the troops preparing for the coming battle would know precisely where they were going and what they would be up against.

There was another new innovation which the Army had been slow to accept. It was the idea that guns could be accurately ranged by aeroplanes observing their fire and sending back instant corrections by wireless, and it was the brainchild of Lieutenant Donald Lewis, a signals specialist of the Royal Engineers on secondment to the Royal Flying Corps. Had it depended on official channels it would never have got off the ground at all, but Donald Lewis had friends, and Lieutenant James, a fellow sapper, was equally enthusiastic. Together they installed a prototype wireless in Lewis's aircraft and that was the easy bit. Neither officer was an expert in speedily sending morse and it took them weeks to work up their speed and efficiency, Lewis in the air and James on the ground. Then they approached another friend, the commander of a 9.2 Howitzer battery, and invited him to join in the experiment. It was a startling success. An aircraft observing a shoot firing blind 'by the map' at a specified target could instantly signal back the result and the correction that would lay the gun accurately on the target. They had worked out a code using an imaginary clock face divided into segments superimposed on the map. It was simple and it was fool-proof. The War Office gave Lewis and James their blessing and sent them with their new system to France where they kicked their heels for a month before they were allowed to try it out.

70

Lt. D. S. Lewis, Royal Engineers, Att. RFC.

We went out with three machines, fitted with 300-watt Rouget sets, run off the crankshaft, and receiving sets with Brown relays. For a month they wouldn't use us, having a very British distrust of things new! At last we got our chance and made about the biggest success of the war. We do nothing but range artillery, sending down the position of new targets and observing the shorts. The results are really magnificent. In this flat country all heavy artillery shooting is utterly blind without aeroplane observation. As it is, during a battle, every enemy battery that opens fire can be promptly dealt with and accurately ranged on. With 'Mother', the 9.2-inch 'How', one can generally hit a target with the first three shots. We signal the shots by a clock method, direction by figures, distances by letters, i.e. C9 means 200 yards at nine o'clock to the true north.

The problem was that in the run-up to the offensive there were precious few shells to spare, not even for the task of ensuring the accuracy of the guns in the all-important bombardment. But not all the guns had yet arrived and the Battery Commanders of those that were in place were none too keen to send precious rationed shells flying into the blue without good reason. Sir John French had calculated that by economising on ammunition he would store up enough for three days' fighting. And a three-day fight would put him on top of the Aubers Ridge.

He was sure of it. It had to, it *must* succeed.

Part 2

~

Into Battle: Neuve Chapelle

How do you feel as you stand in a trench
Awaiting the whistle to blow?
Are you frightened, anxious, shaking with fear,
Or are you ready to go?
All men react in a different way
But few to heroics aspire
But should a man boast that he never felt fear
Then, in my book, that man is a liar.

Sgt. Harry Fellowes
12th Northumberland Fusiliers

Chapter 6

The sixteen thousand men of the 46th North Midland Territorial Division did not share the qualms of the Commander-in-Chief with regard to their ability to fight. They had been ready, willing and waiting for months, weary of training and itching to get into the real war.

But they were not all so experienced as the Terriers who had been rushed to France in the early days. When war broke out not many Territorial battalions were up to full strength and some in country districts had been nowhere near it. In the first weeks of the war they had been forced to enrol new volunteers to make up their numbers and so far as the new recruits were concerned the Territorials were a popular choice. For one thing they were issued with uniforms and rifles right away and for months now they had been swanking over their khaki-less comrades of Kitchener's Mob in cloth caps and civilian clothes. The trouble was that as many as two in ten of the Territorials were as raw and inexperienced as the masses that flooded into the ranks of Kitchener's New Armies. In the early days, this had caused difficulties in many Territorial battalions, not least in the 6th Battalion of the South Staffordshire Regiment. They still remembered one embarrassing incident which, although amusing in retrospect, had not impressed the Colonel at the time.

It had been unfortunate for the Battalion that when the Commander of the North Midland Brigade arrived unexpectedly to confer with Lieutenant-Colonel Waterhouse he was not greeted with the 'military compliments' which a full colonel of the regular army was entitled to receive. The soldier enjoying the sun outside the guard-room merely glanced at him with no apparent interest. It was 12 August, the 'guard-room' was the gate-house of a brewery in Burton-on-Trent, where the South Staffs had been ordered to concentrate, and ten days ago the soldier leaning against the wall had been a tram-driver. Today, by some fluke of authority, he had been told off for guard-duty, and he had only the haziest notion of what this entailed. He couldn't recognise a Brigadier when he saw one and, since the sentry was correctly attired in the uniform of a

Territorial, Colonel Bromilow did not recognise a raw recruit. 'Turn out the Guard!' he snapped. The only response was, 'Eh?' 'Where *is* the Guard?' '*I* don't know.'

The Colonel twigged at once and changed his approach. 'Where are the other fellows?' The sentry jerked his head at the guard-room 'In there.' Bromilow made for the door but the sentry had gleaned from somewhere that the purpose of a sentry was to guard *something* which might well be the guard-room itself, and he sprang to life bellowing, ''ERE YOU! *You* can't go in there!' He even went so far as to shove his superior officer out of the way.

Colonel Bromilow was an old soldier. It was thirty years since he had been commissioned into his parent regiment, the Royal Dublin Fusiliers. He had fought in the South African War at the battle of Ladysmith and been in the legendary charge of the Irish Brigade at Colenso. He had served in Egypt, in India, in the Sudan. And he knew when he was beaten. He turned on his heel and strode off to exchange a few curt words with Lieutenant-Colonel Waterhouse. Next day, for the benefit of newcomers, the regulations governing the duties of the guard were reproduced in Battalion Orders, with the rider that platoon officers must see to it that newly enlisted men were trained to carry them out.

Most Territorial officers in the 6th South Staffs had at least one or two years' service, but this did not mean that they encountered no difficulties. They were perfectly familiar with duties of Orderly Officer of the day but it was natural that in the course of afternoon or evening drills they had never been called upon to perform the routine task of 'inspecting men's dinners', and it had seldom fallen to their lot during annual camps. 'Inspecting dinners' was simply a matter of visiting the cookhouse while the food was being prepared and going to the mess halls when the meal had been served to ask 'Any complaints?' It was at the cookhouse that Lieutenant Langley had come to grief, for when the sergeant-cook ordered the lid of a huge dixie to be lifted for his inspection, he realised that he had not the faintest idea what he was supposed to do next. He peered into the bubbling brew, playing for time and racking his brains. 'What is it?' he asked. 'Boiled beef, sir.' All that occurred to Lieutenant Langley were the queries 'Is it beef?' and 'Is it boiled?' – and he could see that that was ridiculous. The expected response – and universal escape-route in awkward situations – was a laconic 'Very good. Carry on, Sergeant', but these words completely escaped him. The cooks were waiting expectantly. Langley, now uncomfortably enveloped in steam, went on earnestly scrutinising the contents of the dixie. How *was* he meant to 'inspect' the food? He was finally driven by heat and desperation to prodding the beef gingerly with the end of his short Malacca cane. And then, at last, the blessed formula came to mind. 'Very good. Carry on, Sergeant.' The cooks sportingly showed no sign of astonishment. Later a few scornful words from the Adjutant, who had happened to be passing the open cookhouse door (and also happened to be Langley's elder brother), put the over-zealous inspector right.

But, like other battalions of the 46th Division, the 6th South Staffs had been licked into shape and trained for war service. Now they were to have the honour of being the first division composed entirely of Territorials to go to the front and the Commanding Officer of the 6th South Staffs was determined that their arrival should not go unnoticed. He had issued orders to the company officers to ensure that every man was familiar with the tune of the French national anthem and, although he was not so ambitious as to expect them to learn the words, he insisted that they should practise whistling it. The Battalion enthusiastically took to the idea, were encouraged by the officers to rehearse it on route marches and picked it up in no time. They were whistle perfect long before they embarked for France. It was not easy to fit English words to the tune of 'The Marseillaise' but, as the weeks passed, a few wags were moved to vary the eternal whistling by warbling *When are we go-ing, when are we go-o-ing, When are we go-ing to the front?* But they could get no further. Neither, it seemed, could the battalion.

Their departure was delayed so long, and every man had been home on his 'last' forty-eight-hour pass so often that his family, who had bidden him an emotional goodbye on the first occasion, became blasé, if not downright bored, by numerous repeat performances of 'The Soldier's Farewell'. Even the men got fed up with it and it was a relief to all when they finally embarked on 5 March. The departure from Southampton was thrilling.

2nd Lt. F. Best, Army Service Corps, 46 Div. Supply Column.

The sea was absolutely calm. I counted fourteen searchlights looking aimlessly for aircraft and the water was raked by as many horizontal ones on the lookout for submarines while we were gliding down the Solent. The water looked a dazzling blue green in the zone of light. A more gorgeous sight you couldn't imagine – the coloured lights and signals, the still water and the misty land disappearing gradually into the haze. Further south a couple of destroyers escorted us – little black streaks plough-ing along in the dull light. That made us feel very secure. It suddenly occurred to me that *we* were performing the famous tableau I'd seen so often as a lad at Hamilton's Panorama – it was called *Troopship Leaving Southampton*.

We anchored among several other vessels outside the harbour

of Le Havre, with French and English destroyers flitting round us all the time. Then the pilot led us in. We took a short time to land and proceeded to a large shed at the side of the line a mile and a half from the dock. We were joined later by *masses* of others. The troops and citizens in Le Havre were startled by the spectacle of an officer charging through the town at break-neck speed, taking no notice of tram lines or level crossings – sparks flying from the granite setts. This was Eric Milner on a stylish looking charger he'd selected from the Remount Depot at Southampton when his own horse Jingly Geordie died there of cold. He was some miles on the other side of town before he managed to stop the beast!

Lieutenant Milner narrowly escaped being the very first casualty of the entire division and, compared to his dramatic entrance into the field of war, the arrival of the 6th South Staffs was something of an anti-climax. It was also a deep disappointment to Colonel Waterhouse. His men played their part to perfection, marching smartly through the streets to the transit camp, lustily whistling 'The Marseillaise' in compliment to their French allies. But the allies, as represented by the civilian population of le Havre, took not the slightest notice. The 46th Divisional supply column had been longer on the way for it was a laborious job to pack up and move the 200 wagons, 600 men and as many as 550 horses that made up the Divisional train. The men who had reached France before the supply column got there were more than pleased to see it when it finally arrived. No one was happier than Captain Ashwell of the 8th Battalion, Notts and Derby, known to the army as the Sherwood Foresters. Ashwell had drawn what turned out to be the short straw, for he had been sent to France in charge of the advance guard, and if the fifty men who made up this vanguard had been inclined to crow over the laggards who were left behind, they very soon regretted it.

Advance guards were nobody's children. Even at le Havre, while waiting for space in a train going north, no one seemed inclined to find them billets. They were obliged to shift for themselves and bed down in empty trucks and, when they finally did reach their destination, with no transport, and with no Divisional, Brigade or Battalion headquarters to issue orders or to turn to in case of difficulty, they felt more than ever like lost sheep. There were naturally no battalion postal arrangements and one new arrival, anxious to let his family know his whereabouts, scribbled a hasty note and posted it in a village post-box. No one had told him that troops in France were forbidden to use the civilian postal service and the question of censorship had not entered his head: 'Dear Mum and Dad, Well, we got away all right. At the moment I am at a place near Cassel with a few other fellows. I expect the rest will arrive soon. I am in the pink, and hope this finds you as it leaves me . . .' This letter caused consternation, first in his family and later in the Battalion, for his parents looked up Cassel on a small-scale map of Europe, found only Kassel in Germany, and made the natural assumption that their son had been taken prisoner the moment he set foot in France. They wrote straight off to the War Office for information. Later, after the arrival of his Battalion, when the wrath of Whitehall eventually descended on the head of his Commanding Officer, the unfortunate soldier received a wigging he was unlikely to forget.

The task of the advance guard was to pave the way for the Battalion, to find billets for a thousand weary men at the end of their long journey, to select premises suitable for Battalion Headquarters and orderly rooms, places nearby where the cookers could set up, and suitable fields for the wagon lines. Finding billets in the scattered hamlets north of Cassel, Ashwell discovered, was a simple task compared to that of feeding his fifty men. Iron rations were soon exhausted, they had to forage further and further afield for supplies and, in the three days before the Battalion arrived, Ashwell reckoned that he had personally trudged no less than forty-five miles in search of food. They arrived on the evening of 4 March. Ashwell was heartily pleased to see them and even more pleased, when the next move came, to be back in the fold and travelling as one of the crowd.

It had taken ten days for the whole division to congregate. There had been time – but only just – to give a few of the earliest arrivals a brief stint in some quiet sector of the trench-line but soon after the last straggling unit arrived and the division was complete, the order came to move south. This time it was the real thing for they were moving into general reserve for the Battle of Neuve Chapelle. Untried though the 46th Division was, the Commander-in-Chief was forced to use it. There was no other to use.

But neither Sir John French, his staff, nor Sir Douglas Haig, the architect of the battle, was unduly concerned about this lack of experience. As reserves the Territorials of the 46th Division would not be in the thick of the attack. When the Regulars, assisted by their own attached Territorial Battalions, had smashed the line, when the cavalry had thrust ahead through the gap, only then would the soldiers in reserve be brought forward to support the troops who had broken through and to follow behind as they advanced.

It was twenty kilometres from the la Bassée Canal in the south to Bois Grenier further north and Haig's First Army now held this front with six divisions. The Germans facing them held it with two – and those were greatly under strength. Six Battalions had just been

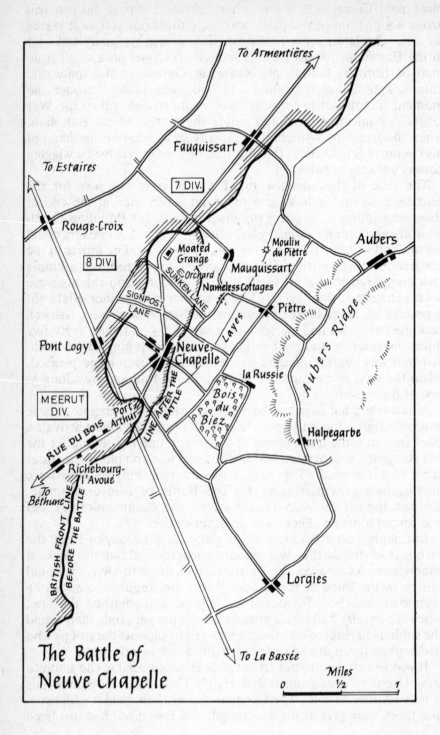

To Armentières

Fauquissart

To Estaires

Rouge-Croix

7 DIV.

8 DIV.

Moated Grange

Orchard

SUNKEN LANE

SIGNPOST LANE

Pont Logy

Neuve Chapelle

MEERUT DIV.

Port Arthur

RUE DU BOIS

Richebourg-l'Avoué

To Béthune

Moulin du Piètre

Mauquissart

Nameless Cottages

Piètre

LAYES

la Russie

Bois du Biez

Halpegarbe

Aubers

Aubers Ridge

BRITISH FRONT LINE BEFORE THE BATTLE

LINE AFTER THE BATTLE

Lorgies

To La Bassée

The Battle of Neuve Chapelle

Miles

0   ½   1

transferred to the front in Champagne, and they had been withdrawn from the precise sector of the line on which the first and most fearsome British attack would fall. Fifteen British Battalions were poised to attack the line held by just one and a half Battalions of German troops. In front of the Indian Corps, where nine Battalions of the Meerut Division were waiting to strike, there were just three German Battalions, and all of them were strung out by companies along the vulnerable length of their ill-manned front. The nearest reserves, a mere two companies, were at Halpegarbe just over two kilometres from the German front line.

It was true that the Germans had local reserves in stronger formations, but they were at least ten kilometres away. Sir Douglas Haig had taken them into account and had impressed on his Corps Commanders the vital importance of getting ahead as quickly as possible before German reserves could get there. Everything hinged on speed. The infantry must not hesitate but must push on as fast as possible. This order was handed down the line and there was no Brigadier, no Battalion Commanding Officer and, eventually, no Company Commander who was not fully aware of its importance.

As Commander of the First Army, General Haig had given a good deal of thought to the disposition of his troops and his plans had been approved by the Commander-in-Chief. He proposed to attack in depth. The attack would be narrow, but at the centre, where it mattered, it would be deep. Everything depended on the capture of Neuve Chapelle and the system of German trenches that formed the salient around it. Once the village had been captured and the line straightened, the troops on either side of it could advance in line with the victors and the battle would be as good as won. With one more push, long before the enemy was able to bring up his reserves, they would be on top of Aubers Ridge. The two essentials were that they should be the very best troops available and that there should be enough of them in close support to pass speedily through the first successful waves and continue the assault. Neuve Chapelle was the crux.

In normal circumstances, with the enemy ranged in a semi-circle around it, a salient is an awkward place to occupy and the men defending it can be harassed by rifle and shellfire coming from two sides as well as from their front. But on the British side there had been neither bullets nor shells to spare. In the months they had been holding it, the Germans had got off so lightly that it was they who had been able to harass the 8th Division who had the misfortune to surround them in this sector of the line. Neuve Chapelle was a sniper's paradise. Its houses, still mostly intact, were full of them and, firing in all directions from behind stout walls, their long-range rifles fitted with telescopic sights had been giving the men of the 8th

Division an uncomfortable time and they looked forward to squaring the accounts.

But a salient is also an awkward place to attack. The original plan had been for two brigades of the 8th Division to attack it in the flank from the north, but the Army had had second thoughts. So crucial was the position, so vital was its capture to the success of the whole plan, that it must be hit so fast and so hard at a single blow that there could not be the smallest possibility of delay or hold-up. To stiffen and deepen the attack, the Indian Corps, the immediate neighbours of the 8th Division on its right, was squeezed up to bring its Garhwal Brigade in front of Neuve Chapelle. The 8th Division squeezed up and moved left to make room. It was just one stage of a wholesale reshuffle.

The thirteen-mile front that ran from Neuve Chapelle north to Bois Grenier was held by IV Corps. It comprised the two Regular divisions that together represented the ace in the British hand – the 7th Division, which had borne the brunt of the Battle of Ypres in October, and the 8th Division composed of Regular Battalions brought back from foreign stations. Now there was the Canadian Division, newly arrived in France, but as willing and enthusiastic as any Commander could desire. They were to take over a quiet sector at the northern end of the corps front to allow the 7th Division to double its strength in front of Aubers Ridge. The reshuffling was complete twelve days before the battle. It was a large concentration of troops to compress into an area of a few thousand yards, and although, in principle, the process was much like ordering a single line of soldiers to form fours, to perform the same drill with some twenty thousand men – and in the face of the enemy – was no easy matter. But it had been done, and the troops were in position. Now the IV Corps, with the 23rd Brigade of the 8th Division on its right, joined hands with the Garhwal Brigade on the left of the Indian Corps. Together they formed a rough V-shape round the apex of the salient in front of Neuve Chapelle and when the battle began they would attack it simultaneously from both sides, linking up triumphantly when it had been captured to pursue the advance. This fateful arrangement was the flaw in a well-laid plan. The two brigades, each from a separate Corps, came under two different commands and this factor, in the place where the attack should be strongest, was destined to be the Achilles heel that would trip it up.

The supporting brigades of divisions in the line stretched far back into the rural hinterland for it had been impossible to find billets for so many in nearby farms and hamlets. They could be moved close up as the battle approached. In any event, it would be injudicious to run the risk of their being spotted by inquisitive enemy aircraft before the preparations were complete.

There was little enough time to prepare for the battle, but miracles were accomplished in a few days. For one thing there was the question of forming up trenches and jump-off positions that would give the infantry the all-important head start that would take the enemy by surprise. They could hardly be expected to climb laboriously across the high sandbagged breastworks that had sheltered them since the appalling weather had forced them out of the trenches. But the weather had improved and the ground had dried out – not so much as had been hoped, but enough to dig new trenches and to reclaim old ones, to pump out water, shore up crumbling walls. There would still be an inch or so of sloppy mud underfoot, but heavy planks could be laid to give reasonably dry standing while the men were waiting, and it was a foregone conclusion that they would be up and away in no time, and streaming far ahead. There were bridges to be constructed – scores of them – to lay across the ditches and culverts the troops would have to cross as they moved to the assault. Miles of telephone wire had to be laid, along the ground, festooned along communication trenches and, further back, strung between newly erected poles. The telephones and buzzers would keep Battalions in touch with Divisional Headquarters, link each Division to its Brigade Headquarters, connect Brigades with Corps, and Corps with First Army Headquarters at Merville where Sir Douglas Haig and his staff would be coordinating the offensive and issuing orders. Most important of all, telephones and buzzers would be the vital link between all of them and the guns.

There was the material to be carried up to dumps close to the line – large quantities of food and water, boxes of small arms ammunition for the rifles, shells for the guns, spades and pickaxes, bales of barbed wire, iron pickets, and the hundred and one items that the army would need to dig itself in as it advanced. None of the preparations could be carried out by day and, in the ten nights before the battle, the groans and curses of a thousand working parties might have been heard in Berlin.

L/cpl. W. L. Andrews, 1/4 Bn., Black Watch (Royal Highlanders) (TF), Bareilly Brig., Meerut Div.

We knew, of course, that we'd have to fight our way across fields so sodden with the winter rain that they were like morasses. Before the battle we had to throw bridges across drains and watercourses running through our own front so that the troops could concentrate quickly. We dragged our way up with ammunition, bombs, rations, sandbags, barbed wire, spare bridges, planks, hurdles and iron pickets, and stored them at dumps in the fields. We were carrying all through the hours of darkness night after night. It took a tremendous time to do this but it never occurred to us to wonder what to expect when we crossed to the fields the Germans were holding where we wouldn't have hundreds of bridges to help us over the watery parts, and we would still have all our fighting material to carry forward.

Soldiers? We were more like sweating coolies. How we came to loathe the sodden tracks, with wire overhead, wire underfoot, every few yards! And we still had to carry our rifles and ammunition with us. That was the military way, although there was no danger of our being suddenly attacked and we'd have been a lot more useful as coolies without them!

The gunners, too, had been hard at it, labouring with whatever material was available – planks and bricks and hurdles – to build platforms strong enough to anchor the guns to the muddy earth. Every gun that could be begged or borrowed had been sited behind the front, and the combined field artillery of the IV and Indian Corps, augmented by light thirteen-pounders borrowed from the cavalry, was positioned in a deep horseshoe mostly in front of Neuve Chapelle. For days now they had been ranging on the enemy's line, taking care not to arouse his suspicion and taking care also to expend as little as possible of the precious ammunition. At the start of the offensive they would fire the hurricane bombardment that would smash the German wire and blow open a path for the infantry to advance. Behind them were the heavy guns that would pulverise the trenches and destroy strong-points in the line – but there were not nearly enough of them. Of the two mammoth 15-inch Howitzers on which Sir John French had depended only one had arrived. It had brought little ammunition, and what it had was faulty.

As the days passed the Commander-in-Chief fumed and fretted. Two batteries of heavy guns were still missing and their eight 6-inch Howitzers would constitute a third of all the siege guns that had been faithfully promised weeks earlier. Far from being in position where they ought to be, they had not even embarked for France. They were the 59th and 81st Siege Batteries, but their high numbers gave a false impression for they did not indicate the number of siege guns at the disposal of the British Army. They were Indian numbers and although the gunners were not ready to embark they had arrived from India three months earlier.

Bdr. W. Kemp, A sub-section, 59 Siege Bty., RGA.

We were at Roorkee when the war broke out. At first it didn't upset the routine in our battery at all, and that really annoyed us because we'd expected to be away to France on the next boat. But we didn't get away until the middle of November and we landed in Devonport about Christmas and marched to Portsmouth barracks. What a reception we got from the crowd! We were heroes already, in their opinion. All *we* were thinking about was getting a feed of fish and chips, and to hell with the cheers! My last taste of them was in February 1909, before we sailed for India, so all I thought about was getting to the nearest chip shop.

We'd left our 25-hundredweight guns behind, but we kept our pre-war numbers and 59th and 81st Batteries kept their old Garrison Artillery numbers, so when we finally *did* get to France in March this caused some confusion to people who didn't know owt about the Royal Garrison Artillery. Other batteries that came out later couldn't understand why the number of our battery was higher than theirs. We went to Fort Fareham at the beginning of January to be equipped with 6-inch 30-hundredweight Howitzers and started to work with them. It was a different cup of tea from India!

For one thing the battery was horse-drawn. Out there we had bullocks, great hefty beasts, and when we went to camp we had elephants to pull the guns out when they managed to slide into a ditch – which was often! Compared to them these horses were ruddy devils! *Now* when we got stuck in a ditch or the mud it was a case of 'Take out the 'osses and put on the drag ropes.' It was some change, because you could say we'd lived in luxury in India. Everything was done for us – we even got *shaved* in bed by the Nappi. He came round every morning and we paid him about fourpence a month. We didn't know we were born!

Of course we worked hard too. I'd started on the old 4-inch gun mounted on an elephant carriage – no buffers, so when it fired it went back about ten yards and had to be wheeled forward to its correct position. We did gun-drill, we did some rifle exercises, a little semaphore, practice in observation, a guard now and again – and that was our life.

One of the things we had to do now was practise firing by the map at targets we couldn't see, and that was absolutely new to *us*. In India we went to Battery Practice Camp once a year. A nice wide area was selected where the 'enemy' guns could be seen from the observation of fire instruments. The enemy very kindly fired powder puffs twice so that we could correct our line. We brought our instrument on to the centre line of the enemy's battery, and when we fired we were able to record the fall of our shots easily, because the enemy always stopped firing so that the observers on our instrument wouldn't get mixed up with the fall of shot and the gun-fire of the very obliging *Enemy*!

This was a wonderful system where the gunners ran with the hare and hunted with the hounds! Even we gunners on the instrument used to laugh at it, but to no avail. Fancy intelligent officers of the Royal Artillery falling for this daft idea which could *only* be carried out in practice camp!

Since mid-February a series of urgent telegrams had been flying between Staff Headquarters at St Omer and Ordnance Head-quarters in England, and they grew more and more fiery as the weeks passed and there was no sign of the two missing batteries. First came the assurance that they would sail on 26 February, then without fail on 1 March. On the 3rd Sir John French was cast down by the news that the batteries had not yet left England. Time was running out. If they did not arrive soon they would hardly have time to dig in the guns or to range on targets before the battle began. Their targets had already been allotted, and both of them were crucial. The particular task of 59th Battery was to smash the German strongpoints around Mauquissart on the front of the 22nd Brigade who would attack it.

Chapter 7

Mauquissart was a cluster of ruined houses on the left of the planned attack. It was clear enough to see for it was barely a quarter mile behind the German line directly in front of Aubers on the ridge a mile beyond. Between them, close to Mauquissart, another landmark rose out of the tumbled grey waste. It was the Moulin du Pietre, a large double-storeyed working mill that had served local farmers for miles around and now doubtless served the Germans as a useful place from which to make observation close to their line. Beyond Mauquissart the enemy line began to curve, dipping back slightly behind the Ferme van Biesen, brooding, abandoned, a hundred yards ahead in No Man's Land. It was a large farm, almost a manor, surrounded by trees and a once-ornamental waterscape that had doubled as a drainage ditch in the low-lying farmland. A hundred yards beyond it, British troops, looking from their own lines into No Man's Land, christened it the Moated Grange.

The line that looked so clear-cut and distinct drawn as a firm black line on war maps in the newspapers was different when looked at from the air or the line itself. The two sets of trench-lines, separated by a hundred yards or so, straggled and meandered through a mish-mash of splintered trees, crumbling buildings, ruined roadways, here switching back to take advantage of higher ground, there jutting out to protect the prize of a fortified village or wood. As often as not the trenches ran in untidy loops and angles where the last loss or gain of a local attack had left them. There was nothing clear-cut about them.

Beyond the Moated Grange the German trenches ran south to cross the track the British called Signpost Lane, and then pushed out to form the salient enclosing Neuve Chapelle. Where that salient ended another began, jutting this time into the German lines. The British called it Port Arthur and it was small, but it was theirs, and this was all to the good, for it enclosed the crossroads where the Estaires road met the Rue du Bois that ran back towards Béthune and these were the vital, the indispensable routes to the trenches. Before the lines had been rudely carved across it the Rue du Bois had also led to the Bois du Biez, a large rectangular wood, half a mile in length and half a mile behind Neuve Chapelle. It was empty and untouched. In early March, as buds on the trees slowly opened, the wood beyond the Indians' front line was gradually turning green.

This, then, was the battlefield. It was such a small stretch of land that an onlooker at a vantage point not much above ground level could have surveyed it at a glance, barely turning his head. The headache for artillery observation officers was that vantage points above ground level near their lines were few and far between. For want of anything better, haystacks were burrowed out to serve as makeshift observation posts and on the day before the battle no fewer than thirty observation officers crowded into a single ruined house at Pont Logy, training binoculars on the trenches of the salient that protected Neuve Chapelle. It was here at Pont Logy that the twenty machine-guns of the Indian Corps would be massed to cover the advance. The ammunition had been brought up and sandbagged emplacements constructed in the front line. All the previous night Arthur Agius and his men had been working. At six in the morning they returned to la Couture and Agius turned in to sleep for a few hours, stretched out on a wooden table. With so many troops crammed behind the front there was neither a bed nor floor-space to be found. But he slept the sleep of the just. In a short time they would be off and so far as his part went, he was satisfied that everything was ready.

At the eleventh hour and some eighteen hours before they were due to take part in the battle, the 59th Siege Battery finally arrived.

Bdr. W. Kemp.

We detrained at Estaires and went into action off the la Bassée Road. We pulled into the orchard of a farm and I was detailed to join the signallers – or telephonists as we really were. There was very little morse code used and visibility didn't allow us to use flags. But we all had to set to and get our heavy guns set up double-quick and it was *some* job, although we were trained to do things double-quick and it seemed like practice camp all over again. It was what we had been used to and the only difference was the country we were in. The detachments put down their double-deck platforms and bulk holdfast – the guns were anchored to them by a volute spring. But the volute springs had been left behind! That was the first panic. The consequence was that when the guns fired they recoiled about ten yards and had to be run-up by hand to the correct position – just like the old days in India.

The line of fire was the next question. What to do? Well, what we did was to ask another battery not far away. We could only see about two hundred yards on account of trees, but we could see the spire of Neuve Chapelle Church. The officer on this job was told to get a line on the church, hit it, and then register this as his line of fire and switch from it to other targets. He set up a plane table with a map of the area, put a pin on the church and another in the centre of the battery position. Then, with a director marked in a 180 degrees left and right, he took a zero line from the pins and then gave individual angles to all the guns, which brought them into parallel lines with the line of his director. One gun fired and hit the church and the others took parallel lines to it. But, needless to say, it didn't fire *that* afternoon, and it was doubtful if we could even be ready to fire a shot in the bombardment next day.

The Colonel of the Brigade came along about this time and spoke to the Major to tell him about the battle tomorrow. They stood at the plane table and the Colonel pointed to the map. I heard him say, 'One division will go in and swing left, the next one will go in and swing right, and then the cavalry will go through.' The Major looked at him and said, 'Like Hell they will!' I heard him say it.

The Major had good reason to be despondent. The Colonel had spared no pains to stress the importance of the role his Howitzers were expected to play, and the Battery-Commander well knew that it would be a near-impossibility to achieve it. Despite the gargantuan efforts of his men, he would be lucky if his guns were able to fire a shot in the next twenty-four hours, let alone hit the target, and on this occasion the enemy would not be so obliging as to fire puffs of signal smoke to help them. But, in the late afternoon, as the troops were assembling for the move to the line, there was hardly another man from Sir John French himself to the most newly arrived Territorial who was not full of optimism and confident of success.

L/cpl. W. L. Andrews.

We felt honoured to think we'd been chosen to serve in the battle. We were eager to fight, smarting to avenge the things that had been said about the Territorials. We might be raw – we'd only been out a couple of months – but we were keen men, intelligent men, and every one a volunteer. We meant to do our best and we were convinced that this was the battle that might end the war! In those days we thought we only had to break through the German front and the enemy would crumple up and we would be done with trenches because, once we had thrust through the trench system the line would be rolled up. That was a favourite phrase then, *rolled up*!

Later on, battles were more mysterious and the ordinary soldier never knew what was happening except in his own bit of battlefield. You could get stuck in a reeking shell pit for a whole day and night and not know whether it was friend or foe in the trench fifty yards away. Of course battle plans were not revealed to a humble lance-corporal like myself, but at Neuve Chapelle we had a good idea what we were after. We had a very fair idea of the ground to be covered and in our stints in the line we studied it as much as we could. The ground slowly rose towards the village of Aubers and we knew that about nine miles beyond was the city of Lille. We were hopeful and innocent enough to believe that there would be cosy billets for us in Lille on the night of the battle.

The men from Dundee knew that they were not to take part in the opening stages of the battle. Their job was to wait until Neuve Chapelle had been captured, only then would they move forward to hold the first captured trenches while the victors swept ahead. Every man knew what he had to do. Alex Letyford had spent most of the day making the scaling-ladders that would take the troops across the enemy's sandbags, but he would be in the thick of it when the battle began. Around the salient, as aeriel photographs had shown, some trenches straggled back deep into German territory to link up with others that could not possibly be taken in the first assault. As soon as the first wave had gained a foothold engineers would go forward to construct barricades that would protect them as they consolidated and dug in, and a thousand Sikhs of the Lahore Division were standing by to repair the surface of the shattered road that ran through the German front line into Neuve Chapelle. As darkness fell and the troops began to gather for the move to the line, the Battalions who held it shuffled right or left to make room for them.

Capt. A. J. Agius, MC.

Until five o'clock we worked on the guns then we pushed up to the front again, via Richebourg St Vaast and Windy Corner. Our brigade was to make the attack on the Indian Corps frontage, four Battalions in the front line, with ours in support, and behind them the remainder of the Corps. The Brigade Machine-Guns were divided into two; half went forward with

their own Battalions just behind the attacking line, the remainder were to bring supporting fire to bear from the trenches on
the left flank south of Pont Logy and this was where I was with
my colleague, Johnnie Sutcliffe.

Lt. C. Tennant.

On 9 March we were still at Vieille Chapelle, because our
brigade had been in reserve. We had received orders on the 8th
to be ready for a move and we spent the 9th packing up and
sending away all superfluous kit to store at la Couture. We took
nothing with us but rations, coats, a spare pair of socks and
twenty rounds per man.

I turned in at 10.30 leaving orders that I was to be woken
at one o'clock. Breakfast for the men was punctually at
2 a.m. and the Battalion was ready formed up in the road by
2.55. It was dry, but cold and rather misty. We marched to
Richebourg and passed through it to a redoubt in an orchard
and the companies were put into trenches and dug-outs and
were all settled by about 5.30. An occasional shot from a
field battery made the morning sound like any other morning
during the last two months.

The troops were packed so tightly, the narrow country roads were
so congested, and their progress was so slow and full of checks
that it was dangerously close to dawn before the last of them
reached the line. It was no bad thing that waiting time was
shortened, for the assembly points were still wet and muddy and
trenches that had been put into reasonable order had been
soaked yet again by frequent showers of rain and sleet. It was dry
now, but it was cold. A light mist carried frost across the
battlefield and in the early hours, mercifully for the men who
would advance across it, the ground froze hard. Stew that was
still more or less hot had been carried up in dixies for the soldiers
of the first wave who had been longest in position and, as they
chewed and waited, they could hear movement in front, a medley
of muffled voices, of chinking and loud twangs, as parties of
Royal Engineers cut wide openings in their own barbed wire. In a
little while the first wave would be charging through them on
their way to the enemy line.

L/cpl. W. L. Andrews.

Snow swept down on us as we waited in the flooded trenches
near Neuve Chapelle. We grew colder and colder – so cold

that I never thought I could be so chilled and still live. It was sheer biting torture. We could hardly drag our feet along when the orders came to move from the trench to the Port Arthur dug-outs for a few hours sleep before the battle.

At five in the morning my platoon was routed out again to move to a reserve trench. We shambled over ground hardened by frost. It was colder than ever. We called it a trench, but it was more of a breastwork like a stockade strengthened with sandbags of earth, my pals Nicholson and Joe Lee and myself huddled together close to each other with our backs to the stockade. When dawn came we peered across at the German lines, wondering if Jerry knew we were coming.

Dawn broke on the day of battle at half past six in the morning. At just about that time the 6th Bavarian Reserve Battalion were marching to billets in Tourcoing. They were weary, for they had spent two weeks in the wintry trenches near Ypres. They had marched ten kilometres before transport met them at Menin and it had been a long cold night. Now they were looking forward to hot coffee, a breakfast of bread and sausage and cabbage soup, a wash to get rid of the mud, and two blessed weeks away from the dangers and discomfort of the front. In the courtyard behind the Dewavrin house a cooker had already been set up, and the family wakened to the sound of tramping feet and shouted commands as a half company of Bavarians marched in.

Lt. C. Tennant.

The daylight, as it strengthened, showed no sign of anything unusual taking place on our front. But at 7.30 punctually the whole sky was rent by noise – about four hundred British guns all opening fire at once in a concentrated bombardment of two hundred yards of German trenches. We had a battery of – I think – 4.7s only forty yards behind us and the din was terrific. The whole air and the solid earth itself became one quivering jelly. After the first few minutes and after I had gone round and told them to keep their mouths open (instead of trying to look grim with clenched teeth!) the men didn't seem to worry much about the row which was enough to give anyone a sick headache. Funnily enough, I normally have a fanatical dislike for mere noise of any kind, but I was conscious of nothing except the extraordinary sense of security the infantry man gets from hearing artillery fire from his own side.

L/cpl. W. L. Andrews.

The bombardment started like all the furies of hell. The noise almost split our wits. The shells from the field guns were whizzing right over our heads and we got more and more excited. We couldn't hear ourselves speak. *Now* we could make out the German trenches. They were like long clouds of smoke and dust, flashing with shell-bursts, and we could see enormous masses of trench material and even bodies thrown up above the smoke clouds. We thought the bombardment was winning the war before our eyes and soon *we* would be pouring through the gap.

Capt. W. G. Bagot-Chester, MC, 2/3 Gurkha Rifles, Garhwal Brig., Meerut Div.

At 7.30 a.m. artillery bombardment commenced, and never since history has there been such a one. I should think for a full half hour our guns, four hundred and eighty of them, fired without the fraction of a second's break. You couldn't hear yourself speak for the noise. It was a continual rattle and roar. We lay very low in our trenches, as several of our guns were firing short. Later I picked up two shrapnel bullets and the bottom of a shell fuse. They'd landed right beside me.

Lt. C. Tennant.

An aeroplane was observing not very far in front of us and flying fairly low down. A very risky job with that tremendous amount of big 'iron ration' flying about. Through all the bombardment and in fact through all the heavy shelling of that day and the next, the larks mounted carolling up to the sky with shells screaming all round them, as though all that devil's din was only some insane nightmare and as though all that was really true was the coming of spring.

Capt. A. J. Agius.

It was hell let loose. The village and the trenches in front of it were blown to bits. The village seemed to melt away before our eyes. The Hun bracketed one of my guns and finally buried it, but no harm done. The infantry assault was launched at 8.05. Nearest us on the right were the 2/39 Garhwals. They went trotting over. Suddenly I saw a fellow stop then spin and spin till he fell. Others pushed on, tried to get through a hedge, eased to their left and got in further along. It was wonderful to watch the two attacks converge and meet.

Capt. W. G. Bagot-Chester, MC.

Our first attacking line of two double companies advanced, and our guns increased their range so as not to hit our men. Our first and second lines reached the enemy's trenches without much loss because the Boche were obviously quite demoralised by the bombardment. I followed close behind with H Company. Last of all Major Dundas brought along G Company. We advanced right through to the front line under very light fire. We all reached our objective, an old trench-line called the Smith-Dorrien Line, with only about 96 casualties in the whole Battalion, and started to dig ourselves in in case of a counter-attack. There was very little firing from the German side and our attack seemed to have taken them completely by surprise. Some snipers left behind in our advance troubled us for some time until they were cleared out by the Leicesters on our right.

Since the 3rd Londons were in reserve for the early part of the action, Arthur Agius and his machine-gunners were the only men of their Battalion who had taken part in the first attack. His guns had covered it from emplacements in the front line and he had seen it all – the dash across No Man's Land when the barrage lifted, the charge into the trenches of the salient and the signal flags that appeared in an encouragingly short time to show that the line had been captured. For the Germans had indeed been demoralised by the bombardment and they were overrun before they could recover. On the left, Captain Peake of the Lincolns, a blue flag held high above his head, rushed along behind his bombers while they cleared the trenches. Away on the right, Lieutenant Gordon of the Berkshires, waving a flag of bright pink, was doing the same thing. It was the signal for sappers to rush to block the captured trenches, and the signal for the second wave to pass across them and rush the defences of Neuve Chapelle.

Lt. C. Tennant.

We got word that all the first line of German trenches was taken and that an attack was pushing on into Neuve Chapelle. At 10.30 we were ordered to move up in support and marched forward to a place near the line. There was a

94

big farm where No. 1 Company sheltered, while No. 2 lay down very comfortably in the sun under the lee of some straw stacks. From here through my glasses I could very clearly see our first line of supports lining an old trench. Presently across the field came trudging a cocky little Tommy of the Leicestershires with fixed bayonet following a dozen young German prisoners. He was munching a ration biscuit and he was yellow with lyddite fumes. Soon other parties began to pass with prisoners, most of them looking very shaken but delighted to be out of the inferno and in comfortable captivity (instead of having been shot at once which – according to their own officers – is the fate of *all* prisoners who fall into our hands!).

The outlying trenches had been captured so quickly and the troops had dashed so speedily through Neuve Chapelle to occupy trenches on the other side that the supporting Battalions following on their heels to secure the village might have had a dangerous time. Snipers lying low in the houses had been trapped there by the bombardment and, with shells exploding all around their hideouts, they had no chance of escaping before the British were upon them. But the snipers were not inclined to give trouble. One Artillery Observation Officer went forward soon after the village had been captured to reconnoitre a new observation post. Two signallers went with him, carrying telephones and the reels of new wire that would connect them with the guns, and he brought along the battery's trumpeter, Jimmy Naylor, to run back to the battery with messages if required. Young Naylor was only seventeen, but he had been in France as a boy trumpeter since the beginning. He had blown the trumpet-call that brought the guns of his battery out of Mons, he had ridden back with them on the long retreat, he had been in the battles of the Marne and the Aisne. It all added up to the most amazing six months of his short life and even the privations of a winter in Flanders had not dampened his cocky enthusiasm. Compared to the Territorials on the battlefield, Jimmy was an old sweat, but this was his first experience of victory and it was the biggest thrill of the lot.

Tmptr. J. Naylor, 23 Brig., RFA, Att. 8 Div.

We came in just at the back of the troops, after the second wave. The first lot had gone on and they'd already consolidated on the far side of the village, and we could hear the guns firing on either side of us, but there was nothing in the village, just the odd burst of small-arms fire. The infantry were clearing the houses and I never saw anyone so pleased as these little Gurkhas! They looked as if they were having the time of their lives. There was one that caught my eye, and it was a really ghoulish sight, but being a boy and full of bravado I wasn't a bit squeamish. I was a cold-blooded little blighter at that time, but I've never forgotten it, because he was carrying the face of a German – not his head, just his face, clean sliced off. And he was grinning like mad, this little Gurkha, which was more than you could say for the German prisoners who were being marched back. It must have given *them* a very nasty turn.

We were standing there waiting, because my officer wanted to get into these houses to bag a position to observe from – we thought we'd be moving the guns forward any minute – but we had to hang about until we were told it was safe to go in. All of a sudden a cheer went up, and coming down the street was *another* little Gurkha driving a bunch of Germans in front of him at bayonet point. There must have been half a dozen of them and they were twice his size! They all had their hands up, and he looked as pleased as punch. It was marvellous! Even the Major laughed to see them. We were exhilarated, all of us.

The Gurkha soldier's name was Gane Gurung and no one was more exhilarated than he, for the Germans had still been firing from one house and he had gone into it alone and captured eight burly prisoners single-handed. It was the 2nd Rifle Brigade who had called for three cheers when he marched them out and, as the Indian Corps Commander later proudly pointed out, there was 'probably no other instance of an individual Indian soldier being cheered for his bravery by a British Battalion in the midst of a battle'. It was Gane Gurung's moment of glory. Another came a few weeks later when the whole brigade paraded and in front of them all Sir James Willcocks pinned the Indian Order of Merit on his chest. But that was only the icing on the cake.

Another Gurkha was just as anxious to show off his German prisoner, and he was so delighted with him that, by the time he had made his way over open ground and was crossing the old front line near Agius's emplacement, he had shouldered his rifle and was walking chummily by the German's side. Now that the advance had gone far ahead the machine-gunners had ceased firing and, as they waited for orders, they had time to look around. This was the first time any of them had clapped eyes on a German and, seeing them stare, the Gurkha stopped and ostentatiously offered his prisoner a cigarette. It was gratefully accepted, and as the German soldier pulled on it he stared back at the machine-gunners. 'Offizier?' he asked, pointing to Arthur Agius. His captor guessed his meaning and nodded, but the German was shaking his head. 'Junge. Junge,' he remarked. Agius, all of twenty-one and recently promoted to the rank of captain, was not greatly flattered by this uncalled-for comment on his boyish looks. He gave the German a frosty glare, indicated to his escort that he should get a move on and was rather pleased that, after only two weeks with the Meerut Division, the two words of dialect he had picked up now came in useful. 'Jaldi Jow,' he ordered. He had no idea which Indian language they belonged to – and they happened to be Urdu – but they worked, and the small Gurkha fell in smartly behind his prisoner and obediently started to hurry him along. Shells were beginning to fall dangerously close and the German showed no sign of being loath to go.

The victors of Neuve Chapelle were not having things all their own way and the Germans were beginning to answer back.

L/cpl. W. L. Andrews.

We thought the German guns must have been swept out of existence, but they soon opened up and we got the benefit of the counter-fire. Nicholson shouted, 'Look, they're shelling *our* fellows!' Sure enough, looking along the breastwork I could see shrapnel plumping down on our own Black Watch Terriers. They were shelling all along our line and every shell came about ten yards nearer Nick and myself. We could see our turn coming and all we could do was lie and wait for it. Nick yelled, 'The next one's ours!' Douglas Bruce, another pal, had crawled up to us for warmth, and he just shouted, 'Och well, if we're for it, we're for it!' I was amazed how calm we were. The shell came screaming over and we wormed down as low as we could. It burst with a great roar ten yards away and we were drenched with earth. Then it was past. A few more fell further and further behind us and it fell quiet. We could even hear birds singing.

Lt. D. S. Lewis.

I saw most of it from the air and I was badly scared. We had about four hundred guns all firing like hell and as we were flying at about twelve hundred feet owing to clouds, we were fairly surrounded by our own shells. It was quite a relief crossing the line to exchange German bullets for British shells. No troops would have withstood that bombardment. I fairly had the wind put up me by seeing a 9.2-inch shell whizz past my tail. Two of my subalterns *were* killed by a shell.

Owing to the weather we couldn't do much in the way of ranging, but we caught most of their batteries firing, which was quite useful. The first part of the show was well run. We'd been registering all the batteries on all important points and every inch of the trenches had been photographed from above, so that every subaltern knew exactly where he was attacking and what trenches there were in front and to the flanks.

L/cpl. W. L. Andrews.

At eleven o'clock the order came: '4th Black Watch, move to the left in single file'. Neuve Chapelle had been taken and we were ordered to move forward to the captured German trenches. We passed many many Indian dead on the way and the ground was a mass of stinking shell-pits. There was a point where we had to jump a ditch in full view of the Germans. They were a longish way off but they must have had a rifle trained on it and they were hitting men as they jumped. Captain Boase was on the other side of the ditch calling on us to hurry, because so many men hesitated to jump that we were in a bunch. There were four in front of me. The first ran as fast as he could and jumped high. Crack! A bullet got him, but it was only a slight wound and he recovered himself and carried on. A little stumpy fellow was next. Crack! He was shot dead. The next man just flopped into the ditch and scrambled out soaking. Then Nicholson jumped and got away with it. Then it was my turn. I thought to myself, 'Now for it!' I'd jumped for my school, so I aimed to jump high, tucked my legs under me and then thrust them forward for landing. Bullets whistled past, but I wasn't hit. It's curious, but that jump is almost the last thing I remember! Everything is confusion after that, except that there seemed to be more and more fire, and I remember the stench of the shell-pits stinging my nostrils.

But Neuve Chapelle had fallen. It had been captured in less than an hour, and everything had gone like clockwork.

Messages flashed from First Army Headquarters. The Cavalry was ordered to move close up, and at mid-day the 8th Sherwood Foresters received instructions to start marching without delay to Bac St Maur. From there only two hours' march would take them into battle and they were warned to be ready to move at a moment's notice.

Chapter 8

The Rifle Brigade had gone so far and so fast that the first men who reached the other side of Neuve Chapelle were in serious risk of running into their own bombardment. They halted reluctantly and, more reluctantly still, returned to join the main body of the Battalion halted a little way in front of the village. But three men could dodge shells where hundreds could not, and Lieutenant Stacke of the Worcesters was not prepared to wait. His Battalion, the 1st Worcesters, was waiting at the old front line, ready to move forward and carry on the advance. His job was to reconnoitre the ground. He had picked two men to go with him, and they were the best scouts in the Battalion. They worked to their left, clear of the village and just clear of the bombardment, and made a dash for it up the remnants of a lane. Ahead there was nothing and no one to be seen, and peering at the Bois du Biez through binoculars, Stacke could detect not the slightest movement. A few stray bullets flew round as they worked their way back, but they were easily dodged and, if anything, they added spice to the adventure. They were in high spirits, hurrying now, for already the Battalion would be moving forward. They were to rendezvous at 9.30 in the village, and move instantly through the captured line to the attack. Stacke would have the satisfaction of reporting that it would be a piece of cake and, as the patrol went back through the captured line, he passed on the good news to the Rifle Brigade. Colonel Stephens could see as much for himself. The bombardment had stopped, there was no sign of the enemy on his front and already he had sent a message to Divisional Headquarters for permission to advance. He was astounded by the reply, but the order was unequivocal. The Battalion was to stand fast – and it was to dig in.

Lieutenant Stacke had reached the rendezvous, but there was no sign of the Worcesters. He moved on to the old line, expecting every moment to meet the Battalion on the way, but the Worcesters were still at the assembly point. They had been told to wait, and Stacke's encouraging report did nothing to quell their impatience. They could not imagine where the difficulty lay.

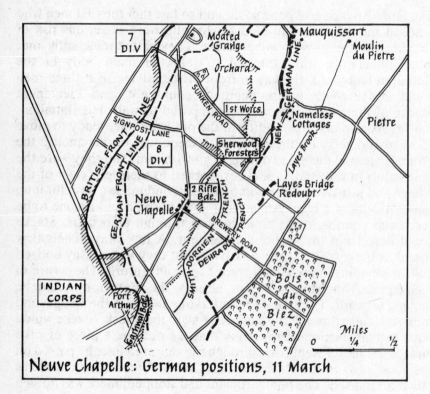

Neuve Chapelle: German positions, 11 March

It lay on their left where the attack had failed, and it had failed because the unfortunate 59th Siege Battery had been unable to destroy the defences in the German line.

Bdr. W. Kemp.

They'd worked in shifts all night, just taking turns for an hour's sleep. You never saw men working like it – and all the light there was to work with was these old candle-lanterns we had, and the worst of *them* was that every time the guns fired the candle went out. Not that they did fire on that occasion! It was getting the blooming things stabilised that caused the trouble, and there were four of these big Howitzers to a battery. You can judge the size of them by the weight of the ammunition – these 6-inch shells came twenty-two to the ton, and of course *they* all had to be manhandled. When it came near daylight I was sent forward with some other signallers to the observation post. Well, it was no observation post! It was a straw stack! The officer got on top of it with his binoculars and we signallers were behind it with the telephones. As soon as it got daylight the guns were supposed to range on the target so the fire could be adjusted before the bombardment started at half past seven. But it was completely new country to us. How could the officer tell from the top of a haystack if the shells were dropping on the target on ground he'd never seen before? It wasn't humanly possible. On top of that, our normal rate of fire should have been one shell every two minutes, but, not being solid enough on their platforms, they recoiled so far that they had to be run up by hand and re-positioned after every shot. Great heavy guns, remember. That first morning we were lucky if we fired two shots in ten minutes, and it was anybody's guess where they were going. The upshot was that, when the infantry went over, the wire wasn't cut at all.

The job should have been so easy that the Battalion Headquarters could hardly be blamed for thinking that it had been a brilliant success. The first wave of 2nd Middlesex went over and disappeared into the mist. A second followed quickly on its heels and, minutes later, a third. Two Battalions were assaulting a line held by only two companies of German Jaegers and it was hardly wishful thinking to assume that they had given up without a fight, for not a single wounded man returned. But the trenches had not been touched by the bombardment and neither had the Jaegers defending them. Few though they were they had plenty of machine-guns. The Middlesex had been mown down long before they reached the enemy trench and no wounded had returned because all of them were dead.

On their right the Scottish Rifles advancing alongside had at first been more fortunate but, while the right-hand companies got forward with comparative ease, one flank was 'in the air', for the companies on the left had been decimated by the same machine-guns that annihilated the Middlesex.

L/cpl. E. Hall, 2nd Bn., Cameronians (Scottish Rifles).

We'd taken our positions in the trenches the night before and we put up climbing ladders for jumping over the parapet. We were on tiptoe with excitement because we were fed up with trenches and living in a sea of mud and we just wanted to get the Germans out in the open. We'd seen them off at Messines Ridge when they attacked in November, but *this* was *our* offensive, the first our army had made since the trench warfare began.

I was company stretcher-bearer and so I had to follow the company as they advanced across No Man's Land. They got up to the German trench, but the barbed wire wasn't cut at all and the Germans were shooting like mad while our lads were crouching down in the mud trying to breach it with wire-cutters, and those that didn't have wire-cutters hacking at it with bayonets. Eventually they did get through and over this high parapet of sandbags – it hadn't been touched by the shells, mark you! – and in they went with the bayonet. They chased the Germans from traverse to traverse until they were all accounted for – at least in *that* part of the line.

But our losses were appalling during the few minutes it took to cut the wire. They went down like ninepins! Every single Company Commander went down leading the attack, and the Major, the Adjutant and the Colonel. They'd all been years in the Army, excellent soldiers, and we could ill-afford to lose such men! All the officers went, killed or wounded. By the end of three days we had just one subaltern left.

Far away on the right, at the extreme edge of the attack, a Battalion of the Indian Corps was also struggling with barriers of bristling barbed wire – but it was not the fault of the gunners. The 1/39th Garhwalis had attacked the wrong objective. Perhaps the mist was to blame. Perhaps they had been misled by the line of the road swinging off at an angle towards la Bassée. Perhaps it was because their old reclaimed trenches did not directly face the line of their attack, or because, as some said, a tree which had been picked out as a landmark was blown to pieces in the bombardment. Whatever the reason, the Company lost direction and the others were propelled by sheer momentum to follow their lead.

Like the Scottish Rifles a mile away on their left, with no bombardment to prepare the way, with no cover on their flanks, and with no friendly guns to cover them as they advanced, they had hacked and clawed and battered their way through the Germans' wire and captured a long length of their trench-line. It was a magnificent feat of arms, but it had scuppered the whole attack. It had also dislocated the plan of Sir Douglas Haig and, when they finally realised just what had happened, it placed both Corps Commanders in a dilemma. Now, where the attack had diverged, there was a gap in the line. On either side of it the troops had surged ahead and, between them, in the trenches that faced Port Arthur, the Germans were holding on, manning their machine-guns, and giving notice of their intention to hold out to the last man.

The battle orders had been precise:

As soon as the village of Neuve Chapelle has been captured and made good, the 7th and 8th Divisions, supported by the Indian Corps on their right, will be ordered by the Corps Commander to press forward to capture the high ground.

The village was undoubtedly secured. In the centre of the assault everything had gone according to plan. The ground in front was clear to the Aubers Ridge – but on either side, at two critical points, each on a separate corps front, the attack had failed and the enemy was still fighting back.

It was difficult for the two Corps Commanders to confer, for Sir Henry Rawlinson had his IV Corps headquarters at Marmuse, separated by eight kilometres of winding country road from Sir James Willcocks' Indian Corps Headquarters at la Croix. For his own part, Rawlinson ordered a fresh attack on the trenches near the Moated Grange. It would be ushered in by a fresh bombardment and this time by guns familiar with the ground. A mile away on the right, Sir James Willcocks would also try again, and until the whole of the German front line had been captured the troops who were waiting to advance must continue to wait.

As the day wore on Colonel Stephens grew increasingly short-tempered, now gazing through binoculars at the tempting prospect ahead, now pacing up and down the length of the Battalion front where his Battalion was digging in. Wherever he turned he was met by a barrage of questions. 'Why aren't we getting a move on, sir?' He fervently wished he knew the answer. The Battalion continued to dig in, as ordered.

It was less a case of digging in than of building up, for no digging was possible on the waterlogged ground and it had not even been feasible to occupy their original objective in Smith-Dorrien trench which had been the old British line before the battles of November. It was a long deep trench that ran clean across the front facing the Aubers Ridge, and the Command had believed that it would make an ideal jump-off for the second phase of the assault. But it was many months since Smith-Dorrien trench had been a trench at all. It was full of water, the Germans had long ago found it uninhabitable, and the bombardment that had been intended to pulverise its defences and cow its garrison had been so many shells wasted. There was nobody there. Fifty yards behind it, on the outskirts of Neuve Chapelle, chafing, fretting and frustrated, the Rifle Brigade was navvying, building a protective wall with bricks and rubble and broken masonry salvaged from the ruined houses and the brewery at their backs. They were working under difficulties. Earlier they had watched the Germans run away, abandoning field guns near the Bois du Biez. Now, seeing no signs of an advance, they had crept back again and were firing at point-blank range over open sights. Shells were bursting among the riflemen as they worked and a machine-gun travelling up and down the road in front of the wood raked them with vicious fire. They replied as best they could, but there were many casualties and the Battalion was dwindling away.

Later in the morning, as they worked, they were encouraged by the sound of British guns firing somewhere behind them to their left. It was the new bombardment on the trenches near the Moated Grange. When it stopped the troops advanced, running past the flung-out bodies of the Middlesex as they went. They could not help but trample on them because they lay in three distinct lines, shoulder to shoulder, just as they had advanced.

By mid morning the trenches had been taken. It was easy going. The new bombardment had been so devastatingly accurate that there was no fight left in the enemy soldiers who survived it. In the wake of the bombardment, as the first lines of Tommies came into view, they climbed out of the trenches behind the Moated Grange and surrendered in droves. The news was slow in reaching IV Corps Headquarters, but it was good when it came and, now that almost all the original objectives had been captured, it was the moment the army had been waiting for to advance on the Aubers Ridge. But the Corps Commander was hesitating. An orchard lay not two hundred yards beyond the captured line and Sir Henry Rawlinson believed that it was so fortified that, if it held out when the line moved forward, it might well be the stumbling block that would endanger the whole advance. When it began there must be no more gaps, no more hold- ups, and he could not afford to take risks. It would be better to wait and bring up reinforcements to attack the orchard in

104

such force that resistance must crumble away. It was the last little bit of insurance that would guarantee success. Two companies of the Worcesters, still waiting at their assembly point, were ordered forward to help secure the orchard. They went off blithely, only too happy to be on the move at last.

General Capper, in command of the 7th Division, was far from happy, for he was equally impatient to get going, and his Division, spread along the line north of the Moated Grange, had been standing by all morning, anxious to get into the fight. There was no resistance in front of them, the church spire in the village of Aubers beckoned tantalisingly across the open ground, and by now they should have been – he believed they *could* have been – ensconced in the village itself. At noon, two and a half hours after the time originally fixed for the advance, in the absence of definite orders, he could restrain his impatience no longer. He managed, with difficulty, to telephone to IV Corps Headquarters and literally begged the Corps Commander for permission to press on. Sir Henry Rawlinson refused, but he took time to explain the situation and General Capper was obliged to be satisfied with a promise that, as soon as the orchard was secured, the advance would begin.

But, even as they spoke, the orchard had already been secured. The troops had strolled across without a shot being fired. The orchard was empty. There were no strongpoints, not even a trench among the tree stumps, and there was no sign that the enemy had ever thought of defending it.

Another hour had been lost. Communications were already slowing down, and it was more than an hour before the news reached corps headquarters. It took twenty more minutes for Rawlinson to prepare his report. At Merville, Sir Douglas Haig was at luncheon with his staff, but despite the excellent food, the well-appointed table, the discreet service of mess-waiters going imperturbably about their duties, it was an anxious meal and the Army Commander was glad to be interrupted when Rawlinson's message arrived. He read his summary of the situation, noted that he proposed to issue orders for a general advance at 2 p.m. and dictated a message of approval. It reached Rawlinson's Head-quarters at twenty-five minutes to two. But now it was Rawlinson's turn to champ at the bit. He had every reason to believe that the Indian Corps, by now, would have captured the segment of line – a mere two hundred yards – where the enemy was still holding out in front of Port Arthur, but a telephone call to Sir James Willcocks at Indian Corps Headquarters swiftly disabused him.

The gap was still open. The trenches had not been captured – but it was not for want of trying. The Leicesters had bombed their way into a section of the trench, at a cost of many men, and had even

105

succeeded in building a barricade before they were forced back. The 3rd Londons had helped too. It was Harry Pulman's company that had dashed through machine-gun fire and struggled in the wire to get at the enemy holding out behind it. Now Pulman was dead, as were Stevens and Bertie Mathieson, and Captain Reeves and 'Evie' Noël had been brought back badly wounded. The Germans still held out.

Now the two remaining companies were to try again. They waited all morning, and half the afternoon for orders.

Capt. G. Hawes, DSO, MC, Adjutant (City of London) Bn., London Regt., Royal Fusiliers (TF).

I went forward to a circular breastwork with Captain Livingston and Captain Moore and their companies on the right and the Colonel went with Captain Pulman and Captain Reeves on the left. Here in this circular breastwork we remained until about 4.30 p.m. I can't describe what the breastwork was like, a mass of blackened, ruined walls of some old farm, built round with walls of earth and sandbags with machine-guns mounted on them, bodies lying about everywhere, dirt and squalor and misery on all sides. By this time the battle was in full blast. The shells were flying overhead, the noise was deafening and the sky was full of our aeroplanes. About 2 p.m. we got word that poor Captain Pulman, Mr Mathieson and Mr Stevens had been killed and Captain Noël wounded in an attack on the left.

Four hours had passed since the Indian Corps Commander had issued orders for a fresh attack. They had reached Brigade and later Division, but they had not reached the 1st Seaforths, already moving up from their support position to Neuve Chapelle, and it was the 1st Seaforths who were to repeat the action of the Leicesters, to attack the trenches from the flank and bear the brunt of the assault. Colonel Ritchie had done his best when instructions finally reached him at mid-day, but it took time to clarify them, to sum up the situation and to brief his Company Commanders. It took even longer to move his Battalion through the shell-fire, across open country, and into position for the attack. The fire was fearsome now and the signallers were having the worst of it. All along the line, and well behind it, the network of telephone wires was being cut to shreds. There was no communication between Battalions and Brigade Headquarters a mile or more away, and little between Brigade Headquarters and Division, who were even further off. Worst of all, there was no communication between the infantry and the guns. News and messages starting from the front line and carried back by relays of breathless runners were inevitably long out of date before they reached the anxious staff at Headquarters in the rear. They were working in the dark, trying to guess the situation as best they could, piecing together scant information and confused reports, hoping – although it was almost too much to hope – that circumstances had not changed by the time they reached them.

General Anderson, in command of the Meerut Division, had guessed wrong. It was well past two o'clock and at that hour, according to his latest information, the Seaforths had intended to attack. No word had reached him of the long delay and he did not know that, once again, the attack had been postponed. The only snippet of news that filtered through (and it was easy to misinterpret) was that the Seaforths had been 'held up'. He ordered the guns to open up to help them forward. It was sixteen minutes to three o'clock. By the revised time-table the Seaforths were due to attack at 2.45 and they were already waiting, concealed by ruined houses on the flank of their objective, ready to charge. As the shells began to explode around the uncaptured trench, Colonel Ritchie could only assume that there had been a change of plan, and could only feel thankful that the bombardment had not begun a minute later. It was a violent bombardment and it was extraordinarily accurate. The enemy guns were swift to reply. All Ritchie could do in such a maelstrom was to wait for further orders and, meanwhile, suspend his attack until they came. A hundred yards or so away crouching behind their breastwork at right angles to the Seaforths, the bewildered 3rd Londons were waiting too.

Capt. G. Hawes, DSO, MC.

I can't tell you what it's like to have these shells whistling over one's head and bursting nearer and nearer. The noise is terrific and the shock of the explosions is terrible. At last it calmed down and about 4.30 we received orders to send Captain Moore and Captain Livingston out of our breastwork to attack.

The Germans *had* to be dislodged from their trench, so our companies climbed over the breastwork in full view of the enemy. They opened a murderous fire, but no one hesitated for a second – everyone went straight on across that awful open country with bayonets at the charge. It was appalling – and it was splendid! No troops in the world could have done better. Crichton was first up. As soon as I gave the order to advance he stepped out in front of his platoon and shouted, 'Follow me!' Before many yards a bullet struck his leg, and he stumbled. One or two of the men following made as if to go over to help

107

him, but he was too quick for them. He struggled to his feet and managed to stumble on. But he got no distance before another bullet caught him. He fell and didn't rise again. Later the stretcher-bearers brought him in, but he only lived for a minute. Many, many men went down on the way across, but the others reached the trench and the Germans surrendered. Mr Sorley was wounded and I can't tell how many of the men were killed or wounded.

After the charge the Colonel and I sat inside that breastwork and helped to tend the wounded as the stretcher-bearers brought them in. It was heart-rending – our first time in action. Those dear lads! I'm not ashamed to say it made the tears run down my face to see them. But they made so light of it! One boy, in great pain, was even smiling. He said to me, 'They can't call us Saturday night soldiers now, can they, sir?' They were simply astonishing. *No* Battalion could have done better and many, I'm quite sure, wouldn't have done nearly so well.

The Colonel and I stayed in that hell until 8 p.m. and then we went forward to a ruined house that had been captured from the Germans. There we tried to collect our companies together, and there we stayed, in reserve.

Like all adjutants of Territorial Battalions George Hawes was a Regular Army officer.[*] Praise from him was praise indeed. It was well deserved, for they had won a small but vital victory. It was not their fault that it came many hours too late.

A mile away on the left, misconceptions and misunderstandings had also dogged the fortunes of the IV Corps. At 2.45, confident of General Willcocks's assurance that the 'gap' on the Indian Corps front was on the point of being captured and filled in, Rawlinson had, at last, felt able to send out the order for a general advance. They were complicated orders, and they were not entirely the orders that had been anticipated by the Battalion Commanders who had to carry them out on the ground. Instead of advancing straight ahead to the Aubers Ridge the leading Brigades of the 7th and 8th Division were to advance north-east, diagonally to their left. It was a sound plan. Although the enemy guns were busy, there had been few German troops behind their immediate front and those who were facing the 7th Division and had not yet been attacked had been keeping their heads well down. One Brigade of the 7th Division would remain opposite the enemy, while the others advanced across

---

[*] This was the pre-war custom, which was still in force in early 1915. As the war progressed and casualties increased the practice could not be maintained.

the ground behind the hostile trenches. General Capper ordered that, as soon as there were signs that the Germans in it were 'unsettled', the remainder of the 7th Division would swing out, capture their trenches, and join in the advance.

It was a complicated manoeuvre, for it meant that the 8th Division would advance behind the German line and across the 7th Division's front. But it might have worked. It might have worked at three o'clock when Rawlinson had sent orders for the advance. It might even have worked in the daylight that remained after 3.30, the hour at which Rawlinson had directed the infantry to cross the old Smith-Dorrien line and move to the attack. But he had underestimated the time his orders would take to pass through Divisional and Brigade Headquarters to the Battalions waiting at the front. It was almost four o'clock before they reached them. Low clouds had been thickening all afternoon. The light was dull now, and threatening early dusk. Even so, it was not too late – but still the infantry waited. The 8th Division was to begin to move forward as soon as the 21st Brigade of the 7th Division came into line on its left. Time passed. There was no sign of movement in the 7th Division and it was hardly surprising, because the 21st Brigade had already moved forward to its position beyond the orchard, and there, a quarter of a mile away, the infantry had been marking time in accordance with their own Divisional Orders. These were that they were to advance as soon as the 8th Division moved into line beside them. It took many runners stumbling and slithering over the ditches and sodden ground, many exchanges of messages, much fuming and puzzlement, and precious time wasted before they could make sense of the situation. It was half past five before the leading Battalions of the 8th Division moved forward and into position to the right of the orchard. It was fully five hours since it had been captured and the enemy had made good use of the time.

Sir Henry Rawlinson had been right in suspecting the existence of a German redoubt, but it was not in the orchard and there was not one, but three. In the weeks before the battle the Germans had been tracing out a second defensive line behind their front. Most of it was still on paper, but they had made a beginning by constructing scattered strongholds and later, when the ground dried out, a new trench system would link them up. They had placed them with care. Houses in the hamlet of Mauquissart, sandbagged and loopholed, were encircled with breastworks, strongly wired, with machine-gun emplacements that commanded a wide field of fire. A little way south, and just east of the orchard, another group of cottages had been fortified in the same way, and there was a third redoubt where a bridge – a mere

109

culvert – crossed the Layes between these nameless cottages and the Bois du Biez.* The nearby reserves had been swiftly brought forward. They only amounted to two companies of Jaegers but during the lull in the afternoon they had ample time to bring up more machine-guns and to filter into the line to reinforce the strongholds. They were ready, and they were waiting.

The redoubt at Mauquissart and the stronghold at 'Nameless Cottages' were directly in the line of the 8th Division advance. During the afternoon, after the capture of the first German trench-line, they were spotted and the guns were instructed to deal with them before the troops advanced. The gunners had done their best, but these important strongpoints, undiscovered until now, had not been registered, and in the deepening gloom they were not easy to pinpoint from the old observation posts. It was almost six o'clock before they finally set off, and it was very nearly dark. Even in daylight it would have been difficult for eight Battalions to keep direction, to pick their way over the sullen ground, floundering through water-ditches, clambering through hedges, wading, sliding and, where there was a foothold, twisting and wrenching ankles on the rotting remains of unharvested turnips and beets. It was hardly a charge. It was a disaster. They barely advanced five hundred yards, and it was a miracle that they had got as far as that in the face of a hail of fire from the redoubts. The German machine-gunners had little light to aim by, but they hardly needed to aim. They were traversing the guns, spraying fire non-stop, small orange jets from the muzzles of eight Maxims jabbed into the gloom, bullets flew into the massed, disorganised ranks, and the attack ground to a halt.

It began to rain. No orders came. Advancing blind, and at an angle, across unfamiliar ground the formations had become hopelessly mixed up. After a time, the machine-guns stopped, but intermittent bursts of warning fire kept the attackers at bay. Even that was hardly necessary. They were finished. The survivors could only stop where they were, huddling down as best they could to pass the long hours of the night, hoping for better luck in the morning. It was half past six. It took runners three hours to crawl back to report the position.

Beyond the Layes Bridge, in front of the Bois du Biez there were no redoubts, no defences. The Indian Corps had advanced with ease and the Gurkhas were lining the road along the near edge of the wood, cheerfully digging in by the light of a burning cottage on the edge of the wood. As they did so the first of the German reserves, under cover of darkness, were starting to file

---

* They were termed 'Nameless Cottages' on British trench maps.

into the wood from the opposite side. They sent scouts ahead of them, and one of them had the misfortune to run into a Gurkha patrol. They captured him with glee, and sent him back to be interrogated. The information was disquieting, for the prisoner declared (or so the interpreter understood) that two German regiments were in the Bois du Biez.*

It was past seven o'clock when this information reached Brigadier General Jacob, and it faced him with a dilemma. His troops were on the right-hand extremity of the battle, his left had been held up by long-range fire from the Layes Bridge and, since there was no sign of the 2nd Rifle Brigade advancing to assist them, both his flanks were 'in the air'. His men at the Bois du Biez were well ahead of their comrades on either side and with what seemed to be a significant force of Germans immediately in front of them. General Jacob was forced to a hard decision. His Brigade had waited all day to advance but, for safety's sake, he had no choice but to order them back again. Shortly after nine o'clock, as the German reserves began to consolidate their position in the wood, the Gurkhas moved back across the Layes and began to dig in thirty yards behind it.

The 4th Seaforths, who had at last been able to move forward, were obliged reluctantly to move back in their wake.

Lt. C. Tennant.

We moved forward to the River Layes – a ditch about three or four feet deep and just too wide to jump in the dark. Some wading, some jumping (or trying to!) and some crossing by a small planked bridge we got across and advanced another hundred and fifty yards towards the Bois du Biez, when we received orders to stand fast and allow the Gurkhas who were in front of us to retire through us. While this was going on we lay down flat and watched a large house burning brilliantly a hundred yards away on our right front. To the left and right of us firing was still going on and a great many German flares were going up. We could see by their position that the attack on our flanks had not got nearly so far forward as where we were. Our position was so precarious that we were sent orders to retire after the Gurkhas and to dig in fifty yards behind the old Smith-Dorrien trench.

My own feeling is that if we and the 9th Gurkhas had been

---

* Whether or not he meant to mislead, the German prisoner had been misunderstood. A much smaller force of two Battalions was moving into the wood, although each one did belong to a different regiment.

allowed to go on and take the risk of being cut off we would have carried the wood. The shelling of the morning had so demoralised the Germans that I am fairly confident that a determined advance at the Bois du Biez, which would have threatened the German rear on the right and the left, would have demoralised them even more and made it possible to advance along the whole front. As it was we reached the new position about 9 p.m. We sent a party back for rations which only arrived at 2 a.m. After getting the men to work I borrowed an entrenching tool and dug a scrape, where I lay down and slept for half an hour at a time from 3 a.m. until 5 a.m.

During the hours of darkness long-delayed messages and orders began to trickle through bottlenecks in the chain of communication and finally reached Battalions in the line. One order had been a long time on the way. It had gone out from Sir Douglas Haig's Headquarters the previous evening, just too late to inspire the assaulting troops whose morale it was intended to boost. They were already on the move, it would be days before it could be posted up to be read by the rank and file and, by that time, the words rang painfully hollow. Most Battalion Commanders, obliged even so belatedly to make it public, only had the heart to display it in an obscure corner of the orderly room.

SPECIAL ORDER
To the 1st Army

We are about to engage the enemy under very favourable conditions. Until now in the present campaign, the British Army has, by its pluck and determination, gained victories against an enemy greatly superior both in men and guns. Reinforcements have made us stronger than the enemy on our front. Our guns are now both more numerous than the enemy's are and also larger than any hitherto used by any army in the field. In front of us we have only one German Corps, spread out on a front as large as that occupied by the whole of our Army (the First). We are now about to attack with about 48 Battalions a locality in that front which is held by some three German Battalions. It seems probable also that for the first day of the operations the Germans will not have more than four Battalions available as reinforcements for the counter attack. Quickness of movement is therefore of first importance to enable us to forestall the enemy and thereby gain success without severe loss. At no time in this war has there been a more favourable moment for us, and I feel confident of success.

112

The extent of that success must depend on the rapidity and determination with which we advance . . .

(Signed) D. HAIG (General)
Commanding 1st Army.

9th March, 1915.

But the fact was that everyone had spent the day waiting for a move – and waiting for someone else to make it. By midnight, almost all the infantry were back on the line which had been captured in the first rush of the battle fifteen hours before. Sir Douglas Haig's special order had accurately summed up the situation of the morning but while the troops rested and cat-napped as best they could in the hours of darkness, the Germans were gathering their resources and the situation was changing. The bulk of their reserves were still on the way, but two Battalions which had been reasonably close at hand had moved into position as darkness fell – and there were no cat-naps for them. They were labouring through the night to stiffen their defences, to haul up more guns, to set up machine-guns, to dig a snaking line that would link up the redoubts and create an unbroken front. Every man was working flat out and in front of the Bois du Biez, where there was no stronghold nearer than the Layes Bridge, they took particular pains. Creeping stealthily from the wood across the ground the Gurkhas had given up, the German soldiers began to dig fifty yards in front of it. Long before dawn they were lining the new trench just half-way between the wood and the Layes Brook, thankful for the chance to ease aching muscles as they waited wearily for reinforcements and the chance to get their own back in the morning.

Chapter 9

The German Command, with no disruptions of their own communications, had no difficulty in transmitting orders to the front and they were precise and unequivocal. Within three hours of the launch of the battle they had ordered that 'The 14th Infantry Division will recapture Neuve Chapelle', and at 10 p.m. that evening more precise instructions arrived:

> Major-General von Ditfurth will carry out the attack on Neuve Chapelle. In case the troops at his disposal are not sufficient for the recapture of our former positions west of the village, the 14th Bavarian Reserve Infantry Brigade is placed at General von Ditfurth's disposal. This Brigade must be in position in the Bois du Biez at 6 a.m. on the 11th.*

But they were not in the line by 6 a.m. Before midnight the troops from Lille had all arrived at the nearest railheads, three hours' strenuous march from the front, but the night had been so dark, there were so many battalions travelling along narrow roads through unfamiliar country that they had been a long time on the way. As they assembled behind the Aubers Ridge dawn was reaching up the eastern sky behind them. Fog lay across the low ground but it might easily disperse, it was almost half-light, and it would clearly be madness to string a large body of troops along the skyline and march them down the ridge in full view of the British lines. General von Ditfurth had no alternative but to postpone his counter-attack and to order the troops to fan out into the villages behind Aubers, to hide from reconnaissance planes and lie low until dusk. Without them, even though the Germans had been able to double their numbers in the line, there were still only four Battalions facing the British troops and it would be twelve clear hours before darkness fell and reinforcements could come to their aid.

---

* 6 a.m. was by Berlin time, one hour ahead of Greenwich mean time used by the British Army.

114

Twelve hours was enough, and more than enough, if all went well, for the British Army to sort out yesterday's muddle, to keep up the pressure and thrust forward from the Rubicon of yesterday's success. If all went well. But the second day of the battle was destined, like the first, to be a day of lost opportunities, of misunderstandings, mounting confusion, and unforeseen fatal delays.

The attack was due to take place at seven in the morning and at 6.45 the guns would open the bombardment. They had specific orders to destroy the strongpoints which had caused the infantry to founder in yesterday's advance, but it was easier said than done. Peering into the foggy morning from their old observation posts, luckless artillery officers found it almost impossible to pinpoint targets. Firing blind and mostly by guesswork, they were horribly aware of the danger that they might be firing on their own troops – the ragged lines of survivors lying somewhere in front of the redoubts that had brought them to a standstill when they had first advanced. No one knew precisely where they were. And no one had the shadow of an inkling that a new defensive line was concealed in the mist beyond. When the guns lifted and lengthened range to cover the infantry's advance the redoubts had hardly been touched – and the new trench that ran the length of the battle front had not been touched at all. At seven o'clock when the troops tried to advance they ran into an inferno. The air tingled with bullets streaming from machine-guns and the very earth seemed to explode beneath their feet as the German guns answered the bombardment with a bombardment of their own. It was fierce and it was accurate and the shells pounded the front for three hours. By the time it tailed away some thousands of British soldiers had been killed, Neuve Chapelle was a heap of smoking ruins, every line and wire had been severed in a dozen places and communication, even the sketchiest, was non-existent. The signallers had done their best, frantically repairing wires that were ruptured in another place even as they were mended, but the odds were against them.

Bdr. W. Kemp.

We signallers were still in the straw stack. We'd been there all night trying to keep the lines open to the battery. I'd been issued with wire-cutters – proper wire-cutters, the same as they used for barbed wire. They weighed about one and a half pounds, and I was supposed to use these on the D-3 telephone wire! I soon lost *them*. We had one pair of pliers for all of us. I don't really know at this stage how we did manage to cut and mend the phone wire. I do know that the telephone we had was a C-Mk-11 magneto and you had to ring it by hand, but the batteries were six large cells in a wooden box. They had to be excited by adding water and leaving them for a few hours before they were any use. Well, *some* of them were ready to use when the battle started, but next morning when all hell was let loose it didn't matter anyway.

The fog was lifting from the battlefield but it still hung thick around Brigade and Divisional Headquarters where the anxious staff were groping for vital information. Messengers were slow in coming and, when they did, the news they brought was mostly out-of-date and often contradictory or untrue. It was not the fault of the troops. The Grenadier Guards, starting off close to the Moated Grange, were brought to a halt at a stream not three hundred yards ahead, and the runner who struggled back through the bombardment reported in all good faith that they had been held up at the Layes Brook. It was the first good news General Capper had received, for here, on the left, the Layes ran well behind the German line and he joyfully ordered up the guns to bombard beyond it to clear the way for the Grenadiers to advance.

The Layes Brook (described ambitiously on local maps as a river) was an artificial drainage ditch, inexpertly dug by local farmers, and it straggled across the fields in front of the Bois du Biez and the Aubers Ridge to join a tributary of the River Lys. On the staff officers' maps it stood out as an unmistakable feature which could safely be described as an objective on terrain that was singularly short of landmarks, but to a man on the ground itself the Layes could not easily be distinguished from a hundred other ditches that trickled in all directions across the dead and battered marsh. Few of them were narrow enough to leap, even without the weight of extra ammunition and equipment, and they were filled to the brim with filthy brackish water. It was deep enough to lap the chins of all but the tallest guardsmen as they floundered through. Now, soaked and shivering, they were digging in on the other side, and, even if most rifles were clogged with mud, trying to reply to the fire that pinned them down. Waiting for supports. Waiting for the guns. Waiting to get forward.

But the deep ditch they had forded was not the Layes Brook, and the guardsmen had advanced only half as far as the unfortunate Worcesters the evening before. When the bombardment began the shells fell far ahead of their position, far behind the strongholds that faced them, and far, far behind the enemy line. And there they stopped when the bombardment lifted. There was nothing else they could do.

The Meerut Division was stuck in front of the Bois du Biez. The

116

opening bombardment had done them no good at all, for Corps Headquarters, knowing nothing of the new trench that now lay between them and the wood, had instructed the guns to bombard the edge of the wood and the wood itself, well behind the enemy and the enemy, safely entrenched on ground that had been occupied and given up without a fight, were unharmed.

Lt. C. Tennant.

The repellent facts are that the Germans (who were now well entrenched on this side of the Bois du Biez) at once opened a hot rifle and machine-gun fire both on the Gurkhas in the front trench and ourselves behind it. Our first orders were to attack again at 7.15, but owing to the want of support on our left, the colonel of the 9th Gurkhas came back to report to our Battalion Headquarters that he found it impossible to get forward with the heavy rifle and machine-gun fire, and he was ordered to stand fast. We had several casualties and our own colonel was wounded in the thigh at 7.30. One of the stretcher-bearers going to fetch him was shot stone dead through the head. His body fell back into my scrape in the ground. I'd left it just a moment before and moved to a neighbouring shell-hole where I'd started to dig a new shelter. Minchin very pluckily at once came out of his scrape and took the stretcher-bearer's place and brought the C.O. in, but the firing was so heavy that we couldn't send him back to the field ambulance post for some time. When he did go, he was unlucky enough to be hit again in *almost exactly the same* place high up in the thigh.

All morning the batteries kept up a very heavy fire against the Bois du Biez, and the Germans replied with high explosive, shrapnel and Jack Johnsons. A great many heavy shells were being fired with great effect into Neuve Chapelle. There was nothing we could do and, in spite of all the row, I managed to sleep very soundly for a good forty-five minutes in my shelter.

It was the first of the unfortunate misconceptions which, before the end of the day, were to cause the Commander of the Meerut Division to tear his hair and reduce the staff of the Dehra Dun Brigade first to bafflement and then to a state of despair. For Brigadier General Jacobs's instructions, passed down to him from Indian Corps Headquarters, had been perfectly clear. From their forward position the leading Battalions of the Dehra Dun Brigade were to attack towards the Bois du Biez as soon as the 8th Division on their left arrived alongside them. But the Battalion of the 8th

117

Division which stood immediately on their left, although slightly behind them, was the 2nd Rifle Brigade. The riflemen were still holding the trench on the outskirts of Neuve Chapelle and Colonel Stephens was not the only one who was fed up, because the Battalion, or what was left of it, was due to be relieved and to move back into support with the remainder of the 25th Brigade. The relief had duly taken place but, by some oversight, no one had appeared to take over from Stephens's battalion. At eight o'clock, forty-five minutes after the Dehra Dun Brigade had tried vainly to advance, Major Walker, its Brigade Major, braved the storm of shelling to go personally to Colonel Stephens to demand the reason for the delay. He found him in the cellar of a tumbledown house behind the RB's trench. Its brick walls had been white-washed by the Germans and 'Gott Strafe England' had been scrawled in many places and signed with the initials of the bored German soldiers who had once sheltered there. Half a dozen runners, sunken-eyed with fatigue, slumped near the cellar stairs, each awaiting the order that would send him out to take his chance in the inferno, dodging to the line or to the rear with the next urgent message. Inside, under the anxious eye of the Colonel, signallers hunched over their instruments were ringing and buzzing repeatedly without much hope of making contact. They worked by the light of candles that flickered and dimmed with close explosions. The circumstances were not conducive to pleasantries or the exchange of the usual courtesies; although a mug of lukewarm tea was offered it was brusquely refused and, from time to time, the two officers had to raise their voices to be heard above the thunderous explosions that were rocking Neuve Chapelle. Perhaps it relieved their feelings of frustration, for they were both equally in the dark. Colonel Stephens was obliged to confess that he had received no orders from IV Corps, from Division or from Brigade, that contained any mention of an advance. Quite the contrary. His last instructions had been to stand fast and consolidate and, in the absence of any others, he could only obey.

Major Walker returned in bewilderment to report to his Brigadier and it was some hours before his unpalatable news travelled up the chain of command and arrived at Indian Corps headquarters where it baffled Sir James Willcocks, for in a subsequent conversation with IV Corps he was assured by the Corps Commander that the 8th Division *had* advanced and, without the support of the Meerut Division on their right, had failed to get forward. It was a sad mix-up, they agreed, but it was vital to retrieve the situation and to try again. A fresh attack was arranged for 2.15 – but only the timing was changed and the new orders were precisely the same as the old ones. In the Indian Corps the Meerut Division was instructed, as before, to advance to the Bois du Biez as soon as the 8th Division

118

was seen to be advancing alongside, and IV Corps had assured them in all good faith that the 8th Division *would* advance. No one passed on the vital information – and at that stage perhaps no one at IV Corps Headquarters knew – that the Battalion of the 8th Division which happened to be standing immediately beside the Meerut Division had been ordered to stay where it was.

The mistake over the relief of the 2nd Rifle Brigade had caused some irritation at 8th Division Headquarters and it was too late now to put it right. After the failure of the early morning assaults it was highly likely that the Germans would counter-attack in the wake of their devastating bombardment and, if the Germans were to launch it while troops in the front line were changing over, the consequences did not bear thinking about. The orders, when they finally did reach Colonel Stephens, were surprising – if not downright contradictory. The RBs were to stay where they were but, although they were in the forefront, they should consider themselves to be in reserve. However, if the counter-attack developed, then (and only then) Stephens could attack in his turn.

The Colonel lost no time in sending a reply that was more than a mere acknowledgement. Even before he received the message the heavy German bombardment had tailed away, the shelling had become spasmodic, and he was able to inform the staff that there was no movement in the enemy line and no sign whatever that they were preparing to attack. He reported his casualties and, putting his case as forcibly as brevity and military etiquette allowed, he requested permission to attack the enemy's guns, near the Layes Bridge. They were only a short way ahead and Colonel Stephens was convinced, as he had been convinced the previous day, that the position could easily be captured and the guns knocked out. The reply, when he eventually received it, was stiff and coldly categorical. He was on no account to make any attack whatever without orders or permission. All the Battalion could do was to wait. They were still waiting at two o'clock when British guns began to thunder on the Bois du Biez. When the bombardment lifted the Gurkhas would go over. Two hundred yards behind their line close to the Layes Brook, the 4th Seaforth braced themselves to dash forward to reinforce the trench as the Gurkhas left it.

Lt. C. Tennant.

Just at this time the Germans got the range of our trench exactly and did some damage with high explosive and shrapnel. On seeing No. 1 Company move forward I ran across to get final instructions from Major Cuthbert, who was now in

119

command. He was sitting in a shell hole with the adjutant, Macmillan and Sergeant Ross of the machine-gun team. Just after I had got there two shrapnel bursts clanged close beside us. Poor Macmillan got a terrible wound right across the forehead, and Cuthbert fell forward with the blood streaming from his head. I could see it was only a flesh wound and, as soon as I had put a field dressing on, the bleeding stopped, but Macmillan was in a bad state – so bad that the adjutant thought he was dying. I saw that his lungs and heart were still working, though part of his brain was laid bare, and I was going to put a field dressing on him too, when the adjutant said that as No. 1 Company had started off some time before, I should go on at once. So I got out and, having got hold of Jim, we gave a yell to the platoon and started off hell for leather across the open.

We took breath under cover of the Smith-Dorrien trench, fifty yards in front, before starting off on the hottest bit of our advance – the hundred and fifty yards of open ground, sloping slightly towards the front, between the Smith-Dorrien trench and the Gurkha trench which we were reinforcing. About twenty yards before we got to it the ground was practically dead and there we flung ourselves down and crawled the rest of the way up to the trench. With my head well down in the mud and my pack in front of it I had a look round to see how the boys were getting on and I only realised when I saw how many of them had been stopped on the way what a hot fire we had come through. A nice cheerful Londoner, Appleton, was blown to pieces by a shell just as he was getting out of the trench, handsome Macdonald, the piper, was killed stone dead by a bullet through the heart, and Speer through the head, and a dozen or more, including my jolly little batman Simpson, were wounded.

Jim had been close to me during the advance and we settled down together in a cramped but safe corner of the Gurkha trench to take stock of the position and to pull ourselves – literally – together. Both our kilt aprons had been practically torn off and I had lost my watch bracelet. Luckily I saw it lying only a yard or two back, so I rolled out at the back of the parapet and recovered it. Jim had a bullet right through his pack (there was hardly a man in the company who had not got a hole through him somewhere) and, generally speaking, it looked anything but tidy.

I naturally expected that as soon as we had brought up supports the Gurkhas would go ahead but their colonel, after discussing the matter with Cuthbert, reported to Brigade HQ and was ordered not to advance further until the people on our left came up.

120

This time it was Brigadier Jacob himself who made his way, fuming and incredulous, to confront Colonel Stephens in his cellar. What had caused the hold-up? Why had his troops been left out on a limb? Why had the 8th Division not advanced? The Brigadier was quivering with fury and frustration and when Stephens produced the order – the order that forbade him under any circumstances to attack – Jacobs read it, and then re-read it, hardly able to believe the evidence of his eyes. There was no more to be said. The Brigadier returned to his Headquarters and, angry, perplexed, and none the wiser, he called off his attack.

But the 8th Division *had* advanced – or, at least, some of them had.

It was almost a quarter to three when the orders for the attack reached Brigadier General Carter at 24th Brigade headquarters and he knew very well that, in the thirty-three minutes that remained until zero, it was useless even to hope that a runner might reach the troops in the forefront of the line where the Worcesters, the Northants, and the Sherwood Foresters were still lying out – still taking punishment, if they raised so much as a finger, from the fortress strongholds between Mauquissart and Pietre. Already the guns which were meant to destroy them had begun to fire. When they stopped the men must be ready to spring forward and capture the redoubts. They were barely five hundred yards away from their support line, but it was five hundred yards of open ground without a tree, without a bush, with no hollow, no incline, no single feature that would conceal a running man from the fire of the enemy, alert and watching in their line beyond. And yet the attack must go in. The Army Commander himself had insisted on it and such direct orders had to be obeyed.[*]

With deep misgivings General Carter issued his instructions. They were addressed to Colonel Woodhouse who waited with the two remaining companies of the 1st Worcesters in a captured German trench on the northern edge of Neuve Chapelle. The Colonel had spent an anxious, sleepless night and his anxiety had not diminished in the course of his restless morning. It had been hard to concentrate on routine duties, hard to hide his concern at the lack of definite news from his two companies in front, harder still to conceal his impatience at the absence of orders. He had spent much of his time in the line scanning the ground beyond and had seen for himself the faint flutters of movement in the distance, had guessed at the futile attempts to get forward, had heard for himself the lethal rap of the machine-guns that laid every attempt to waste. When the orders finally reached him from Brigade Headquarters they were not much

---

[*] Haig's order.

to his liking, for General Carter had resorted to desperate measures. The advance was to be made at once. Under cover of the bombardment Woodhouse must push his two reserve companies up to the outpost line, scoop up the survivors of the three Battalions, and by their own impetus carry them forward to the assault.

It was well past two before the message reached Colonel Woodhouse and the bombardment that was to lead the way had finished five minutes earlier. It was all too clear that it had been intended as the prelude to an attack and the Germans were prepared for it. Shells were falling thick and fast across the open ground and machine-guns blazed out as the three hundred soldiers of the Worcesters began to cross it. Fewer than forty of them made it. They brought little in the way of impetus but they did bring the message that ordered the attack. A dozen copies had been distributed for fear of misunderstanding, and one of the men who carried it had managed to get through. It was passed to Major Winnington and, as second-in-command, it was his responsibility to decide what must be done. It was also his responsibility to pass it to the Northants on his left and the Sherwood Foresters on his right. A little later, from his position in the shallow trench in front of Nameless Cottages, he heard the faint sound of whistles, and the fire and the fury as the Sherwood Foresters tried to go over the top. They tried once, twice, three times to make headway, but, at the fourth attempt, they were successful, for they managed to get forward close to the Mauquissart Road and seized two abandoned buildings close to the German line. It cost many men to gain that hundred yards and the line beyond remained impregnable.

The Worcesters also tried to advance. Two platoons started out on a leap towards a ditch thirty yards from the German trench. Only a handful of them reached it. Lieutenant Conybeare was the only officer who had survived the rush, for Lieutenant Tristram, like so many of the men, had been killed on the way across. All he could do was to gather the shaken survivors of two platoons, to crouch squelching in the mud up to their knees in water, waiting for the rest of the Worcesters to come up. They waited a full half hour but no help came. And then the shells began to fall, coming closer and closer, and they were British shells. At last the guns had got the range of the German line and were exultantly bombarding it. At least it kept the Germans' heads down and stopped them firing at the few survivors on their long crawl back.

The Northamptonshires on their left did not advance at all. Colonel Pritchard had lost half his men that morning, his Battalion had been cut to shreds, and the order that three hundred exhausted men should now renew an attack that was clearly futile was the catalyst that reduced him to cold fury. He did not try to dodge the issue and, with an angry disregard for discipline, quite at odds with his long service and training, he took pains to make his feeling perfectly clear in his reply.

> I received a note from the Worcestershires, 'We have *got* to advance. Will you give the order?' I answered 'No! It is a mere waste of life, impossible to go twenty yards much less two hundred yards.' The trenches have not been touched by the artillery. If artillery cannot touch them the only way is to advance from the right flank. A frontal attack will not get near them.

When it finally arrived at Brigade Headquarters and wound its way up to Division, Corps, and Army Headquarters this message caused deep disappointment and put paid to any hopes of success that day. In front of Mauquissart and Nameless Cottages the survivors clung on, digging deep and toiling to improve their perilous positions. They were completely isolated. Far on the right the Dehra Dun Brigade precariously situated with both flanks 'in the air' retired after dark to a safer position behind the first of the captured trenches. The British line had advanced by hardly an inch since the morning.

Lt. C. Tennant.

At about sunset we received orders to retire to our last night's position and as soon as the light began to fade I went back to look after the wounded. Thank Heaven I am not a thirsty person and though my water bottle had not been replenished for two days, it was more than half full and I was able to supply the terrible need of some of the sufferers. Poor John Allan (whom I have always liked best of all my NCOs – and he was in my opinion undeniably the best soldier of them all) was hit in three places – the leg, shoulder and stomach, and was in a bad way. Luckily an officer of the Gurkhas had some morphia tabloids with him and he gave them to the men who needed them most. As soon as I had done all that I could for the wounded I hurried back to get stretchers, but it was a desperate task as our casualty list during the afternoon had been very heavy, and moreover our first aid post was a long way back. It had been shelled out of the houses on the Neuve Chapelle Road and had had to go back into safety, so the few stretchers we had took a long, long time on the way. Finally we rigged up stretchers with puttees and greatcoats and rifles, but they were not very satisfactory and it took three hours and a lot of time and trouble to get the wounded carried down. Poor Allan died on the way, to my great sorrow.

In the early evening Sir Douglas Haig went forward to assess the situation for himself and to find out from personal meetings with his Generals and Brigadiers closer to the battlefront what had gone wrong. The reasons were all too clear. The breakdown in communications, the difficulties of relaying messages to and from the line, could not easily be rectified – but something could be done. The guns could be brought closer to the line – dangerously close if need be – and positioned to make such an all-out effort to destroy the German defences that, with one more push, the infantry would be able to sweep across and carry the day. To make doubly, trebly, sure, to give the gunners ample time and the advantage of good light to register their targets, the attack this time would be scheduled for ten thirty in the morning. The night lay before them, and four full hours of daylight. There was time, and surely time enough, for even such feeble strands of communication as there were to carry instructions to the front, to move the guns forward, to bring up the reserves, and to ensure that every infantryman was prepared to play his part tomorrow morning.

But the Germans also were preparing for tomorrow. Under the cloak of the darkness the movement of many men was masked by the enemy guns as the six battalions which had been skulking out of sight all day crossed the Aubers Ridge and took their places in the German line. They were well fed and well rested and it was all to the good for there was not much left of the night. Just before dawn they would launch the counter-attack.

The 4th Seaforths were out of it but they had waited six hours for their relief and it was a long, weary wait. Charles Tennant had formed up his men on open ground behind their trench and it was two in the morning before the HLI arrived to take over.

Lt. C. Tennant.

The C.O. told Jim and me to show their officers our line. By this time I was beginning to feel very sleepy – consequently stupid, though not really tired – and I felt as if I was handing over an unsolved Chinese puzzle in pieces instead of a fairly simple position, complicated only by the rather vague whereabouts of the shattered remnants of the Garhwalis and the 9th Gurkhas in front. Why we should have been ordered to hand over the old line to the HLI instead of putting them into the front trench with the Gurkhas I'm still at a loss to understand, but the whole strategy (or want of it) throughout the action was utterly incomprehensible to the lay mind. As a result on the following morning the Gurkhas (who for some unknown reason were not relieved that night) were driven in by a German counter-attack and the HLI lost heavily in men and officers recovering the position we could have put them into with no difficulty on the evening before. Such is war – at least under anyone but a Napoleon!

About 2.45 a.m. we roused the men who were sleeping like logs on the bare ground and marched back to la Couture – an uncomfortable march over smashed-up roads dodging shells and being chased by shrapnel. One burst on the road just before we passed and left six or seven wounded and moaning Gurkhas in its train: another passed over the rear of the column just clear of No. 3 Company. It was five o'clock by the time we reached la Couture and the men were pretty well done up but the transport had got hot tea and rations ready for them which cheered them up and then they turned in for a short hour's rest. I made some Oxo in my mess tin and then lay down on some straw and had a glorious sound sleep for twenty-five minutes.

There were fewer of the Seaforths now as they marched away from the line and as they re-formed on the road it was all too clear that they had left many men behind them. As they closed up the thinned ranks and continued on the journey back to blessed rest and billets, the sound of the battle, carried west on the wind, followed them along the road. It had been raging for hours past.

The Germans attacked through the morning mist in the half-light of false dawn.

Capt. A. J. Agius, MC.

We'd been building up the parapet and, just before dawn, we got back into the trench and stood to. At this moment the Hun attacked. It was still dark but round the horizon it was growing light so that the enemy's legs were clearly defined. It was an extraordinary sight to see this mass of legs coming forward. The mist was lying just above the ground, and at first, you couldn't see their bodies. In our immediate front and half-right, they'd been able to get up through their trenches to within forty or fifty yards of us before they delivered their assault. Sutcliffe was with my left gun firing to the right, I was with the right gun firing to the left. We aimed low and just sat down to it. The

125

guns fired beautifully. The Germans came on in dense lines about eight to ten yards between each line. We absolutely caught them in the dim light, in enfilade.

L/cpl. E. Hall.

I was in the front line attending to wounded men who needed attention, and so I had a good view of the Germans as they were advancing. They came over in mass formation. Our reinforcements had come up after dark and they'd brought several machine-guns, so we were prepared to give the Germans a fight to the finish. There was thick wire in front of our position and our officers knew that the Germans would never be able to break through it under a hail of lead, so they gave strict orders that no one was to fire until the Germans were up to the entanglements. The idea was that at such short range the slaughter would be much greater, and fewer Germans would have a chance of getting back to their own lines when we forced them to retreat.

There wasn't enough room on the firestep for all our men, because it was only a short length of trench on that side of our redoubt, and the unlucky ones left standing at the bottom of the trench were so excited while we were blasting them that they were actually dragging some of the men *off* the firestep, so they could get up there themselves and get a few rounds off to settle old scores with Fritz. What with the rapid fire of machine-guns and rifles the Germans were simply *mown* down. They tried to turn tail, but hardly any of them, not even their swiftest runners, managed to make a home run.

Capt. A. J. Agius, MC.

Later as it grew light we counted over five hundred dead in our front. The guns must have done most of this for they were just lying in rows, one behind the other. On the left there were about eight rows of dead, just like swathes of corn. On the right they were scattered – the ground was more broken. Thank God I got a little of my own back and helped to avenge the death of our poor fellows.

There were two points that wanted watching – on our left front a collection of houses on the road with orchards about two hundred yards away, and on our right and running right into us, the Boche system of trenches. Of course they worked up these trenches, sniping and bombing, and it was hot for a bit because they were able to get completely round our flank. But we drove them off – we had a little gas-pipe bomb gun but most had to be done with hand grenades. The Black Watch in our rear helped with rifle fire and later they sent out and got in some prisoners.

Capt. W. G. Bagot-Chester, MC.

When daylight began to appear there was nothing to be seen except lines of dead Germans. We counted about a hundred on our immediate front. There were lots more to our right and left, and the Dehra Dun Brigade's evacuated trench in front of us was full of them. Only a few live ones remained there, and a company of the HLI turned them out by an attack at 1 p.m. The first line advanced through us under fairly heavy rifle fire – they lost about twenty men before they reached the trench. The second line was just about to advance, and the officer in command of it jumped up near me and shouted 'Second line, advance' when he suddenly dropped, shot through the head. The second line never advanced. On our right the 4th Gurkhas advanced and took up their position on the right of the HLI in the trench ahead of us. Our artillery all this time was firing heavily, and we were also firing. Suddenly white flags began to appear in the German trenches and they got up and began waving to us to cease fire and on both sides we stood up to see what was happening. Some men in the Gurkhas on the right started sending back Germans into our lines with their hands up, many of them badly wounded. More followed, until about a hundred or so passed through our trench and there were many more who wished to come from further to the left. They put up white flags but it was difficult to send anyone to bring them in as the Germans were firing from behind and they themselves didn't dare to leave the cover of their trench altogether. However, we got a pretty good bag.

The Germans had been flung back all along the front – even in the shaky line near Mauquissart where the Northants and the Worcesters clung to their precarious foothold.

2nd Lt. E. B. Conybeare, 1st Bn., Worcestershire Regt., 24 Brig., 8 Div.

The Germans came on in a great mass. Their officers were in front waving swords, then a great rabble behind followed by a fat old blighter on a horse. There was a most extraordinary

127

hush for a few seconds as we held our fire while they closed in on us. Then, at last, we gave them the 'mad minute' of rapid fire. We brought them down in solid chunks. Down went the officers, the sergeant-majors and the old blighter on the horse.* We counter-charged, and back the rabble went full tilt for their own trenches four hundred yards away.

The Worcesters had done more than drive the Germans back – they had followed behind, forced the enemy to abandon part of his position and captured the machine-guns that had caused such havoc in their ranks. And they had rescued the Sherwood Foresters when their weak line broke, swinging to their right to recapture it and to retake the ruined cottages when the Germans forced the Sherwood Foresters out. In the wake of the counter-attack the Worcesters thrust forward their fragile line and at last reached the objective they had strained in vain to capture more than thirty-six hours before.

Colonel Woodhouse made haste to send a message back to Brigade Headquarters on the other side of Neuve Chapelle. He was more than happy to be able to report that the Battalion had advanced. But, with unpleasant recollections of yesterday's mis-understanding, he made a point of requesting that the artillery should be warned that the Worcesters were now occupying a part of the German line. He took pains to give a specific map reference, stressed that the Worcesters were now isolated and hanging on by the skin of their teeth, and added a plea for reinforcements to help them consolidate and continue the advance.

The Worcesters beat off three counter-attacks and held on for three despairing hours of shelling – mostly by British guns. No reinforcements arrived. By ten o'clock it was clear that they could hold on no longer and, with bitter reluctance, Colonel Woodhouse ordered the battalion to leave the captured buildings and fall back to the old line. It was a disciplined retirement. They fell back by platoons, each one endeavouring to give covering fire as the others ran the gauntlet through a horseshoe of crossfire from rifles and machine-guns ranged round them on three sides. One after another, as they dashed and dodged across the open ground, the platoons melted away. By the time the remnants of the Worcesters reached the trench they had left at dawn the ground was strewn with dead and wounded. The Colonel was gone, so was the Adjutant and the

---

* The Germans who attacked the Worcestershires belonged to the 21st Bavarian Reserve Regiment. Their regimental history states, 'During this advance Major Eberhard commanding the first Battalion was killed and his body was not recovered.'

last surviving company officer. The Battalion had lost nineteen of its twenty-six officers and platoons had dwindled to fragmented knots of men with only corporals or lance-corporals to take charge. By 10.30, when the new advance was scheduled to begin, the Worcesters, like the Northants and the Sherwood Foresters, were far too weak to make a move. As it was, the attack had been postponed for, yet again, the thick ground mist had prevented artillery officers from making the final, vital observations that would pinpoint the enemy's positions and guarantee the accuracy of the guns. This time they could not afford to take chances. This time the attack must succeed.

It was hard on the front-line troops to wait. They were flushed with their victory, anxious to get on, to follow up the demoralised Germans and hit them hard while they were still stunned and shaken by the failure of the counter-attack. If, like the Worcesters, the whole line had advanced, and chased the Germans into their line, if the reserves had followed, and the opportunity had been seized, their defences might easily have crumbled. But the enemy had been given a breathing space and made the most of it to re-organise the line and bring up support troops to defend it. They were hardly able to believe their luck as the hours ticked by and the British made no move.

Chapter 10

The Army Command had no idea that a golden opportunity had been missed. Reports were long delayed on the way to First Army headquarters and when they did arrive, scanty and incomplete, they gave no idea of the magnitude of the counter-attack, nor was it possible to assess the enemy's numbers from scraps of information gleaned from isolated stretches of the front. But it was plain that the enemy had been brilliantly repulsed and heart-lifting news of prisoners surrendering en masse confirmed the impression that the enemy was demoralised and on the point of giving up the fight. Only the artillerymen were unhappy, still hampered by the mist and now frankly doubtful if the guns could be ranged with any hope of accuracy by mid-day when the bombardment was due to open.

Shortly after eleven General Rawlinson telephoned Sir Douglas Haig to pass on this disquieting news and discuss its implications. It was decided to take the risk and send troops forward as planned. But the plan was not altered in the slightest particular from the orders of the previous evening.

At long last the 2nd Rifle Brigade were to have their chance and they were to be in the vanguard of the attack moving forward with the Royal Irish Rifles to knock out the guns and the redoubt at the Layes Bridge. Forty-eight hours previously, when Colonel Stevens had begged to be allowed to assault that very objective, it had been manned by a skeleton force and was theirs for the taking. Now it was a bastion, and behind deep barricades of barbed wire fifteen machine-guns were poised to rake the battlefield. They could have held an army at bay and against them two Battalions had no chance at all. It was a sorry climax to the long impatient wait.

The first men to leave the trench were pulverised by a tornado of fire – from machine-guns at the Layes redoubt and the field guns behind it, from machine-guns and rifles in the new German trench. Even the guns behind the Bois du Biez, and the machine-guns in front of the wood itself were able to swing right and concentrate fire on the unfortunate riflemen, for the Indian Corps on their front was ordered to stand fast until the Layes Bridge redoubt was captured.

Hardly a man survived to advance so much as fifty yards. Bullets whipped across the trench where the men of the next wave crouched low beneath the parapet, teeth clenched as the ground rocked, white knuckles clamped round rifles, waiting with fixed bayonets for the command that would send them over the top. They knew full well that it would be slaughter. The Colonel knew it too and, on his own responsibility, cancelled the attack.

As the artillery officers had feared, the noon bombardment that preceded the general attack was a disaster and on most of the front the troops failed to make any headway. But where it had succeeded, on the northern edge of the battle, the 7th Division did manage to advance the line and the Germans surrendered in droves. Some ground had been gained but beyond it the enemy fought back hard. The shelling reached a crescendo, movement was impossible and information dried up altogether. Desperate for news, the anxious British staff had to depend on reports from artillery observation officers trying to pierce the mist from positions of small advantage, and endeavouring as best they could to piece together what was happening out in front. The messages that got through to headquarters were long out of date and gave a completely false impression.

At one o'clock the welcome news that the Worcesters had captured part of the German defences near Mauquissart was received at First Army Headquarters to the satisfaction of Sir Douglas Haig. In the absence of other information he could have hardly have known that they had been forced out again and had been back on their old line for a full three hours. As staff officers pored eagerly over the battle-map, pinpointing the Worcesters' supposed position, more news came through. Fourth Corps headquarters confirmed that the 7th Division had advanced and added, 'Observation officer reports having seen British troops crossing the Mauquissart Road.'* That clinched it.

Sir Douglas Haig was an imperturbable soldier, but even his air of unruffled calm hinted at inner excitement, and the air of anxious speculation that had clouded the deliberations of his staff all morning was entirely swept away in moments. Haig was determined to take advantage of the promising situation. The attack must be pressed home and there was no time to be lost. Headquarters signallers, who had spent much of the day waiting for news or transmitting stern demands for information, were as busy now as their Commander could desire, tapping his order along the wires to

---

* The 7th Division had been stopped well short of the Mauquissart Road and the British soldiers seen by the artillery observation officer were later thought to have been captured British soldiers passing, under escort, through the German lines.

the Corps and Divisional Commanders. 'Information indicates that the enemy on our front are much demoralised. Indian Corps and IV Corps will push through the barrage of fire regardless of loss, using reserves if required.' It was just after three o'clock and it would clearly take time before dispositions could be made and instructions passed on to the Battalion commanders at the front, but General Haig was optimistic.

In the light of the good news, he telephoned personally to Sir John French at GHQ and, with his agreement, ordered the 5th Cavalry Brigade to move forward into battle. Then, impatient of impotent waiting, and perhaps with the idea of stiffening his subordinate commanders with his own encouraging presence, he rode the five miles to Indian Corps headquarters at Marmuse. He looked at the map and listened courteously as Sir James Willcocks explained the failure of the Indian Corps and, jabbing his finger at the Layes redoubt, traced the line of fire that could not fail to catch his left in enfilade if his troops even attempted to advance. Haig understood his dilemma but, fired by the conviction that the line at Mauquissart had been breached, sure of his opinion that the Germans were on the verge of disarray, he impressed on Willcocks that a similar breakthrough at the opposite end of the line was the single factor that would break the enemy's resistance and bring about his downfall. Even if Willcocks could not risk the left of his line, then the right must go forward without it and, if the whole of the Bois du Biez could not immediately be captured, they could take the southern part. He urged him to proceed with all possible speed, offered to bring up more cavalry to exploit the gap and, once they had passed through it and began to harass the enemy's rear, the battle would be won and even the Layes redoubt would collapse as the enemy line crumbled. Such tactics were sound, the situation was crucial, and the moment, it seemed, was ripe.

General Rawlinson had also been on the move. As soon as he received Sir Douglas Haig's signal he went first to 8th and then to 7th divisional headquarters to relay the orders in person and to stress to both divisions the urgency of carrying them out. It would necessarily be some hours before the Divisional Commanders would have made their dispositions, issued their instructions and passed them down to Battalions in the line. Before the troops went over, Rawlinson ordered, the Layes redoubt must be attacked and this time 'at all costs' it must be captured.

Capt. R. Berkeley, MC, Rifle Brig.

At 4 p.m. Colonel Stevens was sent for and ordered to make a second attack at 5.15 p.m. There was no opportunity to make

132

Three types of early machine-gun photographed before the war. Left Gardner, centre Maxim and on the right the Nordenfeldt, which so captivated the Kaiser (*Imperial War Museum*)

Spring 1915. Well-constructed front line dug-outs in the 'quiet' sector near 'Plugstreet' Wood (*Imperial War Museum*)

Winter in Flanders. Men of the London Rifle Brigade behind the breastworks at 'Plugstreet' Wood (*Imperial War Museum*)

Neuve Chapelle. Front line trench at Mauquissart looking towards Aubers Ridge (*Imperial War Museum*)

Neuve Chapelle. 'I can't tell you what it's like to have these shells whistling over one's head and bursting nearer and nearer. The noise is terrific and the shock of the explosions is terrible.' Captain George Hawes, 3rd (City of London) Bttn. German bombardment falling behind British line (*Imperial War Museum*)

The pre-war 5 inch breech-loading gun the 11th Howitzer Battery took to France. On left Major 'Steinthal' who was suspended from command while his German antecedents were investigated and who returned as Major Petrie.

Artist Norman Tennant's drawing of the episode when the 'nasty little short-arsed' Major who took Steinthal's place put him on a charge for 'cruelty to a horse'

An artist's impression of the battlefield of Neuve Chapelle

Neuve Chapelle. For want of anything better haystacks were burrowed out to serve as makeshift observation posts and also, as in the photo, Divisional or Brigade headquarters (*Imperial War Museum*)

Memorial to Arthur Agius's friend Cyril Crichton erected on the spot where he was killed at Port Arthur, Neuve Chapelle

Neuve Chapelle. The German machine-gun post that decimated the Scottish Rifles, photographed after its capture . . . (*Imperial War Museum*)

. . . and the bodies of the men mown down by its lethal fire (*Imperial War Museum*)

Site of the once-infamous Layes Bridge redoubt

This was the shell-scarred crucifix from Neuve Chapelle churchyard, now inside the church

A German dug-out later erected on the site of the strongpoint that thwarted the troops at Neuve Chapelle. The village is in the background

German 'stinkpioneren' experimenting with gas before the attack at Ypres on 23 April (*Imperial War Museum*)

British gas equipment similar to that used at Loos, ready for discharge in 1916 (*Imperial War Museum*)

The Regular Army. Troops of the 2nd Lancashires in a mine crater blown during the battle for Aubers Ridge (*Imperial War Museum*)

Kitchener's Army. Officers in the making (*Imperial War Museum*)

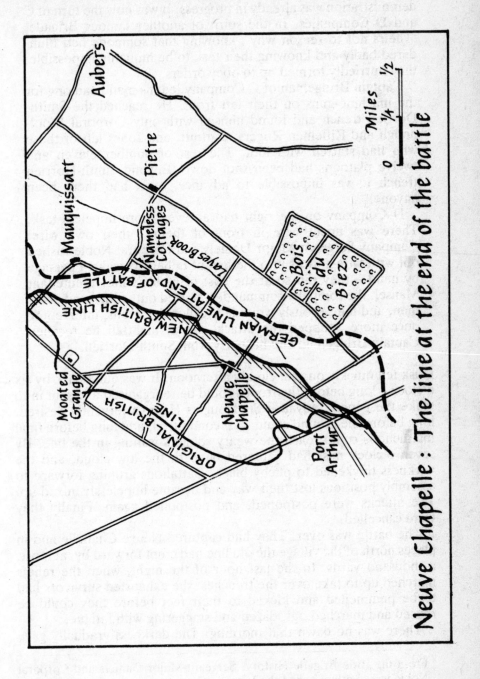

Neuve Chapelle : The line at the end of the battle

any plan. By the time he had reached his Battalion with the order it was nearly 5 p.m. and a small and inadequate artillery demonstration was already in progress. It was now the turn of C and D Companies. In the spirit of another famous Brigade, 'Theirs not to reason why', knowing that someone had blundered badly and knowing their task to be humanly impossible, they hurriedly formed up to obey orders.

Captain Bridgeman of C Company led his men headlong for the machine-guns on their left front. He reached the Smith-Dorrien trench and found himself with only Corporal Woolnough and Riflemen Rogers, Carbutt, and Jones left of those who had started with him. The rest of number eleven and twelve platoons had been shot down. Beyond Smith-Dorrien trench it was impossible to advance, even had there been anyone.

D Company on the right had an even more hopeless task. There was uncut wire in front of them – their own wire! Company Sergeant-Major Daniels and Corporal Noble rushed out with wire-cutters into the hail of bullets to make a passage by hand – they did so at the cost of Noble's life. Lieutenant Mansel, the company commander, started out at the head of his men, and fell seriously wounded. Colonel Stevens, intervening once more, stopped the attack and at nightfall he recalled Captain Bridgeman and his party from Smith-Dorrien.*

Dusk fell quickly on that cloudy afternoon. It was quite dark by six o'clock – long before the troops could be reorganised and sent in to make the general advance Sir Douglas Haig so fervently desired, long before the ground could be reconnoitred, and long before final instructions could reach the weary soldiers waiting in the line. By seven o'clock mist had gathered beneath the low cloud, and the darkness thickened to pitchy black. Battalions groping forward to assembly positions lost their way and became hopelessly mixed up. The attacks were postponed, and postponed again. Finally they were cancelled.

The battle was over. They had captured Neuve Chapelle and in places north of the village the old line had crept forward by, at most, a thousand yards. In the last hour of the night, when the reliefs marched up to take over the trenches, the exhausted survivors had to be pummelled and kicked to their feet before they could be roused and marched out, dazed and staggering with fatigue.

There was no dawn that morning. The darkness gradually gave

---

* From the Rifle Brigade History. Sergeant-Major Daniels and Corporal Noble were both awarded the Victoria Cross.

way to a strange yellow fog, thick with the fumes of lyddite that stung the eyes and burned the throat. Mercifully it shrouded the ground in front, so that the parties of stretcher-bearers could move freely in the open to search for any wounded who had survived the night. They prowled like phantoms in the gloom, picking their way through the carnage and the debris – the terrible litter of rifles torn from dead hands, ripped caps, German helmets, tatters of uniform, khaki and grey, the tumbled contents of pockets and haversacks, razors, pocket mirrors, photographs, smashed pipes and scraps of food, fragments of letters, tobacco pouches, crumpled packets of cigarettes. And everywhere distorted bodies, dead faces of livid yellow pallor staring blank-eyed into the yellow fog. Here and there a feeble movement caught a stretcher-bearer's eye and another man was rescued before the fog began to thin and the German guns thundered out in anticipation of another attack.

L/cpl. E. Hall.

For two days I carried the stretcher without a rest until at last I collapsed under the strain and had to rest for a few hours. How many men I carried I do not know, and the last few hours seemed like a dream, broken with the cries of the wounded.

My clothes were saturated with the blood of the men I bandaged and carried, and when I was finally relieved, I had to get a new suit from the quartermaster's stores.

L/cpl. W. Andrews.

I was stationed with my section to guard a pump at a brewery on the edge of Neuve Chapelle, and right beside it there was a notice-board still standing with just one word on it. It said 'DANGER'. Nicholson laughed and laughed as if it was the greatest joke of the war! He couldn't stop laughing. I was too tired to laugh. By that time I was absolutely stupid with fatigue and cold and the strain of it all.

Not all the troops had been relieved and those who were forced to remain until nightfall in the trenches passed a long and gruelling day under bombardments that were heavier than ever. They were not aware that the offensive was at an end and the enemy, no wiser than they were themselves, and still fearful of a new attack, pounded the British lines all day long. The British guns were firing back and the troops were kept on the alert, for it was perfectly possible that each German bombardment might mean a German counter-attack.

135

Already Sir Douglas Haig was in conference with his staff and his Corps Commanders outlining his plans for the next stage of the offensive. Now that they had lost the advantage of surprise it would be pointless to continue the campaign in the same sector but, once the troops had been re-shuffled (and more were expected any day) while the Germans were still disorganised (as they surely must be), they would launch a new British attack on another sector of the line and approach the Aubers Ridge from slightly further north. Sir Douglas Haig confidently expected to be ready in a matter of days. He ordered his Corps Commanders to prepare detailed plans and put forward his proposal for the sanction of the Commander-in-Chief.

It was true that there had been some unfortunate setbacks but, on the whole, Haig was not displeased with the outcome of the three days' fighting. The British Army had shown that it could penetrate the invincible German defences and, with only a little more effort, the original objectives could surely be achieved.

Sir John French was at first inclined to agree, but when the artillery returns reached his headquarters at St Omer, he had an unpleasant shock. The expenditure of ammunition during the three days' battle had been many times higher than the most extravagant estimate. It was the work of a moment to calculate that the ammunition available in reserve was not nearly enough to replace it and it was clear that there was no possibility of pursuing an offensive of any kind until supplies had been replenished and considerably augmented. In order to drive the point home, the Commander-in-Chief lost no time in dispatching a telegram to London. He did not beat around the bush: 'Cessation of forward movement is necessitated today by the fatigue of the troops, and, above all, by the want of ammunition . . .'

Bdr. W. Kemp.

We signallers worked for seventy-two hours straight off and I was down and out at the finish. When the battle died away the battery had fired two hundred and forty rounds of 6-inch ammunition and we only had *five* rounds left between all four guns. They each kept one round 'up the spout' for three weeks, ready to give the Germans hell!

Tmptr. J. Naylor.

One of my jobs was to go up to the Battery Headquarters with dispatches and bring back the returns and I remember that day very well. I went up to one of the batteries and the Major said

136

to me, 'We've got—' – I forget exactly how many rounds of ammunition they had per gun, but it was almost single figures. When I got back to headquarters the Colonel was talking to another battery commander who happened to be there, and he must have had a similar shortage of shells because the Colonel was saying to him that on no account was he to fire them except in a case of a really bad attack. I can't remember what the Major said, but I remember the Colonel's answer. He said, 'Well, if the worst comes to the worst, you'll just have to bloody well turn yourselves into infantry!' I suppose it was a joke, but it really impressed me at the time. We were frightfully short of ammunition, but I don't think it affected the morale at all. The British soldier is an extraordinary bloke and it takes a hell of a lot to get him down. I suppose we were worried but we always thought that something was going to happen that would put things right.

For many miles behind the line the narrow roads were stiff with traffic and the passage of many men. The reserves who had been stood down were moving back and reliefs were still moving up, for it had not been possible to relieve all the front-line troops in the early hours of the morning. Even the 4th Seaforths, who had got out the night before, were making slow, slow progress and they were still a long way from their destination.

Lt. C. Tennant.

What a road it was, blocked with traffic every two hundred yards, troops passing up to the front and ambulances passing down away from it. Progress was incredibly slow and in spite of the endless halts we were never able to get our packs off. Consequently the six miles seemed like sixteen and it was eleven o'clock before we got in. The men were billeted in the brewery and the officers were shown into a small cottage containing three very small and very lousy looking rooms full of dirty straw and filth. However a yard at the back provided a small barn full of clean straw and there we made ourselves fairly snug for the night. I rose at seven o'clock and after breakfast we paraded by companies for rifle inspection and checking of casualty rolls. Having heard several of the men repeating the old question 'Why was all this waste made?' I seized the occasion to check my platoon for the fault which I had been committing in thought myself ever since the action – namely criticising the wisdom of orders. But there was a well-deserved spoonful of jam administered with the pill, so they took the medicine well. The C.O. detailed me to take a party of forty men back to Neuve Chapelle to check casualties' kits as far as possible, but he countermanded this later, because the Germans were shelling all the roads very heavily all day and he didn't want to risk men's lives for the sake of dead men's belongings. Rightly!

At 5.45 p.m. we marched off and after another incredibly tedious march – we were held up for over an hour by a blocked road – we reached our destination where we have the best billets we have had for many a long day. We arrived at nine o'clock without blankets or valises, as the transport had got hopelessly stuck up on the blocked road, but we were all tired enough to sleep anywhere, and after a good meal we turned in at 10.30 and had our first real sleep since Monday night. This was Saturday night. So ended our share of the week's fighting.

At nightfall, as the Seaforths were thankfully nearing their billets and the prospect of food and rest, the remaining Battalions of the Indian Corps were at last preparing to move.

Capt. W. G. Bagot-Chester, MC.

At 5 p.m. we got news that we were to be relieved. Oh, how pleased we were! All my men bucked up, and started chattering away. One can have too much of a good thing! We hoped to go at dusk, but a message came to say that a German attack was expected, and we must remain for the time being. However, I got away at about 8 p.m. on being relieved by the HLI. Off I went with my men, pleased as could be, but I only got as far as brigade headquarters about a mile away when the General said he was very sorry but we had to stay in reserve to the Brigade which had taken over from us. This was rather hard after five days and nights, with not a wink of sleep for anyone, for all night we'd had to work at improving our trench and in the daytime it was almost impossible to sleep for the artillery bombardments and the fear of a German attack. However, there was nothing for it, so I explained the situation to the men and almost cried for pity for their disappointment. They took it very well, turned about without a word and marched back. No sooner had we got back to Battalion Headquarters than a staff officer came up, and said it was a mistake and we were no longer required. So, it was 'about turn' again and back we went at a snail's pace, for we were all dead tired, and couldn't walk straight. I halted at one place for water (the men had been short of it the whole time in the trench) and further on I halted again and gave the men an hour's sleep on the roadside.

Capt. A. J. Agius, MC.

We were relieved on Saturday night. It was late and pitch dark and very muddy. We managed to get to Port Arthur through the debris and struggled down a trench. It was filled with Connaught Rangers coming up and we finally had to get out and try to go across country. It was dark country, strange country, with any number of hedges and ditches to get through, bullets and shells coming over, men fagged out and laden with heavy kit. The men couldn't keep up. We finally struck a road, turned to our right and, thank God, at last got to Windy Corner – our rendezvous. We were the last out and they were all waiting for us. We had to wait some time trying to gather in stragglers. Before we arrived, Windy Corner had been shelled and my limber had bolted so I dumped spare ammunition in a house and off we trekked.

We marched for hours and hours. Every hour we lay down where we were in the middle of the road and slept for ten minutes – then on again. The men were awfully tired but full of buck and laden with loot, German helmets, etc. It was a perfect spring dawn and the peace of the Sunday morning was wonderful as we passed the Locon road. A lark sang. We finally got to our old billet at 6 a.m. only to find someone else in occupation! We waited some time for orders, and finally we were dispersed to our units. On we plunged down the road to les Lobes. The rest of the Battalion had been in for some time. We finally got to Harry Pulman's old billet, which we were to share with the remains of A Company.

So few of A Company were left that there was ample room for them all and when they had slept and were rested, and awoke hungry, despite their ravenous appetites there were far too few of the Londons left to consume even half the food the company cooks had prepared. The officers ate together. It was a subdued meal, with long silences and, when it was clear that no more stragglers would come in, there was a roll-call. After it, while the men cleaned up and prepared for kit inspection, the officers dispersed to begin the task of writing the difficult letters of condolence to the next of kin of the men they knew for certain had been killed. And there were personal letters to be written too, for the first time in many days.

Charles Tennant settled down to write to his fiancée, Lucy Hilton:

Darling, Heaven only knows when this letter will reach you, but I hope it will eventually, and as I want to put down, before I forget them, some of the details of our share in the Neuve Chapelle fight I will seize the opportunity afforded by a lazy Sunday morning to do so. I went to Communion at 8 a.m. and so have cried off Battalion Church Parade. As a result I have the morning free, and what a lovely morning, the sun shining, the birds singing and the buds in the hedgerows visibly swelling before my very eyes. I am just going to jot down the bare facts and some day beside a comfortable fire I will fill in all the details . . .

Walter Bagot Chester brought his diary up to date: 'I must thank my stars for being spared to see my birthday after such an action as we have had. Today was a day of rest for all.'

The weather had cleared up, the sun shone and, away from the stench and clamour of the battle, there was time to take stock and time to exult in the good fortune of being alive.

Lt. D. S. Lewis.

I've had huge luck in escaping being hit. My machine was hit eighty times in three days during the battle. One well-aimed shrapnel accounted for fifty-odd, and the rest were rifle bullets. Beyond a graze on the thumb and a bullet through my coat, I've never been touched. I've been brought down twice, once a bit of shell in the engine, the other time a smashed propeller, but each time I was easily high enough to get back. I can tell you I'm *some* nut in the artillery world! If only the initial push had been continued we should have broken through, I believe, and then anything might have happened.

In the aftermath of the battle, the delays that brought the first day's fighting to a standstill were gone over again and again in the course of endless conclaves and discussions at General Headquarters. Reports, flooding in now, were collated, digested, compared and analysed a thousand times. Even so soon after the event it was glaringly obvious that the breakdown in communications, the inevitable lack of speedy reaction to the situation at the front, the shattering of the telephone lines between observers and the guns, had been almost wholly responsible for the frustrations and delays. But there were other factors which the staff could only ascribe to misfortune – if only the weather had been kinder, if only there had been no mist, if only orders had not been misinterpreted and certain Divisional Generals had been less hesitant, if only there had been enough shells. The qualifying arguments, even excuses, came thick and fast at every meeting and were reiterated over and over.

The blame had to be laid somewhere. It could not be laid on the shoulders of the troops, for they had been magnificent and the Command was full of praise, particularly for the prowess of the untried Territorials. It could not be shouldered by the staff, for they were confident that all their assessments had been correct and that the battleplan should have succeeded. In their view it *had* succeeded, and if their reasonable hopes had not been fully realised it was surely no fault of theirs. In the final analysis the fault lay with the pundits and politicians whose backing had been so singularly lacking, and whose lamentable failure to supply sufficient men and munitions had thwarted outright victory. The situation showed no signs of improving and the returns that showed the high expenditure of ammunition were far less shocking to Sir John French than the knowledge that production of ammunition in factories at home amounted to a fraction over seven miserable shells a day for every gun on his front. Three days after the battle he shot off another indignant telegram to London:

The supply of gun ammunition, especially the 18-pdr. and 4.5-inch howitzer, has fallen far short of what I was led to expect and I was therefore compelled to abandon further offensive operations until sufficient reserves are accumulated.

But, even if the battle had not led to the hoped-for result, the British commanders were nonetheless elated by success. They had penetrated the formidable German defences and broken the enemy line. They had confounded the pessimists who said that it could not be done. Best of all, they had demonstrated to their sceptical French allies that the British Army was capable of mounting a successful offensive. And if they had done it once it followed that, with very little modification of the same tactics, they could do it again.

The spectre of 'success' at Neuve Chapelle was to haunt the hopes and blight the plans of British commanders for the best part of the war. But the British public was heartened by news of victory and the newspapers made the most of it. A *Times* leader encouraged its readers to rejoice.

For the first time the British Army has broken the German line and struck the Germans a blow which they will remember to the end of their lives. The importance of our success does not lie so much in the capture of the German trenches along a front of two miles, the killing of some 6,000 Germans and the taking of 2,000 prisoners. It is the revelation of the fact that the much-vaunted German army-machine on which the whole attention of a mighty nation has been lavished for four decades is not invincible.

The politicians in the War Council were less enthusiastic and less sympathetic to Sir John French's demands than he had hoped. Far from galvanising the War Office into activity, his telegram complaining of shortage of ammunition received a brusque reply in a letter from Lord Kitchener himself. He could promise no immediate increase in supplies; in his opinion the use of ammunition in the first sixteen days of March had been profligate, and he punched the point home by ordering that, in future, 'the utmost economy will be made in the expenditure of ammunition' To the Commander-in-Chief, basking in the glow of partial victory and anxious to exploit it, this edict was a severe blow.

The War Council was gratified by the reports of Neuve Chapelle and since, according to their information, the army had only narrowly failed to achieve a big success, its members were prepared to overlook the fact that Sir John French had undertaken his offensive without their full approval. But they were not over-impressed with the result. Seen from London, the situation on the western front was still unchanged, the prospect of all-out victory was still remote, and there was nothing to alter the opinion of the sceptics that the war could only be won elsewhere. They had other things on their minds and, in the course of a long meeting, they spent only a few minutes discussing events in France. Most of their attention and all of their interest was now focused on Gallipoli.

Sir Ian Hamilton was already on his way to the Dardanelles, travelling by fast destroyer, and he was still bemused by the events of the last few days. His appointment as Commander-in-Chief of a cobbled-together expeditionary force had come as a complete surprise. He had been summoned to the War Office on 12 March and, within twenty-four hours, had been sent off with such dispatch that he had only the vaguest idea of what was expected of him. His instructions, so far as they went, were to cooperate with the Royal Navy, to effect a landing on the Gallipoli peninsula and, thereafter, to proceed to occupy Constantinople. He was given no advice on how this was to be accomplished. He had no reliable maps, for there were none. He was given no information on the Turkish garrison or its defences, for no intelligence had been collected. No intelligence officers accompanied him, for none had yet been appointed. He was given no plan, for none had been drawn up, and his staff of thirteen officers, hastily co-opted, were as ignorant as he was himself. The General Staff, who had not been in the confidence of the War Council, had received no hint that a Dardanelles campaign was being mooted, and they were naturally in no position to supply more than the sketchiest outline of conditions on the peninsula. Even those dated from a scheme that had been studied and rejected as impracticable in 1906. The best they could do was to supply him with a pre-war copy of a Turkish Army handbook. It was better, but not much better, than nothing, and it was hardly surprising that Hamilton spent many solitary hours wrapped in his own thoughts as he paced the deck of the cruiser *Phaeton*, pausing at times to gaze reflectively at the inscrutable sea. He had plenty to think about.

The fate of the 29th Division had also been decided, for Lord Kitchener had at last agreed to release them. By 19 March the last man had embarked for Egypt where the Australian and New Zealand Army Corps were training hard. They were burdened with a clumsy title, awkward on the tongue, but the combination of initials was a happy one. Supply boxes, orders, papers, and all the stationery of the Corps was stamped with the letters 'A. & N. Z. A. C.' and it was only a matter of time before the convenient nickname 'Anzac' was universally adopted. One day it would be immortal – though no one knew it then. And it was many months before an army interpreter was struck by the shocking irony that 'Anzac' closely resembled a certain Turkish word. That word was 'anjac'. Its meaning was 'almost'.

But that was in the future. Meanwhile, like pawns in some giant tournament of chess, the troops were on the move. Hopes were high in that spring of 1915. But the battles in Europe, east and west, had been no more than the opening moves in the first rounds of the contest. Before it was concluded half the nations of the world would be vying for the role of grand master.

Part 3

~

'This is the happy warrior – this is he!'

Where are our uniforms?
Far, far away.
When will our rifles come?
P'raps, p'raps some day.
All we need is just a gun
For to chase the bloody Hun
Think of us when we are gone
Far, far away.

Chapter 11

On the first day of spring the weather rose to the occasion and 21 March was bright and warm enough to bring out droves of Sunday strollers. They thronged into the parks to enjoy the sunshine, the early spring flowers, and the sight of young soldiers on weekend leave, swaggering self-consciously in stiff new khaki, accompanied by proud mothers or sweethearts in whose eyes they were already heroes. In parks near military hospitals there was the added attraction of genuine wounded heroes to be smiled at sympathetically as they took the air in suits of convalescent blue. Anything military was a draw. In London crowds streamed down the Mall to Buckingham Palace where the King was taking the salute at a march-past of newly fledged Battalions and, when it was over and the stirring music of the band had faded in the distance, hundreds of people flocked into St James's Park and across Horseguards Parade to Whitehall to linger outside the War Office. There was nothing to be seen except the sentries guarding its austere walls, but the sightseers were satisfied with a fleeting sense of proximity to the seat of great events.

At Knowsley Hall, near Liverpool, where the weather was equally kind, it was the day of days for Lord Derby, for his own troops were on parade. By his own efforts and the expenditure of a considerable sum of money, he had raised and equipped no fewer than four Battalions and earned the title of 'England's best recruiting sergeant'. The locals knew them as 'The Derby Comrades Brigade', their solid silver cap-badges – provided personally by their patron – represented the Stanley family crest and, although some hundreds of admiring friends and relatives were there to cheer as they marched past, no one was prouder than Lord Derby. Lord Kitchener himself was there to take the salute from the steps of Knowsley Hall. It took fully forty minutes for twelve thousand soldiers to pass the saluting base and Lord Derby's own recruiting band was there to play them past. Lord Kitchener was full of compliments. Lord Derby was delighted.

But if the Derby Comrades Brigade drew the loudest cheers of the day, the 15th and 16th Cheshires ran them a close second. They came from Birkenhead and not a man among them was taller than five feet two inches. They were the Bantams, small volunteers who had been thwarted by army regulations in their efforts to join up at the start of the war. When it struck those in authority, aghast at the numbers of would-be recruits rejected on grounds of height, that even diminutive soldiers could be useful, they had been only too glad to volunteer. There was a score of bantam Battalions now, and the Birkenhead boys marching past Lord Kitchener cared not a jot if they raised a laugh as well as a cheer. 'All *they'd* be good for,' remarked one unkind onlooker, 'is to run round the back of a German, bite him in the arse, and make him run.'

Lord Kitchener was having a busy day. He had stayed overnight at Knowsley Hall, where the four thousand men of the Derby Comrades Brigade were encamped in the park, and now, without stopping for lunch, he set off by train to Manchester to take the salute for a second time as thirteen thousand men of the Manchester Regiment and Lancashire Fusiliers marched through Albert Square. The sun shone well into the afternoon, and the crowds cheered as lustily as they had cheered in Liverpool earlier in the day.

The brilliant weather over most of the country came as a tonic, for the euphoria and rejoicing that had greeted early reports of the victorious outcome of the British Army's first successful offensive was tempered now with disquiet. The casualty lists, trickling through to a public encouraged by gloating reports of vast numbers of enemy soldiers killed and captured, were manifest evidence that the cost had been enormous. Sir John French's dispatch had also been published and from his account of Neuve Chapelle, people could judge for themselves that the gains had been far, far less than the first published communiqués had led them to suppose. There was downright fury in some quarters of the press itself and the war correspondent of the *Daily Mail* launched into the attack with all guns blazing:

Sir John French's despatch on the fighting at Neuve Chapelle is the one topic of conversation. On March 10th an official statement was issued that the British Army had taken the important village of Neuve Chapelle and had captured a thousand prisoners and some machine-guns. Two days afterwards a British official despatch described the magnitude of the victory, the effectiveness of our heavy artillery, and the defeat and heavy loss of the Germans when they attempted counter-attacks.

The enemy for the time being was 'beaten and on the run'. The whole incident was painted in *couleur de rose*. There was an outburst of national rejoicing. Then suddenly the rejoicing paused. Casualty figures were published in daily instalments, and were surprisingly heavy. Rumours spread from mouth to mouth. Every man one met had some fresh story to tell, stories not in keeping with the official description. Many of them were false – but they fell like a pall on the public mind.

Now Sir John French has given us the real story, and not before it was time. His long despatch is a splendid tribute to the courage and devotion of the British Army, and it records a real victory. But it is very different from the tale told in the first accounts.

The advance was a success. The Germans were, for the moment, overwhelmed. We might have swept right through, far on the road to Lille. It was clearly Sir John French's intention that the Cavalry Brigade should pour through the breach in the German lines and get the enemy on the run. But our reserves were not brought up in time. The net result was that our real gain – a very important gain – was made during the first three hours of the three days' battle. We did splendidly. But anyone who studies Sir John French's despatch with insight can see that his aim was not to capture a village, but to advance on Lille itself. And, but for the unfortunate mist, he would probably have done so.

WHY NOT TRUST THE PEOPLE? Had the real story been told to us at the beginning, all would have been much better.

When the big advance comes, the big advance that would have started at Neuve Chapelle had things gone as well as was hoped, losses will be much greater. The nation will not shrink back. But our authorities would be well advised not to try to blind the public, even for a time, by telling of the victories and glossing over reverses.

The nation as a whole had no intention of shrinking back. It was clear to most people that the war which optimists had predicted would be 'over by Christmas' would be no brief affair and that it would take a good deal more than flag-waving enthusiasm to win it. Neuve Chapelle kindled a new spirit of resolve. Many men who had hesitated to join the army now hastened to enlist, and mothers and wives, fathers and sisters, uncles and aunts, redoubled their efforts to find ways of 'doing their bit'.

The needs of the army were great and the personal columns of local and national newspapers were flooded with appeals. For flint-and-tinder lighters for the troops in the trenches, where smokers were many but matches were scarce and a naked flame might attract the unwelcome attention of the enemy. For dressing-gowns, pyjamas, hot-water bottles for the wounded, and gramophones to cheer the lonely vigils of ships' companies at sea. And for money, money, money. Money to buy stoves and boilers to provide hot baths for troops coming out of the lines. Money for canteens and rest-huts. Money for splints and surgical dressings. Money for comforts of every possible kind. The public were urged to dig so deep and for so many worthy causes that fund-raisers had to exercise a good deal of imagination to make their particular cause stand out among the thousand others that were equally likely to wring cash from a public-spirited citizen's pocket. The ultimate in personal appeals was directed to the nation's dogs and cats:

DOGS and CATS of the EMPIRE! The Kaiser said, 'Germany will fight to last dog and cat.' Will British dogs and cats give 6d. each to provide Y.M.C.A. Soldiers' Hut in France?

Lady Bushman, who started an ambulance fund, came up with a winner. Her idea was that every ambulance should be known by a particular feminine Christian name and that every woman of the same name should contribute to its cost. This idea was appealing and it caught on like wildfire.

HILDAS – Miss HILDA WARDELL-YERBURGH, Hoole Hall, Chester, and Miss HILDA SMALLWOOD, 14 Oxford Terrace, Hyde Park, have joined forces in collecting for the HILDA AMBULANCE at Lady Bushman's suggestion, and will be very grateful if all HILDAS will send donations, however small, to either address.

LOUISA (or LOUISE) MOTOR AMBULANCE – Will each LOUISA or LOUISE send a donation to Miss Louisa Dawson, Woodlands, Crouch End?

AGNES MOTOR AMBULANCE (in connection with Lady Bushman's scheme) – Will every AGNES HELP? Miss Agnes Randolph, The Almonry, Ely.

All over the country Hildas, Louisas (or Louises!) Agnes's, Madges, Helens, Dorothys, Marions, and women of every popular Christian name, were inspired to do their bit – opening their purses, importuning friends and relations and collecting cash in every way they could think of for their own particular ambulance. Lady Bushman realised enough money for a whole fleet and soon, to the satisfaction of the donors, Hilda, Louise, Agnes *et al.* were lurching in the wake of the Tommies along the rough pavé roads of France.

There were some ladies who were keen to do their bit and provide comfort to the troops on a more personal level. One pseudonymous soldier, who published a *cri de coeur* to a faithless fiancée above a box number, was so inundated by replies that he was forced to expend a further ten shillings on another heartfelt plea, addressed to ladies who were eager to do their bit by consoling him.

> KHAKI CLAD, whose message to BROWN EYES appeared here on Tuesday, much regrets that it is impossible for him to answer personally the hundreds of kind people who offer their services in substitution for BROWN EYES.

Some people found even more remarkable ways of doing their bit and Henry Edwards was one of them. He was eighty-five years old, he sported a venerable white beard, and he spent his days waiting outside Lambeth register office. War weddings were the order of the day and business was brisk. This was gratifying to Mr Edwards. Early in the war he had not only seen an opportunity of doing his bit but had spotted the fact that there was a gap in the market.

In many cases, when the soldier-bridegroom expected to be leaving for the front, registry office weddings were hastily arranged, and sometimes with good reason. The licence would be obtained and the ring purchased well in advance, in anticipation of a forty-eight-hour pass, but when the bride and groom appeared for the ceremony itself they frequently forgot to bring along a witness. Henry Edwards, dapper in bowler hat and well-brushed overcoat, a festive flower in his button-hole, was happy to step into the breach and act as best man. Patriotism had its reward. Mr Edwards was not so crass as to demand a fee for his services, but he invariably received a tip 'commensurate', as he put it, 'with the happiness of the bridegroom'. On one occasion this had only amounted to a souvenir fragment of shell from France, but Mr Edwards had not complained. He could afford to be generous for although, on occasion, he received as little as sixpence, he sometimes got as much as ten shillings, and usually not less than five. Since he had done his bit at several hundred military and naval weddings since the war began, he was doing nicely and was as satisfied with his war-work as his grateful clients. It was almost Easter and weddings were all the rage.

CQMS G. Fisher, 1st Bn. Hertfordshire Regt. (TF).

I came home on my first leave and in those days you only got four days and that included getting there and back. When I

151

came home to St Albans they were just beginning to move the 47th London Division Territorials to St Albans for training and they were billeting these chaps in houses in the town. I was going steady with my future wife then, and she was living in a large flat over a shop. There was a regulation that soldiers would *not* be billeted in the house of the wife of a soldier serving abroad. I said, 'I think we'd better get married. You won't have anybody billeted on you then and you'll get a separation allowance.' So we decided to get married. We were married in the registry office in St Albans, and I was due to go back to France the next morning. I had to report to Victoria Station at half past four in the morning, so that meant I must be in London the night before, because there was no train from St Albans that early. We were married at three o'clock in the afternoon and in the evening we went up to London.

I had no idea where we could put up for the night. YMCA hostels would take a soldier, but they wouldn't take a soldier with a lady friend. I was a bit puzzled, so I went up to a policeman outside Victoria Station and I explained the position and that I had to catch a train at 4.30 in the morning to go back to France. I'd got all my kit – rifle, pack and everything. I said, 'I've got my wife with me and we've got to get in somewhere for the night. Can you suggest anywhere for me to go?' So he looked at me and he looked at my wife, and he must have seen that it was all right. He said, 'Don't worry, chum. I've got a friend just round the corner. I'll get you fixed up all right.'

He took me to his friend round the corner, knocked on the door, had a chin-wag with him and got us a bedroom. So there we stayed for the night. I was up at four in the morning to get to Victoria and my wife came with me to see me off to France. I didn't get my honeymoon for two years, because it was two years before I got another leave. So I had my honeymoon two years after I got married, and there's not many men can say that!

Returning to the front after several months in the trenches, fresh from the subsidiary attack to Neuve Chapelle, Gordon Fisher was an old soldier now. The young soldiers of Kitchener's Army were still impatiently waiting to go, but there was little sign of their going.

Kitchener's Mob no longer presented the raggle-taggle appearance of the early months of the war when the word 'mob' had all too aptly described them. It could hardly have been otherwise, for the army had been quite unable to clothe the first hundred thousand, let alone the second or the third, and for months they had worn the same civilian clothes they had worn on enlistment. They ranged from natty city suits and bowler hats to flannels worn with blazers and summer boaters, to shabby working clothes worn with mufflers and cloth caps, and even the best of them had long ago worn out and been replaced with uniforms of navy-blue material which frequently led to soldiers being mistaken for guards or even porters at railway stations. The government had placed large orders for khaki, and meanwhile scoured mills and factories all over the country to buy up stocks of whatever cloth was available. The stock of blankets was quickly exhausted and when they ran out Welsh troops were issued with bales of Brethyn Llwyd and Scottish troops with lengths of Harris Tweed to keep them warm. The mills were working overtime, turning out khaki serge by the mile, but buttons were another problem, for most factories which had produced them had now been turned over to the manufacture of munitions, and even working shifts around the clock it was many months before the remaining button manufacturers were able to meet the demand. So Kitchener's Army had soldiered on, compensated by a clothing allowance of threepence a day, wearing out their own shoe leather for want of army boots, patching, darning, and inexpertly cobbling together holes that inevitably appeared in elbows and knees of suits that had never been intended for wear when crawling about fields and hedges or to come into contact with barbed wire. Now that the hated Kitchener's blue had given way to soldierly khaki photographers across the country were doing a brisk trade in photos to send home. Many of the soldiers who posed proudly in front of some classical studio backdrop or beside a tasteful marble column supporting a drooping aspidistra, still had no belt or cap, for the equipment arrived in dribs and drabs. They also lacked rifles and, in the army's view, that was much more serious. It was shortage of rifles that was holding Kitchener's Army back, for, without them, training could not be completed.

The stock of efficient rifles had long ago been depleted to make up the losses of the early months and to supply the Territorial battalions who had first call on them, and the best that could be done for Kitchener's Mob was to supply them, if they were lucky, with obsolete practice rifles. They were useless for action, and not much better for training, but they were better than nothing, even if there was no ammunition to go with them. Lacking ammunition, the hard-pressed instructors did their best to carry out such musketry training as could be done without it. The Tommies learned the care of arms, handling of arms, the theory of musketry and the mechanism of the rifle. They did visual training in the open, practised judging distances and drilled for endless hours on fire discipline and control. They did everything that could possibly be done with a rifle except fire it, and when service rifles finally arrived there were usually only enough for one, or, at most, two companies. One by one, after a few days' serious practice, the companies were sent off to fire a musketry course and, to no one's astonishment, the results were seldom spectacular. By the end of March not many Battalions had completed musketry training and, until it had, no Battalion had a hope of being pronounced fit for active service.

But the men were fitter than they had been in their lives despite the rigours of training in all weathers, frequently returning to bell tents that were often far from weather-proof. The healthy, outdoor life had hardened them and the drill, the digging, the marches, the football matches and a dozen other kinds of unaccustomed exercise had brought them to a peak of physical fitness. Boys who had enlisted straight from school had broadened out and added inches to their height, pasty-faced office workers were bronzed and hearty, professional men could dig and heave with the best of them, the under-nourished filled out on the plain but plentiful diet, plump sedentary workers became lean and wiry. Even athletes who had prided themselves on their fitness attained greater heights of prowess on army sports fields than they had ever achieved before the war. The scarecrow mob of the previous autumn could now reasonably be described as 'a fine body of men'.

In the opinion of Kitchener's Mob, marching occupied the minds of their commanders to an obsessive degree. They had marched for literally hundreds of miles in the course of their training, starting with gentle route-marches of five or six miles, gradually increasing in length and difficulty, carrying more and more equipment, until now they could march for up to twenty miles with a full pack and 'ammunition', represented by slabs of lead cut to fit the empty pouches. These were known throughout the army as 'Kitchener's Chocolate' and the passage of a Battalion along a long march was easy to spot by the trail of hated 'chocolate bars' discarded by weary Tommies resting at the roadside.

Capt. Sir F. G. Kenyon, KCB, Inns of Court OTC (TF).

March discipline was important. The foundation of steady marching is observing the regulation hundred and twenty paces to the minute. This was practised in company work as well as when the whole Battalion was together and it was kept to, however short the distance. Guides were expected to check their step by looking at their watches at frequent intervals and not to drop the pace more than necessary going up hills. When a company has learnt to keep the regulation rate without distress and as a matter of habit, the foundation of good marching is laid, and the actual distance covered will not matter, provided the men are in reasonably good training.

We also observed march discipline in the matter of regular halts and intervals and, of course, in forming up the column again and keeping to the proper side of the road etc. The men liked to sing but, in that respect, they certainly did *not* come up to the best standards. The singing was usually spasmodic and none too good! If they had taken the trouble to learn the words of songs, and not merely fragments of choruses, singing on the march would have been far more inspiriting. It was surprising what a large proportion of men could continue to sing contentedly with the beat on the wrong foot, or even attempted to march to rag-time!

But the Tommies were oblivious to such criticisms and carried on singing in their own sweet way. It was their only means of asserting their individual feelings and by now some of the songs were very individual indeed. One Battalion found the tune of 'Diamonds in Amsterdam' convenient to march to, but their version, they believed, was an improvement on the original.

> I've seen maggots in Tickler's Jam,
> Tickler's Jam, Tickler's Jam,
> I've seen maggots in Tickler's Jam
> Crawling round.
> And if you get some inside your tum
> They'll crawl through
> Till they bite your bum,
> So watch what you're sucking
> Next time you eat fucking
> Old Tickler's Jam!

It was crude enough to bring a blush to the cheeks of some younger soldiers in whose schoolboy vocabulary 'Drat it!' had ranked as a strong expletive. But there was safety in numbers, and with repetition their scruples were gradually overcome until they were singing as lustily as the rest. But the battalion reserved this ditty to enliven marches along quiet country roads where there was little danger of offending the prudish ears of civilians who chanced to be in earshot.

The Tommies of Kitchener's Army were popular with civilians. They cheered them as they marched in interminable columns through country towns and villages. They hung around camps watching them at drill, at bayonet practice or marching in formation, and on open land and commons the sight of Tommies digging and revetting trench systems was a popular spectator sport. They dug trenches the length and breadth of the country and they had been digging them for months. By spring there were eight miles of trenches on Berkhamsted Common alone, and it was rumoured that there were more trenches in Great Britain than there were in France.

The civilian population took the Tommies to their hearts and, whenever they got the chance, showered them with kindnesses.

Pte. A. Simpson, 5th Bn. (TF), Yorkshire Regt.

As we got our khaki we became available for guard duties outside our billets. I did one outside the Beechwood Hotel, and a few days later I was detailed for another one. We were only supposed to do one guard a week, so I saw the sergeant-major and told him I'd already done one guard that week. 'What!' he said 'And you've been selected *again*?' 'Yes, sir,' I said. 'Well,' he said, '*you* must be extra good! Do this one and then I'll see you get another.' That was the beginning and end of complaining in the army for me!

If it had been a guard on the big house in Cold Bath Road I wouldn't have complained – no one did! The house was used for isolating new recruits who arrived suffering from scabies, and an old lady in a very large house opposite used to send a servant to a fish and chip shop every night for four fish and chip suppers for the guard corporal and three men. On Sundays when the shop was closed she sent sandwiches across, and often there was a brand new pair of socks for each man. No, we didn't mind a bit doing *that* guard.

Every night some Harrogate churches put on free suppers and provided free writing materials and rest-rooms for the troops, and there were no inquiries about your religion, if any. These kindnesses were particularly welcome to chaps like myself because I made an allotment to my mother which left me with only sixpence a day to provide Blanco, postage stamps, razor blades, and so on.

2nd Lt. W. Cushing, 9th Bn., Norfolk Regt.

In May we went by train to Reigate and spent a most delightful fortnight digging trenches on the hill outside the town. We were under the impression that they were for the defence of London, and a sorry bulwark they would have been! But the whole exercise was an excuse for a good time. We were billeted most comfortably, the men in good houses and the officers with the high society of the town. Two of my colleagues, Glanfield and Everett, were billeted with some well-to-do people in a fine house, really a mansion, and I was invited to dine there one evening. I can't remember their name, but I *do* remember their lavish hospitality! Champagne, port, liqueurs, and *gold* finger bowls. My God, those gold finger bowls! I stared helplessly at mine, wondering what they were and what we were supposed to do with them. (Glanfield and Everett were equally at a loss, because usually we all dined in the mess.) We were saved by the charming daughter of the house. She must have seen that we were embarrassed, because she whispered to a servant and had them quietly removed.

Rfn. W. Worrell, 12th Bn., Rifle Brig.

People were awfully kind. I was invited to tea with Lady Haliburton, but I've never had such an awkward afternoon in my life. I'd thought to get a good tuck-in and that there would be other people there, but I was all on my own in this fancy drawing room, and there was even a footman serving out the tea. I sat on the edge of a little chair trying to balance a tea-cup and eat these dainty little sandwiches, with a lady old enough to be my grandmother asking me questions and me trying to make polite replies and not to talk with my mouth full. I thought, 'No more of this for me!' But as I was going out Lady Haliburton said, 'I don't think you've enjoyed yourself, have you?' I said, 'Oh yes I *have*, and thank-you-very-much-for-having-me' – like a well brought up lad. She gave a half-smile and said, 'Perhaps you'd like to come back next Sunday and have tea with the servants?' So out of politeness I had to say yes, and out of politeness I *had* to go back the next week.

They took me down to this big kitchen where there was the cook and the other maids and they made an immense fuss of me. They said, 'What would you like for tea?' I said, 'Can I have anything I like?' The cook said, 'Yes, of course you can. What would you like?' I said, 'Well, I'd like smoked haddock with an egg on it' – thinking I'd beat them! – but she said, 'Yes, certainly.' So I had poached haddock with an egg on it, and I don't know what-all after that. We had a very jolly time, and I also had a large bag of home-made cakes to take back with me.

Pte. H. N. Edwards, 6th (Bristol City) Bn., Gloucester Regt.

When we moved to Danbury in Essex I was billeted with two other blokes on some very nice people called Lancaster. I shared a room with a chap whose father was the man who cleaned out the dustbins in Bristol. You met all sorts in the army. The other chap was a bit of a snob and he rather looked down on this chap, Billy Williams, but I found out that he was as nice a chap under the skin as anybody else and we mucked in together and got on like smoke.

Mrs Lancaster was very good to us and looked after us really well. She always gave us an onion pudding before the main meal on the Sunday. It was a long roly-poly suet pudding with plenty of onion in it. She'd cut you a good thick slice of that and pour gravy on it. It was an old tradition in big families, because if you had that you wouldn't eat so much meat, but we loved these onion puddings. We thought they were marvellous and, of course, with the exercise and all the fresh air you were getting, you were permanently ravenous. But she'd always put on a meal for us, though the billeting money couldn't have gone far. Oh, she *was* good to us! We thoroughly enjoyed ourselves there. When we left we clubbed together to buy Mrs Lancaster a present, just some small thing but she was ever so pleased. Many's the time when we got to France, sitting in some dirty old trench, nothing but bully beef and biscuits, we'd say, 'Remember those onion puddings at Mrs Lancaster's?' We often used to think of them. We could have done with one then!

If the problem of housing the troops had not been entirely solved it was at least much improved since the chaotic early days of mass enlistment when they had squeezed sardine-like into camps and barracks, town-halls, public houses, even race-courses, sleeping in grandstands, on floors, on billiard tables and occasionally at first in the open. Those who were in private billets usually came off best, and even though the majority had moved into camps and the tents were gradually being replaced by huts, private billets were still in demand as Kitchener's Mob moved around the country. There were few landladies who failed to give full value for the billeting allowance of seventeen shillings and sixpence a week, supplying hearty meals, washing clothes, darning socks and generally mothering their 'boys'. Some even rose from their beds in the small hours to brew cocoa or Bovril for a Tommy returning wet and chilled from a night exercise and to stoke up the kitchen fire to dry his clothes for the morning.

Now that Kitchener's Army had been licked into shape and equipment was trickling through, training was more intensive. There were night exercises at least once a week and they were not beloved by the troops, divided into companies, one to 'attack' the other, stumbling across dark countryside to some unknown rendezvous and not infrequently losing their way. The night on which novice guides led them on a compass bearing was not easily forgotten by one half-Battalion for the guides had omitted to allow for the difference between true and magnetic north. It was a night of torrential rain and the unfortunate Tommies were obliged to wait in the inadequate shelter of a hedge until the error was corrected. This took a long, long time and, as one unfortunate observed, 'It's hard to say how long we were held up – perhaps an hour, perhaps two – but I *do* know that, as we stood there in the downpour, everyone had ample time to reflect on how much he was enjoying himself.' When they finally arrived hours late at the barn they were supposed to 'capture', the 'enemy' who held it had long ago succumbed to cold and boredom and they were all fast asleep. Their opponents were in no mood to wake them gently and the free-for-all that ensued was not precisely the 'attack' their Commanding Officer had had in mind.

But with the arrival of weapons, training was becoming more sophisticated and more interesting.

Pte. H. N. Edwards 6th (Bristol City) Bn., Gloucester Regt.

I joined the machine-gun section when we were at Danbury. At first we only had two machine-guns, and one of them was an ancient old crock. They reckoned it had been used at the Battle of Omdurman! But it had been converted to fire 303 ammunition and it weighed a ton. We all tried to dodge carrying that one because it weighed at least ten pounds more than the other. That was the worst side of it – humping round and carrying these heavy guns and tripods. The glamour side was firing them and we were very proud of ourselves when we got to that stage. But first we had lectures and we had to study and learn all sorts of things, which was easy enough if you had some knowledge of mathematics. But I always remember one occasion when we were learning the use of the clinometer. Now, this simply means that if you're carrying out direct fire, you put this thing on the gun, and you move it, and it registers so many degrees up, so then you can work out how far your bullets will go parabolically. So the officer who was instructing us took us through it a few times and then he left us to practise working it out. He said, 'Carry on, Sergeant, will you?' And Sergeant Mawley looked absolutely baffled and said, 'I'm very sorry, sir, I don't think I can do this. I'm a greengrocer in civil life.' I always remember him saying that! He didn't know anything about mathematics at all. Poor chap, we simply roared with laughter.

In the well-organised peacetime army it took three years to train a soldier to the standard of full-fledged efficiency which the men of Kitchener's armies, grappling with every conceivable shortage and difficulty, were now expected to approach in a mere eight months. But they were men of a very different stamp from most pre-war recruits, drive by poor circumstances or unemployment to enlist. The majority of Kitchener's men had joined up for very different reasons. They were fitter and stronger, they were enthusiastic and keen to learn, and the standard of intelligence was generally high, for the rank and file was made up of men from every stratum of Britain's rigidly structured society. And they were doing well.

Many were professional men who had been encouraged to enlist in the first heady wave of recruitment and it was a matter of annoyance to some in authority that there were numbers of men serving in the ranks who might have been more usefully employed as officers and, since Commanding Officers were reluctant to weaken their Battalions by recommending their best men, the pleas of the War Office for suitable candidates fell on deaf ears. The supply of officers was a headache but although they were desperately needed the hierarchy at the War Office was not yet prepared to compromise on the rules that had governed the granting of commissions to career officers of the Regular Army in peacetime. Although a few exceptional men were occasionally commissioned from the ranks, the military authorities held to the belief that, with rare exceptions, the qualities of leadership and refinement required by potential army officers could only be nurtured in the public schools. In the present emergency the War Office was not prepared to grant even temporary commissions to men who had not enjoyed the benefit of a public school education.

2nd Lt. W. Cushing.

I applied for a commission on the strength of three years in the Cambridge OTC and in due course I was appointed Temporary Second Lieutenant in the 9th Service Battalion of the Norfolk Regiment. I joined my unit at the Old Ship Hotel, Brighton. The officers were billeted in the hotel, which also served as Battalion HQ. In the orderly room I found the C.O., Colonel Shewen, and also Captain Stracey. They were very official, but very courteous – so courteous that they didn't even rebuke me when I failed to salute the Colonel – and, what's more, I even omitted to salute the Brigadier General when I had to report to him. Those officers must have said, 'Upon my word, that's a green one!' Their judgement was true, because the Cambridge Officer Training Corps had not fitted me in any way to be a commissioned officer, and this fact was sharply brought home to me in the following weeks. I got very little training that was of any value.[*]

True, I shouted words of command at an obedient line of strange faces under the eye of a dear old boy. He was a white-haired superannuated sergeant-major and I suppose he had volunteered to come back to help in training the 'awkward squad', for he was far too old to fight. I can still hear him calling to the platoon in his thick Norfolk accent: 'Give me your attention naow, while the orfcer 'ere is a-larning of 'is wark.'

I had no command of my own until I went to France. When I did eventually join the regiment overseas I was given a platoon and was expected not merely to bellow commands on parade, but to know how to feed, clothe and billet sixty men, know all their names and characters, keep a platoon roll, attend to their wants, be responsible for their efficiency *and* the good order of their arms and equipment – clothing, boots, gas-masks, entrenching-tools and a dozen oddments – and also lead them through the discomforts and dangers of trench warfare. My training fitted me for none of these things.

But the apprentice officers were shaping up and what they lacked in experience they made up for in enthusiastic application. As a matter of course, in the leisurely days of peacetime, army officers in home stations spent almost as much time on leave, on the hunting field and in sporting and social activities as they spent in performing their regimental duties. There was a vast gulf between them and the men they commanded, and the day-to-day running of infantry platoons was, more often than not, left entirely in the hands of an NCO.

These regular officers were not dilettantes, and they were certainly not amateurs. The army picked the cream of all applicants, the entrance examination was stiff, the training at Sandhurst or Woolwich was arduous and, even when a subaltern was commissioned into a regiment, promotion came slowly and had to be worked for. The high standard of professionalism in the Regulars had proved its worth again and again since the start of the war, and the Old Army had been decimated in the course of it. There were few enough Regular officers left to hold the fort at the front. There were certainly none to spare for the New Armies and their lack of trained officers was critical. Old officers, often long into comfort-

---

[*] The practice of posting newly commissioned subalterns direct to service Battalions in training was discontinued in the summer of 1915 when young officers' companies were formed and attached to reserve brigades for training purposes. Officer cadet Battalions were formed in 1916.

able retirement, had been brought back as Commanding Officers and adjutants of New Army battalions consisting of a thousand men and a dozen or so junior officers, temporarily commissioned, who were as inexperienced as the men themselves. Often they were the sons of family friends or acquaintances, chosen by the Colonel himself who then put their names forward for temporary commissions. On his recommendation they were usually granted.

But the retired Colonels and Majors were often pleasantly surprised. Although the new subalterns could be shockingly ignorant of traditional 'mess manners' they took a far closer interest in their men than the remote beings who had officered Battalions in peacetime. Junior officers spent eight hours a day with their platoons, they shared the rigours of route-marches, worked far into the night to master the arts of signalling, of map-reading, of calculating distances, and the manifold skills of soldiering that would enable them to keep at least one step ahead of their men and help them in their labours. They took a personal pride in their platoons and it was every subaltern's ambition to make his particular platoon the best in his battalion. And if they occasionally made mistakes, if now and again a young officer lost his way and inadvertently trudged his disgruntled platoon round three sides of a sixteen-mile square, if he was slow to report defaulters and inclined to be soft on discipline, these faults would be rectified with experience. Meanwhile, the trust and *esprit de corps* that was gradually building up between the officers and men of Kitchener's Army as they trained and worked together made up for a great deal.

Most public schools had Officers' Training Corps, and they were popular with schoolboys whether or not they intended to make a career in the army. On one or two afternoons a week they marched and stamped and 'shunned and formed fours, practised elementary rifle drill, and generally played at being soldiers under the instruction of some ex-army sergeant, who usually doubled as the school's PT instructor. The cadets enjoyed field days and in the summer term weekend 'army' camps provided a welcome break from school routine, even though the 'officers' were only their own schoolmasters masquerading in khaki. Most men who could claim to have had even such rudimentary training in a public school or university OTC were automatically given commissions.

But the Officers' Training Corps of the Inns of Court was different. It was one of the oldest, certainly the most respected, and when the Territorial Force came into being in 1908 the Inns of Court was the only OTC to be recognised officially and embodied 'on the strength'. For many years after it was formed in 1859 (as the Inns of Court Rifle Volunteers) it was composed entirely of barristers and students at the bar but, of recent years, it had opened its doors to any university

162

graduate. When the war began the Inns of Court OTC was swamped by new applicants and by past members anxious to re-enlist, and for some time was the only military unit devoted full-time to the training of officers. By the end of the war more than ten thousand men had passed through its ranks and been commissioned.

They made excellent officers.

Lt. Col. E. H. L. Errington, VD, Inns of Court OTC (TF).

Unquestionably our own NCOs did not as a rule have the snap or smartness of the pre-war Regular. Although we tried to keep a certain number rather longer than the usual period, a man generally became an NCO simply as part of his training and, of course, went away as soon as he was fit for a commission. If we had been working on the Sandhurst system, the want of experience in the NCOs might have been a weak point, but our object was not perfect drill, nor were we dealing with boys, or trying to develop a particular type. Our object was a high standard of character. We were dealing with men, and trying to produce officers according to their individual characteristics, and the fact that all of us – officers, NCOs and men – were all of the same class was an enormous asset. The object of an officer's training must be to equip him mentally and physically to play his part in the realities of war. In the military profession failure is paid for in the lives of others.

If our NCOs were inexperienced in the military sense, they were not inexperienced in life or ignorant of the meaning of true discipline. Above all, they had the unfailing advice and guidance of their Regimental and Company Sergeant-Majors, and the CSMs were all men who had declined to take commissions for the good of the Corps. CSM Walters, for example, was an old and famous 'Varsity blue. He was also a born soldier and to see him deal with his company was a lesson in the art of training. He was feared by the slackers, adored by every man of backbone, and a constant source of joy to me as Commanding Officer.

There were few other battalions in the British Army which boasted a sergeant who quoted Cato (and in Latin!) to raw recruits on the parade ground or, when they assembled for a night exercise, addressed them in the words of Catullus, '*Vesper adest, juvenes, consurgite.*'* There were not many Battalions who had a quartermaster-sergeant who amused himself off-duty by turning

---

* 'Rise up, lads, evening is coming.'

King's Regulations into perfect iambics, and there was none in which so many legal minds were bent on dissecting these sacrosanct military laws in search of legal niceties that would admit of novel and more advantageous interpretations. There was very little 'crime', as the army knew it, but on the rare occasions when some miscreant was brought before the Colonel this added a certain spice to the proceedings.

The fertile minds of the rank and file frequently came up with imaginative explanations to excuse their misdemeanours. Two men charged with over-staying weekend leave could not deny that they had missed the train, for an NCO of the Corps had seen them racing at the last minute towards the buffet, and madly racing back again as the train steamed out taking their kit with it. But their 'defence' was original. A band playing on the station had struck up 'God Save The King'. As soldiers and as patriots they had no alternative but to stop and stand to attention, even if it meant missing the train – which, 'to their deep regret', had been the case. The Colonel did not believe a word of it, but he secretly admired their ingenuity, and let them off with a warning.

There was one member of the Corps with whom neither excuses nor legal falderols would wash, and only the most foolhardy private would have thought of trying it on. Regimental Sergeant-Major Burns was a Regular soldier of the Scots Guards, who had been appointed to the Corps a year earlier. His job was to lick the embryonic officers into shape and, barristers or not, he would stand no nonsense from anyone if he was the Lord Chief Justice himself. No one, from the Colonel downwards, ever dreamed of questioning his judgement or his authority. RSM Burns was an awesome figure, and well he knew it.

Lt. T. S. Wynn, 2nd Bn., Suffolk Regt.

The dominating character for the rank and file was undoubtedly the Regimental Sergeant-Major. Burns was everywhere. From the outset he gave us raw recruits a precise idea of our unworthiness to be members of the Corps, and of his great and singular condescension in instructing us. It was he who first expounded to us the great truth that although we might, by some fluke of fate, become lieutenants, or even captains and majors, we should not – we *could* not – become a real RSM. His voice spread desolation all over the parade ground. His eye always seemed to light on us cowering in the rear ranks and spotted a chilled hand straying into a greatcoat pocket. He was the best representative of the Regular Army that some of us ever met either before, during or after the war. It was even rumoured among gullible privates that RSM

Burns was a member of the Army Council, and some of us could well believe it!

Capt. Sir F. G. Kenyon.

Every man entered the Corps as a private, and learned his recruit, squad and company drill as such. What differentiated the Corps from an ordinary infantry battalion came at a later stage in their training when the men began to learn to drill others, so the handling of sections and platoons, and even companies, was not confined to NCOs but given to every man in turn. They were never allowed to forget that they were learning to be privates so that they might learn to be officers. And as the NCOs gained experience they were given command of platoons and half companies in field exercises, with officers accompanying them to observe and assist or criticise later.

Lt. C. S. Wynn.

Battalion field days were an adventure, and if you had a motor cycle and a job as an orderly, it was a joyous adventure. But even lacking this, there were all kinds of possibilities. For instance, you might find yourself suddenly placed in command of a section or a platoon or even of a company. Then you learned in the bitter school of experience why things went wrong in a battle. You learned the importance of information (even 'negative' information) and of 'keeping in touch', and you learned from your own experience how terribly exhausting a ten-mile rearguard action can be to heavily laden men, sustained on bread and cheese. And I recall the Company Sergeant-Major pointing out very effectively that 'fire orders' lustily given and quickly carried out were not likely to produce good results if the sights were not adjusted! Of course you might more often be a mere 'man' (as distinct from an 'officer') and your lot might be to tramp round the Beacon in the snow, or attack it on a boiling hot day. But here again the gods might be kind, and there were worse things in life than being 'reserves' behind a sunny hedge for hours on end, knowing (without much sense of loss!) that you probably wouldn't share in the glory of the battle. These excursions gave us heaps of practice in comparing the ground with the map, which can't possibly be taught by lectures, and later on at the Somme, or at Arras or up the Menin Road, there was many an officer who was able to apply the lessons he'd learned with the Inns of Court, and was thankful that he had.

The War Office looked kindly on the Inns of Court and gave them a free hand. Theirs was not only the most effective means of training officers, it was also the most economical. Until they were commissioned, the men trained and were paid as rankers, and the cost of training a private on a three-month intensive course was a fraction of the cost of training temporarily commissioned officers who went straight into service Battalions to pick up such training as they could from their overworked Colonels and Adjutants.

If the OTC was in favour with the War Office, it was even more popular with distracted Commanding Officers trying to build up Battalions of the New Army with a sadly deficient complement of subalterns to assist them. Week after week, as recruits became efficient and progressed to the 'special instruction class', harassed Colonels travelled down to their training ground at Berkhamsted to look them over and pick out likely candidates as officers for their battalions. The demand was huge and even though the Inns of Court was constantly recruiting, it was hard to keep up with it.

Kitchener's Army was not quite ready to go to war, but it soon would be and the War Office was already looking ahead. It was evident that many more men would be needed, recruiting figures had been tending to tail off, and at the end of March the Parliamentary Recruiting Committee launched a National Patriotic Campaign to bring laggards into the ranks. There were public meetings and special appeals during patriotic shows at cinemas and theatres where some soldiers even appeared on stage in rousing flag-waving finales. Kitchener's Army, which now, in its own view, was fine-honed to military perfection and was sick of kicking its heels, was only too happy to help, and when battalions in training were canvassed for volunteers they were seldom slow to come forward. Recruiting made a welcome change from drills and parades and successful 'recruiters' were given small cash rewards and sometimes privilege leave, but it was not always a sinecure. The fledgling soldiers were immaculately turned out in new unblemished khaki, and when they knocked on doors to inquire if the household included a man of military age they sometimes received a dusty answer from the lady of the house. 'My boy is already out in France. When are *you* going?' It was a sore point.

Cpl. G. R. Daniels, 12th (Bermondsey) Bn., East Surrey Regt.

I had just attained the rank of corporal and one day the RSM on the parade ground said to me, 'I hear you can do a bit of spouting.' I assured him that I was never lost for a word or two and he promptly detailed me the following morning to march with thirty men led by the recruiting band from the town-hall and halt at various points in the district. When people stopped to listen to the music I was to address the crowd in general about the need for men and at the same time my men were to go round individually and tackle likely recruits. I felt extremely cocky leading my contingent at the head of a first-rate military band as we proudly marched up Jamaica Road, but my return to quarters was a different matter. I had lost no less than twenty-five of my thirty men. They'd had the nifty idea that they could best find suitable recruits in public houses and they had fallen by the wayside!

However we did have some successes. We were all well used to wearing our khaki uniforms and puttees by now, except for one poor chap called Ben Pendry. He was a stocky little man with extremely broad shoulders and a torso that by rights should have been attached to much longer legs and nothing had been found to fit him in all the stock of clothing we'd received. Poor old Pendry had to parade every day in a black suit and bowler hat, but we even managed to turn this to advantage. We used to volunteer to attend evening recruiting drives where people made rousing speeches and lads who were willing to join up were invited to mount the platform and do it there and then. Pendry used to go along in his civvies and mingle as one of the crowd and when the speaker asked for volunteers, he would dramatically rush forward up to the platform to set an example. I can't say how often Pendry enlisted in the army before he got his khaki. It must have been a dozen times!

Now that they felt sure that their long delayed departure for France must be fast approaching some soldiers found other constructive ways of passing their leisure hours. Several men of the Argyll and Sutherland Highlanders took advantage of a local schoolmaster's offer to teach themselves simple French. He believed in learning by rote and he favoured kindergarten methods. He did not trouble these awkward pupils with the complicated rules of grammar and construction, nor did he confuse them with French spelling. He chalked up useful phrases in phonetics on the blackboard and the soldiers laboriously printed them into notebooks and learned them by heart to recite in 'class'. It was quite a sight to see the husky Highlanders squeezed into desks designed for ten-year-olds and earnestly chanting parrot-wise:

> Ji sweez onglay
> Amee onglay
> Ji day zeer
> kelki shows a mongjay

They rather enjoyed it until they discovered that 'onglay' meant English, and took offence. There were a few other difficulties for the teacher found it almost impossible to understand the Scottish tongue of his pupils, and this problem was mutual. One of the soldiers remarked, 'I can manage the French all right. It's the English the master talks I canna understand!'

The soldiers were hoping very soon to be able to put their newly acquired linguistic skills into action, and to get into action themselves. As the spring days lengthened and there was still no sign of marching orders, impatience mounted. The 10th Royal Fusiliers invented a sarcastic parody of a popular recruiting song.

> On Sunday they say we'll go to Flanders,
> On Monday we're down for Nice or Cannes
> On Tuesday we smile
> When they hint at the Nile,
> On Wednesday the Sudan.
> On Thursday it's Malta or Gibraltar,
> On Friday they'll send us to Lahore,
> But on Saturday we're willing
> To bet an even shilling
> We're here for the duration of the war!

It brought the house down at camp concerts and it reflected the sentiments of virtually every Tommy in Kitchener's Army.

Chapter 12

On the door of a broken-down barn a little way behind the front, some wag with nothing better to do had chalked a notice: 'LOST, STOLEN OR STRAYED. KITCHENER'S ARMY. £5 REWARD TO FINDER.' This was considered to be a good joke and similar notices, some of them less polite, sprouted up all over the place in villages behind the line. But if the promised flood of men had not yet arrived to help the troops in France, there was at least a hearteningly steady trickle of Territorial Battalions. Their arrival and the coming of spring had lifted everyone's spirits. The air was warming up, the ground was drying out, there were buds on the trees and in places, when the sun shone, Plugstreet Wood took on an air of sylvan beauty. The men who had newly arrived in this quiet sector to take up soldiering in earnest found life tolerably pleasant, if not comfortable, with just a dash of danger to make it interesting. They learned to beware of snipers and to keep their heads down. They learned the importance of silence, to be vigilant on sentry duty, to take bombardments in their stride. But the bombardments were predictable, for the Germans shot 'by the clock' and, barring occasional accidents, casualties were light. There were listening patrols to spice things up and after dark there were exciting forays into No Man's Land, close up to the German trenches. Ostensibly the purpose of patrols was to gather information. Their real purpose, as often as not, was to satisfy adventurous new officers in their desire to make their presence felt and show the enemy what was what.

CSM W. J. Coggins, D.C.M. 4th Bn., Oxfordshire & Buckinghamshire Light Infantry (TF).

I used to go out with my company commander, Lieutenant Pickford. He was a master at Brackley High School and he was a silly sod really when it came to patrolling. Of course, usually you would go out at night and, of course, you were supposed to volunteer for these jobs. But he came to me one morning not

169

long after we got there and he said, 'I want you to come out with me this morning.' It was thick with fog, you couldn't see the German line and it was more or less an order. I was only a bugler then and I'd be just turned nineteen, because I'd joined the Ox. and Bucks. Territorials in 1912 as a bugle boy aged sixteen, so I wasn't going to argue with the officer. I said, 'All right, sir.' He said, 'I'm going to give them a bit of music over there this morning.' I thought, 'What the devil with?' I thought he wanted me to blow the bugle or something, but he said, 'Look, I've got an old gramophone here and some old records.' I don't know where he'd got them from. Of course there were old broken-up houses around so maybe someone had scrounged them. He said, 'I'm going to get out as close as I can to that German trench and shove some records on for them.'

Well, it was a damn silly thing to do, but I was game, so off we went over the top and out into the fog. It was a good long way, it must have been nearly four hundred yards, but we were able to walk most of it because the fog hid us from the Germans. When we got maybe twenty or thirty yards from the German line we stopped and put down this gramophone I'd been humping, and it was a fair weight, because it was one of these old things with a big horn on it. We didn't wind it up (he'd done that before we left the trench) so he fished out a record and put it on and set it going. I can't remember what it was, some old scratchy band music, but the Germans must have got a fair old turn hearing it blasting out through this fog-horn thing almost right next to their trench. But we didn't wait to see. We started back again the way we came, moving a lot faster this time! But on the way the blooming fog lifted and before we got back to our trench a machine-gun opened up. The Germans gave us music all right! You should have heard these machine-gun bullets going swish, swish, swish. We both got down on the ground and you could hear the bullets going straight over the top of you, just above your head. We had to lie there a long time before we managed to get back into the trench and I was glad to get back in one piece.

Lieutenant Pickford was delighted with himself. Not for long though! He got a real bollocking from the Colonel for going out and doing that, because after they fired this machine-gun they started shelling like the devil and two or three of our men were killed. No, he wasn't popular! It was a silly thing to do and we got no profit out of it. But people did things like that in those days before we learned better sense.

Pte. H. K. Davis, 5th Bn., London Rifle Brig.

We were in Plugstreet Wood for about six months and we had a very quiet time there. Of course we had some casualties, but the main difficulty was keeping awake – especially when you were on these listening posts. In the early days, when the weather was bad, that was no joke. They were a waste of time as far as I was concerned. You'd get out of the trenches at Plugstreet, take the bayonet off your rifle and stick it in the scabbard so as not to catch any light that might be going, put one round in the breech of your rifle with the safety catch on, so that all you want to do is slip it off when you want to fire. The most important thing was a water-proof sheet. You take out the waterproof sheet and you put it on the ground and you lie on this thing and start listening to see if there's any activity going on. We always went out in pairs and before very long the man I was lying with would be kicking my legs, because I'd fallen asleep. Shortly after that I'd be doing the same to him, so we kept each other awake. But in the winter months – even sometimes when it came to spring – it was usually wet and while the waterproof sheet stopped the water coming up it also stopped the rain from going away, so before very long you were lying in a pool of water. We did three or four hours at a time like that before we crawled back to the trench. There was no way of getting dry. But, never mind, we just had to put up with it.

Even if the old hands were not so inclined to take risks as the newcomers, they were not lacking in bravado. For reasons of their own the Germans had annoyed the London Rifle Brigade by planting a flag in front of their trenches. It flapped at them defiantly from the other side of No Man's Land two hundred yards away, and this piece of impertinence was not to be borne. It was Corporal Jenkin who crept out on another misty morning to capture the flag and bring it triumphantly back to delight the battalion. Corporal Jenkin was the hero of the day, the flag was sent back as a trophy to London Rifle Brigade Headquarters in Bunhill Row in London and the story went with it. It even reached the 'Charivari' column of *Punch*.

> We are not surprised to hear that Corporal Jenkin of the First Battalion London Rifle Brigade succeeded in capturing a German flag at the front. Corporal Jenkin is an artist, and it was only natural that he should make for the Colours.

It all helped to boost morale, but in the spring of 1915 in this quiet sector, morale was high. For once it was the Germans who were in the open. Facing them from their trenches on the edge of the wood with the sheltering depths of the wood itself behind them, with the undamaged trees coming into leaf and even some shell-shattered trunks showing an irrepressible tendency to push out new shoots, there were times when the British Tommies felt that the war was unreal. There were still civilians in the houses and hamlets close to the line and beyond the communication trenches and support lines that ran through the sun-dappled glades, disfigured though they were by barbed wire and the trampling of many feet, there was still a semblance of normal life.

Just two kilometres to the south, where the railway line ran through the village of le Touret, a local train from Armentieres had puffed into the station bound for Comines and all stations east to Courtrai. It had stood there all winter long, and there it would stand for the rest of the war. The wooden carriages were holed and splintered, the engine was bullet-grazed and streaked with rust beneath a grimy coat of mud, with its wheels rusting into the few rails that still lay on the battered track, and coarse weeds poked through the layer of mud and cinders where the track ran into No Man's Land. The sleepers had long ago been carted off and used to strengthen dug-outs. But every morning on the dot of seven o'clock a railwayman picked his way across the debris and climbed into the signal box. And there he sat, trains or no trains, war or no war, until it was time to go home at six o'clock in the evening. It had apparently not occurred to the railway authorities to pay him off.

Sgt. B. J. Brookes, 1/16 Queen's Westminster Rifles (County of London Regt.).

The station was about three hundred and fifty yards behind the trenches, and the trenches ran through the village, at right angles to the road. To get to the front line one went into the first house along the road, and a passage had been made by knocking big holes in the side walls of the houses. Two of these houses were still occupied, and were open to the troops as estaminets, and it was quite possible to come out of the trenches for a quarter of an hour to get a glass of beer. In one of these houses two old women and a young girl were carrying on the business (which, needless to say, was very brisk) and it was remarkable how they stood the strain. There was a curve in the road which prevented bullets from hitting the house, but they continually whizzed by as it was easily within range and the people didn't dare go out of their house. The beer was brought to them by army transport when it was available. I think I can safely say that in no other part of the line were civilians living so near the danger zone.

Now that things had settled down and to all intents and purposes there was a lull in the war and time to take stock, Sir John French was at last able to accede to General Joffre's request to stretch his line northwards and take over another sector of line from the French. Groups of officers were sent up in advance of their battalions to familiarise themselves with the terrain and to ensure that the changeover would go smoothly. Second Lieutenant Jock Macleod went up with a party of his fellow officers of the 2nd Battalion, the Queen's Own Cameron Highlanders.

This was a Regular battalion, but young Jock was not a Regular soldier. He was a student at Cambridge University and, although he had been commissioned into the Camerons at the start of the war, he was a 'temporary gentleman' of a few months' training who, strictly speaking, was not yet qualified to be at the front at all. But the Camerons had suffered heavy casualties, Jock had wangled his way into a draft of reinforcements and, after two months at the front, regarded himself as an old campaigner. He had had an enjoyable time. There had been a few exciting days in the trenches at St Eloi, three weeks away from the line on a machine-gun course and, having passed out with flying colours, he now had his own command as the battalion's newly appointed machine-gun officer. The battalion had been out at rest when Jock rejoined it, but the machine-gun section had been kept hard at it under the eye of this energetic new officer who was intent on sharing the benefit of his newly acquired expertise. He was having the time of his life and his letters home were virtual paeans of enthusiasm. The only slight disappointment – for Jock was a fastidious young man – had been the discovery that the army did not permit him to send his washing home from the front. But he quite saw the point that, if every officer did so, the weekly passage of several thousand sets of shirts and pants, socks and pyjamas, would overload the mail boats and put an unreasonable strain on the army postal service. In passing on this news to his family, Jock took the trouble to remind them kindly that there was, after all, a war on. To underline this observation he added a gleeful postscript: 'We shall be going into the trenches any day now.'

It was in his new capacity as machine-gun officer that Jock was included in the reconnoitring party that rode out from Ypres and up the Menin Road to Herenthage Chateau where the French trenches ran through the wooded grounds.* It was a warm spring day and there was hardly a shot to be heard. It seemed almost like a holiday

---

* The Camerons renamed the wood during their tenancy and soon it appeared on British trench maps as 'Inverness Copse'. In a matter of weeks they were pushed out of it in the Second Battle of Ypres. When British troops eventually returned, in August 1917, the copse had been reduced to a waste of splintered stumps.

173

outing and the French treated them as honoured guests.

*2nd Lt. J. Macleod, 2nd Bn., Queen's Own Cameron
Highlanders, 81st Brig., 27 Div.*

The first thing that struck you was their light-heartedness. It was most amusing to hear them speaking about the Germans opposite and when a German aeroplane went over they all got excited, and shouted insults, and three officers rushed out of their dug-outs, snatched up rifles from the men, and let fly at them! 'Of course,' they explained, 'it does not derange the German airmen, but it shows what we think about the swine.' We told them we had orders against firing rifles at aircraft, and they said they had too, but it was necessary to show the Boche that they were only Boche! In the afternoon their seventy-fives began shelling the German trenches, and the French officers in the support line leapt and shouted whenever a good hit was made.

They gave us a capital lunch – mackerel, ragout, bread, cold beef, vin rouge, and café with cognac. Our lunch party was very jolly. Four French and three British officers in a sort of semi-circular redoubt in a wood. On one side a roofless dug-out – the parapet protected with sandbags, and covered with branches – the firing trenches about two hundred yards away through the wood, and the Germans eighty yards further on in the same wood, but invisible from where we were. In the middle of the redoubt was a tree, and tied to it was a magnificent gilded eighteenth-century clock from the ruined chateau nearby. It was bright sunshine and the birds were singing and the officers were seated on the rickety remains of gorgeous chairs from the same place as the clock. Just beyond the wood was the shell-pitted remains of a golf-course, with a roller for the greens drunkenly straddling the side of a shell-hole – and all seven officers were uproariously cheerful, eating tinned mackerel with pocket knives, some off beautiful old china, others off war-worn mess tins. Every fourth tree was a splintered stump, for the Germans gave the wood a daily ration of shells. The French soldiers seemed very pleased with themselves, with us, and with everything. You should have heard them whistling 'The Merry Widow Waltz' and 'The Marseillaise' after lunch. They were very kind and polite to our little party, and altogether it was an admirable day.

In the afternoon they found some curtain pole rings. 'Aha!' they cried. 'We'll have a game.' (Doubtless the poles themselves had gone the way of all curtain poles about here – for

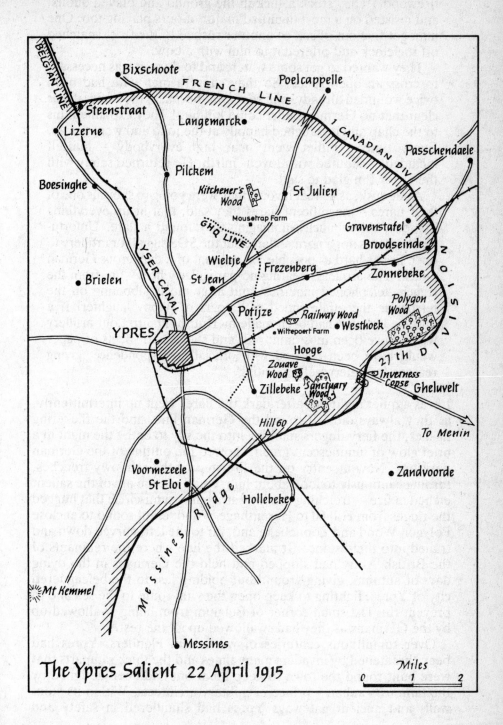

The Ypres Salient 22 April 1915

Miles
0   1   2

firewood!) They stuck a stick in the ground and played quoits, and insisted on a most dignified major of ours playing too. One man got five out of six, so another rushed to the tree, snatched off the clock and offered it to him with a bow.

They wanted to get some water, and to do so it was necessary to cross an open space. So they chose a man who had been twice wounded already, and sent *him*, because, they said, it was clear that no German bullet could kill him! They explained this to the chap and he laughed happily at the joke and went across. Every time a bullet went near him everybody – himself included! – shouted with joyous mirth. He returned safely with the water I'm glad to say!

After dusk, as a great favour, they were going to show us one of their flares – magnificent flares they said, that lit up everything like day. After much rummaging they found a flare. Unfortunately, it was not a normal flare, but the SOS signal for artillery to open fire as hard as possible, on account of a dangerous German attack. The artillery, hearing no particularly heavy fire from the trench, telephoned inquiries, and after much jabbering on the telephone the affair ended with roars of happy laughter! If a mistake like that had been made by British infantry, our artillery would have been most annoyed, and sheets and sheets of paper would have been covered with official correspondence, giving reasons (or otherwise!) in writing.

It was a quiet night but after dark the flares went up intermittently, as they always did, all round the German line, and the flickering flashes, the fiery fingers stabbing into the sky to bathe the night in a brief glow of luminescent green, showed the outline of the German positions. Now a sentry on the fire-step of the shadowy trenches, turning cautiously to look about him, could see the arc of the salient etched in fire – stretching in a long straggling semi-circle that hugged the ridges from Hill 60 to Herenthage Wood, crept round to enclose Polygon Wood and Zonnebeke and, far to the left, curved down and trailed into the distance. It marked the line where the remnants of the British Army had stopped and held the Germans in the dying days of autumn, giving ground but holding fast to the beleaguered city of Ypres, fighting to keep open the vital route to the sea and to prevent this last small corner of Belgium from being swallowed up by the Germans as they had swallowed up all the rest.

Over tumultuous centuries of warfare in Flanders, Ypres had been threatened by invaders many times and the thick ramparts that were built round the town to keep them out had been designed by the famous Vauban – prince of military architects. Within its stout walls and ancient gateways Ypres had slumbered in safety and prosperity. Merchants grew rich on the wool trade and built grand houses, gabled and curlicued with statues and carvings. They raised churches, a cathedral, and fine civic buildings round the wide market square where the great Cloth Hall towered over them all. The towers and spires of Ypres could be seen from every part of the salient but they were sadly battered now, for they presented an irresistible target to the German guns.

There were empty spaces in the streets like unsightly gaps in a fine set of teeth, and heaps of rubble where a house once stood. Here and there a whole wall had been blown down to expose some abandoned doll's-house interior with furniture teetering askew on sagging floors. There were ugly holes that exposed the ancient timbers of steep red-tiled roofs, and broken chimneys that had slithered down and pitched into the cobbled streets. There were sightless windows gazing from the empty shells of burnt-out buildings and others in still habitable houses hastily patched up with wooden panels when the panes and shutters had been blown away. The central tower of the Cloth Hall, blackened by fire, lacked two of its four spires, the embrasures of its high arched windows were innocent of glass and the end wall of the medieval town hall they called the Kleinstadthuis had been blown away. But Ypres still lived and although many of its inhabitants had fled during the November bombardment, much of the population hung grimly on. The town was far from empty and large numbers of the refugees who had flooded in as the Germans advanced across the surrounding countryside had simply stopped there, squatting in the ruins and abandoned houses because they had nowhere else to go.

People managed as best they could, taking their chance by day when stray shells fell from time to time, retiring at night to cellars for fear of heavier bombardments. There was business to be done and there was a large new clientele for the town was stiff with soldiers – headquarters troops, engineers and signallers who lived like troglodytes in the catacomb passages of the old ramparts, troops passing through and briefly resting on their way to the line on the salient, sightseeing groups from nearby rest-camps and billets, curious to see the heroic town for themselves. The fame of Ypres had spread and its name was fast becoming a byword in the British Army.

For the permanent inhabitants life in Ypres was far from easy. The town water supply was drawn from two lakes, Zillebeke to the east and Dickebusch to the west, and they were so polluted – by exploding shells, by rubbish and ordure and, in the case of Zillebeke, even with bodies – that an epidemic of typhoid was unavoidable. It had been raging now since January and despite the valiant efforts of the Friends Ambulance Unit, the nuns at the convent, the RAMC, and the town authorities themselves, it was raging still.

Vaccination was compulsory and more than seven thousand people had been treated – almost five thousand of them at the convent alone. Water barrels were set up at the entrance to the town where the road to Menin and Zonnebeke led through the ramparts and people were forbidden on pain of a heavy fine to use water from any other source. But the epidemic could hardly be contained and every day there were fresh cases. It was rife among the unfortunate refugees, crammed into the doubtful shelter of ruined houses, living in unsanitary conditions. Lacking running water, with no means of washing and often with no possessions but the clothes on their backs, they went down like flies. The refugees were the despair of the town authorities. They could not force them to move on, they could not provide them with adequate shelter, and while they could do their best to ensure that they drank clean purified water, they could not oblige them to change their clothes for clean garments they did not possess.

But at night, when the inhabitants went to ground, when the skeletons of towers and turrets stood silhouetted against the tremulous horizon where the flares flashed and distant guns boomed, when the trundling of wheels and the tramp of the troops echoed across the cobbled square, there was a ghostly grandeur about the place that deeply impressed the soldiers passing through.

Capt. B. McKinnell, 10th (Scottish) Bn., King's Liverpool Regt. (TF), 2 Brig., 1st Div.

A splendid march to Ypres, everybody feeling awfully fit. What a strange sight, a clear sky, new moon, and half the Battalion in kilts lying on the square in front of the famous Cloth Hall, every three or four men clustering round a candle and drinking hot tea supplied by our field cookers. The ruins make a most impressive sight. Silently glides past a battalion of Frenchmen in their quaint uniforms and heavy paraphernalia, which they are invariably encumbered with. Then our pals the Lincolns pass and we get up and follow, our men singing at the top of their voices all the way back.

From 26 March to 4 April we stayed in Ypres and had beautiful weather all the time. I took the opportunity of so much extra leisure to visit all the most interesting sights. Bullen and I climbed up what remains of the Cloth Hall and managed to get up above the clock into one of the small turrets, getting a splendid view of the surrounding country. Some jackdaws were building there and were very much perturbed at our paying them a visit. I also explored the cathedral, which dates back to the thirteenth century. We all meet at a place which we have named 'Marie's' after the barmaid. Any drink can be had there. Dinner or lunch can be got at 'Julia's', and tea at the 'Patisserie', which they say means 'Among the Ruins'. Headquarters billet is a very fine one, 64 Rue de Chien, belonging to a local brewer. The brewery has been smashed by a shell and his private house is all that is left. We have a piano and a gramophone and all sorts of crockery.

All this uplifting of spirits is the result of good weather and in spite of our casualties being heavier this last week than ever before – with every prospect of them becoming heavier still.

Even in the day-to-day routine of the trenches, even when there were no battles and none of the raids or minor actions the army called 'stunts', with the constant shell-fire and eternal sniping, casualties were inevitable. The old hands were accustomed to them and accepted them with dull resignation. To the new men arriving, the first sight of wounded soldiers could come as a shock.

Trpr. P. Mason, 1/1st Yorkshire Hussars Yeomanry.

The first station we landed at where we could get out and water the horses was a place called Hazebrouck. I remember it well. A biggish town in Northern France on the way to Ypres. So we said, 'Who's going to get the water bottles filled?' I said, 'Give them to me.' I was always a willing lad! They put the water bottles around my neck and I had about eight or ten water bottles from the lads in the truck. There were two or three taps in the station yard, you see, and I found my way there. Oh, Christ! I started to walk among wounded soldiers on the ground. Bloody terrible. Some fellows with arms off – and blood! All their clothes were soaked in blood. There were dozens of them waiting for the ambulances and the Red Cross trains. I wanted to be sick, seeing all these poor buggers, some of them with their faces bashed and all. You never saw anything like it. It frightened me to death, I don't mind telling you.

I got these ruddy water bottles filled and put them around my neck again and I had to walk across fellows – pick my way between them to get back to the railway where the trucks and horses and our lads were. I think I was nearly going to faint and Jack Hutton, an old pal of mine, grabbed hold of me. I heard him shout, 'Give us a hand here. This lad's going out, you know.' I broke out in a sweat and was really sick. I had seen such terrible injuries to so many men. I thought, 'My Christ, if this is war!' It makes you think. But, you know, after a fortnight you got hardened to it. That's the funny thing.

The train shunted on to a siding to make way for the hospital train that would carry the wounded to safety, and after an interminable wait it began to trundle slowly north. Their journey was almost over. The odyssey which began the previous August in Middlesbrough and had taken Mason to Hitchin, to Bishop's Stortford, and across the channel to France, at the end of that last long day finally brought him to Ypres.

A little way south-east of Ypres – an easy stroll away across the meadows – was the knoll they called Hill 60, and the Germans were firmly ensconced on top. One could hardly call it a summit, for it was a mere sixty metres high, an artificial hillock, man-made by the engineers who had dug the railway from Ypres to the small country town of Comines and had dumped the spoil on a convenient piece of ground close by. This was the hinge of the salient. It was from Hill 60 that the German line began, on the one hand, to wind north-east across the ridges encircling Ypres and, on the other, to swing south like the leg of a crooked question mark, along the Messines Ridge. These ridges above the flat Flanders Plain, insignificant though they were, gave the Germans an overwhelming advantage and Hill 60 was the keystone of their defence. Ever since they had taken over this sector from the French who had lost the hill to the Germans, the British Army had been anxious to get it back. Skirmishing and infantry attacks had been fruitless and, since conventional methods had not worked, it was decided the unconventional must be tried. In the first days of March they began to burrow into the earth a hundred yards from the German line to construct long tunnels that would reach out to Hill 60 and store up the explosives that would blow the Germans off. It was hard perilous work and, although some professional miners had been recruited for the job, progress was agonisingly slow. They had never before encountered conditions such as these.

Aeons ago, in the millennium before the oceans receded, the plain had been washed by the Northern Sea. Water lay just ten inches beneath the thick unyielding surface that turned to mud with every shower of rain. Far below the miners hacked their way through a stratum of thick clay, close-boarding the tunnels with stout timber as they went, fearful of the layer of running sand that lay underneath and the liquid mud that seeped from above and spouted through the slightest crack or cranny. As the tunnels lengthened it was hard to breathe in the fetid dark, working by the light of candles that sank and often guttered out for lack of air. Their stints at the tunnel face were short – they had to be – but many a man was dragged to the surface, blue and collapsed, long before his shift was due to finish. These miners, hastily co-opted into the army and thrust into uniform, were sent to France in a hurry. They

180

were not soldiers, and many of them were neither young nor fit. But they were paid at a higher rate than the luckless soldiers of the working parties who dragged the spoil back to the shaft-head by day and carried it off by night for fear the Germans would spot it.

The Germans already suspected that something was up and they too were sapping and digging beneath their own line, listening and probing to find the British tunnels and blow them up, if they could, before the British succeeded in blowing up their own positions. There were many false alarms, there were many genuine heart-stopping scares and there was the constant fear of being emtombed if a lucky shell should demolish the entrance and cut off the way out. But the work went on.

As the tunnels drew near the German lines they splayed out in minor branches and six charges were laid. The worst job was bringing up the explosive, more than four tons of it packed in bags that weighed a hundred pounds apiece – half the weight of a hefty man. It took two men to lift a bag on to the shoulders of a third and every hundred yards they had to halt to change over. They were nightmare journeys, staggering by night across dark fields on a track of broken duckboards with bent knees quivering and muscles straining beneath the dead weight of the sacks. They moved as quietly as was humanly possible, praying for the next halt, praying that the enemy was not on the alert, that no flare would pierce the dark to give the show away, and hoping against hope that no shell would land nearby as they stumbled towards the mine shaft.

But at last the job was done. The charges were set, the mines were ready, and the plans were laid. The mines would be exploded at ten-second intervals, the guns were waiting to open the bombardment, and the infantry was standing by to go into the assault when Hill 60 went up.

It was seven o'clock in the evening of 19 April. Everything was quiet and the air was still warm at the end of a fine day. The mines were detonated precisely on time. The infantry watched transfixed and the ground shook beneath their feet as Hill 60 erupted like a volcano, throwing debris and the bodies of the German garrison high into the air. The shock waves were still rippling as the guns began to boom. The infantry sprang from the trenches and the gentle sky of the April evening died in a dense black pall of smoke and fumes. In less than fifteen minutes they were digging in beyond the reeking craters and consolidating their position on the battered crest of Hill 60.

Chapter 13

Jock Macleod had spent a happy day pottering in the garden of the fine house they called 'Goldfish Chateau' on the western outskirts of Ypres where the officers of the 2nd Camerons were billeted while the Battalion was at rest. It was hardly damaged by shell-fire, the garden was a blaze of spring flowers and even japonica and early roses were in bloom. In two days they would be returning to the trenches. There, encouraged by the fine weather over the last few days, a luxuriant display of cowslips had blossomed, and to continue the springtime theme Jock had carefully dug up some daffodils from the chateau garden. He packed them in a flower-pot, purloined from the conservatory, and when the battalion returned to the trenches, he proposed to plant them on the covering of soil that camouflaged the headquarters dug-out. Gardening was still in his mind after dinner, when he wrote his regular letter home, and he was struck by a happy thought: *Please send me some penny packets of summer seeds to sow round the trenches – although I fully expect that we shall be well on our way to Berlin before they flower.* Jock had good reason to be optimistic, for the roar of the mines going up at Hill 60 had been heard for miles and, fired by rumours, dinner in the officers' mess had passed in a buzz of speculation and euphoria. It was Saturday night.

It was true that, at first, the Germans had been completely unbalanced by the explosion. From the high ground at Zandvoorde their guns were firing anywhere and everywhere. It was hours before the situation was appreciated, before the guns settled down to shoot accurately and in earnest, before the shocked survivors rushing back from the hill had been rallied and incoherent reports were understood and evaluated at German Corps Headquarters. By midnight reserves had been hurried to the front and the first counter-attack was launched. It was the first of dozens.

The Germans attacked by night, they attacked by dawn, they attacked by day, making desperate efforts to recover the hill. The fighting and the line swayed back and forth. The shells of both sides pulverised the hill until it was hard to believe that this tortured mound of devastation had ever been a hill at all. Trees and dug-outs were swallowed up. Trenches were obliterated as fast as they were dug through the mangled bodies of British and German dead. The stench was overpowering. Once they had recovered from the first assault the Germans had the advantage, for the British advance had thrust a wedge into their line and machine-guns and snipers concealed on the high ground on either side could sweep their foothold on the hill with deadly accuracy. It was such a small foothold – only two hundred and fifty yards long, and two hundred yards deep – that the enemy hardly needed to take aim and even the most haphazard shots could not fail to find a target.[*]

The first British troops to be pushed back from the hill in the early stages of the assault had caused some disquiet. Although their position had been quickly recovered in a counter-attack it had had to be made by other troops, for the men who had been forced off were finished – choking and gasping, overcome by fumes, they were convinced that they had been gassed, and they were right. But it had been an accident. It was true that the Germans had been planning to attack with poison gas, but they were not yet ready, and the conditions had not been favourable. Nevertheless gas cylinders had been dug into the side of the hill and the Germans soldiers who panicked and ran when the British stormed it, shaken though they were by the explosions, had been less afraid of British troops than of British shells shattering the cylinders and releasing the poisonous gas on friend and foe alike. Only a few had been damaged and the cylinders cracked so that the gas escaped slowly and covered only a small area on the right of Hill 60. It should have been enough to alert the staff to the danger, but so few soldiers were affected, there were so many fumes from the mines and from exploding shells and, since the enemy was known to have fired tear gas shells in the past, the significance of the incident paled against the magnitude of the continuing battle for the hill.

But for those who were not immediately involved in the struggle there were other clues and hints that something unusual was afoot. Strange clanging noises had been heard near the enemy's trenches and patrols were sent out to investigate.

Trpr. P. Mason, 1/1st Yorkshire Hussars Yeomanry.

There was Captain Foster, Lance Corporal Armond, Trooper Mason, Trooper Heslop and Trooper Hutton. There were five

---

[*] On 5 May, when the 5th Division was finally forced from Hill 60, they had suffered three thousand casualties and won four Victoria Crosses. Hardly a body was recovered, and Hill 60 today, still scarred and cratered by this and later battles, is in effect a mass grave.

of us. Our object was to get a prisoner, if possible. It was very, very nervous work, I can tell you, crawling about No Man's Land, you know. Captain Foster said, 'If anybody has the slightest suspicion that he has a cough he's not going.' He had this rule and thank God he did. We would suffocate ourselves rather than give a cough. Well, sometimes when I felt I was going to cough I used to push my face into the ground to stop me. I daren't, you know, because it would give the game away. We got a bit nervy, I don't mind telling you. One night Captain Foster went out carelessly with a luminous wristwatch on his ruddy wrist and Tom Armond said, 'For Christ's sake, take it off.' I remember him saying that. Well, that was dangerous, you know.

It was Captain Foster's routine to call Brigade Headquarters, to see what was needed, any instructions and information. He came back and he said, 'This will interest you. Some of the infantry sentries on forward observation say at night time, just as it was getting dusk, they could hear reports of these iron clangs, metallic clanging, and then the news went around that Jerry was setting up a blacksmith's shop in the front line and would the Yorkshire Hussars find out.' So out we went. Our password was 'Yorkshire', that was the call, and the answer was 'Hussar'. Well, no German of the highest intelligence would ever expect to meet a cavalryman in No Man's Land, would they? So that was the password. Well, we were told on this particular night, up at Ypres, to find out if there was any substance in this claim of the infantry about this metallic clanging.

Well, they must have known that there was a small English patrol along that particular sector and the buggers were waiting for us. I remember very well, Captain Foster drawing on an envelope and saying, 'This is where we're going to be, lads.' He said, 'It's only a farm track across the Ypres to Poelcapelle Road.' Captain Foster and Tommy Armond went over first. I'm in the middle on my own, with Arthur Hutton and big Heslop behind. I didn't get across it because some bugger coughed! We knew it wouldn't be an animal, it was a man, and we knew it was a German, and immediately one or two bombs went over from our lads. Well, when I heard this cough, I knew what to do straight away, because the arrangement was, if there's anybody coughs, throw a bomb where that sound came from. That was my first occasion where I had to throw a bomb and kill people.

Captain Foster and Tommy Armond scurried back as quick as a flash to get away from it and when the Very light went up there were about thirty buggers there waiting for us!

It was the luckiest escape in the world. You know, when you're in a position like that you lose all sense of direction. You've got to lie quiet for a bit and just wonder in what direction to turn – whether you should about turn, or go left, or go right – because you're all confused. Anyway, we all finished up safe and sound back in our own trenches. We could easily have bloody walked into the German trenches!

As it was we were near enough to hear that clanging as plain as a pikestaff, and about four or five days after that they let the gas off.

And there had been other warnings. There was talk that the Germans had already used gas against the French on the Champagne front, but nothing had been heard of it through official channels. But there was other evidence which could not so easily be dismissed. As far back as the end of March the French Tenth Army in the sector north of Ypres reported that they had captured a German prisoner who had been unusually forthcoming under interrogation, pouring out details of preparations for a gas attack. The man had been nervous and eager to mollify his captors, and the French dismissed his ramblings out of hand and did not consider them worth passing on. Two weeks later another prisoner captured in the same sector had told the same story. He gave precise information, meticulous descriptions of the cylinders, fifty-three inches long and filled with chlorine gas. He described how the German soldiers had been trained in their use, showed exactly where the cylinders had been dug in and where the attacks would be launched. He was even carrying one of the respirators which had been issued to protect the German soldiers against the lethal fumes. His story was convincing. But, conferring together, British and French Intelligence Officers, weighing the matter up, concluded that it was a little too convincing. The German had been too easily captured. He had virtually walked into the French lines. Might he not have been sent on purpose?* It might easily be a devious Teutonic ruse to mislead the allies, to persuade them to withdraw troops from the 'danger zone' and allow the Germans to advance in a bloodless victory on Ypres. Or, conversely, if the Germans were preparing an assault elsewhere the ruse might have been designed to *prevent* the allies withdrawing troops from the salient. Who could tell? Even a report

---

* The man was Auguste Jaeger, then a private in the 234 Reserve Infantry Regiment. On 17 December 1932 he was tried at Leipzig on charges of desertion and betraying German plans to the enemy. He was sentenced to ten years' imprisonment.

from Belgian Army Intelligence, which also had evidence that German soldiers had been issued with gas-masks and were being instructed in the use of gas-cylinders, might easily be part of the same plot. War was war, but there were still certain rules to be observed. The use of poison gas was strictly proscribed by the Hague Convention and all civilised nations, including Germany, had signed it.

The Germans were not above employing devious tactics, particularly in the field of propaganda, which frequently backfired despite their best intentions and their desire to adopt a virtuous stance which would impress neutral nations with the justice of their cause. Two days after the capture of the second prisoner and on the very day of the British assault on Hill 60, the German newspapers carried a virulent story, dripping with righteous indignation, which categorically stated that the British had committed the unspeakable crime of using poison gas against defenceless German troops, thus contravening not only the laws of war but the unwritten laws of civilisation itself. It was a cover story, designed to justify the fact that the Germans themselves were planning to use the illegal weapon in an attack which they hoped would be seen at home and abroad as 'retaliation'. It was reported by Reuter, noted in London and disregarded, if they ever heard of it, in France – although General Plumer had passed on the French report to his Divisional Commanders 'for what it is worth'!

The Germans hoped that their new secret weapon would be worth a great deal. Their chemists had been working on it for a long time, and it was weeks since the first experimental cylinders had been dug into position. All that was lacking were the favourable winds that would carry the gas across to the British lines and the Ypres salient had been selected because, according to German meteorologists, the wind in springtime invariably blew in a south-westerly direction. A steady breeze was what was needed. If the wind were too strong the gas would be too quickly dissipated, if it blew in sudden gusts it would be just as ineffectual, and worse, if it suddenly changed direction there was no saying what the result might be.

As the weeks passed, and the wind disobligingly continued to blow from the wrong direction, the German Command began to be seriously worried. Too many people were in on the secret. Special troops, rudely referred to as 'Stinkpionere', had been instructed and trained to operate the gas cylinders, and, since it took eight men to carry one, hundreds of troops had slogged for many nights to carry the cylinders and the cumbersome ancillary apparatus to the line. Thousands of respirators had been manufactured locally in occupied Belgium where spies abounded, and now that they had been issued to soldiers in the Ypres sector, rumour was spreading like wildfire along the line and heavy hints that something interesting was in the offing were carried back to Germany by soldiers home on leave and also in optimistic letters from the front. Musketier Pieter Amlinger wrote home:

> Within the next week we can expect to launch a large offensive between Bixschoote and Langemark. Follow the news bulletins closely. The great offensive about which you wrote is a fact and with some luck there may be peace at the end of May. We also have a 'Dicke Bertha' at our back whose loud voice – although not so beautiful – will be there to support us.

The 'Big Bertha', like the other heavy guns that would support the German attack, was all too necessary, for the German troops on the northern stretch of the western front were still vastly outnumbered by the allies. But the Germans had been heartened by the outcome of the battle of Neuve Chapelle and regarded the failure of the British to push home their initial success as a sign of weakness which could be turned to advantage. But success depended on surprise. As the weeks passed, as the gas attack was continually postponed, as more and more people were let into the secret, the German Commanders grew increasingly edgy. If the allies got wind of their plans, if they were able to take precautions against the gas, all would be lost.

The use of gas was essential to the Germans' plan, for they were well aware that, against superior numbers, the front could not be broken by their infantry alone. They had studied the lessons of siege warfare and they planned a step-by-step advance. First the front-line troops would be overwhelmed by gas. Then the artillery would pound their lines and, pounding behind them simultaneously, would so reduce the salient and pulverise resistance that the Germans, advancing little by little, inexorably pressing on to the next limited objective, would gradually walk over the demoralised enemy and win the day. Pieter Amlinger was not the only German soldier shivering in the wind that so persistently blew from the north who genuinely believed that, when it turned, and before another month was out, he would be marching back to the Fatherland and that the war would be over and well and truly won. Hope was in the air.

Signals were arranged, code words decided on, guns and ammunition in undreamed of quantities brought up to the German front. This was to be an all-out effort. But the obdurate wind still blew from the north, and the German Command, champing on the bit as April dragged on, had to content themselves with ranging the heavy long-distance guns that were brought from the Belgian coast to swell the weight of the attack. They ranged them on Ypres.

The small city of Ypres was far from being the backwater it was to become in later years, when its importance relied largely on its notoriety as a focal point of the war. Tourists, in the modern sense, were few but its fame was widespread and it was a mecca for lovers of art and architecture. Fine buildings lined the streets, erected by a rich and cultured bourgeoisie, rare tapestries and paintings hung in the Cloth Hall. Pilgrims came too, for Ypres had become a noted religious centre in devout Catholic Flanders. There were two important monasteries not far away and several convents in the precincts of the town itself – the 'Black' sisters, the Poor Clares, and the convent of the Irish nuns who ran a private school for young ladies. But the school had closed down, the nuns had been evacuated, and the cubicles and dormitories where generations of virginal schoolgirls had slept and giggled were now inhabited by the heretical kilted soldiers of the 9th Royal Scots who, to their wry and lewd amusement, were billeted in the convent. Bill Hay was one of them, but it was an annoymous private of B Company who recorded their impressions.

Our first tour of inspection degenerated into a hunt for souvenirs. We ransacked the bare attic rooms into which the Sisters had evidently gathered everything in great haste. One brought back in triumph a branching brass candlestick, another a crucifix and a small image of the Madonna – the most impossible things were secreted in packs to be quietly got rid of when we realised the folly of it. One or two lingered longer over the papers and ledgers strewn about the floor – the daily housekeeping of seventy or eighty years written in a clear, fine old-world hand touched us to the quick. What a peaceful, sequestered life, and what an awakening and an end! At first there was a sort of awed feeling at being in a convent, and we thought wonderingly of the schoolgirls and nuns who had lived their quiet life within these very walls. It showed us something of the convulsion into which Belgium had been thrown.

But how comfortable we were! A sacrilegious bunch of kilted heretics! The days we lay in the high-walled garden in the sun – the afternoon teas we gave when some of us struck it lucky with parcels. Even with fatigues – and we were out every night nearly – we had a slack time, for they were properly worked in two shifts, from eight to twelve and twelve to four, and we dug near the town. If anything we worked harder knowing relief was sure after four hours. And there were no bullets and no shells, only the far-off lights and crackle and grumble in the distance. Our unanimous decision was that fatigues at Ypres were a picnic.

We slept or lazed in the forenoon, and in the afternoon we strolled in the town. Walks by the canal, omelette and chip teas, shopping, patisserie-tasting, lace-buying, exploring the Cloth Hall ruins – all these we found time for in glorious weather, and very homely and pleasant it all was. We thought a lot of the gay little town where we had our happiest days since leaving home. For it *was* gay and full of people, the market square lined with booths on one side in front of the larger shops, although in the back streets there were shell-torn roofs and battered houses. And the Cloth Hall towering over it all, a gaunt and empty ruin, but every chipped and battered stone was eloquent, and its pinnacles still proudly cut into the sky.

In its symbolically battered state the Cloth Hall seemed to take on a grandeur it had not enjoyed since the days when Ypres was the centre of the rich Flanders wool trade, and since the wool trade had diminished lacemaking had taken its place. On fine summer days before the war, at open doors and windows all over the town, the ladies of Ypres, lace cushions on their laps, gossiped in the sun as their nimble fingers and flying bobbins worked the fine lace whose beauty rivalled even the coveted lace of Brussels. Their work was in demand all over the world and there were no fewer than twelve lace brokers in Ypres who bought up the lace, distributed it, and grew rich on the proceeds. One of them was Aimé van Nieuwenhove.

This gentleman was not a native of Ypres. He had started his career as a dashing young cavalry officer but fate had brought him to Ypres to its famous cavalry school and there he had met and married Clotilde Brunfaut, daughter of a prosperous lace merchant. Now he was a prosperous lace merchant himself, owner of a fine old house on the Rue de Lille which he had painstakingly renovated over the years, the father of two children, a prominent citizen of the town, a local politician, and one of the public-spirited men who had been co-opted on to the Comité Provisoire to safeguard the welfare of Ypres after the town council was evacuated. Long ago, when things had looked bad at the end of the previous October, he had sent his own wife and family to safety in Paris. But van Nieuwenhove himself stayed on and conscientiously recorded in his daily diary the trials that befell the little town he had come to love. On 20 April, the Germans began to range their heavy guns on Ypres.

Aimé van Nieuwenhove.

20 April Calm until 11 a.m. While I was at the post office counter a dozen shells fell all of a sudden. I took shelter right

189

away in the cellars and went out at mid-day to see what had happened. When I got to the garden I ascertained that a shell had fallen in Lapierre's shops and had destroyed part of the wall that separated them from my garden. A second and third had landed in the garden of M. Desaegher, one against the wall of Mlle Duval's kitchen, the other beneath the carriage porch. When the first shell arrived Marie our washerwoman was in the wash house and dived into our cellar for shelter, where I found her very upset when I got back. The damaged wall belonged to Lapierre, but until it could be repaired, I was obliged myself to block up the hole with planks in order to prevent the English soldiers from getting into our premises.

At two o'clock in the afternoon I attended a meeting of the commission charged with paying the indemnity to support the refugees in the town. We met in the police headquarters building until 4.30, during which time eight huge shells fell on the town. When I came out of the meeting, our uncle, Auguste Liebaert, came to tell me that one of the shells that fell this morning hit the roof of his house and had destroyed one of the rooms. He was terribly upset and emotional. I advised him to go and spend the night in the post office cellars, then to go and find a temporary refuge at Poperinghe. Many more people are leaving the town again and it's as deserted as it was in November. We have no more newspapers and are isolated from the rest of the world. Everywhere there is a feeling of discouragement and, for my part, I'm well aware that my nerves are no longer as strong as they proved to be during the first bombardments.

21 April I went to see the house of my uncle, who had spent a very bad night in the cellars, even though the night was quiet. Not being able to find a car anywhere to take him to Poperinghe, I advised him to take a porter and set off on the Vlamertinghe road, where, by offering a tip, he might be picked up by one or other of the ambulances. This he did.

At mid-day we learned that the eight big shells that arrived yesterday afternoon from the direction of Staden were 380 mm in diameter. This news threw consternation among my friends and it decided some of them to leave the town in case more of the same arrived. Seven civilians were killed on Monday and ten yesterday, besides that, more than a hundred English soldiers and many more wounded. Nevertheless today is reasonably calm. As for the bombardment, only a few shells were heard.

The Germans were ranging their big guns, still waiting impatiently for the wind to change and for the chance to launch their offensive.

The chance came next day on 22 April – but it was well into the afternoon before the wind shifted direction and began to blow gently towards the south-west. The timing was far from ideal. By the time the messages could be passed along the line, by the time the troops could be alerted and in position, there would not be many hours of daylight left. Ideally the gas should have been released in the morning leaving a long day for the German infantry to advance and press home the advantage and dig in by nightfall. But they had waited so long, they had postponed the attack so often, that when the wind turned in the afternoon of 22 April, the chance was too good to miss. The decision was taken. The codeword '*Gott strafe Engelland*' was passed along the line. The assault troops were warned and moved into position, the special troops stood by the cylinders ready to open the cocks, the signal rockets were fired. 222 – '*Everything is ready for the attack.*' 301 – '*Fair Wind.*' 333 – '*Get the troops ready to advance.*' There had been several false alarms, and these preliminary signals had been sent up before – always followed by the dispiriting 6666 – '*Attack Cancelled.*' But this time the front-line German commanders, watching the flares and counting with bated breath, at last saw the signal they had been waiting for. 8888 – '*Open the gas containers.*' The men of the '*Stinkpionere*' pulled on their masks, bent over the cylinders, adjusted the long nozzles that would carry the gas into the wind, and wrenched open the cocks that would release it.

The attack came north of Ypres on the left of the salient and it fell in an awkward place, on the shoulder of the line where the Canadians joined hands with the French in front of Poelcapelle, and all across the French front to the Franco/Belgian boundary on the canal near Steenstraat. The Canadian Division had been holding the line for a matter of days, the French were in the process of changing over and their 45th Regiment had just moved into the line and had barely settled down. It was a regiment composed of French Colonials – native troops from North Africa – and it was on them that the full force of the gas cloud descended. At first, it looked as if it were going to envelop the Canadians. Two companies of the 48th Highlanders were in the front line and from his observation post in front of St Julien Gunner Jim Sutton had a bird's eye view.

It had been a quiet day, almost balmy for late April and, although a few shells had fallen in Ypres, away to the right behind them, only an occasional explosion or short burst of machine-gun fire had disturbed the monotonous routine of daytime in the trenches. It was almost five o'clock in the afternoon, the sun still shone, a pleasant light breeze had sprung up blowing, for once, towards the south-west, and as the soldiers, yawning and stretching, drummed up an early evening cup of tea, some of them were looking forward to nightfall and the prospect of being relieved at the end of their stint in the trenches. The guns of the 9th Canadian Battery were in action east of the village of St Julien on the edge of the Steenbeek stream, and the willow trees that bordered it provided perfect camouflage. Earlier in the day Gunner Jim Sutton had been sent forward to the observation post in front of Poelcapelle to take the place of Signaller-Corporal Lister who had been taken ill. The day had been not without incident for, earlier in the morning, a stray shell had broken the telephone line that connected the observation post with the guns and Sutton had spent most of the morning laboriously tracing the break. He found it eventually in the cemetery just north of St Julien and, squatting between the headstones of long-defunct villagers, mended it and made his way discreetly back to his post. For the rest of the day there had been so little doing that Major McDougall had sent the observing officer and another signaller back to the guns. Together Sutton and the Major whiled away the afternoon, looking out from time to time, from their position behind the Canadian trenches, towards the German front line but, as the pleasant afternoon drew on, with no real expectations that anything untoward was likely to happen. It was almost five o'clock and Jim Sutton was sweeping the German line through binoculars from the roof of a shell-battered farmhouse when he spotted the yellow cloud that rose from the German trenches and slowly drifted towards the British positions. He called to McDougall, 'Take a look at this, sir. There's something funny going on.' The German artillery opened as he spoke and began to pound the line. Major McDougall yelled back above the noise and Sutton leapt to the telephone to warn the guns and pass on the Major's orders to open fire on all targets right and left of the Poelcapelle road. He was only just in time. A moment later both telephone lines were cut but, as they anxiously watched, as the cloud drifted closer and closer to their own trenches, the British guns began to reply, the wind shifted and the cloud which had threatened to engulf the Canadians drifted north and rolled across the front of the Algerian Division, joining with others to form a high impenetrable wall of yellow-green smoke. The unfortunate Algerians had no chance. From their position above the gas cloud Sutton and his officer, staring aghast, could hardly have heard the screams, the gasping and choking as the gas cloud rolled across the troops – but they saw the panic – saw that the Algerians were running for their lives, throwing away rifles as they staggered and stumbled, dazed and terrified, away from the lethal fumes.

Jim Keddie, of the 48th Canadian Highlanders, saw it all from the trench a little way behind the front where H Company was in support. It was his thirty-fourth birthday. He had no means of celebrating, but before they moved forward to take over the front line in the evening Jim was hopeful that the post corporal would deliver a birthday parcel from his mother in Jedburgh in Scotland. Although he had emigrated to Canada some fifteen years ago and was to all intents and purposes a Canadian, Mrs Keddie had never failed to remember his birthday. Now that he was serving with the Canadian Army in France and nearer home, the old lady was hoping at long last to have a sight of her eldest son when his turn came round for leave. Jim was equally keen to get home to his native Jedburgh and had spent much of his birthday in happy contemplation of a warm welcome. It was fortunate for the Canadians that the capricious wind had changed but, even so, the troops on the extreme left of the division on the right of the luckless French Colonials, got more than a whiff of it.

L/Cpl. J. D. Keddie, H Coy., 48th Royal Highlanders of Canada.

My company was in the reserve trenches and it was on the afternoon of my birthday that we noticed volumes of dense yellow smoke rising up and coming towards the British trenches. We did not get the full effect of it, but what we did was enough for me. It makes the eyes smart and run. I became violently sick, but this passed off fairly soon. By this time the din was something awful – we were under a crossfire of rifles and shells, and had to lie flat in the trenches. The next thing I noticed was a horde of Turcos (French colonial soldiers) making for our trenches behind the firing line; some were armed, some unarmed. The poor devils were absolutely paralysed with fear. They were holding a trench next to a section of the 48th, so the 48th had to move in to hold it also until some of their officers came and made the Turcos go back.

Here on the fringe of the attack the 'Turcos', as Keddie was pleased to call them, had not been badly affected. It was natural terror and fear of the unknown that had made them run and, when the temporary effects of the gas had worn off, it was natural discipline that sent them back. But they were the lucky ones, there were not many of them, and the plight of their comrades on their left was pitiable. In the front-line trenches where the gas was thicker they had no time to run, and not many survived. Rolling over the trenches the gas clouds overwhelmed them so swiftly that men collapsed at once. Lying retching, choking, gasping for breath at the foot of the deep ditch where the heavy gas settled and clung thickest of all, they suffocated to death in minutes. From the support lines fifty yards behind, the troops watched in horror and as the wall of smoke rolled forward to engulf them in their turn, as the wind brought the first wisps of the fumes that clutched the throat and stung the eyes, they panicked and ran.

Along four miles of its length, between Poelcapelle and Steenstraat, the line was empty. Fifteen minutes after the gas was first released the German infantry was ordered to don gas-masks and advance. They were prepared for a fight, but there was no one left to fight with. As their guns thundered ahead of them, the German soldiers simply walked forward through the allied line, over the bodies of the dead, lying sprawled out, faces discoloured and contorted in grimaces of agony. Within an hour the Germans had advanced more than a mile and they had hardly needed to fire a shot.

By nightfall the enemy had driven a deep wedge into the allied lines. Flushed with victory they started to dig in.

Chapter 14

Far above the lingering gas, the tornado of explosions and all the horrors below, long trailing clouds turned luminous pink as the sun set in the western sky.

Major McDougall and his signaller had long ago slithered down from their rooftop look-out, for there was nothing to be made of the chaos in front and observation was useless if information could not be sent back. In the first minutes of the attack the telephone lines that linked them to the guns were shattered. It was pointless to brave the inferno to try to repair them for the Germans had already penetrated beyond their position and a machine-gun trained on the back wall of the farmhouse opened up at the slightest movement. There was nothing for it but to try to get back to the guns. They crawled out through a ditch half full of rank, stagnant water but it was shelter of a kind from the ferocious shell-fire. Their hands and arms were plastered with mud, their clothing sodden and stinking, but at length they emerged near the Battery on the outskirts of St Julien, and made a dash for it.

Sgnr. J. E. Sutton, 9th Bty., Canadian Field Artillery.

The major told me that he had heard more shell-fire in one hour than he heard in the whole of the Boer War. When we reached the battery we found that our guns had swung considerably to the left. Gunner Budagier had been wounded and I took his place as number two gunner on number four gun. They were so close together that number three gun was firing almost directly into my left ear. Later when we stopped firing I went with Signaller Macdonald to see if the road was clear so that we could move our guns back to the rear. The German infantry were almost at the edge of the village and the cemetery at the cross-roads, which was filled with ornate memorials and artificial flowers under glass that morning, was completely wrecked. On the main street we saw six Highlanders moving a grand piano from a house. When we asked them where they were taking it, they said they didn't know and they quit the job. Our casualties were six men wounded – four at the guns and two drivers bringing up ammunition.

After dark we moved back to a position on the outskirts of St Jean. Macdonald and I pushed our reel cart which held over two miles of telephone wire, our telephones, reels, pliers, etc. But we lost our kit-bags and coats in the move.

Now it was the Germans who had thrust their line forward into a salient. It jutted southwards from Poelcapelle into the open flank that ran westwards from the Canadian left, and doubled back to run north parallel to the canal bank to enclose the ground left empty by the French Colonials fleeing from the gas. A few were still there holding a straggling tenuous position that ran for a hundred or so yards east of the canal, far behind what had been the French right flank. A few of the others, least badly affected by the gas, had been rallied on the left of the Canadians' original line. But there were precious few of them and four and a half miles of completely open country stretched east to west between the remnants of the line and the canal four miles behind. The first imperative was to close this gap.

In the smoke, in the midst of the confusion and the pulverising shelling, it was difficult to judge exactly what had happened from the muddled messages that filtered from the battlefield, but the panic on the roads north of Ypres told its own tale, and the chaos and congestion near the canal itself was frightening. On the long, straight stretch that ran north from the outskirts of Ypres there was one bridge only behind the British sector and another behind the French at Boesinghe and although the gas travelled slowly, thinning and spreading on the wind as it approached, the fumes now reached as far as the canal and even beyond it, spreading further alarm among the French reserves who had not been close enough to fall victim to gas in the early stages of the attack. As their eyes began to stream, as the sickening fumes were sucked in with each gasping breath to burn their throats and sear into their lungs, as they saw the survivors of their front-line troops dragging their way towards them, some staggering and dropping to the ground overcome with pain and exhaustion, with sickly pallor and blue foam-flecked lips, the reserves turned and ran. The retreat became a rout.

In the struggling mass crowding on to the narrow bridges men collapsed and were trampled underfoot. Some tried to swim for it, and a few drowned in the attempt. Many who made it to the other side could go no further and lay retching and gasping on the far bank or on the road beyond, unable to go further. Those who were still on their feet streamed across the fields and meadows towards Elver-dinghe and Vlamertinghe, progressing more slowly now but still pressing on in desperation to get well away from the horrors behind. Officers mounted on nervous rearing horses were frantically trying to stop the tide of frightened men and turn it back if they could, but they got short shrift, and the few small groups they managed to rally were clearly in no condition to return to the fight, even if they had been able to get through the press of soldiers and civilians streaming across the bridges and along the roads. The people who had obstinately refused to leave farms and cottages close to the battle-line, who had preferred to take their chance among the shells rather than abandon their land and possessions, had taken fright at last. Now they too were struggling to get away, laden with sacks and bundles, pushing hand carts, trailing weeping children, clutching bird cages, pictures, candle-sticks – whichever of their valued belongings they had been able to snatch up. And now that the big shells were thundering into Ypres as they had never thundered before, people were streaming out of the town to swell the mob.

Mme Marie de Milleville.

We lived in a cottage just outside Boesinghe. I was only twelve but I could never in all my life forget that afternoon! It was shocking. I was alone with my mother and the little yard in front of our house was full of coloured soldiers lying on the ground or slumping against the wall. We could do nothing for them but give them water. We had two big metal jugs that held two or three litres apiece and for hours I went back and forwards to the kitchen filling them and filling them again, one after the other, while my mother stayed outside pouring it out for the soldiers to drink. More and more came along, wanting a drink as they passed. I poured water for hours and hours. After a while I had to pump up more from the well at the back because we soon used up what we had drawn that morning. They could not tell us what had happened, but we knew that it was something dreadful and that Germans might come at any moment. We kept on pouring the water, even after it got dark. Much later in the night some carts and ambulances came along to take the poor soldiers away – at least two of them were dead by then. And all the time, although no shells were falling near us, we could hear the guns. They never stopped. I could never forget it.

Even before they knew the full extent of the catastrophe the Divisional Commanders on the spot did not wait for instructions

198

before ordering reserves to the line. By a fortunate chance, two of them had seen the attack for themselves for the Commanding Officer of the Canadian Division had been visiting his gun batteries north east of St Julien at the time of the attack and General Snow, in command of the 27th Division, had been in the observation post above his headquarters in Potijze. Looking across the flat meadows both had seen the thick yellow cloud rolling out from the German lines and although their own lines had been quickly swallowed up in the turmoil of smoke and explosions, it was all too easy to surmise the rest. General Smith-Dorrien had seen it too as he walked back to Ypres after visiting Hill 60, and it was obvious to them all that there was no time to lose.

Had the gas been released and the attack launched early in the day the Germans might easily have poured through the gap and fought their way into Ypres, cutting off the troops in the salient with little resistance to stop them. The anxious commanders, conferring together by telephone, and with General Smith-Dorrien at his headquarters and the French General Putz at his, were fearful that, when morning came, that was precisely what the Germans would attempt.* Darkness came as a blessing, but it was a mixed blessing, for conditions on the roads were still chaotic and the rumours that spread among the civilian population caused more and more of them to take to their heels. It was not easy to get the reserves up. There was still little news to go on, and the scanty information that did reach Headquarters was far from reassuring.

The Canadians had spread out and flung back their line in a sharp angle facing north at right-angles to their original front. The military called it a defensive flank, but it was a short, short line of a few hundred yards and the snout of the German advance had pushed in well behind them. There was no one but Germans between them and Brigadier General Turner in his headquarters at Mouse Trap Farm beyond St Julien. Turner had acted quickly. Almost as soon as the attack began he ordered up his reserve battalion, keeping one company at Mouse Trap, where they had already prevented the Germans from advancing, and sending another two companies to

---

* It is a moot point whether they would have succeeded, or even tried, for, despite their mighty fire power, the Germans had insufficient reserves to make such a wholesale effort practicable. Their intention had only been to advance by bounds to a succession of limited objectives and to some extent they had been surprised by their own success and the cataclysmic effect of the gas on unprotected troops. But nevertheless, given their formidable fire power, situated as they now were within a stone's throw of Ypres whose outlying houses were little more than two miles away, the position of the Allies in the salient was already all but untenable.

defend St Julien as the Germans neared the edge of the village. The 10th Canadians who had just fallen in as a working party were ordered up to help, but it was a long time before they could get there along the roads blocked by fugitives. All round the salient and in the rest areas behind every battalion, every company, every detachment of engineers who could be spared from the line or was in rest behind it was warned to prepare to move to the shattered line.

Pte. W. J. McKenna, 16th Bn., (Canadian Scottish), 3rd Canadian Brig., 1st Canadian Div.

We were in rest billets in a big barn well behind the line and early in the evening when we were just enjoying tea there was a great commotion outside and we saw hordes of people rushing back – French Colonial troops – civilians with every kind of transport – perambulators, hand carts, barrows, all piled with personal possessions. We soon found out what had happened for the result was an order to 'fall in' with skeleton equipment and no overcoats. Extra ammunition was served out, and we had two hundred and twenty rounds. Then we started to march off and did about five miles. It was dark by then and the gas had practically dispersed, but over everything there was the thick smell which affected the eyes, mouth and throat. We lined up in a field and expected to be warned for trench duty but the fates decided otherwise and our battalion was wanted elsewhere. It transpired later on that about two miles behind the original front line which had been vacated by the French Colonials there was a battery of 4.7s of the Canadian heavy artillery. These guns had been abandoned, and the Germans, advancing behind their screen of gas, had taken them. This was our objective. I cannot help thinking that the enemy lost a wonderful opportunity, for surely he could have walked through us like a man could walk through a hoop of paper.

Even by nine in the evening the four and a half miles that ran straight back from the original Canadian left to the canal bank was held in only three places and the gaps between them were wide – two thousand yards, a thousand yards and, longest of all, three thousand yards whose only defence was a single French machine-gun post. Along the rest of the French front, between that one machine-gun and Steenstraat, although the French had formed a straggling line behind the western canal bank, on the enemy side, east of the canal there were no troops at all. The road to Ypres was open. The night was wild with shelling but there was one crumb of comfort. The German infantry had stopped and was digging in. It had been a long twilight but at last it was growing dark and there were seven hours in the allies' favour before daylight. The misty moon was still in its first quarter and there was still some light in the sky as it rose.

Along unfamiliar tracks, across unreconnoitred ground, runners slogged through the night taking messages to and from the outposts, and the signal that finally reached the Canadians hanging on in the old front line was brief and to the point. It came from their Commander, General Alderson, and it could be summed up in two words, 'Don't budge.' Although he was not a Canadian himself, the men from Canada thought a lot of General Alderson. It was barely two months since the Canadians had come to France and the General's speech before they first went into the line had earned their respect. Alderson was a man's man and a soldier's soldier. He did not beat around the bush, nor did he make the same mistake as the Commander-in-Chief who had caused barely suppressed hilarity during his inspection when he addressed the Canucks as 'Men and Canadians . . .' Alderson spoke to them like a father. He pointed out the perils of the trenches, the danger of ever-vigilant snipers, the stupidity of risking a peep over the parapet from mere curiosity and took pains to point out that dead soldiers never won a battle. He advised his men to lie low and sit tight under shell-fire and to refrain from showing 'nerves' by shooting at nothing. And he praised them. He praised their physique, he praised their zeal as volunteers, he assured them of his confidence and his certainty that they would do well. 'And,' he said, 'there is one thing more. My old regiment, the Royal West Kents, have been here since the beginning of the war, and it has never lost a trench. The Army says, "*The West Kents never budge.*" I am proud of the great record of my old regiment. I now belong to you, and you belong to me, and before long the Army will say, "*The Canadians never budge.*" Lads, it can be left there, and there I leave it. The Germans will never turn you out.'

In the Canadian line that night, Jim Keddie was not the only man who remembered these words, and Alderson's latest message, when it arrived, reinforced them. '*Don't budge.*' Hanging grimly on to their straggling line, each man separated by several yards from the next, not knowing what the morning might bring, the Canadians would not budge if they could help it.

The Canadian batteries had succeeded in pulling back their guns but two heavy guns had been lost, for the 2nd London Heavy Battery in support of the Canadians were concealed in Kitchener's Wood behind the French – and Kitchener's Wood, not half a mile from Mouse Trap and St Julien, was now in the hands of the

Germans. The reserves were still inching with difficulty towards the line, or what there was of it, but General Alderson had taken a bold decision. The 10th Canadian Battalion and the 16th Canadian Scottish were filtering towards the gap between Mouse Trap Farm and St Julien, but he did not intend them merely to fill it, they were to plunge forward, counter-attack the Germans, recapture Kitchener's Wood and retrieve the guns.

Kitchener's Wood was a prize worth having. Although its name had a contemporary ring it had nothing to do with Lord Kitchener whose imperious finger had recently beckoned so many recruits into the Army. It was a literal translation from the French '*Bois de Cuisiniers*' ('Cook's Wood') and the origin of the name had been lost to local memory. It was Cook's Wood and that was that. Kitchener's Wood was not large, only a few hundred yards in depth, but in the hands of the enemy, it was a position of huge advantage, lying on the small ridge that ran north from St Julien and protecting the village from the north-west. The Army called it Mouse Trap Ridge, for it ran behind Mouse Trap Farm and overlooked a wide valley of scattered farms and homesteads where only the previous day a soldier could have strolled with impunity. On the far side of the valley the ground rose for two hundred yards or so to the Pilckem Ridge and dropped gently across a mile of open farmland to the Yser Canal.

In Kitchener's Wood the Germans were digging in to consolidate their position but in the morning they would be able to assemble unseen in the concealment of its trees and in the lee of the ridge behind ready to leap forward to renew the attack. A hop, a skip, and a jump would take them to the canal bank. It was vital to regain the wood before that happened.

The Colonels of the two Battalions were no strangers to adventure. Colonel Boyle of the 10th Battalion was a rancher from Calgary and Colonel Leckie of the 16th Canadian Scottish was a mining engineer who had roughed it in the remotest wilds of Canada. But it was another matter to lead a night attack with inexperienced troops, on unfamiliar ground and with no artillery support, for the 'line' was so fluid, the positions of the enemy – and even of their own men – so uncertain, that it would be folly to suppose that guns, newly pulled into unfamiliar positions, could do anything at all to help. A counter-attack seemed an impossible feat to attempt, but daring and surprise might just pull it off.

Like Bill McKenna, Harry Hall of the 10th Battalion was one of the Canadians who slogged up on the long laborious trek to make the attack. Three Hall brothers had gone to war, but the eldest, Edmund, who had been through the battle of Neuve Chapelle, had joined the Argyll and Sutherland Highlanders before the rest of his family emigrated to Canada. It was years since he had seen his younger brothers although they had been not far off, supporting the left of the I Corps during the battle. Now Harry and Fred were both at Ypres, facing another battle and their first real fight.

Sgt. H. Hall, 10th Bn., 2nd Canadian Brig.

Our Battalion and the 16th Canadian Scottish were the only reserves in the whole salient and, as the Germans had broken through, things were looking very black for us. We were instantly summoned to fall in, and soon we were on our way to fill the gap – two thousand men to stop the German divisions in their thousands.

An ordinary general would have posted us in a reserve line of trenches until the Germans advanced the next morning, but not so General Alderson, *our* divisional commander. He tried a strategy which was one of the biggest bluffs of the war, and it utterly surprised the Germans. Instead of waiting for the Germans to swamp us the next morning he ordered us to make a night attack on Kitchener's Wood, where the Germans were massing for their attack.

We made the attack in lines of double companies, five hundred men in each of the four lines. A and B Companies were in the front line, supported by C and D Companies, and then the 16th Battalion behind them.

Pte. W. J. McKenna.

Our objective was not only the four guns in the little wood near St Julien, but also to convince the Germans that we were there in considerable force, and not only to take the guns but to have a strong moral effect on the enemy. Whatever the reasons, two Battalions of Canadian Scottish – the 16th of the 3rd Brigade, and the 10th of the 2nd Brigade – were lined out on a field, on a bitterly cold night nearly at midnight. We were told that our efforts were regarded as practically hopeless and that our work was to be in the nature of a sacrifice charge. At midnight, without bombs, machine-guns or artillery support, we started to advance. We had about two fields to cover and two hedges to pass through and the gaps weren't too many. Presently a bullet whistled past, then another and, before you could close an eye, enemy machine-guns opened about as hot a fire as you could imagine. Men fell in hundreds, but some of us got there, and, when they were facing our bayonets, the Germans were soon beaten and those that weren't killed escaped as fast as they could. We ran behind them through the wood, bayoneting as many as we could catch up with, and eventually we soon cleared the woods of live Germans! The guns were there and we put them out of action.

In order to deceive the enemy in regard to our numbers, we were told to make as much noise as we could and the shouting, swearing, cursing at the top of our voices was terrific! Added to the firing and the groans of the wounded, it made the night hideous. But the effect worked and the handful of us who did reach the enemy were able to drive him before us with the bayonet.

The onslaught on Kitchener's Wood was intended as part of a larger plan, for the French on the left had been meant to advance too. But there was no sign of them and it was clear that, for whatever reason, they had not been able to get forward. The Canadians were riddled by machine-gun fire as they advanced in the dark through the wood across the thick tangled roots of ancient oaks. But they came at last to the abandoned guns and sent back the triumphant message that would bring up the gun teams to haul them back. Long before the teams could get there the German artillery had begun to bombard the wood.

Sgt. H. Hall.

An hour after we had dug in there was a terrible concentration of shells sweeping the wood – it was just like a tropical storm sweeps a forest. It was impossible for us to hold the position. But, instead of retiring, we tried our old tactics of advancing and attacking the Germans again. They were digging them-selves in two hundred yards in front.

We got in a forward position and stayed there until the early hours of the morning. Our Colonel was killed and we only had two officers left, we were still losing men from the German artillery fire, and our ranks were now so thin that we couldn't stay out in that exposed position. What could a few of us do against the German hordes? Sick as we were with the gas fumes and the terrific strain of it all, we retreated back through the wood to an old line of trenches and there we dug in and waited for reinforcements.

Pte. W. J. McKenna.

We worked for dear life to get cover before daylight. Fortunately for us it was a little misty in the morning, and that gave us another hour or so to burrow into the earth. It's hard graft digging with an entrenching tool, especially after an exciting fight and when you're hungry too, but we managed it at last and we were well out of sight when Fritz dropped a few shells among us next day. Our roll-call while we were in our trench was about three hundred and sixty, which means our battalion alone lost about seven hundred and forty men, all in about ten minutes, and we suffered more casualties before we got away.

Sgt. H. Hall.

But our object had been achieved, and the Germans were demoralised. Our first Brigade appeared on the scene and the line was strengthened, and then the Buffs, the famous English regiment, came up at the double after having marched miles from another part of the line.

So the bluff that we pulled off was entirely successful, and the Germans thought that we had about twenty thousand men attacking them. It never struck their cold-blooded unimaginative minds that two thousand men would have the audacity to attack whole German Divisions without artillery support.

Pte. W. J. McKenna.

To withdraw we had to go along a ditch full of wet muddy slime, and bent double. That's no easy job at any time, but it's worse when you're nearly famished and weary for want of sleep. To get out of the ditch meant a bullet, because snipers were on the look-out. We were under rifle fire for about two miles from our trench, and it was a relief when we found ourselves at last out of range. We thought we were in for a rest, but we were told to fall in and go to relieve a battalion that had been in the trenches and had to retire. However, St Julien, the village we reported at, was suffering severely from shell-fire and several houses were on fire. We hung about for two hours before being told to retire.

Of the strength of two battalions, only ten officers remained to shepherd four hundred survivors away from the battle-line. It had been some consolation to find that the guns abandoned in Kitchener's Wood had finally been destroyed by the enemy's own shelling. Even if they had not managed to retrieve them they would at least be of no use to the enemy.

Two nights earlier when they had been relieved from a four-day

205

stint in the trenches the 9th Royal Scots were disappointed to find that they were not to return to their cushy billets in Ypres and had to march on to Vlamertinghe. It was a long, long march and, after four days of inactivity in the trenches, the men were sore and stiff and weary by the time they turned into the field full of black-tarred tarpaulin huts where they were to spend their four days' rest before going back. It was dawn before the huts were allocated and the weary soldiers of the Dandy Ninth were at last able to turn in. They slept most of the day and they binged most of the next night.

Pte. W. Hay, A Coy., 9th Bn., Royal Scots (Lothian Regt.), 27 Div.

We woke to parcels and letters – the height of bliss! Everybody passed everybody else his cakes or sweets, and the bully beef of our daily ration was stacked in a heap – untouched. What digestions we had! One man, whose only vices were cigarettes and tea, and who was bemoaning the scarcity of fags in the trenches and was hoping all the way down that some would be waiting for him, he sat grinning, opening box after box – seven hundred or so cigarettes. According to our tastes, we were all as happy as he was. Soon the tidy hut was strewn with cardboard boxes, paper, string, and luxuries, and what a mess there was to be cleared up when we got the order to move!

They had hardly recovered from the long march, hardly finished stretching after their long-awaited sleep, and had not nearly finished demolishing the contents of the parcels, when the order came. It was barely forty hours since the Royal Scots began the trek out of the line and they were just settling down to enjoy their second evening of relaxation and looking forward to their second long sleep, when rumours began to fly. It came as no surprise when they were ordered to pack up and to fall in at the double.

Pte. W. Hay.

We knew there was something wrong. We started to march towards Ypres but we couldn't get past on the road because it was absolutely solid with troops marching up and with refugees coming down the road. We couldn't pass them so we had to go up along the railway line half-way to Ypres and there were people, civilians and soldiers, lying along the roadside in a terrible state. We heard them say it was gas. We didn't know what the Hell gas was! There were limbers parked at the side, because *they* couldn't get through and it was an absolute turmoil. In fact we had to turn into a field and wait there for a while before we could get on at all. We knew the people must be trying to get away from Ypres, and we could see Ypres up ahead of us all on fire. Blazing! Eventually we got the word to move on, and we had pretty mixed feelings when we got to the outskirts and knew we were going to have to run the gauntlet through the fire, with shells falling all the time. The whole town seemed to be on fire. It was a terrible sight – appalling!

We were split up and we went by platoons, fifty yards between each platoon, and when we got to the big square opposite the town-hall there was blazing and smoking and shells bursting everywhere. We could feel the flames of the fire hot on our faces. Ypres was being demolished – literally razed to the ground with bricks and mortar flying everywhere. I was the Company Sergeant-Major's batman, Sergeant-Major Ferguson, and he'd given me a sandbag to carry with his binoculars in it and the Company roll-book and his shaving gear and all that sort of thing. Of course I was loaded with my own gear, my pack and my rifle, and this sandbag was hampering me, dodging all the stuff that was flying about. Sergeant-Major Ferguson wasn't carrying anything, being the Company Sergeant-Major. So I got rid of the sandbag – I just threw it into the fire, because I honestly didn't think that any of us would get through Ypres the way it was being shelled and bombarded, and fires everywhere and buildings crashing down. You would never have dreamed that you were going to get through that and you'd have even less chance if you were carrying a lot of gear, so I slung the only thing I could get rid of, which was the sandbag. Just slung it into the fire as we passed.

It was a pity really, because we *did* get through. It was miraculous how we did it but eventually we got out on to the Menin Road and there wasn't a single casualty in the whole battalion. I've always thought that was a miracle! Later on I was sorry I'd got rid of the sandbag because it wasn't long before Sergeant-Major Ferguson was calling out for me, wanting his stuff, and I was in trouble. I told him I lost it in the inferno in Ypres, and I couldn't tell you what he said! He gave me a full account of my personal charms, and it wasn't printable what he said. I got dumped out of *that* job on the spot unfortunately, because as a batman you can dodge parades and a bit of fatigues. But of course, all that happened next day. That night we didn't have time to think of anything but getting away from Ypres and getting up to the line. We were up at Potijze Wood by dawn and waited there in bitter cold until the early morning, and of course we didn't really know what was happening. Then we were moved up to Wieltje not far away and it seems the idea was for the battalion to make an attack from there. Then the orders were changed and the battalion was split up and my company, A company, and B company were told to fall in and we were marched off to make up part of a composite force with two companies of the Duke of Cornwall's Light Infantry and we were sent up to fill this gap on the left of St Julien. Of course we were nothing like four full companies, because there had been a lot of casualties. We had to go into ditches and fire a few rounds, and go on a bit further and fire a few more, and come back again and fire again – and this was to give the impression to the Germans that there was plenty of troops there. There were a lot of Canadians lying there dead from gas the day before, poor devils, and it was quite a horrible sight for us young men. I was only twenty so it was quite traumatic and I've never forgotten nor ever will forget it. The first time that I've ever felt really terrified in my heart was when the Colonel gave us orders to fix bayonets.

We were in a ditch in a sunken road and lying there, rifle loaded and all ready, we were told to fix bayonets, and I was really apprehensive. We were all definitely scared thinking that we were going to have hand-to-hand fighting, which wasn't what I thought we'd have to do. I thought we'd be firing rifles – I didn't expect to be going bayonet fighting with the Germans. No, I didn't expect that. There was a temporary sort of cottage they were using as a dressing station at St Julien and I took a look round the corner of it and saw loads and loads of Germans, just like rabbits! There were thousands of them there, a good bit away of course. You could see at a glance that we were very much outnumbered.

We got the order to advance – just to go forward a bit, because there was no barbed wire there and it was open country. However we went no further because it was getting late in the evening so we were told to start digging rifle pits, one to each man, so that they could be joined up to make the forerunner of a trench. We were all up there, because they needed every spare man, there was nobody hanging around, everybody had to go up into action and fill this gap – and I was digging with David Newbury. We were both young men and we didn't know the name of psychology, but we'd both been brought up reading the old schoolboys' magazines and we heard all the tales about Germans being frightened of the Highlanders. We came to the conclusion together that if both of us made for one German it would frighten the wits out of him if he saw two Highlanders come at him with their bayonets. We thought that if we looked ferocious enough as we ran at a German he'd just pack it in and run away, and maybe that would influence the others to do the same. That was our idea, but we never got to putting it into practice.

When we began to advance, their machine-guns opened on us and David got a bullet across his forehead and his blood was running all down his face. I thought he was killed, but even though he was my pal, I wasn't allowed to stop and tie him up. We had to go on, so we went further and we came to a little hollow in the ground and got into it. We couldn't see any Germans then because we were really under cover there in that slight hollow and the Germans were machine-gunning over our heads. And then the Captain got a bullet in his thigh, Captain Taylor. Of course we were stopped then, so I managed to tie it up roughly for him and then stretcher-bearers took him and as he went away, he told us to get on and dig these rifle pits.

We had to get over this stream where all the trees had been knocked down by shell-fire, so we clambered over them, hanging on to the branches to get over the other side and start digging this line such as it was. For some reason the Germans didn't come on. If they had we'd all have been massacred. A few hours later we were pulled out and rushed back to Sanctuary Wood. And that went on for four days. Back and forwards. Out and in. Here and there. We never knew where we were or what we were supposed to be doing!

Hay now belonged to a force of men that was hastily cobbled together, put under the command of Colonel Geddes of the Buffs and rushed to the assistance of the hard-pressed Canadians. It was not much of a force, for it only consisted of a few half battalions, some odd companies, and a few battalions drawn from Divisional reserve, Corps reserve – even Army reserve. Many of them were already under-strength and together they only amounted to seven Battalions, thinned and weakened by casualties. But it was the best that could be done – and it was a dangerous 'best' because although a third of the strength was strung out in a 'second line' just behind the fluid front, every man was in the line. If the Germans made a move and poured through the gaps or broke through the embryo defences of the new flank before reinforcements arrived, there would be no reserves at all to stop them. Forty-two German battalions were on the march and only seventeen battalions of British and Canadians stood in their path. They could be brushed aside as easily as a single finger might push open a well-oiled door and, even with the paltry amount of information at their disposal, the senior officers knew it.

Colonel Geddes's orders were not only to fill the gaps and extend his line to cover the open French front. He was ordered to attack, where he could, to pin the Germans down and, if possible, to push ahead and recover lost ground.

Geddes was as ignorant of the situation as anyone and, with no staff, with only a Brigade Major to assist him, and a platoon of cyclists as a makeshift signalling section, he hardly knew the whereabouts at any one time of all the scattered troops of his command. It was a mammoth task for any Battalion Commander to undertake. But somehow it had to be done.

Chapter 15

All down the line from Ploegstreet to Merville troops were ordered to prepare to move off at short notice but those in reserve or at rest nearest to Ypres were sent for first. They at least could cover some of the distance reasonably fast on foot. Telephone wires hummed and lights burned in Headquarters' offices far into the night – and the next night, and the next. No matter how desperate the situation, Battalions and reserves could not be suddenly withdrawn from the line without first making complicated arrangements to ensure the safety of the line when they had gone. Vehicles had to be provided to carry them north and to follow them up with supplies of rations and ammunition, so transport parks were scoured for lorries and limbers, trains were rescheduled and diverted, and long lines of London buses trundled up to camps and villages behind the front to carry the troops away. No one had the faintest idea what had happened, or where or what they were bound for.

The London Rifle Brigade was rudely interrupted at the start of a spell of rest, made all the more enjoyable by the fact that the weather was fine. A sports day was planned to keep the men entertained, the Adjutant had already been to Bailleul to purchase prizes from battalion funds, and the athletes, excused from parades and fatigues, were spending energetic days training for the various events, sprinting, jumping and pole-vaulting in the mild spring weather.

The train they boarded at Steenwerck jolted first towards Haze-brouck on the first leg of the journey and prompted wild speculation. Various wagers were staked in cigarettes, although the joker who suggested that the war was over and they were bound for Calais and home found few takers. But at Hazebrouck, after much delay and shunting, the engine was reversed, the train began to head north and if there were still any doubts about their destination the trainloads of refugees they passed soon dispelled them. It was clear that something serious had happened and that it had happened at Ypres.

The three squadrons of the Queen's Own Oxfordshire Hussars

were in billets round the small village of Pradelles on the road from Hazebrouck to Bailleul, but when the colonel received the order to turn out his men as quickly as possible he had some difficulty in laying his hands on them. They had already trotted off on various training schemes in different parts of the countryside, but it was a fine morning for a gallop, they had let the horses have their heads, and there was no sign of them for miles. It took more than an hour before dispatch-riders, scouring the countryside on motor bikes, were able to track them down and bring them back and it was well after mid-day before they reached the rendezvous at Strazeele where they were to link up with the rest of the 1st Cavalry Division on the way to Ypres.

Tpr. P. Batchelor, D Squadron, Queen's Own Oxfordshire Hussars.

We waited there for hours before anyone turned up and we didn't have a clue what was happening. Of course we were used to that – all through Neuve Chapelle we'd waited to go into action and nothing happened. We'd had no grub, so Captain Gill let us go off a few at a time for a quarter of an hour to get some coffee and maybe a bit of bread and cheese in the village. It was half-way through the afternoon before we finally moved off, and the road was so packed with troops marching up that we could hardly get the squadron through. It took us more than three hours to cover three miles and then we were dismounted and waited for hours again while they tried to find billets. By the time we'd fed and watered the horses it was past midnight before we turned in ourselves – and we'd hardly got to sleep before we were up again and off on the road to Ypres.

By setting off before first light when the roads were slightly quieter and the weary infantry still slept, by riding across country after daylight, spurred on by the sound of the guns booming louder as they approached, the Oxfordshire Hussars arrived shortly after nine in the morning and unsaddled in fields near Vlamertinghe three miles behind the front. One latecomer got there almost ten hours behind the others and his arrival by taxi-cab caused something of a sensation. Lieutenant Wellesley had been on a machine-gun course at Wisques and on his way back, arriving at St Omer on market day, he had indulged in a little shopping for provisions to enliven meals in the mess. Flanders is renowned for succulent asparagus, in season for a few short weeks in April and early May. One stall was piled high with the pick of the crop – the fattest, whitest, freshest stalks Wellesley had ever seen. Like most officers of the Oxfordshire

Yeomanry, Wellesley belonged to the landed gentry and enjoyed a comfortable income which enabled him to indulge his epicurean tastes. He purchased a capacious hamper from a stall selling baskets, had it filled with a large quantity of asparagus and, leaving it in charge of his servant, strolled off to find a wine merchant. He bought two cases of the best champagne that St Omer could offer and, after a satisfactory lunch in a restaurant, he hired a ramshackle taxi-cab for the eighteen-mile journey to Pradelles. Wellesley's servant sat in front with the driver and Wellesley travelled in the back with their luggage plus his bulky purchases. It was a tight squeeze, but Wellesley did not mind. For dinner there would be champagne and asparagus – dripping with country butter (for he had not forgotten that!) – and he looked forward with pleasure to surprising his brother officers with a rare feast.

It was nothing to the surprise that awaited Wellesley himself at Pradelles when he discovered that billets were empty and the Oxfordshire Hussars had gone. Brigade Headquarters had gone too and, given the situation, the confusion of orders, the congestion of troops, no one could tell him precisely where to find his regiment. He guessed, wrongly, that it might have gone south, and the elderly cab-driver, who was no doubt congratulating himself on picking up a lucrative long-distance fare, changed his mind at Laventie when a clutch of shells exploded on the road less than three hundred yards ahead. He stopped the cab and dived beneath it for shelter, flatly refusing to go on, and it was some considerable time before he could be induced to return to the driving seat. Even then, only a large bribe with the promise of more to come dissuaded him from driving straight back to St Omer. By the time their wanderings ended, by the time they had scrounged petrol, lost their way a dozen times, made a thousand enquiries, and roamed the length of the front within earshot of the bombardments, the driver was a broken man.

It was more than twenty-four hours before they tracked down the Oxfordshire Hussars encamped in miserable bivouacs at Vlamer-tinghe. The champagne and asparagus was unloaded at the entrance to a muddy field in the midst of a bombardment. The taxi-driver, lavishly paid off, set off thankfully to St Omer, and if, in the heat of the emergency, Lieutenant Wellesley did not receive precisely the welcome he had expected from the officers, at least they were impressed by his style. The mess cooks, working in difficult circumstances, were possibly less impressed by the prospect of scraping a hamperful of asparagus in the middle of a battle.

The first task of the Cavalry Division was to reconnoitre and, in particular, to reconnoitre the French front, for the situation was still far from clear and General Wanless O'Gowan, who had crossed the canal expecting to find French positions, had been appalled to

213

discover that there were still large gaps where no troops were to be found. The new British line was fragile and tenuous enough, but the greatest danger zone was along the canal. The bulk of the French troops had fallen back beyond it and four long miles stretched between the British left and Steenstraat where the French joined hands with the Belgian front running to the north. Reports from French headquarters were patchy and imprecise and the British Command suspected that General Putz himself was not entirely sure of the whereabouts of his men. But one thing was certain. The Germans had crossed the bridge at Steenstraat and gained a foothold on the opposite bank. Luck and the Belgians had prevented them going further, and the Belgians had indeed been lucky. By some uncharacteristic mismanagement or misunderstanding on the part of the Germans not all the gas-cylinders at this crucial juncture of the front had been opened and the gas that had been released had so little effect that the Belgians north of Steenstraat had been able to beat back the Germans and bring their artillery into action to help French comrades on their right. But the Germans did manage to cross the canal. Now they were fighting at Lizerne to the west of it and although the French were fiercely resisting, the enemy was within an ace of driving a wedge between the French and Belgian armies. That would bring disaster. Disaster to the Belgians, who would be entirely cut off between the enemy and the northern swamps. Disaster to the French, already in disarray, whose lines could so easily be rolled up. Disaster to the British in their ragged vulnerable line in the salient round Ypres which could be cut off with ease from the rear. As soon as they arrived on the morning of the 23rd, as soon as the horses were watered and fed and rested, British cavalry patrols were sent off to reconnoitre. But one man was ahead of them.

Artur Barbieur was senior policeman at Proven. The bridge at Steenstraat was in his charge and, war or no war, he did not intend to shirk this responsibility. Barbieur was a family man, and his seven-year-old daughter Paula would remember that evening for the rest of her life.

Mevrouw Paula Hennekint.

My mother pleaded with him not to go, but he *would* go. Nothing would stop him. After he set off on his bicycle I remember my mother lighting candles in front of a little crucifix and kneeling down to pray. She was a very pious woman. She did the same every night – but that night I remember especially because she was so terribly anxious. She had done the same when the German Hussars passed through our village in August

1914. I remember how frightened we were. We closed all the shutters and kept very still and quiet, my mother on her knees in front of the crucifix.

Of course the Germans didn't stay then, and the French came when the war really started. I had been going to school since September, and there were soldiers everywhere, French soldiers and Belgian soldiers passing through. The main road was always so blocked with troops and wagons and horses that we had to go to school by the back lanes because the main road was for the military and we were warned not to use it. Next to the police station in the village there was a little prison for soldiers who had misbehaved themselves – nothing serious, but they were under arrest, although it wasn't rigid and they weren't strictly guarded. We used to go and talk to them and take them water, and they asked if we could take them some wine – because the French soldiers liked wine. So my mother used to put a bottle of wine hidden in a big jug of water, and we children used to carry it to them in the prison. They could pay for it. It was all fun to us. The French soldiers were good to us. They used to give us some of their rations and *white* bread, which was wonderful to us.

Then, on the evening of the first gas attack, there were so many rumours going round that no one knew what had happened. All we knew was that something had happened at the canal at Steenstraat and my father decided that he must go to see if the bridge had been blown up, because it would have been his duty to make a report if it had. My mother didn't try to stop him, but she was very worried and upset. I can understand why she was so emotional now, because my brother was born in December 1915, so she must have just recently found that she was pregnant. It must have been dreadful for her. But my father set off, wearing his police uniform and riding his bicycle as if it was nothing out of the ordinary. We children were sent to bed, but my mother waited up all night – and he didn't come back.

Late in the evening, by the time Artur Barbieur reached Steenstraat, the fighting had died down. His police uniform enabled him to pass through the French lines. But the Germans were on the look-out and as Barbieur cycled towards the bridge they opened fire.

Mevrouw Paula Hennekint.

I shall never forget the next day. In the morning two Belgian policemen came to tell my mother that my father had been shot and wounded – but they could tell her no more, only that he had been taken away. My mother was distracted. She kept wringing her hands and saying over and over again, 'What's going to become of my husband!' Mother, children, all of us, we were all crying. He just disappeared and we could find out nothing. Every day we saw trainloads of wounded going away, and there were camp hospitals all around us, but we could find out nothing. We didn't know how badly he was wounded, we didn't know where he was – or even if he was alive or dead. My poor mother! She almost went out of her mind. She thought he would never come back.

Three weeks later he walked in on crutches. He had been badly shot up in the legs with a big shell splinter in his thigh. He'd had several operations in one of the British camp hospitals and when he began to recover they were going to send him on to a military hospital in England. But he wouldn't hear of it. He said, 'No, no. I must get home to my wife and children.' So they let him go. He hobbled in while my mother was on her knees praying. She went wild! We all did! It was the first news we'd had of him since he went out on his bicycle three weeks before.

Early on the morning of 23 April Sir John French drove to Cassel to discuss matters with General Foch at French headquarters. He did not by any means have a clear picture of the situation but he knew enough to judge that it was critical and that the line of the salient might have to be drastically reduced, if not withdrawn altogether. Foch was scandalised at the very idea. His only thought was to regain his original line and, he assured the British Commander-in-Chief, he had every intention of doing so. Reinforcements were on the way and as soon as they were in position the attack would go in. The British *must* support it. He was convinced that they would succeed.

General French was in two minds. The salient was so small, the situation on his left so perilous, the casualties were already so large and his own resources in men and materials so small, that all his instincts as a soldier told him that the sensible course would be to draw back to a line that could be more easily defended – even, in the last resort, to contemplate relinquishing Ypres. But it was difficult to refuse an ally who was so convinced that the situation could be retrieved. French hesitated, and finally, almost against his better judgement, he agreed. But he made one stipulation. If the French did not succeed, with his support, in restoring the situation within 'a reasonable time' he would be forced to reconsider his position and draw in his line. Meanwhile, he would reinforce his Second Army and fight on. Already fresh troops had been ordered to stand by and be prepared to move at short notice. As soon as he returned to his advanced headquarters at Hazebrouck the Commander-in-Chief issued the orders that would send them on their way.

The French Commander-in-Chief, Marshal Joffre, shared Sir John French's misgivings. The unexpectedness of the German attack at Ypres was a disconcerting annoyance and not at all in conformance with his own plan for the prosecution of the war. Joffre had his sights firmly set on the triple attack that would disrupt the German lines of communication – the all-out effort, so carefully planned, that would reduce the huge German salient that swung deep into France, and release the towns and villages imprisoned in its maw. Preparations were almost complete, the British – who had risen in his estimation since their independent action at Neuve Chapelle – were committed to cooperate and, in Joffre's view, the best way of relieving the pressure at Ypres was to distract the Germans with a major offensive elsewhere. Ypres, by comparison, was small beer and had the British 29th Division not been diverted to Gallipoli, thus preventing them from taking over his entire line in the north, Joffre would have had no French troops there at all.* As it was, in the light of the coming offensive, he was reluctant to commit any more of his men and to weaken his armies, poised for the assault, by bleeding them of badly needed resources in men and materials in order to commit them to what, at best, was a distraction and, at worst, might well turn out to be a lost cause. General Foch would have to fight hard to wrest reinforcements from the ample reserves at Marshal Joffre's disposal.

Sir John French, who was equally anxious to participate in a breakthrough and to capitalise on the initial success at Neuve Chapelle, was in sympathy with the French Commander's view. But a promise was a promise. General Foch had been so optimistic, so sure that the French could recover the lost ground, that Sir John French had only a few qualms as he issued the order for the counter-attack that would help them to get it back. General Foch, perhaps with a qualm or two of his own, had already driven to the headquarters of the unfortunate General Putz to urge him to take action as quickly as possible. He must attack, and attack at once. But it was an attack which General Putz was in no position to

---

* There were now only two French Divisions in the line – so few that they were referred to by the French Army merely as the Elverdinghe Detachment – with another two brigades on the coast at Nieuport (the Nieuport Detachment) and, although it would be unfair to say that they were the dregs of the French forces, they were not troops of the highest calibre. Both detachments were under the command of General Putz.

undertake and it had precious little chance of succeeding. The only reinforcements which Putz had yet received – two battalions and two batteries of guns rushed down from his isolated command at Nieuport – had already been thrown in at Lizerne where the French were holding back the German advance.

There was no time for preparation, no time for reconnaissance of the ground, and no exact knowledge of the enemy's position. Nevertheless there was no arguing with a direct order from General Headquarters and, in the circumstances, both Smith-Dorrien and Plumer agreed that if an attack must be made it ought to be made speedily. The enemy front was ominously quiet and that could only be because the Germans were digging in, wiring a line that might soon become impregnable, and bringing up reserves to replace their casualties and increase their strength. But the hold-ups were many, the arrival of fresh troops was delayed by the congestion on the roads and the attack which should have gone in at three o'clock was not launched until almost half past four. Communications were so sketchy that it was all but impossible to arrange for artillery support and the batteries which did receive the message to fire a preliminary bombardment at 2.45 in support of the three o'clock attack did not receive the news of its postponement and the precious ammunition they fired in the general direction of the enemy went for nothing. When the troops finally started off, moving in broad daylight across open country towards the unseen German positions, the guns did their best to support them, but there was not much they could do. The German guns opened up, the infantry vanished into the smoke of explosions and half of those who survived to get within striking distance of the German positions were mown down by close-range fire from rifles and machine-guns. After the attack had started four hundred French colonial troops lining the eastern bank of the canal joined in, apparently spontaneously, but they very soon withdrew and no more was seen of the French. By seven o'clock it was all over and limp bands of survivors were lying low, waiting until darkness fell to cover the long crawl back. All the time the German heavy guns were thundering, as they had thundered all day, raining shells into the battlefield and into Ypres.

But the Commander-in-Chief had kept his promise to General Foch, although at a fearful price. No ground was captured which could not have been occupied if the fresh troops had simply walked forward under cover of darkness and now those badly needed troops who might have served to strengthen the line had themselves been decimated. They had lost most of their officers – including three Battalion Commanders – and more than half the men. It was only some consolation that matters might have been worse for, except at Lizerne, and apart from isolated bombing raids where the outflanked angle of the weak Canadian line turned to join the new extended front, the Germans had not followed up their success of the previous evening with a full-scale assault. But no one had any doubt that sooner rather than later they would, and every man would be needed to meet the attack when it came.

It was Friday night, 23 April. St George was the patron saint of the Northumberland Fusiliers and, as they marched towards Ypres, there was not a man of the 7th Battalion who was not aware that today was St George's Day. It was exactly seventy-two hours since the 50th Northumbrian Territorial Division had landed in France and its 149th Brigade had spent one night in troop trains chugging slowly north, and another in billets around Mount Kemmel. Now they were going into battle, and if any such thoughts as 'lambs to the slaughter' occurred to the mind of their Divisional Commander he kept them to himself.

L/cpl. J. Dorgan, 7th Bn., Northumberland Fusiliers, 50 Div. (TF).

We arrived at the outskirts of Ypres and marched through the square, the market place of Ypres. Shells were dropping on the cobbled stones and some of the lighter shells and the shrapnel were spreading right across the square and the Cloth Hall and the Cathedral were on fire. We had our first casualty in going through the square, Tommy Rachael, who was a postman in Ashington. He was marching behind me and he shouted out, he said, 'I'm wounded.' Nobody would believe him and then somebody said, 'There's blood coming down his legs,' and another fellow said, 'Help him, help him somebody. He's not going to drop out. We're the Northumberland Fusiliers!' That was the spirit we had.

As we reached the outskirts we didn't know where we were going, neither officers nor men. After having an hour or two's sleep just outside of Ypres we marched on in the early hours of 24 April under heavy shell-fire.

Sir Horace Smith-Dorrien had spent an anxious dispiriting evening, counting the cost of the counter-attack and poring over maps, trying as a soldier to read the soldier's mind of his opposite number at German Headquarters. In the position of the German Commander, what would *he* do? It was true that there had been local skirmishes but, from the German point of view, they had demonstrated very little other than their desire to improve their position. The absence of a full-scale infantry assault – which could hardly have been withstood – was a blessing, but the strange lack of movement was ominous. More than twenty-four hours had passed since the Germans had broken the allied line, and still their infantry hesitated. Why? Something was bound to happen. Somewhere the blow would fall. But where?

Knowing, as the Germans must, that the allied line had been broken, guessing, as they surely would, that the scanty reserves had been used up to strengthen the new northern flank, knowing full well the extent of the casualties they had inflicted, Smith-Dorrien reasoned that a German General's inclination might be to attack the southern face of the salient, to break through and take the northern flank from the rear or, by forcing the British to fight back-to-back on two flanks, to gradually squeeze them in and snuff them out. He was dismally aware that it was only one of several imponderable possibilities but it could not be discounted, and he made haste to send a signal to the troops in the thin denuded lines on the east and south of the salient to be vigilant and alert to the likelihood of attack.

But the line on the eastern face of the salient was more vulnerable than the line facing south, and no one knew better than Sir Horace Smith-Dorrien just how inadequate it was. The British Army had only begun to take over this sector from the French in the early part of April, the defences were woeful and even after a lot of hard work they were not much improved. The sector held by the 27th and 28th Divisions ran from the Menin Road, a mile in front of the village of Gheluvelt, lost to the Germans in the autumn of 1914, crept out to enclose Polygon Wood, swung north past Broodseinde east of Zonnebeke, and jutted east again across a slope to enclose the farms the French called Seine and Marne. Here for a few hundred yards the line ran very close to the Germans, a matter of yards away, and from this point the salient began to tail down on its slow curve to the north-west.*

Beyond the tiny copse they called Berlin Wood the Canadians took over the line that ran across the Ostnieuwkerke road half a mile north of the hamlet of Gravenstafel and on, sloping gently above the Gravenstafel Ridge, to the Poelcapelle Road half a mile in front of that village. It was here that the Canadians had joined hands with the French and it was just beyond the Poelcapelle Road that the French line had been forced in by the gas attack. The Canadians had been in the new line for just over a week and the defences they inherited from the French were lamentable. The front-line trenches were constructed of thin sandbagged parapets, far from bullet-proof, and with no sheltering parados to prevent shots striking from the rear. They were

---

* The German line here lay on a gentle slope which two years later would be one of the bastions in their defence of Passchendaele beyond. After the war it was transformed into what became the largest and best-known of all British war cemeteries – Tynecot.

mere outposts grouped together at intervals with nothing to link them but a few shallow ditches, less than three feet deep, running back here and there to flimsy support positions behind. A few tumbledown dug-outs of wood and tarpaulin that were good enough to provide shelter from the rain would give much the same protection as umbrellas against bombardment.

A little way behind the front, on the western edge of the Gravenstafel Ridge, some unfinished trenches straggled across ground that was still littered with the unburied bodies of French and German soldiers killed six months ago in the First Battle of Ypres. The army referred to this sector as 'Locality C'. Canadian working parties, given the distasteful task of scattering chloride of lime in an effort to smother the stench of corruption, referred to it in less printable terms.

But the one bright spot in this pathetically weak front was the deep belt of barbed wire entanglements that protected it and the French had depended on this, on machine-gun posts behind it, and on their excellent quick-firing .75 guns to defend it. And they had constructed another line, far stronger than the first. It was the line of last resort and it ran not far in front of Ypres, from Hill 60 to the Menin Road, across a gradual slope to pass north of Potijze, to encircle Wieltje and cross the low ridge between Mouse Trap Farm and Kitchener's Wood. It was so far back that the British, dearly wishing when they took over their stretch of it that their allies had constructed a line half as strong two miles ahead, little thinking that they would ever need to make use of it as a front, named it 'the GHQ line'. Now, pushing against the newly formed and fragile defensive flank, the Germans were ranged against its northern extremity.

The Germans had made the most of the twenty-four hours' breathing space, and they were thinking on their feet, because the gas attack had been a tactical experiment and had not figured in their overall strategy as the preliminary to a full-scale planned campaign. But the opportunity presented by such remarkable success was too tantalising to resist. Their misfortune was that no reserves had been on hand to exploit it to the full. Even now there were few reserves to call on for their own casualties had not been small and the counter-attacks had taken them by surprise and even demoralised their troops.[*]

---

[*] General Balck, commanding 23rd German Reserve Corps, later wrote of the fighting of 23 April: 'Unfortunately the infantry had become enfeebled by trench warfare and had lost its daring and its indifference to heavy losses and the disintegrating influence of increased enemy fire effect. The leaders and the brave-hearted fell, and the bulk of the men, mostly inexperienced reinforcements, became helpless and only too inclined to leave the work to the artillery and trench mortars.'

The best that could be done in the short term was to depend on heavy artillery fire to soften the British front and create havoc in Ypres, to fight on at Steenstraat and Lizerne, and to warn the tired troops facing the British defensive flank to dig in and stand fast. Even though these troops were in the best position to make a successful assault they were in no fit state to undertake it. But there was still the gas, and with gas they could repeat their success. On 23 April, all during the hours of daylight, through the dusk and on into the dark, while their big guns fired incessantly, the Germans moved up field guns and trench mortars to support their captured front and dug in fresh gas cylinders in front of the Canadians in their unbroken original line still facing them to the east. This time the Germans were determined to make no mistake and to give themselves ample time to press home their advantage.

The wind was steady and blowing in the right direction. Long before dawn they began to bombard the Canadians' vulnerable line. An hour later the gas cylinders were opened and the gas was released across the centre of their front. It was four o'clock in the morning and the moon behind the flashes of the guns had barely begun to wane in the night sky when the first fumes drifted across. Drifting ghostly and lurid in the dim light in a bank fifteen feet high, it rolled across the wire and engulfed the Canadians in the makeshift trenches inherited from the French. They had nothing to protect them from the gas – only handkerchiefs, towels, even cotton bandoliers, hastily clapped across mouth and nose, and soon there was no time even for that, for the enemy was advancing in the wake of the fumes and the men who had not immediately collapsed had to mount the parapets to meet them. Only where the gas was thickest in front of part of Jim Keddie's 48th Highlanders did the line give way after a bitter fight.

L/cpl. J. D. Keddie.

Just before 4 a.m. on the 24th we managed to get a mouthful of rum each. We had no sooner got it down than the enemy started an attack, beginning with gas. They then began to shell the reserve trenches, and they did it to some tune. You could hardly get breath for the concussion! They also had the range, and the loss of life was awful, and oh, the horrors, the sights were dreadful. One poor beggar came along crying for someone to tie up his arm. Nobody seemed to care for the job, so I got hold of him and did my best. The arm was completely off up to the elbow – a fearful sight. While I was attending to him, I got a flesh wound on the head, and, Lord, did it bleed! But it wasn't sore. I'd fired about a hundred and fifty rounds by this time, and I'd sent two men to get more ammunition. I saw them coming back and they only had about thirty yards to go when one of them was shot right through the head. Well, I knew the other couldn't carry it himself, so I crawled out to give him a lift, and on my way I got it through the sole of my right foot. It wasn't very painful at the time. We got the box of ammunition to the trench somehow, then I looked for the quickest way to a First Aid Station and beat it as quick as I could. I could walk on the foot fairly well, and in fact I could sometimes do a little trot. But when I got there I found that an order had been given to retire, so they could do nothing for me.

The previous day when they had been brought up towards the line, the raw inexperienced troops of the 50th Northumbrian Division had only been intended to act as reserves. Now that every man of the reserves was needed, raw or not, they were pushed up into the salient and ordered to press on through the shelling to the front line.

L/cpl. J. Dorgan.

We suffered many casualties on the road up, many, many casualties. I remember a shell dropping when we were lying behind a hedge, and two men had both their legs taken off. One lived a few minutes, the other lived about half an hour. One was called Jackie Oliver and the other was Bob Young. Bob Young was the first to go. When he was hit he said, 'Will you take my wife's photograph out of my pocket?' He was sensible to the last and jokingly, as I thought, he kept saying to me, he says, 'Put my legs straight.' Well, he'd no legs to put straight, and I just made a movement, touched the lower part of his body. What could I do? He died with his wife's photograph in his hand.

Jackie Oliver had a brother in our Battalion and I shouted to our fellows who had to leave me with these two wounded men, 'Tell Weedy Oliver his brother's wounded.' He never recovered consciousness but eventually, some time later, Weedy Oliver came back and was with his brother when he died. No doctors available. No first aid available. I don't know where they were, because our Battalion was still advancing towards the front line. I just had to leave them. I don't know where they were buried. I never saw them or heard of them again. I had to go as fast as I could to catch up with our Battalion.

We went on and on and, as we went up the Canadians and

the Highlanders were retreating from the front line because they had been under gas. There was no gas-masks, nothing for gas casualties, and all they had on was their bandage out of their first aid kit which every soldier carried in a pocket in his tunic, and they had these bandages on their eyes and there they went staggering back. Gas never affected me and there was fellows dropping behind all the time – I must have been one of the lucky ones. We came to the reserve trenches, but we didn't recognise them as trenches, nobody in them, they were all retired. So we just jumped over, but we never reached the front line. The gas was too dense and then we had to retire. We never reached St Julien. I think we only got as far as St Jean but, wherever it was, we had to retire from there. We didn't come out of the line for four days.

The Canadians had finally 'budged' – but only some of them, only in the last resort, and only because the odds against them were not humanly possible to overcome. But, on either side of the gap in the line they had left, others like Jim Keddie were fighting on, manning the parapets with rifles, blazing machine-gun fire to break up the German ranks as they closed in ahead of them, swinging round to pour crossfire on the enemy soldiers as they attempted to advance to 'Locality C'. As soon as the situation was known in the scattered batteries every available gun joined in the fight to beat them off. The Germans took heavy punishment, but they had twenty-four Battalions against the Canadians' eight to envelop the angle of the line that ran in front of Gravenstafel and swung back in front of St Julien to Kitchener's Wood, with a dangerous gap in the eastern face where the Royal Highlanders of Canada had been forced to retire and part of the 3rd Battalion had been overrun in the first onslaught.

L/cpl. J. W. Finnimore, 3rd Bn., 1st Canadian Brig., 1st Canadian Div.

I'd only been four years in Canada when the war started. Before that I was an apprentice at Woolwich Arsenal, but times were slack and I knew perfectly well that as soon as my time was out and I reached twenty-one I would be sacked. It didn't seem worth waiting around for that, so I emigrated to Canada in 1910. Still, I considered myself to be a Canadian, though proud of my British descent, and I considered it my duty to join up. I was glad to do it.

That day, 24 April, was the worst day of my life. It started with a really violent bombardment and then – you could only call it a cloud of death when the gas came over, and this time it was directed straight at us. People were suffocating, but some were worse affected than others and the word was passed down that we were to hold on at all costs. We did our best, but first I was wounded in the leg and then, when the Germans were advancing and we got the order to retire, I couldn't move – naturally. All I can remember much later is a German soldier standing over me pointing his rifle and bayonet at my chest. It was my worst moment of the whole war because, being wounded in the leg, I couldn't get up and I couldn't walk. I thought he was going to let me have it. But he didn't. We were near a deserted farmyard and he handed his rifle to a comrade and went off into this farm and came back a few minutes later with a wheelbarrow. He put me in it and then he pushed me all the way through to their rear dressing station – and it must have been a good mile behind their lines. The German doctors and orderlies were up to their eyes with their own casualties. They couldn't do a lot for *us*. We wounded prisoners were laid down on some straw in a church hall and there we lay from Saturday to Monday. Then they put us in box-cars and took us to Paderborn in Westphalia, a journey of two or three days. They gave us a meal, and I remember thinking it was the first hot food I'd had for a week.

But the Canadians were holding the Germans at one dangerous point they had even counter-attacked, but they could not hold out indefinitely. Nor could the guns. And if the troops were forced to retire, the guns would be in danger.

Lt. Col. P. Burney, 9th Heavy Brig., RGA.

I was commanding the 9th Brigade of Heavy Artillery, consisting of the 71st Heavy Battery of four 4.7-inch guns and the 121st Battery, also 4.7-inch guns. The 121st Battery was in action at Wittepoert Farm, firing in a southerly direction. It was in the forenoon that I got a message by telephone to say that masses of Germans were advancing up the Poelcapelle to St Julien road. I kept Owen's gun teams near his farm billet, to the rear and towards the railway, and had arranged with him for his line of retreat in case of emergency. Just about 11 a.m. my adjutant, Captain Pask, came up to say that numbers of Canadians were coming back from Zonnebeke and that they were not wounded, but he could not get them to turn back, although he had threatened to shoot them! I went down and in the hall of my billet I found about half a dozen Canadians looking very pale, having choking fits and asking for water. Many others were in the road outside, and none could explain what had happened to them.

I went back to my telephone room and called up Owen, told him the situation, and I asked him to turn his guns end for end (no easy job with a 4.7-inch deep in mud), and get on top of his billet at the farm, where he would probably get a view of the Poelcapelle to St Julien road, and keep up a heavy shrapnel fire on the advancing Germans. As soon as he had used up all his shrapnel he was to report to me on the telephone, or if that was cut, to use his own discretion about retiring along our pre-arranged route.

My billet was just outside the Menin Gate and around us were two other field artillery Brigade Headquarters, and one Belgian. The enemy were bombarding Ypres with huge 17-inch Howitzers and the shells were falling mostly on the Menin Gate. Both my horses in a stable across the road had been killed and the stable set on fire, and my Adjutant was somewhat worried and wanted to know whether we had better not shift. I told him to have everything packed and put into the wagon and to be ready to move at once.

About 2 p.m. I heard that the Germans had taken St Julien and were pressing on to Wieltje. Just at that moment Owen called me on the telephone. He said that he had got a good view of the enemy on the Poelcapelle to St Julien road and had kept a heavy shrapnel fire on them until all his shells were expended. He also said that the enemy were now beyond his left rear and asked if he was to retire. I ordered him to move to his wagon lines to the other side of Ypres, as arranged. All the time these 17-inch shells had been causing havoc at the Menin Gate and our billet was being badly shaken by the explosions. The telephone room was an outbuilt room of glass used by the previous owner as a dentistry, and it was literally tumbling to pieces, so I ordered my Adjutant to move to the other side of Ypres and to wait at the Vlamertinghe crossroads until I joined him.

Shortly afterwards it got very unhealthy and I then decided to leave the billet with the two telephone operators who had remained with me. In the street I saw a passing car and hailed it. It was a Staff Officer who was going back through Ypres to Poperinghe, so I got a lift and asked if I might sit alongside the driver, because I knew the best way through Ypres when it was being shelled. As we were passing along one of the streets I heard a shell coming straight for us, so I told the driver to stop. Sure enough, a 5.9-inch burst in the line of houses about two hundred yards ahead of us and blocked the street with debris. Our car was a Ford, and I asked the driver if he could drive over the debris. He said, 'Yes,' so I replied, 'Drive like hell then, before another shell comes.' He revved up the engine and that little car made for the pile of debris and we lurched and bumped and positively *jumped* over it! We got through safely.

At the Asylum Road junction I met General Gay and told him that I had retired the 121st Battery to its wagon lines and just before leaving the Menin Gate billet had heard from Major Owen that the battery had arrived safely with the loss of only two horses killed by shrapnel on the Hooge to Ypres road just where it crosses the railway.

It had been a day of close shaves. The Germans were on the move. St Julien had been captured. The guns were retreating. Every man was in the line. At nightfall the Canadians were ordered to retire from their hard-pressed front to a position further back and the Germans moved forward exultantly into the ground they had given up. But it was not over yet. Ypres and the shrunken salient around it still held out.

Part 4

~

The Desperate Days

The green and grey and purple day is barred with clouds of dun
From Ypres city smouldering before the setting sun.
Another hour will see it flower, lamentable sight,
A bush of burning roses underneath the night.

Charles Scott-Moncrieff

Chapter 16

Until news of the battle at Ypres arrived and the Germans' infamous use of gas caused general outrage, the British public had been avidly following the progress of a sensational murder trial. George Smith was appearing at the Old Bailey on a charge of triple murder in the notorious case of the Brides in the Bath, and it had pushed even the war from the headlines of all but the most ponderous newspapers.

Spring was well under way, the fine weather brought crowds of strollers into the parks and shoppers into the streets, and shipping companies were urging war-weary people who could afford it to book up now for recuperative sea voyages to Cape Town or Madeira. Only Egypt had been struck from their agendas of peacetime destinations.

Harrods of Knightsbridge was preparing a special event to display the new spring fashions which, for one week only, would be sold at promotional prices. Recently, business in the fashion departments had been slow. It was not exactly considered unpatriotic to buy new clothes but unnecessary purchases were looked on as something of an indulgence and Harrods' customers on the whole were shopping with care and with an eye to the practical. In tune with the mood of the moment the advertisements that publicised the new spring fashions featured practical garments – light coloured coats, severely tailored in artificial silk, but in an enticing range of fashionable colours, and plain well-cut blouses in fine crêpe-de-chine – and in all the tasteful window displays there was hardly a frill or a furbelow to be seen. As a further inducement to bring customers into the store the whole event was to have a patriotic theme. In the restaurant the Royal Welsh Ladies Choir would give afternoon concerts, conducted by Madame Clara Novello-Davies, accompanied by her son Ivor Novello at the piano, and weary shoppers enjoying afternoon tea would be encouraged to purchase programmes and copies of the songs in aid of Queen Alexandra's Field Force Fund. There would also be collections for the Red Cross and, as usual, demonstrations of bandage-making and a cutting-out service for flannel bed jackets suitable for wounded soldiers and expert staff would be on hand to give advice on the selection of knitting-wool and patterns for garments for the troops. It was all nicely judged to appeal to the frivolous and the dutiful alike.

When the call came for gas-masks Harrods had several samples made up within the hour and lost no time in replacing spring fashions in a window near the Knightsbridge entrance with a display of home-made gas-masks, showing step-by-step stages of production. Inside the store a special counter was hastily rigged up to sell the gauze, the cotton wool, and tape required to make them up according to War Office instructions and members of staff gave non-stop demonstrations to show the willing public how to go about it.

A face piece (to cover mouth and nostrils), formed of an oblong pad of bleached absorbent cotton-wool about 5¼in. × 3in. × ¾in., covered with three layers of bleached cotton gauze and fitted with a band, to fit round the head and keep the pad in position, consisting of a piece of ½in. cotton elastic 16in. long, attached to the narrow end of the face pad, so as to form a loop with the pad.

These respirators should be sent in packages of not less than 100 to Chief Ordnance Office, Royal Army Clothing Department, Pimlico.

The War Office appeal for half a million gas-masks had been published in the national press and all over the country there was a run on gauze and cotton wool as Red Cross working-parties, schools, and tens of thousands of indignant individuals applied themselves eagerly to the task of making rudimentary gas masks for 'the boys at the front'. The government hoped to be able to send a hundred thousand home-made masks to France within a week. Until they got there the boys at the front would have to manage as best they could.

Emergency measures had been quickly drawn up by the Director of Medical Services and sent out in priority signals to all units. Pending the arrival of gas-masks the troops were instructed to dampen any available piece of material – a handkerchief, a sock, a flannel body-belt – and tie it across mouth and nose until the gas passed over. They believed that a solution of bicarbonate of soda would be the most effective liquid to combat the fumes and Commanding Officers were instructed to obtain supplies locally and to have the solution made up and placed at intervals in buckets or biscuit tins along the trenches. In quiet sectors of the line this instruction was faithfully carried out. At Ypres, where the battle still raged and the 'trenches' were no more than scrapes in the wavering line, it was clearly impossible. Conceding this, the Director of Medical Services advised that, in an emergency, any liquid that was to hand would give some protection against gas fumes. The men in the line, correctly interpreting this suggestion in the personal terms it implied, felt that 'to hand' was a somewhat inappropriate choice of words. But whatever method they used to combat the gas the troops were told to hang on for dear life until the gas cloud passed over, to stand fast and meet the enemy as he came on. It could be done – and the Canadians had proved it.

Although it thinned and dissipated as it went, the gas had left its mark as it travelled. Grass turned yellow. Leaves shrivelled and died. Hens lay dead in abandoned farmyards. Birds fell from the trees, and there were dead rats everywhere. Even quite far beyond the site of the attack the bloated bodies of farm animals lay swelling in the sun. No one had time to bury them. And no one had much idea how to treat the survivors of the gas attack who were carried to the dressing stations and hospitals behind the salient.

The distress of the gas victims was pitiful to see. By the time the lucky ones reached the Casualty Clearing Stations many hours after they had been gassed most had passed into the second stage. Their throats still burned; they were still coughing and gasping, incapable of speech, their chests distended and seared with agonising pain. But the retching and vomiting had passed. The yellow froth that foamed so copiously from the mouth and nostrils in the first few hours gave way to a bright viscous mucus streaked with blood from haemorrhages in the trachea, or reddish-brown where blood vessels had burst and seeped into the tissues of the lung. Now the men were exhausted and weak from lack of oxygen for the lungs had become so engorged with fluid that they swelled to twice their normal size. In the worst cases the skin turned reddish violet, and if pneumonia or pleurisy set in, as it so often did, there was small hope of recovery. Little by little men drowned in their own secretions. It was a horrible death and, try as they would, there was little doctors could do to prevent it.

The doctors and medical orderlies in dressing stations and clearing stations, and in ambulance units run by civilians – the Quakers of the Friends Ambulance Unit, the faithful nuns in the convents – were all frantically over-worked, for men wounded in the fighting and by the incessant bombardments far outnumbered the gas casualties. Stretcher-bearers working under fire performed heroic feats but, even so, men who were wounded in the costly counter-attacks where no ground was gained (or where the troops were forced back) were all too often left to fall into the hands of the Germans if they were lucky, or simply to die if they were not. It was fortunate for Jim Keddie that he

233

could fend for himself, but there were times on his long crawl back when he thought it was touch and go.

L/cpl. J. D. Keddie.

I kept going on and on in a perfect hail of bullets and shrapnel. At last I found an English gun battery. A doctor was there and he put me in a little shed on straw, took off my boot and cut off my sock and dressed the foot. He asked how far I had come and when I told him about three miles he said he did not know how I had got that length. He told me to sleep until he could find a stretcher. I must have slept for hours, but I was awakened by bursting shells, so I thought I'd better get out. But how? was the question. The battery fellows had gone, and now that my boot was off I had nothing to hold my foot together.

There was a farm about two hundred yards away. I saw people moving around so I thought if I could get that length I should be all right. I noticed an old shovel nearby so I hopped over and got hold of it, but it was more difficult than I thought, because my foot started to bleed again, and the blood was dripping through the bandages. The ground was so rough I couldn't hop without falling – and then I found I had a marsh to get over, which I knew was impossible. So here was a fine fix! I could neither go back nor forward, and shells were bursting all around, so I lay down.

Then I saw two soldiers running towards me. They carried me up to the farm and laid me in the barn, gave me some army biscuits and cheese, and a bowl of milk. It was the best they had. I lay there for a while, when, all at once, a shell crashed through the building and killed one of the men billeted there, so they said they would have to try and get me out. There was a Dressing Station not far off, and they said they could take me over, but it was very dangerous owing to the shelling.* I said I would go. I was then carried on their shoulders, and laid on the floor beside a lot more and given an injection for lock-jaw. Later I was taken to a small place outside Ypres, and at daylight next morning to Ypres itself and on by motor from there to a place out of sound of guns and put into a school. Next day I was put on the ambulance train for Boulogne.

Keddie was a fortunate soldier. Those who were more severely

---

* Number 3 Canadian Advanced Dressing Station which had been obliged to move from Hampshire Farm to Wieltje on the 22nd, had been forced to evacuate again and re-open at St Jean.

wounded or were less determined had a smaller chance, because, as the troops fell back and the fighting grew dangerously near, the Advanced Aid Posts, if they were to be of any use at all, also had to pack up and retire further and further away from the shifting line. Even the main Dressing Stations in Ypres itself were forced either to move away or be shelled out of existence. Most of them concentrated near Vlamertinghe, and others from as far back as Bailleul moved up to help them cope with the flood of casualties.

But nowhere was safe from the bombarding shells of which the enemy seemed to have such an inexhaustible supply. His big guns roared and probed, targeted on Ypres and searching for British and Canadian batteries driven back to new positions.

Sgnr. J. E. Sutton.

We pulled back across the main road and went into action behind a wood. After being fired at by enemy guns, which we could see to our rear, we went back to the other side of Potijze Wood. In the wood was a chateau, deserted but undamaged. The occupants must have been heavy champagne drinkers as there were several walls in the grounds built of empty champagne bottles. A direct hit by an enemy shell threw glass fragments a considerable distance. We were hopelessly outgunned. I could count only eight field guns and two 4.7-inch guns in our vicinity. The wood was being shelled by over twenty-four enemy guns, mostly heavies. Some additional field guns moved in, but we were still out-gunned. The enemy were using 17-inch Howitzers to shell Ypres and the shells sounded almost like freight trains as they passed over. Looking back into the city you could see several houses disintegrate when a single shell exploded.

Pte. W. Hay.

We fell back and the chateau in Potijze Wood was our rendezvous. We had one battery of field guns there belonging to the Canadians, eighteen-pounders. And there was a farm ablaze, set alight by a German shell and inside the barn were two big wagons loaded with ammunition shells, and the farm was in flames, blazing. Well, there were two wounded artillerymen, Canadians, in the farm. We had stretcher-bearers (the bandsmen were made stretcher-bearers because they couldn't fight so they were put on a much worse job. A stretcher-bearer is much worse than being in the line, carrying the wounded back under fire) – anyway there was two blokes, Edmondson and another fellow, both of them bandsmen, and they went over with the stretcher and brought these two artillerymen out. The place was blazing – any minute it could have gone up! So two of their gun limbers went in while the place was blazing and hooked up the ammunition wagons and pulled them out, and the two stretcher-bearers went up to the farmhouse and brought out a couple of artillerymen who were wounded. They got no medals for it. Later on you got medals for making a cup of tea for the captain – but not then!*

Sgnr. J. E. Sutton.

Behind our guns was the playhouse for the owner and his meal guests, servants' quarters below with a panelled room above, reached by an outside stairway. There was some beautiful cut glass, but no liquor, also a large oil painting of drinking and wenching scenes. For about a week Macdonald and I slept in the upper room. The building had a thatched roof, which was hit by an incendiary shell. We got out with our belongings in a hurry. Next day Major McDougall said to me: 'Sutton, I have cursed and damned every man in the Battery individually and collectively, and when I was foolish enough to go into a burning building to get a picture, a man from the 9th Battery came along to see I got out safely.' I did not tell the Major that Macdonald had told me that he went back to get the picture but that the 'old man' beat him to it!

Sutton and Macdonald relished the joke. There was not much else to laugh at, and the outlook was grim. In theory the guns were still restricted to firing three rounds of ammunition a day – in practice they had been firing as much as they could lay hands on. But the supplies of shells, so pitifully inadequate to start with, were sinking at an alarming rate. The gunners had done what they could, and

---

* Hay's comment was not quite fair. The Canadians had been awarded their first Victoria Cross. It was won in the aftermath of the second gas attack by Fred Hall, brother of Harry and Ed, who was a company sergeant-major in the 8th (Manitoba) Battalion. In the thick of the battle, as the battalion struggled to hold on and machine-guns sprayed the ground, Fred twice crawled out through the hail of fire to drag in wounded men who were calling for help. He made it the first time, and almost made it the second. As he lifted the wounded soldier into the trench Fred's body was ripped by machine-gun fire. The Victoria Cross was awarded posthumously.

field guns firing at close range had achieved miracle after miracle in helping the infantry beat off the enemy. But heavy guns were scarce, many were obsolete, and heavy shells were scarcer still, so that even when they had been able to pinpoint new enemy positions, their efforts were of little avail. The artillery was outnumbered and out-gunned and in the shrinking salient round Ypres the German guns were clustered round three sides, firing at short range now that their field guns had moved forward to positions on the captured ground which they were labouring night and day to consolidate. And they were consolidating fast.

The new German defences were makeshift, but they were strong and easily able, with the help of powerful artillery, to repel assault by infantry massed in numbers far greater than their own. They might have been smashed by concentrated shelling with high explosive, but there was no high explosive – only shrapnel shell, and the short sparse bombardments that preceded the counter-attacks were as likely to destroy thick wire and heavily sandbagged strong-points as a handful of gravel thrown at a brick wall. And still the counter-attacks went on. Still the ragged battalions were sent forward to wrest back the lost ground, and still they were being ripped apart in the attempt.

The Germans had no lack of heavy guns and apparently no shortage of high-explosive ammunition. Day and night, and with remorseless energy, their big guns searched the salient. Firing from artillery charts on which targets had been accurately plotted from peacetime ordnance survey maps, they shelled every farm that might possibly be defended and every chateau that might be in use as Headquarters – they shelled woods where troops or guns might be concealed – they shelled roads and crossroads to catch transport on the move – they shelled indiscriminately, in the certain knowledge that somewhere in the crowded salient each shell would make its demoralising mark. And there was no means of retaliating.

The slow-moving transport had suffered badly on the shell-racked roads. So many horses had been killed, so many weapons and ambulances reduced to matchwood, so many loads of supplies and ammunition had been lost, that lorries had to be brought up and sent dangerously close to the line to carry rations to sustain the men, bullets to feed their rifles, and the ammunition so sorely needed by the guns. They were nerve-racking journeys.

Driver Rodger Fish, Motor Transport Service, Army Service Corps.

We were just unloading inside Ypres when the bombardment commenced and we had to clear out of it as quickly as possible.

We came back next day, but an officer stopped us, and wouldn't allow us to go in. He said it simply meant suicide, but we had to take the load up as far as possible. I shall never forget the sights in that town. We had to go right through it, dodging dead bodies of men and horses. Then the worst part of the journey came – two and a half miles of open road in view of the Germans. They didn't seem to notice us till we came to the wire entanglements across the road, then they shelled us, but we got into the dug-outs till they eased up a bit, emptied the lorries, and made a dash for it. I don't suppose you have the least idea what it feels like to be close behind the firing line during a battle. As a rule, the lorries deliver to the horse transport, which is a decent way behind, but we weren't allowed to unload in case there might be a breakthrough. This was just at the time when the Canadians made their great stand, and I can tell you it was a night! Guns were going all round us, and when there was the slightest lull I could hear the Maxim and rifle fire, and from the position of the line we were in a horseshoe.

As the battle thundered on, officers in charge of ammunition columns, counting the losses of men and wagons and horses, wrestling with the difficulties of sending up ammunition to the batteries, were miserably aware that the stockpiled shells in the ammunition parks were dwindling away. Lack of transport was only part of the problem, but until more could be spared there was no possibility of replenishing supplies from reserve stock held further back on the lines of communication. And the reserve stock was meagre.

Among Sir John French's many anxieties the lack of ammunition weighed heaviest of all. For months now, and almost daily, he had fumed and raged, begged and pleaded in letters and telegrams to the War Office, pointing out with all the force he could muster that the supply of ammunition – far from meeting his previous demands – had actually diminished. And it was true, although the War Office might have justly claimed that overall supplies had, in fact, increased, if only slightly, and that the discrepancy between their calculations and those of the Commander-in-Chief arose from the fact that Sir John French based his demands on a certain number of shells per gun. He now had more guns at his disposal but guns without sufficient shells were useless. Thrust into a defensive campaign that was neither of his choosing nor his making, French was in despair. Rifle ammunition was also running dangerously low and on 25 April he shot off another protest:

The Commander-in-Chief points out that the average number of rounds per rifle on Lines of Communication has been:

January 216, February 191, March 138, and on 19th April 134. From this it will be seen that the Line of Communication reserve shows no tendency to increase, but rather the reverse, and there will be further considerable reduction when transport has been provided to carry the whole of the rounds allotted to the Field Units. The 22 million rounds for which transport at present is short will, when with field units, reduce that Line of Communication reserve from 134 to 61 rounds per rifle. 200 rounds was the figure which the Army Council agreed would be maintained.

The reserves of shells had fallen in almost the same proportion. With his back to the wall at Ypres the Commander-in-Chief could hardly be blamed for feeling impatient and aggrieved. As the days passed and the clock ticked towards the date set for Joffre's campaign in Artois which French was committed to support (the battle for which he had been so carefully husbanding reserves of the ammunition on which any hope of success would depend) he was more than aggrieved. He was furious with indignation.

At home in Britain people were equally anxious and enraged. They were not yet aware that the troops lacked ammunition – the 'shell shortage scandal' had yet to break – but they were very much aware that the Germans had descended to new depths of 'beastliness' and that the troops at Ypres were in a tight corner. Public confidence had not been shaken, the full story was not yet known, official press communiqués, though bald and brief, stressed the fact that the army was fighting back, and rousing editorials praised the Tommies, damned the Germans, and urged encouragement with impartial enthusiasm. The British Army had seen the Germans off before, and no one had any doubt that it would do so again. But it was clear that matters had taken a new and serious turn for the worse.

It was Sunday 25 April, and in churches all over the country there were prayers for peace – but it must be peace with victory. A large congregation crowded into St Clement's in Notting Hill where the Bishop of London took part in the evening service. He preached a powerful sermon and it was one close to his heart, for he had just returned from a visit to the army in France and had seen enough of the war at close quarters to realise that things were not going smoothly. He warned against the danger of 'facile optimism' and sketched the gravity of the situation – not only on the western front but on the far-off battle-line where the Germans had brought the Russians to a standstill. He stressed the paucity of information and boldly demanded facts and, although his formal text was conventionally drawn from the Bible, his theme was *stick it*. The fortitude of the army was unsurpassed and a source of justifiable pride. They were 'sticking it'. The nation must stick it too.

Father Delaere had a smaller congregation in Ypres that morning when he celebrated mass in front of twelve of the Sisters at the convent, and there was no congregation at all in the church of St Jacques, for the church was a blazing inferno. As soon as seven o'clock mass was over and he had blessed and dismissed the Sisters, the priest ran through the tumbling shells to try to help.

Father Delaere.

We got into the burning houses nearby and carried out the most important pieces of furniture. With huge efforts we managed to contain the fire and saved a few houses. But many others were demolished or fell victim to the flames in the Rue de Dixmude, Rue Jansenius and in other parts of the town. The Palais de Justice went on fire too. The Grand Place, the Leete, the surroundings of the Cloth Hall and the Rue de Dixmude were like an abandoned battlefield.

Five horses, an overturned ammunition wagon, a shattered motor ambulance, clothes scattered around, a big bundle of blankets, three bodies – a soldier and two women lying spread out miserably on the stones covered with dirt beside the pavements shattered and shell-holed.

At my request my devoted assistants Cottinie and Kerrinck, accompanied by Mademoiselle, went to lift the three bodies and carried them to a back entrance of the Cloth Hall, where I went to say prayers over them under a rain of shrapnel and had them buried.

Ypres crumbled and blazed, but for every shell that fell on the town a score were falling in the salient beyond it and long before Father Delaere had finished celebrating mass two thousand men of the 10th Brigade had been wiped out as they advanced to recapture St Julien. Most of the battalions that should have advanced with them had never received the order – and those which did had such difficulty in reaching the line that, of the fifteen battalions which were meant to be in position, only five had reached the rendezvous and even those who had were slow in advancing from the startpoint in the GHQ line through two narrow gaps in the wire. Long before they were able to spread out and deploy across the fields, machine-guns and trench mortars firing from Kitchener's Wood, from isolated farms, and from houses in St Julien, began to mow them down. The German field-guns finished the job. Their own guns stayed silent. It was full daylight. The attack had been postponed from half past three in the morning but, yet again, no news of the postponement had reached

the guns. Yet again the gunners had fired the preliminary bombardment two hours before the troops began to move. All it achieved
was to put the Germans on the alert and when the 10th Brigade
started out the Germans were waiting. Few of the leading waves
returned to tell the tale. The assault had been carried out on the
direct order of the Commander-in-Chief. It was brought to Smith-
Dorrien by a Staff Officer and it admitted of no discussion: 'Every
effort must be made at once to restore the situation about St Julien,
or the situation of the 28th Division will be jeopardised.'

The effort had been made and most of the men who made it now
lay dead or dying among the long rye grass and the newly planted
crops in the fields in front of St Julien. At 9.45 a.m. General Hull
wired GHQ with the news that the attack had failed. He added a
strong recommendation that there should be no thought of renewing
it.

The Germans did not try to press home their advantage by
pushing forward. It was fortunate that they did not for there was
little or nothing to stop them and it was to their credit that they
ceased fire as soon as the British ground to a halt and did not
interfere with stretcher-bearers moving across the open to carry in
the wounded. But the German soldiers had orders of their own and
it was not part of the day's plan to advance beyond St Julien but to
attack elsewhere on the shoulders of the salient. And to bombard,
bombard, and to go on bombarding to beat the allies into submis-
sion and open the road to Ypres. At one point observers, counting
fast, reported as many as sixty-eight explosions every minute. By
nightfall, the Germans had nibbled further into the line. Ground
had been lost and the flanks of some battalions were once again 'in
the air'. A straggle of troops – companies, half companies, odd
battalions of disparate commands – moved up or sidestepped to fill
the gaps as best they could. With only the vaguest of directions to
guide them, marching through shell-fire in the misty dark across
strange country to some indeterminate spot on the map, it was
hardly surprising that some bodies of men lost their way and
appeared at dawn in entirely the wrong place. It was fortunate that
the Germans were not alive to the precarious situation in the British
line. They made no move to advance, but they made use of the
hours of darkness to dig trenches across the ground they had gained,
to wire the new frontages and set up machine-gun posts to stop the
British in their tracks if they tried to hit back. But the shelling went
on and the clouds that hung low across the salient glowed red in the
reflection of the fires that raged in Ypres and in the villages around
it. They could be seen for miles and from the trenches near St Eloi
where the Liverpool Scottish were holding the line, Bryden McKinnell had a grandstand view.

241

Capt. B. McKinnell.

These are very trying days and certainly no rest, the news from the left is not very elevating, what little we get, and we find here that 'no news is bad news'.

The nights are like day, full moon and clear sky; and the days – well, one can only liken them to southern climes – such sunshine, wonderful sunsets and beautiful blue sky all day.

There is a continuous roar of the great battle on the left. Every now and then one of the 17-inch German shells rushes along like an express train, and though this shell is coming towards us from thirteen thousand yards away and is hitting its target in Ypres about three miles away, yet it just sounds as if it was passing along our front, while a cloud of red brick dust flies up and we can feel our dug-outs shake. Every night now we can see a fire in Ypres. So far the Cathedral tower and spires of the Cloth Hall are still standing.

Watching the flames lick into the sky McKinnell found it difficult to believe that barely three weeks ago he disturbed nesting jackdaws by climbing that very tower for a tourist's view of the countryside around. Where were the jackdaws now? What had happened to Marie the barmaid? As the air above their heads trembled in the slipstream of shells thundering towards Ypres, it was hard not to dwell on another question. When would their turn come?

Trpr. G. C. Chaplin, 1st Northants, Yeomanry.

That night another bloke and I were left with the horses not far outside Ypres, and in the distance I could see a church standing out quite clearly. About 1 a.m. the Germans started to shell the area and some shells were incendiaries. One landed in the church porch and started a blaze and in minutes the fire was roaring down the whole length of the place. I could hear the sound of the wood cracking and the glass of the windows smashing in the intense heat. Then the fire reached the tower and we waited to see what would happen next. It was fearful, a terrible thing to see. When the timbers burnt through the spire slid into the tower in showers of sparks and across the fields we could hear the clanging of the church bell as it went down with it. Moments later the whole place was a raging furnace.

The fires could not be doused or even contained, for there was no

242

water to be had. The inhabitants who still remained in Ypres were cowering in cellars hoping and praying that their houses would not catch fire or collapse in a pile of rubble that would block their escape. But Father Delaere was out and about. Someone had braved the explosions and run through the blazing streets to bring him news of casualties. He was not a man to shirk his duty and, even if Ypres was tumbling about his ears, that duty was to succour the dying and give them the last rites.

Father Delaere.

The wounded were at the old wood market. I hurried there with the nurse, and the shells never stopped falling. One woman had her head cut, another her stomach split open, and Alfred Landtsheere had a hand cut off and his knee broken. These last two were mortally wounded.

After having given what aid we could we wanted to go back home. It was dark, but one would have thought that some barbarous assassins not only boxed us in but followed us all the way through the shadows. Many shells and shrapnel exploded just metres from us and followed on our heels through rue Courte de Thourout, Grand' Place, rue St Jacques. We lost ourselves dozens of times, blinded by clouds of dust, and all round us the ground seemed paved with diamonds, for the shrapnel bullets struck the paving stones in a host of tiny scintillating stars, very bright, which sparkled all around us and seemed to spring up beneath our feet. It was very beautiful – but hardly reassuring. These evil little sprites followed us mercilessly. But we got through, and eventually Mademoiselle and I arrived safe and sound at the convent, covered with dust. Deo gratias!

All over the salient there were soldiers on the move and for the reinforcements marching into the salient the sight of Ypres ablaze was an ominous welcome.

Pte. H. K. Davis.

We set off marching towards the front on cobblestones and cobblestones are the most awkward things to march on because they're never level – one will be an inch higher, and the one before it an inch lower. You slip all over the place. To start off with, when we knew we were really going into it, we were paraded and they said, 'It's going to be a bit stiff. Anybody doesn't think he can stand it, one pace forward.' It took more pluck to do that than stand still, I can tell you, so we all stood still.

We started off just when dusk was falling and we kept going until one o'clock in the morning. Anyone who's ever done any marching knows that if the man in front takes a quarter of an inch step shorter than you, you're going to catch up and bang into him, and you've got to stop. And if he takes a quarter of an inch the other way he goes away from you and you have to run to catch him up. All the way we were either bumping or running. It's hard to explain the sound of the guns. The best way is to imagine you're walking up a clock face and you hear batteries firing on your left and your right, going *pop, pop, pop, pop,* and sometimes it was *bong, bong, bong, bong* because it was a louder battery than any of the others. We started off on this clock face, say at six o'clock, and the shells started off bursting, one at five and twenty to seven and one at five and twenty past seven, and gradually as you went on the batteries seemed to go up the scale until the shells were bursting at eleven o'clock and one o'clock, on your right and left. It was unnerving!

This march lasted all evening into the night and every now and again, something seemed to affect our eyesight and we could only walk on by the sound of men's feet in front. I thought it was some disinfectant they had been putting down on dead men and horses but of course it was gas! The whole Battalion marched over the countryside in single file. We were filling up a hole in the line and the C.O. got four of us, one man each from the four companies, and we set off to fill up the line. He dropped me as the first one as a marker for my company. There I was alone in Belgium! He had gone off with the other three and before very long there was a whizz-bang, and then another one, and *that* made me wonder whether I was standing on the skyline and Jerry could see me, so I flopped down. I've never felt so lonely in my life being all alone in Belgium. Eventually the C.O. came back with the others and we were told not to fire because they didn't know who was in front of us. So we got busy and dug ourselves in.

What I remember most is going up to the line, and Ypres was burning. I was crossing number 2 pontoon bridge across the Yser Canal, and just a bit half-right was Wipers on fire. I'll never forget it. It was wonderful. For the moment everything was quite still, no war on so to speak. There was this town on fire with flames and smoke reflected in the waters of the canal, shimmering. It was a wonderful picture. Frightening too, but beautiful. The whole place seemed to be on fire.

Earlier that evening Sir Horace Smith-Dorrien drove from Poperinghe to Hazebrouck to confront the Commander-in-Chief at his Advanced Headquarters. He made a wide detour but for much of his journey the fires of Ypres were clearly visible, flickering in the distance, glowing red against the night sky. As Commander of the Second Army, Smith-Dorrien was deeply anxious about the situation round Ypres. He was concerned by abortive counter-attacks which, in Smith-Dorrien's view, in the light of the failure of the French Army to fulfil bold promises, were not only costly but worthless. The catastrophe that morning had proved it, the virtual annihilation of the 10th Brigade was the last straw, the toll of casualties was frightful and they were men that could ill be spared. As his big staff car inched along congested country roads he brooded on the folly of throwing still more men into the maelstrom to no good purpose. The sight of soldiers on the march did nothing to relieve the mind of their Army Commander as he drove towards Hazebrouck. He was anxious above all to ascertain precisely how the Commander-in- Chief intended to make use of these reinforcements and to dissuade him if possible from dissipating their strength in more fruitless counter-attacks. Behind him, as he well knew, the Lahore Division, newly arrived, was already marching towards the line. The French had promised to launch another strong offensive, but Sir Horace Smith-Dorrien was not so sanguine as Sir John French that they would come up to scratch.

And the war was spreading. Early that morning a force of British, French and Australian troops had been landed on the shores of Gallipoli.

Chapter 17

Sir Horace Smith-Dorrien had not expected to receive a warm welcome and although the Commander-in-Chief received him with impeccable politeness the atmosphere cooled as their meeting progressed. The situation as seen by Sir John French from the eminence of headquarters differed greatly from the situation seen by the man on the spot, but the fact was that it was not possible from either point of view to get a clear idea of the position. Although the shrunken salient that contained them was only five miles deep and barely five miles wide hardly anyone knew where anyone else was. As one emergency succeeded the next and troops were detached from one brigade and hurried pell-mell to assist or reinforce another, or were bunched together piecemeal to make a counter-attack, the very structure of command was in disarray. It was meaningless in the circumstances to refer to corps or even Brigades, and the makeshift formations could only be described by the name of the senior officer in command: Geddes's force, Hull's force, O'Gowan's force. Even the Canadians now had so many 'foreign' troops attached that they could only be called 'Alderson's force'.

But it was easy for GHQ to inform a senior officer prior to an attack that a certain number of Battalions would be *'put at his disposal'*. The troops were there – somewhere – in the chaos of the salient, but they could not be marched from barracks to parade-ground as in peacetime, nor brought together as a body at some assembly point behind the lines. All telephone lines ran through Ypres and since most of them were out of action it was difficult to contact a Divisional Headquarters, let alone a Battalion Commander. The troops might be anywhere, and in the turmoil of events even a mounted man sent off to scour the ravaged salient would have little hope of finding them. All that could be done was to trust to luck – and to pluck and grim determination. There was no shortage of the last two, but luck was in short supply, and so was information. At the end of a long day's fighting, amid a ferocious bombardment, with nothing to go on but scribbled and often contradictory messages, it was difficult to judge precisely how the line stood, what troops were holding it, and how far the Germans had advanced where the line had given way.

Part of the trouble was that there were too many men and too many guns squeezed into one small area. On the map the salient no longer resembled a straggling semi-circle, it was now like a clenched fist at the end of a thick wrist – and far from being in a position to punch a knock-out blow, the Army was fighting with one hand tied behind its back. There was no space to manoeuvre and the loss of material and the mounting casualty lists were ample evidence that a large mass of troops squeezed so tightly together could do little more than provide an inviting target for the enemy's guns. Throwing them in willy-nilly to patch up the front could not staunch the flow of the German advance indefinitely, for the enemy was weaker in men but so hugely superior in firepower and lethal weapons that by merely pressing against the vulnerable salient, by biting into it bit by bit, it could only be a matter of time before it collapsed. Sir Horace Smith-Dorrien wished to reorganise the line and to withdraw the superfluous men and materials without delay. Reason told him that reinforcements could be better employed in relieving exhausted troops and manning and strengthening a shorter front that would be easier and less costly to defend. From this new line, and in due course, a well-planned and meticulously organised offensive could be launched to push the enemy back.

These were the matters he wished to discuss with the Commander-in-Chief.

Smith-Dorrien was not a man who shirked bold action when the situation demanded it. It was only a matter of months since the great retreat from Mons when Smith-Dorrien had averted possible catastrophe by turning to fight the Germans in a brilliant rearguard battle at le Cateau. He had fought it against Sir John French's specific instructions and, although the Commander-in-Chief had initially commended him, there had been an undertone of friction in their dealings ever since. Sir John French did not lend a sympathetic ear to Smith-Dorrien's views although they accorded closely with his own. But he had given his guarantee of support to General Foch and he must fulfil that promise by allowing the French every chance to fulfil theirs. If the French offensive succeeded and they managed to recapture the ground they had lost, it would restore the situation in the salient more quickly than any other course of action, and, in the view of the Commander-in-Chief, speed was of the essence. With his next offensive looming close, he was especially anxious that the salient should be 'quietened down' before it took place. It was perfectly possible, he informed Smith-Dorrien, that the Germans had got wind of the new plan and were merely attacking here in the north in an effort to thwart it. The fighting at Ypres must be concluded – and soon. If the French did *not* succeed, he conceded, it might well be necessary to fall back and tighten the line, but meanwhile, and he stressed the fact, ground must be given up only in the most extreme circumstances – and not at all if it could possibly be avoided. The French must have their chance, even if it was a gamble. 'After all,' he added, 'it was the French who got us into this mess. It's up to them to get us out.'

Smith-Dorrien could only stifle his misgivings and acquiesce, but he was far from happy and, on his return to Poperinghe, a message from General Putz did not lighten his heart, for it seemed that Putz did not share the view of the British Commander-in-Chief that it was 'up to the French' to retrieve the situation with a little help from the British. He proposed to attack at 5 p.m. next day. Two French divisions were already in the line and, for the purposes of the assault, Putz proposed to augment them by less than a whole division.* In the view of General Smith-Dorrien a total of seventeen Battalions was extremely unlikely to achieve a decisive result. He doubted, indeed, if they would succeed in retrieving any ground at all. But the orders of the Commander-in-Chief had been categorical. Reluctantly, and with many qualms, he was forced to commit his troops and send out his own orders for the British to attack on the right of the French. A general plan had already been drawn up in the course of a meeting that morning, but in Smith-Dorrien's opinion the timing was premature. His reinforcements would have no time to rest, still less to prepare and reconnoitre the ground before they were flung into battle. There was worse to come. Well after midnight another message arrived from General Putz, and the news that he had put zero hour forward by almost three hours to five past two in the afternoon came as a bombshell.

By the time his Advanced Headquarters could be contacted the Commander-in-Chief had already retired for the night but at Smith-Dorrien's insistence he was brought to the telephone. With this latest development Smith-Dorrien's fears had increased ten-fold and he spoke eloquently and at length, repeating all he had said earlier and more. He expressed his outrage at the paltry numbers the French proposed to engage, he reiterated his reluctance to fling in weary troops in the most unpropitious circumstances, he begged the Commander-in-Chief to intervene. Their conversation was not a happy one and Sir John French soon cut it short. He gave Smith-Dorrien a direct order to proceed as planned. The attack must go ahead and there was no more to be said.

By the time new orders could be drafted and sent out to the artillery and the scattered infantry it was past two o'clock in the

---

* One of its Brigades had not yet arrived.

morning. The attack was now barely twelve hours away and the fresh troops who were destined to make it had not yet begun to make their way to the line.

The Lahore Division was in bivouacs near Ouderdom, some ten kilometres south-west of Ypres. They had marched thirty miles from Bethune to get there and, undisturbed by the clamour of the distant bombardment, most of them were sleeping like logs. The new orders meant that by 5.30 in the morning they would be on the road again, setting off at half hour intervals to march on Ypres and out to the salient beyond.

Like the Meerut Division the Lahore Division was low in numbers, weakened by sickness, and casualties at Neuve Chapelle had left wide gaps in the ranks and Indian reinforcements could not easily be brought from half-way round the world. The 4th Battalion of the London Regiment was attached to the Ferozepore Brigade to strengthen it, and although they were not the first battalion of the Brigade to set out that morning, Frank Udall thought it was early enough. His feet were still killing him.

Sgt. F. G. Udall, MM (2 Bars), 1/4th (City of London) Bn. (Royal Fusiliers) (TF), Lahore Div.

The day before we left we were all issued with overcoats and a new pair of boots, because they wanted to get rid of these stores and the Quartermaster must have reckoned that the easiest way of carrying them north was to issue them to *us* and let *us* wear them. We moved off on a warm April morning to march from Neuve Chapelle to Ypres and with new boots our feet were so sore and bleeding that there were many, many stragglers. We couldn't *help* but fall out! A good many Belgian women came out of their cottages and bathed our feet and bandaged them up as we sat at the side of the road, and there were so many dropped out that they eventually had to send lorries to pick us up and take us the rest of the way to Ouderdom Camp. The following morning the Connaught Rangers left to go to the line and a couple of hours afterwards, we followed them and marched on to Ypres. We eventually arrived and my feet were still sore, so I fell out again, had a rest and after a bit I struggled to my feet. In the Ypres residential part I looked into a house and saw a table was already laid for breakfast, and so people evidently must have scurried and just left it. They were shelling the place, so you couldn't blame them. Further on I came to a jeweller's shop and the front must have been just blown away. You could see all the stuff lying there in the rubble. Well, there was a Connaught Ranger in front of me. He'd already helped himself and I was about to do the same when a military policeman came along and told me to clear off.

Eventually I caught up with the battalion in an orchard and there was a Quartermaster Sergeant there with his battalion stores. He was giving the stuff away – all of his battalion's rations! He said he hadn't seen his Battalion for three days so we might as well have the stuff. I remember him handing out the tins of Maconochie rations and also big gross boxes of Bryant and May's matches. The Colonel spoke to us while we were resting and said that the Germans had sprung a gas attack and might do it again. He told us, if that happened we should piss on a handkerchief and tie it round our mouths. He said that would do the trick. Then we got orders to move and we started off towards the front. The Connaughts were already in the front line and we were going into support. When we arrived, a few of the boys still had the stuff they'd got from the Quartermaster, but most of us had chucked it away long before.

The Lahore Division was a mixed bag. There were tall Pathans from the north-west territories around Peshawar and Rawalpindi, stocky Gurkhas from the highlands of Nepal, bearded Sikhs from the Punjab. There were soldiers from Bhopal, men of the Frontier Force and, fighting alongside them in their British battalions, Irishmen in the Connaught Rangers, Merseysiders in the King's Liverpools, Scots in the Highland Light Infantry, a Lancashire contingent in the Manchesters, and the Londoners of the Royal Fusiliers. Together they were to launch out from the northern wall of the salient against the German line on Mauser Ridge. And they were to do more than capture it. Advancing with the French troops on their left and Hull's force of 'odd detachments' on their right, they were to batter on and push the Germans back to Langemarck, while the French, advancing from just east of the canal, were to capture Pilckem village on the way.

In the course of the morning Sir John French took the trouble to telephone a personal message of encouragement to Second Army Headquarters. The Commander-in-Chief wished it to be known that he had no doubts about the successful outcome of the offensive as the enemy could not be *'very strong or numerous, as he must have lost heavily and be exhausted'*. These optimistic words did nothing to relieve Smith-Dorrien's anxiety, and there certainly was no time to pass them on to the troops. It was now twenty minutes past eleven and, if all had gone well, even the tail-end of the Lahore Division should now be moving into position ready to deploy.

Major F. A. Robertson, 59th Scinde Rifles, Frontier Force, Lahore Div.

We had orders to make a counter-attack in the direction of St Julien. I had recently been through a course of bombing and had been told to take command of the bomb party of my regiment, but I had no time to put the men through their paces before we marched. Those were the days of frequent changes in the pattern of bombs. As we prepared to deploy I served out the Battye bombs to the sepoys and they looked at them with dismay. I asked them what was wrong and at last a young Sikh remarked, 'But, Sahib, we have never seen a bomb with a fuse like this before! We're used to lighting ours with matches.' So that was a pleasant situation, I must say, when we were just going into action!

It was a bad start, but there was nothing to be done except to give the hastiest of demonstrations and advice, and to hope for the best.

It took a long time to spread the troops of three brigades into formation. They were still well back from the start-line but, apart from the three battalions in the lee of Hilltop Ridge, they were well within view of the Germans, and German aeroplanes, swooping low above them, had shown particular interest in such a large gathering of troops, and buzzed off busily northwards to report that an attack was underway. When the preliminary bombardment started up it could hardly be heard against the roar of enemy guns and the screech of enemy shells targeted on the infantry as they waited to move.

Under cover of the bombardment the infantry moved forward to jumping-off positions. At two o'clock precisely to the minute they began to advance. It was the only movement of the afternoon that went according to plan.

Major F. A. Robertson.

The idea had got about that the German trenches were two hundred yards away. When our front line went over the top they found that there was anything from twelve to fifteen hundred yards to go. Our artillery preparation had not at all shaken the nerves of the Germans, and the two British and four Indian regiments who led the way were absolutely mown down by rifles, machine-guns, and artillery of every calibre. The slaughter was cruel. It was men against every machine that frightfulness could devise. My bombers never even got to grips!

251

It was a miracle that any men did manage to cross that wide shallow valley exposed to a torrent of fire from the German line on the rising ground beyond. Even the men who had started from behind the Hilltop Ridge were mown down in rows as they cleared the skyline. Heavy German Howitzers now had the range and whole platoons were being knocked out by a single massive shell. All across the shallow valley the dead and the dying were tossed into the air and dropped in mangled heaps.* But survivors of the leading waves pressed on until they were little more than a stone's throw from the German wire a hundred yards beyond. A little to their left, where the French were attacking, luck was on the side of the Germans, for gas cylinders had been placed in front of it in preparation for an attack of their own. Like the Canadians four days earlier, the soldiers could see gas clouds passing across French troops, but this time, just as the gas enveloped their leading line, the wind shifted direction and slowly rolled the gas from west to east suffusing the ground where British and Indian soldiers were crouched on the slope beneath Mauser Ridge. All along the line the advance broke up.

Sgt. F. G. Udall, MM (2 Bars).

The Connaught Rangers went over first and we were waiting for the word to go forward, but within a few minutes we saw the Connaught Rangers leaving the line and coming back gassed. They were in no sort of order, and there was greenish colour about their clothing and they were coughing and staggering and some of them were dropping down on the way. I remember hearing an NCO shouting at them, 'Don't let the Territorials beat you!' And many of the Connaught Rangers actually turned round and went back again to their line. Then it came to our turn to advance, so over we went and for the first time we used the entrenching tools for what they were made for and we dug ourselves in within a few hundred yards of Jerry with our entrenching tools. This was at Buffs Road, Hilltop Farm. But the attack seemed to have withered out and we were withdrawn after that. In the evening they came round for burial parties and I volunteered. We buried nine or ten who'd been hit the previous day while we were getting into position. And we'd left plenty more than that behind us in the line!

But the handful of survivors of the Manchesters and Connaughts,

---

* According to German records three Howitzer batteries near Langemarck fired between them at least two thousand rounds that afternoon.

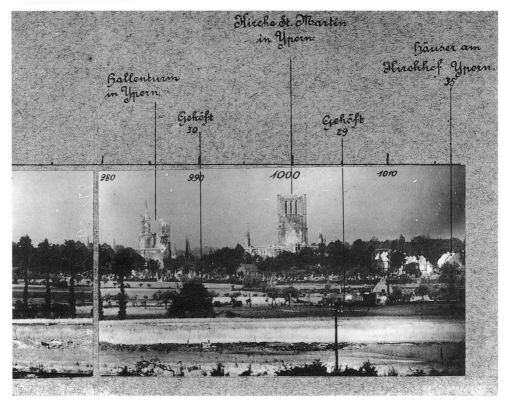

Panorama of Ypres from the German lines, marked with artillery ranges (*Imperial War Museum*)

Ypres, April 1915. 'There were empty spaces in the streets, and heaps of rubble where a house once stood. The central tower of the great Cloth Hall blackened by fire, lacked two of its four spires . . .' (*Imperial War Museum*)

Ypres, July 1915. The safest billets for miles. The soldiers live like troglodytes in the casemates and passages in the old ramparts (*Imperial War Museum*)

Ypres, 1915. 'All of us are deeply dispirited. After battling for six months against all these adversities, we must now resign ourselves to abandoning all our belongings. What will be left when we return?' Aimé van Nieuwenhove (*Imperial War Museum*)

Ypres, 1915. Dead horses in the Cloth Hall Square. 'I have got permission to stay with ten men burying the dead, interring horses. We are virtually alone.' Father Camille Dalaere (*Imperial War Museum*)

Ypres, April 1915. The rue de Lille, The gable of Aimé van Nieuwenhove's house is on the right. The photograph is taken from the Post Office (*Imperial War Museum*)

Ypres, rue de Lille. 'It was a dreadful sorrow to find nothing but burnt-out shells and charred walls. The gable end of our house was still standing, as well as some of the inner walls.' Aimé van Nieuwenhove, July 1915. The ruins of his house are on the right of the photograph (*Imperial War Museum*)

Ypres. In the shadow of the new Cathedral the remnants of statuary from the old church still stand in the cloister garden

Ypres, 1915. The altar still stands inside the ruined cathedral (*Imperial War Museum*)

April 1915. The bombarded cathedral (*Imperial War Museum*)

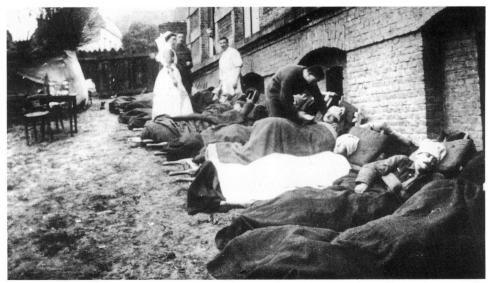

'They took us through Ypres to Vlamertinghe and when we got there, the whole street as far as your eye could see was nothing but stretchers and blankets and walking wounded with blankets over their shoulders and half a dozen doctors working flat out.' Private J. Vaughan, Princess Patricia's Canadian Light Infantry (*Imperial War Museum*)

Sun-dappled trenches at Sanctuary Wood, much visited by tourists – but, according to veterans, approximating the front line of 1915

Memorial on the Bellewaerde Ridge and behind it the ground on which Princess Patricia's Canadian Light Infantry made their stand

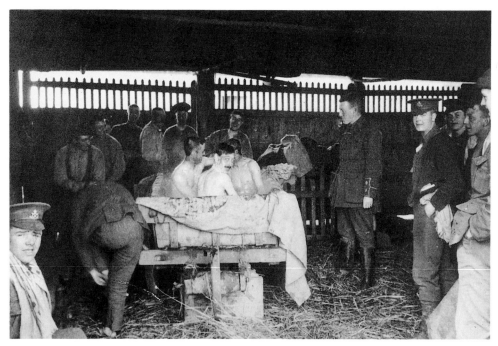

The 6th South Staffordshires solved the bath shortage by lining a farm cart with a tarpaulin and filling it with water from the farmyard pump (*Imperial War Museum*)

'Training, training, training, always bally-well training . . .' Kitchener's army were of the opinion that they had dug more trenches at home than there were in France. The hill behind the bridge is covered in them (*Imperial War Museum*)

On 18 June, Waterloo Day, Sir Evelyn Wood VC inspected the Inns of Court Battalion on Kitchener's Field at Berkhamsted to mark the fact that 2,000 of its members had been commissioned since the outbreak of war (*Imperial War Museum*)

The 7th Battalion Royal Scots at their last pre-war camp – many were to lose their lives in the troop train disaster of May 1915

Marching to Newtonards station, 2 July 1915, 13th Battalion Royal Irish Rifles
en route to France

Sikhs and Pathans, still clung to the ground they had reached close up to the German wire. The slightest movement brought a fresh tornado of fire from machine-guns on the ridge. But they tended their wounded as best they could. At night guides were sent out to bring the survivors back. More than fifteen hundred casualties were left behind – and most of them were dead. The Colonels of three battalions had been killed and two other Commanding Officers wounded. The Connaught Rangers had lost all their officers. So had the Pathans. But, once again, the Germans made no attempt to advance.

Major F. A. Robertson.

It seems that the Germans were expected to walk into Ypres that day, and indeed there was little enough to stop them. But whenever you sprung a surprise on Fritz he would pause while his staff did a bit of thinking. Here he was being attacked by Indians who ought to have been some fifty miles away, as they must have known. An obvious case for consideration! So they stayed where they were and lost their last chance of walking in.

It was an impossibility to take the German trenches but the British line *was* pushed forward and the Germans were held back. The Lahore Division was rallied and for four days, sometimes by ourselves and sometimes working with other troops, we pressed against the German lines. The enemy never advanced one inch during that time and by the end of it the defence had been reorganised and Ypres was safe.

Later they were to call it the Battle of St Julien and in the aftermath of the failure of the first day's fighting Sir Horace Smith-Dorrien took no satisfaction in the fact that he had been right. The absolute necessity of reorganising the line was now occupying his mind to the exclusion of all else. As he had anticipated, the French had failed miserably for, apart from the French troops on the immediate left of his own, the attack that had been promised and intended along the remainder of the French line had never got off the ground, and once again the British had suffered the consequences and footed the bill, as he saw it, for the French. He was not unsympathetic. He knew full well that, just as he himself was being pressed by Sir John French, General Putz was being pressed by Foch, and he knew too that, regarding the reinforcements he had been led to expect and the guns that had been promised to replace the seventy he had lost, Putz had been badly let down. But it was not good enough. The French planned to renew the assault next day and Smith-Dorrien took it upon himself to make it clear to General Putz that he did not intend to order any further offensives in his support unless and until Putz was in a position to make a very much more substantial contribution – and to make it effectively. Then he sat down to compose a longer and more difficult communication to General Headquarters. As etiquette demanded, he addressed it to Sir William Robertson, Chief of the General Staff, but its message was intended for the Commander-in-Chief.

Smith-Dorrien began by outlining the events of the day and, although he scrupulously reported some isolated minor successes as well as the major failure, he was human enough to succumb to the temptation of reminding GHQ of the views he had expressed at Hazebrouck and that he had not anticipated 'any great results'. The French intended to renew the offensive a few hours hence, and the net result of General Putz's latest dispositions, Smith-Dorrien pointed out, would be to add just one battalion to the existing force east of the canal.

> I want the Chief to know this, as I do not think he must expect that the French are going to do anything very great – in fact, although I have ordered the Lahore Division to cooperate when the French attack at 1.15 p.m., I am pretty sure that our line tonight will not be in advance of where it is at the present moment. I fear the Lahore Division have had very heavy casualties and so, they tell me, have the Northumbrians, and I am doubtful if it is worth losing any more men to regain the French ground unless the French do something really big.

Smith-Dorrien was ignorant of the fact that the Commander-in-Chief had already complained to his staff about Smith-Dorrien's 'wordy' missives and messages. Already he had filled several pages and he had not yet come to the purpose of his letter. That purpose was finally to convince the Commander-in-Chief of the need to withdraw the troops and tighten the line as speedily as was practicable. He reminded GHQ that the Germans' guns dominated the salient, that the shelling was intense and that Poperinghe, as well as Ypres, was now within their range. Barely two hours ago his own report centre had been hit by splinters from a shell exploding too close for comfort, and all the approach roads of the salient were constantly swept by shell-fire. If the French were not going to make a big push (and he made no secret of the fact that he was more sceptical than ever about their chances of doing so) 'the only line we can permanently hold and have a fair chance of keeping supplied would be the GHQ line passing just east of Wieltje and Potijze with a curved switch through Hooge and Sanctuary Wood to join on to

254

our present line about a thousand yards north-east of Hill 60.' He added several paragraphs of detailed map references to outline precisely the line he had in mind – a line that would reduce the salient to a quarter of its present size. And he continued with a certain boldness: 'I intend tonight if nothing special happens to re-organise the new front and to withdraw superfluous troops west of Ypres.'

It was clear that in his own mind Smith-Dorrien fully expected that 'nothing special' would happen as a result of the day's fighting – and he went further. They must consider the possibility that the Germans might break through the French lines and gain ground west of the canal. If that happened there would be no alternative for the British but to give up Ypres entirely and the whole of the salient beyond it.

At this point it may have seemed to Smith-Dorrien that he was giving the impression that he himself was pessimistic, for he hastened to assure the chief-of-staff that this was not the case and attempted to enliven the remaining pages of his voluminous letter with an air of optimism. He referred with enthusiasm to the 'big offensive elsewhere' which he knew was dear to the heart of the Commander-in-Chief, and asserted his own belief that it would *do more to relieve this situation than anything else*. He passed on the latest news, reported by the cavalry, that the French had recaptured Lizerne, and that, as a result of his own protest (which he had gone into in detail a dozen pages earlier), General Putz was putting an extra regiment into the line for that day's attack. 'We are to assist with heavy artillery fire,' he added, 'and the Lahore Division is only to advance if they see the French troops getting on.'

By the time Smith-Dorrien signed and sealed his letter it was well into the small hours of the morning and the staff officer who would motor with it to Hazebrouck was unlikely to get there much before dawn.

It was bright moonlight and eight miles away on the edge of the salient the outlines of Mauser Ridge, of Hilltop Ridge, of the jagged spire of the church in St Julien stood out sharp and black against the light of the clear sky. In the shadows below, stretcher-bearers were still on the move among the debris of the battle, picking their way between the deeper shadows of hunched and silent corpses, and keeping their ears pricked for some faint cry or groan or whisper that would guide them to a wounded man. In a few hours' time the guns would start up and the infantry would line up again and attempt to advance across this ground still littered with the bodies of yesterday's dead.

Weary and worried Sir Horace Smith-Dorrien stretched out on a camp bed to snatch a brief rest before the rigours of the day. He had done his best. All he could do now was hope that the letter now on its way to GHQ would induce the Commander-in-Chief and his staff to sanction his proposals. That hope, and with it most of his personal hopes and expectations, was soon to be shattered at a stroke.

Sir John French was furious. But it could hardly have been the content of Smith-Dorrien's letter which caused him to fulminate against its author, for the proposal to withdraw to a safer line made sound military sense and in his heart of hearts the Commander-in-Chief was of the same opinion. But it was the tone of the letter that incensed him, with its apparent lack of confidence, its gloomy view of the French and its lukewarm commitment to the support that the Commander-in-Chief, albeit conditionally, had assured Foch would be forthcoming.

Faced as he was with a triple dilemma, Sir John French was in no mood to be trifled with and, shortly after luncheon, Sir William Robertson sent a telephone message to Smith-Dorrien that made this crystal clear. It was couched in lofty language but it was intended to leave Smith-Dorrien in no doubt that his unfavourable view of the situation was not accepted by the Commander-in-Chief, and it forcibly reminded him that he had more than enough troops and ample reserves to assist the French and trounce the Germans. Smith-Dorrien must 'act vigorously' to assist and cooperate with the French and must attack simultaneously 'as previously instructed' with every gun and every man he had.

This message was more than a slap in the face. It was a body blow. Reading between the lines it was plain that his lengthy letter had caused grave offence, that Smith-Dorrien's analysis, so painstakingly set out, was interpreted unequivocally as lack of zeal, and that the conditional support he proposed to contribute to the latest French counter-offensive amounted to an intolerable contravention of the personal orders of the Commander-in-Chief. So that there should be no possible doubt of his intentions a Staff Officer was sent from GHQ to Poperinghe to repeat the orders verbally and make absolutely sure that Smith-Dorrien understood that they were categorical.

Major-General Perceval was a senior Staff Officer and as sub-chief of the General Staff was second in importance only to Sir William Robertson, but he was junior in rank and seniority to General Smith-Dorrien. He could hardly have relished his task and, in the circumstances, it was doubtless an awkward interview – Smith-Dorrien resentful and icily courteous and Perceval stiff with distaste for an embarrassing task. But worse was to come – and even the signallers at Second Army Headquarters knew it before the Army Commander. Perhaps in error, but not impossibly with calculated disregard for Smith-Dorrien's feelings, the wire from

GHQ was not encoded but was sent 'in clear' for all to read:

> Chief directs you to hand over forthwith to General Plumer the command of all troops engaged in the present operations about Ypres. You should lend General Plumer your Brigadier-General, General Staff, and such other officers of the various branches of your staff as he may require. General Plumer should send all reports direct to GHQ from which he will receive his orders.

It was repeated, also 'in clear', to the V Corps Commander, and Smith-Dorrien's subordinate, Lieutenant-General Sir Herbert Plumer.

It was a humiliating insult and Sir Horace Smith-Dorrien was deeply wounded. Within two hours he left his advanced report centre and drove back to Second Army headquarters. After the hustle and bustle of Poperinghe the chateau seemed very quiet. Most of his staff had already gone to V Corps and there was precious little of his army left – only a single corps in the line south of the salient. He was unmoved by the news that the French counter-offensive had failed again. In the early hours of the morning he had written to GHQ: 'I am pretty sure that our line tonight will not be in advance of where it is at the present moment.'

And he had been right.

Chapter 18

Lieutenant-General Sir Herbert Plumer was now master of the Ypres salient and so that there should be no room for ambiguity GHQ announced that the conglomerate force that had passed into his command would henceforth be known as 'Plumer's force'. Plumer was no intriguer and his appointment had come as a complete surprise, but the fruits of Smith-Dorrien's efforts fell promptly into his hands and did a good deal to lighten his onerous task for, although Sir John French had dismissed Smith-Dorrien almost out of hand, he had not dismissed his assessment or his suggestions. That evening the removal of 'superfluous men and materials' from the salient began, just as Smith-Dorrien had proposed, and the instructions that reached Plumer later the same evening, while they ordered him to consolidate his present line, also directed him to prepare to withdraw to a line closer to Ypres.

The failure of the latest French venture had put things in a new light and early next morning a note from Sir William Robertson warned Plumer that 'in all probability' it would be necessary to begin to take measures for withdrawal that night. Sir John French had made up his mind and he drove to Cassel to inform General Foch. Foch was far from pleased. In the course of a long discussion he urged the Commander-in-Chief to change his mind, or at least to agree once more to postpone his retirement and give the French troops one more chance to retrieve their lost ground. Foch was very persuasive. In the face of his arguments – and they were many – Sir John French pointed out in vain that his troops were tired, that his casualties were large and that resources were being used up which could not be spared in the light of 'the scheme further south'. Foch out-argued and out-manoeuvred him at every turn. He pointed out the tactical disadvantage of holding a line on lower ground overlooked by the enemy and insisted that retirement would be an admission of weakness that would simply invite the enemy to attack to push the allies even further back and possibly capture Ypres itself. He made much of the 'moral ascendancy' that would inevitably pass to the Germans. He admitted previous failures – admitted even that the attack planned for that same day might 'not be important' – but a large force of heavy artillery was expected hourly. Tomorrow they *would* succeed! There was no doubt of it – but they would succeed only if the British supported them unstintingly. Sir John French gave in, though not without misgivings. As soon as he had driven off, as if sensing his ambivalence, Foch drafted a letter to GHQ to summarise their discussion and to drive home the point that, rather than ordering retirement, a retirement should be positively forbidden. In conclusion he begged the British Commander-in-Chief to 'be good enough to keep to his present intention and to support the French offensive to retake the Langemarck region at all costs'. The last nine words of this typewritten letter had been heavily underlined by General Foch himself.

In Sir John French's absence another communication had arrived at GHQ, this time from General Plumer, and, although it formally confirmed acceptance of his new responsibilities, it pulled no punches with regard to the situation in the field. He gave his opinions more concisely than General Smith-Dorrien, but they were nevertheless identical to his. The present line could not be permanently held. Further attacks could only result in more loss of life and the longer the retirement was delayed the more difficult and costly it would be. Plumer accepted that 'the French should be given a certain time to regain their trenches' before the retirement began but, like Smith-Dorrien, he was prepared to give only artillery support unless French troops were seen to be making 'appreciable progress'.

It was difficult to argue with this line of thought, but Sir John French had been swayed by Foch more than he might have admitted and Foch had painted a lurid picture of the consequences of retirement, emphasising the possibility that it might set in motion a train of events that would lose them Ypres itself. And that would be unthinkable.

Sir John French had not been infected or influenced by the belief, passionately held throughout the French Army, that every centimetre of stricken France should 'at all costs' be wrested from the grip of the hated invader and defended to the last man. His long military experience rebelled at the very thought and he knew full well that the cost and effort of clinging on to an awkward salient in defence of a ruined city was worthless in military terms. But nevertheless there were cogent reasons why the loss of Ypres would be disastrous.

If the British Army was not to risk diminishing its stature in world opinion it badly needed a decisive victory which, in the view of the Commander-in-Chief, his part in Joffre's offensive would supply. It could certainly not afford a defeat, and the loss of Ypres – even the minor retirement that commonsense dictated – would be looked on as defeat by the rest of the world. The Germans would see to that.

Every German communiqué since the start of the war had trumpeted even the paltriest gain as a great victory and presented the slightest loss by the British as a resounding defeat. In the last fateful week the names of inconsequential Flemish villages and even of hamlets that were little more than crossroads – Langemarck, Pilckem, St Julien, Gravenstafel – had appeared in German communiqués as victories comparable to Austerlitz and Waterloo. If Ypres had to be abandoned it was excruciating to envisage how the enemy would crow!

The Germans were greatly given to crowing and, just as the British delighted in caricatures of sauerkraut-guzzling Germans, the effete Englishman was a figure of fun in Germany and this character was the leitmotiv of a smash-hit comedy that had been playing for months in a score of theatres in cities as far apart as Hamburg and Breslau, Munich and Stettin. In Frankfurt, where no theatre was large enough to contain the audiences clamouring to see it, it had transferred to the amphitheatre of the Circus Schumann which could seat four thousand people. It was packed out almost every night. With heavy irony the play was entitled *Wir Barbaren* (*We Barbarians*) and the comedy leaned heavily on ridiculing tales of atrocities committed by the German Army which had been widely published abroad and reprinted in the German press. No one in Germany believed them. This was, after all, the land of Schiller, Schumann, Goethe, home of all those *Gemütlich* homely virtues, so foreign to the natures of the cold English and dissolute French but dear to the hearts of the honest burghers of the Fatherland.

The piece opened on a typically domestic scene with mother, father, their daughter and her sweetheart, manservant and cook, all united in simple domestic bliss. Then a lusty postman arrives with the shocking news that the Fatherland's foes have simultaneously and treacherously declared war on their beloved homeland. Cue for the strains of '*Deutschland, Deutschland über Alles*' to come drifting through the window and the tramp of marching feet from the street. Mother, starting up in horror and, for some remarkable reason, speaking in English, exclaims: 'Ze English gentlemens – can it be?' The men on stage proceed to stamp and snarl, repeating her words many times in tones of scorn, 'Ze gentlemens! Ze gentlemens!' English, of necessity, then gives way to German for a series of impassioned speeches extolling the justice of the German cause, followed by a rousing rendition of 'The Watch on the Rhine'. The audience delightedly joins in, and the curtain falls to resounding cheers. But this is nothing by comparison to the scenes that follow. They drip with lofty sentiments and blatant sentimentality that reduces susceptible members of the audience to tears – not least in a trench scene depicting the sufferings of the noble and tender-hearted troops. For now a shivering prisoner is brought in, cowering in abject terror of the 'barbarians', grovelling and pleading for his life. He naturally receives a kindly, reassuring welcome – he is given food (he has not eaten for days!). He is showered with smiles and sympathy and wrapped in the overcoat of a noble German soldier who is only too happy to give it up and shiver in the prisoner's stead in the freezing cold. Even this is tame stuff. Presently a postman arrives in the trench with a bundle of newspapers, eagerly handed round. It must contain a good few back numbers because the headlines bawled out in turn by the excited troops encapsulate the triumphs of many months. *'Russians defeated by von Hindenburg!'* (Audience explodes, shrieking, 'Hoch, Hindenburg! Napoleon Hindenburg! Hurrah!') *'Belgrade fallen!'* (More vociferous cheers, this time for Austria.) *'Belgium crushed!'* (The cheering almost raises the roof.) *'Line broken at Ypres. French and English in disarray. Our troops advance.'* (The house explodes in a frenzy of patriotic fervour.) When the play ends with many encores of patriotic songs the audience has reached such a pitch of euphoria that almost every night the house lights have to be dimmed before they can be induced to go home.

Although British audiences took their pleasures less vociferously, patriotism was not absent from the London stage. The play *Alsace* which, before the war, had been banned by the Lord Chamberlain for fear of giving offence to Germany, was now enjoying a successful run at the Court Theatre. This, naturally, showed the other side of the coin, but its special interest lay in the script, translated from the French and hardly altered from the pre-war version. It highlighted the hatred that had been simmering in France since it had lost Alsace and Lorraine to Germany forty years before. It also revealed that the French had long foreseen the war that would restore the lost territories to France.

This was no comedy but, like the German play, it portrayed a family circle of father, mother, son and fiancée, but with one difference – the fiancée is German and, although the son has been forced into service as a reservist in the German Army, the family remains fiercely loyal to France. War erupts. The German Army marches into Mulhouse en route to destroy France and this throws the parents into panic. Will their son go and fight for the Kaiser? Where do his loyalties lie? With the German girl he loves or with his true homeland?

The question is not resolved until the last act. Scene: a street in Mulhouse. Sound effects off-stage: heavy marching feet and raucous German voices. The boy and his sweetheart look on as a dozen spike-helmeted soldiers, the vanguard of a regiment, march into the street. The sound of marching reaches a crescendo as if trampling on the very soul of France, and the boy, unable to resist the temptation, shouts out fervently, 'Vive La France!' The furious Germans raise their rifles and shoot him on the spot and he staggers home bleeding and dying to his sad but proud parents. 'Truly,' declaims the mother, 'the love of country is stronger than the love of woman.' The curtain falls on a touching tableau as the parents bend sorrowfully over the corpse wrapped in the flag of France. The orchestra strikes up the 'Marseillaise'. Loud applause and a tear or two from the audience which leaves the theatre in a buzz of righteous indignation.

Such theatricals in Britain, as in Germany, were commercially successful in their appeal to the popular mind but they were meaningless in terms of the real propaganda war and its efforts to influence international opinion and impress the neutral nations. There were more subtle ways of achieving such results and everything that came out of Germany, in the form of reports by neutral journalists and diplomats as well as from official sources, was weighed up, considered, and frequently given credence. In Sir John French's opinions this was too often the case at the War Office whose frequent requests for 'clarification' thinly concealed a suspicion that his reports took too rosy a view and showed an irritating tendency to prefer the German version of events to his own. This did nothing to improve the stormy relations between the Commander-in-Chief and the General Staff in London, and it was yet another reason for his reluctance to be seen as the man who abandoned Ypres. But although such a cataclysmic failure would not be easily forgiven, much more than personal honour was at stake. There were overwhelming strategic and political considerations why such an event would be a disaster.

Ypres was the focal point of the last small corner of Belgium which had not been overrun by the German Army. To the south, the French border was a mere ten miles from its gates. Westwards the French port of Dunkirk was barely twenty miles distant, a half hour's drive from Calais down the coast, and Calais, on a clear day, was within sight of Dover twenty miles across the English Channel. If Ypres went it was not impossible that the German Army would be able to occupy these vital ports in a matter of weeks. And, moreover, if Ypres went Belgium would have gone too – 'gallant little Belgium', and it was to save gallant little Belgium that Great Britain and her Empire had gone to war. Apart from its military significance, which could hardly be over-estimated, defeat in Belgium would have a catastrophic effect on opinion in neutral nations – Italy, Bulgaria, Rumania, Greece – still teetering on the verge of entering the war and just as likely to throw in their lot with one side as the other.

Belgium must be held. Therefore Ypres must be held. And that was that.

Miraculously the German bombardment had tailed off. As quiet days succeeded peaceful nights people in Ypres emerged bleary-eyed from cellars and began to creep warily about the streets between crumbling walls and smouldering embers, fetching water, foraging for food. A few shops opened up. They had little to sell, but a few dry-goods and provisions remained and one baker had managed to produce a batch of bread. They queued up to buy it with one ear cocked for the sound of approaching shells, and queued up again with basins and jugs to fetch water from the safe official supply at the Menin Gate. At night when the full moon rose and the ruined towers and gables cast crooked shadows across the pitted streets the citizens of Ypres prudently returned to their cellars for the night. But the nights were strangely quiet.

The weather continued fine and warm. Green shoots began to thrust through the rubble, even blighted trees burst into full luxuriant leaf and there was blossom everywhere in the ravaged gardens. From time to time a stray shell did explode in the town raising a haze of dust that hung for a long time in the sunshine. To the distress of Aimé van Nieuwenhove one of them fell in the Rue de Lille.

Aimé van Nieuwenhove.

Friday 30 April Not many shells during the night, but in the morning small-calibre shells arrive in great quantities. About half past one, while I was dining in the cellars of the post office, Paul Baekelandt came to tell me that a shell must have fallen on my house and that thick smoke was coming out of the windows. I rushed home immediately, but I could not go into the house because the smoke was absolutely suffocating. After a quarter of an hour I was able to ascertain that the shell had fallen on the second floor. The damage was confined to the room where I keep my papers, the roof was seriously damaged and fragments of shell had pierced the floor of the dining room where I usually spend my time. The whole house was filled with a thick layer of dust. I took my courage in both hands and immediately started the work of clearing up.

The Army had taken a hand in clearing debris from some streets to give a clear passage to the wagons that rumbled past all through the night with rations and ammunition and with the tools and sandbags, the wooden stakes, the bales of wire that were needed to construct and consolidate the new line. Every man who could be spared was digging in the moonlight, strengthening the GHQ line, carving out another ahead of it and constructing a switch line that would reach out to loop round Hooge, tracing communication trenches, making new gun positions. On the northern flank of the salient where the line would more or less follow the existing front they were working within sight of the Germans, but the Germans themselves were busy wiring and consolidating and allowed them to work undisturbed.

The Germans had been ominously quiet and, at least for the moment, seemed to have given up the initiative, using their efforts to defend their positions and their guns to repulse the attacks in which the French persisted. But they were feeble attacks and, although British artillery lent supporting fire and the heavy guns promised by Foch had belatedly arrived, they were no match for the German artillery and each new assault was as easily thwarted as those that had gone before.

Over three days of confusion, delay or failure, Sir John French postponed the retirement for a second time, and then for a third, in accordance with Foch's wishes. But he was not a happy man and on 30 April he paid a visit to First Army headquarters to discuss various matters with Sir Douglas Haig, who recorded their conversation in his diary.

Friday, April 30 At 11.30 a.m. Sir John French came to see me to tell me of the situation generally, and to ask my opinion regarding the withdrawal from the Ypres salient. Lee, MP, arrived while we were talking, with a letter from CGS (Robertson) and enclosing one for Sir J.'s signature to Foch. Sir J. read me the letter. It was of the nature of an ultimatum, and stated that the withdrawal of the British troops from the salient would commence tonight, unless the French had succeeded in advancing their line . . . As to the policy of retiring, I said that I had no doubts in my mind as to the wisdom of such a step if the French did not regain the old front but continued in their present position. Our troops are now in a very sharp salient. This will be untenable under hostile artillery alone, while they will find it most difficult to withdraw, when forced to do so. They will also suffer most terribly from hostile artillery, *which almost envelops them at the present moment*. I considered that it was the Commander-in-Chief's duty to remove his men from what was really a 'death trap'.

Sir John also told me Smith-Dorrien had caused him more trouble. He was quite unfit (he said) to hold the Command of an Army and so Sir J. had withdrawn all the troops from his control except the 2nd Corps. Yet Smith-Dorrien stayed on! He would not resign! French is to ask Lord K. to find him something to do at home . . .

He added he could not express what he felt for the staunch support and help I had been to him throughout the war. He had never had any anxiety about my Command. He also alluded to Smith-Dorrien's conduct on the retreat, and said he ought to have tried him by Court Martial, because, on the day of le Cateau, he 'had ordered him to retire at 8 a.m. and he did not attempt to do so, but insisted on fighting in spite of his orders to retire'.

If Sir John French had finally made up his mind to send Foch something that was 'in the nature of an ultimatum', it was never sent, for Marshal Joffre had also had enough. He ordered Foch to abandon his plans for an all-out offensive and to confine himself to small-scale local attacks. The following morning Foch himself brought this news to British Headquarters to the great relief of Sir John French. A new 'all-out' attack was even then under way. Like the others it was a costly failure, but even before the outcome was known, the decision had been taken. Sir John French thankfully sent General Plumer instructions to begin the retirement that night.

The cost of the counter-attacks had been enormous. It had cost the French four thousand casualties to recapture the village of Lizerne and that number was multiplied many times along the French and British lines. Shell-fire alone had accounted for thousands killed and wounded. Everyone was tired, but the first priority was to relieve the most exhausted and, where possible, the units that had been hardest hit. Jack Dorgan's battalion was one of the first to be withdrawn and it was a sorry sight.

L/cpl. J. Dorgan.

It was exactly a week after we'd landed in France – just *one* week to the day – and the next afternoon when we were assembled as a Battalion after all that hectic week in Flanders, we found ourselves with four hundred and odd men out of nearly twelve hundred men who had landed in France. It was terrible, terrible. Most of my pals were gone, either killed or wounded, and I don't remember whether it was the Adjutant or Colonel who sent for me and he says, 'You are now a corporal.' By then practically all the officers and NCOs were wiped out. And it was just *one* week since we'd come off the boat. All gone!

The retirement had to be carried out methodically step by step, with caution and with stealth, for if the enemy got wind of it, if they were to attack en masse while the troops were actually on the move, the retirement could quite conceivably turn into a débâcle. The very last to go would be the men who had furthest to travel from the firing line at the very apex of the salient, at Inverness Copse, Broodseinde, Polygon Wood. During the crisis some companies, and even whole Battalions of the 27th Division, had been rushed to sectors where the fighting was fiercest, but all of them were exhausted because the battalions which had remained to hold the vital front while the salient was shrinking behind them had been in the line now for up to twelve days. Some men were drunk with fatigue.

Pte. W. Hay.

I was sent in front, maybe about fifty yards. It was a covering party, meaning that so many men went out in front to lie there and watch for the Jerries in case they made a sudden counter-attack. If you heard them coming you were supposed to fire a few shots and warn the blokes behind. We were all dead beat. A young man falls asleep quickly when he's tired, and I fell asleep when I was supposed to be wide awake, and Sergeant McGill, he was my platoon sergeant, he came rushing over and woke me up. He said, 'You could be shot for falling asleep over your post! Get back in, back where you were. Send another chap out.'

He was a great chap, Dave, he was a great friend of mine really. So of course he wouldn't put me on a charge, but if he had I would have been court martialled for sleeping at my post and endangering the whole company which I *was* doing really. But I was exhausted, like everybody else. We'd had no sleep, no hot drinks, for four days and we had practically nothing to eat.

Despite their exhaustion and the privations of a week's grim fighting the men of the 27th Division could not be pulled out completely, for the line at the tip of the salient had to be held until the last. The best that could be done, while the retirement continued behind them, was to rest them in relays a little distance behind the support lines. It was not a relief, but it was at least a respite. There was no chance of a wash or a clean-up, but there was food to eat and time to have a sleep, and time at last to write home to families waiting apprehensively for news. Jock Macleod had spent eight sleepless days and nights in the line.

2nd Lt. J. Macleod,

We are having a so-called rest in rear of the firing line, but we are still heavily shelled all day. It will be grand when the Huns run out of ammunition. In the last thirty days we have only had our clothes off three times, have never been out of shell-fire and have lost very heavily in casualties, officers and men.

My valise unfortunately had to be abandoned along with heaps of other stuff in the much bombarded town of Ypres. When things get quieter it may be possible to recover it but for the time being please send me a toothbrush and tooth powder, some soap and a towel, and some socks.

You would be rather astonished if you could see me now. Buttons have been shed galore. My hands are dirty. So is my face! I am unshaved and my bonnet has lost one of its ribbons. We are lying in a dug-out which contains some British officers and native telephone orderlies! The dug-out is in the remains of a charming country house estate, with statues and busts, and ornamental water. The natives all wear their shirts outside their trousers, a somewhat astonishing habit, and a good few have starched white cuffs, which look absolutely incongruous in these surroundings!

The many postponements had at least given General Plumer a breathing space and an opportunity to work out detailed plans for the retirement but it was no easy task to disentangle the scattered troops. Parts of the 4th Division alone were attached to six different divisions under five different commands in five different sectors. It would be days before they were reunited.

Mercifully the night was peaceful, the moon sailed high, the weather stayed fine and the first stage of the withdrawal went like clockwork, unharassed by the enemy. It was a luminous dawn and behind the German line on the ridge above Polygon Wood the sun rose early into a sky of pale, cloudless blue. The silence continued well into the morning, but it was an unnatural silence and it was too good to be true. The Germans had been biding their time and preparing another attack. It exploded just after noon on the front of the 4th Division and on the French on their left where the line ran towards the canal.

The German casualties had been lighter than those of the British and French, but they had been heavy enough and, while some reserves had been able to fill some of the gaps, there were no reinforcements to swell the ranks to a point that would guarantee success. But they had guns, and they had gas, and they were depending on the formidable strength of these weapons to sweep them through the allied line. Bombard the ground, pulverise the defenders, release gas to finish off the few who were left and, last of all, send the infantry forward to walk in and to mop up and consolidate almost without a fight. The quantity and even the calibre of their infantry would be secondary in terms of success. In the German view it was a war of materials now and their tactics had changed accordingly.

Lacking nine-tenths of the materials and resources at the disposal of the enemy, the Allies were depending on the men, first, last and always, and the British had changed their system of defence. The line had been reorganised and there were reserves close behind the trenches, ready to move swiftly to take the place of the supports when they dashed forward to assist the front-line troops. The bombardment that day was devastating and lasted for more than four hours. It was 4.30 p.m. when the gas came over but, happily, the clouds came low, they were thin in many places and, although the only respirators were improvised affairs, the men knew how to use them. They also knew what to expect and this time they did more than stand fast. But it took courage to take the initiative, to move forward through the waist-high deadly fumes to meet the German infantry preparing to come on, and they met them with rifle fire, so pitiless and so accurate that the attack faded away. In places it had been touch and go and there were many casualties, but they had held their ground.

It was a disconcerting setback to the German commander who later reported (erroneously) that *the enemy position was very strongly fortified and protected by deep entanglements. Another gas attack was therefore planned.* They assumed that the concentration of gas had not been strong enough and resolved to make sure that next time they would make no mistake.

The news of the assault was equally disconcerting to General Plumer but by eight o'clock in the evening all was quiet. He waited a little longer to make quite sure before giving the go-ahead for the second stage of the withdrawal. Spasmodic shelling during the night did little to interrupt it and by morning the men were safely installed in their new positions. It was not easy to move several thousand men over rough bombarded country in the dark, but at least they could move on their own feet. Trench stores had to be manhandled – tools, rations, boxes of ammunition, and the manifold equipment that sustained a battalion in the line had to be removed and humped for weary miles. But it had finally been accomplished by stealth and in silence. Two thirds of the withdrawal was now complete and the Germans still had no inkling that it was under way. In the evening of 3 May the last stage of the retirement would begin and, in the most dangerous move yet, the front line itself would be evacuated.

Chapter 19

On the evening of 3 May Princess Patricia's Canadian Light Infantry were waiting to move back from their position in the front line on the edge of Polygon Wood. Despite its name this regiment was not part of the Canadian Expeditionary Force. It was part of the 27th Division of the British Army composed almost entirely of Regular battalions and the Patricias were not alone in the belief that they were just as good as the professionals. They were a unique force, and well they knew it, although it was only nine months to the very day since they had been conceived in the imagination of a Montreal businessman, Hamilton Gault. On 3 August, the eve of the declaration of war, he had travelled to Ottawa, where an emergency military conference was taking place, to ask permission to raise a Battalion of Canadians. Hamilton Gault was a prominent citizen and a wealthy man with the entreé to influential circles. He had also done service as a soldier and there was no difficulty about seeing Sir Sam Hughes during a recess in the conference. But it was a certain Colonel Farquhar who was fired by the idea and joined enthusiastically in Gault's efforts to get it off the ground and proposed they should aim at recruiting experienced soldiers who would settle down quickly to military life and need minimal training – a mere refresher course – before they were ready to go to war.

Thousands of ex-servicemen had settled in Canada in the decade before the war and since they were self-evidently young men of adventurous spirit, they were the right type or, as Farquhar himself put it, 'the best of the breed'. So many of them flocked from all over Canada to join up that, even among these desirable recruits, the regiment was able to have the pick of the bunch. There were prospectors, farmers, professional and business men, lumberjacks, even some cowboys and a prize-fighter or two. Fifty, who called themselves 'The Legion of Frontiersmen' banded together and arrived in a body and the Edmonton pipe band in full Highland regalia, played themselves into the recruiting office and joined up en masse, announcing that they had 'come to play the regiment to France and back again'. The band was enrolled even before the

269

Battalion was complete. Hamilton Gault himself contributed $100,000 to set the ball rolling and the Battalion was raised and equipped in the short space of ten days.

Only one in ten of its members had been born in Canada. Sixty-five per cent were English, 15 per cent were Scots and 10 per cent had been born in Ireland, some had been in Canada for as long as twelve years, some for a matter of months, but they considered themselves Canadian to a man. Of 1,100 recruits 1,049 had served in the Army or the Navy, almost half of those had seen war service and between them they wore the ribbons of 771 campaign and service medals. There were two sections of ex-guardsmen, two of ex-riflemen and two of ex-public school boys. They were tough and they were fit. They also had royal patronage. Colonel Farquhar was Military Secretary to the Duke of Connaught, the Governor General of Canada, who had not only released him so that he could take command of the battalion but had also agreed to part with his ADC and another member of his personal staff, to form a nucleus of officers. Gault himself was appointed senior captain and other officers had been found among the hundreds of willing volunteers.

The Duke of Connaught had also, in a sense, given his daughter and the Battalion, now bearing her name, basked in the distinction of having the prettiest and most glamorous Colonel-in-Chief of any Battalion anywhere. Princess Patricia of Connaught took her duties seriously and intended to be more than just the figurehead of her Regiment and she began by making them a unique and personal gift. On Sunday 23 August, while the British Expeditionary Force was in the thick of its first engagement at Mons, Princess Patricia presented the Regiment with its own colours. She had designed the banner herself, cut out the red material with her own hands, fringed it with gold and embroidered her own entwined initials as a centrepiece. It had taken the princess a week of hard work and late nights to complete it but the pleasure and pride of the men made it more than worthwhile. Five days later the colours, escorted by a guard of honour, were carried proudly at the head of the Regiment as the Patricias marched on board ship to the skirling strains of their own pipe band. The anticlimax came when they were forced to disembark again at Quebec. The Patricias, as they were now called even on the parade ground, finally sailed on 27 September and despite the disappointing delay they were still the first of the Empire's troops to arrive at the war – or, at least, to arrive in the United Kingdom. The 27th Division was in the process of being formed by Regular Battalions brought back from overseas and there was no question that the Patricias were good enough to join them. Before they left England for France they were inspected by Lord Kitchener who was deeply impressed by the medal ribbons displayed on chest after chest as he passed along their ranks. 'Well!' he exclaimed to Colonel Farquhar. '*Now* I know where all my old soldiers went to!'

In four months at the front the Patricias had earned a high reputation and not a few more medal ribbons to add to their collection. There had also been casualties for they had been in the gruelling close-fighting in the trenches at St Eloi and when they left to come to Ypres many of the originals were left behind in their own small regimental cemetery. The last to be buried was their Commanding Officer, Colonel Farquhar, shot by a sniper as he was handing over to the Colonel of the Battalion that relieved them. That had been a blow, and it was felt personally by every man, because now the Patricias were more than a regiment, they were a family. Major Gault had been wounded and, in his absence, Captain Buller had taken temporary command and a hundred reinforcements had arrived from Canada. Among them was Jimmy Vaughan. On the night of 3 May he was almost the last man to leave the line.

The Patricias had not expected to take part in the withdrawal, for they were long overdue for relief, but the 2nd Shropshire Light Infantry who should have relieved them had been hurried away to assist elsewhere and the Patricias had been twelve days in the line in front of Polygon Wood, fifty yards from the German trenches. Now they were to fall back, in the trickiest part of the whole retirement, and they were very tired, for each company, when it was not engaged in the firing line and was nominally 'in support', had been engaged in back-breaking labour helping to dig the new line three miles in the rear. The rudimentary trenches were far from complete, but it was time to go.

Like nine tenths of his comrades Vaughan was not Canadian born. Four years earlier he had left Stockton-on-Tees to work on a farm in Canada.

Pte. J. W. Vaughan, Princess Patricia's Canadian Light Infantry, 80 Brig., 27 Div.

I joined up with my pal Jack Bushby and we didn't join with the first lot because we were working near Winnipeg on a farm and it was harvest time. Well, the harvest was hard work but it was two dollars a day and that was good money so naturally we didn't want to miss out, but we joined up in November when the Patricias called for reinforcements. We were young and we had the same idea that everybody did, 'Oh, the war will be over in about three months, so we'll get a nice trip home out of it and we'll soon be back.' Well, how wrong could you be? We didn't get much in the way of training. We were shipped out in January, had a bit of training at Tidworth in England, and we

271

joined the regiment in the field on 28 March and by 19 April we were in the front line at Polygon Wood, and there we stuck until we had to retire. We didn't worry about the fact we had to retire, didn't think we were losing out or anything, because it was all explained to us.

They started on the move as soon as it got dark and, of course, we had the wood behind us, quite a thick wood that time, so there was no problem about concealment or anything, and over a period of a couple of hours they moved off a platoon at a time. But they'd told us just how important it was that the Germans shouldn't be given the idea that we were clearing off. I was one of thirteen men left behind as a rearguard and we were told exactly what we had to do. What we did was fire a shot – and of course at night you could see the flash of the rifle, the Germans could see it – then we would walk along the trench, maybe for about ten yards, and we would wait a few seconds and fire another shot, and then another chap would come along and do the same and I'd come back to another place and fire off again. That led his nibs across the road to figure that the trench was still fully occupied. Of course I was scared, but we were all very conscious of the responsibility and that we had to stay in the front line until the officer figured that the main part of the regiment had taken up the line at Frezenberg and Bellewaerde Ridge a few miles away. That was the idea. Eventually he came along and he said, very quietly, 'All right, boys, I think they've had long enough now. We'll be off', and he went along the line getting the men together. Out we got, into the communication trench and back to the main trench we had in Polygon Wood. Everything was quiet at first and then, after a minute, all hell broke loose because, as soon as they didn't hear any more firing from the front line, the Germans figured that we were coming over. They thought it was the lull before the storm. Well, that hurried us on our way, all this firing going on behind us and bullets coming right through the wood, knocking twigs off the trees. But we never got a scratch, nobody got hit, and eventually we cleared the wood and started going across country to the new position. It didn't take us as long as it did the main body of the Regiment because there weren't so many of us. It took about an hour and we got there about maybe half past three in the morning.

Well, there *were* trenches, I suppose you could call them that, but they were only about two and a half feet deep because there had been no time to do any more, and the boys that were already there were trying to build up a parapet, filling sandbags and piling them along the trench, so we had to forget any idea we might have had about having a kip, because we had to start in too, digging and such. We didn't get them very deep either before the next morning. It was a beautiful morning. It's funny, but the weather we had during all that battle was beautiful, beautiful, beautiful weather. Next morning there wasn't a cloud in the sky and pretty soon after it got light some German planes came over looking for us, and of course they'd found we'd gone by then but they had no idea before the morning, because all night and when we were going back, we'd heard them bombarding, wasting their shells on these empty trenches, and *that* gave us some satisfaction, even a laugh. But how they found us was this. When these planes came over and spotted us they dropped smoke bars over the side of the plane, and the German artillery officers would naturally have their glasses trained on the plane, you see, and these smoke bars came down in streaks and they just hung there above our position. No clouds, no wind to blow them away, they just hung there plumb above us – and then it started!

It started with the German infantry. It was the first time the Patricias had seen anything approaching open warfare and it was an impressive spectacle to see long lines of Germans pouring down over the Westhoek Ridge at the double – so impressive that some men incautiously stood up on the parapet to get a better view. As it approached, the great mass of grey-clad soldiers thinned, split, separated, and mounted officers galloped up and down the lines directing the deployment.

The Germans were beyond the range of rifles, and the guns that might have created havoc could not easily find the range from their new positions before the enemy went to ground and began to dig in. They had pushed machine-guns forward to protect them and they were firing at close quarters, raking the half-built parapets with streams of bullets that kept the Patricias' heads well down. There was nothing they could do but grit their teeth and stick it out. And then the shelling began when the Germans had got the range. The 'smoke bars' had done the job well, and they had the range to the inch. The shallow trenches crumbled beneath the onslaught, machine-guns were buried, whole bays disappeared and, by the end of the day, 122 men had been hit.

It was the last and the worst of the Patricias' twelve days in the line. Later in the evening the Shropshires came up to relieve them and the Patricias gathered up what remained of their belongings. Dog-weary, hollow-eyed with fatigue, carrying their dead to be decently buried and their wounded to be tended, they trudged out of the line.

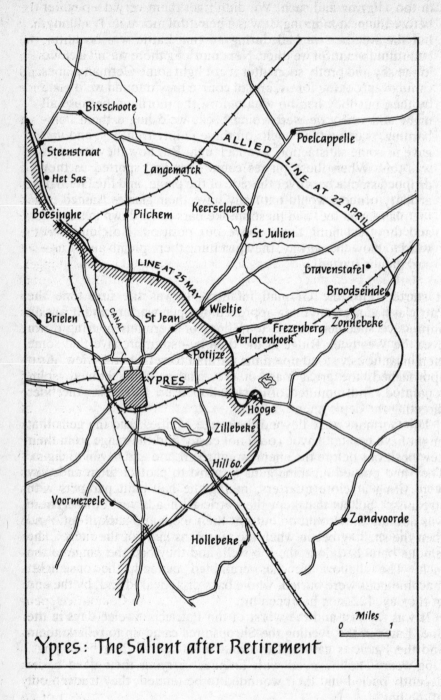

Bixschoote

Steenstraat

Het Sas

Boesinghe

ALLIED

Poelcappelle

Langemarck

LINE AT 22 APRIL

Keerselaere

Pilckem

St Julien

Gravenstafel

Broodseinde

LINE AT 25 MAY

Wieltje

Zonnebeke

CANAL

Brielen

St Jean

Frezenberg

Verlorenhoek

Potijze

YPRES

Hooge

Zillebeke

Hill 60.

Voormezeele

Zandvoorde

Hollebeke

Miles

0   1

Ypres: The Salient after Retirement

The Shropshires set to work to do what little they could to shore up the defences before dawn, and in the shifting dark beyond the battered line the Germans were busy too. All night long, as they waited on the alert, the Shropshires could hear the chink of iron, the faint sound of voices on the breeze, and knew that the enemy was on the move. But the Germans were hard at work, digging and consolidating their new line, and they made no attempt to advance further.

The retirement had taken them completely by surprise. Now, at last, it was complete.

In Ypres too it was time to go. The Provisional Committee met for the last time in the house of the secretary, Aimé van Nieuwenhove. It was a dreary meeting. There were no minutes to read, for his notes had been destroyed by the shell that demolished his study, but no one needed reminding that the main topic of discussion had been on the number of bodies in the streets and the fear that if they were not removed the typhus epidemic could not be contained for much longer. A start had been made in the intervening week and three labourers engaged to dispose of the bodies at the rate of ten francs for a dead horse and three francs for a human corpse. The horses were buried in the largest shell-holes and the human remains interred, with little more ceremony, in temporary plots within the ramparts.

There had been no difficulty in finding people willing to undertake even this unpleasant job now that the economy of the town had come to a halt and there was no work to be had. But there were nevertheless rich pickings, and for the last few days posses of soldiers had been roaming the ruined streets, searching cellars for wine, breaking into abandoned shops and houses and helping themselves to objects they regarded as 'souvenirs'. The officials of the town regarded them as stolen property and there were reports that civilians venturing to protest had been threatened with rifles and even bayonets. People were complaining bitterly and demanding that the Committee should press the military authorities to stop the pillage. Even in the midst of the débâcle, such a request had to be made through the proper channel, and the 'proper channel' was the departed civilian Commandant of the town. No one knew precisely where he had gone, perhaps to Watou, perhaps to Poperinghe, possibly even further afield, but the Committee spent most of the afternoon drafting a letter urging him to take the matter up. It also asked for the prompt dispatch of a force of workmen to assist with the removal of corpses from the streets.

It was sent off by messenger to the Commandant's last known address in the hope that it would find him. It never did, but it hardly mattered now. Next day Ypres was ordered to be evacuated of all civilians and the order had to be obeyed. It was a hard blow to stomach.

Aimé van Nieuwenhove.

Tuesday 4 May All of us are deeply dispirited. After battling for six months against all these adversities, having been deprived for so long of our comfortable everyday lives with the sole object of trying to hold on to our homes, we must now resign ourselves to abandoning all our belongings. What will be left when we return?

Last night was reasonably quiet, but in the morning a huge number of shells fell from different directions. About eleven o'clock the bombardment eased off and I started to make my preparations for leaving. I took everything that remains into the wine cellar for safety and blocked up the entrance with boxes and crates. About three o'clock I heard that two motor ambulances will leave about ten o'clock to take the Committee to Abeele. So, here we are, and this is the last night I shall spend in Ypres. I feel deeply discouraged. Even the anticipation of seeing my dear ones, and the satisfaction of emerging from this furnace with my dignity intact, makes up only a very little for my sadness in having to leave my house.

The town was being evacuated section by section and for three consecutive days the Friends Ambulance Unit ran a shuttle service to transport the old and the sick, while the able-bodied made their way on foot to Poperinghe where trains were waiting to convey them far from Ypres. Ahead of them lay a journey of many days, for they were to be sent well away from the danger zone, away from Belgium itself, deep into France to be billeted on strangers and to manage as best they could. It was a bleak prospect. More fortunate citizens who had relatives in France or who, like Aimé van Nieuwenhove, were people of substance, could make private arrangements, but it was small consolation. Everyone had to go.

Aimé van Nieuwenhove made a last tour of his beautiful, battered house. During the night the glass of the drawing-room windows had been shattered by an explosion. He removed two leaves from his dining table to nail across the gaps but without much hope that they would prevent any determined person from getting in. He went upstairs, looked into the bedrooms and locked the doors. Last of all he went to the kitchen where his children's three canaries chirped happily in the morning sun, unhooked the cages, carried them one by one to the garden and opened the doors. The canaries, as reluctant as van Nieuwenhove himself to quit familiar surroundings, were in no hurry to fly off. He watched them for a few minutes, sick at heart, and then he turned away.

Aimé van Nieuwenhove.

Wednesday 5 May The members of the committee met at my place for departure. During the whole period of the bombardment I have seldom seen my colleagues so well-groomed as they were today. At last, the cars having arrived, everybody got in and I double-locked my front door. What a lovely day it was. I hadn't seen the outskirts of the town for six months now. I sat up in front with the driver.

I cast a last look at the Grand' Place and the Place Vandenpeereboom and finally on the rue Elverdinghe. The shells escorted us out of town as if to pay us their farewell compliments. It was extraordinary how frightened we felt at these explosions, just as we were leaving the places where so many other shells had fallen without much bothering us.

Our first stop was in front of the hospital on the Vlamertinghe road. I got out of the car and looked towards the derelict railway station. I could still see the shells exploding on the town, then, as I got back into the car, I bade a sad, tearful farewell to our dear little city.

The Committee were almost the last to go but, despite the official order, a few obstinate souls remained although the bombardment had started up again only a little less furiously than before. Now that the town officials had departed Father Delaere had taken charge.

Father Delaere.

6 May I have got permission from the English Commandant to stay in the town with ten men who are working under my orders, burying the dead, interring the horses, putting out fires and patrolling the streets to prevent pillaging. We are virtually alone.

The weather has turned rainy. I wish to heaven that it was only raining rain but, alas, shrapnel shells are also raining down, three or four every minute. There are no more than twenty of us left in the town. Ypres is well and truly dead! There is a terrible emptiness but I do not let it depress me. I will not submit to this enforced evacuation without trying every possible means to resist it. I have decided to stay to the end – dead or alive. God have pity on me!

7 May The fire that reduced the church of St Nicolas to

cinders spread to the boys' school next door and it too fell prey to the flames. In the rue Carton many houses went on fire, among them Judge Tyberhien's with all his treasured antiques. My men, who had gone out to look for bodies, triumphantly brought back a poor old man of eighty-six whom they'd found in an abandoned house where he would certainly have died of hunger. They have been doing a good job in finding bodies. Between 27 April and 7 May they buried thirty-two civilians and many, many horses – seventeen of them in a single enormous shell hole.

Our life is very strange. We have enough meat now to last us a long time because my men killed a calf they found abandoned and wandering along the street. We have bread too. There is no longer a baker in the town but we have the key to his house and there's plenty of flour so, this afternoon, my men managed to bake some bread in his oven.

8 May Towards seven o'clock in the morning the shelling started up furiously – deafening crashes of big guns and the constant whistling of shrapnel shells. While I was praying in the chapel there was an enormous bang and a shell demolished the best part of the neighbouring building which was newly built. Nevertheless, my men arrived with three bodies, one of them a woman found in the Café Reubens. We thought we'd be here for a long time but suddenly I heard that permission to stay in the town had been withdrawn and we were ordered to leave before six o'clock in the evening. The police showed me a telegram saying that the evacuation must be completed with no exceptions whatever. Three of my men, who had gone out to bury the bodies, did not return so I went out to look for them. It was truly terrible! All the time shrapnel was exploding above the town. Four horses lay bathed in their own blood in the Grand' Place at the corner of the rue de Lille and all along the length of the rue au Beurre we could see bloodstains every-where, but not a living soul. Everything is in flames, nothing but ruins and it's rare to see a whole wall standing among the heaps of brick and rubble. Hardly a cellar has not been broken into and there are many strong-boxes forced open and tossed among the debris. The houses that have escaped the fire are all holed and splintered, at the mercy of the four winds, ripe for pillage. It is truly the abomination of desolation.

I searched in vain for my men, for they had been arrested by the police and taken forcibly to Poperinghe.

The shells that rained that day on Ypres were not directed at the few

278

defiant civilians still lurking in the ruins. It was the start of a new offensive.

Creeping forward within a stone's throw of the new allied line the Germans were able to judge that it was crude and sketchy, that its defences were weak, and it was easy to tell from the sparse bombardments that the British were short of shells and heavy guns. And there in front of them was Ypres, almost within spitting distance. The Germans still lacked troops, but the retirement had given them new heart. Surely with one more push Ypres would fall into their hands.

It was 8 May, and that same morning General Plumer sent an order to the troops around the salient. It urged them to hold the line tenaciously and, at all costs, to avoid the necessity of calling for reinforcements. In the light of 'the big scheme further south' there would be no one to spare to help them out of trouble.

It was Plumer's first official order as Commander of the Second Army. Thirty-six hours earlier Smith-Dorrien had at last been forced into resignation. In a personal letter to the Commander-in-Chief he had pointed out, in tones of injured dignity, that the evident lack of trust in him 'constituted a weak link in the chain of command' and that for the general good, it might be better if he were to serve elsewhere. It was delivered on the morning of 6 May and, although his letter was addressed personally to Sir John French, Smith-Dorrien did not receive the courtesy of a personal reply, or even an acknowledgement. That evening a curt order arrived from GHQ, instructing him to hand over command of the Second Army to General Plumer and to return to England.*

---

* This was effectively the end of General Smith-Dorrien's distinguished military career. Shortly afterwards he was side-lined to a post in East Africa. He retired from the Army shortly after the end of the war and died, aged seventy-two, in 1930.

Chapter 20

The morale of the Germans was high. On 6 May they had finally pushed the allies off Hill 60, with another devastating gas attack. Now they were ready to launch a fresh attack which they believed might secure Ypres itself. They intended to attack all round the rim of the shortened salient, but the full force and the brunt of the assault would fall on the apex of the British line where it ran across the Bellewaerde Ridge to Frezenberg. Princess Patricia's Canadian Light Infantry were back in the line, holding the rudimentary trenches that were traced across the eastern edge of the Bellewaerde Ridge.

In peacetime this small stretch of high ground, this circle of low ridges that swelled up like an amphitheatre from the flat Flanders Plain, had been a desirable place to live – and there were half a dozen chateaux and small country estates, in as many square miles. Their wealthy owners had planted woodlands, hedged off fields, made roads to link up farms, built chapels in the hamlets and laid out water-scapes and pleasure-grounds round their fine country mansions.

All but one of them were now in the hands of the Germans. Previously the allies standing round the salient had invariably had another ridge at their backs and the advantage of dead ground, invisible to the enemy, where supplies could be brought up and troops could move unobserved to and from the line. Bellewaerde was the smallest ridge of all – and it was the last. Beyond it the ground dipped to meet the flat-lands that ran round Ypres and rolled off into the distance to meet the sea.

Across the ridge behind the Patricias' trenches a finger of woodland curved round the edge of an ornamental lake in the grounds of Hooge Chateau concealing it from view. This was a favourite spot of the Baron de Vinck for it was well stocked with fish and he enjoyed relaxing there on a summer's evening, drifting in a small boat on its placid surface with the trout rising to his bait. Tame swans sailed on the lake, birds nested in the trees and across the grassy parkland peacocks screeched and strutted on the chateau

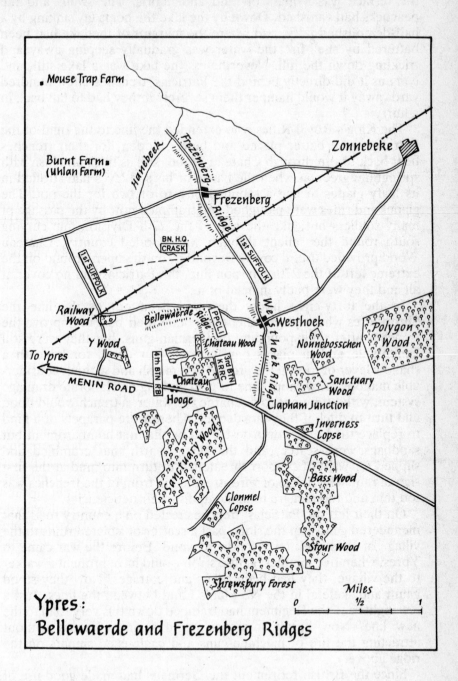

Mouse Trap Farm

Burnt Farm
(Uhlan Farm)

Zonnebeke

Hanebeek

Frezenberg Ridge

Frezenberg

BN. H.Q.
CRASK

1st SUFFOLK

1st SUFFOLK

Railway
Wood

Bellewaerde Ridge

PPCLI

Westhoek

Polygon
Wood

Y Wood

Chateau Wood

Nonnebosschen
Wood

Westhoek Ridge

To Ypres

4th BTN RB

3rd BTN KRRC

Sanctuary
Wood

MENIN ROAD

Chateau

Hooge

Clapham Junction

Inverness
Copse

Sanctuary Wood

Bass Wood

Clonmel
Copse

Stour Wood

Shrewsbury Forest

Miles

0   ½   1

Ypres:
Bellewaerde and Frezenberg Ridges

terrace. Now beneath the shattered gables and glassless windows the terrace was a mass of mud and debris. The swans and the peacocks had vanished. Down by the lake the boats lay sinking by a half-demolished jetty, and where the margins of the lake had been battered by shell-fire the water was gradually seeping away and trickling down the hill. Nevertheless the lake was a lake still, and lying as it did directly behind the Patricias' trenches a few hundred yards away it would hamper them severely if they had to fall back in a hurry.

The King's Royal Rifles who extended the line to the right of the Patricias were better placed and better hidden, for their trenches bent back to run through Chateau Wood, still as thick and lush with springtime green as when the baron or his son Yves had strolled in its leafy glades to bag a rabbit or a bird or two for the pot. The glades and rides were ploughed and trampled now by the passage of many soldiers but, like the rest of the 27th Division line curving south round the salient through well-wooded country, Chateau Wood provided useful cover. Beyond it, on the open ground on the extreme left of the 27th Division line, the Patricias had no cover at all and they were badly in need of it.

In the forty-eight hours they had been out of the line the Shropshires who replaced them had done their best to improve the trenches after their pounding by German guns, but they were still lamentable and in places barely three feet deep, for beneath a shallow layer of topsoil the ground was marsh and without considerable manpower, without time to plan and dig an elaborate drainage system, without pumps to discharge the water, a trench would flood and turn to ditch if they dug deeper. There were parapets of a kind to replace the breastworks destroyed by the first bombardment but sandbags were scarce, and the claggy earth that crumbled and slipped for want of support threatened to turn into mud at the first sign of rain. The tangle of wire stretched in front of the trenches was too thin and too meagre to make up for their deficiencies.

On their left the Patricias' trenches rested on a country road that meandered gently up the slope past a scatter of isolated ruins to the village of Westhoek on the ridge beyond. Before the war came to Ypres, when five minutes' gentle stroll would have brought a walker to the village, they had been barns and cottages. Now they stood gaunt and skeletal in the No Man's Land between the lines. Just a few nights ago the Regiment had tramped down this very road to the new line. Now hardly a mouse could scamper across without attracting the fire of machine-guns and eagle-eyed snipers on the ridge above.

Since the British retirement the Germans had made good use of their time. With the advantage of the newly won ridges and a hinterland of dead ground they had moved up large quantities of supplies – tools, wire, timber for revetments – and although their new trenches were not yet constructed to their customary standard of perfection, they had built strongpoints at intervals along the ridge, from the corner of the Menin Road which British Tommies had cheerily christened Clapham Junction to the ruins of Westhoek village, and across the open to the high ground above Frezenberg a mile beyond it. And they had sited them carefully to command the British trenches and everything that moved behind. There were guns well dug in and concealed in the woods close behind their line – in Clonmel Copse, in Nonnebosschen Wood, in Inverness Copse where so recently Jock Macleod had enjoyed his alfresco lunch with the hospitable French and where the gilt chairs and flamboyant clock salvaged from the chateau were doubtless now adorning the dug-out of German gunners.

The Patricias were still tired, for their time out of the line – and less than a mile behind – had been too short to restore men stunned by the ferocity of the bombardment that had decimated the Battalion, and too short to stiffen it with reinforcements. A draft of new men had arrived with Hamilton Gault, newly returned from hospital in England, but there were far too few to begin to fill the gaps. Even the Colonel was gone, shot by a sniper during the 'rest'. Major Gault was now in command but there was no officer above the rank of lieutenant to assist him. Battalion headquarters was only an apology for a dug-out – a few rough boards thrown over part of the second-line trench a hundred yards behind the first – but Princess Patricia's colours were there and they did a good deal to hearten Gault crouching with the signallers, and hoping against hope for the best.

If the Patricias' trenches were badly placed they were marginally better off than the 28th Division on their left. Their position, bulging slightly forward to form the true apex of the new salient, ran across open ground on the forward slopes of the Frezenberg Ridge where they had no cover at all, for trenches could only be sited for concealment if there was high ground behind them where observers could direct bombardments on to No Man's Land at the first sign of an attack. But there was no high ground behind, no more ridges for observation, no concealed artillery positions, few enough guns and not nearly enough ammunition.

On the flat land beyond Frezenberg village the 1st Suffolks were in the line and Signaller Harry Crask was at Battalion Headquarters in one of the dug-outs hastily constructed near the straggling stream they called the Hannebeek. It was Colonel Wallace's own dug-out and it was not much of a place but from what Crask was able to gather he was a good deal better off than the men in the trenches in front. They were having a miserable time. The battalion had gone into the trenches on 17 April, and the battle had begun on the very day they were due for relief. They had been on the go ever since, attacking, counter-attacking, growing weaker in strength after each costly encounter. Shelling had also taken its toll and the Suffolks now were a pale shadow of the sun-bronzed battalion of Regulars which just a few months ago had quit garrison duties in Egypt to sail for Europe and the war. On that morning of 8 May there were fewer than four hundred of the originals left, and long before nightfall the Battalion would have ceased to exist.

But a company of Cheshires had been sent up to help them and, although shell-fire had accounted for some seventy casualties, the last few days had been comparatively quiet. Crask was not alone in suspecting that something was brewing and that the lull was only the calm before the storm for, working as they were at close quarters, he could sense that Colonel Wallace was worried and on edge. Captain Chalmers was a frequent visitor to the HQ dug-out, struggling back with difficulty from the front line, where the bombarded banks of the stream had given way and the water had spread to turn the low ground from a morass into a swamp. Conditions in the trenches were worse – much worse – and so Chalmers explained to the Colonel several times a day. 'Pitiable' was the word he used. The line was a pitiable mass of mud and blood, the men were 'done up' and in a pitiable condition, constantly asking when they were going to be relieved. There was nothing the colonel could do about it.

It was Crask who received the signal when it finally came through and, suppressing his own delight, handed it poker-faced to the Colonel. The battalion would be relieved that night. Colonel Wallace gave an audible sigh of thankfulness. 'Thank God for that!' he said. Then, turning to the Adjutant, 'Let Chalmers know – and say he can tell the men.' The message was logged in the small hours of the morning of 8 May. But in the darkness behind the enemy trenches orderlies were dishing out coffee, bread and sausage to long lines of German soldiers waiting to attack.

Pte. H. J. Crask, MM, 1st Bn., Suffolk Regt., 84 Brig., 28 Div.

I'd been on the telephone all night. About 6 a.m. a message came through that the 69th Battery would open fire on the whizz bang battery that had been bothering us. Whether it did or not I don't know, for the Germans immediately opened an attack. Shells were raining all over the shop – especially round about us so as to prevent our supports getting up. I was in the dug-out with the C.O. and the Adjutant, working the telephone and making ready for breakfast – but *that* part of the business didn't come off! All remained intact for about twenty minutes. Then number 1 dug-out next to us was struck by a shell, badly wounding Drew in the head and burying all the rifles, so everyone there scattered for the exit. Sergeant Crabb came into ours. Our dug-out lasted out for about another ten minutes, *then* a shell exploded just in the rear of the dug-out and knocked the telephone, me and Crabb out of our positions and wounded the Adjutant who was directly behind us. We hardly knew what was happening for a few minutes or how we had got off so lucky. The telephone, chair, table, *all* had disappeared – with a hole a few yards in circumference staring at us in their place. We all cleared out to the emergency trench which had been dug in the rear of a ditch and which turned out *far* worse than the shattered dug-outs because we were up to our waists in water – and up to our necks after ducking down with shells raining all around! During all this they had also dropped one on number 3 dug-out, shattering a beam which struck Corporal Pugh and smashed his right leg just above the ankle and also wounded him in the head and left arm. It was the hottest shop I had ever been in! I just had time to get properly soaked through, shaking with cold, when a shell dropped right on the edge of the trench, burying me and Lance-Corporal Game. I was lucky again for, after being helped out, Game was found to be horribly wounded with two large holes in the back, one on either side of his backbone. I took him back to number 2 dug-out (which hadn't been hit again) and there I done him up as best I could.

All round the salient the air was whirling in a ferment of smoke and flying mud. The din was deafening, shock waves vibrated along the front, and the earth quaked and heaved and blew apart with the force of the explosions. Fields disappeared. Trenches disintegrated. Men were blown to bits. Two miles away from the Suffolks, and separated from them by the front of the 83rd Brigade, the Princess Patricias were having just as gruelling a time. Shortly after 6.30 a.m. Major Gault had managed to scribble a message to Brigade HQ reporting '*very, very heavy shelling*' – but Brigade hardly needed to be told. In Brigade Headquarters dug-out, half a mile away at the western corner of Railway Wood, they were taking punishment on their own account, for the German guns were searching wide and probing deep and there was little doubt that this was the prelude to an all-out attack. It was hard to credit that the bombardment could possibly get worse but at seven o'clock the fire grew even stronger, the shells flew thicker, and every gun seemed to be trained on the sector where the Patricias and the Suffolks and the unfortunate battalions of the 83rd Brigade were clinging on at the crest of the battered salient. The Patricias' front line was all but obliterated by high-explosive and shrapnel shells that, bursting high, rained red-hot fragments of metal that wiped out whole sections of men at a stroke, while machine-guns on the high ground, sweeping methodically from side to side, sprayed the trenches with incessant fire.

At eight o'clock Gault dispatched a second message to Brigade Headquarters:

Have been heavily shelled since 7 a.m. Sections of front trenches made untenable by enemy's artillery, but have still about 160 rifles in front line. German infantry has not yet appeared. Should they rush our front trenches will at once counter-attack if possible . . . In lulls of gunfire there is heavy fire from rifles and machine guns. Please send me 2 machine guns if possible. I have only two left in the front line. None in support . . . Most of my wire gone.

The runner managed to dodge through the bombardment and safely reached Brigade HQ. It was the last direct news of the Patricias and already it was out of date. Even as the Brigadier was reading it the German infantry was swarming down the Westhoek Ridge to attack the British trenches. And they were whooping as they came.

Looking back on it, even the Patricias themselves found it difficult to believe that they had beaten the Germans back. The line was feeble, their front-line trench was almost non-existent, but every man, even the wounded who were still capable of raising a rifle, poured such accurate and such deadly fire into the German infantry as they advanced that the attack hesitated, faltered, and finally petered out as the survivors began to work their way cautiously back up the hill. When they saw that their infantry attack had failed the German guns opened up again more furiously than before and machine-gun crews which had managed to reach the ruined buildings in the first rush were firing in unison at almost point-blank range. The silence when the guns stopped was almost as stunning as the noise of the bombardment. Then there was a throaty rumbling from beyond the ridge that rose to a roar as the Germans poured down in a mass, running and shouting as they came. The front line was almost obliterated now and there was little point in trying to hold on. In the lull small groups of men had begun to make their way back to the support line and although the rearguard did their best to hold the enemy off, this time the attack was unstoppable. Watchers, peering anxiously from the support line a hundred yards behind, saw with astonishment a row of small white flags appear in part of the line where the fire of a few desperate survivors kept the enemy pinned down but the optimists whose first incredulous thought had been that the enemy was surrendering were soon disillusioned. The Germans were signalling their position to their own guns, warning them to lengthen range, to punish the second line as they had punished the first, and to finish the job.

Pte. J. W. Vaughan.

We were hit dead centre with heavy guns and machine-guns and then we were enfiladed from the right and enfiladed from the left along the trench both ways and it seems that they were using tear-gas too because your eyes were smarting and watering and you had quite a time fighting that off. All the officers practically were gone and of course these trenches weren't much good even to begin with. Then they blew what there *was* to pieces and there was practically no protection at all.

You didn't have much chance. I was hit with a shell splinter and I was just laying there in the trench, what there was of it, and Lieutenant Papeneau came along. He was a wonderful man from Quebec. He came from one of the oldest French-Canadian families, so he came along, and he had his automatic in his hand ready for the Germans to come on, but he stopped and knelt down beside me. One of my buddies had already ripped my puttees off and slit my pants down because I was hit in the leg and my leg had started to swell. Lieutenant Papeneau looked at it and he shoved a cigarette in my mouth and lit it, and he said, 'Don't worry, Vaughan, we'll get you out just as fast as we can.' I said, 'That's fine, sir.' But I lay there for six hours. That's as fast as they could get me out. Six hours! I was lucky to get out at all. One fellow had just been leaning over talking to me and he stood up and the next minute *he* got it, and he fell down dead nearly on top of me. That really upset me because he was one of the married men. In fact that's when I began to get scared. It was all hell let loose, and laying there at the foot of that trench you didn't know what was going on – except that it was bad!

Now that the Patricias' front line had been withdrawn the support line was literally the line of last resort – and things *were* bad. But they were not so bad as they might have been. The 4th Rifle Brigade, in reserve in the lee of the Bellewaerde Ridge, took advantage of a brief pause in the shelling and managed to send

287

forward a company to help out. They walked upright, for they were heavy laden, and the Patricias cheered them on as they came. 'I don't know if there were angels at Mons,' remarked one soldier later, 'but we saw angels that day at Bellewaerde, and they had RB on their shoulders.' They brought boxes of ammunition, and, best of all, two machine-guns. And they also brought hope and fresh heart to the hard-pressed Patricias, for it was not enough merely to save their line – already it was clear that it was up to them to save the day.

Hamilton Gault, wounded for the second time in two hours, and this time seriously, was forced to send a message to Captain Adamson instructing him to take command of the Patricias in the line. He hardly needed to add that he must hold on 'at all costs'. But the situation was worsening by the minute. Adamson himself was wounded and as he crawled along the line, supervising the setting-up of the machine-guns, and handing out rifle ammunition, he was well aware that there was a huge gap in the line on their left. Cautiously raising his head to scan the Frezenberg Ridge, even through clouds of swirling smoke he could see British troops of the 28th Division streaming back to the rear. It could be only a matter of time before the Germans followed to take up the lost ground. When they did the Patricias would be out-flanked.

It was the line of the 83rd Brigade that had given way – only a small part of it, but enough to allow the enemy first to penetrate the gap then to widen it by creeping to the rear of the troops on either side. From the rear, through the smoke and confusion of the fighting, it was hard for Brigade Staff to make sense of the situation, but the sight of retiring troops told its own story and it was clear to the anxious Staff Officers that reinforcements attempting to cross the open slopes of the Frezenberg Ridge would either be mown down or entrapped in their turn. All that could be done was to pray that the flanks would hold, to stiffen the GHQ line, and to hope against hope that the small bodies of men still holding out would be able to contain the enemy until his assault ran out of steam and they could rally the men to counter-attack.

Much closer to the crumbling front, where Harry Crask crouched with the remnants of the signallers in the ruins of his Battalion HQ dug-outs, the position was no clearer.

Pte. H. J. Crask.

Not one of us knew what was happening in front but we more or less knew what to expect. Young French eventually turned up from the front line about 11 a.m., slightly wounded in the head, and stopped with us since the shelling was getting wild again. He reported that our fellows were still holding out in the trenches, but we could see men retiring on our right.

A few minutes afterwards Germans appeared to the right of us, so we had to get out of the trench or we would have been enfiladed. We went back, or rather we struggled back on our chests to the dug-out dragging Game, but all the nine of us were in a helpless condition. There was the Colonel, Sergeant Crabb, Brown, French, Manton, Hayward, Humphreys, Lance-Corporal Game wounded, and myself – and we had not a weapon amongst us.

If Colonel Wallace could not go down fighting, he intended at least to go down with dignity. He had a box of fine Havana cigars in his pocket and he was equally determined to give no German the chance of filching them. He handed the box round and forced a smile to reassure his bedraggled men. 'Smoke, lads? Might as well make the best of things.' The cigars were large and opulent. It took a little while to set them well alight and the men had hardly begun to puff before the Germans were upon them.

They loomed up and circled the shell-hole shouting '*Hände hohe*' and even if the words were incomprehensible the message was clear enough for they stood with rifles and fixed bayonets aimed at the entrance to the battered dug-out. One by one the men clambered out wreathed in clouds of cigar smoke and raised their hands. The air sang with bullets and they had hardly cleared the dug-out when French was shot through the heart and collapsed at Crask's feet. 'The direction of the shot,' Crask noted sadly, 'was from Burnt Farm.' Burnt Farm was, or had been, behind the British line, but the line was so chaotic and the Germans were advancing so fast that it was hard to tell if it had been fired by friend or foe. Crask had his suspicions and so perhaps had the Germans, for one German soldier bent down to pick up French's cap and placed it gently over the dead man's face to hide the staring eyes.*

Pte. H. J. Crask, MM.

They immediately pulled the remaining lot of us down amongst them and we had to lay there roughly two hours in their front line (we were captured about 11.45 a.m.). During that time a party of King's Own tried to retire about eighty or a hundred yards away, but they were simply mad! They were mowed down like so much corn by rifle and machine-gun fire. A few that were left put their hands up, and the Germans in our line

---

* Burnt Farm was later marked on British trench maps as Uhlan Farm.

289

ceased fire immediately. They were good fellows all round that captured us. They were 77th Hanoverian Regiment and they kept us from fire as much as possible by making a parapet in front of us as well as for themselves. They also gave us meat and bread and coffee, and did their best for our wounded. At 1.30 p.m. we were all put in a dug-out. Two guards stayed with us and their line then began to advance towards Ypres. We all had the same opinion – that they were simply making a walk of it to Ypres, then on to Calais, and that they'd finally reach London. The Germans hardly seemed to know as much as I did. They undoubtedly thought that we were all that was left of the Contemptible Little Army.

But it was not quite all – although, after three weeks' fighting in the salient, such reserve battalions as there were were so pitifully low in numbers that they were battalions in name only, and a third of the men in the ranks of the 1st Yorks and Lancs – the only battalion that was anywhere near full strength – had arrived just three days earlier as a draft of inexperienced reinforcements. The 1st Welch, like the Territorials of the 12th London Rangers, were barely the strength of a single company. The 2nd East Yorks and the King's Own could muster fewer than six hundred men between them and the 1st East Lancs were only three hundred and fifty strong. The reserves could not achieve much, but they had to try. Far out in front some ragged remnants were fighting on but they were isolated and would soon be surrounded and a great gap yawned across two miles of open ground between the Patricias at Bellewaerde and the Northumberland Fusiliers at Mouse Trap Farm.

Although by mid-afternoon the Germans had paused in their advance there was no possibility of a counter-attack because the fight had been taken up by their artillery and the British reserves could not hope to penetrate the curtain of deadly fire, but even in the teeth of the bombardment the five hundred men of the East Yorks and the King's Own managed to advance as much as a thousand yards in an attempt to fill the gap. They were just half-way to the old broken line, but they could go no further. The advance had cost them dear, and still they were nowhere near the Germans. Behind their curtain of exploding shells the Germans were entrenching across the gap but mercifully on either side of it the flanks held. They did more than hold. East of Mousetrap Farm the Northumberland Fusiliers clung on, decimated by shelling, beating off attacks in front and on their open flank far into the evening. It was the Germans who gave up first.

Two miles away, the Patricias had every available man in the line – every signaller, every batman, every pioneer, every cook and every orderly. Earlier, with the help of the 4th Rifle Brigade, the left-hand company swung round at right-angles to their front, spread out in a thin line facing the gap, and attacked the enemy troops as they appeared. For the moment at least it seemed they had scared them off, and now help had arrived to extend the flank line further and to form a line of reserves at the Patricias' backs. Even so, it was still touch and go and a determined attempt by the Germans to widen the gap further and 'roll up the line' would have been hard to withstand. But the Germans were still short of men and the one heartening piece of intelligence in an otherwise catastrophic day came from the Royal Flying Corps. Pilots, vigilantly patrolling the skies beyond the salient, could see no large-scale troop movements, no unusual number of trains rushing towards the German railhead and no fresh divisions making for the front. After their initial triumph the Germans seemed content to depend for the moment on the protection of their artillery while they dug in, re-grouped, and used the breathing space to bring up local reserves, to evacuate their casualties, and to marshal prisoners and send them tramping to the rear in long despondent columns.

Pte. H. J. Crask, MM.

We started back just before dusk and our own artillery gave us a parting shell or two which caused more than a little wind amongst us – at least Sergeant Hart of the Cheshires put in a certain amount of gymnastics after the style of the ostrich dance! I could not at all estimate the strength of the Germans. Zonnebeke was simply crammed with them and our own artillery seemed to be lost.

They made any amount of sarcastic cowardly remarks as we passed, calling us swines, etc. One sneering idiot called us 'cousins from over the Channel', telling us also that we were prisoners – we hardly knew that I suppose! – finishing up with a sneer and also spitting at us. We were halted again on the other side of Zonnebeke by some dirty little officer and made to carry the German guards' packs. We had to leave behind our two badly wounded men, Corporal Pugh and Lance-Corporal Game, in two separate dug-outs – apparently dying and left entirely on their own, but with no stretchers they had to be left.

We halted several times before finally reaching our first night's quarters and were questioned by any amount of officers trying to pump us. If they had not asked so many questions they would not have had so many untruths told to them! They thought we were all Kitchener's men. We told them that *they* were still in England – and didn't they look shocked! They had the impudence to tell us that our own Regular Army was absolutely wiped out during the latter part of 1914 and they were more surprised than ever when some of us showed them our pay books and told them that there were lots more Regulars to come from India. Then we were taken charge of by Uhlans and settled down about 10 p.m. at a place called Beclaeare and were put in the church which they had made something like a pigsty. But I was only too glad to get down after such a day and then a march of four miles.

For most of the day Jimmy Vaughan had been lying wounded and helpless in the Patricias' line through the clamour and tumult of the battle, but at last he too was out of it.

Pte. J. W. Vaughan.

Do you know how they got me out? It was the roughest, readiest thing you ever saw, but they had no other way to do it. There was no parados at the back of the trench – well, there practically wasn't a trench by that time! But normally you build up the front to fire at the enemy and it helps to shelter you, and you also should build up the back of the trench a certain amount, what they call the parados, but we had no parados, none at all, and with nothing to conceal you the stretcher-bearers couldn't get up, couldn't carry you back anyway for that matter. So what they did was this. When the first-aid men got to me a couple of fellows said, 'Now, Jimmy, there's an artillery dug-out just fifty yards straight ahead. Now, you've got to crawl over there, crawl to that dug-out and get down in there.' And do you know how they did it? One took hold of my shoulders, the other took hold of my legs – and one leg was wounded, remember! – and they threw me over the back of the trench. That's the only way they could get me out. When I got my breath back and got myself together, I crawled along and crawled along, and it felt like fifty miles not fifty yards. Well, I made it to the dug-out and when I did get in it was full of wounded men, packed with wounded men, and the moans and groans all over were something terrible. I squeezed in and lay down where I could and waited there for the dark, for the stretcher-bearers to come up.

Well, eventually it did get dark and I remember the stretcher-bearers picking me up and getting me out of the dug-out and they carried me to the field dressing station which was about three-quarters of a mile away from the front line.

There was a Red Cross ambulance truck there and the doctor happened to come out, and whether the dressing station was full up or not I don't know, but he looked at me and he said, 'Put him in the ambulance and when she's loaded, take him to Vlamertinghe.' So they took us through Ypres to Vlamertinghe and when we got there, the whole street as far as your eye could see was nothing but stretchers and blankets and walking wounded with blankets over their shoulders, and there must have been half a dozen doctors or more working flat out.*

Darkness was a long time falling on that fine May evening and when it did come it brought little respite from the flash of the guns and the thunder of explosions. The air was heavy with fumes and smoke that thickened as they mingled with the night mist. The situation was still desperate but the Patricias were now in touch with the 85th Brigade, for fresh troops had succeeded in advancing a short distance and stiffening the last few survivors of the earlier advance in their forward position, while across the ridge near Mouse Trap Farm where the hard-pressed Northumberland Fusiliers were still standing firm, as late as 7.30 in the evening the 1st Royal Warwicks and the 2nd Royal Dublin Fusiliers had extended the front and even dashed forward to push the enemy back. Coming after the advance of the 85th Brigade this feat so unsettled the Germans that they actually abandoned some positions they had captured and drew back. It was some small encouragement and these precious footholds made it possible in the hours of darkness to form a tenuous line between the flanks. It was a flimsy enough bulwark and it ran a full three-quarters of a mile behind the front-line positions of that morning, but it was complete. The gap was closed. The tension had slackened.

It would be hours, even days before, they could begin to count the cost but already it was obvious that it had been enormous. Whole battalions had been wiped out, like Harry Crask's, for of the 1st Suffolks only one officer and twenty-nine men returned from the fight. Only two officers and a hundred and twenty men of the 3rd Monmouths survived, and fifty-three men and a sergeant of the 12th London Rangers. Next day the six thousand men of the 84th

---

* Vaughan's wound finished his army career. After many months in hospital in England he was shipped back to recuperate in Canada where he received his discharge in 1916. Seventy years later, on 8 May 1985, as the guest of Princess Patricia's Light Infantry, then serving in Germany, and on what he claims to have been the proudest day of his life, he was able to march through the Menin Gate in the front rank of his old regiment.

Brigade could muster only fourteen hundred of their number. The Patricias had four officers and a hundred and fifty men left.

They had fought like lions to the limit of their endurance and far beyond it. They were drained and exhausted, and it was time to go. The guns rumbled on but the fire was thinner now for the Germans had relaxed their efforts, as worn out as their opponents by the fearful day.

A young moon rose in the hazy sky above the battlefield. On both sides of the line they were carrying out the wounded and relieving the men who had survived the worst of the onslaught.

When the Patricias' turn came in the early hours of the morning they dragged themselves thankfully back to assemble behind the trench. In the light of the first streaks of dawn Lieutenant Niven formed them up and placed himself at the head of the column. He was carrying Princess Patricia's colours. They had not escaped entirely unscathed and the rich red of the banner was smudged and streaked and slightly torn. But the Princess's colours had stayed in the line throughout the battle and now the colours led the survivors of her Regiment out. They marched down the track that led past Bellewaerde Lake, down the hill through Railway Wood and round to the Menin Road. In the shallow-scraped trenches reserve troops of their own 80th Brigade stood up to cheer them as they passed and some called out, 'Well done the Pats!' They were too weary just then to savour either the moment or the accolade, but it soon passed into Regimental history.

Chapter 21

~

Less than twenty miles to the south where the troops were assembled for the start of the 'big show' on which the French and British Commands had pinned their hopes the night was clear and starry. From the Aubers Ridge, a thin pencil line against the luminous sky, past the black-etched slag heaps of the Loos coal fields, across the chalky foothills of Artois to the ancient towers of Arras at the limit of the French attack, the French and British armies were poised and waiting for the morning. They had assembled by stealth, but it was an open secret, for the preparations for battle and the movement of tens of thousands of men could hardly be concealed and only yesterday the Germans had erected a taunting notice in their trenches in front of Aubers Ridge that was clearly meant to rile the British a hundred yards away: *'Attack postponed until tomorrow.'* The implication that the enemy was ready and waiting was clear and the snipers had relieved their feelings by firing at the notice and reducing it to matchwood.

In a front-line trench on what was once the road that led from Sailly to Fromelles Charlie Burrows was sound asleep for, like all old soldiers, he had learned the lesson of resting when he could. Charlie had been in it from the start, he had landed with the 7th Division at Antwerp, he had fought through the first Battle of Ypres, and he had been fighting ever since, but as a gunner this was his first experience of being in the front line with the infantry. It was hardly surprising that he was exhausted for they had moved up earlier in the evening, man-handling the guns into positions that had been secretly prepared for them close up to the German trenches. The wheels were fitted with rubber tyres to reduce the noise as far as possible, but it was nerve-racking heavy work to drag them in under the very noses of the enemy. But every man was a volunteer and nobody had grumbled. Now, there was nothing to do but wait. They had been left in no doubt of the part they were to play and they were well prepared for it.

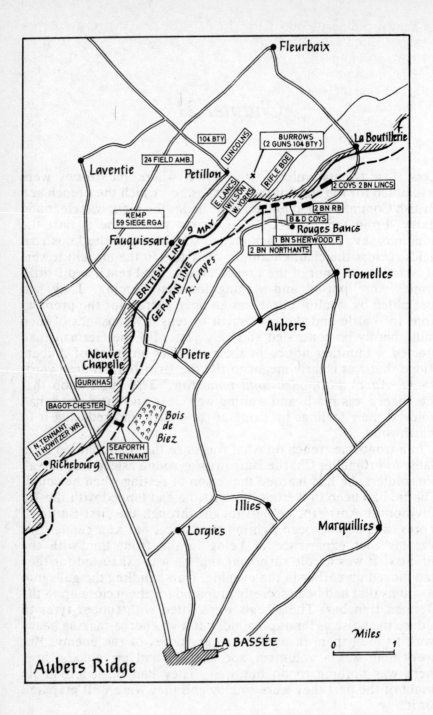

Fleurbaix

Laventie

24 FIELD AMB.

104 BTY

Petillon

LINCOLNS

×

BURROWS
(2 GUNS 104 BTY)

RIFLE BDE

La Boutillerie

KEMP
59 SIEGE RGA

E.LANCS

WILSON
W.YORKS

2 COYS 2 BN LINCS

2 BN RB

Fauquissart

B & D COYS

Rouges Bancs

1 BN SHERWOOD F.

2 BN NORTHANTS

BRITISH LINE 9 MAY

GERMAN LINE

R. Layes

Fromelles

Aubers

Neuve
Chapelle

Pietre

GURKHAS

BAGOT-CHESTER

Bois
de
Biez

N.TENNANT
11 HOWITZER WR.

SEAFORTH
C.TENNANT

Richebourg

Illies

Lorgies

Marquillies

LA BASSÉE

Miles

0   1

Aubers Ridge

Gnr. C. B. Burrows, 104th Bty., 22nd Brig., RFA.

They'd pulled us out of the line on 28 April to somewhere about three kilometres north-west of Merville and we stayed there for four days. Our left section of two guns did some experimental firing on barbed wire entanglements there. We heard that it was an exact replica of the German front line immediately in front of us in our old position. Dozens of Generals and Staff Officers came to watch us firing and after we'd finished they went to inspect the result. We practised and practised, and moved back to our old position on 2 May and on the night of 8 May we went into action right on the front-line parapet. Plenty of excitement. We are to cut the German barbed wire with our shrapnel shells the same as we experimented with at Merville in front of the Generals. We get the guns into position all right and cover them as best we can. I bet we will cop it hot here – there's only about a hundred yards distance between ours and the enemy front line. All our gunners are eager for the fray. The 7th Battalion Middlesex Regiment are in the trenches behind us – they belong to the 8th Division and this is their first attack. We are to attack in the morning.

Not since the Battle of Omdurman had guns been deliberately positioned in the front line with the infantry, but desperate measures were called for if the battle was to be won. Guns were scarce. Ammunition was scarcer still and three weeks of fighting at Ypres had depleted reserve stocks to an alarming level. There were not enough guns and there were certainly not enough shells to cut the wire and batter the German line across the length of the battle-front, so a full-scale frontal attack was out of the question. It was useless, in the circumstances, to attempt to repeat the tactics employed across the same ground in the Battle of Neuve Chapelle two months earlier, and Sir Douglas Haig and his staff had come up with a new plan. The guns would be concentrated in two groups and, firing as fast and as hard as they could, would attempt to cut the wire and pierce the line in two places, on the left in front of Fromelles and on the right to the south of Neuve Chapelle and the Bois du Biez. Then the troops would dash through the gaps, fight their way beyond and sweep round across the Aubers Ridge in a pincer movement that would trap the Germans behind them. The troops had also been placed with care – the Meerut Division, well blooded and experienced, on the right, and the 8th Division two miles to the north. When the battle began every gun would be trained on the German line in front of them. The gunners would drive the breaches, but it was up to the hardened and experienced infantry to follow through and exploit the gains.

Between these two vital sectors the troops holding the front line that looped round Neuve Chapelle and ran north in front of Fauquissart to meet the 8th divisional sector were neither hardened nor experienced. The West Riding Territorials had been in France for exactly three weeks and two days but they had already had one casualty.

Cpl. A. Wilson, 1/5 Bn. (TF), West Yorkshire Regt.

We went more or less straight into the trenches in front of Aubers Ridge, about ten days before the battle. Of course it was all quiet then compared to what came later, with just the odd bit of shelling and sniping, and we went in in batches to get us accustomed to it. The very first night we were there my Company Commander, Captain Lansdale, was shot in the neck. He hadn't been in the trenches half an hour and out he went! He wasn't killed, or even very badly wounded, though I remember we were horrified seeing him streaming with blood. I wasn't far away when it happened, but it could only have been a flesh wound. Anyway, out he went, and that was our first casualty. Strangely enough he came back several months later, again as our Company Commander, and he hadn't been in the trenches another night when he was shot in the shoulder! We could hardly believe it! His total service in the trenches didn't even amount to a day and he ended up with *two* wound stripes. We thought it was a great joke the second time it happened – of course we were a bit blasé by then – but the first time he never got anywhere near the Battle of Aubers Ridge. We had another temporary Company Commander for that show.

The West Riding Brigade did not expect to play a very active part in the 'show' a few hours hence for, if all went well and the Germans in the trenches on their front were cut off by the troops converging behind, they would surely give up with no more than a token fight. The night turned chill as they waited for the dawn and the start of the battle, and sitting with their backs to the wall of the trench Arthur Wilson and his friend Walter Malthouse huddled together for warmth. Despite Arthur's elevated rank of Corporal the two boys were inseparable. It was almost exactly a year since they had joined the Territorials and Walter, marginally senior in age if not in rank, was still apt in moments of levity to annoy Arthur by calling him 'little lad'. This was a reference to the day of their mobilisation.

Cpl. A. Wilson.

We were at Scarborough on our annual camp on the Saturday of the August bank holiday weekend and I happened to be promoted to Corporal and that day I was acting Battalion Orderly Corporal, so I was with the Colonel in the Battalion office. In the afternoon a motor-cycle dispatch rider arrived with special sealed orders to say that the Battalion had to mobilise immediately and strike camp and return to York. There were loads of us there – West Yorks 5th and 6th Battalions, 7th and 8th Battalions, Leeds Rifles, and also the West Yorks Rifle Regiment from Leeds. Well, we packed up and we marched into Scarborough late at night. Of course with all the troops going through the town, and all the excitement, people were coming out of their houses to see what was going on – some of them already in their night attire. I was marching behind the Colonel, who was on his horse, and I had four men each side of me with fixed bayonets. Well, being Battalion Orderly Corporal I was carrying dispatches and *my* rifle was put in a truck, so that I was marching through Scarborough with these four armed men round me, while *I* was carrying the boxes. One old girl looked out of her door and she was standing there in her nightdress and she shouted out, 'Yon little lad's off to prison!' Well, that was me of course. Walter thought it was a huge joke and he never let me forget it.

The Yorkshiremen had also brought their guns and, although they were hardly up to date, they were thankfully received. They were better than nothing but, like many others, the guns of Norman Tennant's battery had seen service in the Boer War and also at the Battle of Omdurman.

Gnr. N. Tennant, 11th Howitzer Bty., West Riding Brig. (TF), RA.

They were five-inch breech-loading Howitzers – great, clumsy old weapons. And they fired 56lb high explosive shells. You had to thrust the shell into the breech, ram it home, and then push in the charge that would fire it, which was explosive held in a canvas bag shaped something like a mushroom with two smaller charges in canvas bags behind it. They were called the 'cores' and it was hard physical work. The gun-drill was just as it had been in the old days and the weapon was really obsolete. Once you'd loaded the gun it was fired by pulling a lanyard and, of course, the guns themselves took a fair bit of man-handling. I did my share of gun-drill in the early days, but I was more than happy when I was made a signaller.

Major Paul Petrie was our Commanding Officer, and actually we'd lost him a few weeks before we went to France. It was a strange affair, because he wasn't called Petrie then. His name was Steinthal, a German name, and he'd been forced to leave the battery, because the powers that be were suspicious about his antecedents and thought he might have German sympathies. He was in the wool trade in Bradford, and there were a lot of families in that business who were German from generations back. Anyway, he was forced to give up the command while they checked all this out and we got a nasty little fat short-arsed fellow in his place. Nobody liked him. He had a high opinion of himself and he used to give orders in a high-pitched, snarling voice. I remember when we were on the march on the Great North Road, he called out, '*Battery will trot.*' Well, away we went at a fair lick and I don't suppose this little fat fellow was a very experienced rider because he was bumping up and down in the saddle looking extremely uncomfortable, going redder and redder in the face, and it was as much as he could do to hold on. It wasn't long before he'd had enough. But he could hardly get the order out because he was thudding up and down so hard that he couldn't get breath. Eventually he managed to jerk out the order, '*B . . . b . . . b . . . battery w . . . w . . . walk m . . . m . . . m . . . march!*' We were most amused. I was delighted myself because I didn't like him at all. He'd just given me fourteen days' CB and the worst of *that* was that it lost me my embarkation leave.

It was all over a piece of nonsense. At stables one morning one of my horses was restless and started kicking the one next to him in the stall, so I picked up a broom – only a light affair – and gave the horse a whack to move him away. Well, as luck would have it, just at that moment this little Major came along, and he went absolutely purple in the face. He screeched, 'Sergeant-Major, take that man's name!' Well, the Sergeant-Major, Billy Brown – a lovely chap – knew perfectly well who I was, but he had to come up and solemnly ask my name – as if he didn't know! – and I was up before the Major on a charge of 'cruelty to a horse'. And that's how I lost my embarkation leave. All I managed to get was twenty-four hours' compassionate leave, because I wrote to my parents and asked them to send a telegram saying my presence was needed to sign some business paper or other. Fortunately our own Major came back to us just before we left. He came back as Major Petrie.

Someone who knew him said Petrie was his wife's name and he'd adopted it to avoid any more trouble.

The Battery was dug in across the fields behind Richebourg St Vaast but Tennant and his fellow signaller Vallender were on permanent duty at the observation post in an empty house in the partly ruined village half a mile away on the main road to Neuve Chapelle. This suited them well. The Observing Officer seldom came to the post and in his absence the signallers amused themselves by scrounging, exploring, and souvenir hunting in the empty barns and houses. In the course of their wanderings they found an old drain-pipe and were struck by a brilliant idea for an emergency signalling system, and when they were next off duty they hastened to share this discovery with two gunners from the Battery. The first experiment was carried out next night, and it took them the best part of the day to prepare it. They built a bed of sandbags for the drain-pipe, laid it carefully in the direction of a pre-arranged fixed point to the left of the Battery, wedged it firmly into place and piled more sandbags on top. Morse code signalled through this narrow channel – a mere pin-prick of light – would surely be invisible to all but the recipients of the message and if the unreliable telephone line were to fail the drain-pipe would be worth its weight in gold. They were extremely pleased with themselves.

Unfortunately it was a large drain-pipe. The light that emerged from the other end was somewhat larger than a pin-prick, and when they began to signal at the appointed hour, the flickering beam flashed like a searchlight across the fields. The answering flash from the gunners at the battery was clearly visible in the observation post and doubtless just as visible to the Germans, since the gunners in the Battery were naturally signalling towards the enemy lines. The gunners had some difficulty in convincing the Military Police that they had not been signalling to the enemy and were not spies. Still chastened by the effect of a severe wigging from Major Petrie the signallers dismantled their ingenious apparatus, resigning themselves to conventional methods – and also to the weary prospect of crawling across the fields to repair the telephone line in the all-too-likely event of its being broken.

In the early hours of the morning Major Petrie himself had come to the observation post with the Observing Officer, anxious to see the bombardment and the battle for himself. The OP was crowded. The atmosphere was tense, but it was the tension of excitement for every man in the battery from the major downwards was thrilled at the prospect of taking part in the real war at last. From their post on the main road Tennant and Vallender had watched the build-up to the battle as the fighting troops trudged past towards the trenches.

They were behind the Indians and their guns were to help to pave the way for the assault of the Meerut Division. In the last few days the fields and orchards round the village had been transformed into a panorama of the East that would not have been out of place on an Indian cantonment and from the tall bearded Sikhs to the cheerful little Gurkhas the Indians were a source of endless and colourful interest. They were troops of the Garhwal Brigade waiting in reserve for the coming battle.

Gnr. N. Tennant.

I can remember how excited I was that night. We all were. Of course, in the run-up to the bombardment – our *first* bombardment – there was no question of going to sleep. We couldn't have slept anyway! You had the feeling that something tremendous was going to happen. Of course we had no idea what it was and we'd been told nothing. I hadn't the faintest inkling that they were going for Aubers Ridge. I'd never heard of Aubers Ridge and I didn't hear it mentioned for a long time afterwards. All we knew was that we were going to take part in the big breakthrough and we were going to push right through to Lille. That's all we were told. I didn't even know that the French were attacking too. We were raw and inexperienced, but we were wildly enthusiastic and we had no doubt that we were well on the way to winning the war!

Not all the gunners were so sanguine as the enthusiastic new arrivals.

Bdr. W. Kemp.

When the ammunition came up it was sealed in strong heavy boxes which could only be opened by hefty men with pickaxes, and it took *some* time. There were not many rounds. Next week the Battery was turned out one night to unload ammunition. There was one wagon and when it was all unloaded there were *ten* rounds – and they were all armour-piercing shells from the coast defence batteries. That's all they could give us. We didn't find it reassuring. We thought it was a disgrace.

The heavy guns were intended to fire on specific targets where strongpoints had been spotted in the German line. The task of the massed field-guns was to batter the line itself, to cut the coiled barbed wire that protected it and to carve a passage for the infantry. The bombardment was timed to last for thirty minutes rising for the last ten to a crescendo of concentrated fire. It had worked initially at

Neuve Chapelle, and although reports had indicated that the Germans had now improved their line Sir Douglas Haig had little doubt that it would work again.

The full extent of the 'improvements' was not visible from the air. Pilots, and even observers on the flat ground opposite, could see that the belts of wire were thicker than before but they could hardly guess that beyond them lay another obstacle. The breastwork parapets of the trenches had been built up and widened – they were seven feet high and as much as fifteen, even twenty feet across. It had all taken a prodigious amount of labour and throughout March and April hundreds of working parties from troops supposedly at rest, helped by squads of recruits brought from depots as far away as Lille, had shifted incalculable tons of earth to fill the sandbags that made up the new defences. Between the parapets and the visible belt of wire the excavations they had left behind were filled with sunken barbed wire, close-coiled and lethal. Even if the outlying belts of wire were blown away these man-traps lay beyond. They were invisible. And they were almost indestructible.

The trench-defences were constructed with equal skill and forethought. Every few yards in both parapet and parados large wooden boxes had been buried cave-like, deep into the thick wall of sandbags, each one large enough to shelter two men and calculated to protect them from even a direct hit from all but the heaviest of high explosive shells. A whole garrison could survive bombardment uninjured and largely unperturbed. And there were machine-gun posts ingeniously constructed from V-shaped wooden frames burrowed deep into the protection of the sand-bagged parapet with the embrasure at the point of the V, with its steel-rail loop-hole directed towards the enemy. They were placed every twenty yards, carefully positioned at corners and traverses to increase the field of fire, and they were entirely invisible from the British lines.

With ten times as many guns and fifty times as many shells, and had the bombardment lasted hours instead of minutes, it would still have been a tough nut to crack. As it was, many guns were old and of obsolete design, many more were inaccurate, suffering from such wear and tear that their shells failed to reach their targets in the enemy line, and many were of too small a calibre to make much impression on it when they did. To add to the difficulty a great deal of the ammunition was faulty.

Bdr. W. Kemp.

We opened fire at twelve hundred yards behind Fauquissart at targets spotted for us by an aeroplane, and we put out a very

303

large letter L, with the long shank on the line of fire to assist the observer in the plane. What we fired at during the battle I just don't know. My bombardier watched the attack and he said that the infantry were met with machine-gun fire as soon as they showed themselves. They never even took the first trench at Fauquissart.

Firing at point-blank range from the British front trench a hundred yards from the German line Charlie Burrows's guns had done well – better even than the gunners realised, for if they had not made the only gap in the wire it was certainly the most effective. They were so close to their target that it would have been difficult to miss.

Gnr. C. B. Burrows.

Attack starts at 5 a.m., our section fire for about an hour and blow all the wire entanglements to blazes. They then lift their fire further on, and the infantry go over. Enemy reply with intense fire. Heard that our infantry were doing well and that some prisoners have been taken by the 2nd Lincolns, and that in parts they have reached the enemy second line. Fighting lasts all day, the infantry do not seem to make much headway. They have plenty of casualties. Our section very lucky up to now, only two gunners wounded out of eight. The German artillery could not have spotted them yet. Heard that our Captain is wounded in two places, but he still carries on.

It was the two leading companies of the 2nd Rifle Brigade who had got through the breach, but they were almost on their own. Then things began to go wrong.

Capt. R. Berkeley, MC.

A number of 'shorts' caused severe casualties in the advanced sap where B and D companies were assembled to lead the attack. At 5.40 a.m. undismayed by this misadventure, they swept across to the German trench taking it in their stride and pushed on to the battalion objective, followed by A and C companies who occupied and consolidated the German trench. Battalion Headquarters crossed immediately behind the support companies but the enemy machine-gun fire was terrific and they had heavy casualties. The battalion machine-guns were unable to get across. Battalion Headquarters were dispersed and the bombing and blocking parties, so carefully organised beforehand, were at once broken up and could not be reassembled. Nevertheless, the task had been performed swiftly and well, and they were just enjoying the afterglow of success when they suddenly realised that, apart from a handful of the Royal Irish Rifles, they were entirely alone. Where were the turning movements to right and left that were to enlarge the gap? Where was the advanced guard *including some mounted troops* that was to press on as soon as the first objective was secured? The Rifle Brigade were on the first objective. Where were the East Lancashires on the right, and the Sherwood Foresters beyond them?*

The answer was not hard to find. As Captain Berkeley sadly recorded, 'They were lying out in No Man's Land and most of them would never stand again.' From their burrows, well protected by many square yards of earth-filled sandbags, the German machine-gunners had begun to fire even before the bombardment ceased, catching troops like the East Lancs as they crawled out from their trenches preparing to assault. The battle orders had made no bones about the fact that success depended on *a continuous forward movement of fresh troops*. Most of the 'fresh troops' of the second wave and support battalions were shot down as they cleared the parapet. The battle and the troops who fought it died in No Man's Land.

Bdr. W. Kemp.

I was asked to go forward with some signalling gear, because the Major had asked Lieutenant Brian to go forward and observe the fire using his periscope. We were nailed down for a start by a 77 mm battery. So the officer spoke to them and said, 'I can't move from here. They're shelling where I want to go.' Well, we got into the line and it was terrible there. There *we* were with our *ten* rounds, and the German shells raining down in hundreds! It was all so hopeless and useless. I didn't like my position where I was with the telephone. I don't know why, I just had a feeling I didn't like where I was. So I moved a little bit away from the officer, and it must have been a premonition, because next minute a shell came over, there was a terrible explosion and Lieutenant Brian was killed. We should both have gone if I hadn't moved.

What a waste of life! He couldn't do anything or even see anything. I was with him at the OP and all *I* could see was that it was all a dismal failure.

---

* From the Regimental History.

Away on the right beyond Neuve Chapelle, the attempt to exploit a second breach in the line had been no more successful. By seven in the morning both attacks had come to a standstill and as more and more troops were sent forward, as the casualties mounted and the hours passed, the battle-field descended into chaos.

Capt. W. G. Bagot-Chester, MC.

It soon came through the telephone to say the first line had been taken, only to be contradicted afterwards. We waited in the redoubt from 3 a.m. to 2 p.m., when we were ordered forward. We had to advance about two thousand yards across open country to start with, but we were not fired on until we reached a long communication trench leading up to the front trench-line. Of course we advanced in artillery formation. Toward the last hundred yards or so German 'Woolly Bears' began to burst overhead, and 'Jack Johnsons'* close by, but I had only one man hit at this point. We then got into a long communication trench leading up from Lansdowne Post to the Gridiron Trenches. Here we were blocked for a long time, shelling increasing every moment, wounded trying to get by us. After a time we got into the Gridiron where it was absolute hell. Hun shells, large and small, bursting everywhere, blowing in the parapet here and there, and knocking tree branches off. Here there was fearful confusion. No one knew the way to anywhere. There was such a maze of trenches, and such a crowd of people, many wounded, all wanting to go in different directions, one regiment going back, ours trying to go forward, wounded and stretcher-bearers going back, etc. I presently went on to a trench called the Pioneer Trench. There I had twenty-six casualties from shell. Havildar Manbir had his leg blown off, and was in such agony that he asked to be shot.

As one got further to the front trench, the place got more of a shambles, wounded and dead everywhere. Those who could creep or walk were trying to get back; others were simply lying and waiting. The ground in front was littered with Seaforth bodies and 41st Dogras. From the Pioneer Trench I went on to the front trench, occupied by the 41st Dogras, who, however, had very few men left so heavily had they suffered. One of their British officers had completely lost his nerve, and was rather a

---

* 'Woolly Bears' were shrapnel shells which burst in a cloudlike explosion. 'Jack Johnsons', nicknamed after a famous Negro boxer of the time, were high explosive shells which burst with a thick black cloud.

pitiable sight. I tried to comfort him a bit. We had to set to work at once to try to clear up the trench. It was full of killed and wounded, equipment of all sorts, and the ground in front was strewn with dead Seaforths, who made the charge this morning at 5.40 a.m. from this trench, also 41st Dogras, who made a second attempt. Towards dusk the 41st moved out. Through the night we were at work repairing the trench and cleaning up generally, while out in front, parties were at work searching for their wounded.

One of the dead Seaforths was Lieutenant Charles Tennant who had written his last letter to his 'Darling Lucy'.[*]

Between the two assaults, in the trenches in front of Fauquissart, Arthur Wilson and Walter Malthouse had hardly enjoyed a grand-stand view of the battle for the incessant shelling had kept their heads well down. All they had heard was the noise of the guns, the spit of machine-guns not far ahead and a spate of rumours that died away as the day wore on. It was late in the afternoon when a shell exploded in the trench.

Cpl. A. Wilson.

Of course we were standing to all day, ready to go, but about three o'clock in the afternoon we were stood down and told we could rest a bit in the trench, and it was fairly clear that nothing much else was going to happen. Well of course we were exhausted, and I got down in the trench next to Walter and I dropped off right away. All of a sudden there was an almighty explosion, right in the trench, a direct hit just a little bit further along from where we were. I was right next to Walter – touching him even. I was stunned of course, but when I got my wits together I could hardly believe it. I was covered in blood – saturated – and I really thought I'd bought it. But it was Walter's blood. I didn't have a scratch myself. Walter had taken the full blast and somehow or other it hadn't touched me. He was blown to bits. A terrible sight. I don't think there was a bit of his body bigger than a leg of lamb. I gathered up what I could, put him into a sandbag and later on when it got dusk, a few of us got out of the trench and buried him a little way behind, about twenty-five yards back, because we couldn't go far. I had my prayer book and I read the burial service – the whole thing, prayers and everything. We had several men to

---

[*] Lt. Tennant's body was never identified and he is commemorated on the le Touret Memorial to the Missing.

bury of course but we saw that they got a proper burial. We were all friends in the Territorials, joined together, been together all along. We felt pretty bad about it. The worst of it was that from the direction of the shell we felt almost sure it was one of ours. Of course the authorities wouldn't have that! But I got a few of the men digging and it only took us half an hour to find the nose-cap. Sure enough it was marked 'WD' – War Department. It was from a naval shell fired by one of our long-distance guns mounted on an armoured train. So we proved the point. But it didn't do Walter any good.*

Many hours before, the remnants of the 2nd Rifle Brigade had been pushed back to the German trench where they had first made the breakthrough and held a hundred yards of it in the face of assaults from either side. It was the only small gain of the day. But at two o'clock in the morning of 10 May the enemy attacked in force and from three sides. A little later, Colonel Stephens, arriving with troops to relieve his Battalion, found that there was no battalion left to relieve. The Germans had made good their losses and closed up their line. The battle was over.

Capt. W. G. Bagot-Chester, MC.

Everything is fairly quiet now. At night parties from regiments behind who took part in the attack come up to my trench and go out in front to search for their dead to bring them in and bury them behind. We don't fire much by night or day. By day there is nothing to be seen to fire at, and by night it would only be a chance shot.

Gnr. C. B. Burrows.

Nothing much doing on the 10th. Our guns have narrow shaves, but do not do any more firing, and we pull them out of action about 8 p.m. in the dark. The battery move off at 11.15 p.m. and march all night to Festubert. There we heard that the French had done good near Arras, and that our attack had been a washout. Heard we were supposed to have been after Aubers Ridge. Well, all I can say is that concludes the Battle of Aubers Ridge and no mistake.

The stretcher-bearers, as always, had done sterling work and they

---

* Walter Malthouse's grave is in Fauquissart Military Cemetery.

had rescued most of the wounded, for the men of the second waves and succeeding attempts had been hit as they advanced from the assembly trenches across open ground.

Pte. L. Mitchell, 24th Field Ambulance, 8 Div.

I did my share of bringing men off the battle-field but by the time it came to Aubers Ridge I'd been transferred to the nursing Division, working in the main dressing station a little way back from the line. I remember watching the infantry going up for the battle and they were singing '*We beat the Germans every time, we beat the Germans at Mons. We beat the Germans at Neuve Chapelle and now we're going to give them hell.*' They weren't singing the same at the end of the battle. It was a real disaster, that attack was. The Germans smashed the whole thing up.

Our division, the 8th Division, had the heaviest casualties of any of the divisions that took part in the attack and it was an appalling affair. For three days we never stopped dressing the wounded men as they were brought in, and at the end of those three days we still had something like sixty or seventy stretcher cases outside. We just didn't know what to do with them. The Major I was with dropped on the floor exhausted and I had to give an anaesthetic for the removal of an arm and I had never given an anaesthetic in my life. I didn't actually see very many die because as soon as you dressed them they were taken out and put in ambulances and lorries and taken away down to the Casualty Clearing Stations. The vehicles were packed jam-full, and sometimes they were coming *back* full from the Casualty Clearing Stations because *they* were full up and the ambulance drivers didn't know where to take the wounded.

I never saw any attack with so many men who had bullet wounds as at Aubers Ridge. The Germans just mowed them down and most of the bullet wounds were through the legs. We had a lot of splinting to do, splinting, splinting, splinting. But one man was brought in with his face covered with a bandage and when the Major came in to look at him and see what was the matter he went out and was violently sick. When he took the bandages off we saw the man had no eyes, no nose, no chin, no mouth – and he was alive! The Sergeant called me and said, 'The doctor says I've got to give him four times the usual dose of morphia.' And I said, 'You know what that will do, don't you?' And he said, 'Yes. And I can't do it. I'm ordering you to do it.' So I had to go in and give him four times the dose of morphia. I laid a clean bandage on his face and stayed with him until he died. That stayed in my memory for a very long time. It stays in it now.

It isn't very nice to go and kill a man, is it? And I had to do it again after that. A man was brought to us with a piece of steel, a big chunk of shell, sticking out of his breast-bone and sticking out of his back. He also had an arm smashed up and very severe head wounds – and *he* was still alive, how I don't know because the steel was running right through him. Well it was quite impossible to do anything for him, and I was only too glad to put him out of his misery. Of course I didn't do it off my own bat. The Officer tells you to do it and you do it – but you don't forget! When I got home after the war I sometimes used to have a nightmare and wake up in the night thinking my arms were covered with blood. It wore off eventually.

For the troops like the West Yorks who remained in the line, the most enduring memory was the sight of the countless rows of dead. The battlefield was one vast charnel house and although many bodies lay where they had been struck down between assembly or support trenches and the British front line, so long as the German machine-gunner ruled the battlefield it was risky work to attempt to bring them in for decent burial.

It was a beautiful month of May, and as one warm day succeeded another and swallows dipped and soared in the cloudless sky the sickly smell of putrefaction seeped into every trench and dug-out, permeated every article of clothing, and tainted every morsel and every mug of tea that the troops consumed.

Chapter 22

Despite the disappointing results of 9 May, Sir Douglas Haig was determined to 'press on vigorously' on the 10th, but an early morning meeting with his Divisional Generals, at which he intended to finalise details of the next assault, forced him to the reluctant conclusion that it would be futile for the moment to attempt to renew the attack on Aubers Ridge. One day's fighting had resulted in the staggering loss of four hundred and fifty-eight officers and more than eleven thousand men, and the surviving troops were in such a state of confusion and disarray that it would take days to reassemble them as an orderly fighting force. But it was not so much the toll of casualties that influenced him, nor even the vehement opposition of some of his field officers. The deciding factor was the want of sufficient ammunition to guarantee a decisive result.

It was a hard pill to swallow – and all the harder in the light of the glowing reports that had reached his Headquarters trumpeting the success of the French Army on his right. The French had prepared the way with long heavy bombardments and in the first hours of the battle their success had been phenomenal. They swept across the hill of Notre Dame de Lorette, captured the defences round the chapel on its summit, thrust down into the Souchez Valley and across it towards the lower slopes of the Vimy Ridge looming ahead like a bastion to guard the Douai Plain. And there they had stopped. The French reserves were held too far back and in the time it took them to reach the front to replace the casualties and pursue the battle, the advance had slowed, the Germans had recovered from the first blow and the impetus was lost. But Marshal Joffre was far from despondent. Encouraged by the first heady success it was natural to suppose that the set-back was only a hiccup on the road to certain victory. With one more effort Vimy Ridge would be sure to fall and the Germans would be just as surely on the run. It was self-evident that the British must continue to give support by keeping the enemy busy, by pinning down his reserves and carrying out their commitment to the letter. National pride, even national

311

honour was at stake. If the attack on Aubers Ridge had to be called off, how were they to be vindicated?

One crumb of encouragement lightened the weight of Haig's dilemma. On the extreme right of the attack where the British sector met the French, the 1st Division had succeeded in advancing the line in front of Festubert. It was a small comfort to Sir Douglas Haig that here, where it would be of greatest use to the French, a concentrated effort stood the greatest chance of success. A decision was swiftly reached. The 7th Division which had played only a minor part in the battle of Aubers Ridge would march south to Festubert. In a matter of days, when the troops had been reshuffled, when resources had been concentrated and the plans and preparations had been made, the assault would be renewed.

In the midst of this reappraisal and recasting of his tactics Sir Douglas Haig was in no mood to spare time for any journalist, not even for Colonel Tim Repington who, as military correspondent of *The Times*, was the only representative of the press who was *persona grata* with the Army. He referred him brusquely to GHQ and there Repington met with better success. From the point of view of Sir John French, Repington arrived at an opportune moment. The Commander-in-Chief had watched the attack on Aubers Ridge from a church tower in the village of Laventie and although his view was necessarily limited and the full facts had not yet come to light, he was convinced in his own mind that, despite his careful husbanding of shells, lack of ammunition for the guns had been a major cause of the disappointing result. The War Office telegram that awaited him on his return to GHQ could not have come at a worse moment. It ordered him peremptorily to release twenty thousand rounds of ammunition from his meagre reserve for immediate dispatch to Gallipoli. It was the last straw, and although the telegram had added that the shells would be replaced 'in a few days' French was seething with indignation and only too willing to seize the chance to publicise his grievances by unburdening them to Repington. Six days later the explosion erupted in *The Times* and the shock waves travelled the length and breadth of the country. The story pulled no punches and, as Sir John French intended, the message came through stark and clear: '*British soldiers died last week on Aubers Ridge because the British Army is short of shells.*'

Lord Kitchener was furious. Mr Asquith was equally put out by the unconventional means chosen by the Commander-in-Chief to appeal direct to the public above the head of the Government. And it was not the first time. Towards the end of March, in the disappointing aftermath of Neuve Chapelle, French had complained of shortage of ammunition in two interviews to journalists which had caused considerable anxiety in the Cabinet and in the country as a whole. Lord Kitchener had categorically denied that it was true. Of course there were difficulties, but they would be resolved in time, and meanwhile, he reassured Asquith, the supply of shells was quite adequate for present requirements. The Prime Minister could hardly doubt the word of this distinguished soldier who was his own Secretary of State for War and he was easily convinced. Only three weeks earlier in a public speech at Newcastle he had set out to quash the rumours and convince the country that the stories were untrue and that all was well. Now he had been made to look a fool, and it was difficult not to lay the blame squarely at Kitchener's door.

Lord Kitchener was not a dishonourable man but he was not above misleading, and perhaps not above hinting that the Commander-in-Chief might be making much of the lack of ammunition in order to distract attention from his own tactical failures. With every appearance of righteous indignation he denied that Sir John French had ever informed the War Office that he was unable to undertake offensive operations for lack of munitions. Even if this was true in a literal sense, it took no account of French's many pleas and complaints. Nor did it take account of the fact that his plans and expectations for offensive operations were based on estimates of supplies which had been promised by the War Office and that the promises had not been kept. But Kitchener stood his ground. In his opinion supplies were adequate and the expenditure of shells was extravagant. Asquith was in no position to challenge him: he had no other first-hand information to enable him to form an independent judgement. While all diplomatic papers and communications received by the Foreign Office were copied, as a matter of course, for the Prime Minister, on the pretext of secrecy no communications of any kind were passed on by the Admiralty or the War Office, or even exchanged between themselves as interested parties.

Three weeks after his Newcastle speech, in which he had denied in all good faith that there was a shell shortage, and two days before the story broke in *The Times*, information had come into Asquith's hands. Even before the bombshell exploded – and he had purposely asked Repington to delay publication for a day or so – the Commander-in-Chief sent two trusted members of his senior staff to London. They carried three copies of a secret memorandum in which Sir John French clearly and concisely set out the situation and stressed its gravity. They also carried copies of all correspondence and communications which had passed between GHQ and the War Office over the previous months, and were instructed to show this evidence to Lloyd George, and also to two leading members of the Opposition, Bonar Law and Arthur Balfour.

The difficulties had many strands, but the major problem boiled down to the fact that management of the war was in the hands of one man and the Secretary of State for War, Lord Kitchener, was disinclined to relinquish it.

Kitchener had seen long and distinguished service but he was a soldier of the old school. His active soldiering had been far from home and his custom, traditional since time immemorial, had been to get on with a mission and to dispatch news of the outcome when it was over. The news had taken days, and occasionally weeks to reach London but since it was invariably satisfactory in the long run, and since transport and communications were so slow that consultation would have been out of the question, successive Governments had been content to leave military matters to the professional military men. Lord Kitchener had devoted his whole life to the army. He was unmarried, he was a successful commander, he enjoyed the confidence of the nation which had covered him with honours, and he saw no reason to alter the status quo.

But the times and the circumstances had changed from the days when small-scale wars and the national interest could safely be left to the professional army. Now that the whole nation was engaged in a far wider, far greater conflict on the nation's very doorstep, now that the 'national interest' was also the personal interest of millions of individual citizens who were being individually urged to do their bit to help to win it, the old system simply would not do. The 'Shell Scandal' when it broke made this abundantly clear to everyone but Lord Kitchener himself. He was displeased, to say the least, that in defiance of cast-iron military etiquette and his own authority Sir John French had seen fit to go direct to the politicians and, worse, to use the ungentlemanly medium of the press to air his complaints and stir up trouble. It breached every canon of military etiquette, it flouted the authority of the War Office, and moreover Kitchener clung to the view that the whole tale was a gross exaggeration – and so he assured the Prime Minister. But the Prime Minister was not easily reassured.

Lord Kitchener's duties were weighty and manifold and far beyond the capacity of a single man to carry out. The vital matter of recruitment and expanding and equipping the Army, a mammoth task on its own, had fallen entirely on his shoulders. It was his responsibility to coordinate the command, to oversee the conduct of the war and to consider its political as well as strategic aspects. A million and one unforeseen details demanded his attention and, since the most able officers of the General Staff on whose experience he might have drawn had decamped to GHQ in France, the onus fell almost entirely on Lord Kitchener himself. The officers of the General Staff had been replaced by 'dug-outs' – elderly officers brought out of retirement – and, to a man, they were so much in awe of Lord Kitchener that the boldest among them would have hesitated to proffer advice, still less to cast doubt on the judgement of his illustrious chief. Even apart from the supply of munitions Asquith fully realised the difficulties that taxed his Secretary of State for War, but it was clear that the situation was critical.

On the question of munitions output the Government had done its best to be helpful. As far back as the previous October, largely at the instigation of Lloyd George, then Chancellor of the Exchequer, Asquith had set up a Cabinet committee on munitions with Lloyd George himself as chairman, but any moves that it made to widen the scope of the manufacture of munitions, by mobilising as much as possible of the engineering capacity of the country and inviting engineering firms to apply for Government contracts, were frequently thwarted by the War Office. Sir Stanley von Donop, Master-General of Ordnance, backed by Kitchener himself, had no confidence in any but the Government contractors who had furnished the lesser requirements of peacetime, and was unwilling to place orders elsewhere. He was only reluctantly persuaded to allow a certain amount of sub-contracting of minor components to private firms and to acquiesce in the placement of a few orders with armament firms in the United States of America. With the cooperation of the Board of Trade, the War Office preferred to concentrate on obtaining manpower, and where possible clawing back skilled workers now serving in the Army and sending them back to the work-bench so that the capacity of the existing armaments manufacturers could expand.

Lord Kitchener, always impatient with what he saw as the interference of civilians, had finally killed off the Munitions Committee by refusing to attend its meetings on the grounds that he had no time. It had not met since early January, but Lloyd George, never afraid to speak out, had continued to voice his misgivings. It was to this ally that Sir John French had turned, and now that the matter was in the public domain the fat was well and truly in the fire. It was the catalyst that caused the underlying friction in the Government to blow up into a full-scale political crisis. It had become glaringly obvious that a modern war could not be run, as in the past, by separate departments with no supreme authority with sufficient knowledge to coordinate the strands.

The Opposition, which until now had been patriotically cooperative, was beginning to voice its unease, and shocked public opinion showed signs of becoming hostile. Both had to be mollified.

The situation of the Liberal government, now ten years in power, was a peculiar one. Its present majority in the House of Commons depended on a pact with the smaller National and Labour parties, while the Conservatives (the official opposition) made up the largest single party in the House. The Conservatives, therefore, had to be treated with consideration and Asquith had sought to circumvent party politics and gain their goodwill by co-opting into the War Council two of their leading members, Balfour and Bonar Law, and occasionally inviting others to attend its meetings on an *ad hoc* basis. This was as far as he could go. There was no question of making the Opposition privy to the detailed deliberations of the Cabinet, even in so far as they affected the war. Party politics ruled that out of court, for with such a narrow margin in the House, Liberal Cabinet Ministers would never have countenanced relinquishing or even sharing their power with Parliament.

The War Council was another matter. Since it was merely an extension of the long-established Committee of Imperial Defence the appointment of members was traditionally left to the discretion of the Prime Minister of the day. The War Council was not concerned in the day-to-day running of the war. It met infrequently and, like its parent committee, its function was confined to discussing and determining matters of long-term policy. It had last met eight weeks previously on 19 March, the day after ships of the Royal Navy launched the attempt to force the Dardanelles, but it had not been summoned to discuss the details and implications of a military attack on Gallipoli and, by the time Asquith next called them together on 14 May, a great deal of water had flowed under the bridge. It was a gloomy meeting. A review of the situation showed impasse on the western front and signs that things were going badly with the Russians in the east. Worst of all was the situation in the Dardanelles. The naval attempt to force the straits had failed, there was little chance of renewing it, and the gamble of a military attack (which, had it been launched simultaneously, might easily have succeeded) seemed already to have been lost. The far-reaching strategy to relieve the pressure on Russia, open the road to the Danube and encourage the vacillating neutrals to come in on the side of the allies was in ruins. What was to be done?

The War Council considered four options, but, now that the troops had been committed, the possibility of withdrawing them was unanimously dismissed and there were only three real alternatives: to push on rapidly to victory, which they recognised was impossible without substantial reinforcements; to settle down to a siege, which would strain available resources to breaking point; to send out reinforcements for a new all-out assault, to which the same objections applied. After many hours' deliberation the War Council came to no decision other than to ask Sir Ian Hamilton what size of force he would require in order to guarantee the capture of the Gallipoli peninsula, and Sir Maurice Hankey sourly noted that this was '*a question that ought to have been put to him before ever a man was landed*'.

It was the last important meeting of the War Council for the political crisis was boiling up. Asquith now realised that there was no alternative but to form a Coalition Government, to disband the War Council, set up a Ministry of Munitions with full powers, to dissolve the bickering Cabinet and re-form it on non-party lines even if it meant that some of his closest colleagues would have to go. The Shell Scandal was one factor in the fall of the Liberal government, but it was the Dardanelles fiasco and the resignation of the First Sea Lord, Lord Fisher, that had finally brought matters to a head and forced the Prime Minister's hand.

It was not the first time that Fisher had threatened resignation. For months now there had been growing hostility between the First Sea Lord, the naval man, and his chief, Winston Churchill, who occupied the political post of First Lord of the Admiralty. The idea of subduing the forts that protected the Dardanelles and forcing the straits by sea-power alone had been Winston Churchill's baby.* Fisher's baby was the Navy. As First Sea Lord in the pre-war years before his first retirement he had nurtured its growth, had scrapped obsolete battleships, introduced the mighty Dreadnoughts and fast modern battle-cruisers, and modernised its structure. Now, at the age of seventy-four, he was not prepared to risk his ships under pressure from a landsman thirty years his junior, in what he increasingly viewed as a hare-brained scheme.

Fisher had been lukewarm about the scheme from the start and his attitude changed to tight-lipped hostility. It had been one thing when the plan involved a swift blow, a short commitment and a high probability of success. Now that the naval attempt had failed with the loss of two of his battleships and the disabling of another, now that the 'disengagement' in the event of failure, which had been the attraction of the original naval plan, was no longer on the cards, now that the Dardanelles enterprise had drifted into what showed every likelihood of being a long drawn out campaign requiring the Navy's continued presence, he was no longer prepared to support it by risking any part of his fleet. In Fisher's view the Royal Navy should bide its time, blockade German ports, tempt the German Navy out to fight and ultimately decide the war in the Baltic. He might have been persuaded, as he had been earlier in the year, but despite the genuine efforts of Churchill to mollify the old Admiral his simmering resentment had grown over the months to something

---

* In view of the fluid situation in the Balkans, with Bulgaria, Greece and Italy uncommitted and Russia cut off from the allies, the idea was visionary and had it been adopted when Churchill first mooted it in September 1914, when it would have met little opposition, it might well have shifted the focus of the war and possibly changed its course.

approaching hatred. He hated what he saw as Churchill's high-handed attitude in pressing ahead with his own plans, in taking his own soundings, in communicating with Naval Commanders over the head of his First Sea Lord and above all he hated his unbridled enthusiasm. The First Sea Lord saw no alternative but to resign. It was the cue for a shake-up all round and, together with the munitions crisis, an unmistakable signal that it was time for the politicians to get a grip on the war.

Lord Kitchener had become increasingly awkward to deal with and it was tempting to take advantage of the re-shaping of the Cabinet to replace him as Secretary of State for War, but although Kitchener's star was waning in political quarters, he was extremely popular with the rest of the country. To most people Kitchener *was* the war. It was his face that stared from every bill-board and gazed up from the pages of every magazine. Kitchener's imperious finger had beckoned the nation to war and it was the first of Kitchener's Armies that was on the point of leaving for the front to win it. To the public at large Kitchener himself seemed to personify stern British determination, and the desirable virtues of honour and duty had been the hall-mark of his distinguished career. Plans were already afoot to celebrate his birthday on 24 June with a mammoth recruiting campaign, and arm-bands stamped '*Kitchener's Birthday Recruit*' were being turned out in thousands ready for the occasion. Lord Kitchener was a national hero and a large segment of the female population of the United Kingdom was partial to heroes and would not be content until every eligible young man in the country was wearing heroic khaki.

Much of the recruiting propaganda was aimed at stimulating women to encourage their men to enlist. There were posters depicting noble matrons – '*Women Of Britain Say Go!*'; white-haired old ladies at cottage doors drawing the attention of a reluctant son to troops marching on the road outside – '*It's Your Duty, Lad!*'; young girls arm-in-arm with a soldier – '*Is Your Best Boy In Khaki?*'; and many women regarded it as a personal mission to accost every young man in civvies to shame him into joining up.

Jeremy Bentham and his friend Bob Southin had been favoured by the attentions of one such lady on a train journey from Harwich to London, and somewhat to their astonishment for they had been in the war from the very beginning. It was true that they could be loosely described as wearing civilian clothes, but 'loosely' was an appropriate word for their suits fitted where they touched and, on that particular day, five days after their escape from the internment camp at Groningen in Holland, they were already coming apart at the seams. Bentham and Southin were two of the fifteen hundred men of the 1st Brigade of the Royal Naval division who had entered neutral Holland when they were cut off by the advancing German Army after the Battle of Antwerp the previous September, and they had been languishing in internment ever since.*

Able Seaman J. S. Bentham, Benbow Bn., 1st Brig., Royal Naval Div.

It was an elderly lady who got into our compartment and tackled us and did she feel small when Southin told her we were escaped prisoners of war! Of course we were very pleased with ourselves, but we must have looked like a couple of scarecrows. At the camp the Dutch officials opened and inspected all our large parcels but they didn't bother about small ones, so I wrote to a friend of mine to send out a couple of suits folded up small, a bit at a time. I think his sister cut out the pieces and he sent them one at a time, a sleeve, a trouser leg or the front of a jacket, and thread and some buttons. It took us some months to collect all the pieces and then we had to sew them together, not very expertly.

Groningen wasn't like being in a prisoner of war camp in Germany. We weren't short of food, though the diet was pretty dull, but tradesmen came to the camp with barrows selling cake and fruit and chocolate and cigarettes and we had plenty of money to buy things, because we were paid a certain amount by the Dutch authorities and I also got a monthly pay-cheque from the Dutch agents of Cocks-Biddulph, the bank I'd worked for in London. We also used to make photograph frames out of Dutch cigar boxes which we sent to Selfridges in London and in return they sent us out cigarettes and anything we needed, so we were quite well off, and the local people were very good to us. In fact the camp was open to civilian visitors every Sunday, and whole crowds of them used to come to see us just as though they were visiting the zoo and we really felt like caged animals. But I got quite attached to a Dutch girl who used to come and talk to me through the barbed wire and we got so friendly that she persuaded her father to write to the Commandant to ask if I could visit their house for a meal now and then. We got so friendly that one evening, just before I was due to go back to the camp, her elder brother asked me when I was going to give his sister a ring! Well that really scared me and it certainly speeded up our plans to get away.

Of course, we'd been planning it for months, and the first

---

* The story of Bentham's experiences and capture at Antwerp is related in *1914* by the same author.

thing we did was to change our religion. That meant that instead of attending church parade in the camp we were marched down every Sunday to the Walsche Kerk in the town, accompanied by a guard who waited outside during the service. There were about ten of us in the party and either the others had the same idea of getting away or perhaps they just wanted a change of scene and a breath of air. I'd also done my best to learn a bit of Dutch but there were a lot of words I didn't know. However, the following Sunday we put on our civilian suits under our naval uniforms, and we were jolly glad of the baggy trousers for we could stuff our caps into our socks. Half-way along the road to the church I stopped to do up my bootlaces and then Southin and I dashed into a wood alongside the road, tore off our blouses and bell-bottoms, hid our seamens' uniforms under some thick bushes and got back on the road further up as a couple of very disreputable civilians. We avoided the town and found the road for Assen which was about twenty miles away, and of course we were terrified we would be picked up on the road, but we got there late in the afternoon and went into a café and I ordered two beef steaks with potatoes. We were starving by then! But the man was suspicious and right away he asked us if we'd escaped from Groningen and he also told us that the police would give him fifty guilders' reward if he reported us. So I said, 'Well I'll give you a hundred if you don't,' and I showed him the money. His manner immediately changed and he said we should be safer upstairs and showed us to a bedroom and said he would cook us a meal if we paid extra. We were a bit worried when he went out and locked the door from the outside, but he played fair and came up with two plates with gorgeous steaks and vegetables and two glasses of lager and he said that in the morning he would take us to the railway station and told me what tickets to ask for and made me repeat it in Dutch. He would walk in front of us next, he said, but we were on no account to try to speak to him. I told him that if he did this I would give him an extra fifty guilders.

Next morning after we'd had a good night's sleep and some coffee, he was as good as his word. When we got to the station I asked for 'Twee kartyes naar Rotterdam,' which I had practised saying. I bought a paper and pretended to read it when we got on the train and Southin closed his eyes and pretended to be asleep. We should have changed at Utrecht but we stayed in the train because we saw some Dutch police on the platform and eventually we arrived, *not* in Rotterdam, but Amsterdam! Well, of course, our idea in going to Rotterdam was to try to get on a ship, so we hadn't the faintest idea what to do next. We started walking round the town and after a while I spotted a shop with an English name. It was called 'Bell's Asbestos Company' so in we went and I put on as casual an air as I could. When the man came forward to serve us I said, 'Is Mr Bell in?' He laughed and said the place was part of a chain of shops in Europe and there was no Mr Bell. So I then spilled the beans and explained who we were. He was very nice, and an Englishman, because Holland being a neutral country there were any number of English people living and working there, but he told us that if he were caught helping escapees he would be expelled from Holland. However, after he phoned the British Consul and the Consul said that on no account were we to go near his office and that he didn't wish to know or hear anything about us, he decided to help us himself. Needless to say this was a huge relief.

He didn't like the look of our scruffy caps so he went out and bought us two straw hats and then took us to a café in a side street and bought us a meal. Then, the same way as we'd done in the morning, we followed him to the station where I bought tickets for Rotterdam and then followed him on to the platform where he stopped and watched from a discreet distance as we got on the train. We reached Rotterdam without any other mishap but the next problem was to get into the docks because there were police at the entrance. So we hung about and then we saw a man with a huge load on a barrow pushing it towards the docks, so we whipped off our straw hats and bent down and helped him to push the barrow through the entrance. He was quite pleased about that and *we* were delighted. Nobody challenged us, and the police took no notice.

Our friend in Amsterdam had found out that the SS *Cromer* was leaving that night and told us to make for it. We waited until no one was about, then ran up the gang-plank on to the ship and were met by the cook who was lounging about the deck. I greased his palm quite considerably, but I think he'd have helped us anyway. The cook was the only man on board and he hid us below until the Captain and the crew came back. Then our troubles were over! The Captain had us dressed in greasy overalls and told us to look busy when the police came round to inspect the boat before she sailed. When they came into the engine room the Captain came with them and he kept telling them to hurry up, because he didn't want to miss the tide. What a night that was, for the cook had used the money I gave him and sent ashore for a *lot* of beer, and next morning we were up on deck feasting our eyes on dear old England as we approached Harwich.

321

HMS *Maidstone* was the guard ship at the entrance to Harwich Harbour and our Captain signalled across and in no time a ship's cutter came to fetch us over to the *Maidstone* and the Captain himself was waiting to meet us on the deck – two such scruffy individuals that it must have given the matelots quite a turn to see him shaking hands with us, because the Captain of a ship is nearly God to them. He took us to his cabin for a drink and gave us a fright by reminding us that, as from the time we had escaped, we were officially deserters. But he said, 'Don't worry about it, just contact your headquarters and report as soon as you can,' and he gave us travel warrants for the train journey to London. It was the happiest journey of my life! We were in such high spirits that we simply couldn't stop laughing – it was so marvellous to feel free and back in our own country again. Best of all was arriving at Liverpool Street. We could hardly believe that we were really back in dear old London!

'Dear old London' had changed considerably since Bentham had left it in August the previous year and the war had laid its mark on the streets. There were fewer young men about and most of those there were seemed to be in khaki. There were newspaper-sellers on every corner – far more, it seemed to Bentham, than ever before – for Londoners were avid for news, and recruiting posters met the eye wherever they turned. Flag-sellers were out in force collecting for war charities and the bill-boards advertising West End plays showed that theatreland too was working for the war. Basil Hallam (soon to enlist himself) was appearing in *The Man Who Stayed at Home* and *Alsace* was still enjoying a successful run. Along the Strand and Shaftesbury Avenue diligent ladies, bent on personal recruitment, haunted stage doors to accost young actors and any likely passers-by, and any civilian-clad young man who managed to escape their clutches still had to run the gauntlet of recruiting offices liberally sprinkled across the West End. There were half a dozen between the Strand and Haymarket alone, each with an eagle-eyed recruiting sergeant pacing the pavement outside on the look-out for potential recruits. All of them were conspicuously decorated with flags and posters, but it was the recruiting office of the Royal Naval Division that drew the biggest crowds for they had thoughtfully filled a window with a display of shells and rifles and various interesting items salvaged from the battlefield plus a life-size wax figure in the uniform of the Royal Naval Division.

Since Jeremy Bentham's uniform was still lying hidden beneath bushes far away in Holland he was anxious to obtain a replacement.

He presented himself at the depot at Blackfriars in the role of returned hero and not only persuaded the storekeeper to fit him out with new clothes but, feeling that he richly deserved promotion, also induced him to hand over a Leading Seaman's badge. This at least would prevent him from doing sentry duty when he reported to the Royal Naval Division at its base in the Crystal Palace. Suitably arrayed he made his way to Sydenham to report for duty, was welcomed with open arms and awarded fourteen days' leave. It was some compensation for the anticlimax of his home-coming.

Able Seaman J. S. Bentham.

I went home expecting a hero's welcome, but when I arrived at the house I couldn't make anyone hear, so I went next door and the neighbours told me that my father and stepmother were away on holiday in Newquay. So I had to set off to my married sister's in Wembley and she was suitably pleased to see me so unexpectedly. My father cut short his holiday and came home but *he* was far from glad to see me and instead of a welcome I was told I was an exceedingly silly boy. There I was, he said, safe in Holland for the duration and now due to my stupidity I would have to go back into the war. I told him that was the whole point of escaping. However he soon came round and I rather think he was quite proud of my exploits because that night he took me down to the local pub and spent the evening telling his friends all about my adventures. That was another good night, because everyone wanted to treat me.

But my real moment of glory came at the first pay parade after I'd returned to the Crystal Palace. On pay parade your name was called, you took a step forward smartly and advanced to the table with your cap extended to receive your pay. Of course the average sailor had only a week or two's pay to draw, but when it came to me there was quite a bit as I had only been paid one guilder every ten days and I had eight months' pay owing. Well! My cap was *covered* with golden sovereigns and you could hear the gasp from all the rookies as I marched back, for they didn't know me from Adam, or where I had come from. I had more than twenty golden sovereigns in my cap. Did I feel rich! Of course I didn't say anything about my self-appointed promotion, but no one questioned it, and I was never ordered to take the Leading Seaman's badge off. Best of all, I was told that my application for a commission had been granted and I started training right away. I was cock of the walk and no mistake!

I knew I was a lucky man because I soon found out about the

terrible casualties my Division had suffered in Gallipoli, and I knew full well that if our Brigade hadn't been interned after Antwerp, I might easily have been one of them.

The five weeks that began on 22 April with the German attack at Ypres accounted for the highest casualties since the start of the war and the full cost of the landings at Gallipoli was only beginning to be known. Every day fresh casualty lists told the tale of the push at Aubers Ridge and Festubert. Nothing had been gained and all there was to show were the long, long lists of soldiers killed, missing or wounded that filled so many columns of the daily newspapers, and the shower of official telegrams that were dreaded by every family with a boy at the front. Even the sight of a telegraph boy cycling down a street could strike terror into a nervous heart.

When a telegram arrived for Jock Macleod's family his mother was at the local VAD hospital where she worked three afternoons a week.

Miss Betty Macleod.

Friday May 21st. Both parents were out when the wire came, Mother at the hospital and Daddy playing bowls in the Trinity Fellows' Garden, so Mollie and I set off on our bicycles to find them. Of course they both had fits. They saw us coming waving a telegram – poor Mother turned as white as a sheet and couldn't stop shaking for ages, and Daddy got a shock too, though after the nasty turn she'd had herself Mother warned us to call out as soon as he saw us to say it was good news. The telegram was from Jock to say that he had leave and was arriving in Cambridge by the 6.15. The whole family tootled up to the station to meet Jock. He looked tired and pale but quite fat, and he was very cheerful. Went out with him and Daddy after supper to see the war telegrams at the library in a sort of triumphal progress down the middle of the street – so many people stopped us and wanted to speak to Jock.

When we got home we settled down to make swabs for the hospital while we all chatted to Jock. What we gleaned was this. On May 19th Sir John French inspected three Battalions of his Brigade and congratulated them. He said they had been subjected to the most intense shell-fire ever known in the history of war. He would not have blamed them, nor been at all surprised, if he had found them on the other side of Ypres and if it had not been for them saving Ypres Italy would not have come into the war. Ypres was to be added to the names on their regimental colours. Jock says there are only seven officers left

324

in his Battalion and he is second in seniority now. He told a tale about one of the men who said, when he was bayoneting a German, 'This is for the *Lusitania*' – prod – 'And there's another for me' – prod. Laughed and talked until very late.

Saturday May 22nd. Jock slept on till eleven o'clock and then had breakfast in his dressing-gown. Meanwhile we went out to buy him sweets and fruit. He ate nearly the whole lot before dinner! In the afternoon we took him up to tennis and tea at the club and Mother came to watch, but Jock got weary soon so we all went home. A few more tales came out. One sergeant sang '*Here we are, Here we are, Here we are again*' all through a bayonet charge and he has been recommended for the VC. Glorious day. Supper in the garden.

The warm May evening, the gentle pleasures of a quiet Cambridge garden, were in sharp contrast to the miseries of battle in the Ypres salient and, in the bosom of his admiring family, with teenage sisters hanging on his lips avid for 'tales', a soldier who had endured its privations could be forgiven for feeling that mild exaggeration was preferable to the truth.

Jock Macleod had a glorious leave. He dined with his father at Caius College, picnicked with his mother and sisters on the river, showed off to admiring friends and acquaintances, consumed gargantuan home-cooked meals and still found room to eat fruit and sweets galore. On the last full day of his leave the whole family went up to stay with his grandmother in London.

Miss Betty Macleod.

Tuesday May 25th. We travelled in state – First Class! – and went straight to 22 Harley Street, then went out a little walk with Jock who bought an electric torch. A great family dinner, all of our lot and Grannie and aunts and uncles. About 9.30 Mother, Uncle Arnold, Jock, Mollie and me went in a taxi to the West End Cinema and spent an interesting three-quarters of an hour. Saw pictures of the Italian Army, cavalry and artillery, coming down mountains etcetera. Everybody cheered!

The news that Italy had declared war on Austria, if not yet on Germany, was almost the only cause for satisfaction in the whole dreary month. In German-occupied Brussels, where for obvious reasons the population was not able to celebrate openly, grocery stores packed their windows with mountainous displays of macaroni and their customers demonstrated their patriotism by purchasing large quantities. In London, where there was a sizeable Italian community, crowds of flag-waving expatriates paraded through the streets, scooping up so many Londoners as they went that the police had to be brought in to control the march to the Italian embassy where the ambassador obligingly appeared on the portico waving an outsize Italian flag. The following morning Victoria Station was mobbed by hordes of excited straw-boatered Italians bound for Italy to join the Army, each with a large excited family to see him off. The shrieking, the cheering, the unrestrained weeping, the shouted farewells, almost raised the roof. There were women with babies in arms and a brood of dark-eyed children at their heels, there were stout mothers and moustachioed fathers, aged grandmothers in voluminous black, and troupes of uncles, aunts, cousins, nieces, nephews. Small girls wore hair-ribbons in the national colours, small boys waved flags, and adults of both sexes were decked out in sashes of red, white and green. Some carried baskets, also beribboned in Italy's colours, and filled with flowers for the women to throw, Italian style, as the men went off to war.

Even after the noisy emotional farewells, when the travellers had passed through the barrier to board the train and were craning out of doors and windows for a last wave and a last look, hundreds of their relatives, impelled by a single impulse, charged the barrier and poured on to the platform, running the length of the train in search of some particular Luigi or Marco or Antonio, to bombard him with flowers, to claim one more embrace, to call one more *arrivederci*, to hold up a child for a last fraternal or fatherly kiss.

It was beyond the power of the single bewildered guard to control them and it required the assistance of several policemen before the crowd was induced to stand back and the train doors could be banged shut. When order had been restored, and the flustered guard managed to summon up sufficient breath to blow the final whistle, the train steamed out a full ten minutes late.

The Government would dearly have liked a similar demonstration of enthusiasm that would inspire more Britishers to enlist. The casualty figures alone, at Ypres, at Aubers Ridge, at Festubert, and also at Gallipoli, spoke for themselves of the continuing need for men. Lord Kitchener had let it be known that he would need a million and a half new recruits before the year was out and, setting aside the difficulty of equipping such an army in the immediate future, no serious politician believed that anything like the required number could be found without introducing conscription. But, fired by the success of his recruiting campaigns in the first months of the war, Kitchener remained stubbornly wedded to the principle of voluntary service and the army had now lowered the obligatory height for would-be soldiers by two inches in order to encourage smaller men who had been rejected once to try again. They also raised the age limit to forty.

Some imaginative newspaper readers came up with bizarre ideas to swell the ranks and one letter outlining a proposal that verged on the sadistic appeared in the *Daily Mirror*. It was boldly headed 'A Chance for the Unfit':

> There are some thousands of men in this country in the early stages of consumption who are willing to fight, but cannot pass the medical test. Why not form a battalion of them, train them to shoot (no long marches or strenuous exercises) and let them go to the front? We should then have a body of men to draw on for those hazardous enterprises which sometimes have to be undertaken, and which practically mean certain destruction. These men would vastly prefer such a glorious end to the prospect of a lingering and miserable death at home.

It was signed with the pseudonym 'TB'. No one, least of all unfortunate victims of tuberculosis, was much taken with the idea.

Before the end of May the battle at Ypres had fizzled out. Even the Germans were temporarily short of shells. The attempt to capture Festubert had been given up. Thousands of soldiers had died and the hospital ships plying back and forth from France to England and from the Dardanelles to Malta, were carrying ever-increasing loads of wounded.

Towards the end of that momentous month of May the Coalition Government formally took office. One of the first decisions of the new Cabinet was to set up a Cabinet Committee solely concerned with sorting out affairs in the Dardanelles.

Something had to be done.

Part 5

—

'Damn the Dardanelles – they will be our grave'

(Admiral Fisher)

The moon shines bright on Charlie Chaplin.
His boots are cracking,
For want of blacking,
And his little baggy trousers they want mending
Before we send him
To the Dardanelles.

Anon.

Chapter 23

The Territorials of the 7th Royal Scots were glad to be on their way. Although they had in theory been 'on active service' since the outbreak of war and had volunteered to a man for foreign service, most of their soldiering had been spent guarding coastal defences within shouting distance of their home town of Leith and while they appreciated the home comforts that were still within easy reach, it was hardly the adventure they had anticipated. It was almost a month since Leith had given them a huge send-off. Even the Provost and Town Council had turned out for an official farewell and the battalion marched to the station through crowds of people who mobbed the pavements to cheer the local boys leaving, as they supposed, for the front. It was something of an anticlimax to find that the move took them no further than Larbert, a mere twenty-five miles inland along the Firth of Forth. But now they really were off to the front. Rumour had it that they were bound for the Dardanelles, and rumour for once was right.

It was a complicated business to embark a whole brigade of four battalions at the small station at Larbert and it was no less complicated for the railway authorities to filter numerous troop trains into the mainline network without unduly disrupting the normal flow of goods and passenger traffic. It had been a long day of parades and roll-calls, blankets to be handed in, kits and rifles to be inspected, iron rations to draw for the long journey to Liverpool, and, for the officers, a thousand and one last-minute details to be seen to before the Battalion moved off. It was almost midnight before the first half of the Battalion, A and D Companies, marched out of camp to entrain. The five hundred men of B and C would follow two hours later in another special train.

By the time a fatigue party had loaded the ammunition, by the time a final roll-call had been held under the dim station lights and the two companies were divided into platoons and formed fours to entrain in batches of eight to each compartment, the night was far advanced. The pipe band that played them aboard the train, and would play them off again at the other end, piled into the front carriage with their drums and instruments and had the luxury of having it to themselves. The battalion signal sections and machine-gunners were together in the second coach, and the colonel and the officers took their places in the first-class compartments immediately behind. It was a quarter to four in the morning before the train finally got up steam and pulled out of the station and by that time the excitement had died down. A few enthusiasts set up card schools. Most were glad to relax and by six o'clock on a fine May morning, as the train trundled through the Borders towards the station at Kirtlebridge, almost all of them were sound asleep. This was a great disappointment to Ella Plenderleith.

Mrs Ella Smith, née Plenderleith.

My father was the signalman at Kirtlebridge. We lived at the station and he always used to tell us when the troop trains were coming through, because we liked waving to the soldiers as they went past. I was fifteen at the time. It must have been about half past six when the train went through, because my father was on duty at six o'clock and it was a while after that when he shouted to us that the train would be coming past. We hurried up and got dressed and went outside to see it go through, but we were a bit disappointed that morning because a lot of the soldiers were sleeping and not many waved back to us. It was my father's first job that morning after he went on duty to clear that train through and signal to the next box down the line that it was on its way. The next box was Quintinshill. It was about six miles away just outside Gretna village – the last mainline signal box in Scotland.

Not long afterwards there was a tremendous crashing noise. We heard it six miles away! A few minutes later my father called out from the signal box to tell us what had happened.

What had happened was the worst rail crash in history. Like William Plenderleith at Kirtlebridge, signalman James Tinsley should have come on duty at six o'clock, but he had a private arrangement with his night-shift colleague, Meakin, which allowed him an extra half hour's sleep before catching the local train from Carlisle and arriving at work nearly forty minutes late. Trains passing through in the meantime were 'logged' by Meakin on a scrap of paper, usually the back of a telegraph form, and transferred later in Tinsley's handwriting into the official log. Tinsley returned the favour when it was his turn to work night-shift and the arrangement had worked to the satisfaction of both parties. But it failed to work that morning. The London to Glasgow express was forty-five minutes late on its journey north, and because the two loop lines were occupied by stationary goods trains Meakin had put the slow local train temporarily on the down line to wait until the fast express went through. Meakin was in a hurry to get off at the end of his long night's stint and he had hardly left the signal box when Plenderleith rang through from Kirtlebridge to 'offer' the troop train travelling south on the down line. Tinsley had arrived moments before in the very train that now stood before his eyes on the main down line but he claimed later that he 'forgot' about it. He accepted the troop train without demur and pulled the lever that would drop the arm of the signal half a mile up the track to indicate that the line was clear. The troop train had picked up speed on the downward gradient from Kirtlebridge and was hurtling fast towards Gretna. It was almost a quarter to seven in the morning.

L/cpl. G. McGurk, 1/7 (Leith) Bn. (TF), Royal Scots (Lothian Regt.).

We were packed together like herrings in a barrel. Some were fast asleep, and most of those who were awake were so weary that when the disaster came it caught them at a disadvantage. Some of our chaps were leaning out of the windows at the time, and naturally they were the first to see that something was wrong.

One of the men in our carriage – Glass, I think, was his name – suddenly drew in a scared face and shouted, '*We're running into another train.*' The words were scarcely out of his mouth before there was a terrible crash, and the carriage seemed to leap into the air. We were all pitched on the floor in a heap.

I was one of the first to go down, and three other chaps all fell on top of me. They squeezed the breath out of me, but otherwise I was unhurt.

Sgt. J. Combe, 1/7 (Leith) Bn. (TF), Royal Scots.

The first two or three carriages were telescoped. I was travelling with Pipe-Major Ross and we felt the carriages coming up in the air and we held our legs up and when the crash came we were shot into the air and the roof of the carriage collapsed and fell down on Ross's back. He was pinned down and shouting to me to help him. I myself was covered with debris and before I could help Ross I had the job of my life to wriggle myself free. I pulled the Pipe-Major by the head for all I was worth. It seemed like hours before I managed to get him free.

Pte. A. Thomson, 1/7 Bn. (TF), Royal Scots.

We were eight to each compartment and the doors locked! The last stop was Carstairs where some of us exchanged a little light-hearted banter with a few girls who were making an early start to work but nearly everyone else had settled down to sleep. Suddenly there was a terrific crash. The carriage rose up and sank down again listing dangerously over a steep bank. The cries and screams and the hiss of steam escaping from the engine was deafening! One by one we climbed out through the window of our compartment and on to the line. What a sight met our eyes. The wreckage was piled at least thirty feet high and terror-stricken men were staggering about. Worse still were the men who were trapped in the twisted metal of the wreckage.

L/cpl. G. McGurk.

The wreckage of the carriage was dropping on us, and the cries of the men that were injured were heart rending. One man had his neck broken by the fall, while others had their arms broken, heads cut, and legs twisted. I managed to get out from the wreckage, and, along with other uninjured men, went along the train to see what could be done. The scene was sickening.

The job was to know where to begin, but some officers got us organised and spread us along the train at intervals, and we started to dig out the dead and dying.

Men who managed to get out in the first moments after the crash were the lucky ones. The initial impact had derailed the engines of both trains and sent them teetering across the up line in the path of the express thundering north. A minute later the first of its two powerful engines ploughed into the wreckage with a roar that was heard for miles.

The troop train got the worst of it. The fire which had already started in the wooden coaches immediately behind the engines burst into an inferno. Carriage walls splintered. Bogies collapsed. Men were trapped. Soldiers who had managed to clamber out a minute before and were staggering dazed on the embankment, or trying to free trapped comrades, were killed or injured as the wreckage buckled and flew apart with the second impact. The fire took hold and began to spread along the rest of the train and behind the ear-splitting blast of escaping steam the cries of panic from men buried beneath the debris chilled the blood.

Sgt. J. Combe.

The shrieks and the moans of the men as they were being slowly roasted to death was terrible to hear. The cruellest thing I've ever seen in all my life was the body of one man hanging high up on part of the wreckage with his arms outstretched. He had no head. But the worst was one fellow whose legs were horribly burned and he was pinned down and it was impossible to get him out. The flames were simply eating him up and getting nearer to his face. He must have been in terrible agony. He kept shouting 'For God's sake, shoot me!'

Young Gordon Dick was one of the lucky ones. He had been thrown clear of the third coach and knocked unconscious in the first crash. When he came round he found himself lying on the track between the rails with both feet caught up in the wreckage, and the flames creeping closer, burning his face and arms as he struggled to get free. It was the second crash that released him and it took all his strength to crawl to the embankment before he passed out again. Only one other man of the eight in his carriage escaped.

Mrs Ella Smith, née Plenderleith.

It was a terrible accident! When my father called out from the signal box a few minutes after we heard that awful crash and told us what had happened I simply couldn't believe that just ten minutes before we'd stood waving to the train. Another girl and I set off right away to see it. It would be well over an hour's walk but we ran a lot of the way. What a terrible sight it was, engines and carriages were piled high and it was still burning. Soldiers were being burned alive because they couldn't get them out. One of the officers was sitting in the field among the dead, looking round about him to see how many of the lads were left. There didn't seem to be many. It was a most terrible tragedy. I'd never seen anything like that. You couldn't *imagine* anything like it!

By the time the single local fire engine appeared it could do little to staunch the flames. As they begun to spread, a shocked NCO was still cool-headed enough to organise a group of the survivors to run to the rear and unhitch the ammunition wagon and to roll it back by sheer muscle-power to a safe distance. But there were explosions just the same, for the train was lit by gas lamps and, as the flames spread along its length, gas tanks beneath the carriages exploded in the heat, flinging burning debris across the field and spreading more carnage among the helpless rows of newly rescued casualties.

There were not many civilian casualties, for the troop train had taken the worst of the collision, and passengers from the other two trains scrambled down the embankment to do what they could to help. Women from the village, running across the fields to find out what was happening, rushed home again and returned with piles of sheets and tablecloths to tear into bandages and to cover the bodies of the dead. Two hours after the accident an ambulance train came up from Carlisle, but long before then Dr John Edwards was at the scene, working close to the burning wreckage, amputating limbs to free men who were trapped, while the firemen did their best to keep the flames at bay.

Stretcher-bearers made countless back-breaking journeys, carrying the injured to the ambulance train for the short journey to Carlisle, laying the still bodies of the dead in empty goods wagons. It was many hours before they were all taken away – and many more before the wreckage cooled and salvage workers toiling by the light of arc lamps could begin the fearful job of recovering bodies.

Pte. A. Thomson.

I was detailed for stretcher-bearer duties. What a job for a lad not yet eighteen! I wept. I saw many a battlefield after that, but I never saw anything like the things I saw on that terrible day.

It was afternoon before we'd rescued everyone we could and there was nothing more that could be done. A lot of the men lay down in the field, they were so exhausted, and some of us thought about the folks at home and how worried they'd be when the news got out and they walked to Gretna post office to send telegrams. Then there was a roll-call. Fifty-seven of us answered our names out of nearly five hundred who left Larbert that morning. About five o'clock they put us on a goods train and took us to Carlisle and then up to the castle for a wash and a meal. A while later they took us back to the station and there was a special train waiting to take us on to Liverpool.

In the confusion of the emergency with all effort concentrated on finding space for the wounded in Carlisle's overflowing hospitals, and the sad task of identifying the dead, no one had time to give much thought to the uninjured survivors. They were still in a state of shocked exhaustion, bedraggled in smoke-blackened uniforms, they had neither rifles, caps nor kit, they had been up all the previous night and had suffered an appalling experience. They should never have been asked to complete the journey they had begun nearly sixteen hours before –

but no orders had been issued to the contrary.

Despite long delays on the journey the second half of the Battalion had reached Liverpool early in the evening at the end of an anxious day. They knew that there was trouble.

Pte. W. Begbie, 1/7 Bn., Royal Scots.

We left Larbert in the second train. After a while we stopped at some station for a long time. We were allowed to come out of the train but not to leave the station. We all felt that something was wrong but it was not until Captain Dawson told us that we knew the first train had been in an accident. He didn't know the details. When we got on the train again to finish our journey to Liverpool, we were really worried – especially the men who had relatives in the first train. Later anyone who *had* a relative on the first train was sent back home.

Like all locally raised Territorial Battalions the 7th Royal Scots was a family. Pipe-Major Ross, who had been left behind in hospital, had a son in the band who was more seriously wounded. The two Duff brothers, George and Robert, had been killed. The Salvesen brothers were both casualties, one killed and one wounded. Some families had three or more relations in the Battalion. As the news trickled through and spread from mouth to mouth and street to street in Leith where Saturday shoppers were out in full force, friends and relatives rushed to the battalion's headquarters. Soon there was a crowd of thousands.

Miss Anne Armstrong.

My father was a sergeant in the 7th Royal Scots. How well I remember that Saturday morning. As soon as we heard about the accident Mother rushed off to the Dalmeny Street Drill Hall. She took us children with her – in fact all the family went – and we waited there nearly all day for news. I'll never forget straining to hear as they read out the names of the men who'd been accounted for. They came through just a few at a time – and, oh, the relief when we finally heard my father's name called out. He was injured, it's true, but he was alive!

I went three times with Mother to visit Father in Cumberland Infirmary before he was moved from Carlisle. The first journey was the worst. I don't know who organised the visit, but a lot of the wives and parents went, and travelling down in the train in the morning most of the women were in tears – it was only the day after the crash – and no one knew what to expect. But when we met up again for the journey home they were all smiles. As a child I couldn't understand this change. I remember Mother explaining that they'd all been through a terrible anxious time. My father had a badly fractured ankle which left him with a permanent limp, and he was badly cut about the nose and face.

Mrs A. Marshall, née Duff.

My family lived in Musselburgh, and there was quite a bunch of Musselburgh boys in the battalion. All the relatives went rushing to the railway station, but they were told to go to the post office and wait there for news. My mother was in a state, for she had a baby eleven months old in her arms (which was myself) and my brother, who was just three, and they said that my granny was in an even worse state because, of course, she had two boys in the same company. They were both killed – my father and my uncle. My father was twenty-seven and my mother was twenty-five, and there she was, left on her own, a widow, with the two of us to bring up. But it was a good while before they got definite news.

The anxious crowd was still waiting for news at nightfall. At long intervals a window was flung up and a name called out. Then it slammed shut and the waiting began again. The names they called were only those of the survivors, and there were few enough of them. Some people who could not stand the suspense made the tortuous journey to Carlisle by branch lines and local trains to find out the situation at first hand. Bob White's father took with him Bob's last letter from Larbert by way of identification, for it was written on notepaper headed with the badge of the 7th Royal Scots. In it Bob had written delightedly, 'I put my name in for the signalling and I and Sinclair were accepted, so I do no duties until further orders! The sun has been very hot and we have played football all day.' But the signallers had all gone. The pipers had all gone. Three officers and two hundred and eleven men had been killed, and two hundred and forty-six seriously wounded.*

Mrs A. E. Cowley.

My father was the Reverend William Swan, DD, minister of

---

* The two railwaymen, Tinsley and Meakin, were tried on charges of culpable homicide and found guilty. Meakin was sentenced to eighteen months' imprisonment and Tinsley to three years with hard labour.

338

South Leith Parish Church, and he was also the local chaplain of the 7th Royal Scots. He was summoned to Carlisle at once, and he had the heart-rending duty of comforting the wounded and the relatives after the dreadful train disaster. How well I remember it! He didn't come home until very late the next night and he was deeply upset. He told us that he had to stand on a chair on the platform at Carlisle station and had to read the casualty list to the anxious relatives who had rushed to Carlisle. It was the saddest thing he ever had to do in his life. Then a few days later he held the mass funeral at Leith. It was almost too much to bear.

The hospitals were overwhelmed. Church halls were commandeered, GPs from miles around rushed to Carlisle to help, and surgeons, doctors, nurses, worked right round the clock attending to the injured. Some of them died in the night and to Dr Edwards's distress one was the drummer boy of sixteen whose legs he had amputated to release him from the burning train. Near the boy's bed another badly burned man lay dying. He tossed and turned and muttered all night. Edwards, bending over him, caught his words: 'If only we could have had a fight for it!' He muttered it over and over again.

In the early hours of Sunday morning Colonel Peebles led the remnant of his half battalion of 7th Royal Scots up the gangway to board the *Empress of Britain* – six officers and fifty-seven dazed, dishevelled men. Their Brigadier was waiting on the deck. He returned Colonel Peebles's salute then shook his hand in silence. At that particular moment neither man was capable of uttering a word.

Pte. A. Thomson.

Early next morning we were put to work sorting out blood-stained equipment salvaged from the wrecked train. It was a gruesome task and I'm quite sure that there was flesh stuck to some of it. Later we were diverted to carrying ammunition aboard ship. Then we were mustered and allocated our mess decks for the voyage.

Perhaps some officer had thought it best to keep the men busy after their ordeal, but the Divisional Commander thought differently and Major-General Egerton had wired with some indignation to the War Office. Shortly before sailing time a reply came back. The survivors could be sent back north and other Royal Scots whose relatives were known to have been killed or injured in the crash could go home too.

Pte. A. Thomson.

We were lined up on the quayside and marched off through the streets to Lime Street Station. Believe it or not, some children playing in the street threw stones at us. We had no equipment and we looked so bedraggled and disreputable that they took us for German prisoners!

The officers had volunteered and been given permission to stay on board, but Lieutenant Riddell was sent home in charge of the party of survivors. The men were unusually silent and subdued. Riddell tried to cheer them up with the news that the General had decreed that they should all be given fourteen days' leave, but they were too tired and worried to care. Most went to sleep or stared blankly out of the windows.

As the train cleared the outskirts of Liverpool and began to pick up speed on the journey north, the *Empress of Britain* cast her moorings and began to slip down the Mersey carrying their comrades on the first stage of the voyage to Gallipoli.

The voyage was pleasant and uneventful. A collection for the dependants of the men who died in the disaster raised £612 which was cabled home from Gibraltar on the day of the mass funeral. Most of Leith and half of Edinburgh turned out for it and the Reverend William Swan who conducted the ceremony was assisted by the Dean of the Thistle and Chapel Royal. Two hundred and fourteen bodies were carried to Rosebank Cemetery in Leith, and so many were charred beyond recognition that all of them were buried together in a mass grave. All the survivors were present.

Afterwards they went home on leave, but few had the heart to enjoy themselves. One man, Private William Roach, spent most of his time composing a eulogy to his shattered battalion. He called it 'The Heroes of Gretna':

> We had been for some ten months in training,
>   And we found it was work and not play;
> You may guess that each man was delighted
>   When we learned we were going away.
>
>
> Off we sped, never thinking of danger;
>   Ah! I see every happy face still -
> Now a joke, now a laugh, now 'Where are we?'
>   'Yes, the next box will be Quintinshill.'

And 'twas just then the terrible smash came;
  Heavens! It caught us like rats in a trap,
Just when some of our boys, a bit drowsy,
  Were enjoying a quiet little nap.

I was thrown to the right of our carriage,
  My head and right arm were held fast;
Horror! Here were the flames coming near me.
  What a death! Was next minute my last?

Yes, I shouted for help – and I listened,
  'Oh, God!' I heard dying men shout;
And midst that came a second collision!
  I can tell you no more! I got out.

Ask me not of the sights I beheld there,
  As I lay on the ground all alone;
But I'll tell of brave lads who leapt into the flames
  And saved lives at the risk of their own!

Oh their deeds will aye live in my memory,
  Their praises I sing them aloud,
But to soldier with such a Battalion,
  It's of that most of all, boys, I'm proud.

Yes the scenes of that woe-stricken morning
  From my vision I never can blot;
But 'twill ever for me be the boast of my life
  That I once was a Seventh Royal Scot.

In the early hours of 13 June the remainder of the 7th Royal Scots
landed with the 156th Brigade of the Lowland Division on the
shores of Gallipoli.

Whatever was in store for them they, at least, would have a 'fight for
it'.

341

Chapter 24

Gallipoli was the most ancient and, to a classical scholar, the most romantic of battle-fields. More than six centuries before the birth of Christ the Greeks had colonised the peninsula and founded a city on the site of the modern town of Gallipoli and christened it Heliopolis. The Turks called it 'Gelibolu' and it lay on the eastern coast of the peninsula looking towards the coast of Asia across the Dardanelles – the narrow seaway that reached north towards Constantinople on the Sea of Marmara, and flowed south to meet the waters of the Aegean. Long ago the ancient city of Troy had stood guard at the mouth of the Dardanelles, controlled its seaborne trade and grown rich and powerful on the proceeds. For this was the Hellespont of history and legend.

It was across the Hellespont that Leander swam each night for a lovers' tryst with Hero, priestess of Aphrodite, who flung herself into its waters when he drowned. The legendary Helen of Troy, heroine of Homer's *Iliad*, might have looked across these straits from those fabled 'topless towers of Ilium'. Five hundred years before the dawn of Christian history Xerxes built a bridge of three hundred boats to carry his army across the Hellespont and up the peninsula on a march that ended at Thermopylae, and a century later Alexander the Great crossed to Asia on his way to conquer an empire. The Dardanelles had witnessed the passage of scores of armies and over the centuries, and as recently as the Balkan Wars a mere twelve months before, the peninsula had been lit by the campfires of soldiers and echoed to their curses and the tramping of their feet.

Few of the modern soldiers were classical scholars, but looking out from the western shores of the peninsula to the islands floating beneath a turquoise sky on the blue Aegean Sea, they were impressed by its timeless beauty.

On the small island of Bozcaada near the toe of the peninsula, British warships were anchored in the harbour of Tenedos where, according to legend, the thousand black-prowed vessels of Agamemnon's fleet had sheltered long millennia before. Bozcaada

342

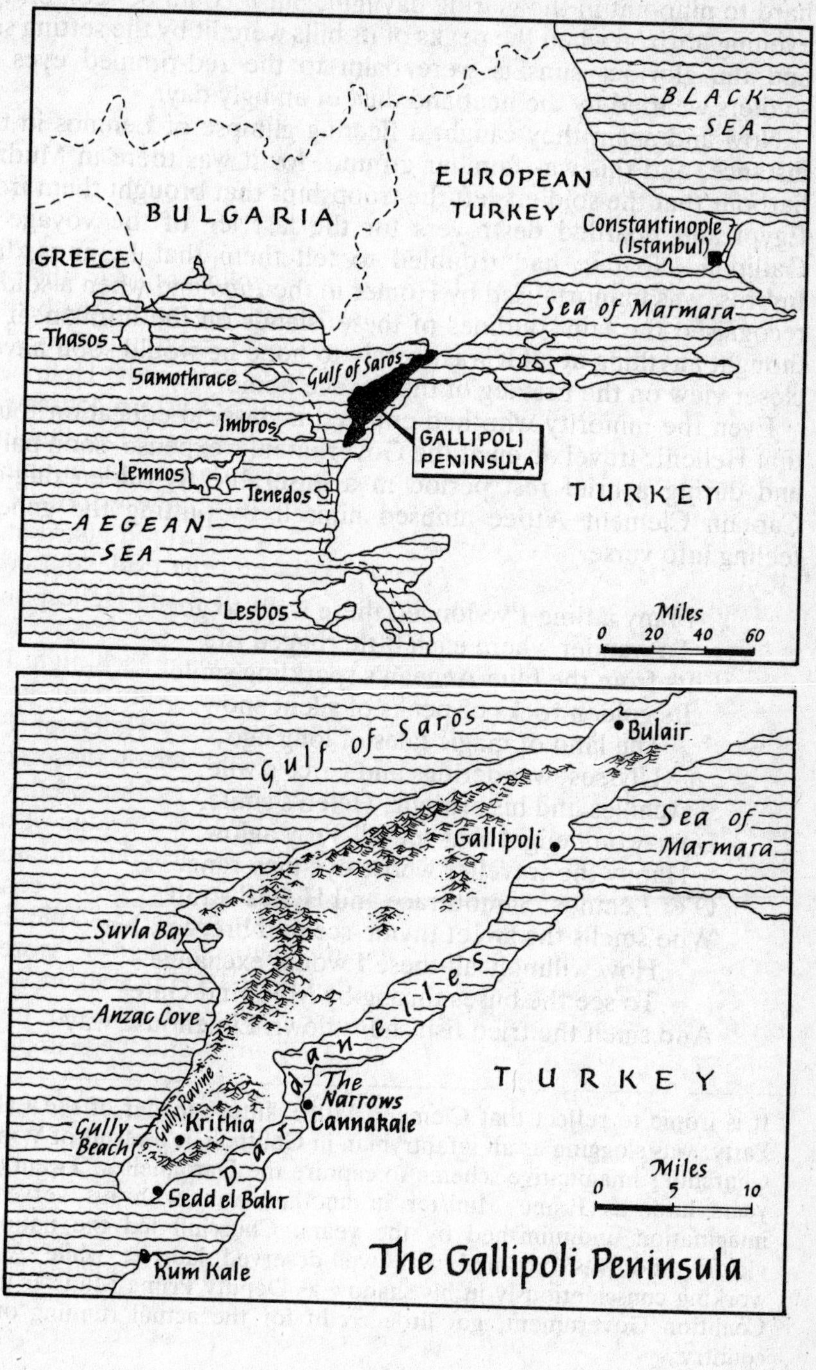

The Gallipoli Peninsula

just ten miles to the south was easily visible to the naked eye. Away to the west Samothrace, once home of the sea-god Poseidon, was hard to pinpoint in the glaring daylight, but it could be seen on the evening horizon when the peaks of its hills were lit by the setting sun and the glorious sunsets were balm to the red-rimmed eyes of soldiers wearied by the heat and dust of an ugly day.

Now and again they caught a fleeting glimpse of Lemnos in the distance, and this was familiar ground, for it was there in Mudros harbour that the soldiers left the troopships that brought them from Egypt and boarded destroyers for the last leg of the voyage to Gallipoli. No one had troubled to tell them that Lemnos, like Imbros, was immortalised by Homer in the *Iliad* and when a soldier recognised the faint outlines of these islands on the horizon, if he thought anything at all it was merely to hope he would soon have a closer view on the first leg of the voyage home.

Even the minority who had enjoyed a classical education found that Hellenic travel, even at the Government's expense, soon palled and during a brief rest period in a miserable fly-ridden dug-out Captain Clement Attlee amused himself by putting the general feeling into verse.

> Many a time I've longed these ways to go,
> To wander where each little rugged isle
> Lifts from the blue Aegean's sparkling smile
> Its golden rocks or peaks of silent snow,
> The land of magic tales of long ago,
> Ulysses' wanderings and Circe's wile,
> Achilles and his armour, Helen's smile,
> Dear-won delight that set tall Troy aglow.
> Happy the traveller whose eye may range
> O'er Lemnos, Samothrace and Helles' strait,
> Who smells the sweet thyme-scented breezes. Nay,
> How willingly all these I would exchange
> To see the buses throng by Mile End Gate
> And smell the fried fish shops down Limehouse way.*

---

* It is ironic to reflect that Clement Attlee, future leader of the Labour Party, was slogging as an infantryman in Gallipoli as a result of Winston Churchill's imaginative scheme to capture the Dardanelles. Twenty-five years later as Prime Minister in another war, with his verve and imagination undiminished by the years, Churchill led the nation to victory and was crowned with well-deserved laurels, while Attlee, working conscientiously in his shadow as Deputy Prime Minister in the Coalition Government, got little credit for the actual running of the country.

Not a single man at Gallipoli would have disagreed, although most would have put it in robust and less elegant terms. By mid-June they had all had more than enough of it. The Gallipoli adventure was not going according to plan and it had gone wrong from the beginning.

The unsuccessful attempt by the Royal Navy to force the straits in March had put the Turks on their guard, and the long lapse of time before the landings gave them ample time to take precautions, to send a strong force to the peninsula and to build and strengthen its defences. They had no doubt that they would be needed, and needed soon, for the plan to invade Gallipoli was the worst-kept secret of the war.

While Sir Ian Hamilton and his staff were still in Egypt letters were arriving from the War Office by the regular mail openly addressed to '*The Constantinople Expeditionary Force*' to the horror and fury of its Commander-in-Chief who, before leaving London, had specifically requested that it should be known as '*The Mediterranean Expeditionary Force*'. Well before the end of March Egyptian newspapers were not merely reporting the arrival of troopships, but were making no bones about the fact that the troops were bound for the Dardanelles. The Army had money to spend and officers of the advance guard were buying up mules and donkeys by the score and scouring the bazaars for milk-cans, canisters, and any other containers that could possibly be used to carry water. In Port Said they were even purchasing vessels by the dozen – the flat-bottomed lighters that sailed out to unload big ships and bring their cargoes to the shore, and the lowly hoppers that worked alongside dredgers and carried away the silt or gravel. No matter how old or slow or decrepit the boats were, so long as they were reasonably seaworthy the Army was willing to pay a good price. Their owners drove excellent bargains and the word spread. It did not require a high degree of inquisitiveness to guess that something big was underway, nor a high degree of intelligence to guess what it was.

The Greek government was not yet fully committed to the cause of the allies but it was common knowledge that Greece had been glad to allow them to use the islands of Imbros, Lemnos and Bozcaada as forward bases in the interest of wresting Constantinople from the hands of their old enemies the Turks. Destroyers and battleships were concentrating in the harbour of Tenedos on Bozcaada and at Mudros on the island of Lemnos. The lighters and hoppers that would take the troops from the ships through shallow water to the shore were towed across the Mediterranean to cluster in swarms round the island of Lemnos. Hospital ships steamed into position. The preparations could not possibly be concealed, and with small boats scudding between the islands on their everyday business of fishing and trading there was very little that did not reach the ears and even the eyes of the Turks. Looking out to sea from vantage points on the peninsula they watched British warships diligently patrolling a few miles from the coast, guessing perhaps that Staff Officers on their decks had their eyes fixed on Gallipoli, peering through powerful binoculars and trying to form an impression of the lie of the land. It was the closest they could get to reconnoitring.

From the sea the Gallipoli Peninsula was a sight of remarkable beauty. Beyond the narrow bays and escarpments at the toe of the promontory, at Cape Helles where the Dardanelles met the Aegean Sea, a low plain rose behind the seashore village of Sedd-el-Bahr, cupped in a saucer between low cliffs, and stretched north to the inland village of Krithia. Beyond it crouched Achi Baba, a deceptively unimposing hill with a broad-breasted summit just high enough to command a view of the Aegean across its western shoulder and the narrows of the Dardanelles to the east. Further north on the western coastline, the land took on a wilder aspect. Sheer cliffs scarred with deep gullies and ravines swept down almost to the water's edge and towered up to rugged heights of formidable grandeur. To the officers planning the campaign it was obvious that they also constituted a formidable obstacle which could not be tackled head on. They would have to be outflanked. The ideal landing place was far further north on the Gulf of Saros, near Bulair at the neck of the peninsula, where the waters of the Dardanelles began to open into the Sea of Marmara and where an isthmus of land only a few miles wide divided them from the Aegean shore. If the Army could seize the isthmus the Turks in the peninsula would be cut off and trapped, the Army would be in command of the Dardanelles, and long before Turkish reinforcements could possibly arrive from the north, the Navy would be in Constantinople and Turkey would have thrown in the towel. It was obvious. It would be equally obvious to the Turks – and it was precisely because they would be ready to meet an attack that the idea of landing at Bulair was rejected.

The plan was cleverly conceived to deceive the Turkish Army, and it envisaged more than a single landing. Streaming ashore from an armada of shallow-draught lighters and cutters, troops would be punched into the blunt southern nose of the peninsula and advance to capture Krithia village and beyond it Achi Baba. Then forces previously landed on the western beaches north of Cape Helles would link up to widen the advance as it swept across the narrow ankle of the peninsula to the straits beyond. They were under no illusion that it would be easy. All along the coast, in places where the cliffs were lower and the ground beyond was easier to cross,

346

tell-tale streaks of newly turned earth showed that the Turks were busy digging trenches, and banks of new barbed wire shone bright when they caught the sun. After one reconnoitring voyage aboard the battleship *Queen Elizabeth* Sir Ian Hamilton reported in a letter to Lord Kitchener, 'Gallipoli looks a much tougher nut to crack than it did over the map in your office.'

The only available maps of the Gallipoli Peninsula were old and rudimentary. They were also inaccurate. They gave no impression of the precipitous terrain, no hint of the deep gullies, the dried-up water-courses, the narrow razor-edged ridges, the deep chasms beyond. And they gave no idea of the thorny, impenetrable scrub that covered the ground and which looked attractively green and lush seen from a distance. It grew thick on the slopes that rose sheer from the sea above a small cove that was nameless before the landings. One day they would call it Anzac – and before long it would be as well known in Australia as the names of Sydney and Melbourne.

The men of the Australian and New Zealand Army Corps who went ashore at Anzac Cove were not intended to land there at all and they were never intended to scale the heights that soared up from the beach. They should have been landed on the wide and sandy expanse of a beach, code-named X beach, a mile to the south, where easier country ran north of Achi Baba across the peninsula to the waters of the Dardanelles. But the small boats that carried the soldiers from the big ships were cockleshell-light and no one had realised that once they had cast off and were making for the shore, the undertow of the swift current would carry them well to the north. The moon had set. A faint phosphorescence gleamed on the water. Once or twice, as distant search-lights on the Asian coast routinely searched the Dardanelles, the outline of the land ahead flickered momentarily into view, but the darkness was inky black. With no light to guide them and with the treacherous current dragging at their hulls, it was almost inevitable that the leading boats of the covering force should drift to the wrong beach. And once the men of the covering force had landed and were scrambling up the heights that loomed directly ahead, once they had come to grips with the enemy and the main body had landed to reinforce them and daylight revealed the full measure of the misfortune, it was far too late to bring them back.

Captain Herbert Kenyon was one of the first men ashore. He was not an Australian, but he did belong to the staff, and as Staff Captain of the 7th Indian Mountain Artillery Brigade, he was vital to the success of the operation. These would be the first guns ashore and Kenyon's task was to find the positions from which they could best support the troops. The Indian Mounted Brigade consisted of two batteries, the 21st and 26th.*

Capt. H. Kenyon, DSO, Royal Artillery, Att. 7th (Indian) Mountain Art. Brig.

It was a perfect night when we started out from Mudros, warm, bright moonlight, not a ripple on the water. I had my greatcoat with me, revolver, haversack, electric lamp, small cap, three days' rations and two waterbottles full of water and tea. Almost exactly at midnight the destroyer glided off with about two hundred and fifty Australians on board, and Colonel Maclagen, commanding the covering party, with his brigade major and staff captain plus Colonel Parker, Kirby, Thom and myself.

We sat where we could on deck – not a light – not a sound – no smoking – no talking. I guess we were all thinking too deeply to talk. We had some excellent cocoa, biscuits, cigarettes, and then had quite a good sleep. I was woken by the destroyer stopping about 3 a.m. The moon was nearly down then but I could just make out the dark mass of four battleships which looked enormous in the dark, and behind them were one or two destroyers. About 3.30 a.m. we got the order to go and the four destroyers glided between the battleships in *absolute* silence. I went down below, and there was a curious feeling in the air, which can only be produced when a party of friends are definitely committed to what all realised might be death in an hour.

We could not sit still and periodically one or other of us went up on deck and could just make out the land. Suddenly the telegraph rang out (which we thought must be heard in Egypt!) and then they ordered 'full speed astern', and I don't think any noise has sounded so noisy before. The boats were immediately lowered and filled and there wasn't a sound from the shore or from our boat. We were in the second lot to go. It was completely dark and silent, then suddenly there was a lot of firing from the shore.

We filled the boat quickly. Some bullets fell near us and one knocked a hole below the water-line. Then the coxswain said, 'Shove her off and pull steady together,' but a sailor said the boat was making water pretty fast. All the boats were provided

---

* The 7th Indian Mountain Artillery Brigade comprised the 21st (Kohat) Battery with one 4.7-inch gun and the 26th (Jacob's) Battery with three 6-inch Howitzers. They were the first guns ashore at Gallipoli and were the only guns of the Indian Artillery to serve in Europe during the war.

with a pail and wooden plugs in case of emergency. The pail was at my feet, and I was jolly glad of an excuse to put my head down and look for a plug! Bullets were falling all round us then. All the plugs were too large and a sailor cut one to fit. The whole of this took I suppose one or one and a half minutes. Then we shoved off. The coxswain stood the whole time and it was magnificent the way he worked the crew. 'Stronger – all together – keep her moving – nearly there. *Now* let her have it!' And we bumped on the beach.

The row lasted about three minutes I think, and I had undone the laces of my boots in case we sank. As we grounded a man was knocked over and wounded. Just before we got there we heard a cheer ashore and we all joined in. The moment we touched, the coxswain shouted, 'Tumble out boys and get at 'em! We'll get the boat back. Don't you wait!' And out we tumbled – literally! The men were carrying tons of kit. We grounded in about three feet of water, and as they jumped out practically every man went headlong full-length under! It made me really laugh, and the Colonel and I got out more carefully.

It was about eight or ten yards from the water's edge to the foot of the hills and we all doubled in under the bank and then up we went after the others, shouting, yelling, cursing, tumbling down and tripping over bushes and holes. It was impossible for the men to climb in their kit so they chucked them as they scrambled up.

Even though most of the men had abandoned almost everything but their rifles, the climb would have taxed the agility of a mountain goat, and Norman Scott from Melbourne was not the only man who blessed the weeks of arduous training as much as they had cursed it – slogging with full packs across the desert under the hot Egyptian sun – and he was not the only one to boast that they were 'so strong and so well trained that we could almost walk up a vertical wall'. It was just as well. In one way a vertical wall might have been easier. At least they would have travelled in a straight line.

Negotiating gullies, edging round sheer overhangs, hauling themselves up the steep crevices of dried-up water-courses, grasping at thorny bushes with bleeding hands, scrabbling through sandy soil that crumbled and slid beneath booted feet, it was literally every man for himself. The possibility of keeping together in sections or platoons, let alone in companies or battalions, was laughable. The wonder was that they managed to reach the top and when they did, they were scattered piecemeal across a wide and hostile landscape. It was daylight now. Looking back, down the long haul to the beach and the sea beyond it, crowded with battleships and destroyers, the

349

men of the vanguard saw string upon string of small boats approaching in long tows to the shore and, far below, an ant-like khaki swarm as the men of the next wave ran up the beach to tackle the climb in their turn. They might also have heard a strangely incongruous sound coming faintly across the water. Now that the fighting had started and there was no need for silence the men in the tows were singing on their way to the shore. They were singing the song some patriot had composed before the war was a month old.

Rally round the banner of your country
Take the field with brother o'er the foam
On land or sea, wherever you be
Keep your eye on Germany!
But England Home and Beauty have no cause to fear
Should auld acquaintance be forgot?
No! No! No! No! No! Australia will be there
Australia will be there.

Even if they were not familiar with all the words, the Anzacs all knew the last few lines – and they seemed singularly appropriate to the occasion.

If they had stopped to think about it the soldiers who had already scaled the heights might have realised that they were facing a dilemma. In front of them was no gentle undulating country, no flatland, no recognisable objectives, no sight of the waters of the Dardanelles. All they could see were more hills, other valleys, deep precipitous slopes thick with scrub and bush. And Turkish snipers and machine-gunners, well hidden in the scrub, were determined to make sure they got no further. The Turkish guns were firing from behind their line and as yet there were no British guns to answer back.

Capt. H. Kenyon, DSO.

The Colonel and I ran with the men to the top of the first hill, and then the Colonel stopped to look round, because of course our job was to reconnoitre for positions for the battery. Eventually he sent me off in one direction whilst he went in another. I rejoined him later and we both decided there was no place for the Battery there. Then Thom and Kirby joined us and we moved along the beach to our right. By then it was daylight and a gun from Gabe Tepe began enfilading straight down the beach. We walked in that direction keeping as far under the cliff as possible. There were a fair number of dead and wounded on the beach but no one moved the wounded. Everyone was too busy.

We then climbed a little hill or spur, called Hell Spit later, which is where one side of Shrapnel Valley ran down to the beach. We looked round there and then the Colonel sent me off to look at what seemed a possible position while he had a breather. However it was no good, and then he went off and told me to wait till he came back. There was a Turkish trench there and a little sentry dug-out, and as some shells and a good many bullets were coming along I got inside this and was practically hidden. Presently I heard someone coming along, so I looked out and at once a voice shouted 'Who's that!' and pointed his bayonet at me. I didn't take long to answer him in language which convinced him I was English! And then I realised how foolish I had been, so I left my retreat and sat down in the open. *That* was a narrow escape!

Presently the Colonel came back and told me which way 26th Battery was to start off when it arrived, and told me that, when I had seen them all off, I was to try and get news of 21st Battery and then bring the Brigade Staff along.

At about 8 a.m. 26th Battery began to land. I told Kirby where to take them and then helped to hurry the mules away as the beach was being badly shelled. Twenty-sixth started about 10 a.m. up the hill, but there was no news or sign of 21st disembarking, so I left word with Thom to bring them along the same way, and then I collected the Headquarters Staff and telephone mule and started off. I got on a wrong track and found myself at an unhealthy spot marked by some undiscovered snipers in the brushwood. I put the men under cover where some of our infantry were and had a look round and presently I found the track again, so I came back and brought them along. It was a longish steep climb and the whole time bullets were singing everywhere. I was going up the edge of a nullah and the enemy's shrapnel were fairly well pouring down it. I wasn't one little bit happy, and all the time was wondering, 'Shall I get as far as that bush, or that mound?' It didn't occur to me that I should get up the whole way!

We had to take one or two breathers where there was any cover. Starting off again was the hardest part, and I wished I didn't have to give the order! At last we got up to the battery mules, right at the top of the nullah, which ends on a small grassy hill we later called the Razor Back.

I went to the Colonel and found him very much agitated as Bruce had been up for an hour and hadn't yet brought the

Battery into action. At 11.50 he said, 'If the Battery isn't in action by 12 I will take command myself.' Just before 12 however it came into action. Almost at once a Turkish Battery which had been shelling down the nullah switched onto the Battery, and it was pretty nasty.

Even without Turkish marksmen firing from the topmost heights and machine-guns sweeping the slopes it would have been hard going and, although the men clinging to the slopes were still in shadow, as the dawn spread slowly up the sky behind the Dardanelles there were shouts of alarm behind the crackle of the bullets, and the sickening thud of tumbling bodies as a bullet found its mark and a wounded man lost some precarious foothold and crashed back down the hill.

The three guns, dragged and man-handled to a perch well up on high ground, were at least able to give the troops some local help, but it was the big guns on the battleships standing off the peninsula which were meant to fire the artillery barrage that would help the troops to get ahead. It was not their fault that they failed. Signal stations on the landing beaches were to transmit messages to the ships and bring their guns to bear on the places where they were most needed. The difficulty was that the signallers on land had no idea what was happening on the high ground behind them and it was impossible for observers at sea to make anything of the situation for themselves. Even on the clifftops it was hard to see what was happening for the troops were so split up and units so confused that there was little or no cohesive command. Even where officers had managed to keep control, or to gather together a significant number of men, the command broke down. The low, thick scrub, so useful to the enemy in their defence, was of little use to soldiers creeping through it to attack across unfamiliar ground, and the officers leading them were so often obliged to stand up to find direction that snipers were easily able to pick them off as soon as they appeared. Deprived of leadership, with no specific objectives and with no clear idea of what was expected of them, driven on by the simple knowledge that they were there to capture the peninsula and kill any Turks in their path, the men acted on their own initiative and charged ahead into a hundred private battles of their own. The men at their backs followed their lead. They plunged down sheer slopes into clefts and found no way back and no way out on the other side. They clambered into gullies and hauled themselves up slopes, breasted knolls and pressed on, sometimes in groups of as few as a dozen men, and they put the fear of death into the Turks.

Three men got further than any others. Lieutenant Loutit and two scouts actually ran three and a half miles across country to the top of

352

a rough hill and reaching the summit, found themselves looking across the waters of the Dardanelles. They were the only soldiers to catch so much as a glimpse of them for many months to come. As they worked their way back, it was plain to see that no one else had managed to make much headway. But it was a magnificent effort and it was not the fault of the troops that it had not wholly succeeded. Later the logs of the signals exchanged between the battleships made tragic reading.

Goliath to Sapphire: 'What is the position occupied by our troops?'
Sapphire to Goliath: 'No news from the shore but northern limit appears to be square 176 R3 . . .'

Goliath to Dublin: 'Are any of our troops dressed in blue?'
Bacchante to Galeka: 'Have we landed any cavalry?'

Amethyst to Sapphire: 'Have you any idea how things have been going?'
Sapphire to Amethyst: 'No news at all!'

All that the gunnery officers could see from the ships was the smoke of Turkish shells exploding along the line of the advance beyond the high escarpments. For fear of hitting their own troops scattered haphazardly behind them, they could do nothing to help them.

Capt. H. Kenyon.

Presently I started off to see what information I could get, but got held up by a big nullah so came back again. It was not a pleasant walk alone. When I got back to the Battery I found Chapman had been wounded so I went to him, helped with the bandaging, and started him off down the hill. Then the Colonel called me and said ammunition was running short, and not coming up quick enough, so I was to go down and get it along. I went down considerably quicker than I came up! I found Rossiter running the ammunition but as he did not know the situation I took it on and hustled it up as fast as it came along. I found the beach packed with wounded, and they were coming down in a steady stream. Chapman arrived when I was there looking jolly bad. All his colour had gone and he could hardly talk. I sat with him while he was being dressed by the doctor and tried to cheer him up, and then saw him carried off to the boat.

I then remembered I was hungry so sat on the beach with

General Lotbiniere and some other fellows, took off my belt and revolver and electric lamp and had some lunch. In the middle of it a shell burst all among us, so we bolted back under the bank.

It looked then as if there could hardly be a whole man left in the force, and crowds of the men who came back told all sorts of tales from which one gathered matters were pretty serious.

Serious though the position was at Anzac things might have been worse still had it not been for the feint attack at Bulair the previous evening. Men of the Royal Naval Division had embarked in small boats and rowed towards the shore just before dusk while there was still enough light for the Turkish observers to spot them. After dark they had rowed back again to the big ships and later under cover of the darkness Lieutenant Freyberg had volunteered to swim from a small boat a mile off shore to light flares along the beach. It was a feat worthy of Leander himself, and it rightly won him the Victoria Cross for it did more than anything else to convince the German Commander of the Turkish forces that the main force of the invasion would strike here. Even though there was no sign of them in the morning except for the ominous sight of British battleships standing off the coast, even though there were reports of landings at six other places a good day's march away, Liman von Sanders was so convinced that they must be feints intended to mislead him that he kept the bulk of his manpower standing by all day at Bulair. It was well after nightfall on 25 April before he realised that he had been duped and sent troops marching south to reinforce the far more thinly defended sectors of the peninsula where the landings had actually taken place. It was von Sanders's first and only gaffe of the campaign, and it was that little bit of luck, in a day of endless setbacks, that gave the allied troops the chance to dig in and consolidate their hold on the peninsula.

But it was only a toe-hold. And the sea was at their backs.

Chapter 25

Three weeks and one day after the rail crash that wiped out half the battalion, the two remaining companies of the 7th Royal Scots landed on the shores of Gallipoli. For some of them, and particularly for the Commanding Officer, the voyage to the Mediterranean had hardly been a rest cure. The signal section had been wiped out at Gretna, so Captain Wightman, no expert himself, took on the job of training a new one, and the men who volunteered to replace the dead signallers had spent long hours training, swotting up morse code, practising semaphore on deck, and attempting to master the art of flashing by signal lamp. They were still far from expert, but they would have to do. The machine-gunners had gone too and Alex Elliott, co-opted as machine-gun officer in place of Lieutenant Christian Salveson who died in the Gretna crash, had spent every waking hour training new machine-gunners as best he could in the confines of a ship at sea and, he fervently hoped, keeping one step ahead of them, poring over instruction manuals through night after wakeful night, doing his utmost to prepare for the day when his cursory knowledge would be put to the test.

In the early hours of 13 June they came ashore at V beach at Cape Helles. It was Sunday morning, and it was five weeks and all but a few hours since the 29th Division had landed at the same spot on the first day of the Gallipoli campaign. The trawlers that brought the Royal Scots to the shore tied up alongside the *River Clyde*, a beat-up old collier grounded near the beach to act as a pier that would carry the troops across the deep water to dry land. At the landings five weeks ago the *River Clyde* had been a vital part of the plan, for the main thrust of the attack was to be launched at Cape Helles at the toe of the peninsula from the beaches that were code-named V, W and X, and it was vital that the largest possible number of troops should be landed in the shortest possible time. As at Anzac the spearhead of the covering force would be carried in strings of open boats, ships' cutters or lifeboats, towed by trawlers or steam-driven hoppers to the shore, where the tows would turn about to return to the waiting transports to fetch the second wave.

Each tow could carry perhaps three hundred men – but not nearly enough to ensure success in the first vital hour of the assault, and it was at V beach that the situation would be critical.

V beach at the foot of a natural amphitheatre of gently sloping land looked deceptively innocent – a narrow strip of sand, perhaps three hundred yards long with low cliffs on the left, and a ruined fort above the village of Sedd-el-Bahr on the right, on the headland where the peninsula turned back towards the mouth of the Dardanelles. It was here that the *River Clyde* was to play a part not unlike the part played by the legendary wooden horse at the siege of Troy in Agamemnon's war. The shabby old tub, sailing in towing a hopper and with three lighters in her wake, carried two thousand soldiers who were to storm the beach in the first vital stage of the attack. The plan was to ground the *River Clyde* close to the beach, the hopper moving ahead of her to act as floating bridge. As soon as it was in position beneath the prow the men would pour out through wide sally-ports newly cut in her sides, along broad gang-planks to a platform beneath her bows, on to the hopper and off again, splashing through shallow water to dry land to secure the beach and open the road to Krithia. The final objective for that first day's fighting was Achi Baba. The Staff were by no means unduly optimistic in supposing that the doughty regular soldiers of the 29th Division would easily reach it.

Because of the strong currents that dragged at the sea where the Aegean met the Dardanelles, the Royal Navy was fearful that the tows might lose direction and could only guarantee to land them safely by daylight. It was a perfect spring morning. As the flotilla set off for the shore just after six o'clock the peninsula still seemed to be slumbering under a pale cloudless sky. Lieutenant-Colonel Williams, of the General Headquarters Staff, had his eyes fixed on the quiet coastline ahead and he could hardly believe their good fortune. There was no sign of life. As the first Staff Officer ashore it was part of his job to make a record of events as they happened. Standing on the bridge of the *River Clyde* with a grandstand view of the tows as they bobbed towards the bay, he made hasty minute-by-minute jottings in his notebook.

> *6.10 a.m.*   Within ½ mile of the shore. We are far ahead of the tows. No O.C. troops on board. It must cause a mix-up if we, 2nd line, arrive before the 1st line. With difficulty I get Unwin (Captain of the *River Clyde*) to swerve off and await the tows.

> *6.22 a.m.*   Ran smoothly ashore without a tremor. No opposition. We shall land unopposed.

But the Turks were holding their fire and in their trenches well hidden

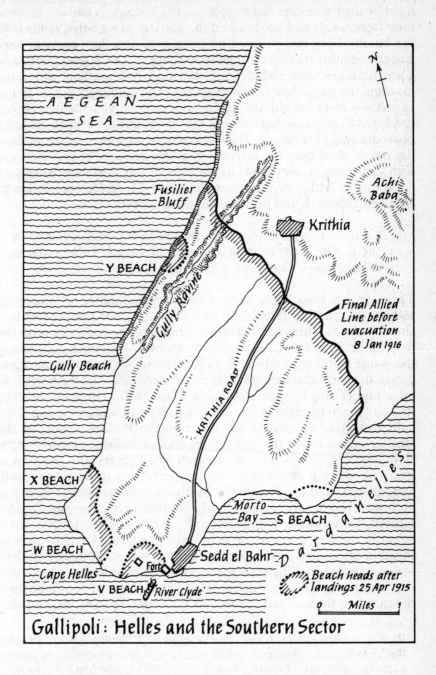

AEGEAN
SEA

Fusilier
Bluff

Y BEACH

Krithia

Gully Beach

Gully Ravine

Final Allied
Line before
evacuation
8 Jan 1916

Achi
Baba

KRITHIA ROAD

X BEACH

W BEACH

Cape Helles

V BEACH

Fort

River Clyde

Sedd el Bahr

Morto
Bay

S BEACH

Dardanelles

Beach heads after
landings 25 Apr 1915

0   Miles   1

Gallipoli: Helles and the Southern Sector

by folds in the rising ground they too were blessing their luck. They had stayed cool under the thundering of the thirty-minute bombardment by the battleships standing off on the horizon. It had not touched their trenches. It had not touched the barriers of wire that ran behind the beach. They had suffered no casualties, and they could ill have spared them for there were only two companies to defend the beach. Their defences were rudimentary, but they had machine-guns commanding the beach from the high ground and cunningly placed to fire in enfilade from the old fort. Even so, it took nerve to wait, to watch the *River Clyde* steaming towards the shore and the armada of small boats drawing ever nearer. They waited until they were within yards of the beach. And then the machine-guns opened up. At that distance, with such a target, they could hardly miss. It was sickening carnage.

From the bridge of the grounded *River Clyde* Colonel Williams watched appalled, and his hand shook as he scrawled:

> *6.25 a.m.*   Tows within a few yards of shore. Hell burst loose on them. One boat drifting to north, all killed. Others almost equally helpless. Our hopper gone away.

The men on board the *River Clyde* were standing at the open sally-ports ready to double up the gangways, but the hopper that should have run forward beneath the bows of the collier to form the floating bridge had swung broadside and was wallowing helpless in the water frothing in a lash of bullets streaming from the machine-gun in the fort. The lighters on the starboard side of the *River Clyde* were higher and less manoeuvrable than the tiny hopper and they had only been brought in as a failsafe to help to bridge the gap if the collier chanced to ground too far from the shallow water for the smaller vessel to do the job. In the hail of bullets, and with little time to spare, it was not easy to inch two lighters into position in front of the big ship's bow, to connect them precariously with gang-planks, and even when this had been managed they still yawed and wavered treacherously in the current. It was the Captain himself, Commander Unwin, who dived into the sea to steer them towards the shore and drag them into position. An able seaman dived in after him to help and there the two men stood, up to their waists in water, pulling on a rope to hold the lighters steady so that the troops could disembark. Bullets from two machine-guns mounted on the bows of the *River Clyde* sprayed over their heads.*

---

* Both Commander Unwin and Able Seaman W. C. Williams were awarded the Victoria Cross. Williams, unfortunately, was one of the many casualties, killed by a shell fired from the Asiatic shore. His VC, the first to be awarded to a naval rating for over fifty years, was awarded posthumously.

Apart from the rifles carried by the infantry they were the only weapons there were to answer the lethal fire and the rifles, in the circumstances, were useless. Not many soldiers survived to fire them.

Few of them even reached the shore. They were shot down almost to a man as they ran down the gang-ways. In minutes the lighters were piled deep with dead and dying men and the water turned red with the blood of the wounded staggering off the gangways to sink and drown beneath the weight of their equipment. The handful of men who reached the beach dashed to the shelter of a low sandy bank and watched in horror as line after line of their comrades were struck down and the tows of open boats bobbed aimless and adrift on the water.

Somehow, despite his own horror, Colonel Williams managed to carry on recording the calamity.

6.35 a.m. Connection with shore very bad. Only single file possible and not one man in ten gets across. Lighters blocked with dead and wounded. Maxims in bows firing full blast, but nothing to be seen excepting a Maxim firing through a hole in the fort and a pom-pom near the sky-line on our left front.

9.0 a.m. Very little directed fire against us on the ship, but fire immediately concentrates on any attempt to land. The Turks' fire discipline is really wonderful. Fear we'll not land today.

When almost a thousand men had been lost attempting to disembark from the *River Clyde*, realising that no more could be done until nightfall they called a halt. It was nine o'clock in the morning and, as the sun climbed higher, conditions in the dark hold of the ship where nine hundred more men were waiting were already uncomfortably hot and cramped. For the moment they had been reprieved, but settling down restlessly in the stuffy gloom, lit only by a few hanging lamps hastily rigged up, they could hear the muffled sound of firing from the land, the spatter of machine-guns from the deck above, the thud of big guns firing from the Asiatic shore and the crump of shells exploding on the beach. They could only guess what was happening.

Waiting on the deck of a small transport that had seen civilian service as a cross-channel steamer, Brigadier-General Napier waited impatiently for the return of the tows that would take him and the second wave of his 88th Brigade to the shore. They were a long time coming and some of them never arrived at all for, like the soldiers in the open boats, many of the sailors manning them had been killed within yards of dry land. The tow that did eventually arrive had landed some of its men but the boats were crowded with dead and wounded. It was several minutes before they were unloaded and the General with his Staff and the second wave of soldiers were able to clamber down to take their places. They sat down gingerly, for the seats were still wet and slippery with blood but in his frustration at the delay, assuming with some irritation that his tow had been used to transport *all* the casualties, Napier made no inquiry. It was not the sailors' job to decide that a landing was hopeless or to volunteer any such opinion to a Senior Army Officer. Their job was to convey the Army to the shore and whatever their trepidation they did not intend to shirk it. Stoically, trailing the little boats behind them, they headed back to the beach and back into the maelstrom.

On board the collier the Commanding Officer of the 2nd Hampshires had just seen one of his own companies wiped out in a vain attempt to land and watched incredulously as Napier's tow neared the open beach. Snatching up a megaphone he called to it to come alongside and the naval officer in charge obediently changed course. But General Napier was on his mettle. From his position in the leading boat, just a foot or so above the surface of the water, he could see that the lighters were full of men and he poised himself to spring on board and lead them ashore. But the men were all dead. Carington-Smith bellowed from the *River Clyde*, 'You can't possibly land!' But Napier yelled back, 'I'll have a damned good try!' And then the machine-guns started up. General Napier and his staff reached the hopper, but they could get no further. Soon their own bodies were lying dead among the rest.*

When night fell many hours later, although the Turks continued to fire haphazardly, the troops in the *River Clyde* were at last able to land and with only a small number of casualties. Under cover of darkness a makeshift jetty was flung out to link the ship to the shore. It was built from the piled-up packs of dead men. Even by

---

* The Official Historian later wrote: 'Thus died the very man who by his rank, his nerve, and his knowledge, would have been of priceless value to the troops in the southern area during that vital day.' It was a telling point. In a conventional battle, Brigade and Divisional Commanders would properly have conducted it some distance behind the fighting line with the advantage of an overall view. At the Gallipoli landings, where there was no hinterland but the sea, so many senior officers were obliged to be at the front and so many were killed that the loss of the very people who would have been in a position to take decisions according to circumstances on the spot contributed decisively to the failure of leaderless troops to progress in the first vital hours in places where they could easily have done so and, as a result, had a significant effect on the long-term outcome of the campaign.

morning the water lapping the beach was still red with blood. Exactly two months earlier, on 26 February, after the bombardment of the fort at Sedd-el-Bahr, while the Royal Navy was engaged in its attempt to secure the Dardanelles, a party of Royal Marines had landed on this very beach and reconnoitred it unchallenged and at their leisure.

V beach and some ground beyond it had long ago been secured, but the beaches were still in full view from the high ground and HMS *Carron* which brought the 7th Royal Scots from Lemnos prudently cruised just over the horizon until after dark. The tows of open boats were a thing of the past now, but in the dark and in a choppy sea it was not entirely easy to transfer the men and their brigade stores to the three trawlers that were to take them across the last few sea-miles to land on the peninsula. In the early hours of the morning the Royal Scots filed off the trawlers, up the gangways of the *River Clyde* alongside and on to the platform beneath her bows. Now it was linked to the beach by a proper jetty but, even so, it was hard work to man-handle the stores ashore and it was daylight before fatigue parties had finished stacking them on the beach.

Compared to the bloody Sunday morning of 25 April, V beach was peaceful. The village of Sedd-el-Bahr was reduced to ruins, but the belts of wire had been cleared away. The rising ground was criss-crossed with new tracks, with freshly dug trenches, and there were sandbagged bivouacs burrowed into the slopes and dumps of supplies in the shelter of the cliffs and the old fort. During the night a procession of ration parties and pack-mules had come and gone laden with food and water and ammunition for the men in the line. A Red Cross flag flew above a cluster of tents and shelters near the beach and, not far from the dressing station, a crop of white crosses marked the graves of the soldiers who had died of their wounds.

They were just a few of the casualties. In the five weeks since the landings, the small Gallipoli force had spent most of its strength. Two pushes towards Krithia had advanced them a mile or so up the peninsula but Krithia itself was still in Turkish hands, Achi Baba remained inviolable and the losses, by comparison with the strength of the force, had been staggering. For every hundred yards gained a thousand men were lost. Not all of them were killed or wounded in battle. Many were falling sick with dysentery. Conditions were worsening and although it was still early summer the heat was already trying and the men were plagued by flies that swarmed and thrived by the million in trenches and dug-outs, and preyed on the bodies of the dead lying unburied between the lines. The spring flowers that carpeted the peninsula in April had withered away and so had the sweet-scented blooms on the thorny scrub that was now so brittle and tinder-dry that it could be snapped off and used as firewood. The burst of a shell, even the scorch of a flying bullet, could set it alight. Everywhere the ground was arid and the nullahs and trenches were thick with dust that rose in clouds at every step, inflamed every eye, filled every nostril and rasped mercilessly at the back of every throat parched for lack of water. Later, as the summer drew on, it would be worse. Even now it was no picnic.

Sgt. H. Keighley, 29th Div., Royal Artillery.

The food was bully beef and biscuits with apple jam and cheese, and you had dried vegetables which had to be soaked overnight in the dixie to boil next day. It were like eating rubber! The potatoes were the same. The food was almost nil. If we did get any bread, which later on we did perhaps once a month, we got just one loaf between eight men for a day's ration. We'd no fresh water. The water that we drank was brought by boat to W beach and water-carts collected it and brought it up so far. We were on the west side of Y ravine and it was a very high cliff. You had to climb a winding path to the top and we had to carry dixies full of water from water-carts up to this gun position.

I was put on as latrine orderly and we had to dig a trench for the latrine and you had to stand astride to do your business, and then you had to cover it with soil because the flies were, oh, dreadful! The latrine was like a hole in the ground. I had to cover it with a ground sheet pegged above the hole and at night if I struck a match to light a candle in the dark the ground sheet was just black with big flies, and when you were eating jam or biscuits you had to knock flies off to get them to your mouth. Most of us got dysentery. That was the biggest scourge we had on Gallipoli, dysentery and ill-health from lack of fresh water and lack of proper food. I got dysentery very badly. I hadn't the strength to go up and down the cliff, across the ravine and up the hill to get to the Medical Officer (he was on the other side) and in the end I lost two or three stones. I was dreadful! I practically had to sleep alongside the latrines, my tummy had so much trouble.

I used to go with an officer on observation post duty. We hadn't trenches, we only had parapets built up with sandbags, and we were going up one day to the front line to do OP duty and he stopped to talk to somebody. We stopped about two minutes and that saved us from being blown to bits, because the Turks blew a mine just at the top of the ravine and when we got up there, there were infantrymen laying dead and badly wounded all over the place. A proper mess – and we should have been there if the officer hadn't stopped. He was a ranker officer, and he seemed to sense that I was fed up with not being one of the gun crew and being sent on mucky jobs all the time, and he used to take me up to the OP when it was his turn to go. I loved it for all it was dangerous, because No Man's Land was very short and you daren't put your head above the sandbagged parapet, but to me it was what I joined up for – and that was to see action.

With constant grappling between the lines there was plenty of action, but there was little progress and after the costly battles for Krithia the fighting had settled down to trench warfare. The troops were weak and debilitated, ammunition was scarce, and with no real prospect of advancing until more reinforcements arrived there was no alternative but to mark time, knowing that when the chance did come it would be harder than ever to break through. It was plain to see that the Turks were using the respite to dig more trench-systems, to bring in more troops and to strengthen the defences. Since the guns were strictly forbidden to fire more than two rounds a day unless the Turks attacked, there was precious little that could be done to impede them.

The French contingent, on the other hand, was well-off for ammunition and fresh stocks of high explosive shell were arriving regularly from France. The French had played a vital role. On 25 April their diversionary landing on the Asiatic shore had helped to confuse the Turks and appreciably assisted the landings on the peninsula. Now they had taken over the sector running north of Morto Bay where the toe of the peninsula turned into the Dardanelles and in a series of costly attacks between 21 and 25 June they had advanced their line and gained high ground which would give the allies a head start when the time came to push ahead towards the vital objectives of Krithia and Achi Baba. But there was still a huge stumbling block on the Aegean shore. It was Gully Ravine. And before there could be any thought of going further the situation there had to be resolved.

Like all the soldiers of the 156th Infantry Brigade the Royal Scots were soft after weeks of inactivity on the journey. A few days after their arrival they were pushed into the reserve line to acclimatise, to become accustomed to shell-fire, to tone up flabby muscles and get back into shape. They dug communication trenches until they were sick of it and they were only too happy when the time came to march into action. They marched by a tortuous route over rough country to the high ground above Y beach.

Behind the trenches steep cliffs led down to the beach. Inland, less than half a mile away, was Gully Ravine, a deep declivity two miles long, many metres wide and, in places, as much as a hundred feet deep. The British trenches bisected it half-way up its length and just above Y beach and to the north a network of enemy trenches formed a redoubt on the clifftops, spanned Gully Ravine and stretched away on the inland side as far as Krithia. Staring across at the bristling new defences it was difficult to believe that the landing at Y beach had been unopposed and that Colonel Matthews, commanding the Y beach force, had walked with his ADC to the outskirts of Krithia only a mile away. He had not been asked to capture it alone, though his troops might have easily done so. His orders had been to wait for the troops advancing from V beach and, when they reached him, to join in on the left of their advance and thus widen the front of the attack. Lacking any other orders, in the absence of any news, and with no message of any kind reaching him from higher authority, he dutifully went on waiting while his troops kicked their heels on the clifftops enjoying the pleasant spring sunshine and admiring the view. The Turks had ample time to muster and march to Y beach to oppose them. Much later Matthews was criticised for failing to act with initiative, but his orders had been explicit, and it had apparently occurred to no one to suggest how he should act if the troops at V beach failed to make headway.

Directly across the peninsula at the northern tip of Morto Bay it had been the same story. The South Wales Borderers landed unmolested at S beach and they were waiting too. There were no Turkish troops within miles, and on 25 April the British troops at S beach and Y beach outnumbered by several times the entire Turkish force – only five battalions – in the sector south of Achi Baba. The two British contingents were just five miles apart on either side of the peninsula. They might easily have advanced and spread out to join hands across it, walked into Krithia and pushed on to Achi Baba. By cutting off the few Turkish troops who were so gallantly resisting at the beaches at Cape Helles they might very well have altered the course of the campaign.

The day after the landing, when V beach was finally secured and the village of Sedd-el-Bahr was stormed and captured, a copy of a desperate message fell into British hands. It had been hastily scribbled by a junior Turkish officer and it reeked of panic:

My Captain, either you must send up reinforcements and drive the enemy into the sea or let us evacuate this place because it is absolutely certain that they will land more troops tonight. Send doctors to carry off my wounded. Alas, alas my Captain, for God's sake send me reinforcements because hundreds of soldiers are landing. Hurry up. What on earth will happen my Captain.

364

But there were no reinforcements within reach to be sent. The following day, dazed and weakened by casualties, the remnants of the eight Turkish companies at V beach streamed away up the hill. There was no pursuit, for the landing force was too exhausted to do much more than consolidate hard-won positions and steel themselves to meet the counter-attacks they believed would surely be launched. But there were no counter-attacks at V beach or anywhere else, for the south of the peninsula was being evacuated. The night after the landings, under cover of darkness, the weary Turkish soldiers who had fought so hard to thwart the landing pulled back several miles to meet reinforcements from the north and, with Achi Baba behind them, they started digging a line of strong defences in front of Krithia.

Recently they had been considerably strengthened and, by late June, a succession of strongly defended redoubts and trenches ran across the spur of land that dominated the beaches on the seaward side of Gully Ravine and across the ground on its inland side barring the road to Krithia. Unless they could be pushed off the cliffs, unless Gully Ravine could be captured, there was little hope of making progress towards Achi Baba, and no hope at all of linking up with the Anzacs, still battling it out on the heights above Anzac Cove. No one was under any illusion that the task would be easy.

A less formidable series of unconnected trench-lines on the Krithia side of Gully Ravine might have presented a lesser problem had it not been for two difficulties. After the battles for Krithia men were scarce and guns and ammunition were scarcer still, and it was evident that the highest proportion of such resources as they had must be concentrated in the vital sector on Gully Spur where the 29th Division were detailed to make the assault. No other troops could easily be spared to attack inland on their right, and if the assault of the 29th Division was widened, if they were thinned out to attack across both sectors on either side of the ravine, it was doubtful if they could possibly succeed.

Sir Ian Hamilton was not anxious to commit the raw Territorials of 156th Brigade, but there was no one else and he was reluctantly forced to attach them to the 29th Division at the urgent request of its Commander. They would attack on the right of Gully Ravine. 'If necessary', a brigade of the 29th Division would support them. But, looking over General de Lisle's dispositions for the battle, the Corps commander was worried. He was particularly unhappy with the arrangements for artillery support, for almost all the guns and ammunition were to be directed on the 29th Division sector. Only four batteries could be spared to assist the Royal Scots and their comrades in their first experience of battle. They could only hope for the best – but the Corps Commander was not alone in fearing the worst.

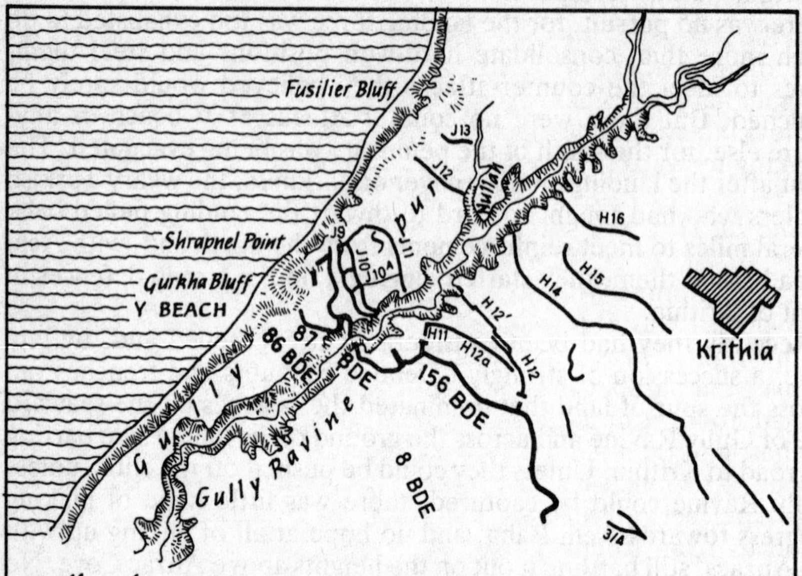
Fusilier Bluff
Shrapnel Point
Gurkha Bluff
Y BEACH
Gully
Spur
Nullah
Gully Ravine
86 BDE
87 BDE
156 BDE
8 BDE
J9
J10
J10A
J11
J12
J13
H11
H12
H12a
H12'
H14
H15
H16
3/4
Krithia

Gallipoli : Gully Ravine, 28 June 1915

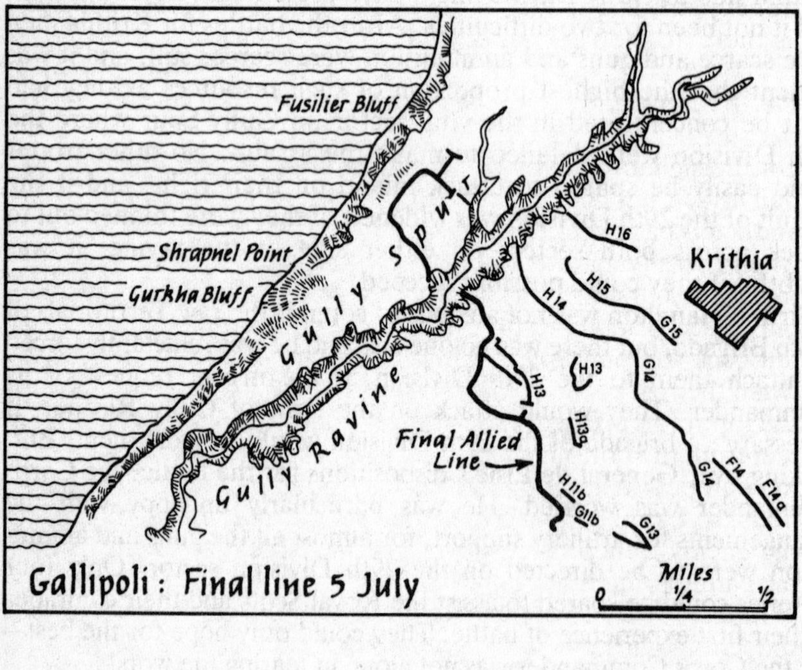
Fusilier Bluff
Shrapnel Point
Gurkha Bluff
Gully Spur
Gully Ravine
H16
H14
H15
G15
H13
G14
H13
H13a
Final Allied Line
H11b
G11b
G13
G14
F14
F14a
Krithia
Miles
0
1/4
1/2

Gallipoli : Final line 5 July

A third of all the ammunition on the peninsula was allotted to the seventy-seven guns available for the bombardment and the guns of the big ships were to join in. It started at nine o'clock in the morning of 28 June and although most of it was concentrated on the far side of Gully Ravine the noise was thunderous. Huddled at the foot of the Royal Scots' trench young Willie Begbie had never heard anything like it. When it lifted at eleven o'clock the infantry would go over the top, and he was not looking forward to it. They were all nervous.

2nd Lt. D. Lyell, 7th Bn., Royal Scots (TF), 156 Brig.

I was standing with my eye on my watch, and just on eleven o'clock I was about to give the word to advance when from the right I saw a movement, so I shouted 'Come on,' and over the parapet the whole company went like one man. We had about a hundred yards to go to the first trench to take that, and then about two hundred and fifty yards to the next one. As soon as we started the Turkish artillery opened on us – a perfect rain of shrapnel, and some machine-guns turned on us from somewhere. The chief thing I remember about the charge was the awful noise. The first trench took some taking. I know I loosed off all six chambers of my revolver! Then the Turks bolted and then we went to the second trench, still under this awful fire. The Turks didn't wait for us there at all. They all flew!

Pte. W. Begbie.

On the signal to charge I caught hold of a root and started to pull myself up, but near the top the root came away in my hand and I fell back into the trench. Before the charge order came when I was lying in the bottom of the trench with the noise of the shells bursting and the machine-guns and rifles firing, the only place I did *not* want to go was over the parapet, but when I fell back the only place I *didn't* want to be in was the trench when the rest of the company were shouting and charging over the top. I ran up the trench till I came to a firing step about two feet from the bottom of the trench so it was easier to climb over the parapet. When I got to my feet I remembered our instructions, so I kept yelling, rifle at the ready, and ran like hell into the enemy trench. Before I reached it I could see some Turks retreating to their next lines.

In later years I have to smile when I think of that, a boy of sixteen, making a three-hundred-yard charge, all on his own!

A little way to the west, on the seaward side of Gully Ravine where the 87th Brigade of the 29th Division dashed across at zero, there were five lines of well-fortified trenches to capture. Here where the bombardment was heaviest the results were everything they had hoped for. The trenches in places were devastated, there had been many casualties, and when the guns lifted and the 87th Brigade went ahead, the unfortunate Turks were too stupefied to make much of a stand. But the Turkish guns were firing back furiously now, and waiting in the reserve trenches with the Royal Munsters, although Captain Robert Laidlaw had been careful to warn his platoon to keep their heads well down, he set them a bad example. It was impossible to resist the foolhardy temptation to stand up to watch the show as the 87th Brigade dashed across to the first trench. He was still gazing fascinated when they reached the second and then, sweeping all before them, raced on to the third. He could hardly blame his men for doing the same thing. They were cheering like supporters at a football match. It was quite a sight.

Capt. R. F. E. Laidlaw, 1st Bn., Royal Munster Fusiliers, 86th Brig., 29th Div.

At 11.30 a.m. our passive role of reserves was finished and we were ordered forward to the lines of trenches already taken by the 87th Brigade. Our whole brigade went across the open in long lines of companies, each battalion in depth, one company following the one ahead as soon as it had gained the enemy trench. By this time the Turkish guns had our range to an inch and men were falling all round as we dashed across to the trenches. As we got into the third trench I lost my platoon and, unthinkingly, ran along the parapet amongst bullets and shells, looking for it. The men in the trench, who were mostly of the 87th Brigade, shouted at me '*Get down you fool*' and, realising my stupidity, I jumped down and continued my search in the trench itself. What with Turkish dead and British dead and wounded, as well as the men on the firestep, it was pretty full, but I soon found my platoon, which had only had a few casualties.

On the opposite side of Gully Ravine the Territorials were having a more difficult time. Their own sparse bombardment had had little effect on the enemy's trenches for the few guns had not been allocated a single round of high explosive shell and shrapnel shells were a poor substitute. Although the Turks had abandoned their front line in the first rush, they were fighting back hard and their own guns were pouring fire on the ground between their trenches as the infantry tried to get across. It was their first experience of intense shell-fire and, in their first taste of battle, it was a gruelling ordeal. Only three subalterns and some eighty men of the 7th Royal Scots reached the second trench unwounded. On their right, the 8th Scottish Rifles had fared even worse, for they had been caught in a deadly rain of machine-gun fire. In a matter of minutes twenty-five of their twenty-six officers and four hundred of their men had been knocked out.

Pte. W. Begbie.

From the time we left our trench the enemy bombarded us with everything they had. After a short halt while the supporting waves closed up, we began to advance on the final objective. By this time the Turks had recovered from their panic and they delivered such terrific fire that our company fell in *bundles*. Halfway across Major Sandeman dropped and Captain Dawson and Lieutenant Thomson were killed as they neared their goal. By now men were falling on my left and right. I then felt as if a horse had kicked my right thigh. I fell and when I got up I had no feeling in my leg, so I fell again. When I felt where the pain was, I saw my hand was covered with blood. When I started to move I heard bullets striking the ground. I lay still. I didn't feel very much pain, but the sun high in the sky threw down intense heat on the sand which was crawling with insects of every shape and size. The worst thing was the craving for water – mouths were so parched by heat and sand that tongues swelled.

There was not a breath of wind. The heat was fierce and now, in the middle of the day, as the sun burned relentlessly in a cloudless sky and the troops sweated and panted with the heat of the action, it was almost insupportable. In some parts of the battlefield the ground itself took fire. The brittle bushes caught light, flames travelling from one to another crept across the earth, and men, too badly wounded to drag themselves away, panicked and screamed and died.

By mid-afternoon the 29th Division had captured all the Turkish trenches to the west of Gully Ravine, and they were holding on – but only just. The first waves had lost so many, they were so thinly spread that, although they were toiling to consolidate as fast as weary men could in the terrible heat, the most critical hours of the battle were yet to come. The unremitting bombardment gave notice that the Turks had by no means given up. Even now they must be regrouping and, even now, reinforcements must be hurrying to their support. In a matter of hours they would counter-attack, and the attack would inevitably fall at the furthest point the British had reached. The trenches of the final objective were code-named J13 and there the tiny garrison of survivors was too meagre to withstand a determined onslaught. The J13 trenches ran across the cliff-top less than three-quarters of a mile from the starting point, but four rows of captured trenches lay across the rough ground between, and the Turkish guns were assiduously shelling. It would take hours for reinforcements to travel that short distance, and speed was of the essence. They were obliged to look for a short-cut.

Lt. R. F. E. Laidlaw.

We were to get out of the trench, cross Gully Ravine just ahead of us at a run, and then make our way by a path on to the cliffs where we were to turn right along a cliff path and then go on until we received further directions from Colonel Geddes the Commanding Officer. We rushed over the open, down into, then out of a very shallow gully ravine, and found ourselves on a narrow path half-way up the cliff, running along the coast above the beach. Reed's platoon was winding its way ahead in single file and another platoon followed us close behind. The path was only wide enough to pass one man at a time. It wound its way along the cliffs, going down into ravines and up over humps, I could see the long line of men ahead and behind me and, out at sea and apparently only half a mile from the shore, a large warship moving slowly along the coast firing as she went. Round and round her chased four destroyers, each one firing as her guns were brought to bear on a target a mile or two ahead of us.

Suddenly, as Reed's platoon was negotiating a ravine just in front of me, a salvo of shells burst in the ravine. I saw Reed, tumbling over and over, go down the face of the bluff and then get caught in some bushes and lie still, while most of his men appeared to be hit. The call for stretcher-bearers went up and just then, another salvo of shells came over and exploded, so I halted my platoon on the edge of the ravine and told the men to lie down. The stretcher-bearers, who had miraculously appeared from nowhere, went by carrying Reed and the other casualties of his platoon, and Reed mustered a smile for me as he passed, though one of the bearers told me that his leg had been blown off at the knee. (I never saw him again, but heard later that he had survived.) The other casualties looked pretty bad.

The shelling stopped as suddenly as it had started and I led my platoon forward again. The path descended on to the beach into a sandy cove and there, standing against the cliff, was our C.O. Colonel Geddes.

Owing to Reed's platoon being almost blown out of existence, and to my halting my own platoon until the shelling ceased, a long gap in the line of men plodding along the path had developed, and Geddes gave me a short and very sharp dressing-down. Did I realise that because I had halted, I had stopped the whole advance and that men badly needed up forward might not get there in time? I was not to halt again and was to get up to the front trenches as quickly as I could. I felt like a whipped cur. I realised that Geddes was right, and felt that I had let down the whole side.

Pte. W. Begbie.

When I fell for the second time I must have turned my arm because I found I was lying on my rifle with the butt about a foot from the front of my head. I was wondering what would be the best thing to do when I felt the rifle rocking and when I looked up I saw the butt had a piece of shrapnel embedded in it. I turned round and crawled back passing men of our company, some dead, and some with ghastly wounds who were obviously dying.

When I reached a trench I threw myself into it. As I was struggling to get my equipment off I heard voices, then two first-aid men came. They straightened me out and bound up my thigh. One of the men helped me to stand up, and with his help I was able to hop along the trench to the aid post. The MO said to the orderly, 'This man's dressing seems to be OK, so if he thinks he can manage to hop to the wagons he can do so.'

The ambulance wagons were well down the cart track the engineers had gouged in the bed of Gully Ravine and it led to Gully Beach where doctors and orderlies were working flat out to save the wounded who had managed to get so far, and many did not, for no stretcher-bearers could be spared to assist them. They had their hands full on the battle-field where the worst of the wounded lay helpless waiting for rescue, and those who could hop or stagger or crawl had to shift for themselves as best they could to reach the wagons that would take them to safety. It took them a long, long time.

It had taken the Munsters a considerable time to negotiate the cliff path to the newly captured line and it was late in the day before they reached it. The worst of the heat was past. The sun was low in the western sky, lighting the peaks of Samothrace, etched clear and pink on the horizon.

Lt. R. F. E. Laidlaw.

We found ourselves in a circular trench running in a hook from our path, round and down to the sea. It was at least twelve hundred yards behind the original Turkish front line and was only connected with our new front line by a single hastily dug trench running along the top of the cliffs. It was the furthest point ever reached by our troops and, because it was captured and held mostly by the 86th Brigade, it was later known as Fusilier Bluff.

When we got into this trench it was still light enough to see it and its surroundings, as well as the many bodies lying all around. Many were Gurkhas, who had crawled far behind the enemy lines on previous days and dealt out destruction with their kukris before being killed.

I just had time before daylight failed to go round the trench, see that it was properly manned, the NCOs distributed, and a proportion of men in holes behind the parados to take their turn of rest and to act as reserves. Then the Turks made their first attack on us. They came forward out of Gully Ravine, about a hundred yards ahead, literally in masses. The men reacted wonderfully and poured in a terrific fire, rapid, well aimed and low. It was like a threshing machine going through a field of corn. None of the Turks came within twenty yards of us that time, and as they reeled back we saw what appeared to be hundreds of bodies on the ground, many of them burning, and some being blown up by the bombs they carried. Then, and in later attacks, these little fires seemed to be burning all over the landscape and the writhing bodies they lit up did not add to our joy.

At his General Headquarters on the island of Imbros twenty kilometres west of the peninsula Sir Ian Hamilton had passed an anxious day waiting for news from the front. It was sparse and fragmentary and it was five o'clock in the evening before he received definite information and learned with delight and relief that Gully Spur had been captured. But he was soldier enough to know that was not necessarily the end of the story. At ten o'clock he turned in, weary with the strain and tension of the day, but his mind was with the men grappling through the strenuous night on the peninsula, and sleep refused to come.

Seventy years on, Ralph Langley at
the grave of his brother Charlie,
Lovencourt Military Cemetery France

Ralph Langley: 'I joined up when I
was seventeen. Everyone thought we
were great lads, but when my brother
was killed a few months later, my
Mother fetched me out . . .'

2nd Lieutenant Jock Macleod on the
eve of leaving for France

'Being Orderly Corporal I was
carrying dispatches with these four
armed men round me. One old girl
shouted out, "Yon little lad's off to
prison!"' Corporal A. Wilson, 1/5th
Battalion West Yorkshire Regiment

Ed's brother, Sergeant Harry Hall, who served with the Canadians at Ypres

Lance-Corporal Ed Hall who served as a British stretcher bearer at Neuve Chapelle

Norman Tennant. Off to battle, 1915

Norman Tennant. On the old battlefront seventy years on

Douglas Pankhurst RFA. 'My Father said, "I know you'll do your duty, but don't forget Mother will be worrying about you". So I had to do my duty, if only for him – and my Mother'

2nd Lieutenant Bryden McKinnell, Liverpool Scottish, killed at Bellewaerde Ridge, 16 June 1915

The troop train disaster. 'We were eight to a compartment and the doors locked. Suddenly there was a terrific crash. The carriage rose up and sank down again listing dangerously. The cries and screams and hiss of steam escaping was deafening.' Private A. Thomson, 1/7th Royal Scots

The troop train disaster. 'The shrieks and moans of the men as they were being slowly roasted to death was terrible to hear.' Sergeant J. Combe, 1/7th Royal Scots

The troop train disaster. 'It was afternoon before we'd rescued everyone we could. Fifty-seven of us answered our names out of nearly five hundred who left Larbert that morning.' Private A. Thomson, 1/7th Royal Scots

The troop train crashed into a local train; two minutes later the London express crashed into them both

The plaque on the memorial to the Royal Scots on their mass grave
(*W. Paterson*)

Private Duff's 25-year-old widow was
photographed with her two children a
month after the disaster. The
photographer framed the sitters
carefully, leaving a gap in which to
insert the photograph of the dead
father of the family

Frank Quiller, one of the few men of
the signal section who survived badly
wounded

Gallipoli. The landing from the *River Clyde* at V Beach. Painting by Charles Dixon RI

'Lighters blocked with dead and dying . . . fire immediately concentrates on any attempt to land.' Lieutenant-Colonel Williams GHQ (*Imperial War Museum*)

Gallipoli. The Anzac HQ dug-outs beneath Plugges Plateau (*Imperial War Museum*)

'Dick got a bullet through his head and fell at our feet. We think an enemy sniper must have been just out in front. I made sure I got that sniper later on.' Corporal G. Gilbert, A. Squadron, 13 Australian Light Horse (*Imperial War Museum*)

Walking wounded at Gully Beach. 'The MO said to the orderly, "This man's dressing seems to be OK, so if he thinks he can hop, he can do so."' Private William Begbie, 7th Battalion Royal Scots (*Imperial War Museum*)

General Sir Ian Hamilton.

Midnight. When I lay down in my little tent two hours ago, the canvas seemed to make a sort of sounding board. No sooner did I try to sleep than I heard the musketry rolling up and dying away, then rolling up again in volume until I could stick it no longer and simply had to get up and pick a path through the brush and over sandhills, across to the sea on the east coast of our island. There I could hear nothing. Was the firing then an hallucination – a sort of sequel to the battle in my brain? Not so. Far away I could see faint coruscations of sparks, star shells, coloured fireballs from pistols, searchlights playing up and down the coast.

Our fellows were being beset to hold on to what they had won there where the horizon stood out with spectral luminosity. What a contrast! The direct fear, joy and excitement of the fighting men out there in the search-lights and the dull anguish of waiting here in the darkness, imagining horrors, praying the Almighty our men may be vouchsafed valour to stick it through the night, wondering, waiting, until the wire brings its colourless message!

Lt. R. F. E. Laidlaw.

The Turks attacked us four or five times that night but only once did a few of them get into the trench. None of these got out – our men were as good with the bayonet as they were with the rifle!

We had plenty of ammunition, brought up earlier, and a few jam tin bombs, but most of the men had drunk their water during the strenuous day and were now very thirsty – and thirst is not a pleasant thing, especially when you are fighting in a sandy and hot country. All along the trench I could hear cries of 'Water, water' and water there was none. My own water bottle was empty. There was none even for the wounded men and somehow I had failed to get any message through to the destroyers when their boat came ashore to pick up the wounded. They were only able to do this two or three times during the night and one never knew when or where they would come. No regular arrangements had been made to deal with the wounded as far as I knew. I saw later when our General's diary was published that he knew that we *were being hard beset to hold on to what we had won*. A little more imagination might have suggested that the prayers for 'valour' might have included a few for the transport of wounded and for a little water. Better still, the necessary arrangements might have been made beforehand!

With every attack the toll of dead and wounded mounted and fewer and fewer men were left to beat them off. All night long they stood at the alert, peering across the parapets of the captured trenches into the shadows where the vicious little fires darted and flickered in the scrub, coughing in the acrid smoke, watching, listening, waiting for the enemy to make a move. Every man was needed and even if any could have been spared it would have been out of the question to carry away the wounded over treacherous country in the dark. They could only bind up their wounds and lay them down in the trench, to wait patiently, parched, suffering, and sometimes dying before the first light of morning.

Willie Begbie was one of the lucky ones. He had got out just before dark, but it had taken him hours to limp back and, lying on Gully Beach, he marvelled that he had made it.

Pte. W. Begbie.

I must have lost my way because when I first saw the wagons I was high on the side of a ravine and the wagons were down below. The ravine was dry and full of stones. I sat on the edge and putting my weight on my left leg, I tried to slide down the side. It was very steep. When I started to slide I dug the heel of my left boot into the sand but I hit some stones and finished up rolling down. Some men who were loading the wagons ran to help me. After they found that my bandage was still in position I was laid on a stretcher and carried to a wagon, which was already half full. The stretchers were laid side by side and the walking wounded sat on any small space available or on the side of the wagon. The side of the wagon and the back were only about two feet high – the wagon was pulled by four mules. We were told to hold on tightly because we could be seen by the enemy. The driver pulled off a long thin branch of a tree, mounted, yelled, and we were off as fast as four galloping mules could go. The enemy front, back and sides but fortunately we had no casualties. This lasted till we reached the beach where we were hidden from view.

As the night wore on, Gully Beach was an eerie sight, lit intermittently by the beams of search-lights reflected from the sky and by the glow of bobbing lanterns as orderlies moved among wounded lying on the sand. There were three Field Ambulances at the mouth of Gully Ravine, but they were soon swamped and the men were moved quickly through as soon as their wounds were dressed and carried to the beach to be evacuated. Some of them had to wait for many hours. Now and again a ship's signal lamp flashed out of the dark from the open sea, now and again the splash of oars, the low splutter of a motor engine, a call from the shore, warned that a tow had arrived to carry the wounded away, and stretcher-bearers waded through the shallows to load them aboard the flat-bottomed boats that would take them out to the ships. They could carry, at most, twelve stretcher cases apiece and, inevitably, progress was slow. Shortly after dawn more and more wounded began arriving from the line. At nightfall they were coming still. Very early on the hospital ships were swamped and the wounded were loaded, willy-nilly, on troop transports, on ammunition or supply ships, on any rusty bucket in the area that could be guaranteed to keep afloat on the short passage to Mudros. But the camp hospitals at Mudros were soon filled to overflowing and with nowhere to put the wounded there was no alternative but to leave them where they were. Some stayed on board for many days. On the ill-equipped transports, where there were no bunks, no dressings, no bedpans, no medical facilities of any kind, conditions were frightful. Despite the efforts of frantic medical officers rushing from ship to ship in Mudros harbour, many wounds turned putrid. Many men died.

Willie Begbie survived. But back on the peninsula the remnants of his Battalion found, after the battle, that they were a battalion no longer. With their two sister battalions of the 156th Brigade and with little or no support from artillery they had, at least partially, succeeded in capturing and holding their objectives in the Battle of Gully Ravine. It was a considerable feat for the untried Territorials and the Divisional Commander, General de Lisle, had sent them a special message. It simply said, 'Well done the Royal Scots!' But it was only a small consolation. In the five weeks since they had set out, of eleven hundred officers and men who had boarded the trains at Larbert, only seven officers and two hundred and seventeen men remained. It was crushing to reflect that, of those five weeks, three had been spent at sea.

But they had indeed had a fight for it.

Part 6

~

Slogging On: The Salient to Suvla

It is midday; the deep trench glares . . .
A buzz and blaze of flies . . .
The hot wind puffs the giddy airs . . .
The great sun rakes the skies.

No sound in all the stagnant trench
Where forty standing men
Endure the sweat and grit and stench,
Like cattle in a pen.

Robert Nichols

Chapter 26

By the end of June the Gallipoli campaign had cost some forty-two thousand casualties, killed, wounded and sick. The support of the government was still half-hearted and, although Sir Ian Hamilton had been promised another division, it had not yet been decided to go all-out for Gallipoli or to send reinforcements in sufficient strength to tip the scales. With the military effort divided between two theatres of war the politicians were in a dilemma and there were those who believed that, in the light of the disappointing results and the heavy cost, it would be best, even now, to cut their losses. The decision was postponed, and postponed again. The question of supplies was a major problem – and particularly of supplies of ammunition. Scarce as they were, was it wise to split them? In the second week of May, when the Gallipoli force was battling for Krithia, when the soldiers on the western front were attacking Aubers Ridge, when hopes were pinned on the result of these two battles thirteen thousand miles apart, the lack of ammunition had stymied them both. If the eighty thousand shells fired at Aubers Ridge had been available for the attack on Krithia the troops on Gallipoli might well be in possession of Achi Baba, if not the whole peninsula. And if the shells that were fired on Gallipoli in the first two weeks since the landing had been available at Aubers Ridge, it was not entirely impossible that the troops on the western front would have broken through to open the road to Lille.

After what, in the circumstances, had been a profligate expenditure of ammunition in the battle for Ypres and the attacks on Aubers Ridge and Festubert, ammunition was scarcer than ever. On 28 May, after the battles in north and south had petered out, Sir John French was forced to order the First Army to limit its operations to 'small aggressive threats which will not require much ammunition or many troops'.

East of Ypres the line had settled down. But it had settled down to the disadvantage of the British Army. The Germans had captured the whole of the Bellewaerde Ridge and north of the Menin Road their front line was established well down the slope. From their observation posts behind it the skeleton of Ypres was in full view and, although the battle had died down, the guns never ceased to shell it and the ruins shivered and shook and tumbled, crumbling a little more with every explosion. Ypres was a dead city, but now that the civilians had cleared out it was also a happy hunting-ground for the troops in the line nearby. Looting was strictly forbidden by the Army on pain of severe penalties but, since the goods left behind in the half-ruined houses were there for the taking, when they could be of no possible use to their departed owners and were likely to go up in smoke with the next explosion, why should a provident Tommy not help himself? His philosophy was as clear as his conscience, aptly summed up in the shoulder-shrugging phrase picked up from the French: '*C'est la guerre.*' In recent months fate, in the shape of '*la guerre*', had not been particularly kind, and now that she was doling out a crumb or two to set against a soldier's normal tedious lot, it was only right to take it in the same spirit as he put up with leaking billets, miserable trenches, inadequate rations and the persistent attentions of the enemy.

The first fortunate scavengers, exploring prosperous dwellings through holes conveniently blasted in their walls, had quickly become connoisseurs of fine wines and expensive cigars, and some entrepreneurs among the engineers and transport drivers with handy wagons at their disposal, had managed to remove sufficient bottles from the cellars to set up a profitable sideline with shop-keepers in surrounding villages.

Capt. B. McKinnell.

Tuesday 1st June. We had to go and inspect trenches, so Thin, the Adjutant, Dickie, Rennison, Graham and self rode off on horseback. Got a great send-off, the last three being anything but accomplished horsemen; Graham's last steed had been a donkey, and it was only *my* third ride. We had a most painful hour's ride and then a mile and a half walking across country, where we were shelled twice. We left the huts at 2.30 and got back to where we left our horses at 9 p.m., having had a bad shaking with shells en route on the way back. Going through the village of Kemmel we met 'Buster' Birkett, who was looking for a wine shop, the one and only within miles and miles. We all found it and had the best of claret (possibly and very *probably* 'salvage' from Ypres) at two francs a bottle. All sorts of stuff could be bought at a price. We only had three bottles between six of us, but we'd had nothing to eat since mid-day, so when we got out of the shop horses held no terrors for *us*. I learnt riding in an hour, as I trotted and even galloped the whole way home in the dark!

No one felt inclined to look a gift-horse in the mouth, and even if the Military Police took a different view, qualms were easily overcome. But when the opportunity arose, some bolder spirits were not averse to giving fate a helping hand when they came across items whose owners – though absent – had not, strictly speaking, 'abandoned' them.

Sgt. G. Butler, 12th Machine Gun Coy., 4 Div.

It was my first guard as a lance-corporal and I took the responsibility very keen. About 2 a.m. the sentry reported to me that a 36-gallon barrel of vin blanc was stood on a farm cart at the back of the estaminet. We couldn't see the sense of it being out in the cold all night so we decided to move it. We got some old bags out of the warehouse we were billeted in, and a brush. It took about five of us to get it off the wagon, and we rolled this barrel along the cobbles on bags all the way to a well, just past the village, one man sweeping the road behind, so you couldn't see any marks where the barrel had been. When we got to the well, a dixie and half a dozen mess tins suddenly appeared – of course the lads only took a drink just to confirm that it *was* vin blanc! Then they put the bung back into the barrel and we lowered it down with some ropes and the chain attached to the well handle.

When morning came I had difficulty getting the guard up. Of course, I put it down to the smell of that stuff in the barrel. The fumes must have gone to their heads! About nine o'clock we heard a hell of a noise and two gendarmes and three or four men appeared. They informed us, to our *great* surprise, that they had lost a barrel of vin blanc so, of course, we helped them to look for it. Well, they searched here and they searched there – they even looked down the well, but there wasn't a Sherlock Holmes among them. We *watched* them look down the well! The following night we pulled the barrel up again to see how it had fared, down under. You never saw such a game! But that was the last of it for our lads. We went in the line next night and we never saw the barrel again. We never got back to that billet again, that was the trouble.

Lt. J. D. Pratt, U Coy., 4th Bn., Gordon Highlanders (TF), 8th Brig., 3rd Div.

I had to send a platoon from my company into Ypres – a party of sergeant and seven men, and they went in and they were supposed to be relieved after twenty-four hours. But the sergeant came to me and he said, 'Can we stay another twenty-four hours?' And I said, 'Why, Arthur,' I said, 'do you like it?' 'Oh,' he said. 'We're having a wonderful time! You see, the population's all fled and there's any number of people from all sorts of regiments in there. They're grabbing stuff like hell and we're getting plenty of booze all over the place. We're having a grand time!'

I believe that lots of lads pinched quite a bit of valuable stuff from Ypres and they went and buried it and hid it away in various places where they thought they would find it later, and a lot of them – probably most of them – got killed. So it's likely that for years to come people will be unearthing all sorts of caches of jewellery and other stuff, quite accidentally.

The army called it 'plunder'. The soldiers called it simple common-sense. Even though the first rich pickings had run out there was still a treasure trove of desirable booty going begging (as the Tommies saw it) in the ruined streets of Ypres, and if officers seldom overtly encouraged theft it was not in their interest to ask searching questions when a mattress, or an armchair or a much-needed table was found for a Headquarters billet, or even for some damp and smelly dug-out near the line. On the whole they shared the Tommies' view that, when welcome creature-comforts were so easy to come by, only a fool would refuse to take advantage of it. Even senior officers found it convenient to turn a blind eye and were occasionally not above conniving to arrange a few unofficial acquisitions for themselves.

Major Cowan, who was in charge of 175th Tunnelling Company and had just been forced to move from the pleasant village of Terdeghem to an undesirable dug-out in Vlamertinghe close to Ypres, was only too happy to take any opportunity of improving it.

Major S. H. Cowan, 175th Tunnelling Coy., Royal Engineers.

About 11 a.m. Hart and I set off. We called first of all at 171st Company to see my NCO in charge of stores and then on into Ypres to the HQ of the 7th Brigade which was established in some old casemates under the ancient ramparts of the town. Beds, tables, carpets even, had been salvaged from the ruins and the place was really very comfortable indeed. As we were coming up towards the square where the Cloth Hall was, Fritz began to unload some 'hate' and we turned off hurriedly into a more secluded route. Just as we had started along there was a deuce of a bang fifty yards away and a badly wounded horse rushed past us. I took refuge with Benskin who gave me tea, and I stayed till the row stopped and Hart reappeared for me. He had a tale to tell! He had just got a very nice stove out of a ruined house and into the lorry, and very luckily the tailboard was up, when round the corner came a Brigadier and a Provost Marshal. Now, looting was a crime of the first water, but Hart had a real flash of genius and he ordered the two Army Service Corps drivers to get under the lorry and start 'tinkering'. 'What is this lorry doing here?' said the Provost Marshal. 'We're waiting for Major Cowan of 175th Company, RE,' replied Hart, 'but something has gone wrong with the lorry and the drivers are trying to find out what it is.' And as soon as the Staff were round the corner, would you believe it, that lorry seemed to get better all at once and was off and away out of Ypres by another route. I got back to the car where my intelligent driver had found time to souvenir a coffee-mill for our mess! The stove was a great acquisition, and if *we* hadn't got it, a shell would probably have damaged it beyond repair the next week.

An ordinary soldier of the line whose duties did not take him into Ypres had little opportunity for souveniring expeditions. Off-duty, the town was strictly out of bounds and on their way to and from the trenches it was an unhealthy place for troops to linger.

Sgt. A. Rule, U Coy., 4th Bn., Gordon Highlanders (TF), 8th Brig., 3rd Div.

A party of us detailed for fatigue duty went through Ypres on our way to the front line. Brick dust from shell-shattered buildings lay thick in the streets, muffling our tread, and as we marched on in this silent, almost ghostly, fashion, we felt like mourners assisting at the funeral rites of a city of the dead. Tumbled masonry, and occasional street barricades, constantly slowed us up. In some cases the front of a house had been sheared off as if by a gigantic knife. Floors, precariously supported by splintered joists, looked as if they only needed a touch to topple them into the street. Even the foliage of the trees in the streets had been blighted by shell-fire, and there was a foul stench of corruption from neglected sewers. The great Cloth Hall with its magnificent facade had also suffered badly. Its square tower offered a splendid ranging mark for the German guns, and at the base of it lay the clock, a twisted maze of works. The interior was completely gutted.

Near the Grand' Place, we came on the Church of St Martin, where an altar among a tangled wreckage of oak pews had miraculously escaped destruction. In front of the church stood a vacant pedestal, and at its base, just as if it was in the act of taking cover, lay the stone statue of some civic dignitary – staff in hand and complete with robes and chains of office. To our irreverent minds it appeared as if the old boy had gone to earth, and must now be cursing the corpulent stomach that had doubtless been his pride in many a bygone civic function. That wonderful tummy alone prevented his lying flat.

The sight of the statue so unceremoniously cast down caused many sniggers and ribald remarks in the ranks of U Company whose spirits were never cast down for long. They were a light-hearted lot. Although officially Territorials of the 4th Gordon Highlanders, 'U' stood for University and they were all undergraduates of Aberdeen whose studies had been abruptly interrupted by the war. Although they had been soldiering more or less in earnest for the best part of a year they still considered themselves to be students rather than soldiers and claimed licence accordingly whenever they could get away with it. The officers, all graduates who not so long ago had been students themselves, were remarkably tolerant.

Lt. J. D. Pratt.

On parade – discipline all the time – you addressed an officer as 'Sir'. Off parade you could call him 'Jimmy' or 'Jock' or whatever his name was. There was no ceremony.

The senior officer was Colonel Ogilvie, and Tommy Ogilvie was, I think, a solicitor. He was a very human individual, hail- fellow-well-met, and he was the life and soul of the party in the mess when we were at camp in peacetime. Freddie Bain, who later was Sir Frederick Bain and who died a good many years ago when he was chairman designate of ICI, he was sergeant of the guard, and Tommy Ogilvie was Captain of the Day. So Tommy went down to the guard tent and said, 'Sergeant, anything to report?' So Freddie said, 'Yes, sir, I've got a prisoner.' 'Oh, what's the trouble?' 'Oh,' he said 'he's drunk.' Tommy said, 'Let me see the prisoner.' So he went into the tent and there was a fellow lying completely helpless, completely blotto. So Tommy stood swaying backwards and forwards, looking down at the fellow, and he said, 'Sergeant, that man isn't drunk. I saw him move!' That gives you the idea of Tommy! But when we mobilised and he became Commanding Officer he cut the whisky bottle right out, and he cut down very heavily on his officers drinking in the mess. Complete change.

Our own Company Commander who commanded U Company was Captain Lachlan McKinnon. He'd been a student – a law student – and he'd graduated about three or four years before. He was a tall, awkward-looking fellow, a little hunch-backed, but terribly conscientious, and he had absolutely no sense of humour whatsoever. That was his great weakness. Well, we did this joke on him. He issued an order that there was to be no smoking of cigarettes on parade. On the first morning after that we marched off from our billets and after a few hundred yards he said, 'March at ease.' So with one motion every member of U Company took out a clay pipe and lit it up. I was Company Sergeant-Major at the back. He came back to me and said, 'Sergeant-Major, do you see that? *Do* you see that? Members of U Company smoking pipes like ordinary council workmen. What will people think about my university men if that's how they behave?' So I said, 'Well, I'm terribly sorry but, after all, you know, you barred smoking of cigarettes on parade but you didn't say anything about clay pipes.' Anyhow the order was countermanded. Poor old Lachie!

He was going round the cookhouse one day and there was a fellow called Chatty Donald – who I may say, when he died, was a Harley Street brain specialist and a Brigadier in the Territorials, and Lachie said to Chatty, 'What are you doing?' 'Oh,' he said, 'I'm cooking the spuds.' 'Well,' Lachie said, 'how do you know when they're properly cooked?' 'Oh,' said Chatty, 'that's easy. You take one up, you biff it against the wall and if it sticks it's cooked and if it bounces back, it isn't!' The Company Commander didn't know what the bloody hell to do, or whether his leg was being pulled or what. In fact, it's a very good rough test!

Looking back now, U Company should have been a reservoir – a first-class reservoir – for officers. Because when we mobilised, I myself, as Colour Sergeant, had two honours degrees and all my sergeants had degrees – some of them honours – and we had about a dozen fellows in the ranks who had degrees and had already got jobs and had come back to the company.

But the Commanding Officer, Ogilvie, set his face against anybody applying for a commission. 'Because,' he said, 'if I once start allowing members of U Company to go for commissions,' he said, 'I admit they'd make good officers, but we shall never get overseas because *they* are the backbone of the battalion.' And, of course, you must remember that, at that time, the talk was that the war would be finished by Christmas – or would be finished early in 1915. And everybody was, naturally, anxious to get out to France. And for that reason nobody was allowed to apply for a commission.

But nobody cared much. U Company was high on enthusiasm but, on the whole, distinctly short of military ambition, and few of them had any desire to be 'temporary gentlemen'. They were perfectly content to be temporary soldiers, to rough it, to stick it out together and, on every possible occasion, to enjoy themselves as best they could. Their singing was renowned and their repertoire was wide. They knew every chorus in the Students' Songbook by heart, they were well-versed in traditional Scottish airs, they could harmonise like angels, and their impromptu performances in estaminets at la Clytte were generally appreciated by their comrades-in-arms in the 8th Brigade, even if they were not always understood by the men of the Suffolks and Middlesex. For some reason which was hard to fathom, the Sassenachs were especially fond of one particular song in the dialect of U Company's native Aberdeenshire which rejoiced in the title of 'The Muckin' o' Geordie's Byre'. It had a catchy tune, it went fast and furious, and it had a long string of verses, not one word of which the English soldiers could possibly have understood, still less joined in. But they could stamp their feet in accompaniment, faster and faster as the pace quickened, and when it reached its thunderous climax and Geordie's byre had been well and truly mucked, they raised the roof with cheers and applause. But the 'language problem' caused occasional misunderstandings. 'Give us another one, Jock,' a Suffolk man called out in the course of one jolly evening. 'Give us "Where's Me Fourpence Charlie?" ' This, after some puzzlement, was interpreted as a request for a plaintive Jacobite song, more familiar to U Company as 'Wae's Me for Prince Charlie'. The story quickly spread, U Company sportingly adopted the revised version, and if the song thereafter lost some of its Highland charm it was always good for a laugh.

But since they had come to the front in February U Company's sojourn had not been entirely carefree. They had had their share of discomfort in the trenches in bitter weather and pouring rain and out of them, on what the Army was pleased to describe as 'rest', they had spent weary hours on irksome fatigues, supplied scores of working parties, staggered up to the line with sacks of coke, with rolls of wire, with timber, with stakes and ammunition, and the thousand and one weighty loads of supplies that were needed in the trenches. They had dug and dug and dug. They had also had their share of excitement – going out with wiring parties into the shifting shadows beyond the parapet, when the ping of stretched wire released by a nervous hand or the muffled thud of a mallet, even the click of a rifle bolt, seemed loud enough to rouse the whole German Army, let alone a German sentry in the trenches across the way. And there had been patrols when men crept deep into No Man's Land, fighting the instinct to run when the flares went up, freezing in the brilliant light in the mild hope of resembling a tree, or playing dead among the grisly scatter of corpses lying between the lines. They had buried their own dead too, and in early May, when U Company marched off from the 'quiet' sector in front of Kemmel on their way to the less desirable sector at Hill 60, they had left a dozen or so of their comrades behind in their own small cemetery. Many more had gone home wounded, and in such a small cohesive company the gaps were all too noticeable.

Now U Company was on the move again and marching through Ypres towards the salient they had no illusions about what lay ahead and, for once, they marched in silence. Even if they had felt like it, it seemed inappropriate to sing in the awesome desolate streets of Ypres. But there was one light moment. Rounding a corner they passed the remains of a large building. It was roofless and the walls were battered, but the doorway was intact and above it, in letters of brass, was the inscription 'English Ladies' Seminary'. As U Company crunched morosely through the dust and rubble one man began to whistle. He was whistling '*Gaudeamus Igitur* . . .', and he broke off after the first few bars, but it was enough to bring a smile to every face. There wasn't a man among them who had not lingered after lights-out outside the women students' hostel in Aberdeen whistling that well-known signal, guaranteed to bring girls to the window to indulge in a little banter and flirtation. Grinning broadly, U Company marched past the ladies' seminary and on through Ypres.

Sgt. A. Rule.

Our route towards the Menin Gate was blocked at intervals by wrecked limbers and by the swollen dead bodies of horses, stinking to high heaven and covered with loathsome flies. We breathed more freely when we had passed through the city wall and crossed the moat.

Near a water tower (it later became a well-known landmark) we dodged an enormous shell-hole flanked by an abandoned perambulator, and skirting the shelled cemetery we carried on across country on tracks which the German gunners seemed to know by heart. Finally, after many delays and a wearisome march, we reached the trenches south of the village of Hooge, and almost at the tip of the salient.

They marched past Hell Fire Corner and moved into trenches on the right of the Menin Road at the place they called Birr Crossroads. The 8th Brigade was not to be in the forefront of the attack. But the 7th and 9th Brigades were, and for the past ten days they had been

387

busily engaged in training and practising in fields behind the line –
advancing wave by wave in 'open order', attacking imaginary
trenches, represented by rows of sticks in the ground and
'consolidating' while the next wave passed through in their turn
to attack the imaginary enemy with bombs and bayonets. It made
a change from the monotony of weary stints in the trenches the
weather was fine, the exercise was healthy, and although Bryden
McKinnell, commanding Y Company, was pleasantly fatigued at
the end of each strenuous day, he even managed to put in a little
badly needed riding practice in the twilight of the long June
evenings. Occasionally there were thunderstorms and it was then
that Y Company blessed their company quartermaster – and not
for the first time. QM McFie took good care of his company and,
insofar as the limitations of active service allowed, he was
solicitous for their comfort. He made sure that they were well fed
and, returning damp and ravenous to their field outside Brandhoek, they discovered with joy that the Quartermaster had
arranged to have tea dished out on their arrival to tide them over
while they waited for the evening stew, and had thoughtfully
arranged for tent and blanket bivouacs to be erected in their
absence. It was some compensation for the fact that it continued
raining all night. Parading in damp uniforms in the morning,
McKinnell's men were only slightly cast down by the news that
the leave they had been eagerly awaiting was indefinitely postponed. It was Sunday 13 June, and at least there was a day off to
look forward to. That evening the colonel called the officers
together for a conference.

Capt. B. McKinnell.

Sunday June 13th 10 p.m.   Our orders are definite now and we
know what we are in for, though not in detail. I think we are all
very glad now the suspense is over. It had to come sooner or
later, and very much better that it has come as an honour,
namely, to be among the chosen few to do a special job, than to
be among a crush. Strange to think, will I see next Wednesday
at 10 p.m.?

Tuesday June 15th.   We have got all our instructions. We have
a trench to take, in fact the enemy's second line, together with
the help of the Lincolns. I'm afraid it's going to be a very
difficult job. The men are all cheery and we all rag each other
as to how we will look with wooden legs, or tied up in an oil
sheet for burial. All the plans have been explained today,
Tuesday 15th, to all ranks.

All stores have been issued and we are waiting to march off. Hope we win! Unfortunately the Huns must know almost everything, as it has been so widely discussed. I am beginning to suspect it is done with an object. Sacrifice a brigade here and push hard somewhere else. However we are going to justify our existence as Terriers and men – we middle-class businessmen!

God Save the King!

Early in the afternoon the Liverpool Scottish marched out of camp on their way to the line. The field cookers had gone ahead and McFie had arranged for them to halt on the far side of Ypres to give the men a hot meal while they waited for darkness to cover the last mile of their progress to the front. He had been on the go since early morning, riding with his wagons to the dump near the transport line, checking long lists in the Lieutenant-Quartermaster's office, drawing supplies, seeing that they were speedily stowed in the wagons and properly sorted out when they returned. By the time Y Company had breakfasted the stores had been set out at intervals along one side of the field. McFie had detailed extra men to help and two of them stood by each pile to hand out the goods, while Y Company paraded to receive them in a long crocodile, moving along the field, a platoon at a time. As one man remarked when he got to the end, they were 'loaded like blooming Christmas trees'. Every man was issued with two extra bandoliers of ammunition to be slung cross-wise across each shoulder, two empty sandbags, a waterproof sheet and a day's extra ration in addition to his iron ration to be stuffed into his haversack. The trench-stores had been seen to. There were hand-grenades to issue to the company bombers, wire-cutters to distribute, and shovels to be carried up to the front by one unlucky platoon. It all took a long time. Then there were overcoats to be rolled and stowed on a wagon, and packs to be dumped, for Y Company was to go into action in 'light order'. At last it was finished, dinners were served, and Y Company was ready to go.

They lined up on the road to take their place in the battalion, and McFie went to stand at the fence to wave them off. They were in high spirits. Even before they got well into their stride mouth organs had been produced and some of them were singing as they went by. They broke off to wave and shout as they passed the quartermaster. *'We'll bring you a souvenir, QM. What'll it be?'* 'We'll bring you back a Hun or two to cook for breakfast!' 'Keep the cookers going, Quarters, we'll be back soon'*, then, *'Are we down-hearted?'* and the obligatory answering roar – *'NO!'* It may have been bravado but they gave every indication of being glad to go. Marching at the head of the column, smiling as he returned the Quartermaster's salute,

Bryden McKinnell was to all appearances as happy as his men. There was no time now, on the eve of the battle, to brood on the thought he had recently confided to his diary: '*Will I see next Wednesday at 10 p.m.?*' It was Tuesday evening and at ten o'clock, as darkness began to deepen, they moved into trenches in front of Y wood. The 'special job' was to recapture the Bellewaerde Ridge. It was an important objective in itself but the attack had a secondary purpose which, in the view of the Commander-in-Chief, was of the utmost importance – to divert the attention of the Germans from an important assault on Givenchy in the First Army sector some thirty miles to the south. The attack on Bellewaerde was referred to as 'a minor operation'.

The British front line now lay across the longest arm of the Y-shaped copse north of the Menin Road and ran across open ground to bisect the wood that lay immediately south of the Ypres–Roulers railway. It was a long time since any trains had run along that track for the town of Roulers a dozen miles away was well behind the enemy lines* and there the railway was busily working for the enemy. Roulers was an important junction and from it the lines led south into France, north into Holland and linked up through Brussels with lines that ran to the heart of Germany. But if Roulers was an ace in the German hand, in the salient the Bellewaerde Ridge was a trump card.

A month had wrought many changes. Chateau Wood, the lake, the farm, the ridge itself that Princess Patricia's Light Infantry had fought so hard to hold, were now part of the German defence system. Their front line now ran along the farther edge of Y Wood to the top of Railway Wood. It was linked by a web of communication trenches to two other fortified trench-lines, one midway up the slope, the other on the crest of the ridge itself. Even Hooge Chateau was in the hands of the Germans – if it could still be called a chateau now that only two walls were left standing. A stone's throw from it, no more than fifty yards away, the British held on to the chateau stables and to the pulverised brick heaps that were the ruins of Hooge village. But they only just held them, for here the line looped out across the Menin Road and swept back in a deep semi-circle across the fields to Zouave Wood, and round again to Birr Crossroads. It was a nasty kink in the line for, as the British trenches ran back, so the German line ran forward, curving across the lower slopes of the ridge with all the advantage of high ground behind them. The task of the 3rd Division was to straighten the line and capture it. Between and beyond the two small woods that marked

---

* Roulers is the modern Belgian town of Roeselaere.

the limits of the attack, the slopes were entirely open with little dead ground and no cover. Captain McKinnell had been right in surmising that it would be a difficult job.

But hopes were high. This time a good deal of thought had been given to the possibility of a breakdown in communications, and lines as far back as brigade headquarters had been laid in triplicate. Eight rows of jumping-off trenches were prepared, so that consecutive waves could move speedily into action, but they were dug, unavoidably, in full view of the enemy, and the enemy had conveyed his displeasure by shelling them by day as fast as the working-parties had dug them by night. They were still discernible as shallow tracings on the ground, but they offered little shelter to the assaulting troops as they waited uncomfortably for morning. The attack was timed for dawn.

The barrage started just before three o'clock and, for once, it was a good one with sufficient high-explosive shells to wreak havoc on the German trenches, and the noise of the shells flying close overhead, the boom of explosions not far ahead, was a distinct comfort to the men, crouching tense and sleepless, waiting for the guns to lift, for the first light of dawn above the Bellewaerde Ridge, for the sound of the whistles that would send them over the top. Seasoned soldiers though they were, after four months in France, not a single man of the 3rd Division had gone over the top before. Excitement hung so thick in the air that it might have been cut with a knife.

At zero hour the first wave went over the top and took the German front line with ease.

The bombardment had done its work. The German wire was shattered. The enemy was in disarray. The barrage had lifted from the first German line to start thundering on the next, and the second wave was waiting to go. When the signal came they were to rush forward to follow the first wave, now in the front enemy trench, and to pass through them and over it to attack the next one. When the signal came the 1st Battalion of the Lincolnshire Regiment went forward with the Liverpool Scottish to do the job. Captain Bryden McKinnell led Y Company across the open ground, through the skeleton trees on the edge of Y Wood, and started up the slope past the communication trenches where a few cowering German soldiers had been cut off by the barrage. They should have halted there, close to the second enemy line, waiting for the barrage to lift before they tackled it. But things had gone wrong. The 7th Brigade, in reserve behind the 9th, were only intended to go forward if they were absolutely required to help. No signal was given but excitement, like panic, easily spreads. A few men started it, carried away by the thrill of the moment, and, seeing the Liverpool Scots and the

391

Lincolns rush on and disappear into the smoke, they leapt forward and ran after them, cheering and yelling and desperate to get into the fight. After that there was no stopping it, and soon the whole 7th Brigade was on the move, running like the wind to catch up. They leapt across the first wave in the captured German trench and caught up with the second, waiting beyond it for the barrage to lift. And they carried them forward by sheer impetus, breaking into their spread-out ranks so that companies, platoons, even sections were split up. Now they were all running – and they ran into their own barrage. In the confusion of smoke and dust, the Artillery Officers observing the bombardment had no means of knowing that the shells were falling on their own troops. When the barrage finally lifted the survivors of the carnage advanced and took the second trench. But it was the death-knell of the attack – so promising in its beginning – that might have won them back the Bellewaerde Ridge.

Even the first wave, reorganising in their newly captured line, was so confused by the sudden appearance of the third wave passing through them that they too had advanced soon and joined in the melee. The result was total confusion. A small group of Royal Scots Fusiliers managed to reach the final objective on the top of the ridge, but under fire from their own artillery they could not possibly hold it for long. All along the line small groups of men were fighting the enemy with bombs and bayonets, but by half past nine the survivors were forced to fall back to the first captured line of German trenches. They had been beaten by their own artillery, by their own bravery and, tragically, by their own blind enthusiasm.

The German guns were bombarding furiously to prevent reinforcements getting up, and U Company was ordered forward from the trenches across the Menin Road.

Sgt. A. Rule.

We crossed the Menin Road under a steady hail of machine-gun bullets. In our old front line we were up to the knees in liquid mud and all but trampling on the dead and wounded on the floor of the trench. The badly wounded – poor devils! – moaned agonisingly at the slightest touch as we squeezed past, and we were sniped at continually when we mounted the firestep to avoid treading on them. Our attack had disturbed a hornets' nest for, in addition to the deadly hail of bullets, whizz-bangs were bursting on the parapet every few yards and shrapnel fairly sang about our ears. Some of the attacking troops were now falling back in disorder, and we received instructions to move forward on Y Wood in order to provide a stiffening effect and help to allay panic. Our line of advance was a partly dug communication trench running towards our objective and it was unhappily chosen, because we became a concentrated target for whizz-bangs and its bottle-neck entrance from our own front line gave unlimited sport to the German gunners. I remember vividly pausing there under cover for a moment, while a brace of whizz-bangs crashed just ahead, and then hurdling the parapet with a desperate rush and *just* missing the next salvo. Two men following me hesitated just a fraction too long and mistimed their jump. A whizz-bang caught them fair and square. Littered as it was with dead and wounded, the trench was even more congested with two streams of men moving in opposite directions.

By this time our casualties were fairly heavy and the two platoon commanders who led us in had both been wounded, but our NCOs carried on. Of course, the Germans counter-attacked but they were beaten off, mainly by the heroic efforts of our solitary machine-gun team, and it stayed in action when, by the law of averages, it should have been blown sky high! Salvo after salvo rained down and, although many of us were buried more than once, we escaped without much harm because our soft crumbly parapet seemed to smother the shell-burst. But often we had to lie low, clinging on grimly, and praying that the next one would miss us.

Sandy Gunn was U Company's hero of the day. Sandy had left his native Caithness two years ago to enrol as a medical student at Aberdeen University. He was now a lance-corporal and although he was no athlete and was not even officially a company runner, he had run like the furies across the dangerous shell-swept ground to take messages back and forward. It was a dangerous job and a man had to move fast and take his chance, but even on his last trip when the Germans had recovered and were spraying machine-gun fire in every direction from the trenches up the hill, Sandy spared a thought for his thirsty comrades and, although it slowed him down considerably, he brought back a gallon can of water to slake their thirst. Later, although they were pleased that Sandy had been Mentioned in Dispatches, there wasn't a single man who didn't firmly believe that he deserved at least a DCM.*

The new line was consolidated – and at least it had been advanced a short way. They had paid a heavy price for it in this 'minor operation'. The attack on Givenchy had been equally expensive and

---

* Lance-Corporal Sandy Gunn was killed in action on the Somme on 1 July 1916 and is buried in Serre Road, No. 2 Cemetery.

only partially successful but, like the men who had fought at Bellewaerde, no one among the survivors doubted that they were still on the winning side.

The rest of the 8th Brigade moved up to join U Company in the trenches beyond Y wood to take over the captured line and the remnants of the 9th and 7th Brigades were relieved late in the evening. The Quartermaster had been waiting for many hours for Y Company to come back.

CQMS R. S. McFie.

Towards evening we packed up rations for the trenches and set out for a place on the other side of Ypres where we expected to be able to hand them over to our men. Outside the town, shells were dropping rather uncomfortably near the road, but we reached the chateau used for a dressing station, which was our destination, without accident. There we waited, and as we waited men of ours stumbled haltingly down the road to have their wounds dressed. We did not believe their stories! Only one officer, possibly two, was left. So-and-so is killed, so-and-so wounded. The total strength of the battalion could not be more than ninety, and so on.

After a time, orders came that the Regiment would be relieved and that rations were therefore not needed, but that the camp was to be pitched at once in readiness for the return of the men. We hurried back and found the shelters and tents all pitched and set to work to prepare a good reception for the boys. A friend at home had sent me about thirty fine boxes of delightful biscuits, so I put them in the tents, a box for every five men. We set out the letters and parcels, candles, food, and prepared tea and pea soup on the cookers. Of my own company a hundred and thirty men had gone to the trenches and I was ready to feast them all when they came back.

At last we heard the distant sound of pipes and after a while there passed through our gate a handful of men in tattered uniforms, their faces blackened and unshaved, their clothes stained red with blood, or yellow with the fumes of lyddite. I shouted for Y Company. *One man* came forward! It was heart breaking.

Gradually others tottered in, some wounded, all in the last stages of exhaustion, and when at last I went to lie down at about 5.30 a.m., I had only twenty-five of my hundred and thirty who had gone out thirty-six hours before.

I fancy there was a great deal of bungling. At drill an attack can be practised in an hour that in real warfare should take two days, and I fear that in their eagerness our men rushed forward much too far and much too quickly. It is terrible! The Regiment is practically wiped out.

The whole of the 3rd Division had suffered badly. The 9th Brigade alone had lost seventy-three of their ninety-six officers, and more than two thousand of three and a half thousand men. The Commanding Officers of four Battalions were wounded, and another had been killed.* The total casualties of the 3rd Division, killed, wounded and missing, were more than three and a half thousand.

The exhausted survivors sank thankfully into bivouacs to sleep, and far out in the line U Company held on to the trenches captured the previous day. They cleaned up as best they could. They carried out the wounded, and munched on iron rations in lieu of a hot meal. They posted sentries every few yards and the rest settled down to snatch what sleep they could in the few remaining hours of the night. Presently the gun-fire tailed away. The night was almost quiet, but there was a rustle of movement in front. Reinforced by fresh troops the Germans had crept back down the hill, and the clink of shovels and a stealthy stirring in the dark told that they were working through the night to strengthen their battered line. Out in front, where the ground was littered with the silent dead, Bryden McKinnell's body was lying among the scattered bodies of his men. They had been killed before ten o'clock in the morning.

---

* They were Lieutenant-Colonel B. F. B. Stuart of the 3rd Worcesters, Lieutenant-Colonel E. Treffry of the Honourable Artillery Company, Lieutenant-Colonel R. G. Hely Hutchinson of the 4th Royal Fusiliers, Lieutenant-Colonel C. Yatman of the 1st Northumberland Fusiliers and Major H. E. R. Boxer, commanding the 1st Lincolnshire Battalion, who was killed.

Chapter 27

Scott McFie passed a miserable day. A few more men had straggled in, but there was not much to do. The survivors slept. There was tea on tap all day, and bully-beef sandwiches for any who woke up, but it was almost evening before they roused and began to stumble bleary-eyed out of bivouacs. A meal had been prepared, and the stew had been simmering since dinner time. McFie stood beside the boiler as it was dished out with hefty hunks of bread, and with so many absent there was more than enough to go round. There was good strong tea to wash it down, and afterwards he saw to it that the men had a ration of rum and walked round with the Sergeant as he measured it out, murmuring the suggestion that he might be generous. And he lingered to chat with the men. They were eager to talk and the Quartermaster marvelled at their spirit. When the camp had settled down for the night, he retired to his own office-tent and, weary though he was, wrote a letter to his father.

They told tales of the greatest heroism and tales of unutterable horror. Excepting the mistake of great haste, our men did nobly – but the gains are not very great, and the cost is terrible. They are queer chaps. You would imagine that our camp is plunged in gloom. Not a bit of it! After a good sleep and a good meal the men at once recovered their spirits and they are peacocking about in German helmets, taken with their own hands, and proudly showing their souvenirs, and showing off the rents in their clothing and recounting how they bayoneted Huns, or how they had narrow escapes. Of course this disaster has brought much work to me. Will you please tell Cyril Dennis that his biscuits arrived safely, Jenny that her parcel came and is now in the process of consumption, and Charlie that I received his letter in the tent in which I am writing at 11 p.m.! And now to bed in my other tent – the rough and ready blanket one.

The 'rough and ready' blanket bivouac was exactly the same as the men's but McFie was perfectly happy with it. He was never a man to

396

pull rank, and certainly not in the present circumstances. The blankets, and packs and overcoats had been retrieved and next day when the hospital returns came in and the first rough casualty list was made up, he and his storemen would begin drawing up an inventory of unclaimed possessions. There was a large quantity and it was the Company Quartermaster's responsibility to sort them out, to return those that were the Army's to battalion stores, to go through the packs of the dead and the missing and, in due course, when all hope of news had been given up, to see that their personal effects were sent home. It was a dispiriting task which McFie was not looking forward to, and when he woke to another glorious day, even the fine weather did little to cheer him.

It was 18 June, and the hundredth anniversary of the Battle of Waterloo. Across the Channel at Berkhamsted the Inns of Court Battalion was drawn up on Kitchener's Field for a special parade. There were thirteen hundred of them, but more than half as many again had passed through the ranks and were now serving as subalterns in almost every Battalion of the New Army. They had recently reached the remarkable total of two thousand commissions, and it was to mark this achievement that Colonel Errington invited their honorary colonel, Field Marshal Sir Evelyn Wood, VC, to inspect the battalion. The Field Marshal had set 18 June as a suitable date, not merely because it was Waterloo Day but because it was a date he had particular reason to remember, 'For,' as he explained in his letter of acceptance, 'I got a big hole in me that day sixty years ago.'

Sir Evelyn Wood was eighty years old, he had got 'a big hole' at the siege of Sebastapol in 1855, and to the men in the callow ranks of the Inns of Court he was a historic figure. He had been in the Ashanti wars, had won the Victoria Cross in the Indian Mutiny, risen to be Commander-in-Chief of the Egyptian Army and had retired a mere twelve years earlier with the rank of Field Marshal. He took the keenest interest in the Army although, to his bitter regret, he was considered to be too old to serve in the present war. But on Waterloo Day the Field Marshal was in his element. He insisted on taking the salute mounted, stopped frequently during his inspection to speak with gruff good humour to numerous soldiers, and later cantered round the field, as the Colonel remarked admiringly, 'as if the day *had* been really sixty years ago!' He addressed the troops in the most complimentary terms, and if his speech was a little rambling as he recalled his own bygone days of soldiering, and if his voice cracked at times and did not quite carry to every corner of the field, the Inns of Court were delighted and rewarded him with three hearty cheers.

There were other Waterloo Day parades and celebrations in various parts of the country, and especially in schools, but the centenary was not celebrated as it might have been in peacetime. It passed virtually unnoticed at the front, but on the same day, by coincidence, a shell exploding near Essex Farm on the Pilkem Ridge uncovered an ancient cannon-ball, buried since Marlborough's wars. The following evening the 4th Gordon Highlanders were relieved and U Company thankfully handed over the trenches in Y Wood and went back to rest. There were many faces missing on the march back to the fields round Brandhoek and they only got there in the small hours of the morning, dog tired, but extremely happy. Their glorious rest was to last for almost four weeks.

Their casualties, though bad enough, had been less severe than those of the battalions in the forefront of the attack, but their 8th Brigade had held the trenches on the Menin Road for the best part of four weeks, and Colonel Tommy Ogilvie intended that his Battalion's rest should be a good one. Muscles were soft from lack of exercise and the Army decreed that when men were relieved from the front there should be a stiff programme of training and exercise to toughen them up for going back again. Captain Hopkinson, who now commanded U Company, interpreted this order in liberal terms and the platoon commanders taking their cue from him were determined that the men should enjoy themselves so long as the fine weather lasted.

Sgt. A. Rule.

We were camped in hessian bivouacs and we enjoyed a spell of almost unbroken sunshine and glorious summer mornings. The term 'early morning parade' was broadly accepted by our Platoon Commander as embracing gentle strolls past promising field crops, and physical exercises in the morning sunshine, just strenuous enough to stimulate our digestive juices. Training took place after breakfast and our Platoon Commander had taken a university course in agriculture so perhaps for that reason he had an eye for a well-sheltered training field. Through pastures green he led us where, instead of wearisome drill, we could enjoy a private sun bathe and a siesta. Unfortunately, after about a week of this pastoral idyll, the commander of another company blundered into our preserve and, although he and his men did have the good sense to follow our example, our sanctuary was robbed of its privacy.

There was good food, plain, but plenty of it. There were estaminets in Brandhoek where the beer was thin but abundant, there was money to jingle in their sporrans – four weeks' unspent pay – there were letters from home and parcels galore whose contents included

398

the occasional bottle of whisky which certainly helped to enliven camp sing-songs in the warm evenings.

Best of all there were baths. Baths were arranged at Poperinghe for one company at a time, and although water was plentiful and U Company had been able to wash regularly, a cold water wash in a bucket could not be compared to a bath – even if the bath was a communal one in the vats of a brewery. U Company's turn came at the end of their first week's rest and it was a red letter day. It was their first trip to Poperinghe and, after a blissful scrub, a lot of horseplay, and an invigorating cold douche from a two-inch hosepipe, the men were allowed the indulgence of two hours to explore and to enjoy the novelty of a town that still contained shops and civilians and was only slightly battered by shell-fire, for many of the refugees and tradesmen had returned. Since they had existed entirely on army fare for the past five months, most of them explored no further than the cafés and restaurants in the square, and once the novelty of being presented with menu cards had evaporated, and given the limitations of time and money, they set to and did their utmost to work their way through them. Stew was not popular, but there was good hearty soup, gargantuan omelettes, veal, steak, sausages, and mountains of golden chips, so cheap that even the less provident, who had spent the lion's share of four weeks' deferred pay on beer, could afford several large portions of chips, if they could afford nothing else.

By the time they fell in for the three-mile tramp back to Brandhoek, U Company were new men. They were pleasantly replete with decent food, washed down with quantities of beer and wine, but best of all they were clean – and felt properly clean and spruce for the first time in weeks. During the past days they had spent hours smartening up. Kilts and tunics had been dried off and brushed clean, buttons and boots were polished, puttees were free of mud, faces were scrubbed and shining beneath khaki Tam o' Shanters perched at a jaunty angle on gleaming slicked-back hair. They stepped out smartly, for the pipes were playing them along the road to the lively strains of 'Cock o' the North', and U Company, who knew a variety of versions, was in excellent voice. It would have been hard to find a happier-looking bunch of Jocks. Just as the tune came to an end they caught up with a battalion of Kitchener's Army. They were the first New Army men they had seen and they were not an alluring sight.

Sgt. A. Rule.

They were resting by the wayside and looking unutterably weary and dispirited. We later learned that they had just

399

received their baptism of fire on the Menin Road and had been relieved – after just forty-eight hours in the line. They were probably misled by our 'shining morning faces' and took us for a newly arrived Territorial unit, anyway they began to shout caustic comments and we catcalled back at them. One woebegone-looking sergeant called out, 'Just wait till *you've* been up there, lads, and you won't be singin' then!' Well, we soon put *him* right. I'll never forget his look of utter incredulity when we informed them we'd just come back after holding the Menin Road for *weeks* on end. It sent us into roars of laughter.

To add spice to the joke someone sang out in a high falsetto voice *'We don't want to lose you, but we think you ought to go . . .'* It set U Company off again and when they had recovered they favoured Kitchener's unfortunate soldiers with another mocking ditty which struck them as peculiarly appropriate, bellowing as they swaggered down the road:

> Send out the Army and the Navy,
> Send out the rank and file,
> Send out the good old Territorials,
> They'll face danger with a smile!
> Send out the Boys of the Old Brigade
> Who kept Old England free,
> Send out my brother, my sister and my mother,
> But for God's sake, don't send ME!

It was a touch unkind, and the Kitchener Battalion shouted insults and imprecations until U Company was well down the road. They were the 9th Battalion, the Rifle Brigade, of the 14th Light Division – the very troops who had relieved U Company's own brigade a few days before. The riflemen had been in Flanders for just over a month and, if they did not at present appreciate the joke, they looked forward to getting their own back. As the second of the New Army divisions to reach the front they too would be acting the old sweats before many weeks had passed, lording it over newer arrivals as the pace gathered momentum and Kitchener's Army began to arrive in significant numbers.*

The vast bulk of the 'First Hundred Thousand' of Kitchener's Army were champing at the bit. In their opinion they had been ready for months, and the last weeks of waiting had been weary. They were

---

* The 9th (Scottish) Division left for the front on 9 May, the 14th (Light) Division on 19 May, and the 12th (Eastern) Division on the 29th of the same month.

sick of drilling, sick of route-marching, sick of training, sick of mock attacks and if they were not exactly sick of the Army, they wanted to get on with the war. It had not been easy to equip them but now, at last, they were garbed in respectable soldierly khaki and could say goodbye to the suits of 'Kitchener's blue'. At long last they had rifles, and some who were natural shots could fire them. Others had been dragged through the final musketry tests on which the proficiency of the battalion depended. It was an open secret that a well-meaning instructor, seeing that a man was firing an unacceptable number of outers – or even missing the target altogether – had his own system. 'I think there's something wrong with that rifle, lad,' he would say. 'Let *me* try it.' And, on the pretext of testing the weapon, he would pump enough inners and bullseyes into the target to make sure that a soldier got the required score. They would improve with practice – and they would get plenty of opportunity to practice in France. But they were fit, and they were keen and, ready or not, in the opinion of many Commanding Officers, as eager as their troops to get to the front, they were in danger of going stale with the long delay. Now that things were hotting up and there was a real prospect of getting going, the anticipation was unbearable as the days dragged and the troops chafed at the bit, waiting for the final inspection that would signal their departure.

The King was working hard, for he was anxious to inspect as many Kitchener's Brigades as possible to wish them Godspeed. He was a modest man and he regarded this as a duty, for Kitchener's men had been exhorted to join up in his name 'for King and Country', and even if he was exhausted by the end of June, his effort had given enormous pleasure and satisfaction.

Sgt. J. Cross, MM, 13th Bn., Rifle Brig., 37 Div.

King George was coming down to inspect the Division before we left and we'd been told that we had to keep a sharp look out. Well, at ordinary times the police used to do the guard for the camp because we were busy with our training, but this particular week we had to do camp guard for twenty-four hours and this particular day I was in charge of it (I was paid Acting-Sergeant at the time) and of course the other lads pulled my leg about this because I'd never done a guard in my life before, not even as a rifleman, because we hadn't been anywhere to do one. I told my sentries, 'You keep your eyes peeled. And if you see a cavalcade of horses come along there and if His Majesty is there there'll be a chap riding along with the Royal Standard, so don't forget to give us the word right smart!' Well, suddenly a voice rang out, 'Guard, turn out!' And we jumped out and

401

stood to attention. The King's party passed along between the road and the camp, riding on the grass. When they got round more or less to my front, I pulled the guard to attention, 'Royal salute. Present arms!' – and the bugler sounded the royal salute. They stopped and the King wheeled his horse round and he saluted the guard and something was said to one of the aide de camps, and he came galloping across to me at the guard post. He said, 'What regiment are you, Corporal?' I said, 'Thirteenth Battalion, Rifle Brigade, sir.' 'All right,' he said, 'you can stand the guard at ease.' So I gave the order. 'Guard – order arms. Stand at ease!'

The Orderly Sergeant came round at night. He says, 'Jack, you're for orders in the morning. Belt and side arms,' he said. 'Do yourself up well.' So, next morning's Orderly Room, before they saw the prisoners, I had to go in. Colonel Pretor-Pinney sat at the table and he looked at me straight. He said, 'I'm very pleased with what happened yesterday and the way you conducted the guard as His Majesty passed by.' I said, 'Thank you, sir.' He said to me, 'What is your rank now?' I said, 'Paid Lance-Sergeant, sir.' So he said, 'From now on, I promote you to full Sergeant,' and that come out in Battalion Orders that night. So I went to France as a full Sergeant.

Jack Cross's comrades of the 13th Battalion, the Rifle Brigade, had been gratified by the King's visit, but the visit of Duggie Jones's mother had given even greater pleasure to at least a dozen of his particular chums. They thought it was particularly civil of her, for Duggie was only sixteen, although his large bulk and his height of six feet had easily deceived the recruiting sergeant. Unlike many mothers of under-age boys, she had sportingly connived at the deception, and even more sportingly arrived two days before their departure to give Duggie and his friends a memorable send-off. Mrs Jones was rich, her son Douglas was a public schoolboy, but he was 'one of the lads' – and what a night the lads had! Duggie's mother had reserved a private room in a local hotel and treated the boys to such a dinner as they had seldom enjoyed. There was smoked salmon, there was caviare, there was turbot followed by a joint of beef large enough to go round half the battalion. There was trifle, there was ice cream, there was even a savoury of roasted cheese. There was good wine to wash down the meal and, as if that were not enough, Mrs Jones presented each of the dozen guests with a half-bottle of whisky to take away with him. It was a wonderful evening. She had also had the tact and foresight to charm Colonel Pretor-Pinney in the course of a personal visit and to beg his acceptance of a case of champagne for the officers' farewell dinner, thereby ensuring that there were no recriminations when the merry diners returned to camp, long after lights out.[*]

Kitchener's Army had basked in the glory of the first weeks of the war, when the flags waved and the bands played and every volunteer was hailed as a hero, but the euphoria had evaporated over the weary months of slog and marching and training – and waiting, waiting, waiting. Now, on the eve of their departure, now that they were real soldiers at last, and now that they were on the brink of the long-awaited adventure, there was a new sense of bravado in the air and it came through proudly, if a little self-consciously, in farewell letters home.

Rfn. J. Hoyles, 13th Bn., Rifle Brig., 37th Div.

My Ever Dear Mother and Father,
I started writing a letter this afternoon, dear Mother, but in the meantime I have been so busy drawing ammunition (a hundred and twenty rounds) and other jobs.

First of all dear Mother I wish to thank you for the cake and socks. The cake was ripping and I thoroughly enjoyed it. My chief news, dear Mother, is to tell you we are going tomorrow morning after breakfast either to Southampton or Folkestone and we embark on Sunday for the front. The King sent a message down, which the Colonel read out on parade, in which he wished us every success in the future and by the grace of God his protection over us, at which our Colonel broke down. He is such a nice gentleman, a man liked by everyone, and we cheered him to the echo.

Dear Mother, we had our photographs taken yesterday and if you should see it in the illustrated papers I am just behind the Marquis of Winchester.[†]

Mother dear, I know at times you must feel sad, but I know you will keep a cheerful appearance for my sake. It does not seem that we are going out, somehow we cannot realise what lays before us, the hardships and dangers of real warfare. Mother dear, I ask of you that you will say a prayer beside your bed (every night) for me, asking God to protect me through all

---

[*] After the war Douglas Jones became a well-known actor under the stage name of Aubrey Dexter, and appeared in many films and West End productions, including *The Mousetrap*. His last appearance before his retirement and untimely death was with Sir Laurence Olivier in *The Entertainer*.

[†] Major the Marquis of Winchester was an officer of the 13th Battalion, the Rifle Brigade.

the dangers I have to traverse. As you say, Mother, you will leave me in the hands of God, which is a kind thought from you for me. Take care of everything of mine at home as I prize everything I possess.

Dear Mother, I am glad to hear you are going to Liverpool for a change, but I am so sorry to tell you, owing to the rotters not paying us the billeting money, I shall be unable to send you anything as they are going to credit it to us in our pay books. I think the reason is because of the men getting too much drink and kicking up a row before we go. They owe me £2.

Frank's division is following us out in about a week's time. Tell him, dear Mother, I am gone.

Well, dear Mother and Father, I think I have told you all and I will write as soon as we land. Kiss all the children for me and Goodbye to Jack and all friends at home and look for the time when I, Frank and all are reunited again after this war.

Goodbye to all. With fondest love and my first thoughts for you, from your ever loving son,

Joe (of the Rifle Brigade).*

Gnr. D. A. Pankhurst, Stokes Mortar Bty., RFA.

We were given twenty-four hours' leave and I went home. Father left for work very early in the morning and he came into me before he went and woke me and said (these are his exact words. I shall never forget them), he said, 'I know you'll do your duty, but don't forget, Mother will be worrying about you.' Those words went with me through the whole of the war. 'I know you'll do your duty' – so I had to do that if only for him. And my mother.

The first two hundred thousand were ready to go to war. The problem that faced the Government was where to employ them to the best advantage – whether to send large reinforcements to the Dardanelles in the hope of tipping the scales and ensuring success, or to concentrate resources on the western front in the hope of eventually breaking through the German line. The long-postponed decision had at last been taken – but it was still in the nature of a compromise. Three New Army Divisions would be sent to the Dardanelles, with more to follow if necessary. The political crisis had caused four weeks' delay and the first of the three embarked in

---

* The subsequent story of Joe Hoyles and the 13th Battalion, the Rifle Brigade, is told in the author's book, *Somme*.

mid-June, the third on 7 July. The voyage was long, the temperature on the peninsula was rising, the new troops could not possibly take the offensive before August and by then the blistering heat would have reached its peak.

In the early evening of 5 July a special train left Victoria Station carrying the Prime Minister, with Lord Kitchener and other members of his Cabinet, to Dover en route to Calais for a meeting with their French counterparts. Sir John French travelled from his GHQ at St Omer to join them. It was not an entirely satisfactory conference, for the proceedings were in French, a language in which not all the British delegation were fluent, but they believed that certain agreements had been reached. The Dardanelles campaign would be continued and, in the near future, there would be no large offensives on the western front, although 'local attacks' would be carried out vigorously, as the British understood it, to harass the line – but not to break it. In view of their still-meagre stocks of rifles and ammunition and the amount required merely to hold the line, they calculated that no all-out offensive would be possible within a year. Lord Kitchener had forecast that by the spring of 1916, he would be able to have seventy divisions in the field – although in the opinion of Lloyd George this optimistic estimate showed a cavalier disregard for the problems of equipping them with rifles or supplying them with the guns and ammunition without which, as he acerbically pointed out, they might as well stay at home. Nevertheless, the army in Flanders had now swelled by three divisions of the New Army, and thirteen more would follow before autumn. The British were therefore able to agree to hold a longer front and to extend their line north of Ypres and south towards the Somme.

The meeting ended amicably. If Marshal Joffre still nursed ambitious ideas for renewing the offensive on the western front he did not succeed in communicating them to the British staff and their political masters, and they departed well pleased. The Prime Minister, wishing to have a look at the war for himself, stayed on in France, with Lord Kitchener and the Secretary to the Cabinet, Sir Maurice Hankey. The highlight of their short stay was their visit to Ypres.

General Plumer was not at all happy about it. For one thing, protocol demanded that he should personally escort the visitors, and he could ill spare the time, and for another, Ypres was far too dangerous for sightseers although the Prime Minister did not seem to appreciate the risks. He lingered for a long time at the Menin Gate chatting amiably to some soldiers while Plumer, standing by on tenterhooks, could only express his displeasure by 'looking daggers' at his hapless Chief of Staff, General Milne, who had arranged Mr Asquith's programme. The Prime Minister lingered even longer in the square, shaking his head over the ruins, asking an inordinate number of questions which might as easily have been dealt with in a safer place, cocking his head as he listened for shells and inquired about their calibre. He even insisted on personally measuring the largest of the shell craters. Lord Kitchener was rather more interested in casting a connoisseur's eye over two small statues which still stood miraculously intact in their niches, on the wrecked facade of the Cloth Hall. He was clearly itching to get hold of them and his interest was so unabashed, his desire so palpable, his dilemma so obvious, that General Milne and Hankey shook with silent mirth. 'I rather think,' murmured Milne, 'those statues are in greater danger now than they've *ever* been from German shells!'

Fortunately for General Plumer's peace of mind the few shells that came over that morning exploded well away from the centre of the town, but he was heartily thankful when the party drove off with General Milne to tour the heavy gunline and to inspect some reserve trenches at a good safe distance from the line.

Visitors to Ypres were not encouraged. Civilians could not enter the town without the permission of the military, and could not even come into the war zone without a pass from the civil authorities. It had taken Aimé van Nieuwenhove ten wearisome days of form-filling and string-pulling before he managed to secure an official permit that allowed him to spend three nights in Poperinghe and another that enabled him to spend six hours and no more in Ypres. He fervently hoped that it would be long enough to retrieve the family fortunes.

It was more than two months since he had locked his front door for the last time and wondered, 'What will be left when we return?' In view of the news that had reached him in Paris he had a fair idea that the answer to that question would be 'Not much.'

Aimé van Nieuwenhove.

The purpose of my journey was to excavate in the garden of Uncle Pierre Liebaert, to find all the stocks and bonds the old man had buried in August 1914, which he had had to leave behind and which added up to hundreds of thousands of francs.

Although I wished to perform this service for Uncle (also a refugee in Paris and becoming more and more miserable each day at being parted from a large part of his fortune) I also had a strong desire to see for myself the ruins of our home and of our unhappy town in general. On 17 July, three days after leaving Paris, I came into Ypres at seven in the morning, with a one-horse wagon and two workmen I had picked up in Poperinghe. On reaching the outskirts of Ypres, I confess that I felt apprehension flooding back. Of course I had lost the habit of risking life under bombardment. Fortunately for me it was not very heavy that morning, although the previous evening a policeman had been killed by a shell near the prison.

It is impossible to describe the appearance of the town. It was a dreadful sorrow to find nothing but burnt-out shells and charred walls where there once were houses. At last we arrived at the site of our house in the rue de Lille. The gable-end of the house facing on to the street was still standing, as well as some of the inner walls. I quickly clambered in to inspect it. The cellars were filled up with a pile of bricks and debris. With the help of the workmen I started to dig, but everything I found was charred and useless – even the bronze of the clocks that I pulled out of the debris had melted and the bottles in the wine-cellar turned to cinders as soon as one touched them. After that I dug up a big zinc container buried in the garden which contained books of designs for lace. Then I went round to the rue de Chien to Uncle Liebaert's house and there we started to dig. Although I myself had buried three strongboxes containing his stocks and bonds and part of his silver, I couldn't find the most important strongbox because one of the party walls we had used as a marker had disappeared. The shell which had struck the wall had left a huge hole where the wall had been – and where I believed the box had been buried as well. However, after digging in it for less than an hour in drizzling rain and with shells coming over from time to time, the box came to light. It must have been because of the great depth at which it was buried that the shell had not reached it – although it very nearly had. 'Well,' I thought to myself, 'Uncle's in luck!'

It was not quite ten in the morning. The men took their cart to the water-tower to load up some furniture belonging to one of them, and I had still three hours in hand before I was obliged to leave at one o'clock. I spent them walking round my garden to see if anything was left of my plants and trees and on the lawn I found the three cages of the canaries just where I had left them at the time of my departure. The big garden seat is still at the foot of the garden. Despite the rain I wanted to make the most of my time so, with a full heart, I tore myself away from all that had once been my delight and, accompanied by the Belgian policeman I had been obliged by the authorities to bring as an escort, I took a melancholy walk round all the streets of the town, ending up at the water-tower. We went into an abandoned house while we waited for the men to finish loading and made a snack of some food which we had had the forethought to bring with us.

We left Ypres about half past one and arrived at Poperinghe

at five in the evening, just twelve hours after leaving it. It had been some job! Nevertheless that evening I felt great satisfaction at having succeeded so well, and looked forward early next morning to sending a telegram to Uncle Liebaert to let him know that all his fortune had been retrieved intact. I spent the whole of Sunday in Poperinghe with friends I met there.

It took the whole morning running hither and thither to get my passports stamped for the return journey, and in the afternoon I went to see a servant of ours at Crombeke. At last, I set off at one o'clock on Monday for Hazebrouck and from there caught the train for Paris the following morning, arriving at seven in the evening.

After having placed Uncle's possessions in his hands I took another train for Neuilly-Plaisance where, happy and pleased with my journey, I found the whole family at the station. I brought back a suitcase containing our jewellery and table silver which a fortnight earlier I had asked a friend, R. Clinckemaille, to dig up from our garden, because at the time I had not expected to be going to Ypres myself. My journey was not accomplished without difficulties on every side, but its result made quite a few people happy – and even more will be happier still when the war at last gives way to peace.

That time was a long way off, and it was just as well that van Nieuwenhove had managed to recover the hidden money and valuables, for living in Paris was expensive. It would be almost four years before he came again to Ypres, and by then it was almost razed to the ground. It had taken exactly seven days to accomplish his mission. He reached Paris on 19 July. In the Ypres salient, two hundred miles to the north, it was a day of notable excitement. They intended to blow up Hooge.

Major Cowan of 175 Tunnelling Company was in charge of the project, Lieutenant Cassels was in charge of the work, and a detachment of coal-miners, newly co-opted into the Royal Engineers, was responsible for actually doing it. They were not young men, they were untrained and, to say the least, unskilled in soldiering. They were also unused to marching and it had been a wearisome business getting them from the railhead to the front. But they were experienced miners and once they had reached the line and were given a job to do, they knew precisely how to do it. The pit-men were not particularly enjoying their strange surroundings and when the Germans shelled, which was most of the time, they were clearly happier underground – and that was all to the good, for the tunnels had to be dug at top speed and there was no time to be lost. After several false starts and many alarms the work was completed in less than a month. But there had been anxious moments.

Major S. H. Cowan.

A wire was brought to me saying that Cassels had heard mining under our own trenches. After convincing himself that the Germans were under us, he had reported to the infantry officer in command and had organised a retrenched line round their probable 'crater'. It was too late to attempt to blow their mine as they were already under our feet. Cassels then withdrew his men – who are not trained soldiers – to Battalion Headquarters, then, on the advice of the Colonel, to their back billets. I consider he did right.

It would be pathetic, were it not so absolutely absurd, to count how many people there are who are willing to swear that the Germans have actually mined under our trenches from no other evidence than lying *on* the ground and listening to every blessed overground noise there is. One case we traced to a sentry kicking his heels together twenty yards away. Two other scares were traced, one to a nest of young rats, the second to a loose shutter in a ruin about a hundred and fifty yards away which kept on 'dabbing' irregularly in the wind. But I must own that everyone's nerves are at their very worst between midnight and the very welcome dawn.

There is only one way of hearing real underground sounds and that is, dig down about six feet, then forward for about ten feet under your own parapet. Next, hang a curtain to shut out noises from your own people, who should be sent away for twenty yards or so. Then, at last, lie down and perhaps you'll hear the Germans. If you do, it's time to send for the Corps Travelling Company, but meanwhile, you'd better keep on listening, remembering all the time that so long as you do hear him you are safe. When he stops work all you can do is to clear out and wait, ready to rush his crater before he arrives.

It was one of many false alarms, but it was an understandable mistake, for the Germans were indeed working underground – but they were working beneath their own line, burrowing dug-outs and constructing the first of the concrete strongpoints they believed would make it impregnable. It was perfectly obvious to the German Command that their tenancy of the high ground around the salient would not go unchallenged for long. The British had tried once to wrest it back, and they would certainly try again. Since the capture of their old front line on the lower slopes of the ridge, the Germans had been working day and night. They had built a tangle of new trenches, strong and deep, looping back on themselves to form four-sided redoubts, girded with stout wire, and pushed forward to enclose the remnants of Hooge Chateau, left in No Man's Land after the fight on 16 June. All that was left of the chateau was a few tumbled walls, little more than fifty yards from the furthest point of the British front line where it reached out round the ruins of the old stables. The chateau was the original objective, for it was suspected that the Germans would regard it as a stronghold. But every day, as his men worked in the lengthening tunnel below, Lieutenant Cassels made a point of visiting the front-line trench and peering through a periscope at the German line, looking for the tell-tale signs that would show that the ruins were being fortified. After several days of close observation, he concluded that they were not. But he spotted a still better target – two newly completed concrete redoubts, a little way apart, each big enough to hold a company, and pierced with threatening apertures, wide enough to provide machine-guns with a deadly field of fire.

The plans were changed, and the tunnel was diverted to run towards the new objective. It was to be a Y-shaped tunnel now, with a subsidiary arm running from the main passage and two chambers packed with explosive, one under each of the redoubts. But the time was short, the work was necessarily hasty, and on the left, the minor tunnel deviated so far from the second redoubt that the charge was bound to miss it altogether. This was a severe blow. There were only days to go. The plans had been made, and the infantry was standing by to follow up the explosion, to consolidate the crater while the enemy was still staggering from the shock, and by breaching his stoutest stronghold, to pave the way for the capture of the ridge.

In desperation, Cassels came up with a bold plan and managed to persuade his superiors to agree to it. He proposed to pack all the explosive into a single charge beneath one redoubt in the hope that the force of a single mighty explosion would also destroy the other. To make quite sure of success, it was also decided to use an explosive not commonly used by the Army. It was three times as powerful as gunpowder and, knowing perfectly well that there was a stock of it in France, Major Cowan sent an indent to GHQ for three and a half thousand pounds of ammonal.

This request caused consternation, and not a little puzzlement at GHQ. No one was familiar with ammonal and the indent was passed to the V Corps Quartermaster, with a request for clarification. He was equally at a loss, but he was struck by the idea of consulting the Medical Officer at Corps Headquarters, and the MO replied without hesitation. Ammonal, he informed the startled Quartermaster, was a sedative drug prescribed to subdue cases of abnormal sexual excitement. He added, thoughtfully, that so far as he knew, no such cases had yet occurred among V Corps troops.

This provided food for thought. It was hard to fathom why 175th Company was demanding almost two tons of the stuff, presumably for the use of its two hundred men! The Quartermaster might have been forgiven for wondering in bafflement what manner of men they were.

Further inquiries disclosed the difference between the use and effect of the explosive ammonal and the drug ammonol and cleared up the misunderstanding, but it all caused delay. The mine was to be fired just before the infantry attacked on 19 July. Three days before the deadline, the ammonal had still not arrived and Cassels frantically set about begging and borrowing whatever explosive he could lay hands on from neighbouring companies and local stores, which – for obvious reasons – did not hold large stocks of such dangerous material so close to the line. He scraped up less than fifteen hundred pounds, and although it contained a small quantity of ammonal, the rest was conventional gunpowder and gun-cotton – poor stuff by comparison. It was nowhere near enough, but the attack could not be postponed and it would have to do. But he doubted whether it would do the job. The miners worked all through the night of 16 July, pulling the heavy bags of explosive down the long tunnel, and tamping them into the chamber beneath the largest of the German redoubts. Next day when the long-awaited wagon-load of ammonal arrived, the probability of failure became in an instant the certainty of success, for now Cassels meant to use the lot, augmenting more than half a ton of explosive, already laid in the mine, by more than twice that quantity of three-times-as-powerful ammonal. It would be the heaviest mine ever fired in the war, possibly in history, and, fired at a depth of only twenty feet, no one was quite sure what the effect would be.

But Major Cowan stifled his qualms and Cassels set to work. In the afternoon of 19 July, with less than five hours to go before zero, he reported that the job was finished and the mine was ready to blow. Cowan immediately left for the line to see the show.

Major S. H. Cowan.

At 2.30 p.m. Hart and I set out. We motored to Ypres and left the car close to the old Lille gate. Then up by a road I'm seriously beginning to dislike. Luckily there was no shrapnel, but even before we got to the village (Zillebeke) we got into the belt of country where all the German bullets which come over the top of our parapets generally settle down – hence their

411

name 'overs'. It's a funny sound, an 'over', a high-pitched whining buzz followed by a *whit* into the earth or a louder noise against a tree or a wall. Shrapnel is my pet abomination when in the open. They are quite pretty to watch when their noise increases *and then diminishes*, but if it keeps *on* increasing most people prefer the view of a ditch dry or wet.

At Hooge I found everything all right, but everyone *very* excited. I tested our firing leads – they were OK – and gave my final orders to Cassels, then went back for a thousand yards to join the Brigadier whose men were to do the attack.

The charge was due to blow at seven o'clock just as the sun was sinking. The last few days had been showery but although it was a fine evening, Lieutenant Cassels was in no position to admire the sunset. Counting the minutes to zero as he crouched in a dug-out not far from the front line, he was waiting to fire the charge, when, with minutes to go, the worst happened. A German shell bursting close by ruptured the electrical leads that ran from the dug-out, down the shaft and along the tunnel to fire the mine. With trembling hands Cassels tested the leads. They tested negative.

It was the signaller-corporal scrabbling frantically round the edge of the smoking shell-crater who found the break, and it was providential that the leads were cut clean and were speedily mended. There was a minute to go now. Watching anxiously from Brigade Headquarters Major Cowan was sweating.

Major S. H. Cowan.

A shell arrived near the work, and for two *centuries* my hair stood on end. But in eight actual *seconds* there was a cloud of smoke and dirt five hundred feet high, and an explosion and a real shake, even under *our* very feet. Then Hell was let loose and for twenty minutes every gun we had made a curtain of fire just beyond our objective.

If the ground shook a thousand yards from the line it positively rocked beneath Cassels's dug-out. He was stunned. The explosion was far greater than anything he had imagined. Tons of earth, bricks, stones, rose into the air. Uprooted trees whirled like matchsticks in the smoke. Bricks, timber, iron bars, whole slabs of concrete were tossed sky-high in a shower of splintered rifles and fragments of flesh and bones, and even the guns that immediately opened up could not muffle the crash and rumble of debris falling back round the colossal crater.

It was an awesome sight.

⌐

Chapter 28

The crater was a hundred and twenty feet wide; it was twenty feet deep and the lip on the circumference was more than twice the height of an extremely tall man. The main redoubt was blown out of existence and the second was damaged and buried, just as Cassels had hoped. Unfortunately, the fountain of debris had also buried a dozen men of the 4th Middlesex waiting to dash forward to capture the crater, and waiting a little too far ahead. But the rest of their Company made it and the Brigade bombers were poised to dash ahead. Skirting the reeking crater almost before the debris had subsided, they disappeared into the smoke and pushed on, bombing their way through trenches, capturing strongpoints, sending back a few stunned prisoners, hurling grenades when they met opposition and driving the bemused Germans back three hundred yards. They advanced so rapidly that they ran beyond the protection of their own guns, and when the German bombardment thundering behind them threatened to cut them off they were forced to go back. There was no sign of anyone coming up to support them. In any event, they had run out of bombs.

It seemed as if every gun in Belgium was pouring fire on this one small corner at the head of the Ypres salient. But the British guns, firing hard, were no match for the enemy artillery. There was no hope of sending troops forward – no means of following up the bombers' advance. Not all the bombers got back, and among several who did not, was Sergeant Allardyce of U Company. But the troops in the line held fast.

Sgt. A. Rule.

The Germans retaliated with great gusto. Their barrage wrecked our parapet in many places and caused heavy casualties – but their counter-attack failed. For the next three days our trenches were strafed continuously with missiles ranging from hand grenades to whizz-bangs and 5.9s. We were even peppered one evening with machine-gun bullets from two wicked-looking taubes as they flew back and forward along our front line. A huge Minenwerfer trained on the mine crater sent over its dreaded aeriel torpedoes until it was silenced by our artillery. Sniping went on continuously and there were frequent 'wind ups', and there at the extreme tip of the salient we were vulnerable to deadly enfilade fire and it often appeared as if we were being fired on from our *own* support trenches in the rear. Our parapets only consisted of a *single* thickness of sandbags, and shells bursting in the soft earth in front blasted them inwards. As soon as dusk fell we had to set to work repairing the breaches – generally under fire from a German machine-gun – and all the time we were digging for material to fill sandbags we were digging up dead bodies.

Despite the spectacular success of the mining operation the existence of the crater had not improved the position of the infantry. It had not been possible to capture more than the crater itself with bombing posts on either side and the trenches that tenuously linked them were awkwardly placed. It was difficult for the companies to keep in touch with each other, and much too easy to keep in touch with the enemy, now uncomfortably close in the uncaptured trenches which were almost a continuation of their own. The infuriated Germans were clearly determined to give no quarter, and the unfortunate Tommies who were taking the brunt of their displeasure were inclined to think that the blowing of the crater had been a good deal more trouble than it was worth.

The explosion had been heard for miles and ecstatic rumours flying round the villages behind the line had done a good deal to uplift the spirits of civilians on the eve of Belgian Independence Day. In peacetime it had been a national holiday and a day of celebration. This year, with seven-eighths of little Belgium under German occupation, 'independence' had a hollow ring, but there were flags outside a few houses and estaminets, there were services in village churches and the patriotic prayers had never been more fervent.

It was a far cry from the celebrations of peacetime when Independence Day had been the holiday of the year and country people flocked to the towns and larger villages to enjoy themselves. There were *Te Deums* in churches, there were parades and pageants, and there were travelling fairs set up in village squares. Town bands played, flags flew everywhere, and knots of ribbon in the national colours were worn in every button-hole or Sunday frock. Cafés and restaurants were packed with citizens celebrating the fête by consuming gargantuan meals, but enterprising restaurants set up stalls on the pavements and sold legions of sausages, mountains of shrimps, pancakes by the stack, and chips daubed with golden mayonnaise by the ton. Even if these delights were no more, at least the population in this small remaining corner of Belgian Flanders, racked and battered through it was by the war, were free to mark the occasion as they saw fit.

In German-occupied Belgium it was very different, and in anticipation of a possible surge of nationalistic feeling on Belgium's national day, the occupying power had issued stern edicts and made it clear that severe penalties would be exacted if their orders were flouted. The Germans were particularly anxious to avoid demonstrations in Brussels where the civilian population was adept at finding subtle ways of cocking a snook at the authorities. There was the matter of the season of Wagnerian opera which had recently been held under official German patronage. Two years earlier, a similar event had brought all Brussels to the Théatre de la Monnaie and the operas had played to glittering houses for a full week. This time all Brussels had shunned it and, apart from a handful of German officers and their wives, the audiences stayed away. Even the ambassadors of neutral countries had refused official invitations with polite excuses and, to the fury of the German 'Governor General', the whole thing had been a flop. Brussels was not to be so easily placated for the many indignities its citizens had suffered at the hands of the invaders, and they kicked back in any way they could.

It was a point of honour not to keep Berlin time, and people obstinately continued to order their days by '*l'heure des alliés*', one hour behind the hated '*heure boche*' which had been imposed by the Germans in the first days of the occupation. Inevitably this caused confusion, especially since the proprietors of all public clocks were obliged to show Berlin time and, although the order could not be openly defied and it was explicitly forbidden to stop them altogether, the clocks of Brussels developed a bizarre tendency to run so fast or so slow that it was entirely pointless for passers-by to consult them. Only the clock of the Hotel de Ville (now occupied by the German Kommandatur) showed the 'correct' German time and this was a godsend to officials keeping appointments. It was the Spanish ambassador who conveniently noticed that to state a time according to *l'heure de l'Hotel de Ville* could not offend the Germans because it was *their* time, and could hardly offend the Belgians because it was *their* clock.

After almost a year of occupation Brussels was a gloomy city. Food was scarce, spirits were low and the only entertainment to be found in the one-time 'Paris of the north' was the pastime of duping the Germans. As the day of the national fête approached people turned their minds to new ways of outwitting them. The Germans had already prohibited the flying of Belgian or Allied flags and the wearing of national colours, and on 18 July a new edict was posted up.

NOTICE

I warn the public that on July 21, 1915 demonstrations of all kinds are expressly and emphatically prohibited. Assemblies, parades, and the decoration of private buildings fall within the scope of this prohibition. The offenders will be liable to punishment of imprisonment not exceeding three months and a fine not exceeding 10,000 marks.

The Governor of Brussels,
Von Kräwel, Lieutenant-General.

But the Germans had not thought of everything. They had not forbidden the Belgians to wear flowers and the flower-vendors were out in force selling posies of red and yellow blooms which, worn in the lapel of a black frock-coat or pinned to a black dress, represented the colours of the Belgian flag. Almost everyone was in black, for Brussels was observing the occasion as a day of national mourning. Black-bordered handbills distributed clandestinely had mooted the idea and everyone took it up. Shops, cafés, restaurants, closed their doors, offices shut up for the day, householders drew their blinds and closed their shutters. Everyone went to church and in every parish the churches were full from early morning. This year there was no great *Te Deum* at the Cathedral of Ste Gudule, but the packed congregation heard high mass, and as it finished, the great organ began to play. It played the National Anthem, faintly at first, and people stood straining to listen, silent and a little unsure how they ought to react. And then the organist found his courage, pulled out the stops to give the great organ its voice, and began again. As the music of the 'Brabançonne' swelled and rolled round the cathedral the people went wild. They cheered, they laughed, they wept. They stood on chairs and called for their national anthem again and again, and when it began for the fourth or fifth time they joined in. They shouted rather than sang the words, and when they reached the last line – '*Le Roi, la Loi, la Liberté*' – they positively raised the roof. The music tailed away but the people went on shouting: '*Vive le Roi! Vive Belgique! Vive la Liberté!*' The atmosphere was electric, and it changed the mood of the day.

There was almost an air of carnival, just like old times, and it quickly spread. Now nobody wanted to stay indoors behind drawn blinds and soon it seemed that the entire population had thronged into the streets and parks. They ignored edgy parties of German troops, trailing machine-guns as they paraded the streets, and were careful not to provoke them. They jostled and chattered and laughed, they congregated round the statues of Belgium's national heroes and removed their posies to pile around their pediments. It hardly mattered that the cafés were closed. The people of Brussels were already drunk on a heady cocktail of patriotism and defiance.

The shut-down in the city had infuriated the German authorities but their face-saving effort was belated and somewhat unimaginative in its conception. Late in the afternoon German soldiers were sent into the streets to post up yet another edict. It informed the citizens that, by order of the occupying power, the shops, cafés and restaurants in Brussels were to close on 21 July. It gave all Brussels a hearty laugh to cap the emotions of a satisfying day.*

The Belgian national fête had, not unnaturally, passed unnoticed in the trenches, although it ought to have been a day of celebration for the men of the 3rd Division who were due to be relieved. But the situation round Hooge was still fluid as the Germans relentlessly pounded the captured ground and it was thought best to postpone the relief for twenty-four hours. It was a night of teeming rain and the 4th Gordons were not happy. To crown the miserable day their relief was late and the men were exhausted long before it arrived.

Sgt. A. Rule.

For four days we hadn't had more than two hours' sleep at a time and there were a lot of cases of shell-shock among the men who were more highly strung.

Our relief was due at dusk, but the weary hours dragged on towards midnight and still there was no sign of it. The rain that

---

* The shops and cafés stayed open, by order of the Germans, on Independence Day the following year, but the population of Brussels retaliated by boycotting them, and shopkeepers colluded by asking outrageous prices of the few customers who were injudicious enough to enter them – fifty thousand francs for a cap in one case. The wearing of flowers was also forbidden, but the Belgians replied by wearing green leaves, the colour of hope, and went so far as to strip the blossoms of house plants in their windows so that only the green foliage was left. One lady went one better, to the admiration of her fellow citizens, and paraded the boulevards all day accompanied by her three little girls, one dressed entirely in yellow, another in red and the third in black.

had set in about midday became heavier and heavier and our spirits flagged with the increasing emptiness of our stomachs. When the long-expected relief finally did arrive, well after midnight, we were quite past caring what happened to us.

We were heavily shelled all the way out, some of the shell-bursts were so close that we could actually feel the vicious hot blast of the explosions and every blinding flash seemed to make the darkness even more intense than before, so that the column sagged and stumbled in all directions. We were still in the danger zone when dawn broke and although we were by now entirely dead beat we kept plodding along like automatons without a solitary breathing space. We picked up our company pipers at Kruistraat, but our progress along the Vlamertinghe Road was more of a stagger than a march – we scarcely knew whether the pipes were playing or not. I was parched with thirst and I vividly remember sucking the moisture from the lapel of my greatcoat, which was saturated by the teeming rain. At times I actually fell asleep on the march and, imagining that the files in front of me had performed a right wheel, I would wake up with a start to find myself in a ditch by the side of the road and the column going on straight ahead!

Our first halt came at Vlamertinghe and after that nightmare journey of six miles that had taken us *six hours*, a drink of water tasted like the nectar of the gods! We covered the last two miles to Brandhoek at a more respectable pace, and in a final supreme effort we even attempted to double to get into camp ahead of another company that had left the trenches an hour earlier. But it was beyond us!

Our camping ground was sodden and cheerless, but our weary company, with faces haggard and drawn in the morning light, lay down prepared to sleep anywhere and in any position! It was just my luck to be detailed as company mess orderly with another companion in misfortune! By the time breakfast duties were over we were both fairly shivering with cold. Having no groundsheet or blankets, we attempted a lugubrious duet outside the QM store – '*If the sergeant drinks your rum, n—e—ver mind . . .*' – but we only got curses in reply. So there was nothing for it but to lie down on the cold wet ground and keep on shivering until the sun rose. Eventually it warmed our chilled bodies and we slept like logs.

It had been their worst stint yet. Late in the day when the Battalion medical officer held a sick parade a long straggling queue of men waited to consult him with a string of ailments. There were men whose feet were blistered and painfully swollen after the long wet march in boots and socks they had worn for almost a week. There were men with high temperatures, men with sore throats, men with cuts and scratches, even a few who had been lightly wounded by flying shell splinters on the way out. But there were not many malingerers, for the MO had the reputation of being a hard man and lead-swingers got short shrift. He was as tired as his patients after four gruelling days in the line dealing with a steady stream of casualties, and too tired perhaps to recognise a case of shell-shock. The shell-shocked boy had queued up with the rest, but when his turn eventually came and he stood pallid and trembling in front of the MO he was incapable of describing his symptoms and Captain Maclaren's glare was not calculated to reassure him. All he could do was gibber and eventually blurt out what was certainly the least of his troubles, 'I've lost my hat, sir. My hat! I've lost it. It's my hat . . .' They heard Maclaren's roar two fields away. 'And what do you take *me* for! A bloody milliner? Get out before I have you put on a charge!'

The MO's own nerves were none too good, but a few days' rest would work wonders. At least they were out of it for a while and it was enough to live for the moment, away from the grinding anger of the guns, the splutter of machine-guns, the incessant vigilance of enemy snipers, the constant apprehension of an enemy attack. Even the toughest of them were thankful for the respite.

The 14th Division had taken over the line round Hooge and across the Bellewaerde Ridge. For some of these Kitchener men it was their first experience of the trenches and, although Corporal Willie Lowe was a reservist, his last experience of active service had been in South Africa more than a dozen years before. Until now his company had escaped trench-duty, though the men had grumbled mightily about fatigues, but compared to the other men in his section Lowe was an old hand.

Cpl. W. F. Lowe, 10th Bn., Durham Light Infantry, 43 Brig., 14 Div.

I had to hold a barrier on the railway and, as we had sixty-seven whizz-bangs over even before our Captain visited us, ration carrying in retrospect assumed new and tremendous advantages. When daylight came, a further novelty was introduced by persistent sniping from the Huns. When the rations came in we learned the cheerful history of the post from the men who brought them up. The last corporal in charge there had his head blown off and seven men were maimed – then another lance-corporal and five men were killed or wounded.

419

'One shell,' they said. 'They've got the range to an inch. Wouldn't let *us* stop here!' Well, when they heard that, the change in my men was laughable. It was a 'post' when we first arrived. Now they decided it was a 'guard', and on a guard they should be relieved at such and such a time after so many hours. However, I compromised by putting as many as possible into the trenches at either side and keeping only the sentries and myself at the barrier. In the little I've seen of fighting, the dangerous post is the safest – it's the getting to and fro where the peril is – so I slept and ate and lived as close to my post as possible.

Rain fell heavily all night, and the day following it rained shells as well! In the afternoon they got my poor old shelter. The sand and bits of bag covered me, my tea, the 'McConachie' ration, and my *best* pipe which I'd laid on the butt of my rifle while I was eating. I regret to say that it's buried there yet! The weary vigil crept on till about half past three in the morning. Then the whole barrier seemed to lift and we were almost smothered with sand and dust and terrible fumes.

You need an unnaturally callous nature to live under shell-fire. You can stand it for a while – especially if you are engaged in work that requires any concentration of thought, but the men whose minds were on nothing else really suffered. They ducked badly at even the furthest-off shell and looked very nerve-worn and jumpy. For the next two nights, just for a change, we suffered most from rifle fire and we were warned that our company was to make a charge to stop this. Lieutenant Peate asked me to go over the parapet and locate the wire and arrange for cutting a road.

I noticed the grass was long, so that there was little risk once I got safely over the parapet. I got the men to lay sandbags to make steps, and then I just ran up them and jumped over. Well! If it had been arranged for a cinema film it couldn't have been better timed. A shell burst *just* as I landed and blew me back against the parapet. I thought a giant had given me a thundering kick in the chest, and it was a while before I came round (afterwards I found I had splinters in my wrist, my head and my right boot). Lance-corporal Nelson came out and brought me in and later on when I was feeling better I went out and followed the wire right round. But we had no need to move after all, because the Germans were pushed back slightly on our left and the tables were turned a bit. We were relieved that night by the Ox and Bucks. I didn't trouble to tell the corporal who relieved me all the trouble there had been. I just informed him, quite truthfully, that we had lost no men *at the post*!

But there was a far worse ordeal in store for the battalions who were moving up to relieve them. The Germans had been biding their time. Knowing very well that a garrison was at its weakest during and just after a relief, they were waiting for this precise moment to make a determined effort to recover their lost ground. They reasoned that it could hardly fail, for they had a new weapon to sweep the British out of Hooge. It was their intention to roast them alive with liquid fire.

They had had no difficulty in surmising when the relief would take place, and to judge when troops who had not had time to settle down and were unfamiliar with the ground would present far less opposition than soldiers who had been in the line and on the alert for days. Even so early in the war the Germans were far more technically advanced in the use of wireless and were easily able to overhear British plans and dispositions by tapping into their communications. They knew to the hour and the minute when the relief was due to take place, and they also knew that their adversaries of recent weeks would be replaced by inexperienced troops. Having laid their plans they settled down to wait. It was the night of 29 July and, as the relief marched up to take over the trenches, it was ominously quiet.

2nd Lt. G. V. Carey, A Coy., 8th Bn., Rifle Brigade, 41 Brig., 14 Div.

I remember having a strong presentiment as I plodded up to the line that night that I should never come back from it alive. (In the event I was the only officer in my company to survive the next twenty-four hours.) We had two or three miles to cover before we reached the line, with the delays inevitable to troops moving over strange ground in the dark, and the difficulty of getting into the broken-down trenches while the 7th Battalion was getting out of them was even greater. I remember feeling certain that the tramp of feet and the clatter of rifles must have given the show away. I need not have worried – we knew afterwards that the Boche learned from more reliable sources when a relief was to take place! There was very little shelling on the way up – for which we were duly thankful! – but the absence of snipers' bullets as we filed up the communication trench from Zouave Wood was more surprising, and the silence after we got into the line became uncanny.

About an hour after we were settled in and the last of the 7th Battalion had disappeared into the darkness I decided that a bomb or two lobbed over into the Boche trench running close to my own near the crater might disturb him if he were up to mischief. So I got one of the bombers to throw over a hand-grenade which looked as if it carried about the right length. It exploded well. We waited. No reply. He sent over two more. 'This ought to rouse them,' we said. But again, no reply. There was something sinister about this. It was now about half an hour before dawn and the order for the usual morning 'stand-to' came through from the Company Commander. I started on the extreme right of my bit of the line to ensure that all my men were lining the trench with their swords fixed. Working down gradually I decided to go on along the stretch of trench which bent back from the German line almost in the form of a communication trench. There were servants and some odd men from my platoon in so-called 'shelters' along there, and I wanted to make sure that these people who are apt to be forgotten at 'stand-to' were all on the alert. Just as I was getting to the last of these there was a sudden hissing sound, and a bright crimson glare over the crater turned the whole scene red. As I looked I saw three or four distinct jets of flame, like a line of powerful fire-hoses spraying fire instead of water, shoot across my fire-trench. For some moments I was utterly unable to think. Then there was a terrific explosion and almost immediately afterwards one of my men with blood running down his face stumbled into me coming from the direction of the crater. Then every noise under Heaven broke out! There were trench mortars and bombs in our front trench, machine-guns firing, shrapnel falling over the communication trenches and over the open ground between us and the support line in Zouave Wood and high explosive shells all round the wood itself.

It was impossible to get up the trench towards the crater, so I got out of the trench to try to get a better idea of the situation. The first thing I saw was men jumping over the edge of the crater in C Company's trench and, deciding that they *must* be Boches, I told the few survivors of my platoon to open fire on them, which they promptly did. But by this time the Boches were in *my* bit of trench as well, and we saw that my handful of men couldn't possibly get back into it, and it was a death-trap to stay where we were under a shrapnel barrage. MacAfee, our Company Commander, had rushed up for a hasty consultation, and he reluctantly gave the order for me to get the remnant of my platoon back to the support line. About a dozen men of 2 Platoon were all that I could find, and we started back over the open. (Those who had faced the flame attack were never seen again.)

A retirement is a miserable business, but I have nothing but praise for the men in this one. There was *nothing* approaching a run, and every few yards they lay down and fired at any Boches we could see coming over into our line. There was a matter of four hundred yards of open ground to cover under a regular hail of machine-gun and shrapnel fire, and I've always marvelled how *anyone* got over it alive! As it was, most of my fellows were wounded during that half-hour's retirement, if not before. Eventually I literally fell into the main communication trench about twenty yards ahead of our support line. It must have been then about half past four in the morning.

B Company was in support and their OC, Cavendish, when he learned that our front line was lost, suggested that we should there and then build a barricade in the communication trench – for we still expected that the Boche would come on. So my small party set to, using sandbags from the side of the trench and it was rather ticklish work when it came to the *upper* part of the barricade, because the Boche was firing shrapnel very accurately and there were a lot of rifle and machine-gun bullets flying about.

But the men in the support trenches behind us were having a worse time – they were being heavily bombarded. We continued to stand by our barricade. I borrowed a rifle and tried to do a bit of sniping and we could see the Boche throwing up the earth in *our* front line. It now looked as if he were going to stay there! About an hour and a half later Mac came back with the grievous news that Michael Scrimgeour (commanding 3 Platoon) had been killed while reorganising his men in the wood. He also began to fuss about *my* wound, and eventually gave me a direct order to go back to the dressing station. I had to go – and that was the last I saw of poor MacAfee. He was killed that afternoon leading his men in the counter-attack.

The immediate small-scale counter-attacks were only partly successful. Despite the unexpectedness and horror of the attack the survivors rallied, and men of the 7th King's Royal Rifle Corps, who had been attacked in their turn, charged back into the carnage, into the stench of oil and smoke and burnt flesh, and fought across the charred bodies of their comrades to wrench back the remnants of part of the trench-line they had lost on the fringes of the attack.

By some miracle the Germans had stopped to consolidate and, at least for the moment, they made no attempt to press on. There was time to reorganise. Time to send for help.

News of the disaster spread quickly.

Major S. H. Cowan.

30th July. On the way to 8th Brigade about 8 a.m., Hart and I were stopped. No traffic through Ypres – and why? Roads had

423

to be kept clear for troops on their way to make a counter-attack. But where? Hooge, he thought! The first thing was to impress on the sentry that being an officer of the Corps Staff (which was a lie!) I was not affected by the order. That was quickly accomplished. And now to think. Well, I knew that our Corps had shifted a little southward leaving one of Kitchener's divisions to the 6th Corps who now embraced Hooge – and I had my own opinion of that Division.

Arrived at 8th Brigade, and Hoskyns told me the truth and we had a swearing trio with Macready (Staff Captain). The facts were: we had been booted out, not only from the biggest hole in Belgium which cost Hoskyns four hundred good men and me six weeks of anxiety, but right off the top of the knoll we'd always had and which we had fortified on all sides, and right back into the edge of the wood itself! The stories were: an attack by liquid fire, etc. etc. But none of us know of a spray that can throw twenty yards and *every* bomber can do thirty. The inference is that the whole blessed lot were caught half asleep, fell into a panic and ran. A *real* bad show. And the worst of it was that at the bottom of our hearts we could not feel very much surprised. But *I* know that if the 8th Brigade had been left there it would not have happened.

Later we had fine view of the bombardment for a counter-attack – which we learnt later, failed. We were not a cheery party by any means.

It was hardly fair. No troops on earth could have stood fast, engulfed in clouds of oily fumes, scorched by jets of searing flame. No measure of experience, no infinite amount of courage, no steadfastness of resolution could have prevailed against the unex-pected horror of liquid fire. No soldiers could have advanced more gallantly when the order came to counter-attack – and in such circumstances no counter-attack could possibly have succeeded.

The order for a general attack arrived in mid-morning from Divisional Headquarters, and the instructions were explicit. It was to start at 2.45 p.m. Fresh troops were already on their way to follow in support, but after a bombardment of forty-five minutes the 8th Rifle Brigade, now holding the edge of Zouave Wood, was to advance across the ground it had lost to retake Hooge. It was easy to understand the thinking of the Divisional Commander, for it was obvious that reinforcements rushed at top speed to the line could not possibly change places in the time available with the troops who had been stricken by the attack in the morning. It was equally plain to Brigadier Nugent, frantically trying to reorganise his shocked troops on the spot, that the 8th Battalion was a battalion no longer.

Such men as were left were at the end of their strength, and apart from the survivors of a few ragged platoons, the 'battalion' now consisted of little more than one organised company. Nugent wired a strong protest to divisional HQ: '*In my opinion situation precludes counter-attack by day. Counter-attack would be into a re-entrant and would not succeed in face of enfilade fire.*' His protest was overruled. It was essential to make a general attack as speedily as possible before the Germans tried to push on, or even the woods might be lost. The Brigadier was ordered to proceed.

Angry and sick at heart, he issued the order, knowing full well that it was fore-doomed to failure, and knowing also, as he later wrote, that:

The utilisation in the forefront of a spent battalion that, on top of the heavy fatigue of a relief, had been fighting throughout the remainder of the night, had obtained no rest, and had been without food and water since coming into the line was, to speak mildly, a serious error of judgement – for the quality of dash, so essential in such an operation, could hardly fail to be lacking.

The 'quality of dash' was not entirely lacking, for the men went forward behind their officers in a way that astonished the Brigadier. But 'dash' was not enough. Most of them were cut down by machine-guns as they started across the open ground. The few who were left when the attack fizzled out were brought out of the line that night. Kitchener's Army had been well and truly blooded. The total casualties were close to two and a half thousand, and the 41st Brigade alone had lost fifty-five officers and almost twelve hundred men. When the remnants limped out of the line at dusk the 43rd Brigade went in to take its place.

The 10th Durhams had been resting for two days in a camp near Poperinghe.

Cpl. W. F. Lowe.

My time was mostly spent teaching the scouts and snipers sketching, and how and what to report, and how to develop their powers of observation. They quite enjoyed it (it certainly gave great satisfaction to the officers) and the lessons might have led to useful results – had the men not met so early with unfortunate ends. As it was, our class was interrupted on the 30th by a 'stand-to' and another exhausting, heavily laden, rush back to Ypres and up to the trenches.

All night we endured heavy shelling, and the next day was

just one long bombardment. I'd had difficulty in keeping men in their firing bays before, but never to such an extent as *this* day. As soon as a parapet is overturned they flock into the next, and then the next, until, of course, when a shell *does* reach them, the casualties are really excessive because they're all crowded together. I can't see why a German gunner would select a battered bay when whole ones are standing, yet you can't get the men to remain after *'she's been blown in'*.

Crowding is *bad*. Lance-Corporal Nelson rushed into my section with the most awful expression of horror on his face I've ever seen in my life, and he shouted at me, 'I've shot Lance-Corporal Fidler!' Now, Lance-Corporal Fidler was his best friend! Nelson was wounded himself, and he was far too agitated to know what I was saying, or even to understand what he was saying himself. What had happened no one can tell but, *if he did shoot them*, it seems possible that he happened to be wounded just as he was loading his rifle, and the rifle went off and the bullet passed through Lance-Corporal Carling's brain, then touched the wood or sandbag on top of the dug-out and entered Lance-Corporal Fidler's arm, *then* his thigh, and then went into Private Jenning's leg, and *then* into another man's stomach!

Again I pointed out the folly of crowding into so-called 'shelter'. By now whole stretches of the trenches were levelled and deserted and any in our section that still had *any* appearance of shelter would soon have been crowded out, had I not stood at the worst end and forced back the men (and NCOs too!) of other regiments who tried to get in. We'd been reinforced (never mind by whom, I'd rather not say!) and the new regiment was all mixed up with ours. This is bad, very bad! However, by now my men were aroused and would let no one through. They could crowd in their own sections as they liked, but budge we wouldn't!

When we were relieved I was surprised to find I could hardly walk. I'd had no sleep and now that all the excitement was over I felt done up. I was warned to attend an inquiry into charges of 'sleeping on duty' made against several of our men. An officer had been down the trench and found no one awake. I cannot say whether the inquiry was held or not. Most of these men were wounded or killed in the afternoon – but I should have been delighted to attend. From my diary I could prove that the men had only been allowed twenty-two hours' sleep in eight days. The Captain had aroused me myself at 4 a.m. and *without* a rifle or hat – and you should never take your equipment off in the trenches! I stood sleeping on my feet, my head resting on my arms folded on the parapet. When he woke me I had absolutely no idea where I was!

Far more work would be done in such a restricted area by dividing the men into two 'shifts'. The 'off-shift' should be left severely alone to make the best of what poor sleep they can get. The 'on-shift' would be fresh and alert for work or fighting. As it is, the wakened men are a nuisance, and a positive danger. The nervous start banging away without inquiry, the dazed wander into the way, and the rest ask absurd questions, which is natural when people are suddenly alarmed from a sound sleep. Six cool well-rested men are worth forty startled into action!

They had stayed for almost a week in the battered line round Hooge, grimly digging in and sheltering as best they could from shell-fire that hardly stopped, for the Germans were alert and determined to thwart any ideas the British might entertain of renewing the attack. But the British Command had belatedly learned the lesson that hasty improvisation would not do and that only a well-organised and well-prepared assault could succeed in pushing the enemy out of Hooge and winning back 'the biggest hole in Belgium', but they had no intention of entrusting it to the inexperienced volunteers of Kitchener's Army.

This calumny was as ill judged as it was unjust. Like the Territorials before them, Kitchener's volunteers had proved that they were no weaklings. The criticism muttered in high places did not reach the ears of the rank and file, and it would not have worried them greatly if it had. They knew they had done their best. They had received high praise and even rare expressions of admiration from the senior officers on the spot, not least from Brigadier-General Nugent. And they had stuck it out. Best of all, one of their number had won the Victoria Cross – the first in the New Army. And the New Army was not a little proud of it.*

When the Regulars of the 6th Division took over the line and managed to recover Hooge, Kitchener's Army did not grudge them their victory.

---

* In the immediate aftermath of the liquid fire attack, Lieutenant Sidney Woodroffe of the 8th Rifle Brigade bombed his way out after his small detachment was surrounded and cut off, rallied his small party and led them back through a hail of fire to counter-attack. He was killed at the head of his men while attempting to cut a path through wire entanglements, and awarded a posthumous VC.

Chapter 29

It was exactly a year since Great Britain had gone to war on 4 August 1914 and the 1st Coldstream Guards had been fighting from the start. They had fought their way back in the long retreat from Mons in a series of brilliant rearguard actions. They had fought in the battles of the Marne and the Aisne and raced north in October to meet the Germans at Ypres in the great battle that brought the German army to a standstill and saved the Channel ports. At the end of the autumn fighting the Battalion had been reduced to a hundred and fifty officers and men. But the drafts of reinforcements from the Reserve Battalion which had brought them almost up to strength were also Regular soldiers and Guardsmen, long-schooled in the discipline and traditions that had forged the reputation of the Guards as the best of all the soldiers in an army that was generally acknowledged to be the best army in the world.

Fighting in the trenches was a sad comedown from the cut and thrust of mobile warfare and the particular length of trench-line the Coldstream were now inhabiting was not one that would have been easily envisaged by a guardsman drilling on the immaculate parade ground at Caterham or mounting the King's Guard at Buckingham Palace in the piping days of peace. It was in a particularly nasty sector of the line at Cambrin near the la Bassée Canal where the tunnellers of both sides had been busy and the frequent explosions had reduced the trenches to a meandering shambles of loops and saps. The British and German lines were barely thirty yards apart and in the sector occupied by the Coldstream Guards the distance was even narrower. Two large mine craters nicknamed Vesuvius and Etna lay between them and the German front line and each side held one lip – a good deal too close for comfort. The Guards had constructed a new front line a little further back with a long listening-sap running forward to 'their' side of the crater. Every sound and every movement could be heard clearly by the troops across the way and although silence was rigidly observed and orders were given as far as possible by hand signals, it was difficult even for the disciplined Guards to make no sound at all in the ordinary way and, no matter how stealthily they went about changing places with an incoming battalion, almost impossible during a relief. A few nights earlier the Coldstream had suffered badly when the Scots Guards moved in to relieve them. The Germans were alerted by the shuffling of movement and the occasional inadvertent clink of equipment and sent over a shower of mortar bombs, giant Minenwerfers fired from close range, which had caused havoc in 2 Company's trench. There were several casualties, including two of the senior sergeants, and the Company Commander, Captain the Honourable Thomas Agar-Robartes was furious.

Lt. G. Barry, MC, 1st Bn., Coldstream Guards.

Tommy Robartes was a remarkable man. He was a Member of Parliament, and one of the very few men I've ever come across who appeared to be entirely devoid of any form of fear. Nobody ever saw him duck for a shell or take cover when bullets were flying around. His company would have followed him anywhere. He was infuriated at the loss of his two sergeants and swore he would get his own back on the Germans.

Now it so happened that while he was on leave in England Tommy had bought a number of musical instruments, including a drum, which he'd had sent over to France with the intention of forming a company band. It numbered about ten men under a corporal and when we were out of the line or in billets they used to practise and they soon became so good that they were even allowed to play on route-marches. So when Tommy's fertile imagination got to work on how to avenge the death of his two sergeants he immediately thought of the band. A large number of Germans would be lured to a certain spot by the music of the band, whereupon they would be well and truly shelled!

Before we went back to the trenches Tommy explained his plan to the Commanding Officer, Lieutenant-Colonel John Ponsonby, and the Colonel was tickled to death at the idea and gave him his blessing. At three minutes to midnight on the following night the band would start a musical entertainment as close to the German line as possible – in the saphead under the lip of Etna. Then the gunners behind would lay down a heavy barrage on the German trenches immediately behind and on both sides of *their* lip of the crater. The barrage would start exactly at midnight. Colonel Ponsonby made only one stipulation – that the front line on both sides of Etna should be evacuated for a short distance before the show started, and the troops moved back to the support line. He was under no delusions as to what the outcome would be!

In order to make a really first-class kill, Tommy decided that, like all good shows, this one would have to be previously advertised. A large notice was prepared and stuck into the ground that night above the parapet of our front line so that the Germans could read it through their periscopes the next morning. It was written in German and read: '*Our Band Will Play Tonight at Midnight*'.

It was 4 August and the Coldstream felt that on this auspicious date the Germans might think that the 'concert' was intended to mark the completion of a year of war.

The instruments were brought up from the transport line, not without difficulty, and at a quarter to twelve they were passed along the front line to the band waiting at the sap-entrance ready to move up to the listening post under the lip of the crater. Robartes had made a point of warning them that it might be a dangerous job, but no one had backed out.

Lt. G. Barry MC.

It was a lovely calm summer evening. Hardly a gun was firing along the front. Quite a number of spectators couldn't resist coming to watch the show, especially myself, since the party was to take place practically in my platoon sector. So, after that part of the front line was evacuated in accordance with the Colonel's orders, I went along to Etna. The band was already there and waiting. It was also clear that the Germans had read our notice for they had begun to collect opposite us, and we could hear movements along their trenches and even see the spiked tops of their pickelhaube helmets against the skyline. From that distance – only about ten to twelve yards – we could hear them talking quite distinctly.

Then Tommy appeared, smoking a cigar as usual, and the men got their instruments into position. It had been decided that the overture to the grand symphony should be 'The Watch on the Rhine' – we hoped that the Germans would appreciate the compliment! I know that I, for one, waited in a state of intense excitement for the curtain to rise, and then, at exactly three minutes to twelve, Tommy nodded to the band and the music began.

It would be difficult to picture a more bizarre scene on that warm summer night – the strains of music from deep down in the ground, the orchestra on our side of a deadly dividing line and the audience, our enemy, occupying underground stalls on the other! 'The Watch on the Rhine' was played through to the end and the band stopped. Immediately from across the mine crater came cheers, and shouts and clapping. Some of them shouted, '*Hoch, hoch*,' and one voice called, '*Long live the Kaiser.*' Tommy looked at his watch and saw that there was still more than a minute to go to midnight and on no account must the audience be allowed to disperse, so he motioned the band to start an encore.

The men struck up again and had got about half-way through when Tommy gave the signal to stop. By this time there were only about fifteen seconds left to get clear of the saphead before the barrage was due to come down. There was some difficulty, I remember, getting the band out of the narrow trench quickly without a lot of noise – especially the man with the drum! The rest of us followed behind and we hadn't even got out of the sap into the front line when there was a swish and a roar and the first shells screamed over our heads and plunged into the ground just behind. A good old scramble then took place to get along the communication trench to the support line! A constant stream of our shells was pouring into the German trenches, and their flashes were lighting up the darkness around. But it wasn't long before we heard a dull report from behind the enemy lines and, looking up into the sky, we saw the lighted tail of a Minenwerfer bomb turning over and over, as it began to fall. It made a noise like the rush of an express train but fortunately it fell behind us and we only got a rain of stones and earth thrown from the crater. More followed in quick succession but by this time the band was out of the danger area and we all reached the support line without mishap.

I can't remember how long our own guns went on firing, probably not more than ten minutes, for no one but a fool would have remained in such a death-trap any longer, but the Germans continued to pound our front line round Etna with Minnies and 5.9 shells for well over two hours. Not once did they think of putting some shells into our support line, and even then they would have got us a second time when we eventually re-occupied the front line, for it should not have been very difficult for them to guess that we would repair it during the first lull and all they had to do was to give us half an hour and then put down their barrage in the same place as before. As it was, we didn't have one single casualty.

Tommy now felt that he had had his revenge and decided he would treat the Germans to a real genuine show. So, before dawn, another notice was put up:

Our Band Will Play Again Tonight
This Time No Danger

That evening the band assembled again but in a different place where the two lines were a little farther apart. They gave a first-class concert, and even sang some songs, but the only response from the Germans was a few bullets overhead! The following morning at stand-to I saw through my periscope that the Germans had put up a notice on *their* front line. It read:

We Have Taken Warsaw and
Captured 100,000 Russian Prisoners

The implication was clearly: '*So sucks to you!*' But the Coldstream were satisfied that they had won on points.

The Germans, never slow to trumpet their victories, flashed news of the fall of Warsaw round the world and a very few hours after they had obliged the Coldstream with this information in their trench-line in France, a similar placard was hoisted above a Turkish trench at Lone Pine on far-off Gallipoli. The Australians of the 5th Battalion AIF read it incredulously and instantly dismissed it as a 'furphy'.

The word 'furphy' had been coined many months before in the training camps at Melbourne, where the rubbish and the contents of latrines were removed every day by carts prominently blazoned with the name of the contractor, which happened to be Furphy. The word 'furphy', meaning (in its politest form) 'rubbish', had rapidly gained currency and on Gallipoli, where rumours abounded, it was particularly useful. Every carrying party returning to the trenches from the beach had a tale to tell: Greece had declared war on Turkey and was going to land a hundred thousand men on the peninsula. Or, Rumania had declared war and was marching through Bulgaria to Constantinople. Or, two hundred thousand French were landing at Helles with the intention of taking over the whole peninsula. All were furphies, but the news of the fall of Warsaw happened to be true. It was serious news, for it meant that the Germans were winning on the eastern front and that the Russians were in retreat. The report reached Gallipoli on the eve of the 'big show' planned for 6 August when the Anzacs were to storm the high ridges in conjunction with a new British landing at Suvla Bay. In the minds of the men who conducted the war it was now

432

more important than ever that the big show should succeed. In a few days, with a modicum of luck, the peninsula might be secured and the Royal Navy might be steaming up the Dardanelles on the way to Constantinople.

The War Cabinet in London was desperate for first-hand information and Asquith had arranged for the Cabinet Secretary, Sir Maurice Hankey, to travel to the Dardanelles to report direct to him on the situation as he saw it, and so that Hankey would not be embarrassed by having to pass his reports through open channels, he also arranged for a King's Messenger to bring them back. Hankey's views would be confidential and he was to pull no punches.

Sir Maurice visited every corner of the peninsula. He spent time at Cape Helles ('I shall have to paint a picture of great discomfort and hardship . . . our men are in good heart'). He rode close to the front line for a view of Achi Baba ('The only difficulty for the Turkish gunner on Achi Baba is the bewildering variety of targets – crowded beaches, horse lines, rest camps, flotillas of trawlers . . .'). He scrambled up Gully Ravine ('Proper sanitation is impossible in places as the Turkish dead lie in heaps, the smell being bad, while the thought of masses of flies in such conditions makes the flesh creep . . .'). He visited every beach ('Really rather horrible. A dust storm rages for a great part of most days, the sun is intensely hot, of shade there is none, the soil is soft sand, very fatiguing to move about in, the flies are execrable, and, worst of all, the Turks shell at frequent intervals . . .'). He went to Anzac ('Several very deep, steep and bare ravines, the sides everywhere scarred by hundreds of "dug-outs" where the men off duty live like anchorites and hermits. The hills, some four hundred feet above the sea, are crowned with the most amazingly complete labyrinth of trenches . . .').

Sir Maurice spent a good deal of time in the Australian trenches at Anzac for his cousin was Second-in-Command of an Australian battalion and escorted him up to the front line for a close-up view. Hankey was deeply impressed. He wrote to the Prime Minister:

I do hope that we shall hear no more of the 'indiscipline' of this extraordinary Corps, for I don't believe that for military qualities of every kind their equal exists. Their physique is wonderful and their intelligence of a high order. Harassed by continuous shelling, living in intense heat, tormented by flies, compelled to carry their water and most of their supplies and ammunition by hand 400 feet up the hills and deprived of any recreation except occasionally bathing, they are nevertheless in the highest spirits and spoiling for a fight.

Since it seemed the only way to get out of their present situation the Australians were certainly 'spoiling for a fight', but their spirits were not so high as the visitor assumed. The Anzacs made no bones about the fact that they were fed up. Perspiring in the baking heat, with frequent, unwelcome visitations of dysentery, with a monotonous thirst-provoking diet of bully beef and biscuits enlivened occasionally by tough unsavoury stew, and with no rest to look forward to but the weary toil of fatigues, it was hardly astonishing that they were sick of the peninsula and sick to death of the war. It was not what they had bargained for.

Pte. W. Carrol, 21st Bn., AIF.

The war broke out when I was up in Queensland and we were shearing and there were no telephones or wireless in those days and the shearer said, 'Oh, there's war. They're going to have war.' They all said it wouldn't last a week. They wanted men to keep Arabs and Turks away from the Suez Canal because it linked England and Australia and New Zealand and China and India and so it was very important to have that channel free with all the food and ammunition and soldiers going backwards and forwards. They wanted Australia to send men – and I was one of the mugs. We all came down from the station, and they said anyone who would like to go to join the Army and go to Egypt to defend the canal was to report to barracks, and there was such a crowd and I didn't expect to get through. We said it wouldn't last a week, or two at the most. What fun it would be. That's what we thought, actually. We were proved to be a lot of suckers.

First of all, I was in the 13th, the Light Horse. Everyone wanted to ride a horse. With sixty pounds on your back, you didn't get much encouragement to join the infantry! But then they must have had ideas that a horse was no good at digging trenches – you must have infantry, so they had to transfer a lot of us. We were all wishing to go. We thought, 'The war will be over before we get there.'

When we got on the boat my sister and father came down to see me off and as I went up the gangway an old aunt pushed a little bag into my hand and there were ten gold sovereigns in it. Just think of that today! The first thing we knew was in the morning we'd slipped anchor and the two big ships, the *Euripides* and the *Ulysses*, both Blue Funnel ships that had been converted to troop carriers, were steaming out on their trip to the Suez Canal. We didn't touch any other Australian port. We went by the Luin, a headland in Western Australia, and that was our last view of Australia. All the troops were on deck and you should have heard all the noise and yelling that went on. We all hung over the rail. It was fairly rough and the lights on shore were getting dimmer and dimmer. I think everyone was fond of their country. They were watching – I suppose they were thinking of their wives and sweethearts. I hadn't a sweetheart, I hadn't a mother, so it was a fairly easy trip for me, but as the lights got dimmer and dimmer they all went down below, and that night I never heard the men go to bed so quietly. The Captain said, 'Have your last look at Australia.' He couldn't have spoken a truer word because 50 per cent of the infantry on board never came back.

If the Aussies had hesitated to treat Sir Maurice Hankey to a recital of their woes they were only too willing to express their views to any other passerby, regardless of his rank.

Cpl. G. Gilbert, A Sqn., 13th Light Horse.

We had no horses at Anzac. We were serving as infantry and we were all crawling with lice, thirsty, hungry and completely browned off. One of our Generals came up to inspect us in our trenches in front of Lone Pine, and he was a fatherly sort, always used to ask the blokes about their family and stuff like that. He spoke to all the troops and he said to one soldier on the firing step, 'Don't forget to write home. How is your father?' The bloke answered, 'He's dead.' A bit later the General coming back along the trench asked the *same* question to *same* soldier, 'And how is your father?' And the bloke said, 'He's *still* dead, the lucky bugger.' We all laughed. I don't know what the General thought! But the tale went the rounds.

Col. G. Beith, 24th Bn., AIF.

I went down to one of my boys, I said, 'How are you getting on, son?' He said, 'I'm not too bad, I'll tell you what, if I could get out of this bloody place I'd volunteer to scrub out the Melbourne exhibition building with a tooth brush!'

Cpl. G. Gilbert.

My best mate and I used to go on the firing step together in Lone Pine. One morning moving into Lone Pine trenches one soldier just ahead of me turned to my mate and said, 'Come on, Dick, you and I will go on together this time.' One used the

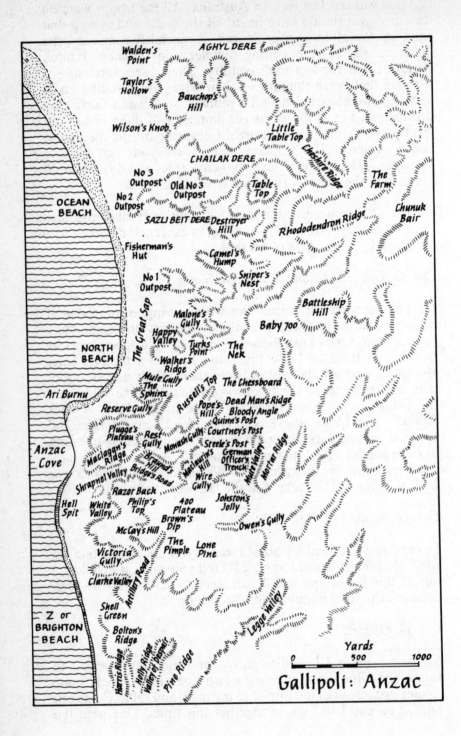

Gallipoli: Anzac

periscope to see what Johnny Turk was doing, the other was ready for any quick sniping at anything that moved (the trenches of the Turks were only thirty or forty yards away and in some places closer). The rest of us waited in an old dug-out, to take our turn. The next minute, *bang*, Dick got a bullet right through his head, and he fell at our feet. He made no sound at all! He was still alive when the stretcher-bearers took him down to the beach to be put on a hospital ship for Malta. But he died there. We think an enemy sniper must have been just out in front using slight ground cover waiting for our relief guard to come in. I made sure I got that sniper later on.

In these high lands where the Anzacs were perched among rough outcrops separated by sheer drops and steep ravines there was no continuous trench-line, only rudimentary support-lines, and few conventional communication trenches. But the outcrops had been ringed and fortified with short lengths of trench, sometimes tunnelled underground and pierced with loopholes to command the Turkish lines. They called them 'posts', and the Anzacs clung to them like limpets.

Pte. N. Scott, 6th (Victoria) Bn., 2nd Brig., 1st Australian Div.

I'll try to describe a fortnight my battalion spent in a place in the firing line known as Steel's Post. To draw it mildly, I might state that at Steel's Post we were in a hell on earth, with all the most fiendish appliances of man thrown in just to spur things on a bit. I had charge of a post of ten men in a position some forty yards in front of the firing line. This position was a maze of underground passages and the fire-trench was also in the form of a tunnel, with ten loopholes looking down the side of a gradual slope towards the Turks. This post was the extreme left of the Australian position and the New Zealanders were on my left. Well the NZs sapped forward and placed a 12-pound mountain gun right alongside our post. This gun fired only ten shots when Mr Turk spotted its position. Then things began to move! For a solid hour the Turks shelled it with every kind of gun they had but not *one* of those shells even touched the gun. My post got the blooming lot! Sixty-four shells dropped into my twelve yards of trench in one hour. They knocked all the tunnel work in, smashed our firing line to atoms and *still* were not satisfied. I received orders to move out all my men except one.

Well, the two of us dodged shells for another hour. One shell burst within four feet of where we were standing and how the

Dickens the splinters missed us, I can't make out. It was a nice big 8-inch shell and it buried us where we stood, right up to our necks. The sensation of being buried by a big shell is terrible. (I know that all the faces of my friends and relations seemed to crowd before me, and I remembered every bad deed of my life in a flash. That's the time you wish you had been a saint all your life!) Well they got me out and told me I was lucky! Lucky mind you!

Before the end of the fortnight I'd managed to get buried three times. One shell didn't bury me, but it simply bashed me up against the side of the trench as though I was a blooming sandbag. I just sagged forward, crumpled up and forgot everything. To give you some idea of what an ordinary 6-inch Howitzer shell can do, I saw a machine-gun smashed to atoms by one, and the crew of a corporal and five men wiped clean off the face of the earth. They were picked up in pieces and carried out in their blankets. That was on just an ordinary 'quiet' day at Steel's Post. We heard later that before we went in Steel's Post had been comparatively quiet, and the Turks must have just opened up all of a sudden. At the end of that fortnight of bashing, tearing, relentless shelling, we were all nerves, every one of us. The stuffing was knocked clean out of us. Steel's went back to its normal state when we left. It was just like the luck of the poor old 6th. We seemed to walk straight into all the music.

Pte. W. Carrol.

We were right against the Turks. You could touch a Turk on the head the trenches were that close at Courtney's Post. That was the first place I was put on, Courtney's Post. The Turks were good soldiers, you couldn't deny that. He's always been a good soldier, right from the Crusaders and Saracens. But the Turks were quite good types. Oh, you don't tell me! He's no harm. Sometimes we'd be talking to each other and we'd say, 'Got any weed?' Sometimes we ran out of tobacco and when you were a smoker and had the feeling to smoke it drove you mad. The Turks said, 'Oh, we've tons of tobacco. Have you got any meat?' They'd got no meat. You could hear the fowls crowing at the back of their trenches. There were no chickens on our side but we had a barter with bags of Turkish tobacco for our bully beef. That's how the war goes on. But it wouldn't do to be getting too friendly with those men, because you might give them the idea that they could do what they liked and break through. You want to let them know they're not welcome in our lines. We put barbed wire all the way along at night time along our trenches, and when we woke up in the morning they'd trained grappling hooks and they'd pulled all our barbed wire over in front of their trenches. All the trouble we went to put all our barbed wire all along and then the Turks grabbed it over in front of theirs and they thought that was a good joke! They were laughing and waving their shovels.

But the Turks were ferocious soldiers and they were prepared to give no quarter, for they were not only fighting in defence of their homeland, they were fighting a jihad – a holy war against the infidel – and they were filled with holy zeal. '*Allah, Allah, Allah!*' they shouted as they plunged forward to attack. During their training the Anzacs, like the British, had also been urged to yell to encourage offensive spirit as they bayoneted the swinging sandbags which then represented the enemy. Now, when they were charging flesh and blood Turks, the New Zealanders dashed into a fight with a war cry shouting the words they had picked up from Egyptian vendors of hard-boiled eggs who shouted their wares round the training camp. '*Eggs is cooked!*' they bellowed. The imprecations that spurred the Aussies on to victory varied, but their favourite expression occurred so frequently that, according to interpreters who interrogated the prisoners, the Turks who invoked Allah as they charged genuinely believed that '*Bloody bastard!*' was an invocation to the God of the Australians. Or so ran the tale, and although it might well have been a furphy, it amused the Aussies no end.

'*Oh my, I don't want to die,*' sang the British soldiers in France, '*I want to go home.*' The Turkish soldiers' philosophy was much the same. Sometimes, in quiet periods, they could be heard singing in their lines:

> In Çanakkale there is a market with looking-glasses,
> Mama, I am going
> to meet the enemy,
> And I'm so young.

> In Çanakkale there is a cypress tree.
> Some of us are married,
> Some of us betrothed,
> And I am so young.

> In Çanakkale there is a pitcher full of water.
> Mothers and fathers have lost
> All they hoped for,
> And I am so young.

439

In Çanakkale they have shot me.
They put me in a grave
While I was still alive,
And I am so young.

Çanakkale was the name the Turks gave to the peninsula the British knew as Gallipoli. Within a few hours, when they had captured the rugged ridges beyond and scaled the heights of Chunuk Bair the Anzacs confidently expected that the Turks would be in full flight and that shortly afterwards the peninsula itself would fall.

On the eve of the attack Divine Service was held for the men of the 1st Australian Brigade who wished to attend. The padre had some difficulty in finding a suitable spot close to the trenches and he hit eventually on a small hollow in Wire Gully near the lines in front of Lone Pine. It was lined with ammunition boxes for it had also been picked out as a suitable place in which to make a reserve dump of rifle ammunition, but there was room among them for the fifty or so men who filtered down from the line to take part. Returning with a carrying party from a laborious trek up from the beach, Sergeant Drummond of the 5th Battalion was astonished to find a service in full swing. '*Hide me, Oh my Saviour, hide,*' they were singing, ' '*til the storms of life are past* . . .' The sergeant did not mean to disrupt the service, but he had a job to do and it was impossible to do it quietly so the rest of the hymn and the prayers that followed were accompanied by the slither and thud of ammunition boxes sliding down a plank into the hollow. The padre, who was about to embark on his sermon, was not pleased and he shouted up to Drummond, 'Are you aware that you are desecrating the first church in Gallipoli?' 'I'm sorry, sir,' Drummond called back, 'but the ammo's just as necessary for tomorrow as your sermon, isn't it?' The padre was a reasonable man. He smiled a little sadly. 'Unfortunately, I suppose it is,' he admitted.

The ammunition was far from plentiful, but it had been garnered with care and now a good supply of shells was piled around gun positions, and rifle ammunition stacked behind the trenches in readiness for the battle. On the offshore islands the British troops were already embarking on the lighters that would carry them to Suvla Bay. At GHQ on Lemnos Sir Ian Hamilton, having made his dispositions, could only wait and hope, and possibly pray, for success in the morning. The King's Messenger was on the point of departure and by the light of a hurricane lamp Sir Maurice Hankey hastily penned a postscript to the latest report he would carry to the Prime Minister. In the event of success rapid political decisions must be taken and Hankey had given this matter deep thought. Since formal peace negotiations with Turkey would take some weeks, a

440

provisional armistice would have to be arranged in the immediate aftermath of a Turkish defeat, which, he suggested, should provide for '*Disarmament of all the Turkish forces . . . The handing over of arms to the Allies . . . An Allied Garrison in Constantinople . . . Disarmament of the forts in the Dardanelles and Bosphorus.*' He offered to stay on to supervise the Armistice arrangements but, being a realistic man, he added, '*In the alternative event of complete failure or partial success involving a further period of trench warfare, I shall come home as soon as I can. The position then will be rather grave.*'

But no one anticipated failure.

Chapter 30

The landing at Suvla Bay should have been easy. The bay was deep and it was wide – a long, curving coast of sandy beaches and a low plain reaching out to the Anafarta Hills more than two miles away. Nearer the shore were a few gentle hills, hardly high enough to be obstacles, and although there was one possible stumbling-block – a large salt lake that lay just behind the shoreline separated from the bay by a narrow spit of land – it was expected to be dry in summer and there seemed no reason to expect that it would present a problem.

To the south, on the right of Suvla Bay, rose the Sari Bair Ridge – less of a ridge than a succession of razor-edged spurs and peaks, with deep cols and gorges covered in dense scrub. It was wild and untracked country, many times more forbidding than the heights of Anzac beyond it. For obvious reasons, the Sari Bair Ridge was almost undefended, but if it could be grasped at the same time as the landing, while the troops were rushing inland at Suvla Bay, the Turks would be outflanked and their positions at Anzac immediately to the south would rapidly become untenable. It would be a mammoth task, and the only chance of success depended on the element of surprise, for only a madman would imagine that it could possibly be approached by the wild unknown terrain where the western end of the ridge dropped to the sea. But this was the feat that the New Zealanders, backed by some unfortunate newly arrived battalions of Kitchener's Army, were expected to attempt, marching by night across the cliff-top tracks and gullies to the foot of Sari Bair. Then they were to climb. The force was divided into three columns and it was estimated that by clambering up by different routes they would arrive simultaneously on top of the ridge well before dawn. After that, as they moved forward unseen to capture the height of Chunuk Bair, the worst would be over and by comparison mere fighting would be easy. From the summit of Chunuk Bair in the first light of day they would at last be in sight of the Dardanelles.

The 'big show' opened on 6 August with two preliminary attacks.

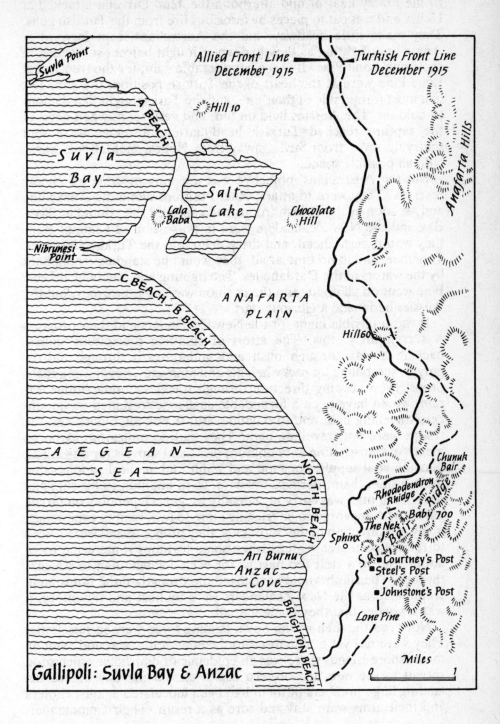

Allied Front Line
December 1915

Turkish Front Line
December 1915

Suvla Point

A BEACH

Suvla Bay

Hill 10

Salt Lake

Lala Baba

Chocolate Hill

Anafarta Hills

Nibrunesi Point

C BEACH — B BEACH

ANAFARTA PLAIN

Hill 60

AEGEAN SEA

NORTH BEACH

Chunuk Bair

Rhododendron Ridge

The Nek

Baby 700

Sari Bair Ridge

Sphinx

Ari Burnu
Anzac Cove

Courtney's Post

Steel's Post

Johnstone's Post

BRIGHTON BEACH

Lone Pine

Miles

0   1

Gallipoli: Suvla Bay & Anzac

In the brassy heat of mid-afternoon the 42nd Division attacked at Helles and was cut to pieces by ferocious fire from the Turkish guns. They made little headway, but the Australians leapt forward at Anzac and, fighting as they had never fought before, succeeded in capturing Lone Pine. It was a considerable gain, for the trenches at Lone Pine were at the heart of the Turkish position, the strongest and most formidable of their line, and the Turks fought like demons to hold on. The Aussies held on too, and very soon, when news of the capture reached Turkish headquarters, reserves were sent scurrying away from Suvla, away from Helles, making for Anzac with all possible speed.

But the Australians' objective was not only to draw off enemy reserves. They were to attack other positions along the Anzac line and, as soon as the British troops had captured the ground at Suvla Bay and the New Zealanders were in possession of Chunuk Bair, they would push ahead, and drive deep into the Turkish defences. Together, and in no time at all, they would be standing triumphant by the waters of the Dardanelles. The fighting and bombing at Lone Pine went on all night, and the position was still precarious, but the Aussies had made a glorious start.

It was a terrible night for the New Zealanders and their progress was cripplingly slow. The effort of climbing precipitous slopes, hacking a way through bush and undergrowth through narrow gorges, scrabbling up rocky heights and pinnacles, negotiating sheer drops, even keeping direction through trackless mountainous terrain, would have been a formidable challenge to skilled mountaineers travelling light and in daytime. But it was pitch dark and the troops were not travelling light. They had no mules, no carts, no means of transporting ammunition, picks and shovels for digging in, plus the vital supplies of food and water and medical supplies that must sustain them, perhaps for days, so in addition to his rifle and pack, each man was carrying a deadly weight. Depending on Greek guides who appeared to be trusting more to luck than to experience, many lost direction in the 'short cuts' they proposed and were forced to retrace their weary steps when some tortuous route came to an abrupt end in a cleft too narrow for even a single man to squeeze through. The climb would have taxed the strength of the fittest men. Debilitated as the New Zealanders were by heat and dysentery, it was a wonder that they made it at all.

Not even the men of the Suvla landing force were in fine fettle. They were not yet acclimatised to the enervating heat and even on the offshore islands there was an epidemic of diarrhoea which soon spread to the new arrivals. To cap it all, on the day before the landing large numbers of them had been inoculated against cholera and their arms were stiff and sore as a result. Their Commander,

General Sir Frederick Stopford, was also under the weather. The three newly arrived divisions destined for Suvla Bay had been formed into a single new Corps and Sir Ian Hamilton had begged the War Office to supply an experienced senior officer to command it, even going so far as to suggest that General Byng or General Rawlinson would admirably fit the bill. But Byng and Rawlinson were serving in France and invaluable though the experience of either officer would be, Lord Kitchener dismissed out of hand the very idea that they could be spared for months – or even days – on end. And there was another point to be considered. In command of the 10th Division, part of the newly formed IX Corps, was one of the Army's most senior generals and under no circumstances could Major-General Mahon be expected to take orders from a Corps Commander less senior than himself. It would be an unthinkable breach of etiquette and tradition and not for a moment could Kitchener contemplate such an outrageous idea. A senior man must be appointed, and that was that.

The difficulty was that officers above the rank of Major-General were thin on the ground. Lieutenant-Generals were only one step below Field Marshals, the highest rank in the Army, and only Generals Ewart and Stopford were available for active service – and even they had only been brought out of comfortable retirement by the exigencies of war. The choice had fallen on Sir Frederick Stopford, and although weighed down with honours earned in more than four decades of distinguished service, mostly in staff or administrative posts, Stopford's experience of soldiering in the field was negligible. He had never led troops into battle, he had never commanded so much as a battalion in an engagement, he was sixty-one years old, and his health was indifferent. But there was no one else. On the eve of the landing at Suvla Bay General Stopford was not a happy man. He had sprained his knee that morning and the Staff Officer sent by Sir Ian Hamilton to ensure that his instructions were understood was startled to find the General lying down in his tent and disturbed by his frankly expressed forebodings. The optimism with which Stopford had originally greeted the Suvla plan had evaporated in the days of waiting and reflection. He was worried in particular by the paucity of artillery support he could expect, for as it dashed inland, the IX Corps was to secure positions for its own guns which would only begin to land when they were consolidated, and although he was reminded that the guns of the warships would be covering the landings Stopford was not re-assured. He dwelt on the fact that experience in France had shown that strong trench systems could only be attacked with the help of large numbers of Howitzers, and was doubtful of the assurance that on the evidence of reconnaissance aircraft no such systems existed, and although it was stressed and stressed again that everything depended on rapid advance to attain the inland heights before the Turks could bring in reinforcements, Stopford doubted that the prowess of the New Army men was up to securing the beach-head in the dark, let alone advancing to seize the first vital positions. Assured that the opposition could not possibly amount to more than five battalions. Stopford doubted the accuracy of the estimate. Finally he said, '*Tell Sir Ian Hamilton that I am going to do my best, and that I hope to be successful. But he must realise that if the enemy proves to be holding a strong line of continuous entrenchments I shall be unable to dislodge him until more guns are landed.*' It was a bad beginning and, with hindsight, the outcome was inevitable.

A little after 9.30 that evening the first contingent of the main force landed at Suvla Bay. By ten o'clock four battalions were ashore and more were on the way. A single rifle shot from the shore had struck one lighter and an unfortunate naval rating was the only casualty. A short way to the north two Yorkshire battalions advanced in the dark and, at far greater cost, captured the main Turkish garrison on the hill of Lala Baba. But there the advance came to a halt.

In the long bitter aftermath of the failed Gallipoli campaign the Anzacs could hardly be blamed for thinking they had been let down, and the impression took deeper root as the decades passed. More than seventy years on, the film *Gallipoli* told the story of just one of the tragic happenings on the fatal morning of 7 August. The framework of the plot was fictional and one-sided but in essence and in all its stark reality it was true, and it came to epitomise the whole desperate endeavour – the microcosm of the Australians' sacrifice on Gallipoli.

The attack at the Nek should have been a minor operation. It was such a narrow causeway of land to cross, only sixty yards at its widest, and it guarded the hill they called Baby 700, a position so strong that a lone assault could not possibly succeed. But in conjunction with a converging attack by the New Zealanders at Chunuk Bair it stood a good chance of success and if together the Anzacs could pull it off, the summit of the Sari Bair Ridge would be in their hands. Both forces were to attack simultaneously at dawn, and long before then the New Zealanders would have captured Chunuk Bair. But by dawn few of the New Zealanders had managed even to reach the assembly position, those who had were waiting for the others still struggling up the slopes and it would be many hours before the last of them arrived and the assault on Chunuk Bair could begin.

But the attack, which was destined to be fruitless and in the circumstances pointless, was nevertheless ordered to proceed.

Three separate waves went over the top into the maw of the Turkish rifles and machine-guns. The force was all but annihilated.

The rattle and thunder of the deathly fire that slaughtered the Australians ripped across the pinnacles of Sari Bair. Marking time on Rhododendron Ridge, glad of the respite after their laborious climb, the New Zealanders listened and wondered as they rested and waited for the late arrivals and the long-awaited signal to advance, and, chafing at the delay, General Johnston wondered more than anyone if the attack which he himself should have supported could possibly have gone ahead without him. On the spur itself everything was peaceful. A short distance ahead, just beyond two more spurs and dips, the tantalising slopes of Chunuk Bair stood out against the sun as it climbed into the eastern sky. All was quiet. Two hours passed. At 6.30 Johnston decided to wait no longer and led his troops forward some five hundred yards to the rocky hillock at the apex of Rhododendron Ridge. They were met by a few shots from the main ridge and halted again. From the apex they were looking down on their left to Suvla, and on their right they could see the Nek where, on a tiny patch of ground no larger than two tennis courts, the morning sun burned down on the bodies of more than six hundred Australian soldiers, lying so motionless and so at one with the earth that to the New Zealanders on their vantage point the Nek seemed to slumber undisturbed in the sun. General Johnston's Brigade Major scanned the view through binoculars and was deeply impressed: *'The situation as seen from the Apex was intensely interesting and indeed astonishing. Looking down towards Anzac all was quiet. At the Nek and Baby 700 not a shot was being fired. Above us we could see the trenches on Chunuk Bair bristling with rifles, and a certain amount of rifle fire was coming from that direction. On Hill Q all was quiet. There was no sign of the Indian Brigade or the 4th Australian Brigade. Away at Suvla the bay was a mass of shipping. Some men could be seen on the beaches walking about freely. Peace seemed to reign everywhere.'*

Peace certainly reigned at Suvla. It was 9.30 in the morning. The first troops had landed twelve hours earlier, many more had arrived in the course of the night, and more still were now making for the beaches, but not much was happening and the worst of it was that no one, least of all the troops, seemed to know what was meant to be happening.

Spr. J. Johnston, 44th (Welsh) Field Coy., RE, 53rd (Welsh) Div.

We were loaded into small boats and rowed towards the shores of Suvla Bay where we had to wade ashore for about sixty yards as the boats couldn't get in any nearer owing to the shallow water. In parts there was a lot of loose barbed wire which had been thrown there by the Turks to impede any landing, however we managed to get ashore about 5.45 a.m. and there were so many boats that we were told to move away as quickly as possible. The Turks had spotted the landing and opened up with shrapnel shell-fire, but we were fortunate to have been in the first boats and had travelled about two hundred yards inland, so the shrapnel shells went right over us towards the beach. This was our baptism of fire and we were all scared out of our wits, and as there were quite a lot of rocks near us we took what cover we could find until the firing slackened off. Then we began to look around for our officers for further orders, but there were no officers near us. It appeared that they had been landed further over from A beach. It was more than six hours before we were able to meet any of them, however like a lot of inquisitive war recruits that knew nothing about war, we went forward to see what was further on. When we had gone about three-quarters of a mile the heat was unbearable and we were thirsty. Then we saw a padre coming towards us with about two dozen water bottles over his shoulder. He was making for the beach to get water for the troops who were ahead of us. He was the padre of the 5th Welsh and generally known as 'Dai 5 Welsh'. He advised us to make for Hill 10 as there were troops gathering there, however when we reached there we were advised to make for Hill 20 as it was considered there were too many troops in one place and we would be a target for the Turkish gunners if we were spotted, so off to Hill 20 we went. We hung around all day waiting for orders. No one told us what to do, so we stopped there all night.

On board the destroyer *Jonquil* where he had slept all night on deck, General Stopford was as ignorant as anyone of the situation ashore and he was certainly in no position to influence events. It had been his intention to land with the troops and set up his Headquarters ashore but he had changed his mind and elected to stay on board – perhaps because of his injured knee, perhaps because he imagined that from the *Jonquil* he would obtain a more coordinated view. Either way it was a fatal mistake. Only half his staff was on board, the ship was not equipped for communication and small boats which might have carried messages to and from the shore were so scarce that it took one officer, desperate to discuss the situation with his Commander on board the *Jonquil*, six hours before he could find a vessel available to make the journey. As for Stopford himself, for all he knew of the situation he might as well have stayed on Lemnos. According to the single message which he succeeded in transmitting to GHQ he was satisfied that the troops had landed, adding with no hint of dismay that they had been unable to progress far beyond the beach. Its complacent tone did little to allay the anxiety of Sir Ian Hamilton, although he was comforted by the assumption that the message had been long delayed and merely described the situation early in the morning of the 7th. But as the hours passed and no news of further progress reached him, his anxiety deepened for he had heard from other sources that opposition at Suvla had been slight and he was desperate for confirmation that the troops had advanced and seized the Anafarta Hills. The fact was that they had hardly advanced at all.

Spr. J. Johnston.

Presently next morning the word came over from someone who appeared to be in charge with orders saying '*Do not retire, stay and dig trenches for yourselves where you are, and hold them as long as possible,*' so after a while we were down in a trench deep enough to afford us some cover. This was done with our entrenching tools, because the picks and shovels had been landed with our tool carts elsewhere! Then we dug towards the others on each end of us and connected up the trenches together. Soon after we had finished a couple of our company officers arrived and took over. At about midnight that night we were told to fall in and form ranks, and we marched under cover of darkness over to a place called Lala Baba where we started again digging trenches. We had come about one and a half miles or so along the edge of the Salt Lake which was a dry bed at the time. We were soon put to work again setting up barbed wire entanglements there, and afterwards at Chocolate Hill.

The order to 'dig in' had not come from Sir Ian Hamilton and it was the last thing he intended, especially in the light of the disturbing news brought back by a reconnaissance aircraft. Strong columns of Turkish reinforcements had been spotted marching towards Suvla from Bulair. It would be some hours before they got there, and there was still time for the troops to advance – but it was fast running out. The previous afternoon a message from Hamilton had urged Stopford to '*Push on rapidly*' and to '*Take every advantage before you are forestalled,*' but it had been couched in terms of such tentative encouragement that it might easily have been read as an expression of Hamilton's confidence in his Corps Commander rather than a direct order from the man at the top. Not for the first time in Hamilton's dealings with subordinates his characteristic gentle courtesy had betrayed him in a crisis which demanded overt bluntness and resolution.

A second laconic message received next morning, 8 August, revealed with horrifying clarity that General Stopford's imagination had stopped short at achieving the landing itself and that, contrary to the evidence, it was still inflamed by the belief that rows of trenches bristling with hostile troops stood in the path of an advance. Stopford had even taken the trouble to send a message of congratulation to the troops on their achievement so far, and he was in high spirits when he met Colonel Aspinall on the deck of the *Jonquil*. Aspinall, the main architect of the plan, had gone to Suvla to assess the situation at the urgent request of the commander-in-chief. 'Well, Aspinall,' beamed General Stopford as they shook hands, 'the men have done splendidly and been magnificent.' Aspinall was taken aback. 'But they haven't reached the hills, sir,' he demurred. 'No,' replied Stopford, 'but they are ashore!' Aspinall never forgot the conversation and two years later, giving evidence to the Dardanelles Commission, he did not hesitate to report it verbatim. All his urging, all his reminders of the necessity for speed, all his arguments for an immediate advance were brushed aside by General Stopford. He answered with some complacency that he was well aware of the situation, but until the men were rested and more guns and supplies were landed it was quite impossible to move. He added soothingly that he had every intention of ordering a fresh advance next day. Next day, and Aspinall knew it, would be a day too late. He had already been ashore with Sir Maurice Hankey and they had found a doleful state of affairs.

Col. Sir Maurice Hankey.

A peaceful scene greeted us. Hardly any shells. No Turks. Very occasional musketry. Bathing parties round the shore. There really seemed to be no realisation of the overwhelming necessities for a rapid offensive, of the tremendous issues depending on the next few hours. One staff officer told me how splendidly the troops were behaving, and showed me the position where they were entrenching! Another remarked sententiously that it was impossible to attack an entrenched position without a strong artillery, and this was not yet available. As an irresponsible critic I do not want to be hard, and I do want to recognise the very real difficulties, but I must confess I was filled with dismay, as was the General Staff man whom I accompanied. It was a delicate situation. His message to Sir Ian had to be sent through the Corps Commander, and it was difficult for him to

450

send an adequate message. We solved the difficulty by doing it through the Vice-Admiral, who was luckily in port!

The message sent by wireless from Admiral Roebuck's flagship read: *'Just been ashore, where I found all quiet. No rifle fire, no artillery fire, and apparently no Turks. IX Corps resting. Feel confident that golden opportunities are being lost and look upon the situation as serious.'*

Col. Sir Maurice Hankey.

What distressed me even more was the whole attitude of the division. The staff of the division and corps were settling themselves in dug-outs. The pioneers, who should have been making rough roads for the advance of the artillery and supply wagons soon to be landed, were engaged on a great entrenchment from the head of the bay over the hills to the sea 'to protect headquarters'. It looked as though this accursed trench warfare in France had sunk so deep into our military system that all idea of the offensive had been killed.

'You seem to be making yourselves snug,' I said to a staff officer. 'Are you not going to get a move on?' 'We expect to be here a long time,' was his reply.

The trouble is it is so difficult to do anything. One could only report to Sir Ian and to his Chief of Staff. It took hours to poke round and find all this out. It took hours to get a boat, and I was not back at Kephalos until 11 p.m.

The soldiers of the Suvla force, the Kitchener's men newly out from England, were equally at a loss. They had done well. They had not been rattled under haphazard shrapnel shelling, they had suffered many casualties, almost entirely due to overcrowding behind the beaches and the failure of the force to fan out, and they had suffered them stoically. They were keen to do well, but they could not advance without orders. In the innocence of their inexperience it was not up to them to reason why, but many of them wondered. Colonel Rettie who, as Commander of a brigade of guns, had rather more experience and did not hesitate to express an opinion, had spent two frustrating days aboard the destroyer *Minneapolis* before lighters arrived to take his guns ashore in the afternoon of 8 August.

Lt. Col. W. J. K. Rettie, 59 Brig., RFA.

At *last* we were told we might start disembarking . . . I was struck by the restfulness of all around. There appeared to be

451

little going on – a good many infantry sitting about or having a bathe. The impression conveyed to my mind was that of a 'stand-fast' at some field day. Having located the Commander, Royal Artillery, on the beach near Lala Baba I was told to bring the batteries into action under cover of that hillock. This was rather a shock, as we had at least expected to go forward to Chocolate Hill. On expressing surprise, and asking what we were waiting for, I was met with the grim reply: 'For the Turks to reinforce!' And so it proved!

When Colonel Rettie finally did move forward with his guns to Chocolate Hill, he found the Brigadier conferring with his Staff Officers. They sat with maps spread out, quite at ease on the open ground. There was no need to take cover.

Lt. Col. W. J. K. Rettie.

There was no firing, beyond an occasional shot from a sniper somewhere, and the sensation of a pause in a field day still prevailed. I was plied with queries as to how things were progressing on the beach, and when we were likely to get a move on – a question I could not answer.

It was a question which has not been answered to this day, and the line has not yet been drawn beneath the final account. The blame has been laid on many shoulders, but the truth that shines through the continuing post-mortems is that it could not be laid on the shoulders of the troops. They had done their best, they had done their duty and many of them died in the doing of it. Golden opportunities had indeed been missed. By the New Zealanders, whose long wait had enabled Turkish reinforcements to reach Chunuk Bair in time to deny them more than a foothold on its slopes. By Kitchener's men at Suvla, thwarted less by the enemy than by the pusillanimous leadership of their own command. Where minutes had counted hours had been frittered away and although the fighting battered on, the seeds of failure had been sown. They had germinated in the lack of coherent orders, in fatal delays and stultifying inaction, in pointless sacrifice and lack of resolve. The 'big show' conceived and planned as a coordinated effort had devolved into three independent battles. It could have succeeded, but it had failed – and it was the death-knell of the grand Gallipoli strategy. Suvla had finished it. As Sir Ian Hamilton would later point out, just as no one would think of pouring new wine into old bottles, the combination of 'old Generals and new troops' was fatal. In the face of much vilification Hamilton kept his dignity and his gentlemanly reserve.

General Stopford was less restrained. In mid-August when he was relieved of his command he embarked on a campaign in which self-justification and vilification of Hamilton played a large part. It hardly mattered now.

Sir Maurice Hankey returned to London saddened and depressed to make his official report.

Col. Sir Maurice Hankey.

It was not without a pang of regret that I bade farewell to de Robeck, Ian Hamilton and my many friends at the Dardanelles. In leaving these brave men marooned on the desolate, sunbaked shores of the peninsula amid squalor, heat and the torment of innumerable flies, with death staring them in the face day and night, encompassed by difficulties, behind them failure, before them the haunting vision of a winter campaign, or the alternative of evacuation, which even the most sanguine anticipated must be a shambles, I felt no small compunction in returning to the comfort of England and home. I also felt a grave responsibility about the report I had to make to the Prime Minister.

But the news had travelled ahead of him and, with the failure of the venture on which so much had depended, a strong body of opinion was already opposed to continuing operations in the Dardanelles. The dilemma that faced the Cabinet was how best to cut their losses without prejudicing British prestige and how best to help the Russians, staggering on the eastern front under the weight of a German army that was steadily pushing them back. The Dardanelles campaign had been partly designed to tempt Bulgaria into the camp of the allies, and now Bulgaria's position haunted the deliberations of the Cabinet. It seemed more and more likely now that she would soon throw in her lot with their enemies. Serbia was already fighting Austria on one front. If Bulgaria went to war and attacked her by the back door Serbia would surely be crushed and men, guns and quantities of ammunition would soon be pouring along a through-route from Germany to Turkey. Even apart from the dire consequences this would have for Russia, the allies would then be ignominiously shelled off the peninsula. The political considerations that had given birth to the Dardanelles campaign were more important than ever, and few but Sir Ian Hamilton clung to a thread of hope that a victory on Gallipoli was still possible. Pending a final decision and in the face of some opposition Kitchener decided to dispatch the fifty thousand reinforcements Hamilton requested, with the thought at the back of his mind that, if necessary and as policy developed, they could be used elsewhere in

453

the Mediterranean to assist Serbia.

The slender hope that fortune might eventually smile on the allies at Gallipoli was slender indeed and, at best, a matter of 'jam tomorrow'. The immediate and most urgent need was to relieve the pressure on Russia and this, in Kitchener's view, could only be done by a new offensive in France on a scale large enough to force the Germans to weaken their army in the east by rushing large numbers of their troops to the western front. Reluctant though he had been to commit his troops to any major battles in the near future, there was now no alternative. Kitchener felt sure that the French would be only too happy to cooperate.

The troops on Gallipoli knew nothing of these developments. The fighting had quietened down. August scorched on. But at last there was blessed relief for some – a whole month's leave for part of the Anzac force when reinforcements from Egypt took over the line and they were whisked off to the islands to rest and recuperate. The rest camps bore little resemblance to holiday resorts. They were almost as arid and fly-ridden as the peninsula, but there was half-decent food, there was water in abundance, best of all there was beer, and although of necessity there were drills and parades they were kept to a minimum. The weary soldiers could sleep undisturbed in the furnace of mid-day, they could bathe in the blue waters of the Aegean without being shelled, they could play cricket or football when the heat lessened towards evening, and at the end of the day they could lounge yarning and singing in the starlight. But day after day the distant rumble of guns firing on the peninsula brought a grim reminder that this was a fleeting respite, and some soldier had time to compose the parody that summed up the general feeling. It was sung to the familiar tune of 'The Mountains of Mourne' and soon it became their anthem:

> Oh, old Gallipoli's a wonderful place,
> Where the boys in the trenches the foe have to face,
> But they never grumble, they smile through it all,
> Very soon they expect Achi Baba to fall.
> At least when I asked them, that's what they told me
> In Constantinople quite soon we would be,
> But if war lasts till Doomsday I think we'll still be
> Where the old Gallipoli sweeps down to the sea.

Verse followed verse and since everyone had a go at adding one, soon almost as many versions as there were battalions were being sung at impromptu concerts. The Scots of the 6th HLI contributed the verse that expressed the basic, unsentimental longing at the forefront of every soldier's mind.

454

We don't grow potatoes or barley or wheat,
So we're aye on the lookout for something to eat,
We're fed up with biscuits and bully and ham
And we're sick of the sight of yon parapet jam.
Send out steak and onions and nice ham and eggs
And a fine big fat chicken with five or six legs,
And a drink of the stuff that begins with a 'B'
    Where the old Gallipoli sweeps down to the sea.

They had some hopes! Soon their holiday would be over, soon they would be returning to the peninsula, to the interminable diet of thirst-provoking bully beef and the sweat and grind of life – or death – in the trenches.

Birds were seldom seen on Gallipoli, but towards the end of August, to the astonishment of the men, large flocks of birds swooped through the sky above the peninsula, migrating from the chilly steppes of Russia to winter in the south. The searing heat showed no signs of abating, but the birds brought a salutary reminder that time was passing, that another season was on the way and that, despite their valiant efforts, they had advanced very little since they had landed in the spring. But it had not been for want of trying.

Part 7

~

Loos: The Dawn of Hope

The firefly haunts were lighted yet,
As we scaled the top of the parapet,
But the east grew pale to another fire,
As our bayonets gleamed by the foeman's wire,
And the sky was tinged with gold and grey,
And under our feet the dead men lay,
Stiff by the loop-holed barricade
Food of the bomb and the hand grenade,
Still in the slushy pool and mud –
Ah, the path we came was a path of blood,
When we went to Loos in the morning.

Patrick MacGill

Chapter 31

During the summer months, in towns all over the United Kingdom, photographers were making handsome profits. On the eve of their departure for the front the first contingent of Kitchener's Army were being photographed in droves, proud and a little self-conscious, for the benefit of their admiring families. Some enterprising firms set up make-shift studios at the gates of army camps and the newly fledged soldiers queued up to be photographed against teetering canvas backdrops of tasteful classical scenes. The exposure in daylight was necessarily long, the sitters emerged stiff and serious, but the results were mostly thought to be satisfactory and tens of thousands of photographs were proudly dispatched through the post or distributed personally on embarkation leave.

After the weary months of waiting, the impatient soldiers of Kitchener's Army were only too glad to be marching out of camp, new rifles on their shoulders and slung beneath their packs the white linen bags of extra rations that marked them out as men bound for the front. The hour of departure was an ill-kept secret so there was always a good turn-out of well-wishers along the road, and even if civilians were not allowed into the railway station itself, the band that had played the departing warriors from camp was there on the platform to perform a farewell medley as they entrained for the journey. As the train got up steam the band invariably struck up the plaintive strains of 'Home Sweet Home' which, in the circumstances, was not an especially tactful choice, but the newly fledged Tommies, who had had quite enough of home sweet home during their long apprenticeship, were far too elated to observe the irony. Even officers renowned as martinets and drill-sergeants of terrifying mien succumbed to the excitement of the occasion and amazed their erstwhile victims by surging to the carriage windows to shake hands, to wish them luck and, wonder of wonders, to salute the cheering Tommies as the train moved off.

Between July and September more than one hundred and fifty battalions of Kitchener's Army left for France. Not many of them had any experience of foreign travel and it was all strange and

459

exciting. A hundred thousand letters home began in the same way, *'Dear Mother, I am living on a farm . . .'*, but the homely picture this painted in the imaginations of families at home hardly fitted the reality, for the troops were not exactly living in comfort. But the farms of Flanders were ideally designed to house numbers of men and even if only the NCOs or occasionally the junior officers had the privilege of a room in the farmhouse itself, there was ample accommodation for the troops in the barns and pigsties that extended from both ends of the farmhouse and turned at right-angles to skirt a village road. In the middle of the square formed by the farm buildings there was invariably a muck-heap, an evil-smelling mixture of manure, rotting vegetation and the contents of crude privies which, over the course of the year, would mature to provide rich fertilizer for the fields in the spring. The Tommies skirted the middens with care and held their noses as they passed but after a time they got used to them.

At first while the divisions grouped they were a good way behind the firing line with only the grumble of guns in the distance to hint at what lay ahead, and across a hundred miles of France and Flanders every available building had been pressed into service to provide accommodation for the burgeoning British Army. The northern-most billet was in the farm and out-buildings of a Trappist monas-tery some miles beyond Ypres. If the silent monks moving imperturbably about their business in their white habits were disturbed by the presence of the British Tommies they gave no sign of it, and the Tommies of the headquarters troops, intrigued though they were by these strange companions, were only too happy to be there. It was a cushy billet, if only because the Trappists supported themselves by brewing a sweet beer, dark and strong, and since the normal channels of distribution had been disrupted, they were only too happy to sell it to the troops. The word soon spread and the men trudged long distances to buy beer from a hatch in the buttery wall. It kept them happy. The Battalion Medical Officer who was billeted in the monastery itself was less happy. He did not object to the sale of beer, but he took strong exception to the insalubrious pond which abutted the walls of the monastery. It was filthy, an obvious breeding ground for disease, and he was fearful of an epidemic among the troops. The Royal Engineers were peremptorily ordered to drain the pond and to remove the danger of infection. A few days later a notice appeared on the buttery hatch, laboriously written in English: *'There Is No More Beer.'* The officers, who had also acquired a taste for Trappist beer, confronted the abbot. Why had the beer run out? The Trappists were a silent order and the abbot the only monk in the monastery with a dispensation to speak, but he was not a brilliant conversationalist. Unclasping his hands from his voluminous white sleeves, spreading wide his arms in a gesture of despair, he looked like some lugubrious bird of prey. 'You have drained the pond,' he said simply. 'There is no water to make beer. Therefore there is none.' The MO was aghast. The Commanding Officer was consulted and the Royal Engineers were ordered to refill the pond, but to keep a close eye on future cleanliness. The beer flowed again – but some of the troops were heard to remark that it had lost something of its flavour!

After years of strict peacetime soldiering, some of the regular NCOs who had nurtured Kitchener's battalions through their training and come with them to France brought with them ideas of disciplined cleanliness which were not entirely appropriate to the new circumstances. During one Battalion's first tour of initiation in the trenches, one such sergeant went so far as to put a soldier on a charge for what he regarded as a heinous crime. The unfortunate Tommy was standing stiffly to attention when the Commanding Officer happened to come round the corner of the firing bay. 'What's the matter, Sergeant?' he inquired. The sergeant was bursting with righteous indignation. 'There's a *fly* in this man's butter, sir!' The Colonel peered into the tin of butter lying open on the fire-step. Sure enough, there was a fly. He gazed at it for some moments then, turning to the NCO, he bellowed, 'Sergeant. Arrest that fly!' The soldier did not dare to laugh, nor did he dare to catch the sergeant's eye, but that was the end of the matter.

The fledgling soldiers of Kitchener's Army were sent into supposedly quiet sectors for their first initiation but there was still occasional shell-fire and there were unavoidable 'wind-ups' when machine-guns spattered and bullets whizzed past too close for comfort. In such moments the voice of a sergeant-major which had terrified them on the parade ground, and his gruff phlegmatic 'Steady lads,' was decidedly reassuring. But Kitchener's Army was no stranger to trenches. They had dug trenches the length and breadth of the country until they were sick of the sight of spades and sandbags. But on the hills and meadows at home they had dug undisturbed by the presence of the enemy. Even now the enemy was invisible and despite repeated warnings it was easy to be over-confident.

Pte. F. Bastable, 7th Bn., Queen's Own (Royal West Kent Regt.), 55 Brig., 18 Div.

Trench digging. That's what we were trained for. If we didn't know anything else, we knew about digging trenches. In fact we won a prize for it, two of my mates and me. When we were training on Salisbury Plain our Colonel offered prize money for digging a quick trench, and me and two mates of mine won it. I think we got five shillings each. But it was a different story when we got to France, and one of those mates of mine, Bill Beckington, was one of our first casualties. We went down to the Somme area, and the first two casualties in the whole battalion oddly enough were two brothers, and they weren't even killed by the enemy. We had no proper baths or anything, so we used to go in a stream or a river and try to keep clean and have a swim at the same time, and these two brothers went out too far in the middle of the river and got caught in the reeds in the bottom and they *both* got drowned. After that the first casualty was my mate. It wasn't very nice. The trenches had been fired on and they'd broke them all up and we had to go in there and make them up tidy again with sandbags. This was right in the firing line so we both went in there, Bill and me, and one had to hold the sandbag open while the other filled it up. We were just arranging it between us, and thought nothing of it – we were well used to digging trenches so either he said, or I said, 'You hold the sandbag open while I put the earth in.' Anyway, when we'd filled a few, Bill went up on the top with the sandbag to where the hole was all broke down to make it up. I was down below while he was standing up doing it and the bullets started coming over. I said to him, 'Look out, Bill, they've got you spotted!' Well, he didn't bob down quick enough. The bullet just missed me and went to the back of the trench, made my ears whistle, the noise of it, and the next moment before Bill could say anything he got it right in the head. It blew his head open and his brains was all coming out. I was right next to him and his brains covered my tunic like the roe out of a herring.

I didn't know what to think. To think we'd got five bob for doing that job before, and now Bill was finished like that. I couldn't believe it. We went up the same night with the padre and gave him a proper burial – all the mates went up to see him buried. It was the first burial in our battalion. The padre said the prayers and some lads let off a round over his grave, it was near la Boiselle, not far away, not far from where he was killed. I couldn't get over it! The first man killed in the battalion and it was my own mate. And all we was doing was sorting out the trench.

Bill Beckington was one of many casualties and there was sometimes panic at home when parents who had indulgently connived at young boys joining under-age were shattered by news from France. Young Ralph Langley was not quite eighteen when his brother

Charlie died of wounds, and the first he knew of it was when he was called out by the sergeant-major on the parade ground shortly before the Battalion was due to sail.

Rfn. R. Langley, 16th Bn., King's Royal Rifle Corps.

I was in the 16th Battalion Kings Royal Rifle Corps – the Church Lads Brigade. We'd all joined up together in our local branch and after months of training I was dying to get to France. We were just on the point of going. Then this particular morning when we were on parade, the Sergeant-Major called out my name. 'Langley! Step forward!' The Sergeant was glaring at me. He had a paper in his hand and he said, 'Langley.' 'Yes, sir,' I said. 'How old are you, Langley?' I said, 'Nineteen, sir.' He said, 'You're a bloody liar! I've got a letter here from your mother. You're under-age – and you're out!'

I was absolutely staggered. They didn't send me home, but I can't describe what it was like staying behind in the barracks and knowing the Battalion would be going without me! Of course I didn't know at that moment my brother had been killed. My mother had got frightened, you see – realised I was in for it too, and she wasn't going to have that. They gave me leave to go home, and then I had to go back to the barracks, and *stay* there. It was awful seeing the Battalion go off. I was miserable. Really fed up. Of course the time passed and I got older and I had to go in the end. I was lucky to get back to my original battalion, but so many of them had been knocked out on the Somme by the time I joined them that if I'd gone out when the others went I might not be here now.

From the start of the war the Church Lads Brigade, like the Boys' Brigade and the Boy Scouts, was a fruitful source of recruits and many local branches like Ralph Langley's had joined up as a body. It was natural that the lads who had not yet reached the statutory age for military service had no desire to be left behind. They had been positively encouraged to lie their way into the Army for although all such organisations laid stress on the virtues of upright manly honesty, the ideal of service and patriotism was no less important. Even in peacetime they were trained in rifle-drill and marching, not as a means of inspiring a belligerent attitude but because the founders saw these activities as a means of banding boys together and inculcating the all-important virtues of 'obedience, reverence, discipline and self-respect'. The Boy Scouts' more adventurous pursuits of tracking and patrolling had not included formal military drill, but scouting was also intended to instil the spirit of patriotism and duty that would impel young men to spring to the defence of their country in time of need and it was more than a year since the War Scouts' Defence Corps had been formed. Thousands of scouts had joined it and even twelve-year-olds were enthusiastically training in rifle shooting, signalling, entrenching, army-drill, first aid and camp cooking, and busily preparing for the day when they too would be tall enough and strong enough (if not officially old enough) to exchange the khaki drill of the Boy Scouts' uniform for the khaki of soldier of the King. Their founder, Lieutenant-General Baden Powell, had inaugurated the scheme, with the words, 'An efficient boy of sixteen in the event of invasion would be worth a dozen grown-up men trained to do nothing in particular.'

Since the start of the war Boy Scouts had been permitted, indeed encouraged, to wear uniform to school and to undertake a variety of patriotic duties. They were to be seen everywhere, from the hallowed corridors of Government offices where relays of boys were acting as messengers, to the forecourts of railway stations or cycling along country lanes in the self-appointed pursuit of suspicious characters who might be German spies, frequently causing annoyance to innocent citizens going about their lawful business. But the zeal of the Boy Scouts was not easily diminished. They were mainly affluent youngsters, for the uniform in which they took such pride was not cheap. The less well off were more inclined to join fraternities whose 'uniform' of cap and belt was more easily affordable and in recent months there had been a huge upsurge in the number of boys aged twelve to eighteen who had enrolled in all such organisations. But a universal source of inspiration for both rich and poor alike was the *Boy's Own Paper*, which was avidly read, even at third or fourth hand, by almost every literate boy in the land. For thirty years it had been a firm favourite, packed with thrilling adventure stories, with articles on science, on new inventions, on hobbies and leisure pursuits, and it was imbued with a healthy 'moral tone' that extolled the virtues of heroism and nobility, well-spiced with the thrills and danger that appealed to a boyish sense of adventure. With the advent of the war the 'moral tone' had soared higher than ever. Out went the jungle adventures, the narrow escapes from ferocious beasts, the quelling of treacherous native tribes, the tales of derring-do in remote outposts of the Empire. In came the young heroes, the barbarous guttural Germans, the noble martyred French, wicked Zeppelin crews, vile and devious spies. They featured in dozens of exciting lurid sagas to be rescued or outwitted, as appropriate, by a virtuous schoolboy hero. A favourite character was the master whose post as teacher of German in an educational establishment was merely a cloak for his nefarious activities as a spy. It was always a public school, and the public school ethic with its stern message of moral duty oozed across every page and filtered through more mundane levels of society to impressionable schoolboys everywhere. So far as the *Boy's Own Paper* was concerned they were all 'England's Boys', and they were left in no doubt that a great deal was expected of them.

> On many a college playing-field,
>   All fleet of foot, and strong of hand,
> They speed the ball, the bat they wield,
>   And win the victory they have planned.
> Across the sward they run the race,
> The air is full of happy noise;
>   Supple of limb, and bright of face,
> The pride of our country, England's boys.
>
> Hope of our country, England's pride,
>   Boyhood of Britain, true and brave;
> Where'er the sun shall travel wide,
>   Across the lands, above the wave,
> The world shall know not, shall not trace
> In Athens' story, Sparta's, Troy's,
>   A fairer breed, a nobler race,
> Than the pride of our country, England's boys!

Under the circumstances, and under such a flattering depiction of their worth, even readers in Scotland, Ireland, or Wales were only too happy to be regarded as 'England's boys' for the duration.

Those who allowed their minds to stray from the obligations demanded of them by the war to the wider question of civilian careers were dealt with briskly in the correspondence columns which, in the past, had been a willing source of advice: '*We would help you if we could but due to the War there are no examinations for the most promising of the suggested careers. Your best plan is to join the Army and when the War is over you will have no difficulty in finding an opening.*' And again: '*You can get all the information you require at the nearest recruiting office. Go there at once. Your country needs you!*'

The editor adopted a milder tone with the many anxious readers who pleaded for advice on developing puny muscles or even increasing their height in order to reach the standards required by the Army. A few eager correspondents were barely in their teens but, as the editor wrote with kindly encouragement, '*You cannot begin too soon.*' It was hardly surprising that so many impressionable readers of these high-minded sentiments had inveigled their way into the Army well below the minimum age and in almost every battalion of Kitchener's Army there were baby-faced soldiers, sometimes as young as fifteen.

Bill Worrell, who had never been nearer the playing-fields of Eton than a boat trip on the Thames near his home in Isleworth, had joined up starry eyed at the age of seventeen and suffered the humiliation of having his mother arrive at camp to fetch him home. Since Bill had merely left a note of farewell on the kitchen table it had taken the distracted Mrs Worrell some days to track him down and by then Sergeant Hubbard had taken a liking to him.

Rfn. W. Worrell.

Sid Hubbard had been in the Oxfordshire Constabulary. He was a man who looked every inch a sergeant-major – he had a waxed moustache and he was over six feet, and big with it. He must have weighed all of eighteen stone and he had a very commanding manner, but beneath it all he was a very decent bloke. I don't know how my mother found her way to me, I think it was just chance, because the platoon was marching along, or *trying* to march, and suddenly there she was! She wanted to haul me out there and then and take me with her to see the Colonel. It was the very early days of the war, before we had uniforms or anything, and Sid Hubbard had been made our section commander and put in charge of our tent. So he took my mother aside and he spoke to her and I don't know how he did it but he talked her round. He said, 'Well, let him stay. We'll look after him.' He knew I was a kid and he always did keep an eye on me. He always called me Willie. To everyone else I was Bill. Before we left for France he was promoted Sergeant-Major and he was very regimental. In fact he was disliked by many blokes because he was so regimental, but he was a good sort – to me anyway.

Under the benevolent eye of Sergeant Hubbard, Bill had survived the training and emerged as a fully fledged member of the Rifle Brigade. In mid-August he had been in France for over a month and he was thoroughly enjoying himself.

Rfn. W. Worrell.

When we went into the trenches at first at Laventie it was fine. Every part of the line wasn't blood and shells and fighting and many parts were comfortable, cushy we called it. You just sat

466

around in the trench and nobody wanted to do anything. The people on the other side were said to be Saxons and *they* didn't want any trouble, so we all just carried on and it was all very new and interesting to us, and very, very novel.

When we came out of the line it was delightful, and of course I was top dog, because I had my schoolboy French and these other lads hadn't any French at all, so when we got into the estaminets and other places, I could do the shopping for them and go into the patisserie and the grocer and get grub, which they couldn't do. My platoon was in the racing stables and the concrete floor was a bit hard for sleeping on, but opposite the billet was the estaminet and the daughter, Julie, was the serving maid. Julie was really 'magnifique' – a big buxom girl with beautiful curves. She was nearly six feet tall and she must have weighed about twelve stone with a figure about 48–38–48 – inches of course, just like an hour-glass! Well, my fighting-weight was about seven stone, but I was first favourite with Julie, because I could talk to her and she could understand what I was saying, so when she was in difficulties with the troops she used to call on me to interpret. She used to call me her 'petit anglais' and her mother occasionally invited me into the kitchen for a bowl of soup after closing time, so I was in clover. We had a very pleasant sort of comradeship. Also I was young then and I wasn't taking the liberties that the other fellows were taking. Most of these chaps were crude. They thought all Frenchwomen were very loose women and of course the women didn't wear any underclothes. *That* was found out pretty quickly and the fellows used to take wicked liberties with Julie, patting her bottom under her skirt and that sort of thing. They didn't do anything worse than that, but that was their game.

One pay day the estaminet was packed and Julie had to squeeze her way through the benches to serve the drinks. One chap, who was a real cad called Shaughnessey, was sitting opposite me and, as Julie passed, he put his hand under her skirt and patted her bare bottom on *my* side. Julie put the glasses down and without turning round to look she threw a vicious back-hander that caught me behind the ear and I went sprawling on the floor. Shaughnessey was roaring his head off thinking he'd got away with it. Of course immediately Julie had twigged what had happened she picked me up and then let rip at Shaughnessey, hit him over the head with her tray and then pushed him under the table and kicked him. *That* wiped the silly grin off his face! It was pandemonium. Poor Julie looked at my swelling ear and was 'désolé'. She knew that *I* wouldn't do such a dirty trick – at least, not in public – so, having put Shaughnessey in his place, she took me to Mama in the kitchen, who sat me in the best chair and said I must rest awhile and stay for soup. Well, I suppose I did put it on a bit, but feminine sympathy was in very short supply in France.

It was closing time and I could hear Julie chucking the troops out. Mama began filling the soup bowls and I began rubbing my tum in anticipation. Then, of all the blasted bad luck, in came the Provost Sergeant, Tim Arley. He was a big raw ex-Irish Guardsman who fancied his luck with Julie and he used to use his exalted rank to get into the kitchen after closing time. When he saw me sitting there he went berserk – grabbed me by the collar and the seat of my trousers and literally threw me through the back door into the stinking midden in the courtyard. I scrambled out, smelling of non-violets! But I had the small satisfaction of hearing Julie roaring that he was a big ugly cochon who was no longer welcome in Mama's house. I almost felt like going back to interpret *that* for him! I scraped off the worst of the muck but it was days before even my best friends would come anywhere near me. The sequel came when I met Tim Arley at the reunion dinner in 1921. I gave him a nasty look and reminded him that he had insulted me in front of a lady in 1915. He pretended not to remember but as I turned away he said, 'Phew. There's a terrible whiff of a midden here all of a sudden.' That did it! 'Choose your weapons,' I said. 'Right,' said he, 'one pint of bitter and thank you very much.' What could you do with a man so lacking in decency! Anyway, he was out of luck with Julie – he told me she never spoke to him again as long as he was at Laventie.

Compared to the innocent enthusiasts of Kitchener's Army now pouring into France, men like Frank Moylan who had been at the front for several months were old hands, but, although the new men had a lot to learn and it would be months before hard seasoning would turn them in the eyes of the Army into useful soldiers, even now the Army was glad of them. There was a lot more territory to cover. The British had now taken over a line that stretched across the downlands of the Somme to meet the right of the French Tenth Army, and on its left they had extended their front from the la Bassée Canal across the coal-fields where the trenches ran among spoil-heaps and mining villages. In front of the trenches of the 47th London Division was the looming black pile they called the Double Crassier.

Cpl, F. Moylan, 1/7th (City of London), Bn., London Regt., 140 Brig., 47 Div.

Let me explain the position of the front line. There was a communication trench leading back to the mining village, a sort of model place, with a brick wall round it and a hole had been knocked in the wall, that's where the communication trench ended, and there were all the miners' cottages there. There was a wide road and these cottages were on a slope each side, most of them with the furniture still in, and little gardens, and if you were in support you were in these houses. We had a company commander, Captain Green, and we used to think he was a bit of a martinet. These cottages had red-tiled floors and he made us clean them while we were in there. Of course you couldn't move out in the daytime, and it kept us occupied, but they had an obsession about cleanliness, these officers. Even the brigadier, Brigadier-General Cuthbert, ordered brooms to be taken from these houses up to the front line and we had to actually sweep the trenches! And not only that, but there was a sandbag pinned up in each fire-bay, stuck to the side of the trench with a spent cartridge, and this was for rubbish to keep the trench tidy. We used to call him 'Spit-and-Polish Cuthbert!' That was his nick-name. Of course, in the summer months when it was comparatively dry it was easier to keep the trenches in good order than it was later on when we had all the mud.

Anyway, when you were in support you were back in these cottages and they all had gardens and they were full of soft fruit, blackcurrants, raspberries, gooseberries, and naturally we wanted to get at them. The only way you could do that was to open the back door and lie flat on your tummy and crawl down the garden and reach up for the fruit. You couldn't stand up because it was on a slight slope and the slope faced the German line and the wall didn't hide you because you were above the wall because of the slope. If you stood up you could see the German trench, but nobody was fool enough to stand up. We used to crawl out into the garden when the officers weren't about to gather this fruit. There were young carrots too and young turnips and they were all just about right, and we used to pull them up and cook them. Of course we couldn't make smoke, but sometimes we got hold of dry fuel that would flame and if we had none and we could get hold of newspaper that would do. (I discovered you could boil water and make tea on one newspaper. You would roll it up and twist it round into tight sticks and that was one useful thing I learnt. I can still do it!) It was fairly quiet there in August so long as you didn't attract the attention of the Germans, but I had one nasty experience. I wasn't company runner, but this day when we were in the front line I had to take a message back to Battalion Headquarters which was in these cottages, a beautiful sunny day it was. I went along this communication trench and I was coming to that hole in the wall and all of a sudden about six whizz-bangs came – one after the other. Not one of them dropped in the trench, just nearby, but by Jove, that made me lie low for a bit. After it was quiet I got up, started going along a bit and it happened once more. Still they didn't drop one in the trench. Then it suddenly dawned on me. They were very profligate with their ammunition and there were balloons, observers, and if they saw some movement it was the old idea: 'If it moves, shoot it.' I was extremely careful about my movements until I got through that hole, believe me, and I was very careful indeed going back again.

Not far ahead of the trenches, easily visible on rising land behind the German line, was the small mining village of Loos. It was an insignificant place, familiar to no one but the local inhabitants of the region, but within a few weeks the name of Loos would be blazoned in the headlines of newspapers round the world. It was here among the pit-heads and the slag-heaps that the British Army was to make its next desperate push.

The planners were busy but it was summertime and although the August weather was unpredictable and a few warm days were often succeeded by a period of rain and thunder storms, the intermittent sunshine was heartening. Barnyard billets, so draughty and inhospitable in winter and chilly spring, were pleasantly cool on summer days. Drilling, parades and route-marches, endured with sullen stoicism in inclement weather, seemed less arduous, and off-duty in the long pleasant evenings even Tommies with nothing to spend in the local estaminets could pass the time pleasantly enough lounging in a field, leaning on a farm gate, or strolling in the pleasant countryside. Some even helped gather in the sumptuous harvest and the women and girls who had been left to run farms single-handed were happy to repay them with an acceptable jug of cider or rough wine. And there were entertainments. Most battalions out of the line took the opportunity of holding traditional field days and sports days just as they did in peacetime and they kept the troops amused and in high spirits.

2nd Lt. F. Best.

The greasy pole over the corner of a muddy pond afforded great mirth, the competitors being dressed in the regulation Army Service Corps swimming costume of honest underpants. The entire population of the village formed up round the water to spectate. The most shouting event of all, however, was the

470

band race. Here all the players were formed up at the starting point and were handicapped according to the nature of their instruments. Triangle and cymbals started at scratch, tuba well forward, and so on, with the big drum ahead. The conductor started them all playing 'Come Lasses and Lads' which is the Staffs march-past and he instructed them to continue until I dropped my stick. I let the bandsmen play on for at least fifteen bars or so, and on dropping the stick at an unexpected moment, the whole mass moved forward at a run while the harmony groaned and slid all over the scale. I was doubled up with laughing at this point, but I learnt that the tenor trombone just overhauled the big drum in the last five yards! Everyone thoroughly enjoyed it.

With so many more men in France baths were becoming a problem but the Army did its best. They had commandeered breweries up and down the line where as many as a dozen men at a time could bathe in relays in the great vats filled with warmish water and until now it had been possible to provide each man with a bath once every week or ten days. Now, with so many more battalions demanding bathing facilities, the troops were lucky if their turn for a bath came round once a month. It was a sore trial for the Tommies emerging hot and sticky and dirty from a stint in the fly-ridden trenches to take up temporary abode in a fly-ridden farm where the scent of the farmyard midden could be cut with a knife. The 6th South Staffs solved the problem by using the only facilities that were readily available on the farm. One officer had the idea of lining a farm cart with a haystack tarpaulin and filled it with water from the farm pump. The 'bath' could only hold three men, four at most, and they were not exactly able to wallow in comfort. It took a long, long time for the men of even a single company to be bathed, the water got blacker and blacker and had to be frequently changed, but at least they were able to scrape off the worst of the dirt and it was marginally better than nothing.

In spite of the sticky heat in the narrow confines of the earthen walls and the discomfort of sudden rain storms that at least had the minor advantage of temporarily laying the dust, life in the trenches between bombardments passed quite pleasantly in the summer months. Tommies with no immediate task to perform could lounge and slumber on the warm firestep or, taking a turn as look-out, gaze through the trench periscope discreetly poked above the sandbags across the desolate expanse of No Man's Land where the weeds and long grass mercifully hid the bodies of the dead, to that other mysterious line of sandbags that marked the parapets of the enemy trenches.

Capt. F. O. Langley, 6th Bn. (TF), South Staffs Regt., 137 Brig., 46 Div.

Our predominant feeling is one of intense curiosity as to what exactly is happening behind those black and white sandbags over the way. Are the Germans at this moment paraded there, being harangued by their officers before attack? Or are 90 per cent of them asleep and the other 10 per cent yawning. Does the spiral of blue smoke ascending to the sunny heavens indicate a deadly gas preparation or the warming up of a tinned lunch? Are there ten thousand Germans there or ten? One of my men writes naively to his sweetheart: 'There's millions of Germans here, but they's all behind bags.' On the other hand Lieutenant Collinson, whose dashing spirits demand an attack, contends that the whole line opposing us has been deserted by the soldiery and is now held by a caretaker and his wife. The caretaker does occasional shooting while his wife sends up the flares.

The tenderfoot Tommies of Kitchener's Army were just as fascinated by the German line, and there was brisk competition for a turn at the periscope. It was weeks before the novelty began to pall and the existence of the invisible Germans was taken for granted.

Occasionally in the quietest sectors there were visitors – curious politicians during the parliamentary recess and once, to the astonishment of the Tommies, a party of bell-bottomed sailors, fresh-faced from service in His Majesty's ships, brought on a conducted tour of the front with the idea of increasing *esprit de corps* between the services by giving the sailors a glimpse of life in the trenches. It did not appeal to them much and they were not slow to assure the Tommies that they were welcome to it. There were parties of civilians from factories, cloth-capped and taciturn, for it was part of Lloyd George's strategy as Minister of Munitions to organise tours of the front for representative groups of trade union leaders and munition workers. Nothing, he calculated, was more likely to inspire industrial workers to eschew strikes and spur them to greater efforts than the opportunity to see for themselves how badly munitions were needed.

The supply of ammunition had improved, but only slightly, and now that the British troops were committed to fighting another great battle on the western front, more – much more – was needed. But after the huge expenditure of shells in the defence of Ypres and the assaults on Aubers Ridge and Festubert, the stocks in France were building up again. This time there should be enough. And this time there would be a new weapon. The Germans' use of gas, although it was loudly denounced by the civilised world, had swept away the rules which the

472

allies had rigidly observed. Now the game was tit-for-tat, and the British Army was preparing to give the Germans a taste of their own medicine. Early in August they began to issue the troops with new gas-helmets that were vastly superior to the earlier primitive model – a simple bag of flannel shirting worn tucked into the collar of the tunic and with a 'window' of transparent mica. It had not been particularly satisfactory. The mica eyepiece had been prone to crack and admit fumes and the helmet itself was suffocating after more than a few minutes, but the new pattern was an improvement. It had glass goggles instead of the mica panel and a tube to breath through, or rather to exhale through for the breath had to be drawn in through the nose and blown out through the tube. This was a tricky operation and the technique took some practice to perfect. To the delight of the Tommies of Kitchener's Army the tube had an unfortunate tendency to produce noises of suggestive vulgarity which convulsed the schoolboy element in the irreverent ranks.

Pte. F. Gowland, 10th Bn., Worcestershire Regt., 57 Brig., 19 Div.

We were on one of those alleged rests when gas-bag no. 3 was issued, and of course, in the interests of military discipline, gas-mask drill by numbers was the order of the day. Our sergeant was a man called Rawlings, one of those gentlemen with a very red face, a large moustache and a pronounced 'chest' hung low. He always seemed rather short of breath, but Sergeant Rawlings liked things done right, and having been initiated into the mysteries of the new gas-drill he proceeded to give us a demonstration. First he showed us the motions in excellent style. Unfortunately however he managed to end up with the wretched thing on backwards and of course this produced an immediate epidemic of mirth in the company. The sergeant snatched off his mask, roared for silence and growled threats about insubordination, but noticing that the Company Commander was approaching he started again. This time he got it right and breathed as he had carefully instructed us. His first inhalation produced a deep growl, '*ur—r—rgh*', followed as he exhaled through the tube by an extremely high and wavering '*peep*' and finally there was a barrage of '*urghs*' and '*peeps*' as he struggled to get it right. The officer looked startled, and beat a hasty retreat in the direction of the mess. Seeing that his demonstration was not being taken in quite the right spirit, Sergeant Rawlings got completely out of tune and lost his grip on the mouthpiece and the whole bag began to inflate and deflate violently. Our demoralisation was now complete and we were doubled up with laughing. The sergeant unmasked hurriedly and gave us a right dressing-down.

When order was restored the whole company donned their masks and the resulting musical effect was beyond description! Every valve seemed to have some peculiar characteristic. Some made a deep gurgle, others a shrill scream, and the snorts and grunts and wails had to be heard to be believed. Poor Sergeant Rawlings. That parade was doomed to failure. But we got the hang of it in the end.

For months now every Battalion Headquarters had been inundated with orders demanding the transfer of men with special skills, now serving in the ranks, who could be more usefully employed elsewhere. GHQ had trawled for mining engineers, for telephonists, for draughtsmen and cartographers, for blacksmiths, carpenters, for men who were qualified in dozens of trades or professions. Now, in the hope of starting up gas manufacturing plants in France, or even floating plants offshore, they were demanding chemists. In the 4th Gordon Highlanders and in U Company alone there were at least half a dozen chemists, but once again the Colonel put his foot down and barked, 'Nil return'. The weary Adjutant, sick of the usual formula, relieved his feeling by sending a sarcastic reply to Divisional Headquarters: '*Unable to supply chemists, but we have a contortionist if required.*' Someone at Divisional Headquarters had a sense of humour and the answering signal put the Adjutant on the spot. '*Contortionist is ordered to report forthwith for duty with Divisional Concert Party.*' But the Adjutant had the last word: '*Regret contortionist was wounded last night and has been evacuated.*'

Not many officers of the administrative branch of the Army had time to indulge in facetious banter. They were working at full stretch with the reshuffling and reorganisation of divisions as more and more men arrived and with the formation of new ones. In August, after the arrival of some second-line battalions and the newly formed Welsh Guards, it was at last possible to create a division formed exclusively of Guards battalions. Delighted though the Guards battalions were there were some sad partings. Since their arrival nine months earlier the 1st Battalion, the Hertfordshire Regiment, had been serving and fighting with the 4th Guards Brigade and as 'mere' Territorials they were extremely proud of the fact.

CQMS G. Fisher, 1st Bn. (TF), Hertfordshire Regt., 6 Brig., 2 Div.

We arrived in France on 5 November, Guy Fawkes Day, right in the middle of the First Battle of Ypres, and of course we ended up in that battle before it finished. But at first we had no idea where we were going. We went up by train to St Omer and the rumour was that we were picked to be bodyguards to the Commander-in-Chief, because St Omer was General Headquarters. But we were spread out in billets round the town and after a few days drilling and so on, we were told that we were to make a practice attack across some fields. There were ever so many officers there to watch us, all mounted, some of them with red tabs. What had happened was this. The old English formation for a Brigade was three Battalions, but to line up with French formations our Brigades were increased to four Battalions and the 4th Guards Brigade needed another Battalion to make them up. So the Brigade Commander, and the Divisional Commander, who was Major-General Horne, had come to look us over to see us doing this attack and to see if we were any good. Of course, we only found this out afterwards. Anyway we did this practice attack and they were there with our Colonel and all these officers from GHQ, and they watched us march in and they watched us do this dummy attack. Apparently we hadn't been at it very long when the General of the Guards Brigade said to our Colonel, 'Well, they're good enough for me. They'll do. I'll have them.' Next day we left to join them at Ypres, and before we went we had a parade and our Colonel spoke to us and told us about this and said what an honour it was and that he hoped that we would live up to it, etc. etc. So there we were in the 4th Guards Brigade, which was the 2nd Battalion Coldstreams, the 2nd Battalion Grenadiers, the 1st Battalion Irish Guards – and *us*, the 1st Battalion the Hertfordshire Regiment. Territorials! I think we did prove ourselves. I think they thought a lot of us. The Guards were marvellous soldiers but I reckon we kept up with them. They used to call us the 'Herts Guards'. The Guards had been well blooded by the time we got there because they'd been through Mons and the battles after that, but that was the first a lot of them had seen of fighting service even though they were well trained and well disciplined.

Everyone has the idea of a Guardsman, but they were human like the rest of us. I remember during the Battle of Festubert the Guards Brigade attacked and we happened to be the supporting battalion in the brigade and we had to follow in. The Guards took two lines of trenches and we had to go in after them and occupy and hold the trenches they'd taken. The Germans had been overrun as the Guards went forward and some of them were in shell-holes and they were sniping at us as we came up. One of the snipers caught my officer, Lieutenant

Daish, and the bullet went through one side of his jaw and out the other, so he was out of it. I was platoon sergeant then so I had to take over the platoon and carry it through the Battle of Festubert, so we went in to occupy these Germans trenches that the Guards had just taken while the Guards went on moving forward. That was the holding line. If the Germans attacked we'd got to keep them back. 'These are *our* trenches now. *You* don't have them!' That was the idea. I went into one of the dug-outs and I found two Germans in there and one was fairly badly wounded and the other, strange to say, was a Swede. Lots of people don't know that during the First World War the Swedes were very favourably disposed to the Germans. I said to the Swede, 'What the hell are you doing in the German Army?' He said, 'I believe they're in the right.' Anyway I got some stretcher-bearers up and they made this Swede carry the wounded German back. That was the routine.

Now, I don't always like to tell this, but it's perfectly true. I went further along and looked into the next dug-out and there was a Guardsman in there. They talk about the psychology of fear. He was a perfect example. I can see that Guardsman now! His face was yellow, he was shaking all over, and I said to him, 'What the hell are you doing here? Your battalion is out in front. What are you doing back here?' He said, 'I can't go. I can't do it. I daren't go!' Now, I was pretty ruthless in those days and I said to him, 'Look, I'm going up the line and when I come back if you're still here I'll bloody well shoot you!' Of course I had plenty to do because you had to reconnoitre the line and reverse the defences, so it took quite a while to get that going, and when I came back, thank God, he'd gone. He was a Coldstream. A big chap six foot tall. He'd got genuine shell-shock. We didn't realise that at the time. We used to think it was cowardice but we learned later on that there *was* such a thing as shell-shock. Poor chap, he couldn't help it. It could happen to anybody. But at that time you either did your job or you didn't. There was no halfway house. I've seen chaps go, but I've never seen anybody go like that. It was horrible. A day or two later we heard that a Guardsman had been shot for cowardice. I often wondered if it was that chap.

But the Guards were wonderful soldiers – marvellous, second to none! Still I think we proved ourselves. I think they thought a lot of us.

A few nights before they left the 2nd Division the Grenadier Guards gave a dinner in Béthune to bid farewell to the divisional staff and Colonel Page-Croft of the 1st Herts was a guest of honour. There were many speeches and many toasts – not least to the 'Herts Guards'. The Colonel of the Grenadier Guards proposed it in a speech of fulsome praise and Colonel Page-Croft made a suitable reply, but he could not resist concluding with the words, 'I suppose now we will have to go and try to raise the standard of some other Brigade.' This remark was greeted at first with boos and cat-calls, but then the Guards rose to their feet and applauded for a full two minutes.

On 19 August the three Guards Battalions marched away. The route was lined with detachments from the remaining battalions of the 2nd Division but, as Colonel Page-Croft proudly remarked, 'A company of the Herts was given pride of place.' General Horne in command of the 2nd Division took the salute, and the brass band played a rousing medley of military marches to speed the Guards on their way. The Hertfordshire men cheered louder than anyone else as the three Guards battalions marched past and they were more than gratified when the Colonel of the Grenadiers gave the *Eyes right*' as his battalion approached and saluted them as they went.

The Territorials had earned their spurs. All of them had done well, and more than well. It was no exaggeration to say that the war would have gone badly without them. But the war went on. Their task was not over but henceforth, with more men in the field, it would be lightened. As the summer crept towards autumn the strength of the British force on the western front was substantially increased and the Commander-in-Chief kept an eye on the swelling numbers with satisfaction. His command was beginning to look something like an army.

Chapter 32

Two new divisions, the 21st and the 24th, arrived in the early part of September in time to enjoy almost two weeks of balmy weather. The 12th Northumberland Fusiliers were scattered round the village of Eperlecques almost on the Belgian border, ten miles from St Omer and twenty-five miles from the front. It was a delightful spot. And the men, on the whole, were enjoying themselves exploring the unfamiliar delights of the French countryside and doing their best to communicate with the locals by sign language.

The officers had billets in the village and Captain David Graham-Pole was particularly pleased with his. He and the padre were in the house of the village curé and the curé and his sister were hospitality itself. They astonished Captain Pole by producing an excellent and liberal dinner every evening and although the four courses were eaten from a single plate they were washed down by three sorts of wine and followed by coffee and brandy. Captain Pole was given the best bedroom and begged to make use of the garden and to help himself to grapes from the vine that clung to the wall and the luscious pears and tomatoes growing in abundance. The curé even carried a chair and a table into the garden so that Pole could interview the company officers and conduct the company's business while enjoying the sunshine. The officers agreed that Captain Pole had struck it lucky and, since he invariably shared the fruit with callers, his visitors were many. Even 'orderly room' held in these attractive surroundings seemed less of an ordeal to defaulters marched through the garden gate and brought before him for the mildly nefarious offences of indulging in straw fights in their barn billets or succumbing to the temptation of raiding an orchard. The 'misdemeanours' were trivial but discipline had to be maintained and already Captain Pole had been obliged to give C Company a dressing-down, for his men had apparently been under the impression that such obligations as saluting officers and polishing buttons could be dispensed with now that they were on 'active service'. C Company had taken it philosophically and were not much perturbed.

Most of them hailed from Tyneside but there were two 'foreign-ers' in the company, Harry Fellowes and Bob Hanson. Given the choice of regiments when they enlisted at Nottingham just a year ago they had chosen to join the Northumberland Fusiliers for two simple reasons. They were avid supporters of Newcastle United and, since neither had ever travelled more than ten miles from Nottingham in his short life, they fancied the long train ride to the north. Their trip across the Channel in the troopship was the first time Harry and Bob had ever seen the sea and they were still revelling in the delights of foreign travel despite long thirsty route-marches when the water-carts stayed with the transport far down the road at the rear of the battalion. C Company had complained long and loudly. 'There are few philosophers among them,' wrote Captain Pole in one of his first letters home.

The Battalion was being toughened up, and if route-marching was not to the men's taste rifle-practice was another matter, and the new short Lee Enfield rifles were a vast improvement on the wooden weapons they had toted for almost ten months. They were heavy to carry on the march and not many of their owners were more than half proficient in using them but they were still a novelty. Marching along the rough country roads with their new rifles on their shoulders they felt like soldiers at last although there was no word of their going to the front. 'We may train here for a month or two I hear,' wrote Captain Pole, 'route-marching, bomb-throwing, machine-gunning, etc.' Only if they listened very carefully when the wind was in the right direction could they hear the sound of the guns.

The guns were never silent but although machine-gun bullets frequently came ripping over the trenches from the other side of No Man's Land and snipers in concealed positions were lying in wait for the unwary, apart from an occasional flurry of shots when there was real or imagined cause for alarm, the eight miles of trench-line that stretched from Aubers Ridge across the coalfields around Loos and Lens was reasonably quiet. It was so quiet that one German sniper amused himself for several days in idle moments by training his rifle on the wall of a ruined cottage near the British front-line trench and 'carving' a cross in the bricks. It took shape over the course of several days and the soldiers of the Post Office Rifles whose trench ran through the cottage garden rather admired his artistry. It was chalky country and the deep chalk walls of the trenches were a positive invitation to bored Tommies manning the support lines and it was not long before the trench walls were covered with graffiti. There were cartoons: 'Know Your Enemy' was a favourite caption, usually under a lampoon laboriously carved out with a jack-knife, and representing some well-known pacifist hanging from a gallows; rough but recognisable. One trench displayed a show-piece that

479

must have taken some patient earth-dweller many hours to carve. It had obviously been copied from the kind of picture post-card which was popular at home and were posted by the thousand to Tommies at the front. It showed a country cottage with roses round the door and a mesh of fine lines to indicate its thatched roof. There was a garden too, with a postman standing at the gate and an old lady rushing down the path to meet him. The outlines stood out boldly in charcoal and the carved caption read 'A letter from Tommy'. But most offerings were less ambitious and the troops generally confined themselves to written slogans or lines of doggerel inscribed with a combination of indelible pencil and spit. 'I have no pain, dear Mother, but blimey I am dry, so take me to a brewery and leave me there to die.' Sometimes they were disgruntled – 'A loaf in the trench is worth ten at the base' – and some leaned towards romance with hearts and arrows and mysterious initials. There were also solitary arrows, usually pointing in an easterly direction and confidently announcing 'To Berlin'.

From a military point of view the chalky ground put the Army at a considerable disadvantage for although the permanent trenches could be reasonably well camouflaged by sandbagged parapets the new trenches could not, and as the Army prepared for the coming battle the long lines of glistening white chalk in full view of the Germans were impossible to miss. Night after night the working parties went out digging. They dug assembly trenches behind the lines, they dug communication trenches, they dug saps that poked into No Man's Land and they dug trenches in No Man's Land itself. In the ten nights before the battle they dug twelve thousand yards of them. The Germans would have been blind if they had not realised that a major attack would soon be launched.

Lt. A. Waterlow, 19th (County of London) Bn. (St Pancras), 5 London Brig., 47 (London) Div.

Our job was a somewhat ticklish one. The whole battalion was to go up to the front line armed with picks and shovels, file out along the various saps which had been extended out into No Man's Land and spread out along a line about two hundred and fifty yards in front of our front line, where patrols usually only crawled about on their stomachs. We were then to dig a *new* front line, which would be previously marked out in white tape by the Royal Engineers. It was to run from slightly in front of our present front line at the Béthune-Lens main road (where the British and Boche trenches were closest together) in a straight line to meet our present front line in front of South Maroc, so straightening out two re-entrants, taking in a consid-

480

erable area of No Man's Land and making a convenient jumping-off trench for the coming attack. We had instructions to carry on with the digging, no matter how heavy the casualties might be. They were expected to be fairly heavy because the London Irish had been digging the new line in front of the right-hand part of the sector on the previous night and, with the new trench running in a straight line and suddenly ending 'in the air', it should have been obvious to the Boche during the day what our game was and to get the exact range of the new line and have us taped at night.

When the time came we filed out of the sap-heads like mice and spread out along the taped line. Every man had to take the utmost care not to jangle the picks and shovels against one another or against his equipment. Any slight noise might give us all away, and if the Boches chose to turn a machine-gun on to us they could have practically wiped us out. We were simply a line of men spread out across No Man's Land with absolutely no cover. The men with the picks got to work at once, while the men with shovels lay at full length on the ground, with the shovel blade in front of them to protect their heads until their turn came. Never have I seen men dig at such a rate! They seemed to be two feet deep in no time.

The policy was for each pair of men to dig a hole to give them both as much shelter as possible and, when this was the required depth, to join up the various holes into one continuous line of bays and traverses. By a marvellous piece of good fortune we only had desultory rifle fire from the Boches, in spite of the fact that they were sending up Very lights regularly which seemed to light us all up so plainly that we could not fail to be observed. In fact it gave one the impression of standing naked and unable to take cover in front of a vast throng of people. But it was two hours before they sent any shells over and by that time the men had dug some cover for themselves. We got a few salvoes at intervals but altogether only two men were wounded. The Boche knew where we were right enough, for all the shells landed only a few feet behind the new line we were digging, so that it passes comprehension of the Boche mentality why he did not turn on a machine-gun or even rifle fire, when he definitely knew that we were there! Our artillery had been given instructions to retaliate with compound interest on the Boche trenches if we got shelled at all but their reply was somewhat feeble. I heard they got 'strafed' by the higher powers.

Dug-outs were being constructed as far forward as possible and although that was a specialised job for the Royal Engineers, hapless working parties of infantrymen were pressed into service to supply the unskilled labour.

Cpl. F. Moylan.

They wanted to reinforce a new big dug-out for Advanced Brigade Headquarters for this coming push so that Brigade Headquarters would be nearer up. There was a big cutting and there was a railway in it connected up with a coal mine, and the Engineers took those railway lines and loosened them and we carried them up. God! That was a working party! I forget now whether it was a hundred men, but it was a hell of a lot. We had to pad our shoulders with sandbags. How we lifted those rails on to our shoulders in the dark I don't know! It took about twenty men to carry one rail. It was a hell of a job. Then you'd go back over this crossing and down into the communication trench.

I was in 11 Platoon and my Platoon Officer, Lieutenant Flower, was in charge. Flower was a very nice chap because I broke a double tooth on an army biscuit when this railway business was going on and it gave me hell, and Flower sent me up to the Regimental Aid Post which was half-way down the communication trench, in a bit of a dug-out. The Medical Officer, Dr Bell, was there and the Medical Sergeant, Gilder. He'd got some empty bully-beef boxes there so he sat me on one and I remember Sergeant Gilder holding my shoulders and the MO – he'd got no anaesthetic or anything! – he just took my double tooth out. It was very painful and he said, 'I'm not sending you back up the line; you get on a stretcher and have a night's rest here.' And I did, and Lieutenant Flower let me take it easy when I got back.

It was peculiar because the same thing happened when I was a prisoner. I broke a double tooth on the opposite side. But there it was a civilian German dentist, who laughed and said, 'I'm not going to give you an anaesthetic because I haven't got one. If you want one write to Lloyd George and tell him to take off the blockade.' That was in 1918. No sympathy then! But Flower was very kind to me the first time, just before Loos. He let me off the working party and that was one good thing anyway.

Night after night the unfortunate troops who were out of the line in reserve or on supposed rest were marched off as soon as darkness fell to navvy through the night. But there were some compensa-

482

tions. After they woke from a long lie-in there was quite often the luxury of a bath parade to scour off the dirt of the night, for with so many mines in the area the men had more chance of a bath, and the pithead baths were equipped with hot water and real showers and the mine owners were happy to oblige the Army with the use of their facilities. There was a hot meal at mid-day and, since men told off for a working party were excused other drills and fatigues when a battalion was at rest, they had a few hours' spare time before they had to parade to set off for the night's work. With luck there might be a football match.

The inter-battalion football matches of the 15th Scottish Division always drew a crowd, not only because their footballers were good but because fierce regimental rivalry guaranteed a lively game. The supporters were nothing if not partisan but the banter and insults they freely exchanged would have mystified a civilian football fan, for their origins lay deep in the mists of military history. They also baffled Kitchener's Army. Few of them had the faintest idea why they were bellowing 'HLI! HLI!' – obligatory if a team which looked like winning narrowly kicked the ball over the touchline in the last minutes of the match – but bellow it they did. None but Regulars – and ancient ones at that! – could possibly have been present at the long-ago final of the Army Soccer Championship in India when the Highland Light Infantry maintained their lead and won the championship by this unsporting tactic. But the most thrilling matches were between any battalion of the Black Watch and any battalion of the Gordon Highlanders. The battalions of the Black Watch now in the 15th and 9th Divisions were service battalions. No member of either had been in France for more than four months, yet any doubtful move on the football field which remotely resembled a foul immediately brought down a bombardment of yells of *'Kaiser's bodyguard, you bastards. Kaiser's bodyguard'*, which was a reference to an unfortunate incident which befell the Black Watch at Mons. This insult invariably brought down howls of retaliation from the supporters of the Gordons: *'Wha took the bite oot o' yer spats?'* Not one man in a hundred was aware that this calumny referred to a long-ago battle against charging Dervishes when the military ancestors of the Black Watch had broken their square and caused the regiment to be disgraced in perpetuity by having a V-shaped incision in their spats. Not that anyone was wearing spats at the front, but this was a point of small importance and often the shindigs among rival supporters carried on for some time after the final whistle blew. But the Military Police were never far away, and the crowds were generally well behaved. The football fans had picked up a new slogan that incorporated their immediate ambition as well as their favourite pastime and it was frequently chanted at half-time. *'Kaiser Bill we're going to kill, I bet our score is twelve to nil.'*

Young Bill Worrell was also helping to prepare for the projected
'killing' of the Kaiser and he was not enjoying himself.

Rfn. W. Worrell.

In the line at Laventie, a number of us were sent for to go back
to Battalion HQ. I went back in fear and trembling because I'd
been in all sorts of trouble in my time, but I couldn't imagine
what I'd done. Anyhow, when I got back I was asked would I
like to take a little job for just a few days. All I should have to
do would be four hours' duty a day. The rest of the time I'd be
off and I'd be in the reserve – no trench work, no trench duties,
no carrying parties. Well of course, when you had an offer like
that the answer's 'Certainly!' Well we moved up, then looking
round I saw that the others were just as skinny as I was – I
weighed 7 stone 6 pounds in those days, and they were all about
the same size as me. There were six of us and we were told,
'Righto, strip off here. Just keep your trousers on.' We were
wondering what on earth it was all about. Then we went into
this sap. We were mining across to put a mine under the
German trench in readiness for 25 September, you see. And we
got in there, spaced out – there was hardly room to get in – you
could just about get in and just sit down. And there we were a
few feet back from the Welsh miner who was working on the
face digging out, with a listener with him, filling up sandbags
with earth as he cut it back, and we had to pass them along and
carry them out. It was awfully hot and it was a good thing they
told us to strip off because we were perspiring profusely. Four
hours of that was a very hard day's work. That was the only
time I ever had anything to do with mining, and I wouldn't want
to do any more of it!

The men who had volunteered to join the special gas brigades were
even more fed up, for their job was no picnic and they failed to see
how by any stretch of the imagination a 'special knowledge of
chemistry' was of the slightest assistance in doing it. Muscle power
would have been much more to the point for it seemed that the main
requirement was for labour and it was no light task to unload the
heavy gas cylinders from the trains at the railhead at Gorre and
heave them on to the wagons that would take them to dumps behind
the line. The only part of the job that demanded any degree of
expertise was the task of unscrewing the boxes and removing the
cylinders in order to loosen their dome covers with a long spanner so
that the cylinders were ready for action and the gas could be

speedily released. This was done on the station platform. It was perfectly safe and there was no possibility of any leakage, but this was not the view of one panicky senior staff officer who came to inspect their progress. He ordered them to stop doing it forthwith. There was no officer of the Royal Engineers of sufficient seniority to argue or to point out the difficulties of opening tightly screwed boxes and undoing the stiff tops of cylinders in trenches in the dark. The General had spoken, there was no more to be said and from then on the weighty boxes were carried straight from the train to the wagons.

The wagon wheels were muffled, and even the hooves of the horses were thrust into partly filled sandbags so that the rumble of wheels and the sound of hooves striking the stone pavé of the roads would not be heard. Sound carried long distances at night, and well the infantry of the working parties knew it as they tramped cautiously humping the heavy gas cylinders from the dumps to the trenches. The cylinders themselves weighed sixty pounds and each contained another sixty pounds of liquid gas. With frequent and necessary halts to rest, it took two men carrying one between them as much as four hours to cover a mile and a half to the front line. They also had to carry other equipment – the seven-foot-long connecting pipes, the ten-foot parapet pipes that would carry the gas well away from the trench to drift towards the German lines and, in case something went wrong, the Vermorel sprayers to be placed at intervals along the trenches to clear them of gas if the need arose.

It was not easy to carry the long pipes through narrow trenches and round traverses but somehow it was accomplished. By 20 September all the cylinders had been carried to the front line and installed by the Royal Engineers in specially dug emplacements, well sandbagged for protection. It had taken many hours of labour and much cursing and swearing to undo the tight domeheads which might easily have been untightened at Gorre. The special gas squads were in charge now and it would be their job to discharge the gas when the moment came. In the course of gas-mask drill officers passed on to the infantry some rudimentary instruction on the effect of gas which they themselves had gleaned sketchily from demonstrations. In the weeks before the battle company officers were sent off in batches for instruction.

Capt. W. G. Bagot-Chester, MC.

Sept. 5. Today being a holiday, Company Commanders had to go to St Omer to see how to kill our fellow creature with gas. So four of us and some from other regiments started off in a motor bus at 8.45 a.m., arriving at the place of demonstration at 12 noon, where we were taken on to a heath where the gas apparatus had been prepared in a trench. Two cylinders were emptied for our benefit, and several smoke cartridges lit which gave forth volumes of smoke. After lunch in St Omer we started back at 4 p.m., and our driver took us hell for leather back, so that we took in returning about half the time as on our way onward previously.

Walter Bagot-Chester's 'holiday' had ended more happily than Lieutenant Waterlow's. Several days later he was still suffering the effects.

Lt. A. Waterlow.

I had instructions to attend a lecture on gas at Houchin in the afternoon and so I borrowed from battalion HQ one of the signaller's bikes, which was a great deal too small for me, and made my way back through Noeux-les-Mines, past the bombing school on its western outskirts – where live bombs were bursting perilously near to the road – to the practice trenches at Houchin where the gas lecture took place. There was a large gathering there, including General Barter and members of his staff. After the lecture we all had to pass through the gas. They had a cylinder of gas on the edge of one of the trenches, hissing it out in our faces as we passed along the trench in single file. We only had the plain helmets on, with the piece of mica for a window, and my helmet was by no means gas proof. After getting a whiff of it which made me cough, I held my breath, but the queue in front was very slow in moving and I got held up with the cylinder blowing the stuff right into my face! But I wasn't chancing a second breath of it, so my lungs were nearly bursting when eventually I got clear. General Barter carefully tied a gaily coloured silk handkerchief round his head before donning his helmet – a mirth-provoking sight.

Troops out of the line were marched to a scale model of the battlefield constructed well away from prying eyes. It covered almost a whole field and was large enough for platoons and even half-companies to walk across the ground that represented their front and, more particularly, the enemy front that lay beyond and the unknown country that would be theirs when they advanced to beat the enemy back. Small mounds of earth were heaped up to represent hills, chalk was sprinkled with careful precision to show

486

the trench-lines, and even the slag-heaps were represented by small piles of coal and buildings by half-bricks. It was far from being a facsimile of the battlefield, but at least it was better than the few yards of ground glimpsed in the mirror of a trench periscope or seen through binoculars from a long way off and it gave the troops a miniature bird's-eye view of the terrain.

It was a coalfield rather than a battlefield. In the centre of the sector, on the ridge that rose immediately above the British line, the Germans had constructed two redoubts in their front trench system. The Lens Road redoubt protected the main road that led to the large mining village of Lens, invisible behind rising ground and slag-heaps. The Loos Road redoubt, some few hundred yards to the north, straddled a country track from Vermelles to the smaller village of Loos across the valley. It was a strange landscape. Wide stretches of fields and farmland where the crops, unharvested when the fighting came in 1914, had seeded themselves and poked up tentative shoots round the trench-lines in the spring – soon trampled into the earth by the passage of troops and wagons on their way to the line. Behind Loos the ground rose to another ridge that carried a road from Lens to la Bassée, following the slope as the ridge dropped towards Hulluch and dropping with it to run arrow-straight to Auchy and the canal beyond. But the unmistakable landmarks were the mine workings and the slag-heaps the French called 'crassiers' that reared up among the villages behind the German line. From the long black fingers of the Double Crassier, across the front of the 47th London Division, to the dumps of the mines round Auchy four miles to the north, it was plain that they would be formidable obstacles. Even the foreign names were difficult for the British to grasp, but the French had originally drawn the trench maps so the Tommies had to put up with them. Not all the slag-heaps were 'crassiers'. Some appeared as 'fosse' on the maps, and the mines themselves as 'puits'. The nearest most Tommies could get to that was 'pits' – and by chance it was a literal translation.

The overhead workings that rose from a pit at Loos doubtless had another peculiar name, but this did not concern the Tommies. It was the most prominent landmark across the front, high twin pylons each topped with an ironwork turret and linked by a long iron walkway. Rearing up beside Loos village it reminded the Londoners forcibly of home. They christened it Tower Bridge.

The whole panorama was well behind the German lines, dug deep, well defended, and protected by what looked to the waiting troops like veritable forests of barbed wire.

In the wire in front of the British trenches gaps were to be stealthily cut during the night before the battle to make passages for the infantry to advance and to rush across No Man's Land to the German trenches where, they fervently hoped, the wire entanglements that protected the Germans would have been cut to pieces by the guns. And guns had been brought up as close as possible to the front line to make sure that there would be no mistake. One was placed near the foot of the slope where the old road into Loos village was barred on the crest of the ridge by the formidable Loos Road redoubt.

Bdr. A. Dunbar, A Bty., 236 Brig., Royal Field Artillery.

After a busy time at Festubert and Givenchy my battery came into action not far from Vermelles, near the main road from Béthune to Loos. Preparations were obviously in hand for a big push. From our battery position we could see the towers of the Hulluch mine-workings, part of Hill 70 and the Double Crassier nearby. Beyond this and out of our sight was the town of Loos. We suspected that it would be one of the objectives in the attack. My gun was detached from the battery and was to be used *only* on the day of the opening attack for cutting the wire of the enemy's trenches to provide spaces through which our infantry could advance. For this to be effective the gun had to be taken as near to the target as possible so that the trajectory of the shrapnel shell and its bullets would be almost parallel to the ground when the shell burst so as to do the maximum damage to the wire.

Alongside the main road and about a mile in front of the other guns of the battery was a row of houses (or partly demolished houses) and their backs looked across open ground to the front-line trenches. Between the German and our front line the distance was about sixty yards. One of these houses had a ground-floor room intact and from the corner of the house we could look straight across to the wire about four hundred yards away. My gun was brought up at night and after cutting through the back wall of the room we positioned it facing the back corner. We then made a right-angled frame of wood and covered this with canvas which we painted to resemble bricks. We cut out the bricks in the corner and replaced them with our 'dummy' – hoping that the Germans wouldn't see the deception! But I went up to our front line the next day and I couldn't distinguish our dummy wall from the real bricks, even with binoculars. It was a perfect match. That was on 15 September and it was my birthday and I was very pleased.

We got up about two hundred rounds of shrapnel and a few high explosive shells and put plenty of sandbags around the gun and the inside walls of the room. All the outside work had to be done at night because the road was under observation from German balloons and there were always plenty of *those* on the watch.

After three or four days a bombardment started up and it seemed to us that all the guns for miles were taking part except us. It went on for a week and we wondered where they got all the ammunition from. It certainly disturbed our rest at night and having finished all our work we were hoping for a little peace.

All through the month of September more batteries of guns had arrived and were moved into freshly dug positions behind the lines. They did a lot for the morale of the troops as they passed to and from the front and a new ditty began to enliven the march and their spirits at the same time.

> There's a battery snug in the spinney
> A French 75 in the mine
> A big 9.2 in the village
> Three miles to the rear of the line.
> The gunners will clean them at dawning,
> And slumber beside them all day,
> But the guns chant a chorus at sunset
> And then you should hear what they say!

Four days before zero, on 21 September, the guns began to bombard the German lines. By comparison with future bombardments and the battles that lay ahead it was meagre, but it was the heaviest of the war so far. Even the gunners were thrilled. Alan Watson, whose daily diary had hitherto contained little more than a bald record of the weather and letters received, scribbled page after page in his excitement.

Gnr. J. A. Watson, 13th Siege Bty., Royal Garrison Artillery.

Sept. 21. The opening of the bombardment. Heavy firing all day by the Field Artillery, continual roar all day – sounds champion after doing nothing and we have great hopes of advancing. Fired twelve rounds off my gun.

Sept. 22. I would like to write a description of what this is like at the time being. It sounds great. Last night about 10 p.m., heavens what a row! It was like hundreds of railway trains going through the air. This is the second day and the big guns began in earnest at twelve. How it is going and what it is like with the

Germans, goodness knows. *They* are dropping a few round here but we are just reading and playing cards, being off duty. Our relief is on. All our chaps in great spirits. I do hope it is a success. I think we are getting seasoned to the war. Don't seem to realise that any minute a shell might put paid to our account. If this could only be transferred to Leyburn for half an hour wouldn't it open their eyes at home! It is worth enlisting for. A chap with the gift could write a book on the impressions this gives. Nothing that I have heard before approaches it. Everyone thinks it is the beginning of the end, but if it is a failure and if the Germans can stand this and what is to come, they will hold out for years yet. Our battery fired about a hundred and sixty rounds today – my gun seventy-two.

Sept. 23. Bombardment worse than ever, especially in the afternoon. I was no. 1 on the gun and it alone fired ninety-two rounds. My head was aching somewhat. Refugees leaving the village, but the Germans are scarcely replying at all. Got complimented by the Captain and Lieutenant on the working of my gun.

Sept. 24. Bombardment still going on. Thunderstorm last night and it was a whisper compared with the artillery fire this afternoon. I have heard some since I came out here, but none to hold a candle to this. Our gun fired sixty-two rounds.

Whatever its effect on the Germans the comforting roar of the guns, the crash of the explosions as shells thundered on the German lines, the exhilarating sensation of giving the enemy 'what for' raised everybody's spirits. An air of optimism rippled like a summer breeze through the ranks of the British Army from the rawest infantry private to General Haig in command of the First Army and even to the Commander-in-Chief himself. But to Haig's irritation General Willcocks in command of the Indian Corps did not appear to share the general euphoria. The two men had crossed swords in the past and for months now he had been a thorn in Haig's side for General Willcocks had many grievances and he frequently aired them. The Indians had fought stoically but in almost a year of fighting they had suffered huge casualties and, in General Willcocks's view, his men had frequently been mishandled. Their numbers had gone steadily down and there was no possibility of getting trained replacements from India. A high proportion of his officers had been killed and arbitrarily replaced by others who were unfamiliar with the character and the shibboleths of Indian troops. There was no leave for the Indians, scant provision was made for their well-being, and General Willcocks was upset that unduly strict

490

censorship had prevented any detailed news of their exploits being published in India. His frequent complaints, his zealous concern for the morale and efficiency of his troops, had not been welcomed and the matter came to the boil at a conference of senior commanders convened to discuss plans for the offensive. Alone among the Corps Commanders, General Willcocks 'made difficulties'. Haig's patience snapped and he sacked him on the spot. It was bad luck on the Indian Corps to lose their Commander and most stalwart supporter just before the battle.

Although a veil was drawn over the details of the quarrel, Willcocks's main concern was almost certainly the fear of incurring excessive casualties in the weakened ranks of his hard-pressed Indian troops, for they were to undertake a 'subsidiary attack', and subsidiary attacks, as Willcocks well knew, were usually denied the support and resources allocated to the main offensive. Their purpose was to keep the enemy guessing, to keep his reserves pinned down and to prevent him from reinforcing his front where the 'real' battle was taking place. But subsidiary actions were real enough to the troops who had to fight them. The Indians were to attack on the left of Loos across the old battleground at Neuve Chapelle. Their objective was Aubers Ridge and this time, with the certainty of success at Loos, they would be carried on to the ridge by its momentum. Or so it was hoped. Casualties, in the circumstances, were unavoidable but this time there was no doubt that they would be worth it.

Twenty miles to the north where another subsidiary attack was to be launched in the Ypres salient, the 4th Gordon Highlanders were out of the line practising for the battle. They had no need of a model battlefield to introduce them to the ground for it was only too familiar. They were to fight yet again at Hooge. They had been out for a week on a well-earned rest, camped round the pleasant village of Ouderdom, far enough from the line to have escaped the ravages of war, and U Company made the most of it. There were new faces in every platoon but there were still enough of the original student members to mark the company out from the rest. There was even an inner core now. During one particularly uproarious evening in an estaminet, a dozen of them had formed the 'Society of Good Johns'. The fact that only three of its members happened to bear the Christian name of John was immaterial. The main object of their exclusive club was quite simply to enjoy themselves.

Sgt. A. Rule.

At our first meeting our wine order was twelve bottles of vin rouge (très ordinaire!). The after-effects of immature wine are extremely potent and we were fortunate that the day following our inaugural meeting was a Sunday. At the second – and as it turned out the last – meeting of the 'Johns', we condescendingly granted admission to three new members who had given evidence of their fitness and one condition was their ability to treat the foundation members to a round of drinks. Our source of inspiration was also augmented by a bottle of whisky and the 'Johns' rapidly got down to business. We opened up with the chorus '*Varsity Y'Gorra*' in full tongue, and then every member in turn sang a song or told a story. Sandwiched in between these items were rousing student songs and army choruses sung with such magnificent gusto that the old pewter pieces on the walls of the estaminet rattled till they threatened to fall. A party of veterans belonging to the Middlesex and the Suffolk afterwards assured us that they would never forget the honour of being present as privileged spectators at a festive meeting of 'real students', as they put it!

We evacuated the farmhouse-kitchen estaminet in reasonably good order and set off on a general bearing that would take us to our billets – although two members were with difficulty prevented from sleeping in each other's arms in a turnip field along the way. The camp was fully warned of our approach by bursts of song, so we sacrificed the element of surprise, but we still managed with great gallantry to make an irregular frontal assault on the bivouacs. A brilliant feint attack on the right flank was carried out by one member who temporarily lost his bearings and rejoined the main party crawling stealthily on all fours, under the impression that he was in No Man's Land! We met spirited resistance from the occupants of bivouacs near ours when we suddenly descended through their hessian walls on top of them. It was pandemonium until an avenging angel arrived suddenly in the person of an extremely wrathful Regimental Sergeant-Major, torn from his beauty sleep at an unearthly hour on a cold, raw morning. We made a wild dive for our bivouacs and silence descended on the camp – though it was broken for a time by sounds indicating grievous internal suffering!

It was the last meeting of the 'Good Johns'. Next day, on the eve of their departure for the front, the Brigade was drawn up in close column and had the privilege of being inspected by Lord Kitchener himself. U Company stood at attention with the rest, spruce and burnished, showing no signs of the excesses of the night before. A band played the National Anthem and if some hung-over members of U Company winced as three thousand or so rifles crashed down

The ruins of Hooge Chateau in the early stages of the Second Battle of Ypres (*Imperial War Museum*)

Seventy years on. The modest modern chateau rebuilt on the margin of the mine crater, scene of bitter fighting, now landscaped as a sunken lawn and lake

The *flammenwerfer*. German experiment with liquid fire which later decimated the troops at Hooge (*Imperial War Museum*)

A ration dump in Sanctuary Wood. The notice board reads, 'No road by daylight' (*Imperial War Museum*)

Part of the line in Sanctuary Wood, known as the appendix, where it jutted towards the German line (*Imperial War Museum*)

Alex Rule of U Company, 4th Gordon Highlanders, lay wounded in a dug-out much like this one after the fight for the crater at Hooge

8 Septr. 1915.

Adj. 3rd London Regt.

Reconnaissance Report.

Reference:
Sketch Map attached.

1. DUCKS BILL.   In a fairly good state - parados weak in many places -

2. NECK TO DUCKS BILL.   Parapet in places only 2'-3' thick - is a breastwork for about 4' above ground.
    Arranged to fire to E. only.
    Traverses non-existent or bad.

3. BRANCH OF NECK.   Unfinished but good where complete.   Little or no parados.

4. ORCHARD.   Thick hedge all round.
    On S.E side ditch between hedge & road - 3'-4' broad, 3' deep dry but muddy in places.
    On N.W side no ditch
    On S.W. side ditch (dry) between SUNKEN ROAD & hedge.

A.J Agius Capt.

Captain Agius's reconnaissance report and sketch of the infamous 'Duck's Bill' prior to the subsidiary attack on 25 September

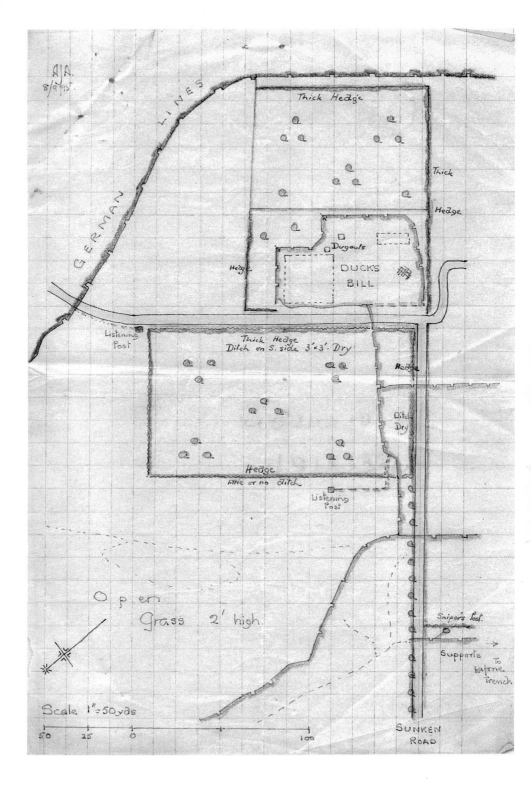

Loos. British bombardment on the German line beyond the newly dug assembly trenches. The long lines of glistening white chalk gave the enemy ample warning of the attack (*Imperial War Museum*)

The Loos battlefield from the British front line (*Imperial War Museum*)

Loos. Looking across from the British line the most prominent landmark on the front was the pithead at Loos. The troops nicknamed it Tower Bridge (seen here before the battle with the Loos Crassier in front and the village below) (*Imperial War Museum*)

Loos. During the battle. 'Tower Bridge had caught it badly: loose iron girders creaked and clanked above the heads of the Northumberland Fusiliers shivering in a field not far away' (*Imperial War Museum*)

Carnage on the Loos road. 'I can't describe it! It was just a mass of holes, and
debris and dead men and horses lying everywhere. Our transport had been
shelled – knocked out!' Harry Fellowes, 12th Battalion, Northumberland
Fusiliers (*Imperial War Museum*)

An appeal to laggards

in a General Salute it was hardly noticeable. All eyes were on legendary Kitchener – the stern face, familiar from ten thousand recruiting posters, the imposing figure, ramrod straight, the chest bearing the ribbons of medals earned in long years of campaigns and service. He moved along the ranks with an escort of staff officers and inspected the men with a critical eye. When he mounted a rostrum to speak to them he did not mince his words.

Sgt. A. Rule.

He bluntly told us that our attack was in the nature of a sacrifice to help the main offensive which was to be launched 'elsewhere'. For that reason, he said, no attempt had been made to conceal our preparations. He congratulated us on the position of honour and responsibility that had fallen to us as a Territorial unit and he wished us '*as much luck as we could expect*' in the course of the next few days. His final words to us were '*Goodbye and good luck!*'

It was part of the plan to delude the Germans into believing that the main attack was to be in the salient and it was clear that they had taken the point. Even before they left the trenches to march to Ouderdom the Gordons had been dismayed to observe a taunting placard propped up on the German wire: '*Why not attack today Jock? Why wait for the 25th?*'

General Haking in command of XI Corps which now included the newly formed Guards Division, was a good deal more sanguine than Lord Kitchener had been about the outcome of the battle. He rode over to meet the officers and senior NCOs of the 2nd Guards Brigade to brief them personally on the plans for the battle. He exuded confidence. He compared the German line to the crust of a pie – one thrust and it would be broken and behind it he expected there would be so little resistance that they would have no trouble in carving a way through. But the Coldstream were old campaigners and the general perhaps noticed a look of scepticism on the faces of the men who had been out since Mons. He paused, then added earnestly, 'I don't tell you this to cheer you up. I tell you because I really believe it.'

The 24th Division was on the move. So was the 21st, somewhat to the surprise of Captain Pole who had expected his battalion to spend weeks or even months in training. They had been just ten days in France, but they were anything but despondent to be marching towards the battle. True, they were only intended to be in general reserve 'in case of need', but at least they would be where the action

493

was. It was a long way to march, but they moved off in the early evening, marched late into the night and rested, roughing it, by day. And the days were sunny and nights were fine. A golden harvest moon hung low, growing bigger on every night of the march. There would be a full moon for the battle.

At their first stop David Pole scribbled an answer to a letter he had been surprised to receive on the day that they set off. It was from the worried wife of his commanding officer, Colonel Harry Warwick.

Collingham
Newark-on-Trent
September 19th, 1915.

Dear Captain Pole

I have only met you once but my husband has so often talked to me about you. I want to ask you if you would try to let me know about Harry if he were not well, or if anything was wrong and he could not write to me himself. There is no one else I know well enough to write and ask this, and it would be such a comfort to me to feel there is someone who would let me know at once if possible. I wish I could be less anxious, but I do find it so difficult in these times. I don't want Harry to think I am worrying so I shall not tell him I have written. I am hoping I may hear from him again soon, but of course he cannot give me any idea where he is and I can't get used to not knowing yet. But I must just be patient and I do realise it does not help one bit to worry and I am one of the lucky mothers with three little children to take up most of my time, so that I can't sit down long and think. I am sure you won't mind doing what I have asked.

Yours sincerely
Margaret J. Warwick

By 23 September, after three nights' marching, the battalion had reached Allouagne, ten miles behind the front. They were 'resting' until further orders. C Company's officers were squeezed into the house of a French soldier who had been at the front for fourteen months and was home on his first leave. It had expired that morning. He embraced his wife and children and shook hands with all the officers before he left, and now his red-eyed wife was doing her best to make them comfortable. After they had breakfasted on rations supplemented by the last of their sardines, and by pears from the garden, Pole went off to scour the local shops for delicacies to replenish the officers' mess box. He returned with some tins of asparagus, mushrooms and peas. It was decided unanimously that they should 'test' them for lunch and Madame was requested, for a small consideration, to use them as a filling for a few twelve-egg omelettes.

It took Captain Pole the rest of the morning to inspect C Company's billets. The men were housed in three large barns and Harry Fellowes, who had been dead to the world for some hours, was having some difficulty in fitting his swollen feet into his army boots. The Tommies had stew for lunch and, since hunger is a good sauce, pronounced it 'not half bad'. They too had pears for dessert, filched from the trees that were reasonably near the roadside, but there were plenty to spare.

Chapter 33

So far as possible the troops who were to be in the first wave of the assault had been relieved and rested for at least three days before the battle. The day before they moved up the line was filled with last-minute preparations. Padres were issued with Burial Registration Books; 'green envelopes' were distributed so that soldiers who wished could put their affairs in order, for such letters containing private and personal information could be sent uncensored by battalion officers, although they might be opened at the base. Extra rations and ammunition were drawn, rifles and feet were inspected, last-minute instructions issued to NCOs. There were sing-songs that night and gambling too, for some troops had been paid and the Crown and Anchor kings set up their boards to fleece them. Mostly they succeeded, but the Tommies didn't mind much. The games had pleasantly passed the time and moreover even the soldiers of Kitchener's Army had quickly cottoned on to the superstition that it was bad luck to go into battle with money in your pocket.

The guns thundered on and the Tommies lying in flimsy bivouacs or on the floors of half-ruined buildings for their last full night's sleep were lulled to rest, or kept awake, by the vibration of the guns pulsing gently through their heads. They were lucky if they slept at all for a spectacular thunderstorm gave way to heavy rain.

Lt. A. F. P. Christison, MC, 6 Bn., Queen's Own Cameron Highlanders, 45 Brig., 15 Div.

Next day men handed in packs and greatcoats and with the C.O. and Adjutant I attended the final briefing for the Battle of Loos. Brigadier-General Wallerstein, a small old man with white hair, gave out the orders clearly enough. The four machine-gun sections were to be brigaded under the Brigade Machine-Gun Company and given the task of protecting the left flank of the division. The Northamptons would be on our left and we were to liaise with them as they advanced. Our Colonel asked whether, if we got our objective easily, we were

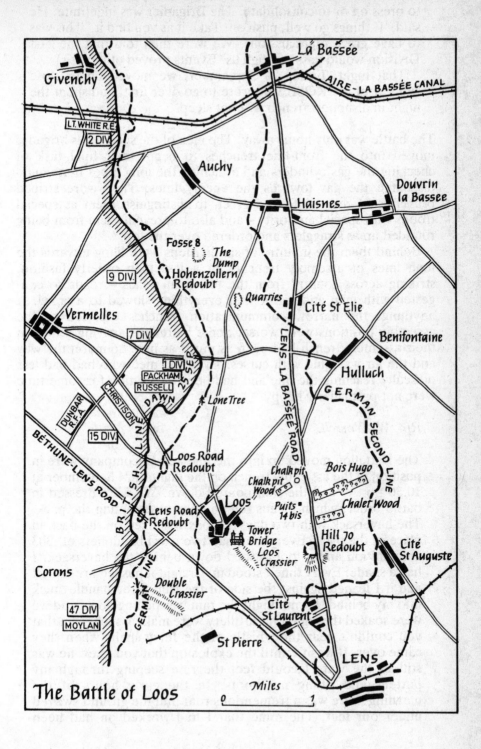

Givenchy

La Bassée

AIRE - LA BASSÉE CANAL

LT. WHITE R.E.
2 DIV

Auchy

Douvrin
la Bassée

Haisnes

Fosse 8

The
Dump
Hohenzollern
Redoubt

9 DIV.

Quarries

Cité St Elie

Benifontaine

Vermelles

7 DIV

Hulluch

1 DIV
PACKHAM
RUSSELL

Lone Tree

GERMAN SECOND LINE

DUNBAR
R.F.A.

15 DIV

CHRISTISON

DAWN 25 SEP

BÉTHUNE-LENS ROAD

BRITISH LINE

LENS - LA BASSÉE ROAD

Loos Road
Redoubt

Chalk pit

Chalk pit
Wood

Bois Hugo

Lens Road
Redoubt

Loos

Puits
14 bis

Chalet Wood

Tower
Bridge
Loos
Crassier

Hill 70
Redoubt

Cité
St Auguste

Corons

GERMAN LINE

Double
Crassier

Cité
St Laurent

47 DIV
MOYLAN

St Pierre

LENS

The Battle of Loos

Miles

0   1

to press on or to consolidate. The Brigadier was indefinite. He said, 'If things go well, push on. Take it as you find it.' This was to have grave repercussions. We were then told that the 21st Division would pass through us. Events proved otherwise.

That night, Friday 24 September, we moved up in close support of the KOSB who were to go over first, and spent the night in a support trench without sleep.

The battle was only hours away. The men of the special gas brigades moved into the front-line trenches to begin their final task of checking the gas cylinders and attaching the long pipes that would discharge the gas towards the enemy lines. They wore striped brassards of red, white and green to distinguish them as special troops with special authority – and also to prevent them from being rounded up as stragglers and ordered over the top.

Behind them the infantry of six divisions were filing towards the long lines of assembly trenches in a less than orderly fashion, striking across country from the few main roads – roads so congested with men and traffic that everything slowed to a crawl. If anything, the narrow communication trenches that led to the assembly positions were worse. Some battalions arriving at last in their assembly trench had been as much as nine hours on the way and the air was blue with curses. Even the men who had had less difficulty reaching the line and had been in position for some time were not particularly happy.

Rfn. W. Worrell.

The Battalion moved up into the line and C Company were in position in the assembly trench on the night of 24 September at 10.30 p.m. – and the rain poured down. We were dressed in battle order, which means full equipment excepting the pack. The haversack with two days' rations was fixed on the back in place of the pack. Every man had two extra bandoliers of .303 ammunition and a tool pushed down behind the haversack. I had a spade. Every time I stood up straight it pushed my cap off and if I leaned against the side of the trench the handle stuck into my behind. By midnight the rain was pelting down and we were soaked through. Our artillery were making such a din that you couldn't hear the whistle of the Jerry shells when they came over. It wasn't until the explosion that you knew he was still in the war. I could feel the rain seeping through my puttees and filling my boots. In the early hours of the morning there was a tremendous roar and the ground swayed under our feet. The mine that I had worked on had been exploded. The artillery bombardment seemed to increase until the noise became painful. Just before dawn the two sergeants, Spud Murphy and Sid Hubbard, came along the top of the trench with a jar and a mug. 'Take a good swig, youngster,' said Sergeant Hubbard. I did that, then gasped, coughed and spluttered. Neat rum, I found out, should not be swallowed in mouthfuls!

There was deep gloom in the trenches where the weary men of the 7th Cameron Highlanders waited miserably for the dawn, for Colonel Sandilands had deprived them of the tot of rum that might have cheered them up. 'If my men are going to meet their maker,' he said, 'they will meet Him sober!' And he had even ordered the sergeants to up-end the jars and pour the precious rum away. They tipped it over the back of the shallow trench and the men got never a sniff of it. Their indignation helped to keep them warm.

For the umpteenth time platoon sergeants checked the equipment each man would take into battle. One particular item was unique to the 7th Camerons and scout Sergeant Tommy Lamb was rather pleased with it. Some of the signallers would be carrying flags or discs on long poles, coloured differently for each division, which they would hold aloft as their battalion advanced to pinpoint the positions of the troops. The flags of the 15th Division were plain yellow, but Tommy Lamb was struck by the idea of cutting a square of Cameron tartan from an old kilt and, with the colonel's permission, having it sewn to one corner of the identifying flag. Now the battalion would go into battle bearing the Cameron colours. Colonel Sandilands was delighted.

General Sir Douglas Haig spent a sleepless night for he was painfully conscious that everything depended on the speed and direction of the wind. Forty gas officers positioned along the front, specially trained to estimate velocity and direction, sent back reports every hour and the wind was also measured in a dozen different places behind the front. Once or twice a night reports came in from Paris collating observations made at various points in France, and weather conditions in the British Isles, monitored at 1 p.m. and again twelve hours later, were wired directly to France. This was standard procedure, for wind and weather were vital to the operations of the Royal Flying Corps and it was the responsibility of the Meteorological Officer, Captain Gold, to see them plotted on a huge chart of western Europe and to produce weather forecasts accordingly. The forecasts were rough and ready, and in the changeable climate of western Europe they could not hope to be accurate for more than the next few hours – but it was the next few hours that mattered. Never had the chart on the wall of the Met. Office been scrutinised more often and more anxiously than in the hours before the battle. As the night wore on, the favourable conditions on which Haig had decided to gamble began to look more doubtful.

The weather forecast at this hour, 9.45 p.m., indicates that a west or south west wind may be anticipated tomorrow, 25th September. All orders issued for the attack with gas will therefore hold good. The hour of Zero will be notified later during the night.

At three o'clock in the morning, after he had plotted the latest reports from the British Isles, Captain Gold went to see General Haig. Near the front the wet westerly wind was still steadily blowing. Usually, Gold explained, the wind began to increase after sunrise but it was impossible, in this case, to rely on it. The wind following the south-westerly was weakening and showing a tendency to turn to the south. General Haig went straight to the point. What time then, in the opinion of Captain Gold, would be the most favourable for the attack? Gold hesitated, reluctant to commit himself. 'As soon as possible,' he said.

'As soon as possible' was dawn, and the order was given at once. At ten to six in the morning the gas was to be turned on and forty minutes later the infantry would follow it over the top. The guns roared on, flashing through the pitch-black night. As the first streak of dawn appeared in the sky behind the German lines the rain eased off. The wind began to drop.

Like the supply of shells, the supply of gas had not come up to expectations. German gas-masks, like those of the British, were soaked in chemicals to filter the lethal fumes and experiments with masks taken from prisoners had shown that they remained effective for only half an hour. After that they had to be re-processed and re-dipped, so it was vital to the British plan that gas clouds should envelop the Germans for at least forty minutes. But such a quantity of gas was simply not available and the plan was modified. For the first twelve minutes six gas cylinders would be discharged, then at two-minute intervals four smoke candles would be lit, then another twelve-minute burst of gas, then six minutes of smoke and, in the last two minutes before the assault, the final and largest burst of smoke would smother the front and cover the infantry as they climbed out of the trenches. It was the best that could be done and this programme would at least ensure that the Germans would still be wearing their masks long after they had lost the power to protect them.

Lt. A. B. White, 186 Coy., Royal Engineers.

My men had previously had the programme explained to them.
By 5.30 a.m. I had everything ready to start at zero and I went
back a short distance to see whether the wind was favourable.
Finding it blowing very lightly from the south south-west and
varying considerably in direction, I decided not to carry on and
warned the men to do nothing without further orders. At 5.40
a.m. a mine was blown up in front of my line. The charge
appeared to have been weak as no debris was thrown up, only
an immense cloud of smoke. From the direction in which the
smoke drifted I was confirmed in my impression that it would
not be safe to carry on.

Lieutenant White was on the 2nd Division front near the la Bassée
Canal, and almost in the same place where Tommy Robartes' band
had treated the Germans to the 'concert'. The mine exploded on the
German line just beyond the lip of the crater they called Etna, but the
Germans were not there. They had retired to another line some fifty
yards behind, and the mine exploded harmlessly beneath their empty
trench. It did at least give a useful pointer to the direction of the wind.
   The light grew stronger. From his position on a high slag-heap
General Gough's French interpreter, Paul Maze, was able to pick
out landmarks coming slowly out of the night. The slag-heaps,
sharply conical or low and lumbering like hump-backed whales; the
skeleton tracery of Tower Bridge rising out of Loos, the overhead
wires above the pits, and suspended coal trolleys 'silhouetted like
spiders entangled in their webs'.

Just before daybreak in front of the Lens Road Redoubt Alex
Dunbar's gun crew had pulled aside the false walls of the ruined
cottage to reveal their gun and were firing point blank at the
German wire entanglements to open a path for the infantry.

Bdr. A. Dunbar.

We ran the muzzle forward into the opening and started work.
Through my telescope sight I had an excellent view of the target
and I could pick out the section of wire I wanted to cut. It was
easy! This was the first occasion I had used direct firing and I
found it much more interesting than laying on an aiming post
and never seeing the target.
   After firing about fifty rounds, I noticed that my eyes were
beginning to water and before long I could hardly see at all. I
put this down to the fumes of the cordite which came from the

breech every time it was opened. The others didn't seem to be affected so I thought that the extra strain of laying was responsible for my trouble. I changed places with my number 2, but after a few rounds *he* was crying his eyes out! Just then we became aware of a beautiful smell of lilac filling the room. This was the last thing we expected. Perhaps there was a field of lilac nearby and a changing wind had brought the smell to us. We were puzzled.

We managed to continue firing by frequently swapping places. We hoped our infantry were keeping their heads well down when we were cutting their wire! With fuses correctly set and with such a flat trajectory there was not much risk of bullets going into our own trenches. At zero plus thirty minutes we ceased fire. We had fired about a hundred and fifty rounds and blown some useful gaps in the wire on both sides.

In the countdown to zero hour, while the guns were doing their best to cut the enemy wire, gas clouds slid across the front like a curtain stabbed by red bursts of shrapnel. But the wind had slowed down. In places it dropped altogether and Lieutenant White on the 2nd Division's front was not the only gas officer who was worried. It took him a long time to get through on the telephone to Brigade Headquarters and it was almost time for the gas to be released. Everything was in readiness. The men were standing by. The iron pipes, ten feet long, had been thrown over the parapet and joined up to the flexible tubes that linked them to the cylinders. At twelve minutes to six, with two minutes to go, White succeeded at last and spoke to the Brigadier-General and informed him that he could not carry on in these conditions. The General made no bones about the situation. Addressing his junior officer with extraordinary frankness he told him bluntly that he had already been in touch with 2nd Divisional Headquarters, that he was aware that all was not well and that he had passed on the information to higher authority. But he had received a direct order to carry on. Under these circumstances he had no alternative but to pass the order on to Lieutenant White. The General's voice was flat and unemotional, but it was clear that the decision was not his. By the time White returned from the telephone in a support trench to the emplacement in the front line it was almost six o'clock. He ordered the gas to be turned on and the cylinders were opened.

Lt. A. B. White.

At first the gas drifted slowly towards the German lines (it was plainly visible owing to the rain) but at one or two bends of the trench the gas drifted into it. In these cases I had it turned off at once. At about 6.20 a.m. the wind changed and quantities of the gas came back over our own parapet, so I ordered all gas to be turned off and only smoke candles to be used.

Punctually at 6.30 a.m. one company of the King's advanced to the attack wearing smoke helmets. But there was a certain amount of confusion in the front trench owing to the presence of large quantities of gas. We experienced great difficulty in letting off the gas owing to faulty connections and broken copper pipes causing leaks. Nearly all my men suffered from the gas and four had to go to hospital. Three out of the five machine-guns on my front were put out of action by the gas.

Very little could be seen of the German line owing to the fog of smoke and gas. Our infantry reached the enemy wire without a shot being fired, but they were mown down there by machine-gun fire or overcome by the gas. One or two made their way back and reported that there were seven to ten rows of wire *uncut*, and that nobody had reached the front German trench. A report also came in that the enemy were not holding their front line, but were firing from their second line.

In the middle of the line, in front of the wire which Alex Dunbar's gun team had been so furiously cutting, the 15th Scottish Division had better luck, for the guns pounding the Lens Road Redoubt had done their job well and here even the capricious wind was stronger. But only a quarter of a mile away, where the King's Own Scottish Borderers stood stifling in gas-helmets as they waited to go over, the breeze was skittish and gas drifted back into their trenches. The German guns were shelling now. As Lieutenant Christison led the machine-gunners of the 6th Cameron Highlanders forward, even through the hiss and rattle of falling shrapnel and even above the sound of his own stentorious breathing in the suffocating mask, he caught the unmistakable wail of bagpipes. He could hardly believe his ears.

Gas was an unknown quantity. The waiting troops had worn their masks rolled up and pulled the hoods down as ordered ten minutes before zero. Already it was hard to breathe. When the gas cloud rolled back to engulf the first line of the King's Own Scottish Borderers it was not surprising that they faltered and hung back. Piper Laidlaw had saved the situation. Tearing off his own mask, leaping on the parapet, he played the pipes for all he was worth. He hardly knew what he was playing but the skirl of the pipes had done the trick. One by one, in a trickle and then in a flood, the men pulled themselves together, clambered over the parapet and began to run across towards the German wire. Machine-guns opened up and sprayed across their lines as they loomed out of the smoke.*

But across most of the 15th Division front the wind had been favourable, the Germans were demoralised, and the Scots battered and bayoneted their way across the first of their lines and swept on into the valley. By nine o'clock they had covered a quarter of a mile and were fighting in the village of Loos.

On their right, where the 47th Division were to seize the Double Crassier and extend to capture the southern outskirts of Loos, the London Territorials were well on the way to success. By the time Frank Moylan jumped off in the second wave, they had already captured the German front line.

Cpl. F. Moylan.

A and B Companies took the front line. C and D were to go through them and take the second one. I was in C. We had the furthest to go. Now, war is peculiar. C Company had the fewest casualties and went the furthest distance. B Company lost every officer – the whole lot on the right, a hell of a lot, got killed. We were lucky. We'd found gaps in the wire. It was all a matter of luck. There's a tremendous amount of luck in war, you know.

We went up the night before this attack. We were pretty tight in the trench and we sat down on the floor of it. I'd got somebody in between my legs and somebody else behind me had got *me* in between *his* legs. There was a fellow named Brockhurst behind me and a man named Emersfield in front of me and Emersfield got cramp and it meant we both had to get up and we changed positions. I was in front then and Emersfield was in the middle. We had ladders in the trench to go up, and when it came to the time we went over and we hadn't got very far when this chap Emersfield flopped down. Must have been a machine-gun bullet. Of course, he was where *I* would have been if we hadn't changed places! I remember thinking that as I saw him go down.

In an attack the whole thing seems a bit like a dream. It doesn't take as long as you think. Crossing No Man's Land, you imagine beforehand what a hell of a journey that's going to be – but it's not, and either the Germans are dead or there's no one there. There were a lot of our dead in No Man's Land as we crossed and more at the places where they'd arrived at the wire and it wasn't cut. Then they were just sitting ducks. We just

---

* Piper Laidlaw was later awarded the Victoria Cross for valour.

went through gaps in the wire, but we weren't in the first wave luckily.

We got to the German front line and they were mopping it up – there were prisoners there being mustered, and there were dead lying about. Then we got to the second line and they'd gone from there. Where we were the gas blew over the Germans and that may have driven them out of that second line. There were some dug-outs there and we went down one of them – deep, long, steep it was, very well made – and I got a terrific fright then. It was pitch black and we were just feeling our way. Somebody had a glimmer of light ahead but where I was it was really dark, and I suddenly felt this arm grabbing me and pulling me flat in the dark. I toppled right over. I nearly died of fright. I must have yelled out because someone struck a light, and there was a wounded German, lying there in the dark. He was alive but somebody must have thrown a bomb down there. He got peppered all over and he was a mass of dried blood. He was calling for his mother and for water. He was muttering, 'Mutter, Mutter, Wasser.' Mother, Mother, water. We got him out and it was a hell of a job up those stairs, and when we got him out it was raining. We laid him out in the trench there and he was taken away after a while.

When we got back in the trench I saw the most extraordinary thing happen. I got up to look over – it was quite safe, because the fighting was a good bit ahead – and there were civilians knocking about. Loos village was on our left, and suddenly out came these civilians. I saw them myself! Of course they were shepherded away as quickly as possible but I remember seeing an old woman wounded, hobbling along and thinking that she must have been shot in the leg. There was a whole bunch of them, at least a dozen, maybe more.

The Scots had broken through so swiftly in the wake of the gas, pushed back the survivors with such determination and battered their way into Loos village with such ferocity that the German troops who endeavoured to make a stand were overwhelmed in the act of erecting barriers in the streets. Soon observers were delightedly reporting back that crowds of Germans were running up the hill towards their second line with the Scots in full pursuit. The village had been captured so rapidly and so unexpectedly that days later German soldiers were still being winkled out of hiding places in attics and deep cellars. The orders were for the troops to press on as far and as fast as possible while a second and third wave followed behind to consolidate the lines they had captured, and the Jocks were carrying out their orders to the letter. They had punched a great hole in the centre of the German line and there was no stopping them.

Further north, on the left of the main attack, things had gone less well and the German line that ran in front of the village of Hulluch, past the outskirts of Auchy to straddle the la Bassée Canal was almost intact.

Paul Maze, Interpreter att. I Corps HQ.

The actual front line was completely blurred. The middle-distance between the front line and our slag-heap was now in constant convulsion, rising in columns of black earth and smoke. The gas which we had released was drifting heavily down across the left of our front, obviously in the wrong direction. We peered and peered through our glasses, trying to catch sight of anything where the smoke had drifted away. Through a gap the horizon showed up like a sinister purple streak. Suddenly someone shouted, 'What's that near Fosse 8?' We all focused our glasses on the slag-heap and for a second figures appeared, as one might see bathers surge up in the troughs of rough seas.

Our telephones buzzed feverishly; messages were coming in on the wires, all more or less confused. Someone caught a visual message and spelt the words out to another who took it down, repeating every syllable with that slow cadence that gives special significance to tidings, and leaves an indelible impression on the mind: '*We – have – no – officers – left – . . .*' Then something happened. The shutter flashing the message had closed. Contact was lost.

Scots of the 9th Division had stormed the Hohenzollern Redoubt, some had even managed to reach a slag-heap beyond it, but on either side of them where the gas had blown back matters had gone badly.

Sgt. F. M. Packham, 2nd Bn., Royal Sussex Regt., 2 Brig., 1st Div.

Our Division's directive was to reach the Loos–la Bassée Road by noon, also the Hohenzollern Redoubt, the village of Hulluch, and to get as far forward as possible by late afternoon. Then we were to hold our positions until reinforcements arrived to carry on with the advance. The right of the Division's line was marked by a lone tree that was growing in No Man's Land. My company was in the second wave of the attack, and

506

the 'lone tree' was our guiding line.

Just before we had to go over the top, an officer gave me a message to take to the officer in charge of the platoon when they reached the front line. I went up the communication trench which was full of troops which made it difficult to make good time, but I was able to get into our front line. There was a gas officer in the trench. He looked ghastly and all the buttons on his tunic were green as if they were mouldy. He was saying that the gas was blowing back into our troops' faces. The wind had turned round on us. The German shelling was terrific and the forward troops had gone over the top, and I thought *my* platoon had gone over the top and caught up with a line of advancing troops, so over I went to catch them up. The gas was now very thick and everybody was wearing gas-masks, just a flannel bag with a mica slot to see through. I had mine on but my mica slot was all steamed up and I couldn't see anything. Also, I was nearly suffocating so I took it off, and to my amazement I saw that there were only about six of us advancing. After a few more yards there were only *two* of us, and as we were both close together we flung ourselves to the ground. The man beside me asked me what we should do. I said that we'd better wait for the next line to come up to us then advance with them.

Very soon we heard the Germans firing again, and looking back we could see a line advancing. We could see men falling so I fired my own rifle at the Germans hoping to keep their heads down. When the line reached us there were only two or three left, and they too went to ground. We waited for another line to come. As we lay there the gas seemed to be getting worse and I had no mask on so I must have breathed a lot of the gas. I found that if I lifted my head up the air seemed to be much fresher. Then the Germans started firing again as another wave came over, but it was the same thing over again! In fact, nobody from this third line even got as far as our position. It was soon after that we heard someone shout for everyone to get back to our front line. As we made our way back across No Man's Land, there were a lot of men wounded or killed laying on the ground and when we reached our front line, the trench was full of troops – including a lot of wounded. I heard that my platoon officer I was looking for was killed within minutes of going over the top.

We heard that the 47th London and the 15th Scottish divisions had captured the village of Loos and had reached the German second line. Also, that our 1st Brigade had reached the Hohenzollern Redoubt and were still fighting there. It looked as if we were the only brigade that had failed to get our objective!

507

All along the left where the 19th Division were intended to form a flank to protect the main attack, it had been an almost complete failure.

Pte. W. H. Shaw, 9th Bn., Royal Welsh Fusiliers, 58 Brig., 19 (Western) Div.

I was about the most fortunate man in France that day. We were almost on the extreme flank of the sector that was going over, on the left flank, north of Loos. I was detailed to go and report to C Company. Each company had three signallers attached to the company – two asleep and one on duty. But an hour before we were due to go over I got a signal to report back to Battalion Headquarters. We were being exchanged and I was to be transferred to B Company, and three signallers from B Company were going to the company I'd just left. Well, the next thing I knew the officer I reported to said, 'We're being attached to the Welsh Regiment.' I had to report to a Captain Davies, a South Wales chap, so I reported to him and off we went, to join up with the Welsh Regiment who were on our right.

We kicked off with a rugby football. That's how we kicked off, chaps with half a dozen rugby balls belted over and in we went. Now there was a Welsh Fusilier chap, and he was the first casualty I saw. You've never seen such a mess in all your life! He was out! He was slumped over the smoke cylinder, and the smoke was pouring out from his stomach. A shell must have hit him directly, and his stomach was completely opened up. Oh! It was shocking. I was only eighteen and it was the first time I'd seen anything like that. You couldn't do anything for him.

As soon as the word came to attack and the whistles blew, the Germans actually shouted to us, 'Come on, Tommy, we know you're coming over.' 'Come on, Tommy, we're waiting for you.' They were that close! The Germans were still shelling us when we went across and, believe me, they didn't half send some stuff over! Of course, the Colonel, this Major Maddox, and the Adjutant, they were carrying their swords! Well, they hardly got out of the trench! They didn't even get to the top before they were hit by the machine-gun. Major Maddox was mown down before he got his feet on the top of the trench. They had their swords flashing, you see! It was absolutely ridiculous because the Germans were looking for officers. They were the main targets.

Well, we dived for cover, anywhere we could get, and machine-guns opened out on us and, believe me, those

508

machine-guns! Whew! Terrific. You couldn't imagine it! I was lying flat on my stomach, trying to make myself as inconspicuous as possible, and this shell came very, very close and a piece of shrapnel came down and hit me on the back of the hand. Now, that piece of shrapnel was perhaps just as big as my hand, and it came flat. It burnt me, but if it had come edge *on*, I'd have lost my hand. That was the first lucky escape I had.

We were held up. We couldn't move. We couldn't budge, and we got the orders to retire to the front line. Well, what we saw when we were trying to get back! It was real sickening seeing the lads, how they were mowed down. I still worry to this day how we stuck it out. Oh, yes, I think about it. I should say that from the time when we went over to when we got back was about an hour, and we were pinned down. We couldn't go any further. It was impossible with all the machine-guns and all the shelling! We were just pinned down and we got the order to retire. Well, there was nothing for us to do. There weren't *enough* left to do anything.

The remainder of us went back to our own regiment and when we got back, the place was in an uproar. The company that I'd originally been ordered to report to, C Company, was completely wiped out. Those three signallers that took our place, they were riddled! And there they were, stuck on the barbed wire. You see, our artillery had been trying to smash their barbed wire and never succeeded. They put a barrage down of shells for about three or four days, then, as the time came for us to go over, the artillery stopped firing but the Germans had time to get up from their dug-outs – and their dug-outs were 60, 70, 80 foot deep. You could get the whole Battalion in some of their dug-outs.

It was our own signalling officer that told us that C Company had been wiped out and that we'd lost the three signallers. We tried hard to get him to let us go and look for them, we were that keyed up. And they were such fine chaps! They were from my own town. Private Edwards, I don't know how he got the name but he was always known as Cosh, and there was Tom Jones and Billy Hughes. But they wouldn't let us go forward. Search parties went out. They wouldn't let me go. I was eighteen – the youngest man in the Battalion.

Pte. C. H. Russell, 14th (County of London) Bn. (London Scottish), 1st Brig., 1st Div.

When I first went up into the front line there were three of us in this fire bay and the sergeant came in to tell us about something and all of a sudden one of these pipsqueaks went off, bang. And, lo and behold, next minute the sergeant was right down in the ground! So of course we all laughed. He got up and he said, 'You're bloody well laughing? You wait until you've been there a month, you'll be quicker than I am in getting down to it.' He was right. My nerves were fine until I got out into the open. When you get out of the trench you feel quite naked. The protection's gone. It's a queer feeling out in the open after being in the trench for about a week.

They told us it would be a bit of cake and all we'd got to do for this attack was to dawdle along and take these trenches which we'd find pulverised by our guns. Every other blooming shot was a dud, I think. You could hear them hit *bomp*, *bang* – that was a live one – but most of them went *bomp* – then dead silence. A dud blooming shell! Lloyd George took it up. Most of the stuff wasn't worth sending out. They said that these trenches were so pulverised that we'd just walk into them and take over. When we did start the attack, my battalion lost hundreds of men in the first hour or so. The whole thing was a waste of lives.

Six of us were going along with bags of bombs. We were to follow the first wave with these bombs, because they soon go and they weigh about a pound each, so the bombers can't carry too many. All Hell was let loose. There were five ahead of me. The chap in front of me had the whole of his face blown away. I've never seen anything so horrible in all my life. It was just a red mass, his face. He sunk down moaning, making a horrible noise and I had to push on. The bag of bombs was blown out of my hand, and I picked it up again and had to walk on with it.

We were all in extended order, waiting to push on further, and a sergeant came in and said, 'You'd better wait until they sing out where they want the bombs.' So we waited there a bit and after a time we went forward again. Reinforcements never came. Another officer joined us. He wasn't one of our officers, quite a decent bloke though, and he said, 'Well, we've got to hang on here, we may have to push forward later on.' But we had to make an orderly retirement back again, because the attack failed altogether. They mowed them down.

The right-hand divisions of the 47th London Division were to steady and form a hinge on which the whole assault could pivot as it went forward. On their right the Londoners were to sweep ahead to capture the Double Crassier and the outskirts of Loos village. They had done just that, the assault had succeeded and now they were in the third German line. They were not intended to advance any further and, having gained their objectives, they were instructed to stop and to form a defensive flank at the southern end of the battle. The orders of the 15th Division had not made this clear to them. They were merely told that the 47th Division would be attacking on their right, and this half-information had given the Jocks the impression that the Londoners would continue to advance alongside them. But, as they advanced looking for the Londoners on their right, they found nobody there. Nor was there anyone to be found on their left, so both flanks of the 15th Scottish Division were 'in the air'. But still they plunged on and, in the excitement of their advance, they drifted well away from the route they should have followed. It was a long time before anyone realised that the Scots had lost direction.

Chapter 34

By nine o'clock in the morning of 25 September the flag of the 7th Cameron Highlanders was flying on Hill 70 and Sergeant Tommy Lamb had planted it there with his own hands. The remnants of two brigades were plodding up the hill and they were horribly mixed up, for the 44th Brigade should have advanced in a straight line due east and dead ahead, past the chalk pit near Puits 14 and on across the la Bassée road to Bois Hugo – a long strip of woodland that ran over the crest of the ridge. There had been nothing, or almost nothing to stop them. But, like iron filings drawn towards a magnet, the fighting in Loos had pulled them to their right and into the joyous mêlée of Scots fighting their way through the village. Now the two brigades whose disciplined ranks should have advanced on a broad front were crowded into a space of some six hundred yards, streaming up Hill 70 in a wild confusion of companies and battalions, and as they went they were drifting further and further to their right towards Hill 70 redoubt.

Hill 70 did not lie directly behind Loos but slightly to the south-east, and already the battle-plan had gone awry, for the whole division had been meant to charge straight ahead over the ridge to the north of the hill and on into the valley beyond to capture the line of defences in front of Cité St Auguste.

Cité St Auguste was not a city, nor was it a village. It was an agglomeration of miners' dwellings and mine workings bordered on the north by farms and woodland, and it was a bastion in the Germans' second line of defence. It had all looked simple and straightforward on the map but once past Loos, with the familiar slag-heaps and the pylons of Tower Bridge behind them, landmarks disappeared, so it was not so easy to keep direction and the Scotsmen's blood was up. Fired by the sight of German soldiers running away over Hill 70 the leaders of the pack could not resist giving chase. Gradually but surely the advance swung to the right and there was no stopping it. The two brigades which should have gone forward abreast with Hill 70 on their right now had the hill on their left and were plunging into the valley towards a strong

512

defensive line that circled Lens through the suburb of Cité St Laurent.

There were fewer of them now, for the ranks had thinned out, and the bodies of the Jocks lay like a tartan tide across the slopes of Hill 70, along the streets of Loos and all across the valley back to the first German line, but the Highlanders were only concerned with keeping the Germans on the run and they followed cheering as they went across the wide open slope down to Lens.

It was Colonel Sandilands arriving breathless on Hill 70 and pausing to take stock who realised that something had gone wrong and that the Jocks were not advancing due east to Cité St Auguste. He managed with some difficulty to rally the troops nearby – men of no fewer than nine different battalions – and to hold back the rest still panting up Hill 70 and, gathering them behind the crest of the hill to await developments, he ordered Tommy Lamb to wave the Cameron flag to bring the Camerons back. Tommy waved it for all he was worth but in the excitement of their plunge down the slope not many looked round or caught sight of it. They were running hell for leather. Already they were half-way to Lens and the dozen volunteer runners the Colonel dispatched to pass the word and bring them back were sucked into the throng and carried along pell-mell.

Sandilands watched in a fury of frustration. From his vantage point on the crest of the hill, looking down into Cité St Laurent, he could see barricades of wire hidden by long grass and invisible to the Jocks racing down the hill. He could also see crowds of German soldiers running through the streets to meet them, swarming into trenches and into houses to fire from the upper storeys. But they held their fire until the Scots were less than three hundred yards away. Then they let rip.

There was nowhere to go. No cover of any kind. No bush, no tree, no dip or dent across the wide bare hillside. No shelter or escape from the deadly fire. No means of answering back. All they could do was lie in the open, hoping for reinforcements and hoping even more for the guns to open up a bombardment that would keep the Germans' heads down and help them to get forward. Some men banded together in small determined groups and made valiant attempts to rush the German wire. Some who survived the storm of answering fire got within eighty yards of it. But it was palpably hopeless, and now the Germans were having things all their own way.

In the confusion of the first advance officers of the 44th Brigade arriving early on Hill 70 had not immediately grasped the inadvertent change of direction and, believing that they were still advancing due east towards Cité St Auguste, sent back reports that troops were advancing on their final objective. The confusion continued all morning, and by the time the error was rectified and the true situation was understood, it was too late. It was certainly too late for the Scots in front of Cité St Laurent, for the artillery bombardment which might have covered their retirement up the hill was thundering down a half mile to their left to assist the 'advance' that Headquarters believed was going ahead. Now every single gun was ranging on St Auguste. At St Laurent the Germans were able to fire with impunity at the slightest movement on the hill, to rake the thin line with machine-guns, to bring in reinforcements and to organise the counter-attack that would retrieve Hill 70.

Colonel Sandilands, who was well aware of this danger and powerless to prevent it, played for time, and set his troops to work digging in on the reverse slope of Hill 70. The two assaulting brigades of the 15th Division were reduced to the strength of a single Battalion, but they were on their mettle and the Colonel had every confidence that they would do their damnedest to hang on.

At First Army headquarters at Hinges, twenty-three kilometres north west of the front, the news that Loos had been captured was greeted with jubilation. The line had been punched open, the troops were through, and according to early reports which staff officers had no reason to doubt, they were advancing as fast and as far as anyone had hoped. The plan was working, at least in part, and from the first optimistic reports that reached Headquarters it seemed that almost everywhere the troops had broken through and were making progress. It only remained to push up more troops to sweep through the gaps and carry on the advance. It was time to call on the reserves and it was a matter of annoyance to Sir Douglas Haig that the reserves were not readily available. The General Reserve was still under the orders of Sir John French and he, and he alone, would decide when, and even if, he would release them to General Haig's command. It was not much of a reserve – only the untried 21st and 24th Divisions and the newly formed Guards Division – but it was all there was. The Commander-in-Chief had strong doubts about the wisdom of employing inexperienced divisions led by inexperienced officers, and strong reservations about what they could be expected to achieve. In his considered view they could be a positive hindrance in a battle. It was true that he had promised them to Haig and true also that he had approved Haig's dispositions for the battle and knew full well that he had put every one of his available divisions in the line and kept back no reserves. But he had also made a promise to the commanders of the raw divisions and he had sent his Chief of Staff to spell it out in person. In no conceivable circumstances, they were told, would the 21st and 24th Divisions be called on 'unless and until the Germans were absolutely smashed and retiring in disorder'. All they need be prepared for was 'a long march' behind the enemy as he retired. Now Haig wanted them badly and, as soon as the first news reached him from Loos, he sent a staff officer with an urgent message requesting the Commander-in-Chief to release them. French was still reluctant, but the news that Haig's First Army had broken the enemy line and was surging ahead was a powerful argument and he gave his consent. It was half past ten in the morning. The information on which he based his decision was already three hours old and the reserve divisions were several hours' march from the line.

It was some time before the order reached the individual brigades and battalions of the new divisions, for twenty thousand men were scattered in bivouacs across the country as much as six miles behind the line. It took longer still to get them on the move and on the march to their assembly positions a mile from the old front line. The men were tired. They had had a long night's march and every battalion had experienced frustrating halts and weary delays along the way. The traffic was heavy, the roads were narrow, often just wide enough for four men marching abreast, and time after time battalions were forced to break rank and spread out to teeter on the edge of roadside ditches while a train of supply wagons trundled ponderously towards the front. Some were held up at level crossings while long ammunition trains chugged towards the railhead. One brigade was actually kept waiting outside Béthune by an officious Provost Marshal on the remarkable grounds that their Brigadier could not produce an official permit to enter the town. There were a thousand and one delays and a few unfortunate battalions only reached their rendezvous, wet, weary and hungry, at six o'clock in the morning.

The 12th Northumberland Fusiliers had at least enjoyed a few hours' rest in the dubious comfort of wet fields. They had also had breakfast. Somehow the cookers had managed to fry quantities of bacon and it was dished out with hefty chunks of bread to officers and men alike. There were no 'ablutions' of any kind, but Captain Pole managed a shave of sorts in an inch of cold water poured into his silver drinking cup, and a sketchy wash with a handful of water from his water bottle. Since Harry Fellowes only shaved at most twice a week he made do with a splash of muddy rainwater from a puddle, and rather wished he hadn't bothered.

It was half past one before they reached the assembly position near Vermelles, for now that the battle had started the roads were even more congested than on the march of the night before. Dispatch riders were scorching up and down the road, ambulances were streaming back, and as they neared the battle-field clutches of prisoners and walking wounded forced them to make way. The prisoners were a heartening sight, and the very fact that they themselves were on the move was evidence that things were going well, but the sound of the big guns pounding and thundering closer and closer as they approached was hardly reassuring and by the time they reached Vermelles where the heavy guns were ranged it was hard for the men who had never heard a shot fired in anger not to jump involuntarily at every ear-splitting crash. But there was worse to come. The German artillery was searching for the guns and as the Northumberland Fusiliers huddled nervously in a field uncomfortably close to a battery of nine-pounders, munching a hasty snack of bully beef, shrapnel shells began to fall close by. The order to fall in and move forward was almost a relief. They had no idea what was expected of them. Colonel Harry Warwick was no wiser than any man in the ranks and even Brigadier-General Wilkinson had made no bones about the fact that he was equally ignorant. His own orders had been ambiguous and when he called his Battalion Commanders together before they moved off he was able to do little more than point out the position of Hill 70 on the map. 'We do not know what's happened on Hill 70,' he told them. 'You must go and find out. If the Germans are holding it, attack them. If our people are there, support them. If *no one* is there, dig in.' No one had reconnoitred the ground. No guides were provided, but in greatcoats and packs, prepared as they had been instructed for a long march, the 64th Brigade began to march in fours, battalion by battalion, down the Lens road towards the line.

It was late afternoon now. The fortunes of battle had shifted since the morning and on Hill 70 they had shifted in the enemy's favour.

The straggle of Scottish soldiers in front of St Laurent held out until midday. When the Germans counter-attacked the few who remained scattered to run up the hill but most of them were killed or captured as they ran. On the hill itself the small mixed force fought hard to hold on but they were gradually pushed back, first from the hastily dug line beneath the crest, then from the Hill 70 redoubt. But they still clung to the slopes and to the high ground to the north, left of the redoubt, where the confusion of troops had at last been reorganised and spread out towards Bois Hugo. The enemy had persisted, and between the salvoes of shells close by it was possible to hear the drum of gunfire to the south where the French attack was at last underway and the fast-firing 75s were supporting the poilus as they stormed the heights of Notre Dame de Lorette. They could almost be said to be supporting the troops at Loos, for now the enemy was in a dilemma. The reserves they might have used to push home their attempt to regain their lost line were diverted to stem the threat to their line further south. At Loos, at least for the moment, there was a breathing space. But the guns thundered on and the troops stood fast, waiting for relief, for reinforcements or, at worst, for nightfall to bring their fragile force a little respite.

Alex Dunbar's gun-team was waiting for the order to move forward, but it was a long long wait, orders were slow to arrive and the gunners had plenty of time to look around and pick up rumours.

Bdr. A. Dunbar.

A lot of traffic was moving up and down the road and there were a lot of casualties coming back. Crowded ambulances were returning from the line and all those who were capable of walking were dragging themselves along as best they could. One thing I shall never forget was the sight of eight sergeants of the Gordons, with their arms around each others' shoulders, all suffering from gas and staggering along holding each other up. A little further down the road was a turning known as Quality Street. There had been some big houses there once but now the ruins held a Casualty Clearing Station, and an infantry brigade HQ and various other units. They were having a busy time.

For light relief there was a large party of German prisoners – well over a hundred – marching eight abreast. The two front ranks consisted entirely of officers, including two or three giants of six feet six inches or more. All the officers seemed to be having a heated argument amongst themselves. Possibly they were trying to find out who was to blame for their capture. What made us really smile, though, was their escort – two diminutive Argyll and Sutherland Highlanders. One was sauntering along with his rifle slung across his back, a cigarette in his mouth, and looking as if he didn't have a care in the world let alone a hundred or so prisoners behind him. The other was just as small, and he had his bayonet fixed bringing up the rear, giving a threatening jab to any prisoner who looked like lagging behind. He looked about as tall as his rifle. We roared with laughter, to the astonishment of some of the prisoners. They couldn't see the funny side of it as we could!

We heard that the 15th Division had been held in front of Lens and were unable to get on because reinforcements had not arrived. Something had gone wrong. But later we saw at the far end of the long stretch of road some troops marching up and soon the whole road was black with hundreds of marching infantry. Their officers were riding on horses in front of each company. We were amazed. This was probably the reinforcement the 15th Division were waiting for. But to come up that road in broad daylight, a road that could be enfiladed by the Germans from end to end! Above all, the German balloons were still there. They must have been able to see that whole road packed with troops. It was beyond comprehension. One of the lads said, 'Perhaps the war is over?' And someone else replied, 'It must be.'

The head of the column was held up and stopped near us for a spell and we spoke to one or two of the men. They told us they had not been in action before and had only been in France three weeks! They said there were two Divisions, the 21st and the 24th. They showed us their Mills bombs as if they were showing off new toys. We were still more amazed.

Ten minutes after, the column got on the move again and the front rank had just reached a slight crest in the road when over came half a dozen whizz-bangs and burst about thirty yards in front. They hit no one, but suddenly the head of the column stopped, turned and began to run back – apparently panic stricken. The movement seemed to spread in seconds as we watched, right down the length of that long line of troops like a wave and in a few minutes they were out of sight. We stood there with our mouths open in astonishment.

What had happened to cause that debacle? Much later when we went up the road to where the trouble started there was a shelled GS wagon in the ditch at the side, and dead horses and three dead men that no one had had time to attend to.

We came to the conclusion that this was the first time those men in front had seen such a sight and at that psychological moment they got their first shelling. The combination was probably too much for them and they broke and ran. Of course those behind them couldn't have known why, but inevitably they became infected and mass hysteria was the result. That seemed to us the only reasonable explanation.

It was not the sight of the dead that had panicked the troops of the leading battalion, it was the salvo of shells that fell among them as they drew closer to Loos. But the panic was soon contained, the ranks were re-formed, and they marched on. Halted a mile behind them the Northumberland Fusiliers had no idea what had caused the hold-up. It was a good half hour before they set off again.

Capt. D. Graham-Pole, 12th Bn., Northumberland Fusiliers, 62nd Brig., 21st Div.

Then I got orders to march on after the Battalion which had already started for Loos. We had just taken it from the

Germans that morning. As we marched along we met most ghastly sights – officers and men lying dead and dying on and alongside the road. Star shells went up and showed us up and shrapnel came crashing amongst us. Horses lay with broken legs and *still* the men marched on steadily. There was no time to attend to the wounded and if your best friend was knocked out you just had to leave him and go on without breaking the column of fours. I was proud of my men; no shouting required, no bullying, only 'Steady lads, steady', and on they came and never even looked back. Then we got to Loos and wherever we went, along streets or more in the open, shells followed us, falling amongst us or into the houses, making them rock and fall or huge pieces fall out of their sides.

But the Battalion had escaped the worst of it. It was the transport column at the rear that caught the full force of the shelling.

Less than a mile away the 24th Division was making for the Hohenzollern redoubt where the 9th Scottish Division was clinging to a wavering foothold.

Pte. G. Marrin, 13th Bn., 73 Brig., 24 Div.

We marched straight into the battle. By the time we got into the front line we were right by the coal mine, Fosse 8, on the left, that's where the Scots got slaughtered, yes, because we saw these men lying around and coming in wounded – thousands of them! The whole thing was an absolute shambles. We were frightened out of our lives. It was terrible. It was our first experience of warfare, and there was machine-gun fire and shelling, and everything seemed to be exploding everywhere. You just didn't know what was taking place. Then we got somewhere – they said it was in the line. *We* didn't know! You were facing one way and they said, 'That's where they are', but *you* didn't know! You put up rifle fire but you didn't know what you were shooting at! You'd no idea what you were doing or *supposed* to be doing. It was just a continual bashing of gunfire. Terrifying! You couldn't think! We were scared out of our wits.

The guns boomed on, but late in the evening the rain eased off. A full moon sailed from behind the clouds and shone so brightly that, squatting in a field outside Loos, Captain Pole could see well enough to write a letter to his sister. It calmed his nerves, and it was something to do to pass the time while his Battalion waited for orders.

519

Sunday 26th September 1915. 3 a.m.
(In action).

A day, Jessie, I shall never forget.

Well, we have been in action right enough but as far as we were concerned with no chance of replying. (I am writing under shell fire by moonlight.) Forgive the writing Jessie, this is being written on top of a map where we have been most of the night and an hour ago it didn't look as if a single one of us would shortly be alive. My servant Holbrook lying by my side got a bullet in his arm and two men in front of me were wounded. I am here with two companies with magazines charged and bayonets fixed and I don't know the minute we may have to go forward and charge another line of trenches.

We were first in the open and although shrapnel and shells were flying they were not concentrated on our small area as they seemed to be an hour ago. Then about nine o'clock I was asked to hold a line of cottages as it was believed there was a gap in our line in front. No sooner had I got in position, digging in and fixing machine-guns, than I was told to go on to a small town and occupy that (Loos). We did so – not without casualties. It is really awful seeing dead and dying lying about and wounded being carried back. It really is Hell. None of us ever want any more of this attacking. That village or town was simply shelled till we had to leave it. I lay down and tried to sleep till orders came to get out into the open and I was to hold this field quite near. I am still holding it – quite calmly, rather hungrily, would give anything for a cup of tea. How and when it will end I can't tell. They are driven back all along the line some four miles.

In the Headquarters chateau at Hinges telephones buzzed busily now, dispatch riders roared up at intervals and it was only now, in the long hours of the night that reports could be properly analysed and the position accurately assessed. The Staff were far from pessimistic, for although things had not gone as well as they had hoped in certain places, the line had been broken, Loos had been captured, almost everywhere the troops had progressed and, with a little more effort, the German defence would surely crumble. And if the subsidiary attacks had not gained much, at least they had achieved the objective of keeping the enemy occupied elsewhere and pinning down his reserves.

In the Ypres salient the turmoil of the day's fighting was over and the night, by comparison, was quiet. An occasional shell came over and now and again a burst from a machine-gun or the crack of a rifle showed that the Germans were still on the alert and fearful that the British would attack by night before the arrival of the reinforcements, marching under cover of the darkness to the line. But there was no fight left in them. Alex Rule lay alone in a sandbagged shelter in Sanctuary Wood drifting in and out of consciousness as he waited to be carried out of the line. His left foot was shattered, he was weak from loss of blood and he had no idea what time it was.

U Company had been in the thick of the fight. Like the other 'subsidiary attacks' it began as night was ebbing towards dawn and the troops at Loos were still filing into position when the guns opened up on the Bellewaerde Ridge. It was still dark, and still raining when the bombers who were to lead the attack crawled into No Man's Land to crouch doggo in shell-holes to wait for zero, and it was a long uncomfortable wait, for the shell-holes were inches thick in squelching mud. The bombers were not objects of envy to their comrades. Shaking hands with Alex Rule as he prepared to cross the parapet, casting a gloomy eye at the dozen bombs that hung in pockets of webbing about his person, Joe Reid remarked, 'Well, cheerio. I dinna wish ye any ill-luck, mind ye, but if ye happen to get in the way of an explosive bullet with a' they bombs around ye, ye'll get blown to buggery.' But waiting in the pouring rain the bombers' thoughts were wholly concerned with keeping the muzzles of their rifles out of the mud and their brassards of thick emery paper from getting soaked. If that happened, and the brassards were too wet to ignite the fuses of their bombs when they were struck, the bombers knew they would be well and truly scuppered.

At zero hour two mines exploded with a roar beneath the German front line, the guns lifted and the bombing party dashed across ahead of the infantry. In the few weeks since the Germans had regained the ground round Hooge, as always they had taken pains to fortify their defences. A length of their front trench-line was devastated by the explosion but the impenetrable tangles of barbed wire in front of it had hardly been touched. Rule and his companions blessed their luck when they found a gap.

Sgt. A. Rule.

Immediately in front of us the belt of wire had luckily been cut in one or two places where an odd percussion shell had landed. Wire-cutters did the rest, and we got to the German front line with comparatively light casualties, thanks to a slight fold in the ground that masked the rifle and machine-gun fire from the redoubt. But elsewhere the wire was practically untouched. Our light shrapnel barrage might have been rain for all the good it did. As we lay on the parapet of the German front line waiting for our guns to lift from our next objective I saw one of the most magnificent sights of the war – a headlong charge by kilted troops! On our flank the 1st Gordons were sweeping forward against the German front line. The wire ahead of them was intact and as they charged into it they were caught in deadly fire. Their line seemed to crumple, almost like a wave breaking on a rocky coast, but they were in such a frenzy that those who survived it kept going and charged right into that belt of terrible wire. Exactly the same thing happened to the next wave. It was all over in a few moments but that picture remains stamped on my memory. But they were 'bonnie fechters', and the few that were left of them worked their way through the wire on part of our front and carried on.

Later, when we were actually in the German line, I saw one private almost going berserk. He was being ordered back to get his wound dressed and he stood there yelling, 'I'm no' goin' back to any bloody dressing station until I've had it oot wi' Jerry! I'd never forgie mysel' if I didnae get the bugger that killed Jimmy.' I assumed that he and Jimmy had been inseparable pals. Another Jock put a clumsy bandage on the wound on his left arm and as soon as it was done he grabbed his rifle with his sound right arm and dashed off into the thick of a bombing scrap a few yards away. I didn't see him again, but I wouldn't have swapped places with any Germans he met that day for all the tea in China.

At first it seemed that they were winning. They had captured a good stretch of the German front line and they sent back a creditable bag of prisoners. Rule's party got well ahead, bombing and capturing dug-outs until their bombs ran out and their numbers were winnowed away. Other less fortunate squads plunged impotently into the fight, trying in vain to ignite bombs on damp muddy brassards, trying in vain to defend themselves with rifles clogged with mud until they were shot at point-blank range.

The 14th Division attacking across the old ground in front of Y wood managed in places to penetrate the German line, but Bellewaerde Farm defeated them. There were no supporting troops, no reserves, no reinforcements, for such reserves as there were had been sent to Loos. Lord Kitchener's grim prophecy of sacrifice and loss had been more than fulfilled, and long before nightfall German counter-attacks had pushed the exhausted survivors back to their start lines. They had not gained their objectives, but they had achieved their purpose. They could only hope that it had been worth it.

Sgt. A. Rule.

I was numb with the pain of my wounds and a cigarette was the only thing in the wide world that I really longed for. After a long time I heard the voice of our medical orderly saying, 'God, there's someone still in here. I thought this dug-out had been cleared hours ago.' He placed me on a stretcher and I asked for the latest news of U Company. From what he said I gathered that all our platoon commanders and the entire rank and file were now either killed or wounded or missing. Three weeks afterwards a letter reached me in hospital from my old platoon sergeant. He said he had called the company's roll at the close of that eventful day and only two or three of its original members had answered their names. Joe Reid got through. He got a large chunk of shrapnel in his left lung, but he kept firing his machine-gun until he was dragged forcibly away from it. When I met him afterwards he confessed that the shell had nearly settled him, but he shrugged it off. He said, 'Anyway, every bloody dug-out in Sanctuary Wood was full of moaning wounded and I refused to die in miserable company. So I carried on.' Months later when we were discharged from hospital a few of the survivors of Hooge came together for a spell at camp in Ripon. After that we drifted our separate ways. And that was the end of U Company.

Bill Worrell was also on his way to hospital. So was Walter Bagot-Chester. Arthur Agius had miraculously survived. All three had been in the attack north of Lens across the old battlefield of Neuve Chapelle. They called it the action of Piètre and the attack at least had a worthwhile objective, for if they could gain a foothold on the Aubers Ridge, link up with the troops attacking on their left at Bois Grenier, and join in with a victorious advance at Loos on their right, they would have been well on the way to Lille. Like the men who fought at Hooge, they were back where they started, but the first two German lines had already been captured when the 12th Rifle Brigade went 'over the top' for the first time.

Rfn. W. Worrell.

At about 8 a.m. on the 25th the order was passed down for 9 Platoon to move up to the front line. Those ten hours of waiting, up to our knees in mud, had certainly dampened our fighting spirit. As we reached the front line I had a shock. My Company Commander was being held up by his runner. He had been shot through the forehead while standing on the firestep encouraging the company as they went over. He must have been killed instantly. Duckboards with every other bar knocked out were being used as ladders. I found myself in front of our barbed wire with Albert Chitty. Every few minutes a Jerry shrapnel shell exploded with a roar and a burst of black smoke just to our right, and we could hear the bullets and splinters plopping into the mud around us and machine-guns and rifle fire were enfilading from the left flank. We decided not to wait for the rest of the platoon but to push on. The safest place seemed to be the German trench! We slithered and scrambled across the long, long two hundred yards between the trenches, found a gap in the German wire and jumped into the trench. Propped up in a corner on the firestep was a huge Black Watch private. He was unconscious and blowing bubbles of blood from his mouth and nose. It was obvious that he was dying fast. There was nothing that we could do for him except hope that the stretcher-bearers would be following up.

We moved forward until we were in the German third line and we were still alone. Albert Chitty said, 'Well, we'll have to wait till the rest of the company come up, they've got to pass by this place, so we'll sit here.' We sat down and while we were waiting there was a terrific bang in front of me on the other side of the trench. A German shell hit the parados and shot the lot in on me. The trench had a wooden revetting frame to hold it in position, and the top of this frame caught me across my face and it was holding me down, pinning me against the back of the trench – broke my jaw top and bottom. The shrapnel went into my tongue and I had a bit of shrapnel in my head. Albert Chitty was just a little farther up and he came rushing down. He got hold of one of the other lads there and they got their rifles in at the top between the revetting frame and the wall of the trench, and they heaved, and I fell into the gap underneath and they pulled me out.

By this time it was a wholesale retreat of our troops. The Indian troops were coming back over the top of us and through the trench. 'Run, Johnnie, run,' they were shouting 'Allemagne coming.' Albert said, 'Come on, boys, we've got to get out of here,' and they dragged me, carried me, pulled me along, and they got me back into our line. It was a nightmare experience. It took two hours. I was suffering from shock and concussion, in addition to my wounds, and I can only remember flashes of that awful journey. I just remember Albert saying to me, 'Come on, keep going. If you don't, you'll die! Come on.' And he kept me going.

The Battalion dressing station was almost in the front line. That was the day that our Medical Officer, Captain Maling of the RAMC, won the VC. He had a little aid post in one firebay of the trench. The back of it had been knocked right out, and there was all sorts of bits and pieces of men lying about there. He looked at me and he said, 'If you can get out, go! Can you walk?' I said, 'I think so.' Well I couldn't walk. My knees were giving way under me, and there was this big Welsh lad who was in my company, big Ben Williams, who was wounded in the arm, and he was making his way out by Winchester Road communication trench. Albert saw him and he said, 'Would you take Billy out with you?' He said he would, so we went on along Winchester Trench, and it was about three feet deep in water! Everybody was trying to get through it, and we kept on feeling things underneath us, which of course were wounded men who had fallen and drowned in the mud. Ben said, 'I don't like to leave you, but I'm going over the top.' Well, I couldn't talk – my face was tied up by then, you see – my stomach was hurting me like hell, I don't know what it was. So he said, 'Right, come and stand over here and I'll climb over you and pull you up.' So he climbed up and got over the top, then pulled me over with his one arm, and helped me down.

We got to the end, where the communication trench came out on the road outside Laventie (it was an awfully long way, I remember!), and there was one of the old horse-drawn ambulances, and the chap was saying, 'Walking cases only, walking cases only.' So Taffy said, 'Well he's a walking case, he can get in.' Of course I was half dead, and the driver didn't want to take me. Anyhow, eventually Ben got me on. The next I knew was when I woke up lying on the floor in the convent at Estaires where the sisters were looking after our people. I had this anti-tetanus jab and this sister came along with a little funnel. My nose was completely blocked up. My mouth was closed up and I was breathing through just a little hole. She put this funnel in and began pouring tea in – kindly meant, but I couldn't breathe and my reaction was to blow, and I blew the tea back all over her! The Mother Superior came round and had a look at me, and had me taken in to her little cubby-hole where she bathed my mouth and eventually cleaned the blood up, and then I was put on the ambulance which took me to a train, then to Rouen.

The 12th Rifle Brigade had covered themselves with glory. They were the only battalion of the 20th Division to go into the attack, and they had not let the division down. They reached and held the third line of German trenches, but they were out on a limb. The Bareilly Brigade on their right had done well too, but when they were driven back the riflemen beside them had no alternative but to retire. It was a bitter blow, and the action cost them dear. Bill Worrell was one of three hundred and twenty-nine casualties – killed or wounded or missing.

The Garhwal Brigade of the Meerut Division had fared worst of all. Their frontage, on the right of the attack, ran south from Mauquissart, and the 3rd Londons were in the support line ready to advance in the second wave when the Gurkhas and the Leicesters had captured the first enemy line. Arthur Agius's company was in position behind the Duck's Bill, where a small rectangle of breast-works enclosed a watery waste of craters and dug-outs. It was thrust out well into No Man's Land towards the enemy line, connected by a long sap to the British front-line trench. Such a fine target for enemy guns was constantly shelled and since enemy machine-gunners seldom left it alone the Duck's Bill was a hot spot. The Gurkhas were to advance on either side to capture the German front line and a Gas Brigade detachment was standing by ready to release clouds of gas and smoke that would smother the enemy before the infantry attacked.

Stand-to, for the infantry, was at 3.30 in the morning. Platoon officers roused their men and called the roll, rifles were inspected with special care, hot tea was handed out. Later, towards zero hour, there would be a rum ration, and meanwhile the men were warned to keep their heads down. The bombardment was well under way, the enemy guns were sending back shell for shell and here in the support line there had already been some casualties. Captain Agius, making his rounds to see for himself that all was well, was constantly called back to the signallers' dug-out. Messages were arriving thick and fast. The one they had all been waiting for was logged at six minutes past four: 'Zero 5.50. Please acknowledge.' But long before zero they were overtaken by disaster.

The shell fell well in front of the trench, but it was near enough to cause the men to duck involuntarily and let out a collective sigh of relief when the fall-out subsided. It was several minutes before Lieutenant Taylor of the Royal Engineers came staggering down the sap and almost collapsed into Agius's arms. He was incapable of speech, he was green and gasping, and he was waving a message which he apparently wished Agius to wire to brigade headquarters: 'Am somewhat gassed,' it read, 'but will attempt carry on at time stated if you wish. Wind one mile per hour southerly direction.' Taylor was quite obviously unfit to 'carry on', and in no state even to tell what had happened but it was not hard to guess that the shell had hit the gas cylinders in the trench ahead and already there was a whiff of gas in the air. There was nothing to be done but to call for stretcher-bearers, to rewrite the illegible message adding *'Lieutenant Taylor incapable of carrying on'* and dispatch it by runner.

Even before Agius could go forward to find out what precisely had happened another message arrived, scribbled with frantic haste, blurred and spattered with raindrops, but its purport was plain enough. *'To Captain 3rd London: one battery of cylinders destroyed by bomb 4.35. Several men gassed slightly, one seriously.'* It was signed *'Figg Acting Sergeant RE'.*

It was the first of Figg's urgent calls for help, and even before Agius had mustered a party of volunteers to go forward another arrived. The messenger's eyes were bulging and streaming as he stumbled out of the sap. *'Must have twenty men at once to cover remaining gas batteries with sandbags. Figg Acting Sergeant RE.'*

Pulling on his gas-mask, Agius went forward to see the situation for himself. It was desperate. The trench was badly knocked about. Despite Figg's valiant efforts gas was seeping steadily from the damaged cylinders. One after another, as the gas spread, men were collapsing wild eyed, vomiting, gasping for breath, and it was obvious that Sergeant Figg himself was on the point of collapse.

Agius's men did their best. It was hard labour working in suffocating gas-helmets to rebuild the broken trench, to tear sand-bags from the sides of the sap, to heave them to the forward post, to pile them round the cylinders in a blinding smog of concentrated fumes. Man after man succumbed. The guns were thundering, time was running out, the gas was still escaping from the damaged cylinders. Now it was hanging thick in front of the trenches and drifting lazily northward enveloping more of their own line as it went, drifting everywhere but towards the Germans.

At zero hour the Gurkhas waiting to go donned gas-helmets and charged through it. It was a bad start.

Capt. W. G. Bagot-Chester, MC.

Clouds of gas blew backwards and we had to tuck our helmets which we were wearing all the tighter. I was wearing two helmets one over the other, but in spite of these my throat became very sore. Even before we started one of the gas men in the traverse in which I was standing keeping an eye on my watch became overcome while working his removal sprayer and was lying at my feet groaning horribly. I was counting the seconds and when I gave the signal to cross the parapet I think we were all glad to get out of our trench full of gas. The air in front was thick with gas and smoke from the smoke bombs and we couldn't see more than a few yards. There was not a shot fired from the Germans and owing to this we were able to slacken our pace to a quick walk and dress our line to a certain extent. The distance to the front German trench was about two hundred yards. For the first eighty yards the air was thick, but as we emerged into view of the Hun they let drive at us. I found my men dropping all round me, and when I reached the German wire I was practically alone and I found myself with one or two others literally running along the outside cage of the German wire searching for a way through.

The wire was not cut, and there was no way through. In a matter of moments Bagot-Chester felt a sharp blow on his right shoulder and fell to the ground close to the German wire. It would have impaled him had he not been flung backwards by the force of the bullet. He thanked his lucky stars for that and rolled into a shell-hole a yard or so away. It was the smallest of shell-holes, gouged by a 'pipsqueak' – too small and too shallow to give much cover. Havildar Budhiman was already there, clutching his wounded arm, and there was just enough room for the two of them lying face to face on their uninjured sides. Raising his head an inch to risk a cautious look across the pock-marked ground Bagot-Chester could see wounded men in every shell-hole, squirming and jumping under a shower of shrapnel and flying bullets. There was a squeal beside him. Budhiman had been hit again. His breathing became laboured, his face turned grey and pallid, he was obviously in pain. Bagot-Chester had morphia in his pocket but the shell-hole was so shallow, the firing was so fierce, the cover was so puny, that he dared not turn to reach it with his left hand, and his right hand beneath his shattered shoulder was useless. There was nothing for it but to lie still, to hope for the best and to wait for the dark.

They lay there for thirteen hours. By mid-afternoon both men were half unconscious with pain, for Budhiman had been hit again in the legs, and a shell fragment had pierced his captain's right groin, and by and by two more splinters wounded his left foot and his left leg below the knee. Late in the afternoon to complete their misery the rain came on in torrents and their shell-hole began to fill with water. But at least the discomfort roused them to consciousness and, better still, the firing eased up as the machine-gunners who had been paying them such assiduous attention sought shelter. All that Bagot-Chester could see from his position just below ground level was the rain running from strand to strand on the black wall of barbed wire looming above him and the merest glimpse of a trench behind it. It was not a pleasant sight but, feeling instinctively that his best chance of survival lay in staying conscious, he forced his eyes to stay open and nudged Budhiman from time to time when he showed signs of drifting off.

It was the longest day of his life.

Capt. W. G. Bagot-Chester, MC.

The rain stopped after a time and dusk began to come on, so slowly it seemed to us. Budhiman wanted to be off, but I was not taking any risks. We had lain about all day and it was stupid to spoil our chance by leaving half an hour too early. I suppose it was about eight o'clock when we started. I had lost so much blood I couldn't get up on my feet, and in trying to do so I was very sick. Fortunately the rain had made the clay soil so slippery that I was able to slide myself along on my back. Every now and then I came up against a dead body in the dark and it was a great effort to me in my weak state to get round them. My progress was very slow. When I got about half-way back to our trenches, I was able to stand on my feet – or rather on one foot and the other heel – but I couldn't walk more than five yards without collapsing, so really I got on quicker on my back. Finally I struck a muddy wet ditch about fifty yards from our trenches, and thinking to get on quicker along its slippery bottom I crawled into it, but I found it worse, and I was too weak to get out again, so I had to give it up. Fortunately the ditch seemed to be a highway for other wounded and unwounded and presently to my surprise an old Colour-Sergeant of mine in the 2nd Black Watch – Sutherland by name – came crawling along with some of his men. He tried to help me to move along, but I couldn't do any more so he went on and let them know in our own trenches that I was out. After waiting some time, wet through and almost frozen stiff, Captain Burton, DSO (since killed), came out, bringing four of his men and a stretcher. I was soon in then, and he gave me some whisky. It was about 10.30 p.m. before I got to our first aid dressing station and after fifteen minutes' rest in our doctor's dug-out he sent me on to the advanced dressing station which meant being carried on a stretcher down a communication trench about eight hundred yards long, and then on a tramway another mile and a half. I was so tired that I kept falling asleep every time the stretcher stopped in the communication trench.

But at least he was alive and on his way to safety. So was Havildar Budhiman, but of Bagot-Chester's hundred and twenty men who had

529

gone into action, eighty-six had been killed, wounded or were missing.*

The firing tailed off as if the enemy too was exhausted by the gruelling events of the day. The troops were back where they started. Sentries had been posted, the men were dozing as best they could but Agius was still awake, still harassed as he had been all day by urgent requests for information. Apart from the fact that the attack on his immediate front had failed he had very little idea of what had happened in the course of the day. He had half filled his message pad in the course of the last twenty hours and responding to the latest urgent request for information he took the opportunity of trying to find out.

Situation unchanged. Mist prevents anything from being seen. Night fairly quiet. We dispersed a German party working on their parapet 3.50. Can you tell me how far the right of the Brigade has got on?

The fact was that it hadn't got on at all.

Just a mile or so away on the Loos front beyond the la Bassée Canal, the shelling went on at intervals all night. Behind the enemy line they were rushing up munitions, gathering what reinforcements they could and reorganising their line. After their first spectacular dash the French had been brought to a halt at the foot of the Vimy Ridge. From the German point of view the situation there was still precarious but with the cessation of the attacks at Neuve Chapelle, Bois Grenier, and Hooge, it was becoming clear to the German High Command that the main push was against Loos. Tomorrow the attack would surely be renewed, and tomorrow they would be ready for it. Scarce though their manpower was, twenty-two extra battalions were rushed to the battle area. By morning the second line would be far more strongly held than their front line had been at the outset of the British attack.

It had been a long day for the gunners, and an exhausting one, but towards evening when Alan Watson's team no longer had a gun to fire, he unexpectedly had time on his hands, and he used it to scribble in his diary.

Gnr. J. A. Watson.

September 25th. A most exciting day. The attack was made

---

* Captain Walter Bagot-Chester recovered from his wounds and returned to the front more than a year later. He died of wounds on 23 March 1918.

with the aid of a very strong kind of gas which killed hundreds of Germans. Our casualties very few. Advanced about three miles. Everybody in great spirits. I will never forget this week, especially today on the gun. We were working all night and started firing at 3 a.m. – wet to the skin. From our gun we fired a hundred and nineteen shells and then the gun burst! Heavens, what an explosion! We were all round the gun and not a soul was touched – a miraculous escape. One piece of steel ploughed through about eighty yards all *trees*, hit a wall and glanced off and cut down a tree about six or eight inches thick. Another one about the same size (about one and a half hundredweight) hit the wheel of a gun carriage about four yards to my right and smashed it to smithereens. It was dusk when that happened and the flash nearly blinded us. It was a truly marvellous escape. Saw a good few German prisoners, a miserable-looking lot, all sorts and sizes. Would not have missed today for worlds – really great!

At First Army headquarters in the chateau at Hinges the lights burned late and the orders that went out to the line were clear and straightforward. Tomorrow where the line had not been broken the troops were to break it, where they had succeeded they were to press forward, and tomorrow they were to recapture Hill 70. Now that they had the assistance of two fresh divisions, in the opinion of the Army Commander there was nothing to stop them smashing the Germans' second line. The assault of 25 September had not been wholly successful but neither had it been entirely unsatisfactory. The official communiqué had already been wired from St Omer to London and although it was too soon to expect detailed information, exultant headlines had already been set in type and the presses in Fleet Street were rolling. In a very few hours the welcome news of victory at Loos would thud on to a million doormats to rejoice the Home Front at the breakfast table.

Chapter 35

Sunday morning dawned bleak, with a grey drizzling mist. The men were cold and wet and hungry, for not one in a hundred quartermasters endeavouring to convey hot food to their men had managed to reach the line, still less discover their battalions. Some soldiers still had the remains of their iron rations – hard biscuits and perhaps a bite of cheese, but most water bottles had long ago been emptied and it was difficult to eat the dry untempting food when mouths and throats were dry and parched with thirst.

Lying out with his machine-guns to the left of Bois Hugo, Lieutenant Christison of the 6th Camerons was probably the first man to catch a glimpse of the Germans that morning. During the hours of darkness a battalion of the Northamptons had come up on the left of his post but the patrol Christison sent out returned with disquieting news. The Northamptons had moved away. Now the machine-gunners were isolated up the hill, some hundreds of yards ahead of their Battalion and well out in front of the ragged line.

Lt. A. F. P. Christison, MC.

We stood-to for a bit but all was quiet, and we brewed up some tea. Suddenly looking to my left I saw a line of Boches running forward and jumping into the trench vacated by the Northamptons. I noticed they were the famous 17th Bavarians. I wished we had some bombers, but all I could do was to pull back one machine-gun and a few men to protect my exposed flank. I felt machine-guns should not be sent out on their own without supporting infantry.

The infantry who might have supported them was still in confusion and efforts to reorganise them during the night and to push forward the new divisions to stiffen the front had only added to the chaos. After dark, plodding through rain and mist in search of some approximate position in strange country, it was remarkable that

532

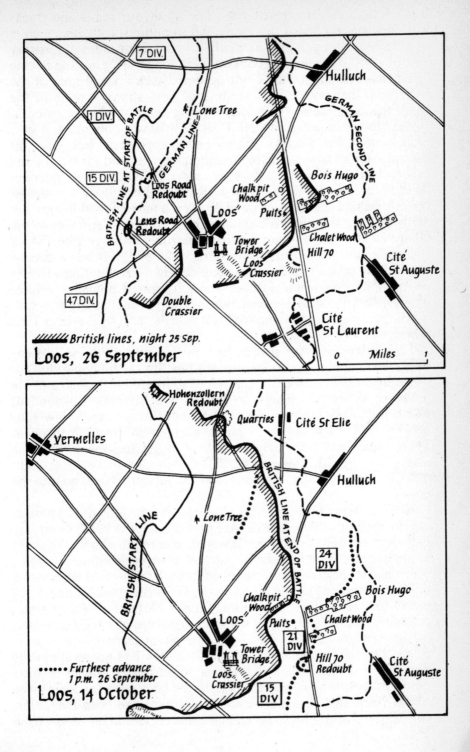

Loos, 26 September

7 DIV.

1 DIV.

15 DIV.

47 DIV.

BRITISH LINE AT START OF BATTLE

GERMAN LINE

Lone Tree

Hulluch

GERMAN SECOND LINE

Loos Road Redoubt

Chalk pit Wood

Bois Hugo

Lens Road Redoubt

Loos

Puits

Tower Bridge

Chalet Wood

Loos Crassier

Hill 70

Cité St Auguste

Double Crassier

Cité St Laurent

////// British lines, night 25 Sep.

0   Miles   1

Loos, 14 October

Hohenzollern Redoubt

Quarries

Cité St Elie

Vermelles

BRITISH LINE AT END OF BATTLE

Hulluch

BRITISH START LINE

Lone Tree

24 DIV

Chalk pit Wood

Bois Hugo

Loos

Puits

Chalet Wood

21 DIV

Tower Bridge

Hill 70 Redoubt

Cité St Auguste

Loos Crassier

15 DIV

•••••• Furthest advance 1 p.m. 26 September

some Battalions had reached the line at all, for roads and tracks were few and the maps the Army had so optimistically issued were of little use, although they helpfully covered many miles of territory east of Loos to guide the troops on their 'long walk' after the fleeing Germans. The immediate front occupied such a small area of the large map that few, if any, landmarks were shown – none of the small tracks, none of the numerous slag-heaps, and only an occasional blob to indicate a wood. Even Hill 70 was only marked by a faint contour line. Faced with the need to appoint a rendezvous 'off the map' for its supply and ammunition wagons, and for lack of any other clearly distinguishable spot, most battalions had independently plumped for the farm of le Rutoire. Le Rutoire lay almost directly behind the front at Lone Tree on a narrow road linking the highway from Béthune to Lens and the road from Vermelles to the village of Hulluch, and not far from the ruined cottage where Alex Dunbar's gun was hidden at the start of the battle. It was a narrow road and in peacetime on a busy day during harvest perhaps five or six farm wagons would lumber along its rutted unmade surface. Now, with fifty, sixty, seventy horse-drawn army limbers trying to make their way to the same spot it was little short of mayhem. The jam stretched back for miles.

The difficulties were just as bad on the main Béthune to Lens road, the vital highway to the line at Loos. It was still being shelled; its surface was so broken and cratered, so littered with dead and the debris of shattered wagons, so choked with streams of wounded, that it had taken hours of sweat and labour to get even a few guns forward and it was almost impossible to get ammunition through. There would not be nearly enough of either to support the new attack on Hill 70. The bombardment was due to begin at eight o'clock in the morning. An hour later the infantry would go into the attack.

At First Army Headquarters at Hinges it was difficult to appreciate the shifting circumstances that prevailed at the battle-front, for they were beyond description. It would have required hours of study to analyse and weigh up the dispatches of seven separate divisions, which had themselves been compiled from the reports of twenty-one brigades, summing up the position – so far as they could judge it – of eighty-four confused and disorganised battalions. Only time, patience, and the exercise of considerable leaps of imagination and intuition, might have resulted in an omniscient grasp of how matters stood. On the maps on which staff officers had so scrupulously drawn the advanced line, battalions stood neatly ranged in their supposed positions as lead soldiers might be ranged for a set-piece battle. Naturally, they were aware that there had been casualties, and Major General McCracken had made it clear in his report from

15th Divisional Headquarters that his division was in no fit state to renew the assault in the morning, but his objections had been overcome. The 62nd Brigade would be detached from the 21st Division to assist him. The advance must be pressed, and before it could go forward, Hill 70 must be retrieved. With that he had to be satisfied.

Tower Bridge had caught it badly during the night. Its battered twin towers were hidden in the mist. But loose iron girders creaked and clanked in the morning breeze above the Northumberland Fusiliers shivering in rough and ready trenches in a field not far away. They had been waiting and shivering for two tedious hours before orders reached them not long before the bombardment began at eight o'clock. Colonel Harry Warwick summoned the company officers to the shack that served as Battalion Headquarters. Two battalions, their sister battalion the 13th Northumberland Fusiliers and the 8th East Yorks, were to follow in immediate support of the 45th Brigade of the 15th Division. Their own role was to follow two hundred yards behind, attacking on either side of the track that led to Hill 70 redoubt. No track was marked on their maps, the ground was unfamiliar, and the Colonel could only point out the general direction and wish them luck. David Graham-Pole returned to C Company to pass on the orders and warn his men to stand by. Harry Fellowes was *not* ready. His Lewis gun which had been loaded on to the transport had not yet reached the line.

Pte. H. Fellowes, 12th Bn., Northumberland Fusiliers, 62 Brig., 21 Div.

Our platoon officer got hold of me, and of course he knew that the transport hadn't come up. There were two of us, so he told us to double back and go as quickly as we could and find the transport and bring back the Lewis gun, because we were going into action. So we set off. It took us a long time to work our way back past the road where the cemetery was and on to the main road we'd come down the night before. That main road – well I can't describe it! It was just a mass of holes, and debris and dead men and horses lying everywhere. We worked our way back and eventually we came to where our transport should have been. Of course, it wasn't there. It had never even got there! We went a bit further and it was only then that we found out that it had been shelled – knocked out! Anything that was left of it had gone back, and of course there was no gun. So we had to turn and go back again. This took a long time and by now the shells were flying over our heads, and now and again we had to stop and

535

duck down. By the time we did get back to where we'd been, the Battalion had moved off, going up to the attack, you see. When I came back from what was left of the transport, I hadn't got my gun, but the Adjutant stopped me. He said, 'What company do you belong to?' I said, 'C Company, sir.' He said, 'The C.O.'s got a message for you.'

He thrust a paper into Harry's hand and said, 'Make your way up to the front and give it to Captain Pole.' The message was written on a sheet from a signal pad and it read, '*The C.O. wishes the attack to be carried out with bayonets in the true Northumbrian fashion.*' Harry thrust the message into his pocket and plodded off towards the hill, following his nose. The bombardment had lifted and the sound of the fighting ahead showed him the way.

When he arrived in front of the redoubt the first waves were well ahead and when he eventually found C Company they were standing with bayonets fixed and on the point of going over the top. The whistles blew, the men clambered over the parapet and began to run towards the redoubt a hundred yards ahead. For a moment the trench was empty then the following wave dropped in from the parados to take their place. Pushing his way through looking for Captain Pole, Fellowes could not see a single familiar face. C Company had gone. Guessing that Captain Pole would be with them, and intent on delivering the message, Fellowes scrambled over the top and ran after them into the fight.

Pte. H. Fellowes.

The whole hill was crowded with men. There was no formation of any description. The whole hill was just one mass of men, moving on, cheering like hell. All the time we were running across the Germans never fired a shot and then it just seemed as if somebody had given the order and they all opened out with machine-guns. Men were just mown down. It was just slaughter, just suicide, all hell let loose. Men began to stumble and fall, and machine-guns were firing from the front of us enfilading from the left-hand side from some other Germans. A lad in front of me was shot in the head and he fell, and I tripped and fell over him. To this day I don't feel any shame. I stayed where I was!

Capt. D. Graham-Pole.

Going up the hill I got a horrible bang on the head, put my hand up and found it covered with blood, so whipped out my handker-

536

chief and tied it over my head and under my chin. The blood stopped flowing – it was only a surface wound – and served as a good hair fixer, as I hadn't had time to do my hair that morning. Then I went on. When quite near the German trenches I found I was still sucking on a cigar. The Germans were perfectly awful with machine-guns – simply mowed our men down.

How long I stayed there I don't know.

Pte. H. Fellowes.

It seemed like hours. Afterwards I knew it could only have been about ten minutes, but I'll remember the sight until my dying day. The whole slope was full of prone figures. Men began to come back. Others never left – like the lad I stumbled over who'd been shot through the head. After a bit I began to crawl back and I got back into the trench. I landed in the same place where I'd left. We wondered what was going to happen to us! We lay there and it was awful listening to the cries of the men on the field. Some were screaming – terrible! The Scots were in a trench that they dug themselves, about four foot deep, and our lads were crowded at the back. It was trickling with rain all the time.

Colonel Warwick went forward himself after his battalion was pushed back, but there was nothing to be done. He could only stop in the trench looking for his own men in the confusion of troops who had fallen back, and hoping against hope that the confusion was such that the few bemused officers and men he could find were not all that was left of his Battalion.

Twice they had charged up Hill 70 and twice they had very nearly succeeded in taking it. The front trenches were overrun but two hundred men in a keep in the centre of the redoubt held out. The keep was constructed with just such an attack in mind. Its trenches were deep and formidable. They faced in four directions and up to twenty machine-guns could pour out fire from concealed positions. They could command the slopes in front when fresh waves pressed on from the captured trenches. They could command the summit of the hill behind if any troops managed to gain it. Not many did, for the machine-guns in the keep also dominated the slopes on either side and the British soldiers attempting to pass were scythed down like meadow grass. The Scots were in the vanguard of the rush up the hill. Some of them survived and almost reached the crest, but it was too much to expect of the half-trained inexperienced soldiers of the 62nd Brigade. The survivors following close behind hesitated, wavered and then began to drift back, crawling, stumbling, even running in a dash for safety. A few remaining Scottish soldiers, unsettled by the sight, or perhaps believing that an order had been given to retire, followed suit.

Lieutenant Christison had been ordered to bring back his guns from the outposts near Bois Hugo and to protect the left flank of the Battalion as the Camerons went forward to the attack.

Lt. A. F. P. Christison.

My chaps were most indignant. They felt they had done well and were in a strong position. Lance-Corporal Campbell even argued we should ignore the message but 'Orders is orders' and regretfully we disengaged and ran for it across the Lens road under fairly heavy rifle fire, losing another gun and one or two men on the way. When we got to a large German support trench near Puits 14 bis, I found a party of about eighty or a hundred Camerons in it without an officer. I could see a battle going on on Hill 70 under heavy fire and I heard that we had taken and now lost Hill 70. It seemed we were trying to retake it and I tried to lead the party in the trench forward to help. But they were unwilling. Seeing most of them were West Highlanders or Islemen I stood on the parapet and sang the first verse of the 'March of the Cameron Men'.

> There's many a man of the Cameron clan,
> That has followed his chief to the field;
> He has sworn to support him, or die by his side,
> For a Cameron never can yield.

He sang it in Gaelic and it was a song that had stirred the blood of the Highlanders for as long as anyone could remember. The men still looked sullen and frightened but there was a twitch of reaction. Christison was dangerously exposed standing at full height on the parapet but he launched into the well-known chorus, roaring rather than singing it to make himself heard above the chatter of machine-guns and the clamour of battle.

> I hear the pibroch sounding, sounding,
> Deep o'er the mountain and glen;
> While light springing footsteps are trampling the heath,
> 'Tis the march of the Cameron men,
> 'Tis the march, 'Tis the march,
> 'Tis the march of the Cameron men.

They were stirring now, standing up, picking up rifles, and Christison knew that he had won. He hardly needed to continue. As he launched on the third verse the Camerons were already scrambling out of the trench and encouraging reluctant stragglers to come on.

> Oh! proudly they walk, but each Cameron knows,
> He may tread on the heather no more;
> But boldly he follows his chief to the field,
> Where his laurels were gathered before.

Hoarse with his efforts Lieutenant Christison led the Cameron men at a trot to pick up what laurels they could on Hill 70.

Lt. A. F. P. Christison.

As we approached the main part of the Battalion I was told the C.O. had led two charges up the hill and gained some ground each time. He was preparing for a final effort.

I handed over the stragglers I had brought forward to Captain Campbell Colquhoun and was told by the Adjutant to get my guns out to the left flank and give covering fire. I do not think there was any artillery support as the situation was too confused. There was no Forward Observation Officer.

The arrival of the stragglers gave Colonel Douglas Hamilton the chance to charge again – and he knew very well it was the last chance, for there were precious few Camerons left. A little way to his right, in the immediate vicinity of Hill 70, there was no sign of another advance. The officers of the 62nd Brigade had bravely tried to rally their men, knowing that they must, but so many officers had courted danger in setting an example, waving encouragement from the rims of the shelter pits where the shocked men were huddled, that most had been shot down in the act. So far Colonel Douglas Hamilton had seemed to be immune, twice charging up the hill ten yards ahead of his men in fruitless attempts to reach the top. Now he prepared to try for a third time. His force was almost spent, but if, with a supreme effort, they could advance, it might do a great deal to encourage others to join in, and one more charge might just succeed in encircling the vipers' nest in the redoubt and out-flanking it.

He was the first man out of the trench. He raised his arm, gave a final shout of encouragement – 'Camerons . . . charge!' – and set off up the hill. As the Camerons began running forward the Germans were lining up and preparing to counter-attack. They met before the

Camerons had got half-way up the hill and, spent and exhausted as they were, they hardly stood a chance. Those who survived the encounter were pushed back well beyond their start-line. The Colonel was hit and, seeing him fall, Campbell Colquhoun dragged him to the shelter of a shell-hole and did his best to bind up his wounds. Douglas Hamilton had been caught across the middle of his body by machine-gun bullets and he only spoke twice more. 'Colquhoun, I'm done!' he muttered as the captain cut away his tunic to staunch the blood. For a time he seemed to be unconscious, then he opened his eyes and began to struggle a little, saying, 'I must get up, I must get up!' Moments later he died.

Christison and his machine-guns had been left behind.

Lt. A. F. P. Christison.

I was left away forward with my two guns. I never discovered what happened to one of them, but a wave of German infantry swept down on us. The gun I was with did some fine execution and then it jammed. I struggled with it while I sent the No. 1 back to collect more drums from the No. 3 and for some reason the No. 2 crawled out of our shell hole and was immediately hit, and I was left alone. The No. 3 crawled up with the last two drums and as he handed them to me he was hit and rolled into the next shell-hole. As I was struggling to release the drum which had jammed I looked up, and there was a German officer with a pistol in his hand. I drew mine and we fired together. I felt as if a mule had kicked me in the groin and he fell dead on top of me while the waves of German infantry swept by. I heaved him off and got a fright when I saw where he had caught me – in the thigh just below the groin. Thank Heaven I had been a medical student and had done an advanced course in First Aid. I suspected that an artery had been severed and I thought I was done. In panic I snatched off my whistle and stuffed it into the wound – which was not hurting then – and fixed and tightened my field dressing with the muzzle of my revolver to make a tourniquet. I tried to remember how many minutes later one had to release it and re-tie. I lay doggo and managed to change the drum.

Until now there had been little shelling for the position was too indeterminate for the Germans to risk hitting their own men, but on the dot of eleven o'clock their guns opened up and shells began to fall on the western slopes of Hill 70 where the remnants of the infantry lay helpless in front of the redoubt now firmly back in enemy hands. And the enemy, intending it should stay there, were pulverising the trenches and the ground for a mile behind to prevent supports and reserves from coming up to renew the assault. But there were no supports, and there were no reserves, and the frontal assault on Hill 70 would not now be renewed.

The plan had been for the 24th Division and the remainder of the 21st to attack side by side as soon as Hill 70 was captured. Even though the attack on the hill had failed, the Corps Commander intended to carry on with the second part of the plan, for the two new divisions were to attack to the left of Hill 70 between Bois Hugo and the village of Hulluch, secure behind the Germans' second-line defences, which the 7th Division had disappointingly failed to capture the previous day. Now the 1st Division was to try again and General Haking reasoned that, if two divisions at full strength could advance alongside them far enough to penetrate the German second line, Hill 70 would be out-flanked and easily enveloped. It was true that the 21st Division was short of its 62nd Brigade, now spent and shattered, but there was still, it seemed, a very reasonable chance of success. The 24th Division was also short of a Brigade. Their 73rd Brigade was with the 9th Division at Fosse 8.

The 21st Division was already in position in the line, the 24th was not, and written orders for the attack only reached them at 5.30 that evening long after it was over. They would have known nothing of it had Brigadier-General Nickalls not gone to Divisional Head-quarters and returned with verbal instructions a matter of minutes before they were due to begin. Long before they reached the line their sister Division had been forestalled by events and overtaken by near disaster.

Since early morning small reconnoitring parties of the enemy had been filtering out of the second-line position a thousand yards ahead and working their way towards the British outpost line concealed by the morning mist. When it cleared there had been skirmishes, and even before larger bodies began to approach there had been many casualties in the fledgling battalions. But they had stood it well, and they had stuck it out with little protection from a heavy bombardment that preceded the German attack. When it lifted, the Germans moved forward and began to take up position for the assault. The 12th West Yorks had done well. They had already repulsed one attempt by rifle fire alone and now they were in action again, in a crude and shallow trench just north of Bois Hugo, firing at a group of enemy infantry moving diagonally across their front some hundreds of yards ahead. Their line was the base of a rough triangle formed by the western leg of Bois Hugo and the Lens–la Bassée road. The West Yorks were firing steadily and well, then a burst of fire from the eastern end of the wood took them by surprise. It

541

ripped along their line, at lethal close quarters, and it caused devastation. It also caused panic. Soon most of the survivors were running back towards the Lens road. They ran fast and purposefully, but they were not an unruly mob; they were merely adjusting to the circumstances, and, with good Yorkshire sense, removing themselves as far as possible from the hurricane of bullets that showed no signs of letting up. Many more were wounded or killed as they ran. It was unfortunate that the colonel had been knocked out minutes earlier by a shell, and although the officers did their best to rally their men on the road and in the Chalk Pit further back, they met with no success. Brigadier Nickalls who saw the debacle from his headquarters at Chalk Pit House ran forward personally to help and was killed as he ran. After that there was no stopping them. One battalion after another, unsettled by the sight of men streaming back from the line, rose up and joined them in the retreat through Chalk Pit Wood and beyond, and the Germans began to follow in a great mass. Then it was their turn to panic. Five heavy shells fell among the leaders as they emerged from the cover of Bois Hugo and, stunned by the explosions and the sight of the carnage, the rest turned and fled back into the shelter of the wood.

As the British troops continued down the hill intent on reaching the shelter of its lower slopes they almost ran into disaster. A battalion of the Durham Light Infantry on its way up saw them approach, mistook them in their long overcoats for Germans, and opened fire. There were several casualties before the mistake was realised and the firing ceased. The men in retreat were not deterred – and neither were the 14th Durhams. They moved on, advancing up the slope to the front through the lines of retiring soldiers. The 15th Durhams were also on the way and, like the men of the 14th, they pushed on steadily to the line. On the stroke of eleven o'clock at the precise moment at which the attack of the two divisions had been planned, the two solitary battalions fixed bayonets and advanced in accordance with their orders. They did not get very far.

The 24th Division was in better fettle. It was true that they had started late and left the support position at the time they should have been going into the attack, and it was also true that, due to the detachment of one brigade and two battalions of another, they were at half strength, but they were full of pep and gave every impression of being delighted at the prospect of getting to grips with the enemy. They moved off in immaculate order down the long bare slope from Lone Tree Ridge into Loos Valley and, circling to their left to bring them parallel to their objective, kept in a perfect alignment. The very precision of their advance, their cheerful demeanour and their resolute step, put heart into men who were still retreating. As they dressed into fighting formation and began to advance up the hill, most of the men who were falling back turned and went back with them. They were still disorganised, the brigadier was gone and there was no one to direct the battalions to any particular objective, but when the whistles finally blew, they began to advance from more or less the positions they had left.

No order had reached Lieutenant Christison. He was still lying wounded far out in front. The tide of battle had flowed past him, and ebbed, and flowed past again. But lying in a small pocket of ground, he still had his machine-gun and it was enough to protect him, and to hold off any Germans who might have captured him. He had accounted for quite a few of the enemy as he lay waiting and hoping for support, or for reinforcements, or for rescue.

Lt. A. F. P. Christison.

Some time later I saw the lines of the 24th Division moving forward and the Germans running back. The Suffolks came through where I was and seemed to be going well. Then they wavered, and to my horror I saw them and the troops on both sides of them doubling back and leaving me isolated again. But one stout fellow, Sergeant A. F. Saunders, refused to retire. He had a Lewis gun he had picked up with a full drum on it. He crawled over to me and said he'd stay and fight. He made to crawl over to the next shell-hole and as he did so a shell landed and blew part of his left leg off about the knee. I crawled over and got him into the shell-hole, putting a tourniquet on his leg and giving him my water bottle, as his was empty. I crawled back to my hole and a few minutes later on looking over the top I saw a fresh wave of Germans advancing. I was wondering what to do – whether to lie doggo or open fire. There seemed no point in opening fire as there were perhaps a hundred and fifty enemy advancing rather diagonally across our front. To my amazement I heard short sharp bursts of Lewis gun-fire coming from the shell hole on my right. This was Sergeant Saunders, more or less minus a leg! The Germans were taken by surprise and bunched up, so I joined in and between us we took a heavy toll and the rest retired out of sight. I took down Sergeant Saunders's number, name and regiment. I did not see a live German again that day.

Before they had been pushed back and pursued by large masses of the enemy, the leading battalions of the 24th Division had done wonderfully well, advancing eastwards north of Bois Hugo and down the long open slopes almost to their objective – the second German line. The line was all but impregnable. It bristled with concrete emplacements and strongpoints and during a night of interminable labour in the dark and the rain the Germans had stiffened its already strong defences, closing the few gaps to present an unbroken front, broadening and heightening the barbed-wire entanglements until they were fully four feet high and fifteen feet wide. Unlike their equally formidable front line which had been stormed so successfully the previous day, the second-line defences had not been shelled before the attack, and the 24th Division's own guns which should have fired some kind of bombardment in advance of their assault were in trouble themselves. In the struggle and muddle during the hours of darkness they had failed to find their proper positions and, when daylight came, the gunners discovered, to their horror, that the guns were spread out on open ground across the Lone Tree Ridge. There was no cover, no means of camouflaging the battery positions, and they were in full view of several of the enemy's guns which immediately opened fire. It was hardly surprising that their fire in support of their own Division was sparse and inaccurate. Some shells had fallen on their own troops. None but a few ranging shots had reached the objective they were about to assault.

The Germans had moved up more men in the night. This time there could be no helpful release of gas to take the fight out of them. As the British battalions ran down the gentle descent they could see the enemy soldiers with heads and shoulders well above their parapets firing on them as they came. They were also being fired on from both flanks – from the line in front of Hulluch, now behind them on their left, and from Bois Hugo as they passed it on their right. Inevitably, as they pressed further on, the enemy was firing at their backs. Not many men had reached the German wire, but a few of them did, and some even worked their way through it, but most of those who tried to cut some desperate passage through the wire were killed in the attempt, leaving a handful of survivors lying out in the long grass waiting for the reinforcements who would help them carry the line. They had waited until they were killed or wounded, or overwhelmed when the enemy advanced for the waves that had started to follow them were forced to retire. It was a gallant effort for untried troops in their first battle.

Now that they had recaptured the whole of Hill 70 redoubt and pushed the troops back down the hill the enemy guns were busy.

Capt. D. Graham-Pole.

The Germans began to bombard us with high-explosive shells. They are the very Devil and horribly nerve-racking. When they hit a man they simply send him into pieces. One lump of the Post Corporal – one of my men – was heaved at me hot and steaming. It was horrible! We were absolutely stuck by want of men and the attack had to be abandoned – the ground strewn with dead and dying – eloquent testimony to the pluck of our men! We got orders to retire about 4 p.m. as the trench was being enfiladed from both flanks. I was the last to get back to our old trench and there I just about collapsed. The Colonel was shot on the way back. About five o'clock I got with some other men to another line of trenches. We helped to hold these until we were relieved between 1 and 2 a.m. on Monday morning.

All along the line attacks had failed – but some German attacks had also been repulsed. On the northern flank the situation at Fosse 8 was still precarious, in the small hours of the morning the enemy had succeeded in reoccupying the quarries half-way between Hohenzollern redoubt and the Hulluch Road, and the situation north of the Hulluch Road was worrying. The 2nd Division which had failed to make much headway on the 25th and was back in its original trenches astride the la Bassée Canal had been ordered to stand fast and had suffered less than some others. Now they were ordered to provide a composite force of three battalions, to move it two miles to the south and to recover the quarries. They were put under the command of Lieutenant-Colonel B. C. M. Carter of the King's Liverpool Regiment, and they called it Carter's Force. Joe Beard was on the left-hand flank of the attack.

Sgt. J. Beard, 1st Bn., King's Royal Rifle Corps, 6 Brig., 2 Div.

Throughout the 26th, a Sunday, we waited in support, eventually getting to the front line by evening. As you can imagine, by this second day it was quite a battlefield scene. Horses were dead around a wrecked field artillery gun which must have been driven across the trench over some temporary bridge. There were other casualties, too, and I can recall looking at them and thinking, 'Some mother's son.'

I was afraid of being afraid, the more so because I had a responsible job as NCO. Actually there was a sense of relief that the inevitable had happened: 'Let's get it over!' I suppose adrenalin flows and a person isolates the mind from thoughts of danger – gets on with the job.

There we are, fixed bayonets, waiting. A while previously Aunt Elizabeth had asked me what would I like in a food parcel. I'd asked her to send me a piece of home-cured boiled

545

bacon and I had a small piece left. I was chewing it when the order came. '*C Company. Over the top.*' Up we jump. Says I, 'Well chaps, I'm not going to waste this,' and there I went, bayonet in one hand, a piece of ham in the other.

Just previous to the command there was heavy enemy machine-gunning along our parapet which would have been murderous. But as we ran forward it ceased – for a spell. From that point I can recall every thought and action. I was thinking, 'Mary, Mary,' just looking at a picture of my lovely sweetheart in my mind. Afterwards I felt ashamed that I hadn't thought first of Mother.

The trenches were possibly four hundred yards apart and half-way across there was a barrier of barbed wire which was supposed to have been blown to smithereens, but in fact we went through a gap in single file. The Germans could easily have wiped out our section. They held their fire, until we were through. Then they let us have it.

I was running by the side of our Company Officer, Captain Sumner. He asked, 'How many are there left?' I glanced around. 'Three.' Very luckily we were on the edge of a captured German trench. At that moment he was shot through the knee and said, 'Jump into that trench.' That was the last I saw or heard of him. Which left Lance-Corporal Priddy, DCM, and myself.

In a dug-out was sitting a lone Captain of a regiment which had unsuccessfully attacked. A wounded man was screaming out in front and the Captain said, 'I wish you could fetch that man in.' Priddy and I looked at each other, then we both jumped out. By this time it was quite dusk, about seven o'clock. I bent down, feeling corpses. Machine-guns were turned on us but I found the wounded man. He was shot through the stomach. I recognised him as a chap in my platoon I'd reprimanded for shooting pigeons. His eyes were pin-pointed towards his nose through shock. I was bending over him when I was shot – a spate of bullets ragged my clothing and the emergency first aid pack sewn into the corner of my tunic was shattered. The feeling was like a red hot poker going through the flesh. I clapped my hands over my groin and I remember shouting, 'Priddy, I'm shot.' I stood like a fool for a few moments then I realised that I was *still* a target, so I fell down and rolled. I am sure it was pure luck that I rolled into what had been a German communication trench.

I could only crawl and drag myself along. The weather had been wet and everyone was covered in greyish-white chalk clay. I had to climb over sandbag barriers – all wet and shiny. Each time I got to the top of one I was above the trench, exposed to shells or bullets. After two of these I reached a barrier of piled-up dead men. I can still feel the thankfulness I felt as I got a good hold of the stiffs' clothing and slid over!

Eventually I fell into a group of our own company. Fortunately I didn't know how bad my wound was. I was soaked with blood. Someone cut off my right trouser leg and I remember a corporal saying, 'Well lad, *I* can't do anything with it.' Lieutenant Adie gave me a drink of brandy from his flask – he was killed later that night. Someone poured iodine into the wound; the pain was so intense I fainted.

Hulluch and the quarries remained in German hands. Now everything depended on the Guards – the last remaining reserves. They had been a long time on the way, for although the order to bring them into battle had been sent out early in the morning it had only reached some of the brigades at noon. But they had made good time marching through the throng of returning troops and vehicles, pressing on, hardly faltering in the shell-fire that sped them along the road. Late in the afternoon they reached the trenches outside Loos.

Pte. W. Jackman, 4th Grenadier Guards, 3rd Guards Brig.

Getting nearer our destination we kept seeing wounded chaps passing us and when we saw a lot of Highland regiments, they had aprons over their kilts, so we knew we were getting nearer to the firing line.

My company was Number 1 Company, leading, and we went up from Vermelles over a ridge. It was like a big valley. In front of us was Hill 70. Then we came under fire. Well, I didn't understand it was fire! It was like a lot of whips cracking. And the order came, '*Get into artillery formation.*' Well, artillery formation is about ten feet between each soldier, and we went down in line like that, straight down the hillside, and it was a most eerie affair because it sounded like whips cracking, and then you'd see the man on the left, he'd just flop down and that was that!

Capt. G. A. Brett, DSO, MC, 23rd Bn., London Regt.

Looking backward from the village into Loos Valley, the late No Man's Land, the straw-coloured ground rose gently up to the ridge and the mining hamlets of Philosophe and Maroc stood against the sky some fifteen hundred yards away. A platoon of troops appeared over the sky-line near Maroc, marching in fours towards us. Another showed to their right, then another and another, until the crest of the ridge was dotted with moving black squares. More and more followed until the whole straw-coloured slope began to look like a gigantic moving chess-board.

Soon after the leading platoons came over the crest German batteries opened fire on them, and quickly every possible enemy gun was concentrating on the chess-board. The platoons never hesitated. They came steadily on, more and more of them, through a real hell of explosion and flame – no halting, every gap filled immediately it was made. 'It's the Guards,' said someone, 'the Guards Division coming into action for the first time.'

Pte. W. Spencer, 4th Bn., Grenadier Guards, Guards Div.

Well, I wasn't really frightened to tell you the truth. We were all marching in fours, you know, the same as we might do in England. Then all of a sudden when the first shell burst near the road as we were marching up, we all deployed left and right of the road and spread out, and we kept on marching. Some were knocked out, but we kept on going and we did feel a little excited but not frightened – that's the impression it gave me. As a matter of fact, I was a bit disappointed with the first two shells. I thought they'd make more explosion. But I found out afterwards it wasn't always the ones that made the most explosion that caused the most damage. No! We advanced roughly about a mile and then we saw some old trenches which had been occupied previously by British troops that had gone forward and they were mostly Scotsmen who were laying about on the ground and I always remember two who were actually hanging on the barbed wire. In kilts. That's very vivid in my memory. We paused by those trenches and then went forward again and our battalion went straight forward for the town of Loos.

Capt. G. A. Brett. DSO, MC.

Our men leapt spontaneously from their cover into machine-gun fire to pull aside barbed wire and throw plank bridges across the trenches, anything to help these magnificent soldiers through. They reached us and passed through us, every man in step, rank closed up, heads erect, probably the finest men the world has ever seen.

Next day, it was hoped, the Guards would recapture the Chalk Pit and Puits 14 bis, and deliver a two-pronged assault that would finally secure Hill 70. Meanwhile they would take over the line from the remnants of the divisions whose men were on their last legs. The 3rd Cavalry Brigade, who had expected by this time to be dashing across the Douai Plain, stabled their horses and set off on foot to help them hold the line.

Pte. W. Jackman.

The people in front was this 21st Division, and we had to try and get in and take over the line from them, but they'd started off by digging a small trench alongside the road, and we all laid down there and the order came to dig in. Well, we only had trenching tools and there was a little mound in front of us what they'd chucked up and we had a bit of cover like that. So we kept on digging away. Where I dropped in the trench there was a dead man, and me and another chap had to hump this bloke out. That was my first experience of a dead man. We dug, and dug and dug, and it was hard chalk and all you could do with a trenching tool was dig into the bank, the wall of the trench. The shrapnel was coming over, and we was trying to make a hole to get our head in there.

Trpr. W. Clarke.

We were practically on top of Jerry's trench and relieving was a dodgy business. It was only twenty or twenty-five yards from them and you couldn't stand up or you'd get it in the noddle. Right, we crouch our way to this trench, start to go in – and by the way I've got my load on my back, plus a huge trench periscope made of sheet steel. I was so loaded I could hardly walk, let alone crouch. We get half-way up the trench and a message is passed down, 'Lieutenant So-and-So refuses to be relieved.' What we heard him called by the men we were to relieve I can't repeat here, but after almost having a riot on his hands he gave in.

Right, we get to our position and I had to go along to the left. When I got there I found I was the only man. Round the corner from my bit of trench it had all been blown in and it was filled with liquid mud, so when I reported this I had orders that every two hours I must crawl along the trench and make contact with the infantry on our left. Which I did . . . now and again! On the way there was a dead Welsh Fusilier, lying on the fire platform, and he wasn't a pretty sight, a great big hefty fellow, about six feet four inches. He was beginning to smell terrible. We reported him and later that night came a message: 'Soames, Clarke, bury that man.' I thought, 'Oh blimey, here we go again.' Anyway we had a go. He was too heavy and bloated for us to get him over the top and bury him, so in the end we dug a hole in the side of the trench, pushed him in and covered him up the best we could. But as it rained the earth washed away and there was our companion again! We kept on having to cover him.

Pte. W. Spencer.

Our company was on the extreme right nearest to Tower Bridge. We got half-way up the hill, there was quite a steep gradient where we were, and then we paused again and got down and we were ordered to take cover as much as we could. But there wasn't much cover at all, and of course we were right in the line for machine-gun fire from the Germans. All we could do was lay out in the open, that's what it was. By then it was getting dusk and we lay down on the ground and there was plenty of firing coming up, and then Jerry started sending these Very lights up to see people who were moving and train machine-guns on them. Well! Next thing a Very light came over and just missed my back and settled on my haversack. I could feel it! It had flared up and smoke was pouring over my head, you see? I could smell it and I thought, 'My God! I'm on fire.' I rolled over quick on my back and rolled back and forward to smother it. No time to get it off – it was blazing! Then I pulled it off when it got to a smoulder. I kept that haversack for years. It had a large hole in it where the Very light had burned through.

Throughout the night as others moved in to relieve them, small parties of exhausted men made their way out of the line and went thankfully back from the battle zone in such an inextricable confusion of units and formations that large numbers of military police had to be posted along the roads to direct them to their various rendezvous and guide them across country in the dark. The remnant of the 15th Scottish Division was to move back into reserve. The 21st and 24th Divisions would be withdrawn and re-formed.

Behind the soldiers plodding wearily westwards the horizon glowed with the flash of the guns and flared into brilliance as Very lights streaked through the sky. A mile or so to the north, where the battle for the slag-heaps near the Hohenzollern redoubt swung back and forth and the position was touch and go, the remaining brigade of the 24th Division was still in the line, and the men were clinging as best they could to trenches along the eastern edge of Fosse 8. There was no relief for them, or if any was planned no word of it had reached George Marrin.

Pte. G. Marrin.

I was ordered to go on a ration party, and four or five of us had to find our way from the front line back to the wagons, or as far as the wagons could get up the line, which would be some long distance really. But you didn't know where you were going and they just gave you that direction, '*You keep going that way and you'll find them because they're looking for you in any case.*' Which was quite true. We found the ration depot, drew our rations and we had to put them into sandbags, and our duty then was to get this food back to the line. We were so exhausted that I can remember we tied the rations to our feet to drag it along because we couldn't walk by that time – we were so tired. But of course we never got to the line, because when we *got* to the line there was no line there! Where we'd been, or where we *thought* we'd been, it had all gone, the men had all gone and everything had moved, so we didn't know where we were. And there we were, back in the line again with these ration bags tied to our feet and everybody had gone. They'd either moved back or forward and there was no means of telling *where* they'd gone, you see? Somebody would come along and say, 'Oh yes, they've moved to so-and-so,' so you'd try and find out where that was, just wandering. Then, when these other relief regiments came through, we were challenged. 'Who are you?' And I said to this officer, 'I'm 13th Battalion Middlesex.' He said, 'They don't exist, get out of it!' I can remember him now, standing there on the trench saying, 'Get out of it, get out the bloody way!' He was bringing in a new posse of troops that knew more about it than we ever did. They were trained soldiers. We did what we were instructed to do. We found the communication trench and we walked through the communication trench and got out at Vermelles, and from there we had to go back and find the base and find our regiment somehow – or what was left of it.

But that was days later. Meanwhile the unfortunate 73rd Brigade stuck it out in the trenches they were soon to lose. It was the end of the second day of the Battle of Loos, and the beginning of a long, hard and ultimately fruitless grind.

551

Chapter 36

Harry Fellowes remembered very little of the long trek back. All he retained was a muddled impression of trudging in anonymous clusters of men, dragging along like automatons, stumbling and limping up the dark road, sometimes falling, sometimes dropping out to slump at the roadside, too weary to curse or complain when passing transport forced them into the ditch. Looking back it seemed to him that they had spent more time in the ditch than on the pavé for there was, as ever, a solid stream of limbers, ambulance wagons, staff cars, motor cycles, attempting to reach the front in the hours of darkness, and working-parties toiling to repair the gaping shell-holes that impeded them. Tempers were short. Everyone on the road that night was engaged on urgent business, and the exhausted Tommies making their way piecemeal from the line came low in the list of priorities. Here and there an equally done-up officer took a group of stragglers under his wing and tried to introduce a semblance of order to encourage them along the road. The leaderless men were kept going by a simple urge to get out of it.

Further back there were Military Police at the road junctions but it was almost mid-day before Harry Fellowes was set on the road to Vermelles with other survivors of the 62nd Brigade, and it was almost nightfall before he found his own battalion. It had taken twenty hours to cover less than six miles from the front, and Fellowes was too close to collapse to sup more than half the hot soup that was ladled into his mess-tin and then crawl into a bivouac tent to stretch out on the naked earth. He slept far into the forenoon of the following day and woke up ravenous.

The Battalion was camped in the field where they had rested on the way to battle. Now the same field might have easily accommodated all four battalions of the Brigade. More stragglers came in during the morning and after dinners at noon the men were paraded for roll-call. They were a sadly bedraggled bunch and there were not many of them. In C Company perhaps sixty men lined up and Fellowes spotted only a few familiar faces. He could see few officers. Captain Pole was there, not in his familiar place in front of C Company but out in front, facing the thinned-out ranks of dishevelled men. All but five other officers had been killed or wounded and Pole was now in command of what remained of the Battalion. He looked as drawn and hollow-eyed as anyone, but he stood the men at ease and addressed them kindly. He knew they had been through a hard time, but they had done well in their first experience of battle. He knew and understood that every man was tired, but very soon they would be moving back to billets. Meantime he urged them to smarten up and to prepare to march out in a soldierly manner as a credit to the Battalion. He would inspect them in the morning. Until then there would be no drills or parades. He nodded to the senior sergeant to dismiss the parade and began to walk away.

Captain, now Acting-Colonel, Pole had started along the road when Harry Fellowes caught up with him. Until a few moments ago he had completely forgotten the existence of the message he still carried in his pocket. 'Excuse me, sir,' he called, and handing Pole the crumpled paper he began to pour out excuses and apologies. Pole read the message: '*The C.O. wishes the attack to be carried out with bayonets in the true Northumbrian fashion.*' Harry said again, 'I'm very sorry, sir. I did *try* to find you.' It was some moments before Pole looked up and spoke. 'It doesn't matter, sonny, now.' Harry never forgot Pole's words nor the tears that were coursing down his face.

The wounded who were fortunate enough to be rescued were well on their way back to safety. Christison was one of the lucky ones, but it had been touch and go.

Lt. A. F. P. Christison.

I was very weak, almost out, and very glad to see bearer parties from the Royal Engineers looking for wounded. They got me and Sergeant Saunders on stretchers and started to carry us back, but shells dropped close and we were abandoned. We were lucky. A bearer party from the Scots Guards picked us up and got us to the advanced dressing station where emergency surgery was carried out. From there I went back in a two-horsed ambulance which was hell, as my wounds were now hurting and every jolt was unpleasant. I had another operation in a base hospital at Choques and was evacuated to the Royal Free Hospital in London, via Boulogne, in the hospital ship *Anglia* on 28 September. Our Battalion casualties on 25 and 26 September had been 8 officers and 102 other ranks killed and

350 wounded. Thirty-six were missing. Sergeant Saunders, now without a leg, was awarded the VC and I was given the Military Cross.

Sgt. J. Beard.

During the night we were collected and laid out in a group. In early morning we were transferred to an Advanced Dressing Station – a schoolroom – about 10.30. I was put on the slab and the surgeon said, 'You're a lucky chap, Sergeant. Can you bear to see it?' I peeped up. There was a hole in my groin you could put a fist in! The surgeon told me I'd had a miraculous escape. It had just missed the femoral artery, and a fraction of an inch any other way and the bone could have been shattered or I could have been emasculated. Lucky me!

I was put on a train to the base hospital at Rouen. On Saturday 2 October, I was taken aboard the hospital ship, *St George*, and by hospital train to Derby. We had a wonderful reception when we arrived at Derby. It seemed as though the whole town turned out to wave and cheer. Women were kissing us and we were showered with cigarettes. How lovely it was to lie in a nice warm bed! By the way, the wounded man I went out to *was* rescued. I met him later at camp in Sheerness.

Young Bill Worrell who, thanks to Ben Williams, had got out early, was taken to a base hospital at Rouen.

Rfn. W. Worrell.

It was a canvas marquee hospital and I woke up – I'd been half-conscious, most of the time – and I woke up and behold, there was somebody I knew. It was Doctor Dowding, a great friend of my aunt, and there he was, to my absolute astonishment. He was in the RAMC then. He'd seen my name on the casualty list and he'd come in to have a look. So he said, 'Well, we'll get you back to England as soon as possible.' My jaw was all wired up by then and I could hardly speak, but I said, 'Do you think I'll get there?' He said, 'You certainly will! Now is there anything you want?' 'Well,' I said, 'I've lost my hat. Could you possibly find me an officer's hat with a Rifle Brigade badge?' Of course we all used to scrounge there, because there were no strict restrictions on dress – and out of the line any time you wore any sort of cap – that was before they issued the floppy cap that you could put in your pocket. But for your best, you'd always try, if you could, to get an officer's hat. That was a mark of complete distinction – an officer's hat with a floppy top, a big rim, and you were made! I don't know how Dr Dowding wangled it but next day, sure enough, he came back with an officer's hat – Rifle Brigade badge and all.

Well! I clung to that hat. I wouldn't let it out of my sight in case it got pinched – in fact at night I slept with it under my pillow. You see, when we went into the line that night we were wearing woollen helmets because of having our gas-masks rolled up over them, which you couldn't do over a cap, though as things were I'd probably have lost my cap in any case. Anyway, Dr Dowding got me a really posh hat, though it was ages before I could wear it because when I got to England I was months in bed in hospital. But I kept it with me all the time. It was my most prized possession and when I did eventually get out in my hospital blue suit I wore my officer's hat and I was as pleased as Punch.

Not all the wounded had been got away safely and the troops could only hope that the injured men they had been forced to leave close to the German line had been picked up and cared for by the enemy. The dead were another matter. They were long past help and it was pointless to risk more lives just to retrieve their bodies. Old soldiers accepted this but there were men in the New Army who did not agree with that precept. A day or two after the opening of the battle Colonel Thuillier commanding the 1st Division's artillery, had a chance meeting that deeply impressed him.

Lt. Col. H. F. Thuillier.

Returning from Loos along the straight Lens Road I met a sergeant and six or eight men of the 7th KOSB near the top of the ridge where the old German front line had been. I warned the sergeant that he would be exposed to enemy machine-gun fire farther along the road, and advised him to take his men across country. He thanked me, and asked how he could get to Hill 70. I replied that he couldn't get there at all, because it was now in the enemy's hands. He said, 'How can that be, sir? The Regiment took the hill and got over the other side.' I answered that there had been a lot of fighting since then, and that the Germans were on the top of it now, and I asked him why he wanted to go there. He said that his Colonel had sent him up to bury two officers of the regiment who had been killed on the top of the hill. I told him that it was out of the question, but he replied that he knew exactly where the officers had fallen and that he and his men proposed to get as near the spot as possible by daylight, creep out at night, and bring in the bodies. I explained that it was impossible, but he said, 'Well, sir, we couldn't go back and face the Regiment when we hadn't even tried to bury the officers, so we'll be getting along and make the best try we can. Thank you kindly for warning us all the same.' His men, who had been listening intently, gave unmistakable murmurs of agreement and the party prepared to move off. I said, 'Now, look here, Sergeant, it's really quite useless. You'll only lose your lives, and we can't afford to lose men like you. I'm not going to allow you to go to certain death. I *forbid* you to go, and I am ordering you back to your regiment.' The NCO, evidently very disappointed, said, 'Well, sir, if you *order* me to go back I must go, but I can't face the Colonel and say I haven't carried out his orders unless I show him in writing the order you've given me. I must also ask you, sir, if you'll excuse me, to give me a note with your name, rank, and regiment on it.' I gave him the documents, and saw him and his party, very reluctantly, turn about and go down the road towards Mazingarbe.

I don't think I have ever been more impressed with the spirit of any men than I was with that of those eight or nine Scotsmen. The NCO appeared to be an old regular soldier, but his men were all youngsters and the story doesn't show half the difficulty I had in turning them back.

It was true that Hill 70 was now back in the hands of the Germans. Even the illustrious Guards had not succeeded in taking it.

The plan was for the 2nd Guards Brigade to recapture the Chalk Pit, circling to approach it from the north, and to carry on to storm the pithead buildings of Puits 14 bis before the 3rd Guards Brigade struck from the west to assault Hill 70. It was late in the day. The light was failing but the Irish Guards of the 2nd Brigade reached their objective and thrust the Germans out of the Chalk Pit and Chalk Pit Wood just as they had planned and, just as it was planned, the Scots Guards swept up behind them to press on to Puits 14 bis. The Irish Guards had not been intended to go with them, but somehow, in the enthusiasm of this first success, they were swept up and carried along across the long stretch of open ground between Chalk Pit Wood and Puits 14 bis.

Just up the slope across the Lens—la Bassée road German machine-gunners were posted at intervals round three edges of Bois Hugo. As the Guards came running across their front they presented a target that was a machine-gunner's dream. They were cut down as they ran. The advance ground to a halt and withered away, and as the 3rd Guards Brigade began moving towards Hill 70 their comrades were already in retreat. It was not a rout. They were the Guards, and although for many it was a first experience of battle they had been trained and disciplined in a hard school. Later some guardsmen insisted that they had heard a shouted order to retire. If they had it had been a ruse by the Germans and, true or false, their retirement was so determined that it took all the efforts of their few remaining officers to stop and steady them.

A handful stood fast in the Chalk Pit. One of them was the son of Rudyard Kipling, an eighteen-year-old Lieutenant in the Irish Guards. A year previously his father had pulled strings and used his considerable influence to wangle John Kipling a commission at the age of seventeen. Now he was shot in the mouth. And there, in the Chalk Pit, he died.*

Despite the fact that Bois Hugo and Chalet Wood had not been captured, the 3rd Guards Brigade went straight in to attack Hill 70. It was almost dark by now, the enemy was on the alert and even the invincible Guards could not get forward.

They stuck it out for three days, repulsing counter-attacks, suffering shelling – and gas shelling too, for the enemy had moved further ahead in the technology of gas warfare. And the Guards tried again to capture the hill, but their efforts were futile and their casualties were huge. Hill 70 held out. It was a bitter blow.

So far as the Staff were concerned the lack of progress was a hard pill to swallow after the success of the first breakthrough. And just as Hill 70 had baulked the British, the operations of the French Army on their right had come to a standstill in front of the bastion of the Vimy Ridge. But neither the French nor the British Command had given up hope. It was necessary to pause, it was even more necessary to reorganise, and it was clearly necessary to bring in fresh troops, but there could be no question of abandoning the offensive. At Sir John French's urgent insistence, and in the light of his concern that his reserves were being so rapidly used up, General Joffre agreed to draw a division from his own reserve to relieve the 47th Division and the Guards and to carry his line northwards to include the Double Crassier, the ruined village of Loos and the

---

* Kipling never recovered from his boy's death and could never throw off his acute sense of guilt. Years later he wrote a bitter couplet: 'If any ask us why we died / Tell them "Because our fathers lied".' Ironically (because Kipling devoted much of the rest of his life to work on behalf of the War Graves Commission) John Kipling lay for many years in an anonymous grave. Recently (1992) his grave was identified and a new headstone bearing his name has been erected in St Mary's Dressing Station Cemetery near Lone Tree.

killing field on Hill 70. And when the relief was completed, as soon as plans could be made for a new, and this time a joint attack, the French would do their utmost to regain it.

Slowly the hardest hit battalions were recovering. They had cleaned up, they were comparatively well rested, and a few square meals had done a good deal to restore them. Most now had a roof over their heads, even if it was only the roof of a barn, but they had not yet fully recovered their morale. Despite the efforts of officers to get up sports and football matches and despite the return to normal routine, the air of depression was slow to dissipate. All too often there were reminders.

Pte. G. Cribley, 8th Bn., Gloucestershire Regt., 57 Brig., 19 Div.

My friend was killed. We lived next door to each other at home. We were boys together. After we came out the line the Post Corporal said to me, 'There's a parcel for your mate, George' – parcels couldn't be sent home so they were divided up between the rest of us. There was a gooseberry pie in his parcel and it was all mildewed and had to be thrown away. I thought of his poor old mother picking those gooseberries as I'd often seen her do, and bottling them, because it was past the gooseberry season, and I thought of how she would feel when she got to hear of his death. The sight of those dead I will never forget. They were a ghastly sight, and I used to think what their mothers would have felt if they could see their boys now. It was that gooseberry pie brought it home to me.

It was quickly brought home to the new drafts, now arriving to make up the numbers, that they had been brought in to fill the gaps. Less than a week after their fight at Hill 70 Carson Stewart joined the 7th Camerons.

Pte. C. Stewart, 7th Bn., Queen's Own Cameron Highlanders, 44 Brig., 15 Div.

A while before I left I went to see a pal of mine in hospital, George Sutherland. He'd been wounded at Festubert and sent home, and he said to me, 'You'd better take your running shoes to France for you'll have to get off your mark at the double.' He wasn't keen on going back. Oh, no! But I was full of beans. I was attached to the 44th Brigade (all Scots Regiments, kilty lads) and we were in reserve at the coal-mining village of Noeux-les-Mines. My battalion hadn't long come out of the attack. It was a very badly arranged attack. The lads that came back said that the Colonel of the 7th Camerons, Colonel Sandilands, wouldn't give them their usual drop of rum before the Battle of Loos. He told them that if they were going to meet their Maker, then he wanted them to be sober and he poured the rum into the trench before they went into action on the morning of the 25th. They talked more about that than they did about their losses. But they told us all about it.

They took the small hill at Loos just beyond the coal-pit, but they met with terrible machine-gun fire – so much so that the 44th Brigade were cut to ribbons. They couldn't hold on to the hill and so they were ordered to retire to our side of the hill. But not many who went over the hill ever got back to our side of it. The machine-gun fire was just *murder*!

I got all my information about the Battle of Loos from our boys after it was all over. I joined the survivors of the 7th Battalion Cameron Highlanders immediately after Loos. Soon after I got there, the next day I think, there was a mail came in. All the boys in my company were crowded round to see what there was for them and the Post Corporal was calling out the names and dishing out the letters and parcels. Half the names that were called out there was nobody to answer them. Then a voice would call out, 'Ower the hill.' Then one or two more, then another name – and there would be silence, then his chum would call out, 'Ower the hill.' That was all you could hear: 'Ower the hill. Ower the hill. Ower the hill.' If it was parcels they dished them out anyway and we new arrivals got a share of the parcels that were meant for the boys who'd got killed.

Letters for men who were wounded were returned to the base and reached them, sooner or later, in hospital. Parcels were shared out among their comrades. Letters addressed to the men who had gone were stamped '*Killed*' and returned to the senders. Sometimes, though seldom, such letters arrived at a soldier's home address before the official telegram informing his next of kin that he was dead.

Orderly room clerks as well as Post Corporals were kept busy, for a great tide of paper flowed out from every battalion in the days after the battle. The soldiers were all writing letters to worried families and sweethearts. 'Dear Mum and Dad . . . Dear Ethel . . . Dear Sarah . . . Dear Aunt May . . .', and, however bald and uninformative, they brought welcome reassurance to anxious friends at home. 'We've been in a big fight, but I've come through . . . I am in the pink and hope you are the same. Hope this finds you as it leaves me.' There were no words to express what they had experienced, no way of telling the relief of being alive. Some day they might have a tale to tell. Not now.

Officers were dutifully applying themselves to the depressing task of writing to relatives of the men who had been killed. As the newly appointed Battalion Commander, David Pole was swamped with paperwork, but he had led C Company into the battle, and he felt that, like any Company Commander, he had a personal obligation to write to the families of the men who had not come back. A personal letter might ease the pain of the terse official telegram. 'Dear Mr and Mrs Craven, It is my painful duty to tell you that your son, Sergeant Craven . . .' It was indeed a painful duty. Later it would become routine. But there was one special letter that took priority: 'Dear Mrs Warwick, You asked me to write if any mishap befell your husband and I must first hasten to assure you that, although the Colonel was wounded in our recent attack, I have every reason to believe that he is going on well and that you may confidently expect to have him home soon . . .' It was 29 September. As Pole wrote the date at the top of his letter he must surely have been struck by the fact that it was just three weeks to the day since the Battalion had landed in France.

Every surviving officer was writing difficult letters, but there were other matters to be attended to and some were pleasanter tasks for they were instructed to send in recommendations for gallantry awards. It was Arthur Agius's impression that every one of his men had earned a reward but, since the authorities were unlikely to share this view and the allocation of medals would be limited, he confined himself to the most deserving.

No. 1783 Private BUTE, WILFRED
No. 1919 Private PEPPER, JOSEPH WILLIAM
(Stretcher-Bearer)

On the early morning of Sept. 25th when an enemy minen-werfer bomb exploded a battery of gas cylinders in the DUCKS BILL, these two men assisted to evacuate the casualties which were numerous and to clear the gas in the trench.

The difficulties and danger of this operation were accentuated by the fact that it was still dark, the trench was full of escaped gas and gas appliances, the officer in charge of the gas and most of his personnel were gassed, and there were two full gas batteries adjacent. This is the first time that these men had experienced gas. The DUCKS BILL is a dangerous spot, 80 yards from the enemy lines and 100 from ours.

Signed: Capt. A. J. Agius

Senior officers were busily engaged in writing their reports and Brigadier-General Jelf, in command of the 73rd Brigade, took particular pains with his. He had taken over command of the Brigade on 26 September after its own Brigadier was killed. He was angry. And he was more than angry. He was incensed. It had come to his notice that the 24th Division, and his Brigade in particular, was being criticised by higher authority. He expressed himself frankly:

No communication of any kind had been established with my Battalions either by wire or orderly, and I attribute this to the fact that all battalions and the Brigade Staff were quite ignorant of the rudiments of what to do in the trenches, how communications were established, the method of drawing rations, etc. They never had been in trenches in their lives before. And I can confidently assert, after many months of trench warfare, that it would have taxed to the uttermost the resources of any Regular battalions with plenty of experience behind them, to have kept themselves supplied, under similar conditions.

The post-mortems and reappraisals had already begun and the thrusting of the two untried and imperfectly trained divisions into battle, even the very fact that they were employed as almost the only reserves, was already a sore point. Sir John French had recognised the value of bringing in fresh divisions whose attitudes had not yet been stultified by the stalemate of trench warfare, but it was for exactly this reason that he was reluctant to commit them until success was certain and a breakthrough assured. He had promised the Divisional Commanders as much, making it clear that all that would be required of them would be to pursue the advance, or more precisely, to pursue the enemy in his flight. It was not his intention that they should be thrown in to attempt to smash the enemy's second line. It was his right and entitlement, indeed as Commander-in-Chief it was his duty to retain a proportion of troops as reserves, but under his own orders, and to release them only when, in his judgement and his judgement alone, it was the right moment to send them in. It had previously been arranged, with the concurrence of Sir Douglas Haig, that the reserves should be held a short distance behind the battle-front, for there was no certainty that they would be required. Everything hinged on success in the first stage of the battle, and as soon as news reached the Commander-in-Chief that the German line had been breached, that the troops were swarming forward and that they had captured Loos, he released his hold on the reserves and placed them at the disposal of Sir Douglas Haig. It was Haig's orders that sent them into the attack, and he had issued them in good faith on the basis of the information he received and in the belief that British troops were already tackling the Germans' second line. But the fortunes of war are fickle and the fog of war grows thicker as confused information travels along the chain of command and across the miles from the front, and, as often as not, by the time news reached Army Headquarters the situation had already changed.

After the relish of a glorious beginning, matters had gone downhill. The self-satisfaction of the First Army Staff had received a severe jolt and the laurels which they believed they had justly earned were beginning to look slightly wilted in the backlash.

The friction between the Commander-in-Chief and the ambitious commander of the First Army had been increasing over the months. Now Haig, affronted as much by the recent failure as he had been gratified by the initial success, settled in his own mind on whose shoulders the blame should be laid. In the course of a meeting on 28 September Sir John French informed him that he was withdrawing the 21st and 24th Divisions for further training. It was a private meeting and there is no record of what passed between them, although shortly afterwards Haig confided to his diary: '*It seems impossible to discuss military problems with an unreasoning brain of this kind. At any rate, no good result is to be expected from so doing.*' Next day Haig wrote a carefully considered letter to Lord Kitchener himself.

Wednesday 29th September
1st Army H.Q.
Hinges

My dear Lord Kitchener,

You will doubtless recollect how earnestly I pressed you to ensure an adequate Reserve being close in rear of my attacking Divisions, and under my orders. It may interest you to know what happened. No Reserve was placed under me. My attack, as has been reported, was a complete success. The enemy had no troops in his second line, which some of my plucky fellows reached and entered without opposition. Prisoners state the enemy was so hard put to it for troops to stem our advance that the officers' servants, fatigue-men, etc., in Lens were pushed forward to hold their 2nd Line to the east of Loos and Hill 70.

The two Reserve Divisions (under C. in C.'s orders) were directed to join me as soon as the success of the First Army was known at GHQ. They came on as quick as they could, poor fellows, but only crossed our old trench line with their heads at

6 p.m. We had captured Loos 12 hours previously, and Reserves should have been at hand *then*. This, you will remember, I requested should be arranged by GHQ and Robertson quite concurred in my views and wished to put the Reserve Divisions under me, but was not allowed.

The final result is that the enemy had been allowed time in which to bring up troops and to strengthen his second line, and *probably* to construct a third line in the direction in which we are heading, viz., Pont à Vendin.

I have now been given some fresh Divisions, and am busy planning an attack to break the enemy's second line. But the element of surprise has gone, and our task will be a difficult one.

I think it right that you should know how the lessons which have been learnt in the war at such cost have been neglected. We *were* in a position to make this the turning point in the war, and I still hope we may do so, but naturally I feel annoyed at the lost opportunity.

We were all very pleased to receive your kind telegram, and I am,

yours very truly,
D. Haig.

Lord Kitchener was obliged to investigate Haig's complaint and he wrote a kind and tactful letter to the Commander-in-Chief. It was marked '*Private and Secret*' and written, as he told him, '*with great reluctance*', but it was insistent. 'Colleagues' had put certain facts before him and he had no alternative but to ask the Commander-in-Chief for his side of the story. Sir John French replied in formal terms stating the facts from his own point of view, but writing privately he was more forthright. 'It is all, of course absolutely false and stupid,' he wrote, 'and *full* explanations have been given.' There was probably little doubt in his own mind as to who the mysterious 'colleagues' were. He was well aware that General Haig had the ear of influential friends in high places, including that of the king himself.

Fresh troops from the Second Army in the north were already marching towards Loos. In a week's time new attacks would be launched and the battle would drag on. But little was gained. Much later, and with hindsight, the Battle Nomenclature Committee decreed officially that the Battle of Loos ended with the failure of the joint Franco-British offensive on 8 October, but it was only on 4 November that Sir Douglas Haig was finally forced to inform the Commander-in-Chief that his efforts must be abandoned. By then many more lives had been lost. Between 25 September and 16 October alone there were more than fifty thousand casualties, and almost sixty thousand if the subsidiary attacks are included, and more than twenty-six thousand of the casualties were killed or missing. A few of the missing turned up later as prisoners of war, but more than half the casualties at Loos, at Piètre, at Bois Grenier and Hooge, had gone 'ower the hill'.

It was too early to count the cost. The full force of disappointment was yet to come and no one could deny that on 25 September the British Army had won its first real victory of the war. They had smashed through the German defences, they had advanced the line, and they were holding on. Surely it was only the beginning. The ground they had gained measured little over a mile but it was better than an advance of yards, it was infinitely better than retreat, and it looked most impressive on the maps that illustrated the glowing newspaper reports which were still being published days after the start of the battle.

Sir Douglas Haig was the hero of the hour and the news of victory spread fast and far. Before long it reached Gallipoli and some senior officers hatched a plan to celebrate. At a certain hour a thunderous cheer would be raised all along the line. The front-line troops were taken with the idea and were quite willing to cooperate. Some introduced a further refinement and fearing that the Turks might not fully understand the reason for the celebration stuffed proclamations of the victory into empty bottles to be hurled at the enemy trenches when the time came.

It was quite a performance. Up and down the line from Suvla to Cape Helles the sky above the trenches rang with cheering and a fusillade of bottles descended on the heads of the unsuspecting Turks. Assuming quite reasonably that they were about to be attacked the Turks replied with fusillades of bullets, thereby – as one officer remarked happily – 'wasting thousands of rounds of ammunition'. Regrettably, there was some casualties. Nevertheless it was an event that was long remembered. Months later a wounded officer of the Royal Scots whiled away the long hours of convalescence by writing an epic that described it.

> With faces flushed and eyes like wine
> The men sat mute along the line,
> And some polemical design
> Was palpably in view.
> A flare soared sudden through the murk
> They turned unflinching towards the Turk,
> And shouted all they knew.

A wilder din you will not meet,
It hit the hills, it shocked the Fleet,
And many a brave heart dropped a beat,
To hear the hideous choir,
While the pale Turk, with lips tight set,
Peered out across the parapet,
And opened rapid fire.

Far down the lines the Faithful heard,
And had no notion what occurred,
But plied their triggers undeterred,
By trifles such as that.
From sea to sea the tumult spread
Nor could a single man have said,
What he was shouting at.

And a despatch in pleasing wise,
Spoke of a daring enterprise,
'Against some enemy supplies',
Adding this tragic note:
'The casualties of the force,
Were sixty men extremely hoarse,
And one severe sore throat.'

Although a few men had paid the price of the celebration with their
lives it possibly did something to raise morale – and the troops on
Gallipoli sorely needed it.

Cut off far from home, isolated on the peninsula, they were
beginning to feel that they were a forgotten army. But they were not
forgotten, for the situation in Gallipoli was very much on the minds of
the men who were conducting the war and opinion was sharply
divided.

The sun still burned warm and bright in daytime but already the
nights had turned cool and offshore there were stormy flurries that
whipped the sea into a frenzy of raging waves that battered the beaches
and presaged worse to come. Piers at Suvla and Anzac were swept
away, small vessels were cast adrift and smashed against the rocks, and
before long it would clearly be difficult, if not impossible, to land the
stores that would be so urgently needed if the troops were to withstand
the winter. Already they were in a bad way. Sickness was rife. Almost
a thousand men were being evacuated every day and the vast majority
were not wounded but sick – with dysentery, with blood poisoning
from infected insect bites, with heart disease, skin disease, or simply
with debilitation. In a very short time huge quantities of supplies would
be required before the onset of the cold weather – warm clothing,

thousands of tons of timber and corrugated iron to build huts and shelters to shield the soldiers in the winter, as well as constant supplies of food and ammunition. If conditions worsened, how were the troops to be supplied? If reinforcements were sent, how were they to be landed? If (and some added 'Perish the thought!') it was decided to give up the peninsula and withdraw the troops, how were they to be safely evacuated? No one could come up with a satisfactory answer.

All through the month of October controversy raged. Public opinion had been roused and there was much criticism of the Gallipoli campaign and, as the arguments continued, the fate and future of the Gallipoli operations swung in the balance. When the Dardanelles Committee met on 11 October two papers lay before them and each one was a bombshell. The first was the report of General Sir Frederick Stopford, now relieved of his command and back in England, who had hastened to present a report designed to defend his actions and disclaim responsibility for the debacle at Suvla Bay. It was a farrago of half-truths and downright lies and it implied harsh criticism of Sir Ian Hamilton's conduct of operations, not only at Suvla but on the peninsula as a whole. It was viciously unfair, but it went unchallenged. Sir Ian Hamilton, who had not even seen it, was given no opportunity to reply, but Lord Kitchener had already made up his mind. Although he had appointed four Generals of the War Office staff to make further inquiries, and despite the fact that they had neutrally reported back that they felt unable to make any judgement 'without much fuller information', Kitchener informed the Government with all the weight of his authority that the Generals' review had resulted in 'considerable criticism of Sir Ian Hamilton's leadership'. It had done no such thing, but this was not all. An Australian journalist, Mr Keith Murdoch (who was to become the father of Rupert Murdoch), had recently taken it upon himself to write a virulent letter to the Prime Minister of Australia, attacking the conduct of all the troops on the peninsula (with the exception of the Australians) and violently attacking Sir Ian Hamilton and the chief of his General Staff. He had shown this letter to Lloyd George and, at his suggestion, had sent a copy to the British Prime Minister. These documents now lay before the Dardanelles committee and they had a considerable influence on their deliberations.

The dilemma which faced them was whether to strongly reinforce the troops in the peninsula as Sir Ian Hamilton had desired, and to make an all-out effort to capture it, or to cut their losses and give it up. Already opinion was split between 'Easterners' who clung to the idea of pursuing the strategy in the eastern Mediterranean and 'Westerners' who subscribed to the belief that the war could only be won on the western front. There were many factors to take into consideration.

Bulgaria, just as they had feared, had now entered the war on the side of their enemies and had already invaded Serbia. At the behest of the French the 10th Division had already been dispatched with a French Division from Gallipoli to the Greek port of Salonika in an effort to break through to help the Serbs, and although it was even now apparent that they had only a slender chance of succeeding the French were pressing for reinforcements. It was a delicate political situation, not least because of the continuing neutrality of Greece. What was to be done? No one could decide.

Eventually a compromise was reached and it was agreed that a strong force should be sent to Egypt 'without prejudice to its final destination'. Gallipoli? Salonika? It was anybody's guess, but at least it would buy time. But the Dardanelles Committee did reach one unanimous decision. Sir Ian Hamilton was to be sacked.

Another head was also destined for the block. Returning by special train from an Anglo-French conference at Chantilly at which the Salonika question had been the main item on the agenda, General Callwell, then Director of Military Operations at the War Office, overheard an interesting conversation in the dining car. Lloyd George, Mr Asquith and Sir Edward Grey were discussing the replacement of Sir John French as Commander-in-Chief of the British Armies in France. They made no effort to lower their voices and since a short train of only two coaches makes less noise than a long one, their words were plainly heard.

Major-General C. E. Callwell, KCB.

The Big Three sat together at one table, whilst we lesser fry congregated close at hand at others. They may perhaps have been somewhat stimulated by draughts of sparkling vintage! But, be that as it may, the Prime Minister and the Minister of Munitions were in their most expansive mood, and after a time their conversation was followed by the rest of us with considerable interest. To the sailors present, also to one or two of the junior officers, it was probably news – and it must surely have been news to the waiters – to learn that Sir John French was shortly to vacate command of the BEF in France. Nor could we be other than gratified at the discussions concerning Sir Douglas Haig's qualifications as a successor. I was expecting every moment to hear Sir William Robertson's suitability for the post freely canvassed – he was sitting back-to-back with the Munitions Minister. Cabinet Ministers certainly are quaint people.

But Haig seemed the obvious candidate for the job of Commander-in-

Chief, and there was little doubt on whom the final choice would fall.

Jock Macleod celebrated his twenty-first birthday in style. After a better-than-usual dinner in the mess, supplemented by a birthday cake from home, the officers drank his health in port wine laid down by his godfather in the year of his birth, and which he had brought back after his last leave with this occasion in mind. It was the eve of the 27th Division's departure for an unknown destination and early next morning the Battalion marched off to entrain. It was a long, slow journey. Mail was collected along the way to be censored and dispatched at the first opportunity, and Jock was able to post a letter home.

> I am now using a new pony.
> Nothing seems to do any good
> to my old pony, which still
> remains lame in spite of
> all bandages. The pony that
> I now have belonged to our origi-
> nal padre, who has left us
> for the Base Camp at Havre.
> On the completion of his year he
> returns to his parish. He had
> merely six weeks to do until then,
> and so the authorities decided to
> retain him in France. It did not
> seem worthwhile to
> employ him with us, and then
> immediately send him back.
> Last night we had a
> long rumour that a Bulgarian gen-
> eral had been assassinated.
> Sorry that I have no news!
> Yours Aye,
> Jock.

The censor passed it without comment for its contents were of no importance. But it was of considerable interest to his family, for it was written in a clever code, prearranged with Jock's father. Added together, the first letters of each line spelt out the news he wished to impart: I-N T-R-A-I-N F-O-R M-A-R-S-E-I-L-L-E-S.

He had no idea where the 27th Division was ultimately bound for. Neither had anyone else. The 27th Division had been sent off 'without prejudice to its final destination'. But they were only too thankful to kick the mud of Flanders from their feet and nobody gave a hoot where they were going.

Part 8

~

The Dying of the Year

Colonel Cold strode up the Line
(Tabs of rime and spurs of ice),
Stiffened all where he did glare,
Horses, men, and lice.

Visited a forward post,
Left them burning, ear to foot,
Fingers stuck to biting steel,
Toes to frozen boot.

Those who watched with hoary eyes
Saw two figures gleaming there,
Hauptman Kälte, Colonel Cold,
Gaunt, in the grey air.

Edgell·Rickword

Chapter 37

On the western front, after a spell of fine autumn weather when the sun shone through the dying days of the Loos offensive, winter set in cold and harsh and early as the troops settled into the monotonous routine of holding the line. After a brief rest the 15th Scottish Division was back in the trenches. This time they were in front of the Hohenzollern redoubt, and it was a bleak initiation for the men of the new drafts.

Even in the best of weather it was not an inspiring spot and wrapped in the dank mist of early winter it was positively eerie. The mist hung above the low plateau of the redoubt and hung in wisps round the unlovely slag-heaps where two battered cranes still sat drunkenly askew on the flat top of Fosse 8. The leaden November skies added to the gloom and the ground between the lines bore miserable witness to the fearsome efforts that had been made to capture it. Among the battered trenches, the splintered stakes that still supported remnants of rusting wire, the dead were lying in rows, just as they had been cut down – as neatly and tidily as if some ghostly sergeant-major had drilled them in their dying as he had once drilled them on the parade-ground. There was no possibility of bringing in the bodies and as they decomposed, the smell of death and decay hung thick about the trenches.

But the dead soldiers were still doing duty of a sort for soldiers creeping close to the enemy lines on listening patrols could lie low among the dead and get away with it. It was not a job for the squeamish.

Pte. C. Stewart.

My first listening party there I'll never forget. We were out there in No Man's Land, crawling out among the dead boys, because the idea was that if we lay close to the dead boys you would think *we* were dead. We spaced ourselves out, so you would be on your own among these corpses and we had to be quiet, no noise, no speaking. After a while, if we couldn't see

571

or hear anything and it was time to come in, the NCO in charge would crawl round and give your foot a kick. That was the only way he could see if you was one of the Loos dead or one of his listening party. If you responded to his kick he gave you the sign to come into the trench again and if there was no response then he knew it was one of the poor boys killed at Loos.

The officer in charge of the listening party was a very fine chap. We just called him 'Algy', because he always wore a monocle. He was a great guy, always for his men and a real good sport when we were out of the trenches. After we got back into our own trench we found that our officer 'Algy' was missing and they called for volunteers to go out again into No Man's Land to get him in. Everyone wanted to go. I wasn't chosen for the rescue party, but the boys *did* get 'Algy' in and he was very badly wounded. We sent him down the line a bit, and maybe he got the length of the big hospital at Etaples, but I am so sorry to say he died. At least he would get a burial. There was nothing you could do for the boys lying out in front at Loos. They were a terrible sight. We used to talk about it afterwards – and even long afterwards, for the rest of war, we would say that something or somebody was 'as quiet as the Loos dead'. It was quite an expression with us.

Trpr. W. Clarke.

It was impossible to bury them all. They lay in the trenches where they'd fallen or had been slung and earth had just been put on top of them and when the rain came it washed most of the earth away. You'd go along the trenches and you'd see a boot and puttee sticking out, or an arm or a hand, sometimes faces. Not only would you see, but you'd be walking on them, slipping and sliding. The stench was terrible because of all that rotting flesh. When you think of all the bits and pieces you saw! But if you ever had to write home about a particular mate you'd always say that he got it cleanly and quickly with a bullet and he didn't know what had happened.

Looking over the top through the periscope we could see old Jerry's line about fifty yards in front. So I thought, 'Blimey, that's within bombing range, isn't it?' We kept our eye on him all night – and by the way, we had no wire in front of our trenches, it was all open! – and me being the left-hand man there was no one at the side of me, so I had to traverse through a lot of trenches to make contact with the infantry on our left, and blow me if I didn't come across the dead Welsh Fusilier again I'd come across weeks before, only there was hardly anything left of him by then. I felt responsible for him, don't know why, so I popped him in the side of the trench again. That was the last I saw of him.

Pte. F. Bastable.

We went in the trenches ten days at a time – sometimes it was twelve days, but if you was lucky it was ten – a day marching up, three days in the front line, three days in support and three days in reserve, and in that weather you was a right mess when you got out. You'd march back to your billet and when you got back your coat was covered in mud, you couldn't lift them hardly sometimes because they'd be dragged down in mud, and you're in mud all the time. Then you had to get these coats cleaned and your rifle cleaned and go on parade next morning. It's impossible, you know, to get all the mud off your coat in that time and go on parade, and I was really unlucky. I was Mess Orderly and I had other duties to do and I suppose I got my coat clean but I hadn't cleaned my rifle. It was loaded, and I went on parade with it loaded. Of course when they inspected your rifle you had to have it properly cleaned and you had to open and shut your bolts so that they clicked all together. Well, I went to pull my bolt and it fired out this bullet! It went right past the bloke's nose next to me – nearly hit him. Well, I got court-martialled for that. I got ten days' number one field punishment, and it was bleeding cold and the worst time of the year.

I got tied up against this cart-wheel. I never knew they was going to do that. I never knew they done such a thing (they don't do it now!). It was done under the Military Police and there were a few of us who'd been court-martialled (not for the same thing) and they gave us orders to go to the wagon-lines and told us to bring up the wagons and clean the wheels, because they were covered in mud. Well, the *old* soldiers might have known what was going to happen, but I didn't. I thought it was just like fatigues and this was the punishment, cleaning the wheels. But it wasn't! After we'd cleaned them they tied us one up against each wheel for a couple of hours a day, an hour in the morning and an hour in the afternoon.

I wasn't none too keen! I wasn't all that eager to do it. I got froze! You had to run round to get warm after that and there was a school there and we used to run round the playground to get our circulation back, because it was bleeding cold. Anyway,

I done this ten days and went back up the line again. When I got back (we were in the reserve line at the time) I laid on the firestep of the trench and went off to sleep. Now sometimes if you go off to sleep in the cold you don't wake up again. They say that sometimes they used to find men dead of a morning, just with lying in the cold. Anyway I went off to sleep and I felt myself, like, sinking, just as though I was sinking down, and I roused myself and woke up. I was covered in snow. It must have been the first snow of winter, in fact we didn't have much more of it until January time, but when I roused myself and woke up it was all snowing. I shan't forget that. I shall always remember that. It was bleeding awful.

Snow before Christmas was unusual, but the bone-chilling night frosts that descended on the trenches were bad enough. Years later they said it was the worst winter of the war – but it was the first winter in memory in which tens of thousands of men had been forced to live exposed to the elements with only holes in the ground for shelter. Women at home were so busy knitting that the clack of millions of needles might almost have been heard in France, but they were knitting socks and there was hardly a parcel that did not contain at least one pair. Now, at the urgent request of battalions in France, there were published appeals for other garments – mufflers, mittens, wrist-warmers, woollen helmets, knitted waist-coats, and yet more mufflers. Many months ago someone in the Quarter-master-General's department had the wit to look ahead to winter and about this time the troops were issued with fur jerkins. They looked extremely odd for they were made from a variety of furs – goatskin, sheepskin, the skins of shaggy ponies and even of piebald cows. They were imported mainly from South America and, since some of the skins had been badly cured, they did not always smell particularly sweet. Wearing these bulky garments fur side out over khaki tunics, with equipment strapped and belted round them, the Tommies closely resembled an army of brigands, but the jerkins were a lifesaver and a bulwark against the Flanders chill.

When the gnawing cold abated, it turned to rain, and in the Ypres salient it rained in torrents. Company Quartermaster-Sergeant Scott McFie was enduring his second winter in the salient and, as he graphically described in a letter to his brother, it was no more pleasant than the first.

My dear Jimmy,

I had a little break in the monotony of life on Sunday night. I still live with the stores in my tents by the side of the farm pond,

574

but the men have been moved about almost every day lately. On Sunday they were at the point of the salient, between the much-contested place where we made our charge and the hill with the numerical name. It is always pretty lively there, the place being almost surrounded by the Germans. Also it is an awfully long way off, a good ten miles at the least, and the tracks, especially the tracks across the fields, were deep in mud with the heavy and continuous traffic after a day of never-ceasing rain. So I put plenty of dubbing on my boots and made up my mind for twenty miles of bad walking in the dark. Fortunately there was a good moon or I don't see how we could have avoided the big shell craters, now full of water and unpleasantly cold.

We reached the wood just behind the firing line where our men were, and were waiting for the fatigue parties to come and carry away the bags of rations when the Germans suddenly began an attack to regain some of the ground they lost lately. The first thing that happened was that a packhorse bolted without its leader. Then all the carts belonging to other regiments fled home at a gallop. Then a lot of soldiers came running from the direction where the attack was and rushed for positions of greater safety – but I think they were only a digging party and not fighters. All the time there was a fine display of fireworks – not only the ordinary white magnesium rocket, but green and red stars, and even clusters of various colours – signals of course – and the bursting shrapnel of high-explosive shells from both sides, an occasional small mine going off, and the rattle of the machine-guns and rifles made a most deafening noise. Everybody who could took shelter in a communication trench close to us, but as I was the senior left I had to stay with the transport. I took the responsibility of unloading all the things on the ground and sending the carts and horses back. They went off in such a hurry, and the ground was so slippery, that two horses fell and two men were slightly injured.

We do not yet know what was the result of the attack. As soon as things grew quieter we handed over the rations and did our muddy ten miles home.

It is a horrible day – pouring and blowing furiously. My 'office' has been trying to go up like a balloon and I have had to sit and watch for loose pegs all day. The groundsheets are covered with mud, little rivers run in at each corner, occasionally a gust of wind gets in and scatters everything. However the other tents are worse, and many have been blowing about the field like autumn leaves in a gale.

I was out last night, first to the town of Ypres with rations,

575

and then to a village about five miles away to attend the funeral of my captain, another officer and two men who had been killed that morning by a shell when out for a walk. I fear he must have been very badly smashed for he was a tall big man and the bundle in a blanket which we buried at night was quite short. Barring the colonel, who is ill, we have no officer with us now of more than a few weeks' standing.

Many thanks also for the big tin of milk, the chocolate, the candles (very scarce just now!) and the handkerchiefs.

Love to Helen and the boys
Your affectionate brother
R. A. Scott McFie

In the trenches there was danger, there were frequent alarms and there were many casualties but it was difficult to decide what was the worst enemy – the Germans, the weather, or sheer boredom.

Trpr. W. Clarke.

When it was quiet, it was so boring. Awake all night. Stand-to just before dawn, which meant that you got up on the fire platform, ready for old Jerry in case he would make a surprise attack, and then at dawn stand-down, hoping you'd get a mug of tea or something to eat, which as often as not we didn't get because being so close to the German lines we couldn't make fires to brew tea. We had to rely on the boys at the back making tea down in the deep quarry and bringing it up. It got very boring during stand-down too if nothing was doing. Funny that, you were bored if there was no danger. Well, there really wasn't anything to do except read, that is, if you were lucky enough to have something. You could write letters if you felt like it, or sometimes you dozed.

At night there was always the fear of the unknown, the threatening shadows in No Man's Land, the rustling of the wind, the occasional crack of a twig or some other unidentifiable sound magnified in the darkness. The small night noises heard behind nervous bursts of fire might be the movement of some animal, for the rats were busy at night, or might just be a band of enemy raiders poised to descend. The first night of a Battalion's stint in the front-line trenches was always the worst. After days of relaxation nerves were on edge and even soldiers with no immediate duties, stretched out on the fire-step or dozing restlessly in funk-holes burrowed into the clammy wall of the trench, slept with one ear cocked in case of danger. It was marginally more comfortable for the officers, but their job was no sinecure.

Lt. R. E. Smith, 7th Bn., Royal Scots Fusiliers, 45 Brig., 15 Div.

We had three officers in the Company at the time, which meant three hours on duty and six off. I'll take the day as starting at 12 midnight, and I'll suppose that I go on duty at 2 a.m. From 11 p.m. to 2 a.m. you have been making desperate efforts to get to sleep. You are sitting in a dug-out, which our fellows have captured. In it there are a couple of chairs, from goodness knows where, and a kind of table, and there are two compartments leading out of it. In one are the company signallers with all their telephone apparatus and the other is used by the gunners as an artillery observation station and is provided with special observation loop-holes. The whole place leaks like hell and you have to keep your oilskins on all the time, but the main things that strikes you about the place is its smell which is reminiscent of a pantry, a stable loft, a coal cellar and the hold of a ship. However there is a brazier and it is warm. All the light is from a pair of candles, stuck in bottles.

At two o'clock *very* punctually, the man you are to relieve comes in and kicks you out of a sort of doze, you get up, swear, and put on some extra wraps, your revolver, electric torch, gas-helmet. The other man, who is now wriggling into your late place on the floor, gives you his report which is something of this sort: '*All quiet. We've got a working party repairing the parapet in Bay 6, and another pumping all along the main trench from Bay 5 to Bay 9. One sentry in Bay 4 is complaining of frostbite, but I think he's skrimshanking. Good luck. It's a hell of a night.*' You walk out into the trench. The air is refreshing after the dug-out, but it's beastly cold and there's a bit of a drizzle.

Your duties are to visit all sentries, generally inspect all work that is being done, and you are responsible for meeting any emergency until some superior person comes along. The men's job is to do sentry and to go on working-parties, etc. As you come up to the first sentry you ask him, 'Have you anything to report?' You get this sort of answer: '*Nothing much doing, sir, I can hear them working just opposite and I think they have a patrol out on the left.*' Alongside the sentry there are two figures wrapped up in waterproof sheets, sitting on the fire-step which is raised about eighteen inches off the floor of the trench. They are two reliefs for that particular bay or traverse and the three take it in turns, one hour on, two off. Poor devils, they have to sit out there all night and in all kinds of weathers.

The bottom of the trench is on an average six to eight inches deep in slushy chalk the consistency of whipped cream, and in some places it is two and even three feet deep in water. After doing the round you give a look to the working-parties. Some of this is beastly work. The sandbags get water-logged and then freeze, and the bags burst, and a mass of parapet weighing three or four tons topples right over. All the debris has to be cleared, new bags have to be filled, and the broken bit has to be built up again. This is a filthy dirty job and a most tiring one – a sandbag filled with chalk is a jolly good weight. You then give a look to the sap – a trench which runs perpendicularly from our line out towards the enemy – and here one has to be rather more careful. The sap may be going to be used for a listening post, or perhaps as the starting point of a future firing trench. Of the three men in it one is at the end and acting as a sentry, the other two with their rifles and bayonets fixed alongside them are quietly and silently working, the one picking, the other shovelling the chalk up to the side. They have to take care not to throw earth up while a star shell is burning as this would give the show away. By the time this is over, two of the three hours have passed, and you can sit down on the fire-step for ten minutes or so and smoke and talk to one of the sentries. Every now and again there is the purring of a machine-gun and the sing-sing-sing-sing as the bullets fly overhead, generally searching for the transport away back behind. One more round of the sentries completes the time, but just before five when the sky is beginning to grow grey there is suddenly a loud whizz in the air, coming yards away. Then five or six 'pip-squeaks' come over together, a pause and then another whizzing but this time louder and slower and a bigger bang, three or four of these and then the 'pip-squeaks' come on again. In a quarter of an hour it is over.

At six o'clock there is a general cry of stand-to all along the line, and everyone turns out and stands-to their post as this is the danger hour. But the feature of stand to is the issue of the rum ration. By this time it is light and you can see the men's faces and clothes and it is really a picture. Everything – faces, hands, clothes – are the same dirty-white colour, and the chalk is lying deep over everything. They have three or four days' growth of hair on their faces and the only things which are clean are the rifles and ammunition which at all costs must be kept clean of dirt. Of course, the poor beggars are pretty fagged out and show it.

Most battalions were low in numbers. Drafts of reinforcements were arriving in dribs and drabs and there were seldom enough to bring them up to anything like full strength and replace the casualties incurred in the daily routine of holding the line. Even in quiet periods there was an average of five thousand casualties a week. Manpower was still a headache and one of the many matters on which opinion in Government circles was divided. Unlike more militaristic nations which required every young man reaching a certain age to do military service and which could call upon huge reserves of trained men in the event of war, Great Britain had always depended on her standing army of professional soldiers and also relied on willing volunteers to augment it in time of need. Now, after fifteen months of war, with greater casualties than had ever been imagined – and, as the war spread, far wider commitments than had ever been envisaged – it was becoming evident that volunteers could not be relied on indefinitely to fill the ranks. Recruiting had slowed down, enthusiasm had waned, and it was time for drastic measures. Conscription had been under discussion for months but there were some to whom the word 'conscription' was anathema. True to his nickname of 'England's best recruiting sergeant', it was Lord Derby who worked out and sponsored a compromise scheme.

The Derby scheme was conscription in all but name, but it retained an element of individual choice that at least paid lip-service to the ideal of a volunteer army. Every man between the ages of nineteen and forty-two was required to register – and it was estimated that there were five million of them. If he was not debarred from military service, either because he was unfit or employed on work of national importance, he then had a choice. He could either enlist immediately in the regiment of his choice, with the possibility of applying for a commission, or he could wait to be called up in his category and sent wherever the Army chose. There would be a six-week period of grace in which men could make up their minds, but the Government gave an unequivocal assurance that married men would not be called upon until all the single men were in the ranks. The call-up would start early in the New Year.

The Territorials had done more than their bit and had lost close to half their strength. Kitchener's 'First Hundred Thousand' had already taken a bad knock. The second hundred thousand, and the third, were trained and ready to go, but a hundred thousand men amounted to barely seven divisions of combatants and support troops and the nation's commitments were growing so fast that far, far more would be needed if the war was to be won. Now that the autumn battles had drawn to a disappointing close the question of whether it was to be won on the western front or elsewhere was back on the agenda. None of the dilemmas that faced the Government had yet been resolved.

It was the end of October before General Sir Charles Monro arrived to take over command of the British forces on the Gallipoli Peninsula. On instructions from Lord Kitchener his first and most pressing duty was to 'report fully and frankly on the military situation', to suggest any means by which the deadlock might be removed, either by attacking with sufficient force to finally trounce the Turks, or by evacuating the troops and cutting their losses. Kitchener, who was personally opposed to evacuation, urged him to submit his report as soon as it was humanly possible and Sir Charles Monro almost immediately set off on a tour of inspection. After long experience of the disciplined organisation on the western front he was astounded by the ramshackle, makeshift conditions on the peninsula, and appalled by the suffering of the troops. Every Divisional Commander he spoke to pooh-poohed the very idea of an offensive and they were unanimous in their opinion that, in their present state of health, the troops were incapable of keeping up a sustained effort for more than twenty-four hours. The Commanders believed that they could hold on to their present positions but only so long as the Turks were short of ammunition. If, as now seemed all too likely, the enemy received heavy supplies of guns and ammunition, they could hold out no promises, except that they would do their best.

At GHQ on the island of Lemnos the staff had drawn up a careful memorandum for the information of the new Commander-in-Chief. A breakthrough *could* be made, but not before the spring and not without the addition of a staggering four hundred thousand men. They gave it as their opinion that evacuation would be feasible, but only if it were voluntarily carried out very soon. If the Turks were to force them off the peninsula into the sea it would be a sad and costly shambles. Sir Charles Monro came down heavily on the side of immediate evacuation. There was no sane alternative. The day after he telegraphed his views to London the destroyer HMS *Louis* was blown ashore by strong winds and wrecked at Suvla Bay.

Everyone but Lord Kitchener was agreed that the evacuation should start without delay. He had an ally in Admiral Keyes who was pressing the merits of a new naval scheme to force the Dardanelles, and Kitchener was tempted. Evacuation would be expensive – Monro had hazarded a likely loss of 30 or 40 per cent – and in the present delicate political climate it would also be seen in the Near East as an ignominious climb-down on the part of the British Empire. '*I absolutely refuse to sign an order for evacuation,*' Kitchener telegraphed to Lemnos, '*which I think would be the greatest disaster and would condemn a large percent-*

age of our men to death or imprisonment.' Lord Kitchener boldly decided to travel to Gallipoli to see for himself, and the Dardanelles Committee decided that the matter should be left in abeyance until his return.

Travelling fast overland to Marseilles and onwards by destroyer, Kitchener reached Mudros on 9 November. Next day it was blowing hard and the destroyer that carried him across the fifteen miles to the peninsula bucked and ploughed through heavy seas and the lighter that carried him to the shore spun like a cork in the whirling currents.

Once ashore, Kitchener did not take long to make up his mind. Standing with General Birdwood at a post high above Anzac he put his hand on the General's arm and said, 'Thank God, Birdie, I came to see this for myself. You were quite right. I had no idea of the difficulties you were up against.' He was as deeply impressed by the spirit of the men as he was appalled by the conditions. 'I think you have all done wonders,' he assured General Birdwood as they shook hands in farewell. Kitchener was now on his way to Greece to review the situation at Salonika, and it was 22 November before he cabled his long-expected report to London and the 24th before he finally set sail for England. Pending the final decision of the Cabinet he had already ordered that preliminary preparations for evacuation should begin. Two days after his departure winter roared down the peninsula and made the final crushing decision for them.

The storm struck with the force of a hurricane and it raged on for three days. The wind howled and hammered, sweeping away piers, dashing small vessels into matchwood, uprooting trees, tearing the flimsy roofs from dug-outs, lashing whirlwinds of stinging sand against the bare limbs of the miserable soldiers still clad in thin khaki drill. And then thunder began to roll, out-thundering any bombardment, lightning flashed, and the heavens opened. It poured in sheets for twenty-four hours. Dug-outs soon flooded, stores were washed away, trenches, gullies, dried-up water-courses, turned to raging torrents so deep that many men were drowned. Hundreds more died of exposure.

Spr. J. Johnston.

Our officer, Captain Newton Phillips, seeing the state of the men, said it was a case of every man for himself and God for us all. Well, I and my pal Dai Morris had previously been employed digging a dug-out for the officer in charge of explosives and cartridges and we knew this might be a good place to take over, so we made for this dug-out which was more than half full of boxes of these bombs. There was about two feet of water in the dug-out but we piled some of the boxes at one end to get above it, then we settled down to sleep. About midnight there was a short lull in the storm and another officer, Buck Adams, came round to inspect if the bombs were all right and he shone a torch into the dug-out and ordered us out of there, so we both decided that we should go down to the beach and walk along the sand which would be better than stamping around in the mud and freezing. On our way we came across a big galvanised tank that had been put up on sandbags to hold paraffin oil supplies. The storm had washed away the sandbags under the tank, the tank had then fallen down and all the oil had run out to sea. We thought the empty tank would be a grand shelter from the storm and would be dry inside and a shelter from the wind and the cold. I started to crawl inside when my head came into contact with hobnailed boots. I shouted to the man to shift up and make room for two more men, but there was no response. Then we realised something was wrong and we found that there were seven men in the tank and they'd all been suffocated with the fumes. They were all dead! We had a real fright at finding this and intended reporting it when we got to our camp. Then we made our way towards our camp and rounding a corner we saw what seemed to be a number of men sitting and sprawling in the mud. We found on getting nearer to them there were twenty-three men all frozen to death. They'd left the front-line trench after being there for thirty-six hours and were making their way to the beach to a boat which was waiting to take them out to a Red Cross boat to give them food and a night's rest and more food supplies before they returned to the front line again, as supplies could not reach them owing to the floods. They had had a ration of rum before leaving the trench – that was all they had there – and the effects of the rum on their way down to the boat had worn off. They had slumped down where they were and had been frozen to death. You see, when the rain stopped a bitter frost set in, and men who'd been soaking wet the previous day had the clothes frozen to their bodies, and if you took off your overcoats they could be put to stand upright frozen stiff. For a couple of days after the storm died down we were on duty digging graves.

The troops were hardest hit at Suvla Bay, where there was little or no shelter. There was less flooding at Helles where the trenches were mostly on sloping ground, and in the high posts on the peaks at Anzac the Aussies with their underground dug-outs and galleries were a little better off. The trenches were virtually abandoned, but it was fortunate that the Turks were in the same plight. The temperature plunged. On the third night the wind dropped and in the wake of the hard frost it began to snow. Not many of the Anzacs had ever seen snow before.

There was an unofficial armistice in places where the soldiers of both sides had been forced out of the flooded trenches and huddled in groups in the open with no attempt at concealment and no stomach for a fight. But the guns were still firing from batteries miles behind.

Col. G. Beith.

I was in command of fifteen posts and I lost thirteen or fourteen of them in the storm. I was conferring with a sergeant and a corporal and *bang*, the next thing I knew I was lying in a trench with two corpses on top of me. There were eight or nine inches of icy cold water and mud in the trench and about eight inches of snow on the parapet. I managed to push the corpses off and I crawled into the dug-out. It was about eleven o'clock in the morning and I wasn't picked up until seven o'clock at night and taken down to the Advanced Dressing Station. All they did was wipe mud off me a bit and send me off to the Casualty Clearing Station on the beach, but the barge that took the wounded out to the hospital ship had been smashed on the rocks during the storm and we had to wait for two days before they could get us off. There were hundreds of us there and it was sheer hell.

I said to a doctor, 'Is it possible to get a drink of water? I'm dying of thirst.' He said, 'I'm afraid we haven't got a drop.' I said, 'Well, does nobody think of scraping that snow off the scrub outside there and melting it?' So he sent someone off to do that and after a while an orderly came down with about half a pint of snow water. When I saw him I said, 'Well, well, well, so it's you, Snodgrass!' Now this Snodgrass was a man I'd sent down weeks before with a self-inflicted wound. I heard this shot and I rushed out and he was sitting on one of the latrines, and he said, 'I've been wounded in the foot.' Imagine that, wounded in the foot sitting on the latrine! Well, he showed me and believe it or not the boot wasn't even undone – it was all laced up, and that fellow's state of mind was such that he had taken off his boot, shot himself, and put his boot back on again! Well, a chap like that is no good to you at all. However, he'd obviously got off with it, and when I saw him there in the clearing station I said, 'There you are, Snodgrass, I told you you wouldn't get off this peninsula until the show was over, but you're much safer down here.' He said, 'I'm all right, sir.' I said, 'It's human nature, old chap, but it's a terrible thing to go

583

SIW and leave your pals behind. Anything's better than that, so you stick to your job.'

As a matter of fact *that* was the thing that was worrying me. I knew that I was very badly wounded, but the strange thing was that it didn't worry me a scrap. It was leaving my men to do a job that I was there to help them to do – that's what worried me most somehow.

But the job was almost over and in a very few days after Gordon Beith left the shores of the peninsula the evacuation would begin and the remnants of the men who had struggled so valiantly for eight long months to do their job would be turning their backs on Gallipoli, leaving all its miseries and the graves of many thousand comrades behind them.

Chapter 38

After the storm that tore the last breath from the Gallipoli campaign there was a long spell of fine weather. The sun shone, there were chilly breezes but they were gentle and the tideless sea that lapped the beaches was mercifully calm. Without good weather the evacuation would have been infinitely more difficult.

It was a difficult operation, later regarded as one of the triumphs of the war, and until it was safely accomplished the Turks had no idea that it was underway. It had taken nerve and cunning and discipline. For only disciplined troops could have padded silently with muffled feet along tortuous pathways from the trenches to the beaches, first from Suvla, then from Anzac, and maintained their silence on the beaches, waiting to board the lighters that glided in from the darkened sea to carry them off. It took nerve for the men waiting their turn in the emptying trenches, seeing their luckier comrades depart, working all the while to do the work of ten, twenty, a hundred men, rushing from point to point to send up flares and to fire the fixed rifles that would delude the enemy, knowing that it would be all up if they were attacked. And it had taken cunning and Machiavellian ingenuity to invent the devices that would send up the flares, explode the mines, keep up the rifle-fire, and keep the Turks guessing and on their toes for hours after the last of them was safely away.

It was some satisfaction, particularly to the Anzacs, that they had at long last succeeded in putting one over Johnny Turk. They bore him no ill will. The Turks had been clean fighters and worthy adversaries, and although at the last moment the main supply dumps were blown up or set on fire, where battalion rations and even prized possessions like gramophones had to be left in dug-outs, notes were sometimes found fixed to the wall with a nail or a spent bullet: '*So long, Johnny. It's all yours. Love from Australia.*' One Turkish officer in charge of a cautious reconnoitring party kept such a note as a souvenir for the rest of his life.

The evacuation went like clockwork. General Monro's estimate of 30 to 40 per cent casualties was wildly wrong. By the

585

combined efforts of the Army and the Royal Navy not a single man was lost and by 20 December all the troops on Gallipoli had been evacuated – with the exception of the unfortunate 29th Division who were ordered to stay for seventeen more days to garrison Cape Helles.

Christmas on Gallipoli was not something to look forward to with unalloyed pleasure. Months ago, before the failure of the August battles, supplies of the 29th Division Christmas card (designed and printed in Egypt) had arrived on the peninsula, and the soldiers had bought them by the dozen to send to friends and families at home. They depicted a British bulldog clinging grimly to the toe of the peninsula. It was strangely appropriate.

The delivery of Christmas mail in the eastern Mediterranean was a headache, for the troops evacuated from the peninsula were scattered far and wide – many in Egypt, some en route to Salonika, some still on the Aegean islands – but the Royal Navy had turned up trumps, and with its assistance most of the soldiers' mail was delivered before Christmas. The Australians on Lemnos received a large consignment on Christmas Eve. There were letters and cards and parcels from home, and every man received a billy-can from the people of Australia packed with acceptable goodies – smokes, and pipes, and razors and sweets and socks and handkerchiefs. Some of the billy-cans were decorated with a cartoon of a victorious kangaroo, feet firmly planted on the peninsula, with the caption '*This part o' the world belongs to US!*' That hurt.

Even the delivery of mail to the western front had stretched the resources of the Army Postal Service to the limit. There were hundreds of tons of mail, mostly parcels containing Christmas gifts and this year there were some interesting novelties. Manufacturers who had been caught on the hop by the speed of events last year had taken pains to design and produce goods to tempt shoppers looking for suitable gifts for men in the forces. Even firms like Goldsmiths and Silversmiths Ltd, who had always supplied their affluent clients with luxury goods – gold cigarette cases, rings, watches and lockets, silver-backed brushes and so on – now offered a range of items designed for more practical use. An officer's whistle in solid silver, which ingeniously combined a detachable compass and silver indelible pencil; a collapsible drinking cup, also in silver and enclosed in a leather case; a luminous wrist watch in silver or gold; silver hip-flasks, matchboxes and tinder cigarette lighters whose discreet glow was guaranteed not to attract the attention of the enemy if lit in the trenches.

Lance-Corporal Jim Keddie of the 48th Highlanders of Canada had recently received a present, of a sort, from a grateful

Government – and it was not before time. It was more than six months since his foot was shattered at Ypres and then amputated in hospital at Huddersfield. Later he went to convalescent camp at Shorncliffe and his stump was healed, but he was still hobbling on crutches, waiting wearily for his turn to be fitted with an artificial limb at Queen Mary's Hospital at Roehampton. The hospital was working flat out but there was a long, long list of maimed soldiers awaiting admission, and it took all the efforts of Jim Keddie's mother, who took it up with her Member of Parliament, and an irate correspondence in the newspapers to shift him up the queue.

Sir,

The question put by Sir John Jardine in the House of Commons last week brought out into clear relief the treatment to which this young man has been subjected by the military hospital authorities. Lance-Corporal James Keddie was one of the heroic Canadian contingent which hastened homewards as soon as the cry reached the Far West that the Mother country needed them. He had the misfortune to be severely wounded at Ypres in May last, and as a consequence a foot had to be amputated. One would have thought that with the least possible delay an artificial foot would have been fitted in the hospital at Shorncliffe. But, no! Month after month has passed and James Keddie has been compelled to limp about on crutches, a very trying and depressing experience for a young man. He appears to have been referred to one authority after the other and all his appeals to have the limb replaced before he returned to Canada, disregarded. Obviously the advantage to him lay in having this completed in this country, so that he might be able to spend a time in his own home at Jedburgh before setting sail for Canada. Lance-Corporal Keddie has not been well treated by the home authorities, in fact very badly. An incident like this is bound to do harm to the call of patriotic duty, and there may be other cases of a similar nature. It is devoutly to be hoped Sir John's question will lead to prompt reparation.

Yours faithfully,
A Border Canvasser.

In late November, and somewhat ahead of his turn, Keddie was sent to Roehampton to be fitted with his new foot and to learn to walk again. Now he fully expected to be home in Jedburgh for Christmas and better still to bring in the New Year in Scotland in the knowledge that he was out of the war for good.

William Cushing was just as certain that he would be spending Christmas at the front, for his first home leave expired on 19 December.

2nd Lt. W. Cushing.

I don't know who it was who suggested that I should bring back with me a turkey, a Norfolk turkey, for the officers' mess Christmas dinner, or whether I made the suggestion myself. At all events I went to a shop in Prince of Wales Road, Norwich. As soon as these good people heard that I wanted to take a turkey to France, they offered me one at cost price. Rashly, I said that in that case I would take *two*! 'And what about some sausages?' 'A good idea,' said I. 'We'll put you those in free,' they said. I thanked them, and some days later just before catching the train at Norwich Thorpe Station, I called to fetch the packages. The turkeys, each weighing some twenty-four pounds, and several pounds of sausages, were beautifully packed in two hampers with handles, and once more thanking these kind people, I set down Prince of Wales Road for the station. Those two hampers! By the time I arrived even at Thorpe Station my arms were aching, and by the time I got back to the battalion, out at rest in the Poperinghe woods, those birds seemed to have increased in weight to about half a ton each! However, they *and* I were welcomed and acclaimed!

Next day the turkeys were cooked for an early Christmas dinner in the officers' mess and Cushing's health was drunk with glowing appreciation. Two days before Christmas the 9th Norfolks marched back to the line. The war had to go on, and to make sure that it did GHQ had sent an edict to every Division.

CONFIDENTIAL

140th Infantry Brigade

The G.O.C. directs me to remind you of the unauthorised truce which occurred on Christmas Day at one or two places in the line last year, and to impress upon you that nothing of the kind is to be allowed on the Divisional front this year.

The Artillery will maintain a slow gun fire on the enemy's trenches commencing at dawn, and every opportunity will as usual be taken to inflict casualties upon any of the enemy exposing themselves.

(Signed) B. BURNETT HITCHCOCK,

Lt. Colonel,
General Staff,
47th (London) Division

19th Decr. 1915.

Just before Christmas the War Office produced a long and detailed memorandum on the future conduct of the war based on a realistic analysis of the events of the past year. They made it clear that the war would not be won by improvisation, and the muddled inception of the Gallipoli campaign proved it, just as the debacle at Suvla Bay demonstrated that determined, experienced leadership was vital to success. No longer would commanders be appointed on the basis of seniority in the army hierarchy. It was plain to the General Staff that Egypt and the Suez Canal must always be defended, but other commitments in the eastern Mediterranean were not desirable, nor was it desirable to disperse the strength of the Royal Navy, so vital to the defence of Britain's far-flung sea routes as well as her island shores. Germany could not be defeated through the back door. As for Serbia and Russia, they could best be helped by a successful offensive on the western front, and the breakthrough at Loos had shown that it could be achieved and that complete success had been within their grasp.

The Staff detailed the lessons that must be learned. The wire had not been sufficiently cut – more heavy guns and shells were needed, more men were needed, more careful planning by a well-trained Staff and less dependence on a single factor like the use of gas to compensate for other deficiencies. They could not rely on luck alone.

There was no criticism of the troops. The Staff, like the senior officers in the field, had been astonished by the prowess and endurance of the soldiers of the New Army, were lavish in their praise of the Territorials, and confident that with more preparation, more experience, more materials, more backing, they would stand 'a fair chance of success'. 'But,' the authors wisely reminded, 'there is no certainty in war.'

Nevertheless the message was clear. Come next year new brooms would sweep aside the debris of the setbacks that littered the chronicle of 1915 and sweep the New Armies to victory in the year ahead.

Sir Douglas Haig was already installed as Commander-in-Chief and on Christmas Eve Sir John French motored for the last time to Calais and boarded a destroyer en route for England to take up his new post in command of the Home Forces. Officially, the Government had *'reluctantly accepted his resignation'*. Privately they thanked him profusely for his valuable services and assured him that no criticism was implied in their desire for a change. He was endowed with a peerage and also with the promise of a suitable pecuniary reward at the end of the war. The deposed Commander-in-Chief, newly ennobled, had given some thought to the choice of a title and decided on 'Viscount French of Ypres' – perhaps with a very natural desire to remind the nation down succeeding generations that his services had been thought to be of value when they were most needed.

Fifteen months of the strain and responsibility of command in a war waged on a scale which had never before been encountered, with anxieties and disappointments at every turn, would have taxed the capacities of a much younger and fitter man. French was now in his sixty-fourth year. He was bitterly aggrieved and indignant, but in his heart of hearts he could not have been sorry to be going home, even if he was not much in the mood to celebrate Christmas.

It was a stormy crossing, for the weather was filthy. At Ypres the rain had turned to sleet and it was bitterly cold. The 9th Norfolks were in wet trenches at Wieltje and B Company was in the front line where even the sandbags were disintegrating into slush and the duckboards were under water. Just before they left camp, Cushing had received a mammoth package of woollens from his Aunt Laura who was headmistress of the Girls' Primary School at Swaffham. It represented months of work by the staff, the girls, and their relatives and it contained enough jerseys and mufflers and helmets and socks and gloves to kit out every member of No. 1 Platoon with at least one additional warm garment. They sorely needed them now and Cushing was sorry for them, for several were new to the platoon and were finding their initiation into trench life a spartan experience. Two inventive spirits thought to improve matters and, spotting some abandoned corrugated iron behind the trench, crawled out at night to retrieve it and propped it over their firebay to make a slightly weatherproof shelter. They were quite proud of their handiwork and actually went to fetch their platoon officer to admire it, feeling quite obviously that what the Army had lacked before their own arrival was brains. Cushing was forced to point out that the purpose of a firing bay was to fire from, and that their splendid roof entirely defeated that purpose. But he told them kindly and without undue blustering. Although he was several years their senior and had been a schoolmaster in civil life, it was not so very long ago that he himself had arrived, green and ignorant, to join the Battalion.

Even in that short time there were new faces in the ranks and in the mess, and every day there were more casualties.

2nd Lt. W. Cushing.

On the morning of Christmas Eve a man in B Company on our right was hit in the head by a sniper's bullet, and died a few minutes later. The new Second-in-Command of the Battalion was in the line on a visit of inspection. He was an energetic and efficient officer but he was also a fire-eater. He made both platoons file past the dead man, saying to each, 'You must avenge this. You must kill two Germans for every one of our dead.' I said nothing, but I felt outraged. The men evidently thought he was mad. The object of war, the aim of a battle, is not primarily to kill numbers of the enemy, but to defeat his forces in battle. The men resented the Major's tactless tactics. It was the mistaken psychology of fire-eating blimps and it made the bloodshed of war evilly bloodier.

In the line at Loos a battalion of the Camerons had a Christmas visit from a Staff Officer.

Lt. G. Barber, 1st Bn., Queen's Own Cameron Highlanders, 1st Brig., 1st Div.

On the morning of the 24th I was sent to D Company, to take command while Gordon went on leave. This time D Company was in a support trench about a hundred and fifty yards from the front line. This trench was in poor condition – narrow, too seldom traversed, and not nearly deep enough. As I had to send two platoons up to the front line every night, it was rather difficult to improve the trench, especially as no work was possible by day owing to the fact that the Hun on Hill 70 could look down and shoot right along it. This fact was not fully appreciated by the Powers That Be who wear Red Hats, until one of them arrived about eleven o'clock in the morning on Christmas Eve and shouted down the steps of my dug-out for me. I went up and found an irate Staff Officer who wanted to know why the devil my men were not doing any work! I pointed out to him, respectfully but firmly, that unless he wanted half the men blotted out it was an impossibility. While arguing the point, he started along the trench and when he was about thirty yards away from the dug-out the Huns put over a covey of 'pip-squeaks'. I've never seen a staff officer hurry so fast in all my life! He bolted into my dug-out like a rabbit, head first. He then stayed so long talking about the impossibility of working by day, that I very nearly had to offer him lunch! Christmastime did not reduce the daily hate on both sides.

But in some parts of the line at least the 'hate' tailed away in the evening of Christmas Eve. It was the Germans' *Weihnachtsabend*, the traditional night of celebration, but there was not much sign of celebration in the trenches. From time to time there was a plaintive attempt at a carol and once in the trenches close to Plugstreet Wood a tremendous voice entertained the trenches of both sides with a selection from *La Traviata*, stopping abruptly in mid-aria as if a door had been slammed shut. Near Wulverghem a Christmas tree ablaze with candles appeared on the parapet of the German front trench. For a few moments the tiny pinpoints of flame flickered uncertainly in the dark until a British officer ordered rapid fire and the Tommies shot it down.

In the first chill light of Christmas morning the guns boomed out.

Cpl. D. A. Pankhurst, Royal Field Artillery, 56 Div.

We hailed the smiling morn with five rounds fired fast, and we kept up slow fire all day. Those were our orders. Some batteries sent over as many as three hundred shells. It was a Christmas present to Fritz, they said. But I do believe myself that it was intended to discourage fraternising.

The 7th Green Howards did not parade until ten o'clock on Christmas morning, and they richly deserved a lie-in for the whole battalion had been out until the early hours working in the rain and the dark filling sandbags with liquid mud and had returned dead beat and chilled to the marrow. A rum ration on their return and a hot breakfast when they woke up restored their spirits and they looked forward to a lazy day with a few festivities to enliven it. Later the Chaplain came over to hold a Christmas carol service in a field near the camp – the third he had conducted that morning – and it was lustily enjoyed by everyone but the Sergeant-Major. There was no music, but the Sergeant-Major was the proud possessor of a fine tenor voice and he volunteered to act as precentor and lead the singing. It was very cold so the service was a short one, but there was time for a number of old favourites before disaster struck. The Colonel saw it coming.

Lt. Col. R. Fife, DSO, 7th Bn., Green Howards.

It went pretty well until the Sergeant-Major started the hymn, 'Once in Royal David's City', to the tune of 'Hark, the Herald Angels'. I saw the awful pitfall yawning at the end of the first verse – and so did the Sergeant-Major when it was too late. The cold beads broke out on his brow. When the last two lines of the verse had been sung and the tune required them to be sung again, there was a brave effort, but it failed, and for the remaining verses the congregation sang any tune each happened to know, with remarkable effect!

We celebrate the glad Yule Tide by moving this evening to the ramparts for three days' cave life before returning to the trenches, also by getting no letters, parcels or newspapers for days.

The fact that it was Christmas scarcely disturbed the routine business of the war. It was a 'normal' day in the trenches, with the normal amount of sniping and shelling, but the 'normal' casualties that were usually accepted with stoic resignation seemed especially poignant in the season of peace on earth and goodwill to men.

2nd Lt. W. Cushing.

Private Wilkerson was killed on Christmas Day. A shell fragment severed the femoral artery. Stretcher-bearers attempted to deal with this mortal wound by using a tourniquet but this caused the poor chap pain, and the MO told us on the field telephone to remove it and let him die in peace. Only *immediate* surgical intervention could have saved him and that was impossible. All the same, the MO was about to risk his own life by coming to us across the open – there were no communications trenches left – but the C.O. ordered him to stay where he was at battalion HQ. It was just as well. We couldn't afford to lose a Medical Officer in a fruitless effort to save life. He couldn't possibly have arrived in time.

The soldiers who were out of danger and lucky enough to be out of the line and off duty kept Christmas as far as possible in traditional style. Regimental funds had been ransacked and in many battalions they were subsidised by officers to ensure that the Tommies had a good Christmas dinner. Turkeys were scarce and only for the fortunate few, but pigs were slaughtered wholesale and they were more than happy with roast pork. There were nuts and sweets and apples and almost a surfeit of plum pudding. So many had been sent

593

by public benefactors as well as families and friends that some soldiers were eating them for days. In some quiet sectors quartermasters even managed to send Christmas pudding with the rations to the trenches (one actually managed brandy butter) and even if it was none too warm and a touch dry without the traditional custard sauce, there was rum at hand to set it alight – and a sergeant-major might be sufficiently moved by the Christmas spirit to issue enough of it to flame each individual portion.

Even cold Christmas pudding would have been welcomed by the 6th South Staffs, munching the eternal bully beef and washing it down with water in a train chugging towards Marseilles. Conversation was desultory for they had speculated on their ultimate destination until there was no more to be said and most of them were thinking back rather than looking forward. Occasionally someone would say, 'Remember this time last year?' How could they forget it! Last year at Saffron Walden they had wined and dined like kings, for due to a fortunate accident, the battalion had received a double allocation of turkeys. The birds ordered by the comforts fund were delayed in transit and were finally delivered on Christmas Eve just as the quartermaster returned from Smithfield Market with a fresh consignment to replace them. Seated on the floor of the railway wagons, jolting and shuddering to the south, they thought longingly of Christmas past.

The soldiers nearing the end of their training at home were having a whale of a time.

Pte. J. Bowles, 2/16th Queen's Westminster Rifles.

Our grand dinner came off at four o'clock. And it *was* a spread too! Turkey and ham, sprouts and potatoes. Christmas pudding of first-class quality – beer, ginger beer, and port wine ad lib, oranges, nuts, bananas and smokes – and all provided by the Colonel. It was a glorious feast and one that I shall never forget. The King's Christmas greeting was then read and we all drank his health amidst a terrific din. Then the Brigadier spoke a few words, and told us what the future held in store for us. He himself was going to France on Tuesday with the Colonels of our Brigade to learn a little of the work we should soon be called upon to undertake. On their return we were going off – probably to Salisbury Plain for a few weeks' final training, and then off for France. The cheering when he told us we were going was enough to loosen the rafters. He paid very high tribute to our Brigade, and although I am in it myself and perhaps should not say so, I do not think that any finer body of men exists. The pity of it is that men of such physique and training should go to this human slaughter-house, and leave beneath the soil of France the product of so many years of toil. Is what they are fighting for worth it? I'm sure the answer is yes.

The Brigadier left amid cheers, and we set to work upon the remaining turkey. Beer was brought round in buckets and some drank more than was good for them and consequently there was a great deal of merriment. One fellow, noted for his camel-like propensities, was about full when he started, and before dinner was over, he insisted on standing on the table and making a speech. He was not very firm on his feet and several times subsided into the arms of those sitting near him. When he did get up he was met with a regular fusillade of bread, potatoes and bones, but somehow they all missed him and did damage to the innocent. His speech was not a success, but he caused great sport.

Not being fond of beer, I specialised in port. To one unused to it, port plays havoc and for the rest of the evening I was quite happy. After dinner we had a concert given entirely by our own fellows and it was jolly good. I left at nine o'clock and spent the rest of the night at the billet where we again made merry.

There was another concert many hundreds of miles away in the heart of Germany at the prisoner of war camp where Harry Crask had been imprisoned since his capture on the Westhoek Ridge on 8 May. Christmas there was an abstemious affair but, with the help of Red Cross parcels and many parcels from home, there was plenty to eat and even a few luxuries, for the five shilling parcels that relatives were able to send through the good offices of the *Daily Mail* contained plum cake and sardines and potted meat and chocolate, as well as tea, milk powder and sixty cigarettes. A few braver souls had attempted to make a vicious alcoholic brew from fermented potato peelings, others had managed to bribe a guard to smuggle in a bottle or two of beer, but most were content to munch on chocolate as they watched the entertainment and the mess hall was thick with the fumes of precious cigarettes recklessly chain-smoked in honour of Christmas. It was a good concert and it was a pleasant break in the frustrating monotony of life as a prisoner in Germany.

Life as a prisoner in Holland where a brigade of the Royal Naval Division was interned was hardly less monotonous, but in the camp at Groeningen they did better than prisoners in Germany. The Dutch were more kindly, food was more plentiful and there was no shortage of beer on Christmas Day. News was still scarce for

Holland was meticulous in observing the rules of neutrality and there was strict censorship, but Arthus Agius had found a way of getting round it. He was spending his own Christmas on a Greek island, having arrived on Gallipoli as a newly commissioned officer of the Royal Naval Division just in time for the evacuation, but before his departure he had organised a dinner in London for sixteen escapees from Groeningen. There was an embargo on news of those who had succeeded in reaching home, but the Dutch authorities had not thought to censor a formal report of the dinner which Agius sent to the editor of the camp magazine. It appeared in the Christmas edition and, since it concluded with a list of the guests who attended the 'escapees dinner', it was of great interest to the men who were left behind.

In Great Britain, since Christmas Day happened to fall on Saturday, Boxing Day was officially postponed until Monday. On Sunday it was business as usual, and business as usual meant Church Parade. The Padre had recently returned from the front, where volunteer clergymen often did a three-month stint, and he undoubtedly meant well, but although the topic he chose for his address was close to his own heart it did not do much for soldiers on the point of embarking for France.

Pte. J. Bowles.

He was a cheerful brute. He told us of the sufferings of the wounded, and the administering of the last sacrament. He went on to show us how difficult a task he had when men who were past all earthly aid were brought to him and confessed that they were not communicants. He was in a painful position and was seeking a solution from a higher source. He also spoke of men too ill to receive the sacrament. What could he do for them? In the Epistle of St James he has discovered that the pouring of oil on the heads of the sick would cleanse them of their sins. It would make them await death without fear, and would give them strength to withstand pain. Such a thing had not been done yet, but would the men think it over, and then when the time came they would know what to ask of the priest who attended them, or know the meaning of it if it were done without their being able to ask for it.

I wonder what Christ thinks of it all, and whether his death has accomplished all he thought it would accomplish. But I am wading out of my depth so will return to things of the moment. One of them is – dinner today. Our landlady has given us a pressing invitation to dinner, so we are getting off dinner parade and going to enjoy Christmas dinner number two.

The Boxing Day festivities and the hospitality of more than one generous landlady quickly dissipated the gloom cast by the sermon of the day before. Everyone was determined to give the Tommies a good time on their last Christmas, before they went off to the front, and even more anxious to spoil the thousands of men in hospitals who had come back maimed or wounded.

In the War Hospital at Epsom Bill Worrell had difficulty in eating his Christmas dinner. He had lost most of his teeth and those that remained were so damaged that as soon as his jaw healed and he was able to 'open wide' they would have to come out. Meanwhile a kindly nurse minced his share of the turkey and mixed it into a slop with gravy and mashed potato. He was able to eat a good deal of it and when the pudding came round he was given a taste of the brandy sauce with a jelly set in a cup to give it the shape of a small Christmas pudding. Someone had popped a sprig of holly on top and Sister herself brought him a glass of champagne.

Every wounded soldier found a stocking at the foot of his bed, which the nurses had filled with sweets, cigarettes, even small toys, purchased from the hospital comforts fund. There was a bottle of beer or stout for each man to drink with his Christmas dinner, and sometimes a glass of wine. Hospitals were showered with gifts of claret and port and champagne, often by the case, and although strictly speaking they were intended for medicinal purposes to build up the strength of the most feeble invalids, in the glow of the festive spirit all but the starchiest of matrons generally decreed that all the patients should be given a Christmas drink. Every ward was decorated, every ward had its Christmas tree, often groaning under the weight of gifts sent by local civilians. There were seldom personal visitors, for not many soldiers were lucky enough to be sent to a hospital near their homes, but the locals came in droves. Carol singers toured the wards, there were lavish teas with Christmas cake and cream buns provided by generous bakery shops, there were concerts got up by school children and plays performed by amateur dramatic societies, there were games and sing-songs. A good time was had by all.- except in wards where celebration was necessarily low-key and the nurses serving the turkey placed the plates in front of their patients with particular care, for men stunned by shell-shock would start at the slightest noise. They too had their Christmas tree and presents, but the worst cases lying dumb or staring blankly at the wall paid no attention.

There had been over a quarter of a million casualties on the western front alone and for every two men who had been wounded, one was killed or reported missing (which amounted in most instances to much the same thing). There were half as many again in Gallipoli. In the streets of Edinburgh and Oldham, Toronto and Montreal, Sidney and Melbourne, black ties, black armbands and the sweeping black garb of sad women were becoming a commonplace sight. It had been a bad year, and as it drew to a close everyone was sadder. Some were wiser.

A letter from Lord Sydenham was published prominently in *The Times* and if its message hardly rated applause in Government circles it struck a chord in the minds of many others.

The immense efforts and sacrifices of the Allies have not been in vain, and must tell heavily in the coming year.

It is when we reflect upon the conduct of the war in all its branches that we find subject for regret and lessons to be learned. We were forced into conflict, not only with armed nations, but with the most powerful machine of government that the world has ever known. Government had become dependent upon the electorate, which was not interested in preparations for war. We had none of the memories which crowded darkly upon the French nation in August, 1914, and served to unloose a flood of burning patriotism by which France was transfigured. The British people, when at length 'the day' dawned, had the direst need of leadership and found it not. To political conditions, methods, and habits of thought we owe the mistakes and the delays, the wavering and the incertitude which have marked the conduct of affairs in the greatest crisis the country has ever known.

Decisions waited until outside pressure was brought to bear, and the coordination of the work of departments accustomed to independence was slowly and imperfectly effected. Even in the case of far-reaching military operations, our methods of arriving at conclusions, judging from the revelations made public, were ill-conceived and unlikely to result in wise counsels.

The main sources of past weakness are plain, and they can be removed if we earnestly undertake the task. For the whole nation there is only one object, compared with which all others are trivial and irrelevant. For the sake of the many thousands of gallant lives that have fallen, and of the bitter sorrows and suffering that remains, we must enter on the New Year with resolutions strongly forged in the fierce fires of war. Heavy sacrifices have come to us in 1915, but also inspiring memories of devotion, cheerful endurance, and true patriotism. If only real organised methods are forthcoming in 1916, we and our true Allies, in growing strength, may fight on with calm

598

confidence 'until the day break and the shadows flee away' in the light of victory and peace.

Hard questions were beginning to be asked and it was not always easy to come up with the answers.

Questions were also being asked in France and, of all people, Lord Cavan was on the mat. GHQ was up in arms. In defiance of the stern edict which forbade any contact with the enemy, fraternisation had occurred and it was the Guards themselves who had flouted the order. Only a few guardsmen left the trenches and in less than forty minutes a horrified senior officer ordered the soldiers back. The junior officer who condoned the meeting in No Man's Land was sent home in disgrace, Lord Cavan grovelled in apology, but still First Army headquarters thundered its determination to get the to bottom of the sorry episode and threatened dire retribution.

URGENT
======
Headquarters,
XIth Corps.

1st Army No. C/497. 28/12/15

---

1. With reference to your C/197, dated 10.15 p.m. 26/12/15, regarding the fraternising with the enemy on Xmas day, will you please forward *at once*, for the information of the Army Commander, evidence on the following points:

   (a) (i) What *exactly* were the orders issued by Lord Cavan?

   (a) (ii) How were they made known to the Brigades?

   (b) (i) What *exactly* were the orders issued by the Brigadiers of the 2nd and 3rd Guards Brigades?

   (b) (ii) How were they made known to the Battalions?

   (c) (i) What *exactly* were the orders issued by the Officers Commanding 1st Scots Guards, 2nd Scots Guards, and 1st Coldstream Guards?

   (c) (ii) How were they made known to the Companies and by them to the men?

2. As the orders appear to have been verbal, some corroboration of the orders is desirable.

3. It is not necessary to hold a Court of Inquiry, but merely to obtain statements from officers who can throw light on these points.
4. The matter is urgent.

Headquarters,
First Army.

(Signed) A. M. Henderson Scoles.
Captain.
D.A.A.G., 1st Army.

The Christmas truce initiated by the Guards was hushed up. No reports of it appeared in the newspapers and they would hardly have been appreciated in the present mood. The comical Germans of the year before were now the hated Boche, progenitors of all the horrors and misery that had dashed the hopes and expectations of a long and harrowing year.

It was the pantomime season again and, like last year, the traditional fairy-tales, the corny jokes and japes, had a topical wartime slant. At Christmas 1914 the crowds had left the theatres happily humming 'Sister Susie's Sewing Shirts for Soldiers . . .'

> Sister Susie's sewing shirts for soldiers
> Such skill at sewing shirts our shy young sister Susie shows
> Some soldiers send epistles,
> say they'd rather sleep on thistles
> Than the saucy, soft, short shirts for soldiers sister Susie sews.

They were already familiar with the words, for they had appeared on a screen lowered from the flies and the pantomime dame had led a dozen jolly choruses in traditional style, dividing the theatre into sections, setting stalls against circle, pit against gallery, ladies against gentlemen, children against adults, and urging each to outdo another, first in volume then in speed. It was great fun, children took special delight in mastering the tongue-twister, and long after the pantomimes ended the sale of sheet music and gramophone records was still earning a fortune for the publishers and the composer.

This Christmas, the pantomime song of the year did not lend itself to jolly entertainment – but it struck home and went straight to the heart:

Keep the Home Fires burning
While your hearts are yearning,
Though your lads are far away
They dream of Home.
There's a silver lining
Through the dark clouds shining
Turn the dark clouds inside out
Till the Boys come Home.

It reflected the sombre undercurrent beneath the determined gaiety
of the second Christmas of the war. Last year there had been hope –
and there still was, but it was no longer the hope of innocent
optimism. If the agony of loss and the pain of disappointment had
caused iron to enter the soul of the nation they had also put steel
into its backbone. No one doubted that the war would be won. But
no one now doubted that it would be a long hard haul – that it was
up to the Boys – and that it might be a long, long time before they
did come home.

Bibliography

Military Operations, France and Belgium 1915, Vol. 1, by Brigadier-General J. E. Edmonds (Macmillan, 1927).

Military Operations, France and Belgium 1915, Vol. 2, by Brigadier-General J. E. Edmonds (Macmillan, 1928).

Military Operations, Gallipoli, Vol. 1, by Brigadier-General C. F. Aspinall-Oglander, CB, CMG, DSO (Heinemann, 1929).

Military Operations, Gallipoli, Vol. 2, by Brigadier-General C. F. Aspinall-Oglander, CB, CMG, DSO (Heinemann, 1932).

The Royal Naval Division, by Douglas Jerrold (Hutchinson, 1927).

History of the Second Division, 1914–1918, by Everard Wyrall (Thomas Nelson).

The Seventh Division, 1914–1918, by C. T. Atkinson (John Murray, 1927).

The Eighth Division in War, 1914–1918, by Lieutenant-Colonel J. H. Boraston, CB, OBE, and Captain Cyril E. O. Bax (Medici Society, 1926).

The History of the 9th (Scottish) Division, 1914–1919, by John Ewing, MC (John Murray, 1921).

The Fifteenth (Scottish) Division, 1914–1919, by Lieutenant-Colonel J. Stewart, DSO, and John Buchan (William Blackwood, 1926).

The History of the Twentieth (Light) Division, by Captain V. E. Inglefield (Nisbet, 1921).

The Story of the 29th Division, by Captain Stair Gillon (Thomas Nelson, 1925).

The 47th (London) Division 1914–1919: By Some Who Served With It In The Great War, edited by Alan H. Maude (Amalgamated Press, 1922).

Canada in Flanders: The Official Story of the Canadian Expeditionary Force, Vol. 1, by Sir Max Aitken, MP (Hodder and Stoughton, 1916).

What the 'Boys' Did Over There, by 'Themselves' (Allied Overseas Veterans' Stories Co.).

With the First Canadian Contingent (Hodder and Stoughton, 1915).

The Princess Patricia's Canadian Light Infantry 1914–1919, by Ralph Hodder Williams (Hodder and Stoughton, 1923).

Princess Patricia's Canadian Light Infantry, 1914–1984, by Geoffrey Williams (Leo Cooper).

The Indian Corps in France, by Lieutenant-Colonel J. W. B. Merewether, CIE, and the Rt Hon. Sir Frederick Smith, Bart (John Murray, 1929).

The Welsh Regiment of Foot Guards 1915–1918, by Major C. Dudley Ward, DSO, MC (John Murray, 1936).

History of the Welsh Guards, by Major C. Dudley Ward, DSO, MC (London Stamp Exchange).

The History of the Cameronians (Scottish Rifles), 1910–1933, by Colonel H. H. Story, MC (printed by Hazell, Watson and Viney, 1961).

The Life of a Regiment: The History of the Gordon Highlanders, 1914–1919, Vol. 4, by Cyril Falls (Aberdeen University Press, 1958).

The Royal Scots 1914–1919, Vol. 1, by Major G. Ewing MC (Oliver and Boyd, 1925).

The Story of The King's Regiment 1914–1948, by Lieutenant-Colonel J. J. Burke-Gaffney, MC (published by The King's Regiment, 1954).

History of the Queen's Royal Regt., Vol. 7, by Colonel H. C. Wylly, CB (Yale and Polden, 1925).

The West Yorkshire Regiment in the War 1914–1918: A History of the 14th, The Prince of Wales' Own (West Yorkshire Regt.), by Everard Wyrall (The Bodley Head).

The Cambridgeshires 1914 to 1919, by Brigadier-General E. Riddell, CMG, DSO, and Colonel M. C. Clayton, DSO, DL (Bowes and Bowes, 1934).

History of the East Surrey Regt., Vol. 2, by Colonel H. W. Pearse, DSO, and Brigadier-General H. S. Sloman, CMG, DSO (Medici Society, 1923).

The Worcestershire Regiment in the Great War, by Captain H. FitzM. Stacke, MC (G.T. Cheshire).

The History of the London Rifle Brigade 1859–1919, (Constable, 1921).

The History of the Rifle Brigade in the War of 1914–1918, Vol. 1, August 1914–December 1916, by Reginald Berkeley, MC (The Rifle Brigade Club, 1927).

The War History of the Sixth Battalion The South Staffordshire Regiment (T.F.) (William Heinemann, 1924).

9th Royal Scots (T.F.), B Company on Active Service: From a Private's Diary, February–May 1915 (Turnbull and Spears, 1916).

Notes and Comments on the Dardanelles Campaign, by A. Kearsey, DSO, OBE (Gale and Polden).

With the Twenty-Ninth Division in Gallipoli: A Chaplain's Experiences, by Rev. O. Creighton, CF (Longmans, Green and Co., 1916).

War Memoirs of David Lloyd George, Vol. 1 (Odhams Press, 1933).

1914 by Field-Marshal Viscount French of Ypres, KP, OM (Constable, 1919).

The Private Papers of Douglas Haig 1914–1919, edited by Robert Blake (Eyre and Spottiswoode, 1952).

The Supreme Command 1914–1918, Vol. 1, by Lord Hankey (Allen and Unwin, 1961).

Khaki and Gown: An Autobiography, by Field-Marshal Lord Birdwood of Anzac and Totnes, GCB, GCSI, GCMG, CIE, DSO (Ward, Lock, 1941).

Experiences of a Dug-Out 1914–1918, by Major-General Sir C. E. Callwell, KCB (Constable, 1920).

Tunnellers All, by Edward Synton (Grant Richards, 1918).

War Underground: The Tunnellers of the Great War, by Alexander Barrie (Tom Donovan, 1961).

Kitchener's Army: The Raising of the New Armies, 1914–1916, by Peter Simkins (Manchester University Press, 1988).

The King's Royal Rifle Corps Chronicle 1915 (The Wykeham Press, 1916).

The Rifle Brigade Chronicle for 1915, 1918 and 1920 (John Bale, 1916, 1919 and 1921).

1915 Campaign in France, The Battles of Aubers Ridge, Festubert and Loos: Considered in Relation to the Field Service Regulations, by A. Kearsey, DSO, OBE (Gale and Polden, 1929).

Official History of the War: Medical Services, Vol. 2 (HMSO, 1923)

British Regiments, 1914–1918, by Brigadier E. A. James, OBE, TD (Samson, 1978).

Army Lists for 1915 and 1918.

Field Service Pocket Book 1914 (HMSO).

World War 1914–1918: A Pictured History, Vol. 1, edited by Sir John Hammerton (Amalgamated Press).

The Great War . . . 'I Was There', Vol. 1, edited by Sir John Hammerton (Amalgamated Press).

Students Under Arms, by Alexander Rule, MC, MA (Aberdeen University Press, 1934).

Behind the Lines, by Colonel W. N. Nicholson, CMG, DSO (Jonathan Cape, 1939).

By-Ways on Service: Notes from an Australian Journal, by Hector Dinning (Constable, 1918).

Mosaic of Memories, by Lieutenant-Colonel Ronald Fife, CMG, DSO (Heath Cranton, 1943).

David Graham-Pole: War Letters and Autobiography (privately published).

Fate is My Shepherd, by R. A. Chapman (privately published).

Diary of Capt. Bryden McKinnell, 10th (Scottish) Battalion King's Liverpool Regiment (privately published).

A Frenchman in Khaki, by Paul Maze, DCM, MM with bar, C de G (Heinemann, 1934).

Van Den Grooten Oorlog, Elfnovembergroep (Volksboek, 1978).

Oorlogsdagboeken Over Ieper (1914–1915), Jozef Geldhof (Genootschap Voor Geschiedenis, 1977).

Author's Note

I wish to acknowledge my debt to all of the
following, without whose valuable assistance this book
could never have been written.

Captain A. J. Agius, MC, 3rd (City of London) Battalion, The London Regiment Royal Fusiliers (TF).

Miss Anne Armstrong.

Private G. Ashurst, 1st Battalion, Lancashire Fusiliers.

Lieutenant F. R. Banks, CB, OBE, Royal Navy Volunteer Reserve.

Private F. T. Barlow, 7th Battalion, Worcestershire Regiment.

Lieutenant G. Barry, MC, Platoon Commander No. 2 Company, 1st Battalion, Coldstream Guards.

Rifleman J. Bassett, 8th Battalion, The Rifle Brigade.

Private Frank Bastable, 7th Battalion, Queen's Own Royal West Kent Regiment, 55 Brigade.

Trooper P. Batchelor, D Squadron, Queen's Own Oxfordshire Hussars (TY).

Sergeant Joe Beard, 1st Battalion, King's Royal Rifle Corps, 6 Brigade.

Colonel Gordon Beith, 24th Battalion, Australian Infantry Force.

Able Seaman J. S. Bentham, Benbow Battalion, 1st Brigade, Royal Naval Division.

Flight Commander R. D. Best, 53rd Squadron, Royal Flying Corps.

Private H. W. Bickerstaff, MM, 19th Battalion, Canadian Expeditionary Force.

Corporal J. L. Bouch, 1st Battalion, Coldstream Guards.

Private J. Bowles, 2/16th Battalion (County of London Regiment), Queen's Westminster Rifles.

Captain G. A. Brett, DSO, MC, 23rd (County of London Regiment) (TF).

Sergeant B. J. Brookes, 1/16th Battalion, Queen's Westminster Rifles (County of London Regiment).

Private T. Brown, MM, 6th/7th Battalion, Seaforth Highlanders.

Private R. Burns, 7th Battalion, Queen's Own Cameron Highlanders.

Gunner C. B. Burrows, 104 Battery 22 Brigade, Royal Field Artillery.

Sergeant G. Butler, 12th Battalion, Machine Gun Company.

Private T. Campbell, 7th Battalion, Seaforth Highlanders.

2nd Lieutenant G. V. Carey, A Company, 8th Battalion, The Rifle Brigade.

Private W. Carrol, 21st Battalion, Australian Infantry Force.

Petty Officer R. C. Chadwick, Royal Navy, HMS *Edgar*.

606

Trooper G. C. Chaplin, 1st Northamptonshire Yeomanry (TY).

Lieutenant (later Major-General) A. F. P. Christison, MC, 6th Battalion, Queen's Own Cameron Highlanders, 45 Brigade.

Gunner S. T. Clark, 108 Brigade, Royal Field Artillery.

Signaller H. J. Crask, MM, 1st Battalion, The Suffolk Regiment, 84 Brigade.

Private H. B. Coates, 14th (London Scottish) Battalion (County of London), 1st Brigade.

Company Sergeant-Major W. J. Coggins, 4th Battalion, Oxfordshire and Buckinghamshire Light Infantry (TF).

Lance-Corporal G. Cole, 4th Battalion, Queen's (Royal West Surrey Regiment).

Private J. Cole, 2nd Battalion, Worcestershire Regiment.

Sergeant W. J. Collins, Royal Army Medical Corps.

Sergeant John Combe, 1st/7th (Leith) Battalion (TF), The Royal Scots (Lothian Regiment).

Corporal W. F. Common, D Battery, 250 Brigade, 50th Division Tyneside.

Driver C. W. Coombs, ASC, 158 Company, 20th Division.

Mrs A. E. Cowley.

Private Tom Coy, 6th Battalion, Northamptonshire Regiment.

Lieutenant T. C. Cresswell, MC, Hood Battalion, Royal Naval Division.

Private G. Cribley, 8th Battalion, Gloucestershire Regiment, 57 Brigade.

Corporal A. Critchley, MM, 1st/7th Battalion, King's (Liverpool) Regiment.

2nd Lieutenant W. Cushing, 9th (Service) Battalion, Norfolk Regiment.

Corporal G. R. Daniels, 12th (Bermondsey) Battalion, East Surrey Regiment.

Pioneer W. A. Daulman, Royal Engineers.

Private H. K. Davis, 5th (City of London) Battalion (London Rifle Brigade).

Private W. Derbyshire, 19th Canadian Infantry Battalion.

M. Pierre Dewavrin.

Mme Germaine Dewavrin.

Lance-Corporal A. F. T. Diamond, Special Gas Brigade, Royal Engineers.

Sergeant William Dixon, DCM, King's Own Yorkshire Light Infantry.

Lance-Corporal J. Dorgan, 7th Battalion, Northumberland Fusiliers.

Corporal W. M. Draycott, Princess Patricia's Canadian Light Infantry.

Bombardier Alex Dunbar, A Battery, Royal Field Artillery, 236 Brigade.

Sergeant S. C. Duncan, 6th Battalion, King's Own Scottish Borderers.

Private H. N. Edwards, 6th (Bristol City) Battalion, Gloucester Regiment.

Driver A. A. Elderkin, 2 Brigade, 1st Canadian Division.

Lance-Corporal G. England, 3rd Battalion, Grenadier Guards.

Private Harry Fellowes, 12th Battalion, The Northumberland Fusiliers, 62 Brigade.

Private B. Felstead, 15th (S) Battalion (1st London Welsh) Royal Welsh Fusiliers.

Lance-Corporal J. W. Finnimore, 3rd Battalion, 1st Canadian Brigade.

Driver Rodger Fish, Motor Transport Service, Army Service Corps.

Company Quartermaster-Sergeant Gordon Fisher, 1st Battalion,

607

Hertfordshire Regiment (TF), 6 Brigade.

Private W. S. Fisher, 1st Hertfordshire Yeomanry (TY).

Private E. W. Ford, 10th Battalion, Queen's Royal West Surrey Regiment.

Lieutenant-Commander J. C. Forster, Hood Battalion, Royal Naval Division.

Private S. Fraser, MM, 2nd Battalion, Honourable Artillery Company (TF).

Sergeant H. G. Freestone, 1st Battalion, Cambridgeshire Regiment (TF).

Corporal F. H. Fuller, MC, 1st Battalion, Cambridgeshire Regiment (TF).

Corporal G. Gilbert, A Squadron, 13th Australian Light Horse.

2nd Lieutenant J. R. Glenn, 12th Battalion, Yorkshire and Lancashire Regiment (Sheffield Pals).

Private F. Gowland, 10th Battalion, Worcestershire Regiment, 57 Brigade.

Private J. Hardesty, 7th Battalion, King's Own Royal Lancashire Regiment.

Private W. Hare, 16th Battalion, West Yorkshire Regiment.

Lieutenant-Colonel P. W. Hargreaves, MC, 3rd Battalion, Worcestershire Regiment.

Captain George Hawes, DSO, MC, City of London Battalion, The London Regiment, Royal Fusiliers (TF).

Private W. Hay, A Company, 9th Battalion, The Royal Scots (Lothian Regiment).

Private J. W. Herring, 3rd Battalion, Honourable Artillery Company (TF).

2nd Lieutenant H. C. L. Heywood, 6th Battalion, Manchester Regiment (TF).

Mevrouw Paula Hinnekint.

Lance-Corporal F. G. Hodges, 3rd Battalion, North Staffordshire Regiment.

Private W. H. Hodges, Machine Gun Company.

Private H. E. W. Hollobone, 2nd Battalion, Prince of Wales' Own Regiment.

Sergeant F. W. Horn, MM, 1st Battalion, Cambridgeshire Regiment (TF), 82 Brigade.

Major G. Horridge, 1/5th Battalion, Lancashire Fusiliers (TF).

Private Joe Hoyles, 13th (S) Battalion, Rifle Brigade.

Private W. Jackman, 4th Grenadier Guards, 3rd Guards Brigade.

Sapper J. Johnston, 44th (Welsh) Field Company, Royal Engineers.

Sergeant Harry Keighley, 147 Brigade, Royal Artillery.

Private S. H. E. Kemp, 14th (County of London) Battalion, London Regiment (London Scottish), (TF).

Bombardier W. Kemp, A subsection, 59th Siege Battery, Royal Garrison Artillery.

Captain H. Kenyon, DSO, Royal Artillery, Attached 7th (Indian) Mountain Artillery Brigade.

Rifleman Ralph Langley, 16th Battalion (Church Lads Brigade), King's Royal Rifle Corps.

Sergeant G. Leach, 12th Battalion, Rifle Brigade.

Corporal Alex Letyford, 5th Field Company, Royal Engineers.

Lieutenant D. S. Lewis, Royal Engineers, Attached Royal Flying Corps.

Private R. Lloyd, 7th Battalion, The King's (Liverpool) Regiment.

Corporal J. V. Lowe, 10th Battalion, Cameronians (Scottish Rifles).

Sergeant W. F. Lowe, 10th Battalion, Durham Light Infantry, 43 Brigade.

2nd Lieutenant David Lyell, 7th Battalion, The Royal Scots, 156 Brigade (TF).

Private D. Macdonald, 6th Battalion, Black Watch (Royal Highlanders).

Private W. Macdonald, 9th Battalion, Gordon Highlanders.

Miss Betty Macleod.

2nd Lieutenant J. Macleod, 2nd Battalion, Queen's Own Cameron Highlanders, 81 Brigade.

Lieutenant R. Macleod, V Battery, Royal Horse Artillery, 2nd Battalion, Indian Cavalry Division.

General Sir G. Macmillan, KCB, KCVO, CBG, MC (2 Bars), 2nd Seaforth Highlanders.

Private Harry de Maine, 1st/6th Battalion, Duke of Wellington's Regiment.

Sergeant H. Mann, MBE, 2nd/4th Battalion, Queen's Royal West Surrey Regiment.

Private George Marrin, 13th Battalion, Middlesex Regiment, 73 Brigade.

Mrs A. Marshall (née Duff).

Trooper Peter Mason, 1st/1st Battalion, Yorkshire Hussars Yeomanry.

Lance-Corporal George McGurk, 1st/7th (Leith) Battalion (TF), The Royal Scots (Lothian Regiment).

Sergeant Neill McKechnie, 14th Londons (London Scottish).

Private W. J. McKenna, 16th Battalion (Canadian Scottish), 3rd Canadian Brigade.

Sergeant J. F. McMahon, 2nd/4th Battalion, Oxfordshire and Buckinghamshire Regiment (TF).

Private H. Mellor, 2nd Battalion, The Manchester Regiment.

Gunner W. Melvin, 49 Brigade, Royal Field Artillery.

Corporal H. C. Merrett, MM, Royal Engineers.

Mme Marie de Milleville.

Private L. Mitchell, 24th Battalion, Field Ambulance.

2nd Lieutenant I. Morgan, 11th Battalion, Welsh Regiment (Cardiff Pals).

Corporal E. Moss, 3rd Battalion, Grenadier Guards.

Corporal Frank Moylan, 7th (City of London) Battalion, 140 Brigade.

Sergeant F. N. Mumford, 7th Battalion (County of London), London Regiment.

Private E. A. Murray, 6th Battalion, Gordon Highlanders, 20 Brigade.

Trumpeter J. Naylor, XXIII Brigade, Royal Field Artillery.

Private W. H. Nixon, DCM, 2nd Battalion, Cheshire Regiment.

Sergeant F. R. Oliver, 5th Battalion, Yorkshire and Lancashire Regiment.

Private S. Oncken, 14th Battalion (County of London), London Regiment (London Scottish).

Sergeant F. M. Packham, 2nd Battalion, The Royal Sussex Regiment, 2nd Brigade.

Corporal D. A. Pankhurst, Royal Field Artillery.

Private R. L. Ponsford, 24th Battalion, Australian Dental Corps.

Lieutenant J. D. Pratt, 'U' (University) Company, 4th Battalion, Gordon Highlanders.

Captain (later Brigadier) Rathbone, 6th Battalion, Royal North Lancashire Regiment.

Lieutenant-Colonel W. J. K. Rettie, LIX Brigade, Royal Field Artillery.

Lieutenant W. O. Rhodes, 6th Battalion, North Staffordshire Regiment.

Rifleman R. H. Rickets, 1st/6th County of London Battalion (London Regiment).

Corporal H. E. Rickman, 15th Battalion (Civil Service Rifles), County of London Regiment.

Lance-Corporal G. E. Rippon, 2nd Battalion, King's Own Yeoman Light Infantry.

Major F. A. de V. Robertson, 59th Royal Scinde Rifles, Frontier Force, Lahore Division.

Corporal F. W. Rozee, 4th Battalion, The Rifle Brigade.

Private C. H. Russell, 14th (County of London) Battalion (London Scottish), 1st Brigade.

Lance-Corporal E. J. Sarah, MM, Royal Engineers.

Private Norman Scott, 6th (Victoria) Battalion, 2nd Australian Brigade.

Private W. H. Shaw, 9th Battalion, Royal Welsh Fusiliers, 58 Brigade.

Private A. Simpson, 5th Battalion (TF), The Yorkshire Regiment.

Private C. Singleton, 15th Battalion, County of London Regiment (Civil Service Rifles).

Mrs Ella Smith (née Plenderleith).

Private H. F. Smith, 3rd Canadian Infantry Battalion, Canadian Expeditionary Force.

Lieutenant R. E. Smith, 7th Battalion, Royal Scots Fusiliers, 45 Brigade.

Private W. Spencer, 4th Battalion, Grenadier Guards, 3rd Guards Brigade.

Private Carson Stewart, 7th Battalion, Queen's Own Cameron Highlanders, 44th Brigade.

Rifleman F. J. Stratford, 2nd Battalion, The Rifle Brigade.

Signaller J. E. Sutton, 9th Battery, Canadian Field Artillery.

Major A. Taylor, MC, 1st/4th Battalion, Gloucestershire Regiment.

Private J. Taylor, Royal Scots Lothian Regiment.

Gunner Norman Tennant, 11th Howitzer Battery, West Riding Brigade (TF), Royal Artillery.

Private A. Truswell, 11th Battalion, Sherwood Foresters (Nottinghamshire and Derbyshire Regiment).

Corporal W. Turnbull, 1st/4th Battalion, King's Own Scottish Borderers.

Sergeant F. G. Udall, MM (2 Bars), 4th (City of London) Regiment, Royal Fusiliers (TF), Lahore Division.

Private J. W. Vaughan, Princess Patricia's Light Infantry, 80 Brigade, 27 Division.

Private R. C. Vodrey, Royal Marine Light Infantry.

Corporal G. Voller, 1st/8th Battalion, Middlesex Regiment (TF).

Corporal J. A. Watson, 13th Siege Battery, Royal Garrison Artillery.

Lieutenant A. B. White, 186 Company, Royal Engineers.

Driver H. Whitehead, Royal Field Artillery, 2nd Northumbrian Brigade.

Corporal J. H. Whymark, 2nd/4th Battalion, Queen's Royal West Surrey Regiment.

Corporal A. Wilson, 1st/5th Battalion (TF), West Yorkshire Regiment.

Corporal G. E. Winterbourne, 1st Battalion, (County of London Regiment), Queen's Westminster Rifles.

Private W. Worrell, 12th Service Battalion, The Rifle Brigade, 60 Brigade.

Lieutenant C. S. Wynn, The Suffolk Regiment.

Index

Achi Baba 346-7, 356, 361, 363-5, 379, 433, 454
Adamson, Capt. 288
Agar-Robartes, Capt. the Hon. Thomas 429-32, 501
Agius, Capt. Arthur J., MC
  in Flanders 43-5, 47-8
  at Gallipoli 596
  at Loos 523, 526-7, 530, 560
  in Malta 38-40
  at Neuve Chapelle 57-8, 88, 90-1, 93-4, 96-7, 125-7, 139
AIF
  5th Battalion 432
  21st Battalion 434-5, 438-9
  24th Battalion 435, 583-4
Alderson, General 201-3, 246
Allardyce, Sgt. 413
Allenby, Gen. Edmund Henry Hynman 14
Alsace 261-2, 322
Amlinger, Musketier Pieter 187
ammunition, shortage 153, 379
  in Flanders 3, 64-6, 71
  in France 472
  Gallipoli campaign 312, 363, 365, 379, 405, 440
  and Neuve Chapelle 84, 136-7, 141-2
  and political crisis 311-18
  and Ypres 236-9, 279, 297, 312
Anderson, General 107
Andrews, L/cpl. W.L. 83-4, 89-90, 91-2, 93, 97-8, 135

Anzac Cove 347-54, 355, 433, 442-4, 581-2, 585
Anzacs (Australia and New Zealand Army Corps)
  1st Australian Brigade 440
  2 Australian Brigade 437-8
  and Dardanelles campaign 143, 347-54, 365, 432-41, 442-7, 452, 454, 583, 585
Argyll and Sutherland Highlanders 167-8, 517
  1/7th Battalion 29
Armstrong, Anne 337-8
Army Service Corps 77-8
  46 (North Midland) Divisional train 470-1
  Motor Transport Service 237-8
Ashwell, Capt. 78-9
Aspinall, Col. 450
Asquith, Herbert Henry 312-17, 405-6, 433, 567
Attlee, Capt. Clement 344
Aubers Ridge 479, 491, 523
  attack planned 51, 61, 71, 81-2
  attempted attack 103-5, 108, 114, 124, 136
  battle 295, 297-310, 311-12, 324, 379
Australian Light Horse, 13th Battalion 435-7
Avon 43-4

Bagot-Chester, Capt. W.G.
  at Loos 485-6, 523, 527-30

at Neuve Chapelle 93, 94, 127, 138-40
at Ypres 306-8
Bain, Sir Frederick 384
Balck, General 221n.
Balfour, Arthur 313, 316
Barber, Lt. G. 591-2
Barbieur, Artur 214-16
Bareilly Brigade *see* Meerut Division
Barry, Lt. G., MC 429-32
Bastable, Pte. F. 461-2, 573-4
Batchelor, Tmptr. P. 212
Bavarian Reserve Infantry Brigade
  6th Battalion 92
  14th Battalion 114
  17th Battalion 532
Beard, Sgt. J. 545-7, 554
Begbie, Pte. W. 337, 367, 369, 371, 374-5
Beith, Col. G. 435, 583-4
Belgium, Independence Day 414-17
Bellewaerde Ridge 280, 287-90, 379, 390-5, 419, 521
Bentham, Able Seaman J.S. 318-24
Berkeley, Capt. R., MC 132-4, 304-5
Berkshire Regiment 94
Best, Lt. (later 2nd Lt.) F. 77-8, 470-1
'Big Bertha' 187
Birdwood, General 581
Black Watch 483
  1/4 Battalion 83-4, 89-90, 91-2, 93, 97-8, 127, 135
  2nd Battalion 529
Boase, Capt. 98
Bois du Biez 99, 110-13, 114, 116-19, 130, 132
Bois Grenier 79, 82
Bowles, J. 594-5, 596
Boxer, Major H.E.R. 395n.
Boy Scouts 463-4

Boyle, Col. 202
Boy's Own Paper 464-5
Brett, Capt. G.A., DSO, MC 547-8
Brides in the Bath murder case 231
British Army
  First Army 59, 79-83, 112-13, 130-1, 379, 390, 490, 562, 599
  Second Army 216-17, 245, 250-7, 279, 563
  2 Guards Brigade 556, 599
  3 (Guards) Brigade 412, 547, 549, 556-7, 599
  IV Corps 82, 84, 103-5, 108, 118-19, 131-2
  4 (Guards) Brigade 474-6
  V Corps 257, 410-11
  VI Corps 424
  IX Corps 445-51
  10 Brigade 240-1 245
  22 Brigade 86, 297, 304, 308
  25 Brigade 118
  59 Brigade 451-3
  85 Brigade 293
  88 Brigade 359-60
  236 Brigade 488-9, 501-2, 517-18
  see also Divisions
Bromilow, Col. 75-6
Brookes, Sgt. B.J. 172
Bruce, Douglas 97
Budhiman, Havildar 528-9
Buffs *see* East Kent Regiment (the Buffs)
Bulair 346, 354, 449
Bulgaria 53-4, 262, 453, 567
Buller, Capt. 271
Burney, Lt. Col. P. 225-7
Burns, RSM 164-5
Burrows, Gnr. C.B. 295-7, 304, 308-9
Bushman, Lady 150-1
Bute, Pte. W. 560
Butler, Sgt. G. 381
Byng, Gen. 445

Callwell, General C.E. 567
Cambridgeshire Regiment 33-4
Cameronians *see* Scottish Rifles
Canadian Army, 1st Division 53,
    55, 82, 192, 198-201
    3rd Battalion 224-5
    8th (Manitoba) Battalion 236n.
    10th Battalion 200, 202-5
    15th Battalion (48th Royal
    Highlanders) 192-4, 197,
    222-4, 234, 586-7
    16th Battalion (Canadian
    Scottish) 200, 202-5
    Field Artillery, 9th Battery 193,
    196-7, 235, 236
    see also Princess Patricia's
    Canadian Light Infantry
Cape Helles 346, 355-9, 364, 433,
    444, 564, 582, 586
Capper, General 105, 109, 116
Carden, Admiral 51
Carey, 2nd Lt. G.V. 421-3
Carrol, Pte. W. 434-5, 438-9
Carter, Brig. General 121-2
Carter, Lt. Col. B.C.M. 545
Cassels, Lt. 408-12, 413
casualties, numbers 311, 379, 395,
    564, 597-8
Cavalry
    1st Division 214
    2 Indian Division 20
    3 Brigade 549
    5 Brigade 132, 149
    at Neuve Chapelle 79, 98
    reliance on 14-15, 34
Cavan, Lord 599
Chalk Pit 549, 556-7
Chalmers, Capt. 284
Chaplin, Trpr. G.C. 242
Cheshire Regiment 284
    15th Battalion 148
    16th Battalion 148
Chrichton, Cyril 44
Christison, Lt. A.F.P., MC 496-8,
    503, 532, 538-40, 543, 553-4

Christmas 1914, truce 3-5, 16, 588
Christmas 1915 586, 588-97,
    599-600
Chunuk Bair 440, 442-4, 446-7, 452
Church Lads Brigade 463
Churchill, Winston Spencer 50-1,
    53, 317-18, 344n.
Cité St Auguste 512-14
Clarke, Trpr. W. 549-50, 572-3,
    576
Clopet, Capt. 21-6
Clopet, Mrs 21-4, 26
Coggins, CSM W.J. 169-70
Coldstream Guards
    1st Battalion 428-32, 599
    2nd Battalion 475, 493
Colquhoun, Capt. Campbell
    539-40
Combe, Sgt. J. 333, 335
'comforts' 26, 30-1, 66, 149-50,
    232, 574, 590
Connaught Rangers 139, 249-50,
    252-3
conscription 326, 579
Conybeare, Lt E.B. 122, 127-8
Cooper, Lt. Teddy 56
Cowan, Major S.H. 382-3, 408-12,
    423-4
Cowley, A.E. 338-9
Cox, Harold, Chief Engineer 24-5
Cribley, Pte. G. 558
Crask , Pte. H.J. 283-5, 288-92,
    293, 595
Cross, Sgt. J., MM 401-2
Crossingham, Private 3
Cushing, 2nd Lt. W. 156-7, 160-1,
    588, 590-1, 593
Cuthbert, Brig. General 469
Cuthbert, Major 119-20

Daily Mail
    on Neuve Chapelle 148-9
    and parcels 595
Daily Mirror 327
Daniel, Cpl. G.R. 166-7

Dardanelles campaign 53-4, 142-3,
217, 312, 342-7, 355-75,
432-41, 442-51
and Battle of Loos 564-5
and Churchill 50-1, 53, 317-18
Committee 327, 566-7, 581
disease 361-2, 444, 565
evacuation 580-1, 584, 585-6
failure 316-17, 324, 353-4, 379,
441, 452-5, 589
landings 245, 347-54, 355-61
new commander 580
new troops for 331, 340, 404-5
political debate over 565-7
reinforcements sent 453-4
unofficial armistice 583
Davis, Pte. H.K. 171, 243-4
De Lisle, General 365, 375
De Milleville, Mme Marie 198
Defence of the Realm Act 27
Dehra Dun Brigade see Meerut
Division
Delaere, Fr Camille 240, 243,
277-8
Derby Comrades Brigade 147-8
Derby, Lord 147, 579
Dewavrin, Germaine 62-4
Dewavrin, Henri 61-2, 64
Dewavrin, Pierre 61-4
Dick, Gordon 335
Von Ditforth, Major General 114
Divisions
1st 312, 541, 555-6
1st Brigade 509-10, 591-2
2 Brigade 178-9, 506-7
2nd
6 Brigade 474-7, 501-2, 545-7,
554
7 Brigade 387-8, 391-2, 394
3rd
8 Brigade 381, 383-7, 390-3,
398-400, 413-14, 417-18, 424,
491-3, 521-3
9 Brigade 242, 387-8, 391,
394-5, 550

4th 267
12th Machine Gun Coy 381
6th 427
7th 82, 103, 105, 108-9, 131-2,
297, 312, 541
21 Brigade 109
8th 81-2, 103, 108-10, 117-19,
121, 132, 297-8, 309
23 Brigade 82, 95-6, 136-7
24 Brigade 121, 127-8
9th Scottish 400n., 483, 506, 519,
541
10th 445, 567
12th (Easter) 400n.
14th 400, 522
41 Brigade 421-5
43 Brigade 419-20, 425-7
15th (Scottish) 483, 499, 503-4,
507, 511, 517-18, 535, 671
44 Brigade 512-14, 558, 571-2
45 Brigade 496-7, 514, 532,
535, 538-40, 543, 553, 577-8
18th, 55 Brigade 461-2, 573-4
19th
57 Brigade 473, 558
58 Brigade 508-9
20th (Light), 60 Brigade 466-8,
484, 498-9, 523-6, 554-5
21st 478, 493, 498, 514-15,
518-20, 541, 549-50, 562
62 Brigade 535-7, 540-1, 544-5,
552
64 Brigade 516
24th 478, 493, 514-15, 518-19,
541, 542-4, 550-1, 562
73 Brigade 519, 541, 551,
561
27th 53, 199, 206-9, 220, 235-6,
266, 269-71, 282, 568
80 Brigade 292-3
81 Brigade 174-6
28th 53, 220, 241, 283
83 Brigade 285-6, 288
84 Brigade 288-90, 291-2,
293-4

614

29th 53-5, 143, 217, 355-6, 362-9, 586
   86 Brigade 368, 370-2, 373-4
   87 Brigade 368
   156 Brigade 365
37th 401-2, 403-4
42nd 444
46th (North Midland) 54, 75-9
   137 Brigade 472
47th (London) 152, 487, 507, 510-11, 557
   5 London Brigade 480-1, 486
   140 Brigade 468-70, 482, 504-5, 588-9
50th (Northumbrian) 223-4, 265
   149 Brigade 219
52nd, 156th (Infantry) Brigade 363-4, 365-7, 369, 374-5
53rd (Welsh) 447-8, 449, 581-2
56th 592
Guards 548-50
   2 Brigade 493, 514
see also British Army
Dodd, C., Chief Officer 23
Von Donop, Sir Stanley 315
Dorgan, L/cpl. J. 219, 223-4, 265
Double Crassier 468, 487-8, 504, 510, 557
Dragoon Guards, 2 Battalion 549-50, 572-3, 576
Drake-Brockman, Lt. Col. D.H. 68-9
Drummond, Sgt. 440
Duke of Cornwall's Light Infantry 208
Dunbar, Bdr. Alex 488-9, 501-2, 503, 517-18, 534
Dundas, Major 94
Durham Light Infantry
   10th Battalion 419-20, 425-7
   14th Battalion 542
   15th Battalion 542

East Kent Regiment (the Buffs) 205, 209

East Lancashire Regiment, lst Battalion 290, 305
East Surrey Regiment, l2th Battalion 40, 166-7
East Yorks Regiment
   2nd Battalion 290
   8th Battalion 535
Edwards, Dr John 336, 339
Edwards, Henry 151
Edwards, Pte. H.N. 157-8, 159
Egerton, Major General 339
Elliot-Hill, Major 21
Elliott, Alex 355
Empress of Britain 339-40
Errington, Lt. Col. E.H.L. 163, 397
Etaples base camp 45-8, 56
Ewart, General 445

Farquhar, Col. 269-71, 283
Fellowes, Sgt. H. 73, 479, 495, 515, 535-7, 552-3
Ferguson, Sgt. Major 207
Festubert 35, 312, 326, 327, 379, 475-6
24th Field Ambulance 309-10
Fife, Lt. Col., DSO 593
Figg, Acting Sgt. 527
Finnimore, L/cpl. J.W. 224-5
fire attack 421, 422-4, 427n.
Fish, Driver Rodger 237-8
Fisher, Adm. Lord John 50, 53, 317-18
Fisher, CQMS G. 151-2, 474-6
Foch, General Ferdinand 216-18, 247, 253, 256, 258-9, 264-5
Fosse 8 541, 545, 551, 571
France
   Tenth Army 51-3, 55, 185, 468
   45th Regiment 192
   Elverdinghe Detachment 217n.
   Nieuport Detachment 217n., 218
fraternisation with the enemy 3-5, 599-600
French, Sir John 7, 173, 405

advocates coastal attack 50-1, 52
and Aubers Ridge 312
and lack of ammunition 49, 64,
    66, 71, 141-2, 238-9, 312-15,
    379
and lack of equipment 33, 49,
    64, 66, 84-6
and Loos 514-15, 557, 561-4
and Neuve Chapelle 51-3, 57,
    59-61, 71, 79, 84, 86, 89, 132,
    136, 141-2, 148-9
replacement 567-8, 590
and shortage of troops 54-5, 61
and Ypres 179, 216-18, 238-9,
    245, 246-8, 250, 253-6, 258-9,
    262, 264-5, 324
Freyberg, Lt. 354
Frezenberg Ridge 283, 288
Friends Ambulance Unit 177, 233,
    276

Gallipoli campaign 53-4, 142-3,
    217, 312, 342-7, 355-75,
    432-41, 442-51
and Battle of Loos 564-5
and Churchill 50-1, 53, 317-18
disease 361-2, 444, 565
evacuation 580-1, 584, 585-6
failure 316-17, 324, 353-4, 379,
    441, 452-5, 589
landings 245, 347-54, 355-61
new commander 580
new troops for 331, 340, 404-5
political debate over 565-7
reinforcements sent 453-4
unofficial armistice 583
Gallipoli (film) 446
Garde Husarien Regiment
    (Hussars of the Guard) 13-14
Garhwal Rifles 527-8
    1/39th Battalion 102-3
    2nd Battalion 68-9, 93-4, 526
gas
    appeal for gas-masks 232

British use 474, 484-6, 498-507,
    526-7, 530-1
first attack 183-7, 192-5, 196-200,
    204, 206, 208, 214-15
further attacks 252, 267-8, 280
and Loos 557, 560
protective measures 232-3, 268,
    472-4, 485, 486, 500, 503, 507
second attack 221, 222-5, 244
treatment 233-4
Gault, Hamilton 269-71, 283,
    285-6, 288
Geddes, Col. (East Kent
    Regiment) 209-10
Geddes, Col. (Royal Munster
    Fusiliers) 370-1
Geier mail-ship 22-5
George V 147, 401-2
German Army
    14th Infantry Division 114
    23rd Reserve Corps 221n.
    234 Reserve Infantry Regiment
        185
    see also Bavarian Reserve
        Infantry Brigade
Gilbert, Cpl. G. 435-7
Givenchy 35, 390, 393-4
Gloucester Regiment
    6th Battalion 157-8, 159
    8th Battalion 558
Gold, Capt. 499-500
Gordon Highlanders 483, 517
    1st Battalion 522
    4th Battalion 381-2, 383-7, 392-3,
        398-400, 413-14, 417-18, 474,
        491-3, 521-3
Gordon, Lt. 94
Gough, General 501
Gowland, Pte F. 473-4
Greece 54, 262, 567
Green Howard Regiment, 7th
    Battalion 592-3
Grenadier Guards 30, 116
    2nd Battalion 475-7
    4th Battalion 547, 548-50

Grey, Sir Edward 567
Gully Ravine 363-75, 433
Gunn, L/cpl. Sandy 393
guns
  ranging 70-1, 130, 273
  shortage 33, 64-6, 84-6, 297, 365, 405
Gurkha Rifles
  2/3 Battalion 93, 94, 127, 138-9, 306-8, 485-6, 527-9
  4th Battalion 127
  9th Battalion 111-12, 117, 124-5
  in Flanders 68-70, 93, 94, 96-7, 110-13, 119-20, 302
  in Gallipoli campaign 372
  at Loos 526-9
Gurung, Gane 96

Haig, General Sir Douglas
  and Aubers Ridge 297, 303, 311-12
  as Commander-in-Chief 567-8, 590
  and Loos 490-1, 499-500, 514-15, 561-4
  and Neuve Chapelle 59, 79-81, 83, 103, 105, 112-13, 121, 124, 130-4, 136
  and second battle of Ypres 264-5
Haking, General 493, 541
Hall, L/cpl. E. 102, 126, 135, 202
Hall, Fred 203, 236.
Hall, Sgt. H. 202-3, 204-5
Hallam, Basil 322
Hamilton, Col. Douglas 539-40
Hamilton, Sir Ian 14, 142-3, 316, 345, 347, 365, 372-3, 379, 445-6
  and causes of Gallipoli failure 449-53
  and Dardanelles Committee 566-7
Hampshire Regiment, 2nd Battalion 360

Hankey, Col. Sir Maurice
  and Gallipoli 316, 433-5, 440, 450-1, 453
  new ideas 31-3, 36
  visits France 405-6
Hanoverian Regiment, 77th Battalion 289-90
Hanson, Bob 479
Hawes, Capt. G. DSO, MC 106, 107-8
Hay, Pte W. 188-9, 206-9, 235-6, 266
Heavy Artillery, 9 Brigade 225-7
Hely Hutchinson, Lt. Col. R.G. 395n.
Henderson Scoles, Capt. A.M. 599-600
Hennekint, Paula 214-16
Hertfordshire Regiment, 1st Battalion 151-2, 474-7
Highland Light Infantry 35, 124-5, 127, 138, 250, 483
  6th Battalion 454-5
Hill 60 176, 180-1, 182-3, 186, 199, 221, 280, 387
Hill 70 488, 512-17, 531, 534-49, 555-9, 562, 591
Hilltop Ridge 251-2, 255
Hilton, Lucy 139-40
Hitchcock, B. Burnett 588-9
Hohenzollern Redoubt 506-7, 519, 545, 550, 571
Honourable Artillery Company 395n.
Hooge 254, 264, 280-2, 390, 408-12, 413-14, 417-27, 491, 521, 523, 530, 564
Hopkinson, Capt. 398
Horne, Major General 475, 477
Howells, Col. 39-42
Hoyles, Rfn. J. 403-4
Hubbard, Sgt. Sid 466, 499
Hughes, Sir Sam 269
Hull, General 241, 250
Hulluch village 506, 541, 544-5, 547

617

Hustler, Cpl. 14

Indian Corps 66-8, 490-1, 524-6
  and Neuve Chapelle 82, 84,
    88-90, 95-6, 102, 105-8, 110,
    130-1, 138-9, 249
  and Ypres 245, 249
  see also Lahore Division, Meerut
    Division
Indian Soldiers, Fund 67
Inns of Court OTC 154-5, 162-6,
  397
Inverness Copse 173n, 266, 283
Irish Guards 556-7
  1st Battalion 475
Italy, enters war 262, 324-6

Jackman, Gdsm. W. 547, 549
Jackson, Admiral Sir Henry 53
Jacob, Brig. General 111, 117, 121
Jaeger, Auguste 185n.
James, Lt. 70
Jardine, Sir John 587
Jelf, Brig. General 561
Jenkin, Cpl. 171
Joffre, General Joseph Jacques
  Césaire 34, 49-50, 173
  and French successes 311
  and Neuve Chapelle 51-2, 54-5,
    59
  and western front offensive 61,
    239, 405, 557
  and Ypres 217, 259, 265
Johnston, General 447
Johnston, Spr. J. 447-8, 449, 481-2
Jones, Douglas (Aubrey Dexter)
  402-3

Kaiser see Wilhelm II, Kaiser
Keddie, L/cpl. J. 193-4, 201, 222-3,
  224, 233-4, 586-8
Keighley, Sgt. H. 362-3
Kemp, Bdr. W. 84-6, 88-9, 101,
  115-16, 136, 302-6

Kenyon, Capt. H., DSO 347-9,
  350-2, 353-4
Kenyon, Capt. Sir F.G. 154-5, 165
Keyes, Admiral 580
King's Liverpool Regiment 545
  10th (Scottish) Battalion 30,
    178-9, 241-2, 250, 380, 388-91,
    394-5
King's Own 289-90
King's Own Scottish Borderers
  498, 503-4, 555-6
King's Regulations 41-2
King's Royal Rifle Corps 282
  1st Battalion 545-7, 554
  7th Battalion 423
  16th Battalion 463
Kipling, John 557
Kipling, Rudyard 557
Kitchener, Horatio Herbert, Lord
  50, 143, 147-8, 270-1, 326,
    405-6
  and French offensive 454, 459-61
  and Gallipoli campaign 54, 347,
    445, 453-4, 566, 580-1
  and Loos 492-3, 522, 562-3
  and shortage of ammunition 142,
    312-15, 318
  'Kitchener's Army' 169, 318, 579
  in Flanders 399-404, 419-27
  in France 459-61, 466-8, 472-7,
    496
  in Gallipoli 442, 451-2
  recruitment and training 152-68
  under-age recruits 402-3, 462-8
  see also Territorial Force
'Kitchener's Chocolate' 154
Kitchener's Wood 201-5, 221, 224,
  240
Von Kräwel, governor of Brussels
  416
Krithia 346, 356, 361, 363-5, 379

La Bassée Canal 79
Lahore Division 90, 245, 249-55

618

Laidlaw, Capt. R.F.E. 368, 370-2, 373-4
Laidlaw, Piper, VC 503-4
Lamb, Sgt. Tommy 499, 512-13
Lancashire Fusiliers 148
Langley, Capt. F.O. 472
Langley, Lt. 76-7
Langley, Rfn. Ralph 463
Law, Andrew Bonar 313, 316
Layes Brook 111, 113, 116, 119, 130-2
Leckie, Col. 202
Lee, Joe 92
Leicestershire Regiment 94-5, 105-6, 526
Lens Road Redoubt 487, 501, 503
Lens village 479, 487, 513, 517, 523
Letyford, Cpl. A. 19-20, 35, 90
Lewis, Lt. Donald S. 70-1, 97-8, 140
Liddell, Col. 13
'Lilliput Lancers' 40
Lincolnshire Regiment 94
  1st Battalion 388, 391-2, 395n.
  2nd Battalion 304
Liverpool Scottish see King's Liverpool Regiment
Livingston, Capt. 107, 108
Lloyd George, David 31, 34, 50, 313, 315, 405, 472, 510, 566-7
2nd London Heavy Battery 201-2
London Irish Regiment 481
London Rangers, 12th Battalion 290, 293
London Regiment
  1/7th (City of London) Battalion 106-7, 468-70, 482, 504-5
  14th (County of London) Battalion 509-10
  19th (County of London) Battalion 480, 486
  23rd Battalion 547-8
  Infantry Brigade
    1st Battalion 38-48, 55-8

2nd Battalion 55-7
3rd Battalion 55-7, 66, 69-70, 90-1, 93-4, 125-7, 239, 526, 527
4th Battalion 249-50, 252
London Rifle Brigade 6, 211
  5th (City of London) Battalion 171, 243-4
Lone Pine 432, 440, 444
Lone Tree Ridge 542, 544
Loos 470-1, 479-95, 496-511, 512-31, 532-63, 571-2, 589
Loos Road Redoubt 487-8
looting 249-50, 380-3
HMS Louis 580
Loutit, Lt. 352-3
Lowe, Cpl. W.F. 419-20, 425-7
Lyell, 2nd Lt. D. 367

MacGill, Patrick 457
Machine Gun Company, 12th 381
machine-gun 9, 11, 13-15, 47, 159
Maclagen, Col. 348, 350-2, 353
Macleod, Betty 324-5
Macleod, 2nd Lt. J. 173-6, 182, 266-7, 283, 324-5, 568
Macleod, Lt. R. 20
Mahon, Major General 445
Maling, Capt., VC 525
Malthouse, Walter 298-9, 307-8
Manchester Regiment 148, 250, 252-3
marching 154-5, 244
Marrin, Pte. G. 519, 551
Marshall, A. 338
Mascall, Capt. Maurice 67
Mason, Tpr. P. 179-80, 183-5
Mathieson, Bertie 58, 106
Matthews, Col. 364
Mauquissart, British attack 86, 87, 109-10, 121-3, 127, 131-2, 526
Mauser Ridge 250, 252, 255
Maze, Paul 501, 506
McCracken, Major General 534-5

McDougall, Major 193, 196, 236
McFie, CQMS R.S. 30, 388-9,
 394-5, 396-7, 574-6
McGurk, L/cpl. G. 333, 334
McHoul, Capt. 56
McKenna, Pte. W.J. 200, 203-5
McKinnell, Capt. B. 178-9, 242,
 380, 388-91, 395
McKinnon, Capt. Lachlan 385
Meakin, 332-3, 338n.
Meerut Division 66, 69-70, 81, 107,
 116-19, 249, 297
 Bareilly Brigade 83-4, 89-90,
  91-2, 93, 97-8, 135, 526
 7 Dehra Dun Brigade 18, 34-5,
  37, 91-5, 111-12, 117-20,
  123-5, 127, 137
 Garwhal Brigade 68-9, 82, 93-4,
  102-3, 124, 127, 138-9, 302,
  306-8, 485-6, 526, 527-9
Menin Gate 226-7, 263, 293n.
Menin Road 173, 178, 207, 220-1,
 294, 379, 387, 390, 392, 398,
 400
Messines Ridge 180
Middlesex Regiment
 2nd Battalion 101-2, 104, 297
 4th Battalion 413
 13th Battalion 519, 551
Milne, General 405-6
Milner, Lt. E. 78
Minchin, 117
Mitchell, Pte. L. 309-10
Moated Grange 87, 103-5, 116
Monmouth Regiment, 3rd
 Battalion 293
Monro, General Sir Charles 580,
 585
Moore, Capt. 107, 108
Moore, Harold 44
Motor Transport Service 237-8
Mouse Trap Farm 199, 201-2, 221,
 290, 293
Moylan, Cpl. F. 468-70, 482,
 504-5

Mudros, and Dardanelles
 campaign 53-4, 344-6, 375
munitions *see* ammunition,
 shortage
Murdoch, Keith 566
music 28-9

Nameless Cottages 110, 122-3, 128
names, Anglicisation 27
Napier, Brig. General 359-60
Naylor, Tmptr. J. 95-6, 136-7
Nek, attack on 446-7
Neuralia 43
Neuve Chapelle
 attack planned 51-2, 57, 79-81
 British capture 79-86, 87-98,
  99-113, 217
 costs 148-9
 failure to advance beyond
  130-42, 148, 187
 German counter-attack 114-29,
  530
 troop build-up 77-9
Nichols, Robert 377
Nicholson, 92, 97, 98, 135
Nickalls, Brig. General 541-2
Van Nieuwenhove, Aimé 189-90,
 263, 275-7, 406-8
Niven, Lt. 294
Noël, Capt. E.V. 57-8, 106
Nonnebosschen Wood 17, 283
Norfolk Regiment, 9th Battalion
 156-7, 160-1, 588, 590-1, 593
Northamptonshire Regiment 121-3,
 127, 129, 496, 532
Northamptonshire Yeomanry, lst
 Battalion 242
Northumberland Fusiliers 290, 293
 1st Battalion 395n.
 7th Battalion 219, 223-4, 265
 12th Battalion 73, 478-9, 515-16,
  518-20, 535-7, 544-5
 13th Battalion 535
Novello, Ivor 231
Novello-Davies, Clara 231

Nugent, Brig. General 424-5, 427

Officer Training Corps 162-6
officers, commissioning and
    training 160-6, 385-6
Ogilvie, Col. Thomas 384-5, 398
O'Gowan, General Wanless 213-14
Owen, Major 225-7
Oxfordshire & Buckinghamshire
    Light Infantry 169-70, 420

Packham, Sgt. F.M. 506-7
Page-Croft, Col. 476-7
Pankhurst, Gnr. (later Cpl.) D.A.
    404, 592-3
Patricia of Connaught, HRH
    Princess 270
Peake, Capt. 94
Peebles, Col. 339
Pepper, Pte. Joseph William 560
Perceval, Major General 256
Petrie, Major Paul 300-1
photography, aerial 70, 90, 98
Pickford, Lt. 169-70
Pilckem Ridge 202, 398
Plenderleith, William 332, 335
'Plugstreet' (Ploegsteert) Wood 6,
    33, 169, 171-2, 592
Plumer, General Herbert 186, 218,
    257, 258-9, 265, 267-8, 279,
    405-6
Poelcapelle 192-3, 195, 197, 225-6
Pole, Capt. D. G. (later Col.)
    478-9, 493-5, 515, 518-20,
    535-7, 544-5, 552-3, 560
Polygon Wood 176, 266-7, 269,
    271-2
Ponsonby, Lt. Col. J. 429-30
Post Office Rifles 479
Pratt, Lt. J.D. 381-2, 384-5
Prettor-Pinney, Col. 402-3
Prichard, Col. 122-3
Princess Patricia's Canadian Light
    Infantry 269-73, 280-3, 285-94,
    390

prisoners of war 595-6
propaganda war 260-2
Prussian Guard 17
Pulman, Harry 44, 57-8, 106, 139
Putz, General 199, 214, 217-18,
    248, 253-5

Queen's Own Cameron
    Highlanders
    1st Battalion 591-2
    2nd Battalion 173-6, 182, 266-7
    6th Battalion 496-8, 503, 532,
        538-40, 543, 553-4
    7th Battalion 499, 512-13, 558-9,
        571-2
Queen's Own Oxfordshire Hussars
    211-13
Queen's Own (Royal West Kent
    Regt), 7th Battalion 461-2,
    573-4
Queen's Westminster Rifles
    1/16th Battalion 172
    2/16th Battalion 594-5, 596

Rawlinson, Sir Henry 103-5, 108-9,
    130, 132, 445
recruiting 147-9, 160, 166-7, 314,
    318, 322, 326-7, 579
Reeves, Capt. 106
Reid, Joe 521, 523
Repington, Col. Tim 312-13
Rettie, Lt. Col. W.J.K. 451-3
Rickwood, Edgell 569
Riddell, Lt. 340
Rifle Brigade
    2nd Battalion 96, 99, 104, 111,
        118-19, 130, 132-4, 304-5, 308
    4th Battalion 287-8, 291
    7th Battalion 421
    8th Battalion 421-3, 424, 427n.
    9th Battalion 400
    12th Battalion 157, 466-8, 484,
        498-9, 523-6, 554-5
    13th Battalion 401-2, 403-4
rifles, shortage 153-4, 405

Ritchie, Col. 106-7
River Clyde 355-61
Roach, Pte. William 340-1
Robartes, Capt. the Hon. Thomas 429-32, 501
Roberts, Lt. 30
Robertson, Major A.F. 251-3
Robertson, Sir William 254, 256, 258, 264, 563, 567
Roehampton, Queen Mary's Hospital 587-8
Ross, Pipe-Major 333, 337
Royal Artillery 362-3
  7 (Indian) Mountain Artillery Brigade 347-9, 350-2, 353-4
Royal Dublin Fusiliers 76
  2nd Battalion 293
Royal Engineers 70-1, 91, 97-8, 140, 460-1, 481-2, 485, 526, 553
  5th Field Coy 17-18, 19-20, 35
  15th Field Coy 33
  44th (Welsh) Field Coy 581-2
  175th Tunnelling Coy 382-3, 408-12, 423-4
  186th Coy 501-3
Royal Field Artillery 451-3, 592
  23rd Brigade 95-6
  104 Battery 297, 304, 308
  A Battery 488-9, 501-2, 517-18
  Stokes Mortar Battery 404
Royal Flying Corps 70, 291
Royal Fusiliers
  lst London Infantry Brigade 38-48, 55-8
  2 London Infantry Brigade 55-7
  3 London Infantry Brigade 55-7, 66, 69-70, 90-1, 93-4, 106-7, 125-7, 139, 526, 527
  4 London Infantry Brigade 249-50, 252
  10 Battalion 168
Royal Garrison Artillery
  9 Heavy Brigade 225-7
  13 Siege Battery 489-90, 530-1

59 Siege Battery 84-6, 88-9, 101, 115-16, 136, 302-6
Royal Horse Artillery, 2 Indian Cavalry Div. 20
Royal Hussars, 10th Battalion 13-14
Royal Irish Rifles 130
Royal Marines, and Gallipoli campaign 53
Royal Munster Fusiliers, 1st Battalion 368, 370-2, 373-4
Royal Naval Division 354, 595-6
  Benbow Battalion 318-24
Royal Navy, and Gallipoli campaign 53-4, 317-18, 345, 353, 355-70, 433
Royal Scots 429, 564-5
  7th Battalion 331-41, 355, 361, 363-9, 371, 374-5, 392
  9th Battalion 188-9, 206-9, 235-6, 266
Royal Scots Fusiliers, 7th Battalion 577-8
Royal Sussex Regiment, 2nd Battalion 506-7
Royal Warwickshire Regiment, 1st Battalion 293
Royal Welsh Fusiliers, 9th Battalion 508-9
Rule, Sgt. A. 383-4, 387, 392-3, 398-400, 413-14, 417-18, 491-3, 521-3
Rumania 54, 262
Russell, Pte. C.H. 509-10
Russia 6, 59-60, 453, 589

St Julien, battle of 199-203, 226-7, 240-1, 251-3, 255, 260
Sanctuary Wood 209, 254, 521, 523
sandbags, making 31
Von Sanders, Liman 354
Sandilands, Col. 499, 513-14, 559
Sari Bair Ridge 442, 446-7
Saunders, Sgt. A.F. 543, 553-4

von Schlieffen, Count 59
Scinde Rifles, 59th Battalion
    251-3
Scots Guards 553, 556
    1st Battalion 599
    2nd Battalion 599
Scott, Pte. N. 349, 437-8
Scott-Moncrieff, Charles 229
Scottish Rifles
    2nd Battalion 102-3, 126, 135
    8th Battalion 369
Seaforth Highlanders, 1/4 Battalion
    18, 34-5, 37, 91-5, 106-7,
    111-12, 117, 119-20, 123-5,
    137-8, 306-7
Sedd-el-Bahr village 346, 356, 361,
    364
Serbia 6, 453-4, 567, 589
Service, Robert 1
Shaw, Pte. W.H. 508-9
shell-shock 417, 419, 476, 597
Sherwood Foresters 305
    8th Battalion 12, 78, 98, 121,
    124, 128-9
Shropshire Light Infantry, 2nd
    Battalion 271, 273-5, 282
Siege Batteries
    69th 284
    81st 84-6
    see also Royal Garrison
    Artillery
Simpson, Pte. A. 156
'Sister Susie's Sewing Shirts for
    Soldiers' 29, 600
Smale, Nellie 63
Smith, Ella 332-3, 335
Smith family 26-7
Smith, George 231
Smith, R.E. 577-8
Smith-Dorrien, General Sir Horace
    forced resignation 256-7, 258-9,
    264-5, 279
    and Neuve Chapelle 199
    and Ypres 218, 219-20, 241, 245,
    246-8, 250, 253-7

snipers
    German 81-2, 94-5, 169, 479
    Turkish 350, 352, 437
Snow, General 199
songs 28-9, 155
South Staffordshire Regiment 594
    6th Battalion 75-8, 471, 472
South Wales Borderers 364
Southin, Bob 318-20
Southport steamer 21-6
Special Reservists 66
Spencer, Pte. W. 548, 550
spies 20-1, 26
Stacke, Lt. 99
Stephens, Col. 99, 103, 118-19,
    121, 130, 132-4, 308
Stevens, 106
Stewart, Pte. C. 558-9, 571-2
Stopford, General Sir Frederick
    445-6, 448-50, 452-3, 566
stretcher-bearers 117, 135, 233,
    241, 308-9, 371
Stuart, Lt. Col. B.F.B. 395n.
Suffolk Regiment 543
    1st Battalion 283-6, 288-92, 293
    2nd Battalion 164-5
Sutcliffe, Johnnie 91, 125
Sutton, Sgnr. J.E. 192-3, 196-7,
    235, 236
Suvla Bay 432, 440, 442-52, 564-6,
    580, 582, 585, 589
Swan, the Rev. William 338-40
swords, superfluous 16-17, 46
Sydenham, Lord 598-9

Tannenberg (battle) 60
Taylor, Lt. 526-7
Taylor, Major 68-9
Tennant, Gnr. N. 299-302
Tennant, Lt. C. 18, 34-5, 37, 91-5,
    111-12, 117, 119-20, 123-5,
    137-40, 307
Territorial Force
    Dardanelles campaign 54, 363-9,
    371, 374-5

in Flanders 66-7, 77, 579, 589
in France 36-7, 75
and Indian Corps 66-7
kindness of public to 155-8
in Malta 38-43
and Neuve Chapelle 78-9, 89-90,
141
shortage of equipment 152-4
training 38-9, 46-7
see also 'Kitchener's Army'
Thomson, Pte. A. 334, 336,
339-40
Thuillier, Lt. Col. H.F. (later
Major General) 555-6
Times, The 141-2, 312-13
Tinsley, James 332-3, 338n.
Tower Bridge 487, 501, 512, 535,
550
Trading with the Enemy Act 28
training 38-9, 46-7, 154-5, 158-60,
161-6, 271, 594
Treffry, Lt. Col. R.G. 395n.
Tsintau steamer 23-4
Turner, Brig. General 199-200
Tynecot war cemetery 220n.

Udall, Sgt. F.G., MM 249-50, 252
Unwin, Cmdr. 358

Vallender, Sgnr. 301-2
Vaughan, Pte. J.W. 271-3, 287,
292-3
Vimy Ridge 311, 530, 557

Walker, Major 118
Wallace, Col. 283-4, 289
Wallerstein, Brig. General 496-8
War Cabinet 31, 433
War Council 49-51, 53-4, 60, 142,
315-17
Warwick, Col. H. 474, 516, 535,
537, 560
Warwick, Margaret J. 494, 560
Waterhouse, Lt. Col. 75-6, 78, 486
Waterlow, Lt. A. 480-1

Watson, Gnr. J.A. (later Cpl.)
489-90, 530-1
weddings, servicemen 151-2
Welch Regiment, 1st Battalion
290
Wellesley, Lt. 212-13
Welsh Guards 474
Welsh Regiment 508
West Riding Brigade 299-302
West Yorkshire Regiment
1/5 Battalion 298-9, 307-8, 310
12th Battalion 541-2
Western front
deadlock 7-9, 15, 31, 34, 49
debate over 579-80, 589
new offensive 60-1, 216-18, 405
Westhoek Ridge 273, 282, 286
White, Bob 338
White, Lt. A.B. 501, 502-3
Wightman, Capt. 355
Wilhelm II, Kaiser 9-14, 26
Wilkinson, Brig. General 516
Willcocks, General, Sir James 66,
96, 103, 105, 108, 118, 132,
490-1
Williams, Able Seaman W.C.
356n.
Williams, Ben 525, 554
Williams, Lt. Col. 356-8
Wilson, Cpl. A. 298-9, 307-8
Winchester, Major the Marquis
403
Winnington, Major 122
Wir Barbaren (We Barbarians)
260-1
Wolseley, Sir Garnet 14
Wood, Field Marshal Sir Evelyn
397
Woodhouse, Col. 121-2, 128
Woodroffe, Lt. Sidney 427n.
Worcestershire Regiment
1st Battalion 30, 99, 105, 116,
121-3, 127-9, 131
3rd Battalion 395n.
10th Battalion 473-4

Worrell, Rfn. W. 157, 466-8, 484, 498-9, 523-5, 554-5, 597
Wynn, Lt. T.S. 164-5

Yatman, Lt. Col. C. 395n.
Yorks and Lancs Regiment, 1st Battalion 290
Yorkshire Hussars Yeomanry 179, 183-5
Yorkshire Regiment, 5th Battalion 156
Ypres, first battle 17
Ypres, second battle

and Battle of Loos 491
British occupation 6, 176-81, 379-95, 405-6, 590
British withstand German attack 211-27, 232-57, 258-79, 324-5, 327
evacuation of civilians 276-8, 506-8
German offensive 182-95, 196-210, 278-9, 280-94

Zouave Wood 390, 424